346

W9-ANY-099

LIBRARY
FLORIDA STATE COLLEGE FOR WOMEN
TALLAHASSEE, FLORIDA

LIBRARY
FLORIDA STATE COLLEGE FOR WOMEN
TALLAHASSEE, FLORIDA

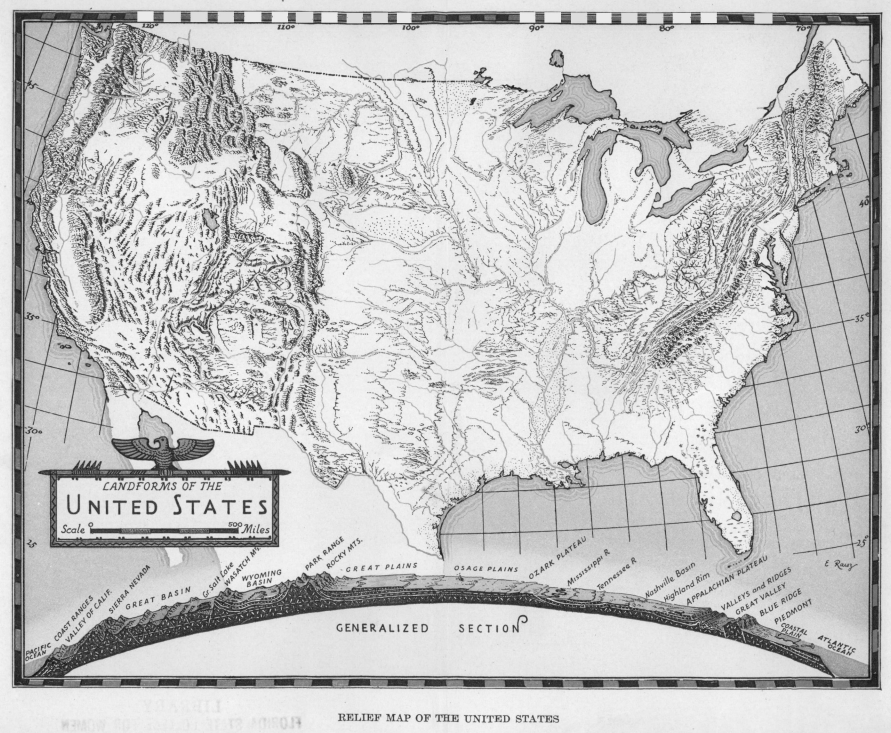

LANDFORMS OF THE
UNITED STATES
Scale 0 ⸻ 500 Miles

GENERALIZED SECTION

PACIFIC OCEAN · COAST RANGES · VALLEY OF CALIF. · SIERRA NEVADA · GREAT BASIN · Gr. Salt Lake · WASATCH MTS. · WYOMING BASIN · PARK RANGE · ROCKY MTS. · GREAT PLAINS · OSAGE PLAINS · OZARK PLATEAU · Mississippi R · Tennessee R · Nashville Basin · Highland Rim · APPALACHIAN PLATEAU · VALLEYS and RIDGES · GREAT VALLEY · BLUE RIDGE · PIEDMONT · COASTAL PLAIN · ATLANTIC OCEAN

E. Raisz

RELIEF MAP OF THE UNITED STATES

LIBRARY
FLORIDA STATE COLLEGE FOR WOMEN
TALLAHASSEE, FLORIDA

THE
Federal Union

★ A HISTORY OF THE ★

UNITED STATES TO 1865

BY JOHN D. HICKS

Professor of History in the University of Wisconsin

FLORIDA STATE COLLEGE FOR WOMEN
TALLAHASSEE, FLORIDA

HOUGHTON MIFFLIN COMPANY

BOSTON · NEW YORK · CHICAGO · DALLAS · ATLANTA · SAN FRANCISCO

The Riverside Press Cambridge

E
178
.H59
1937

973
Hicks

COPYRIGHT, 1937, BY JOHN D. HICKS

ALL RIGHTS RESERVED INCLUDING THE RIGHT TO REPRODUCE
THIS BOOK OR PARTS THEREOF IN ANY FORM

LIBRARY
FLORIDA STATE COLLEGE FOR WOMEN
TALLAHASSEE, FLORIDA

The Riverside Press
CAMBRIDGE · MASSACHUSETTS
PRINTED IN THE U.S.A.

272
3259

★

_____

TO
LUCILE CURTIS HICKS

_____

★

99083

979748

PREFACE

Rec'd as gift N. C. True 12-5-44

For eighteen years it was my good fortune to "give" a survey course in American history for university students classed as "sophomores and above." When at last, with some reluctance, I surrendered this privilege to a junior member of the staff, there was no particular reason why the "course" should not be turned into a book. At least the fear that students might have to listen to the same phrases in lecture that they read in their text need no longer serve as a deterrent.

It is interesting to speculate (no other word will do) upon the sources of information that contribute to the making of such a book as this. That "sources" in the technical historical sense have alone been consulted would be an idle boast. One's store of data begins, doubtless, with the notebooks, once deeply cherished but long since turned to ashes, that were acquired while "taking" certain courses as a graduate student, or even as an undergraduate. Certainly my deep obligation to four great teachers, James Alton James of Northwestern University, Winfred T. Root of the University of Iowa, the late Carl Russell Fish of the University of Wisconsin, and Frederic L. Paxson of the University of California cannot properly be overlooked. Probably one is influenced also, consciously or unconsciously, by the textbooks he has required his students to buy, and has himself out of a distressing sense of duty felt obliged occasionally to read. In this manner I must have absorbed a great deal from Fish's *Development of American Nationality*, Muzzey's *United States of America*, West's *Story of American Democracy*, and Hockett and Schlesinger's *Political and Social History of the United States*. As for the rest, the sum total of one's reading and experience would not be too much to cite.

The foot-notes scattered through these pages are intended as suggestions for further reading rather than as support for statements made in the text. For the most part, only books that are easily available have been mentioned, but an effort has been made to include all the basic secondary works on early American history, and a fair selection of special

[v]

accounts. While references are only occasionally repeated in the footnotes, all authors and titles that have been referred to in any connection are listed at the end of the book. In the case of works that have come to be regarded as classics, the usual practice of citing the latest revised edition has been reversed, and the date of the original edition has been given. This departure from precedent is certainly open to criticism, but it at least avoids the anachronism of citing a twentieth century date for such a writer as Parkman.

In the writing of this book Professor Frederic L. Paxson has been my constant adviser. He has read critically both the manuscript and the proof. His riper judgment and wider knowledge have pulled me out of many pitfalls. He it was, indeed, who encouraged me to undertake this task; and from the first there was a definite understanding between us that the concluding date of my *Federal Union* should be the beginning date of his *Recent History of the United States*, a book which for fifteen years has stood the test of class-room use, and now appears in a new and revised edition. We have not attempted to make these two books alike, either in content or in point of view — each of us has followed his own lead. But we share the conviction, I think, that the historian who would do most to make the present intelligible would do well to keep the prejudices of the present out of the past. If it appears that I have come measurably close to the objectivity that is so characteristic of all Professor Paxson's writing, and that accounts in so large part for the continued success of his *Recent History*, I shall be happy indeed.

A few other acknowledgments remain to be made. Two of my colleagues, Professor Curtis P. Nettels and Professor William B. Hesseltine, have read the parts of my manuscript in which they were most interested, the colonial and the national periods, respectively, and have made valuable suggestions. Professor Max C. Otto, Wisconsin's beloved philosopher, generously gave me the benefit of his criticism on Chapter XXV; Mr. Herman R. Friis, a graduate student in geography at the University of Wisconsin, furnished much needed aid in the preparation of maps; and Mrs. Frances Fries, a graduate student in history, worked long and faithfully over the index.

JOHN D. HICKS

MADISON, WISCONSIN

CONTENTS

CONTENTS

CONTENTS

CONTENTS

CONTENTS

CONTENTS

ILLUSTRATIONS

ILLUSTRATIONS

MAPS

MAPS

CHAPTER I

THE OPENING OF THE NEW WORLD

THE civilization that has grown up in the United States was begun a little more than three centuries ago by groups of European emigrants, mostly English, who crossed the Atlantic in search of new *Europe in* homes in the western world. They were the representatives *America* of a culture that was already ripe, and their task, great as it was, required mainly that they adapt to the new environment a manner of living already well developed in the old. The mingling in America of these representatives of many diverse races, the successful efforts they and their successors and descendants put forth to conquer the continent, and the development out of their great variety of traditions and experiences of an essentially new civilization constitute the main stream of American history.

America before the time of Columbus had developed no great civilization of its own. The Mayas and the Aztecs in Mexico, and the Incas in Peru, shone brilliantly in comparison with other American *Lack of* tribes, but not in comparison with the best that Europe and *a native* Asia had produced. Racial traits may account in part for *civilization* this failure, but the importance of the environment cannot be overlooked. A primitive civilization, if it is to survive the attack of savage neighbors, must have the protection of encircling mountains or seas, such, for example, as nature afforded the Greeks and the Romans. America offered few such settings. Its coast-lines were regular, its islands small and few, its peninsulas hard to defend, its mountain fastnesses inhospitable, its plains too unbroken. Such obstacles proved to be difficult enough for the transplanted Europeans; for the Indians they were insuperable.[1]

And yet that portion of the western world that became the United

---

[1] Livingston Farrand, *Basis of American History* (1904), contains a useful description of Indian society. This volume is the second of *The American Nation: A History*, edited by A. B. Hart. The twenty-eight volumes of this series are still unsurpassed as a general history of the United States. Of merit also is Ellsworth Huntington, *The Red Man's Continent* (1919), which is the first of a set of fifty entertaining volumes, *The Chronicles of America*, edited by Allen Johnson. An early, but scholarly, co-operative work is *The Narrative and Critical History of America* (8 vols., 1884–1889), edited by Justin Winsor.

[1]

LIBRARY
FLORIDA STATE COLLEGE FOR WOMEN
TALLAHASSEE, FLORIDA

States was potentially well fitted to sustain a great nation. Its location *Natural resources* wholly within the temperate zone freed its inhabitants alike from arctic cold and from tropical heat, but because it possessed every other variety of climate, every degree of rainfall, every texture and composition of soil, its agricultural possibilities were limitless. Abundant forests gave to shipbuilders the masts, spars, and naval stores they needed, and to pioneers the timbers for houses, barns, and fences. Wild life offered to hunters and trappers a paradise, and mineral resources of incalculable value awaited exploitation. The time was to come when sixty-six per cent of the world's supply of petroleum, sixty per cent of its copper, forty per cent of its coal and iron, thirty-two per cent of its lead and zinc would be furnished by the United States.

The Indians themselves were incapable of serious resistance, and they taught the Europeans how to live in America. From the experience of natives the colonists learned what seeds to plant, what soils to cultivate, what trails and streams to follow into the interior, what manner of craft to launch upon the inland waters; in short, what wealth the land possessed, and how best to take it.

The fact that America lay so much closer to Europe than to Asia determined that the inhabitants of the New World would be Europeans, *Connections with Europe* not Asiatics, and that for many centuries to come the relations between America and Europe would be closer than the relations between America and Asia. The ease with which sailors soon learned to conquer the Atlantic made that ocean less a barrier between the two continents than a highway. Colonies could thrive in America because during their infancy the all-essential connections with the mother country could be maintained; indeed, dependence upon Europe was so natural that the colonists learned with difficulty to depend wholly upon themselves. The American people remained British subjects for many more years than they have been citizens of independent states, and neither the Declaration of Independence nor the American Revolution sufficed to break the cultural and economic ties that bound the New World to the Old.[1]

Had the Atlantic coast-line of North America been as little indented as the Pacific, doubtless the number of British settlements would have *The coastal plain* been fewer. As it was, ideal sites for colonies could be found on the shores of sheltered bays and landlocked harbors all along the coast. Very often these inviting arms of the sea turned out

---

[1] Ellen C. Semple, *American History and its Geographic Conditions* (1903; new ed., 1933), stresses the environmental influence in history. See also N. S. Shaler, *Nature and Man in America* (1891), and A. P. Brigham, *Geographical Influences in American History* (1903).

[2]

LIBRARY
FLORIDA STATE COLLEGE FOR WOMEN
TALLAHASSEE, FLORIDA

to be also the mouths of rivers which gave access into the interior for trade with the Indians and for the expansion of settlement. The British were thus led to found many colonies instead of a single colony; and each colony, while maintaining close connections with the mother country, developed independently of every other. American political institutions still reveal the influence of this early geographic environment. The thirteen colonies could not surrender their separate political life merely because they had broken with Great Britain. They became thirteen independent states, and the system of government they worked out provided for a federal union, not for a consolidated republic.

The Appalachian mountain barrier also played an important part in determining the future of the American nation. Lying inland at varying distances from the sea, these mountains extend *The Appa-* from Nova Scotia almost to the Gulf of Mexico. They *lachians* offered no protection from the Indians, for they were neither high nor difficult to penetrate, but as a restraining influence against too rapid extension of settlement they were of real significance. Because of this mountain barrier the English settlements tended to densify along the coast before the conquest of the interior was begun. When finally the westward movement swept through and across the mountains, it had behind it the driving force of a permanent and substantial population. The French, on the other hand, let through to the West too readily by the Valley of the St. Lawrence and the waters of the Great Lakes, dissipated their energies over too extensive an area. Sooner than the English they sensed the part that the Mississippi Valley must play in the future of America, but when the final contest for its possession came their scattered villagers were no match for the more numerous and more concentrated English.

The Appalachian mountain barrier served also to promote the development of a strictly American nationality. From the southern border of New York southward the mountains lie in parallel ranges, with fertile valleys in between. Into these valleys and along the foothills, or "piedmont," to the east of the mountains pushed pioneers from the northern colonies and newly arrived immigrants from Europe to mingle with such of the Southerners as had adventured into the interior, and with each other. Separated by the mountains and forests from the people of the seacoast, these men of the "back-country" became a race apart — a new people, not much concerned with local loyalties, and citizens of one nation rather than of individual states. These "backwoodsmen" began early to restrain the particularistic tendencies of eastern Americans, and they bequeathed a common legacy of blood and custom to all future generations of western pioneers.[1]

The interior basin of the North American continent is a vast, undulating plain, bounded on the east by the Appalachians, on the west by the *The Missis-* Rockies, on the south by the Gulf of Mexico, and on the *sippi Valley* north, so far as the United States is concerned, by the Great Lakes. The one great river system which drains this region gives it remarkable unity and a name, the Mississippi Valley. Here lies nearly half the land now contained within the national borders, and far more than half the arable land. Once pioneers began to enter the Valley in numbers, it was inevitable that they should spread all over it. The only mountains to impede their progress were the Ozarks in Missouri and Arkansas, and they were far from formidable. The forests in the northern and eastern reaches were neither impenetrable nor indestructible, and the great central plains offered no more serious obstacle to settlement than an old pioneer prejudice against land that would not grow trees.

Here in the Mississippi Valley the process of racial amalgamation, already begun in the troughs of the Appalachians, was long continued. Here, too, Northerners met Southerners, here travelers from afar met those who had come from regions near by, and here foreigners met natives, all to be absorbed rapidly into one American race. A pronounced similarity of type and culture still exists among the people of the Mississippi Valley. They speak a common language; their institutions vary but slightly from place to place; and their local loyalties, in part because of an enduring mobility, remain weak.

A striking physical feature of the North American continent is the great Cordillera or Rocky Mountain system of the West. The plateau *The Rockies* from which the ranges of this system rise [2] is everywhere from five to ten thousand feet above sea-level; it extends southward into Mexico and Central America and with considerable change of character northward through Canada into Alaska; it spreads out within the United States to a width of a thousand miles, and its peaks rise to magnificent heights. For all their prominence, however, these mountains lack the significance in American history that attaches to the Appalachians, or to most of the other great physical features of the continent. They possessed immense mineral wealth, they offered

[1] F. J. Turner, *The Frontier in American History* (1920), finds in the conquest of the continent the central theme of American history.

[2] W. P. Webb, *The Great Plains* (1931), shows how the pioneering process had to be modified when this region was reached.

valuable grazing facilities, and their valleys could by means of irrigation be made agriculturally productive; but they were unfitted to shelter a large population, such as the Mississippi Valley naturally invited, and they were entered only when the formative period in the life of the nation was over.

As for the Pacific slope, it too had relatively little to do with the making of American civilization. The narrowness of the western coastal plain, and the scarcity of its harbors, precluded such *The Pacific* developments as took place along the Atlantic. Spanish *slope* settlements there were, but they began only when the English colonies were ripe for revolution, and they unloosed few forces of permanent significance. In due time man conquered notably the obstacles that nature here placed in his way, but not until the habits of the American people were already well set, and the nature of the American nation well defined.

During the whole of the Middle Ages Europeans were unaware of the existence of a New World beyond the Atlantic. Eastern Europe lay static under the blight of Byzantine rule, while western *Medieval* Europe, after the decay of the Roman Empire, descended *Europe* gradually into feudalism. Feudalism meant isolation, isolation not only for the peasants who were bound to the soil, but scarcely less for the lords who were bound to their fiefs. While feudalism lasted, each rural community took care of its own simple wants; trade and commerce languished; towns and cities almost disappeared; travel became as unnecessary as it was unsafe. But beginning with the eleventh century a great change came over western Europe. The simple agricultural economy of an earlier age gave way to a city-dominated civilization, the very life of which was industry and trade. Wealth increased, and those who had it demanded better standards of living, sometimes even the luxury of a little learning. Politics reflected the new age, and city governments, or "communes," won by force or purchase their independence of local lords. Isolation broke down, and travel, whether for business or pleasure, became increasingly common and relatively safe.[1]

Because Italy had suffered less from the barbarian invasions than the rest of western Europe, many Italian cities had managed to survive the fall of Rome, and even to maintain throughout the "dark *The Italian* ages" a precarious trade with the Eastern, or Byzantine, *cities* Empire. Naturally these "Italian cities" played a leading part in the

---

[1] On the medieval background of American history see G. C. Sellery and A. C. Krey, *Medieval Foundations of Western Civilization* (1929), and Carl Stephenson, *Mediaeval History* (1935).

commercial revival of the later Middle Ages. By the eleventh century such cities as Venice, Genoa, and Pisa had emerged as vigorous city-states, possessed of considerable wealth and population, and virtually independent of outside control. From ports in the eastern Mediterranean they obtained carpets, sugar, and spices, while from their own workshops came leather, fabrics of linen, silk, and wool, and such articles as glass, paper, and soap. All this produce they sold for good profits to other Europeans. Galleys a hundred feet in length plied the Mediterranean with Italian wares, and Italian traders, seeking markets, found their way by sea far around the coasts of western Europe, and by land deep into its barbaric center.

The Crusades, which began in the eleventh century and continued intermittently for nearly two hundred years, gave a great impetus to *The Crusades* the growth of the Italian cities, and brought prosperity to the merchant class throughout all western Europe. The ostensible purpose of the Crusades was to rescue from the infidel Turks the holy places where Jesus had lived and died, but the real motives were not so pious. The Popes who urged the Crusades were eager to get warring Christians out of western Europe, both for the peace their going would promote and for the ease of mind it would give churchmen who aspired to temporal power. The knights who "took the cross" had often no higher inspiration than the love of adventure and the hope of spoils. Business men looked with favor upon projects which meant for them a profitable trade in arms and supplies. Shippers foresaw that men and provisions would have to be transported by sea as well as by land. Success for the Crusaders promised still greater wealth and prosperity. Colonies would be established in the Holy Land to maintain a lively commerce with the West, and a friendly people would supplant the warlike Turks at the gateway to oriental trade.

The Crusaders were not successful in wresting the Holy Land permanently from the infidel, but for the scheming tradesmen of Italy they did all that was expected of them, and more. Italian traders secured valuable concessions in the towns along the Levantine coast. Their agents were exempt from the usual tolls, held their own courts, and formed in fact if not in name actual colonies of the mother city. The Crusades accounted also for an increased western demand for eastern goods. Returning Crusaders brought back with them the higher standards of living they had learned in the East, and taught these standards to their neighbors. In an age that knew nothing of refrigeration, spices such as pepper, cinnamon, nutmeg, cloves, and ginger won immediate favor for the seasoning of foods. Those who could afford it turned also to display. Prosperous city merchants purchased from Arab middlemen rubies, sapphires, pearls, and diamonds, wondrously wrought rugs and tapestries, "cloths of silk and gold," and all the fineries of the East to adorn themselves, their churches, and their palaces. Kings and prelates caught the spirit, and struggled not to be outdone. So vigorous was the trade thus established that it continued even after the fall of the Latin Kingdom of Jerusalem in the thirteenth century. The victorious Mohammedans did not scruple to give nor the Italian traders to accept the same quarters and the same privileges that they had enjoyed under Christian rule.

Like the Italians, the Levantine traders were middlemen who bought from the East and sold to the West. Many of the articles in which they dealt came from distant lands in Asia, and they were brought *Asiatic trade* to the Mediterranean usually by one of three main routes. *routes* The southernmost of these routes was by water from India and the farther East across the Indian Ocean and through the Red Sea. Caravans completed the journey to Alexandria or Cairo, where the European traders found the goods. The northern route was a tedious relay journey by caravan from the hinterlands of China and India to the Black Sea, and thence to the Mediterranean. The central route was both by sea and by land. Chinese junks, or other native craft, brought the wares to the Persian Gulf, whence Arab traders took them by way of Bagdad to Antioch or Jaffa or occasionally to some Egyptian port. Whether at Alexandria or Constantinople or Antioch the Arab traders were met by Italian merchants. Competitors from outside Italy had little chance because of the greater proximity of the Italian cities to the eastern markets, and because of the special privileges that the Italians had obtained. As middlemen for all the rest of Europe their prosperity was prodigious, and so complete was their monopoly of the eastern trade that the various Italian cities warred for commercial advantages not with others but among themselves.

Efforts on the part of cities outside Italy to break the Italian monopoly could not long be postponed. Italian prices were deemed exorbitant; moreover, the gold and silver with which to pay them was *Jealousy of* hard to find. Western Europe then produced for itself only *the Italian* the bare necessities of life, and it had little to offer in ex- *monopoly* change for the coveted oriental luxuries. Its slender stock of gold was therefore constantly diminished to redress an unfavorable balance of trade. The Italian merchants made sure profits, but the rest of Europe suffered seriously from this situation. Especially unfavored were the people of Spain and Portugal, of France and England, who were far from the Mediterranean trade centers and habitually bought much more than they sold. To these new Atlantic nations commercial vassalage was all the more humiliating because they were no longer feudal states, but centralized monarchies whose kings hoped for self-sufficiency and whose people knew the meaning of national pride. Small wonder that the sailors of these nations dreamed of new routes to the "Indies," routes which the Italian profiteers could not control. These dreams were encouraged by such tales as Marco Polo, the Venetian, told of his long sojourn in Asia during the thirteenth century. According to these tales the original cost of eastern wares was only a fraction of the Italian price, and in the Orient gold itself was easy to obtain. The hopes of sailors were further encouraged by important inventions, the compass and the astrolabe to aid in the navigation of ships, printing presses set with movable type to make available the maps and guide-books of other travelers, and guns and gunpowder to use in warding off the attacks of savages.

The Portuguese were the first to take up the search for a new route to the East. Their theory was that by sailing around Africa they could *A new route* reach the eastern markets, and thus break the Italian *to Asia* monopoly. Prince Henry the Navigator (1394–1460), a younger son of the King of Portugal, is usually credited with arousing his countrymen to this possibility, although his interest was really in the trade of Africa rather than that of Asia. Under his encouragement sailors proceeded farther and farther down the African coast each year, and before he died the vicinity of Sierra Leone had been reached. These ventures were profitable in themselves, for the African coasts yielded gold, ivory, and Negro slaves, but the Portuguese sailors, searching always for greater returns, pushed southward until they passed the Equator in 1472–73, the mouth of the Congo in 1484, and under the valiant Bartholomew Diaz rounded the Cape of Good Hope in 1487. By this time they had the Indian Ocean and the trade of Asia definitely in view, but John II, the King of Portugal, fearing that the route around Africa might never prove feasible, sent out three other expeditions. One was to go by way of Egypt and the Red Sea to Abyssinia, another was to try an overland journey across Africa from the mouth of the Senegal, and a third was to seek a northeast passage around Europe to Asia. These efforts came to nought, and it was not for ten years that the work of Diaz was followed by a successful voyage to the Indies. Finally, in 1498, after completing the long journey around Africa, Vasco da Gama landed at Calicut, erected a monument to commemorate his discovery of the new route, and returned to Portugal with spices, jewels, silks, and tapestries, in proof of his accomplishment. The new route, which eliminated the profits of so many middlemen, was soon in use, and as a result the prices of eastern wares in western markets dropped to much lower levels. The Italian merchants suffered acutely from the new competition, while to add to their distress the Turks grew steadily more powerful and less tolerant of Christian traders. Slowly but surely the splendor of the Italian cities was dimmed, and the commercial leadership of western Europe shifted from the Mediterranean to the Atlantic.

While the Portuguese were first in the field, they were not alone in their desire to find a new route to the East. The Spanish government was convinced through the arguments of a Genoese navi- *Columbus* gator, Christopher Columbus, that the Indies might be found by sailing directly west. Columbus was a well-informed sailor who had lived in the Madeira Islands, had sailed to the north as far as England and perhaps as far as Iceland, and had doubtless heard the gossip of distant lands across the Atlantic, then current among sailors. The common people of the time believed that the earth was flat, but medieval scholars knew well enough that it was round, and possibly one of them, a Florentine named Toscanelli,[1] had some correspondence with Columbus on the feasibility of a western route to the East. Columbus, by underestimating the size of the earth, argued convincingly that this directly western route would be shorter than the route around Africa that the Portuguese were then still seeking, but for a long time he had great difficulty in securing the support of anyone who had means enough to finance a voyage of discovery. At last he won over King Ferdinand of Aragon and Queen Isabella of Castile, the joint rulers of Spain, and under their patronage he set sail in August, 1492, with three small ships and fewer than a hundred men. The Spanish monarchs provided him with letters of introduction to the great Khan of Cathay, and a grant of authority to govern such unappropriated lands as he might discover.

When on the twelfth of October, 1492, Columbus reached one of the small coral islands of the Bahamas, he rejoiced in the belief that he was near the coast of Asia. Exploring farther, he visited Cuba *Discovery of* and Haiti, but he failed to reach the mainland, and he failed *America* too to find the spices and jewels and rich fabrics he had sought. But his conviction that he had reached the Indies was unshaken; he called the natives he met Indians, and he returned to Spain to announce that the new route had been found. Columbus made three other voyages of

---

[1] Henry Vignaud, *Toscanelli and Columbus* (1902), maintains with much learning that the Toscanelli letter is a forgery. A good biography of Columbus is C. R. Markham, *Life of Christopher Columbus* (1892).

exploration to the New World, but he died in the belief that it was a new route to the Orient, not another continent, that he had discovered.[1]

Further explorations, including voyages by one Americus Vespucius, whose name was given to the New World, soon revealed how mistaken *Other explo-* Columbus had been, but trinkets of gold which the Indians *rations* displayed were sufficient to maintain Spanish interest in the new land. Moreover, it seemed reasonable that there must be somewhere an opening through which the journey to the Indies could be continued. For a long time this latter idea fascinated adventurers, French and English as well as Spanish, but early in the sixteenth century it was learned that Asia was far more than a few days' journey from the new land. In 1519 a navigator named Magellan set sail from Spain, discovered and passed through the straits that bear his name, and crossed the Pacific. Magellan himself was killed by Philippine Islanders, but in 1522 one of his ships sailed on by the Portuguese route around Africa to Europe, the first ship to complete a voyage around the world.

Magellan's voyage blasted the Spanish hope of a route to the East that would rival the Portuguese route, but the discovery of America led *Conquest* to an even more valuable source of wealth. In 1519 a *of Mexico* Spanish soldier, Hernando Cortez, pushed his way to cen-*and Peru* tral Mexico and defeated Montezuma, Emperor of the Aztecs. The Aztecs proved to be the most civilized race in North America, and from the rich mines of Mexico they had gathered fabulous treasures of gold and silver. Cortez and the Spanish first robbed them, and then forced them as slaves to work the mines for the benefit of their conquerors. What Cortez did to the Aztecs was repeated about 1531 by another Spaniard, Pizarro, who conquered the equally rich and even more enlightened Incas of Peru. Thereafter for many years Spain drew a tribute from the New World which made her easily the first nation of Europe. Colonies followed conquests, and the Spanish empire in America became the marvel and envy of the whole civilized world.[2]

In keeping with the times the Spanish aimed from the first at a na-*Line of* tional monopoly of all that their sailors had discovered. *Demarcation* When the Portuguese King, professing to believe that Columbus had in reality only touched upon the coast of Africa, threatened

[1] Edward Channing, *A History of the United States* (6 vols., 1905–30), gives in his first volume an excellent account of the exploration of America. In a total of six volumes he carries his history through the Civil War. Based, as it is, upon the results of recent critical scholarship, this work is indispensable to the serious student of American history.

[2] E. G. Bourne, *Spain in America* (1904), covers this subject in detail. See also H. I. Priestley, *The Coming of the White Man* (1929). This is the first of twelve volumes, *A History of American Life*, edited by A. M. Schlesinger and D. R. Fox, which together constitute an admirable survey of the non-political activities of the American people.

LIBRARY
FLORIDA STATE COLLEGE FOR WOMEN
TALLAHASSEE, FLORIDA

LIBRARY
FLORIDA STATE COLLEGE FOR WOMEN
TALLAHASSEE, FLORIDA

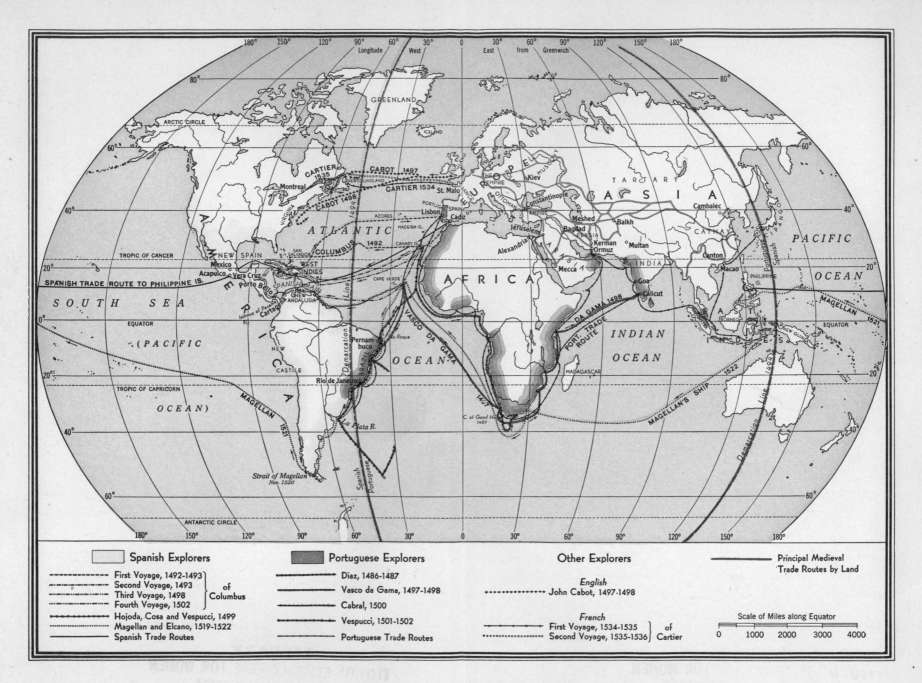

PRINCIPAL VOYAGES OF DISCOVERY

to use his fleets against Spanish trespassers, Ferdinand and Isabella hurriedly obtained from Pope Alexander VI, himself a Spaniard, full confirmation of their rights. By a proclamation issued May 4, 1493, the Pope declared that all heathen lands which lay beyond a north and south line one hundred leagues west of the Azores were by right of discovery the property of Spain. Later, at the insistence of Portugal, this line was abandoned in favor of the famous Demarcation Line, a meridian three hundred and seventy leagues west of the Cape Verde Islands. The new line was intended to divide the whole world, outside Europe, between Portugal and Spain. Both by papal pronouncement and by treaty agreement between the two nations it was stipulated that all discoveries east of this line were to go to Portugal, while all to the west of it were to go to Spain. It happened that the easternmost tip of triangular South America lay on the Portuguese side of the Demarcation Line; hence, when some years later a Portuguese ship was blown out of its intended course down the coast of Africa and touched instead upon the coast of Brazil, the Portuguese King could, and promptly did, claim that part of the New World for his own. Otherwise, the Spanish monopoly on America was for many years practically unchallenged. A Venetian named John Cabot, sailing in 1497 under authority of Henry VII of England, did indeed explore the north Atlantic coast of North America, and in 1535 a Frenchman, Jacques Cartier, carried the French flag up the St. Lawrence to the site of Montreal. But the claims made by these explorers were not immediately followed up. On the other hand, when in 1562 some French Huguenots attempted to found a colony in Florida, Spanish troops under Menendez brought the venture to a bloody end.

The profitable monopoly of the New World by the Spanish and of the new route to Asia by the Portuguese aroused at length the opposition of the English. England under the rule of Queen Elizabeth had achieved a stable government, a satisfactory religious settlement, and a state of domestic tranquillity that *English rivalry with Spain* tempted her merchants and sailors to look well beyond the national confines for new fields to conquer. On every hand they encountered monopolies: the Italians in the Mediterranean; the Portuguese in Africa and Asia; the Spanish in America. One English sea-captain, the pious John Hawkins, defied both the Portuguese and the Spanish by procuring slaves in Africa and selling them at a great profit to the Spanish in the West Indies (1562–68). Others, in a day which knew nothing of international law, attacked the Spanish treasure-ships and brought back rich booty. One such, Sir Francis Drake, in 1577 sailed down the eastern and up the western coasts of South America, plundering as he went, and after advancing as far north as San Francisco turned westward, crossed the Pacific to the East Indies, rounded the Cape of Good Hope, and in 1580 returned to England, the first of his race to circumnavigate the globe. In 1586 Thomas Cavendish duplicated the exploits of Drake, taking many prizes along the Spanish Main and in the Pacific. And then followed a veritable epidemic of piracy.[1]

Long before mere piracy had turned to recognized war Queen Elizabeth was giving her private approval to buccaneers whose raids on Spanish commerce she must publicly denounce. She believed, as did her people, that Philip II, the Spanish King, aimed at the domination of all Europe. He had tried to control England by means of a marriage alliance, and had succeeded in winning one English queen, Mary Tudor, to be his bride. When Mary died young and childless, Philip sought to repeat his tactics and proposed to her successor, Elizabeth. But the new Queen shrewdly rejected his offer, and thus freed the English nation from that particular menace. Philip's ambitions worked out more to his liking with reference to Portugal. He was closely related to the Portuguese royal house, and when in 1580 the Portuguese King died without a direct heir Philip successfully laid claim to the vacant throne. He thus became head of the two greatest empires in the world. Meanwhile his designs on France, then torn by the so-called wars of religion, became increasingly apparent, and he gave even the more remote states of western Europe occasion for alarm.[2]

There was also a religious aspect to the approaching conflict between England and Spain. The Protestant Reformation, which had swept *The Protestant Reformation* over most of northern Europe earlier in the century, found its bitterest enemy in the King of Spain. Philip, as a devout Catholic, naturally looked with horror upon the spread of heresy, but he understood also that the expansion of his own domains must proceed hand in hand with the restoration of loyalty to the Pope. If the Bishop of Rome, as the sole spiritual ruler of Christendom, could not recover his authority, what chance would there be for Philip to secure the temporal supremacy that he craved? If the peoples of Europe would not brook the idea of a spiritual overlord, how much less likely that they would be willing to accept a temporal overlord. It was partly with a view to reviving the rule of Rome in England that Philip sought a marriage alliance with two successive English queens; it was

---

[1] William Wood, *Elizabethan Sea-Dogs* (1918).

[2] E. P. Cheyney, *European Background of American History* (1904), treats every important phase of the subject.

partly because England had proceeded too far along the road of national religious independence to be willing to turn back that Elizabeth refused him. More and more, as the power of England grew, the Protestants of Europe looked to Elizabeth as their champion quite as the Catholics looked to Philip as theirs. A decision must soon be reached. Could Philip, supported by the wealth which he drew from his colonies, obtain for himself the temporal, and for the Pope the spiritual, overlordship of the world? Or could England preserve her own independence in politics and religion, help other nations to preserve theirs, and contrive at the same time to break the Spanish-Portuguese monopoly on all new trade routes and all new lands?

The clash came finally toward the end of the sixteenth century. The Netherlands, which by a succession of royal marriages and births had fallen under the Spanish yoke, revolted in 1566 against the *The Spanish* oppressive rule of Philip's agents, and in the later phases of *Armada* the struggle that ensued received aid from Queen Elizabeth. This interference by the English in the Netherlands, coupled with the wholesale depredations upon Spanish commerce by English seamen, led Philip to dispatch against England his "Invincible Armada" of one hundred and thirty ships, manned by eight thousand sailors, and carrying an army of invasion of nineteen thousand men. The Spanish fleet reached the English coast, but its great galleons were no match for the smaller and more skillfully managed ships of Drake and his kind. The Armada was disastrously defeated (August, 1588), many of the Spanish ships that escaped the English were destroyed by tempests in the North Sea, and less than a third of Philip's splendid fleet ever got back to Spain. Several years later England sent forth a "counter-Armada," which successfully attacked the Spanish port of Cadiz and destroyed a great quantity of enemy shipping (1596). From this time forward it was England, not Spain, who was the "mistress of the seas."

Philip's defeat revealed to all the world that the Spanish-Portuguese commercial and colonial monopoly need no longer be respected. Among the first to take advantage of this situation were the Dutch, *European* whose "sea-beggars" helped themselves to Portuguese *rivalry for* holdings in Africa and the East Indies, and whose traders *America* cast covetous eyes toward the New World. In 1609 the Dutch East India Company sent Henry Hudson, an Englishman, to search for a sea-route through North America to India. Hudson sailed as far as Albany up the river which now bears his name, but he found no northwest passage. What he did discover was an opportunity for fur trade with the Indians, and a Dutch trading-post was soon established on

Manhattan Island. Dutch sailors also wrested from the Spanish some valuable Caribbean islands and a strip of territory along the northern coast of South America. The French, whose sixteenth-century explorations gave them a claim to the St. Lawrence Basin, were almost as active as the Dutch. They, too, discovered the possibilities of the fur trade, established in 1608 a post at Quebec, and in 1610 another at Port Royal. In the West Indies, they occupied Guadaloupe, Martinique, and many minor islands. Even the Swedes, who for the moment had attained a place of prominence in European affairs, planted a colony in 1638 at the mouth of the Delaware, a settlement which the Dutch soon absorbed. Meantime the English, whose defeat of Spain had made all this possible, had not been idle.[1]

The motives which led to the founding of the English colonies in North America were numerous and diverse. A little must be credited *Motives* to the unique pioneering spirit of the age. Sheer love of *of English* adventure led English seamen of the sixteenth and seven-*colonization* teenth centuries to embark in tiny craft for the search of unknown seas, and many landsmen, moved by the same spirit, went along to explore the lands beyond the seas. These adventurers sought gold, it is true, and they sailed often as the agents of commercial companies, but for gold and trade alone they would hardly have risked so much. Their *wanderlust*, so apparent on every page of *Hakluyt's Voyages*, was a striking characteristic of the times, a natural reaction, perhaps, from the insularity of an earlier age.

Nor can the religious motive be overlooked. Protestant England, with the enthusiasm of the novice for her creed, regarded the New World as a legitimate missionary field; and the fact that Catholic Spain, the chief national rival of England, had already won many converts to Catholicism furnished an added incentive. Moreover, there were in England many dissenters from the Established Church whose presence, in an age of religious intolerance, was deemed a menace to the safety of the state. For such as these the New World might prove a haven of refuge; for the government their going would afford profound relief. What better use could be made of dissenters than to permit them to carry Protestantism and the English flag to heathen lands?

Hard times and fancied overpopulation also account for much of the English enthusiasm for colonies. One writer of the period maintained that "unless the three great Imposthumes of the World, namely Wars,

---

[1] Carl L. Becker, *Beginnings of the American People* (1915), contains an interesting account of the partition of the New World.

Famine and Pestilence, do purge the great body, all kingdomes and
countries become very populous, and men can hardly live *Hard times*
in quiet or without danger." Such a condition of affairs *and unem-*
England seemed to have approached. Peace with Spain *ployment*
(1604) left many discharged soldiers and sailors to seek in vain for new
employment. The increasing popularity of sheep-raising within consolidated enclosures threw many farmhands out of work. Henry VIII's
dissolution of the monasteries had made objects of charity of the very
monks and nuns who in an earlier age had been charged with the care
of the poor. The flow of wealth from the New World to the Old had not
proved an unmixed good, for the inflation of the currency by means of
American gold and silver had greatly increased prices, while the abundant labor supply kept wages down. "If the people of this kingdom
were numbered," declared one observer, "I am persuaded there were
never more people, never less employment, never more idleness, never
so much excesse. . . . The poor starve in the streets for want of labor."
Such writers doubtless exaggerated greatly, but their opinions were used
as arguments in favor of founding colonies. If the excess of English
population could only be drawn off to other lands, those who remained
behind need not fear for lack of work.[1]

All such reasons, however, were secondary to the desire of merchant
and government alike to promote English trade. Owing partly to the
invigorating effect of gold and silver from the New World, *English*
English commerce had taken on new life. The well-to-do *trade and*
required now such luxuries as spices, sugar, and tea. They *trading*
built ostentatious mansions for which they must have the *companies*
costliest furnishings of the East. They paid high prices cheerfully, and
merchants made good profits. Capital for commercial enterprise was
thus easily amassed, and with seemingly sure profits ahead it became
extremely venturesome. Dozens of trading companies were chartered
by the government for the purpose of establishing commercial relations
with some foreign region. Perhaps the most successful of these enterprises was the English East India Company, formed in 1600 to exploit
the trade of India; but many others, such as the Levant Company,
which built up a prosperous trade with the eastern Mediterranean, and
the Muscovy Company, which dealt with Russia, paid handsome divi-
dends. America seemed to furnish another such business opportunity,
and companies were soon organized to make profits from the American
trade.

[1] G. L. Beer, *The Origins of the British Colonial System, 1578–1660* (1908), is the standard
authority on this subject.

The generous charters which trading companies received from the English crown reveal a kind of alliance between government and business that is not difficult to explain. The companies' ships left England with cargoes of English manufactures which they proposed to exchange for the raw materials of undeveloped regions. To the business man this meant merely profits; to the government, inspired as it was by the mercantilistic theory of the age, it meant security. According to the mercantilists, the chief measure of a country's strength was the amount of gold and silver it could amass. The trading companies, by exchanging expensive English manufactures for cheap raw materials, might be counted upon to produce for England a "favorable balance of trade," because of which a steady stream of precious metals would flow into the country. By just so much the strength of the nation would be increased. The urgent necessity of promoting national self-sufficiency was another reason why the government gave special privileges to trading companies. At a time when wars were regarded as the normal state of international affairs, and peace only an interlude between wars, each nation naturally aspired to be able to care for itself without dependence on any other. Indeed, economic dependence might easily lead to the loss of political independence.

To thoughtful English officials America seemed ideally fitted to become an independent national source of supply. The Spanish had
Need of a national source of supply found abundant wealth in the New World, why should not also the English? One of Hakluyt's voyagers declared that "gold, silver, copper, leade, and pearls" were available in great quantities along the unsettled coasts of North America. With an independent supply of precious metals England would no longer be wholly at the mercy of a precarious balance of trade. Staple commodities, now purchased from rival nations, were also to be found in America. For naval stores England depended upon the Scandinavian countries, an unfortunate situation which might easily be remedied by the exploitation of the vast American forests. Potash, essential to the woolens industry, came likewise from Baltic lands, but this too might be obtained in America. English fishermen could supply only about one third of the national demand for fish, and the other two thirds had to be bought outside, mainly from the enterprising Dutch. Why should not English colonists in America draw upon the rich fisheries of the western Atlantic? Fisheries seemed particularly deserving of stimulation, for it was already a truism that fisheries and sea-power went hand in hand, and upon sea-power the safety of the English nation must depend. Whatever else England did not produce in sufficient quantity there

seemed reason to hope that America could supply. Moreover, sailors still talked of a northwestern passageway around America to the Orient. If this should materialize, American establishments could serve also as halfway stations to the East, and an all-English route to the Orient would complete the emancipation of the English from any dangerous dependence upon their neighbors.

One other consideration weighed heavily in favor of colonies. England was rapidly becoming a nation of manufacturers, and she was in need of expanding her markets. But other nations, in *Need of* conformity with the popular doctrine of national self-suf- *national* ficiency, raised up just such barriers against her exports as *markets* she also raised up against theirs. Clearly England needed independent markets, markets to which the trade of other nations should not be open, and why could these not be found in a colonial America? Even if the balance of trade occasionally went against England, which seemed unlikely, it would be English colonists who were enriched, not prospective enemies. Freedom of trade for the colonies was, of course, never considered. It was assumed that each colony would send its produce to the mother country, and would make all necessary purchases from English manufacturers.

It is worth noting, however, that the English government, although deeply interested in having colonies founded, never seriously considered founding colonies itself. One reason for this was the fact that the government lacked the means for such undertakings; but far more important was the current conception of colonies as strictly commercial enterprises. Colony founding had to do with the expansion of trade and the making of profits, and so it was considered, for good reason, merely a type of business. The government, according to prevailing economic theories, might foster and regulate every type of business all it chose, but it must not engage in business. It might properly, in order to promote the general welfare, encourage private capital to seek profits from colony planting, but it could not plant colonies.

Why Englishmen, most of whom expected to remain in England, favored the founding of colonies in America is one thing; why certain Englishmen chose to become colonists is quite another. *The call of* Doubtless the love of adventure, the false hope of gold, the *free land* need of a refuge from religious persecution, and the lack of employment at home all sent their quotas to America. But probably no other motive weighed so heavily as the desire for land. In England, and indeed throughout all Europe, landholding was a test of gentility; ordinary people might not even hope to own land. In the New World land was equally open to all. The younger sons of nobles, left landless by the rule of primogeniture, turned to America for recompense; the peasants and artisans, destined if they stayed at home to remain what they were for life, saw in the colonies their only chance to become landed proprietors. Cheap land was the magnet which drew immigrants across the Atlantic to America, just as it was later to draw their descendants, step by step, across the continent.[1]

[1] Among the useful one-volume works on the colonial period are the following: E. B. Greene, *The Foundations of American Nationality* (1922); O. P. Chitwood, *A History of Colonial America* (1931); H. E. Bolton and T. M. Marshall, *The Colonization of North America, 1492–1783* (1920).

CHAPTER II

VIRGINIA AND NEW ENGLAND

Two early colonial ventures which failed made it evident to Englishmen that the exploitation of America was not to be undertaken lightly. In 1578 Sir Humphrey Gilbert was authorized by Queen Elizabeth to hold and govern such lands in America, not already appropriated, as he might choose to colonize. *Gilbert and Raleigh* Gilbert was one of those who believed in the existence of a northwest passage, and his goal was an American colony on the way to Asia. But his first expedition was defeated by the Spanish, who were as yet unhumbled, and his second, bound for the inhospitable shores of Newfoundland, was defeated by a storm. Gilbert's efforts were followed up by his half-brother, Sir Walter Raleigh, who secured a new charter in 1584, and after some preliminary investigations decided to plant a colony along the reputedly rich shores farther to the south, which Elizabeth, the Virgin Queen, now chose to call Virginia. During the next few years Raleigh wasted his fortune on the project. The colony which he had intended to locate in the vicinity of Chesapeake Bay was by a series of blunders established instead on Roanoke Island, an unfavored site from which the colonists fled to the mainland only to lose their lives to the Indians. The ill-fated experiments of Gilbert and Raleigh showed, among other things, that the private resources of any one man were likely to prove inadequate for the financing of so great a venture. Raleigh realized this himself, and in 1589 he organized a company of "Associates" to carry on the work; but he soon lost favor with the Queen, and when in 1603 he was convicted of treason his rights in America were annulled.[1]

---

[1] C. M. Andrews, *The Colonial Period of American History*, I (1934), opens a series that will embody the research of one of the greatest of American historians. The colonial period has already been the subject of many monumental works, among which John A: Doyle, *English Colonies in America* (5 vols., 1889–1907), still takes high rank. *Original Narratives of Early American History*, edited by J. F. Jameson (19 vols., 1906–17), is a valuable collection of sources.

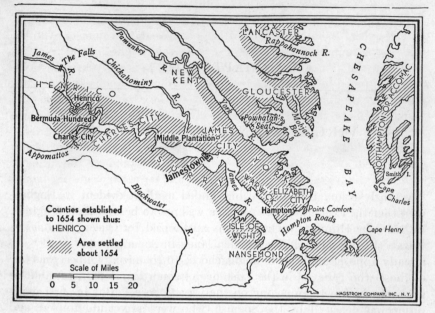

SETTLEMENTS IN VIRGINIA, 1654

The profits of trading companies designed to exploit regions other than America were so good, however, that a group of investors was soon formed to begin where Raleigh had left off. If the initial difficulties

The Virginia Companies

could only be overcome, why should not a Virginia company prove to be the success that the East India Company, for example, had become? Investors in that enterprise were said to have realized profits in a single year equal to the principal they had risked. Accordingly, in 1606, King James I, who had succeeded Elizabeth on the English throne, was persuaded to issue a charter to some London and Plymouth merchants who had in mind the establishment of new outposts of trade in Virginia. By the terms of this charter the stockholders were subdivided into two companies, the London Company and the Plymouth Company, each of which was promised a tract of land along the Virginia coast a hundred miles in width and extending a hundred miles into the interior. The charter stipulated further that the land of the London Company should be located somewhere between the thirty-fourth and the forty-first parallels, while the land of the Plymouth Company should lie farther north, between the thirty-eighth and the forty-fifth parallels. Neither company might establish a colony within one hundred miles of any colony established by the other.

[20]

The London merchants were the first to take advantage of this grant. In December, 1606, they sent out three shiploads of colonists, who the next spring founded Jamestown at a point thirty miles inland from the mouth of the James River. Thereafter for seventeen years the Company continued to send a steady stream of colonists and supplies to Virginia. Of profits there were none, but the stockholders hopefully invested in the project a sum which today would be reckoned at not less than five million dollars.[1]

The mortality among the early colonists was frightful. Out of the one hundred and four adventurers who reached Virginia in the spring of 1607 only thirty-eight were alive that fall, and for many years one half to two thirds of any given lot of immigrants were doomed to *The James-* death within a few months from the date of their arrival. *town colony* Captain John Smith, one of the world's most picturesque characters, stands out in these early years as the man who, more than any other, furnished the common sense that saved the little colony from extinction; but as late as 1616, by which time over sixteen hundred emigrants had left England for Virginia, the population of the colony was only about three hundred and fifty. In spite of the unfavorable odds, however, including an Indian outbreak in 1622 which took a heavy toll, the number of Virginians grew, and by 1624 there were probably as many as twelve hundred people in the colony.

During these years the Virginia experiment was carried on as a strictly business enterprise. The local managers, or "governors," acted as agents for the company and directed the work of the company "servants," who constituted the great majority of the settlers. These servants had usually been paupers or convicts in England. They came to Virginia under "indentures" or contracts which bound them to work for the company from four to seven years in return for their passage across the Atlantic and the prospect of receiving a small tract of land when their term of service came to an end. Such supplies as were brought from England and such provisions as the plantations themselves produced were kept in common storehouses, and were doled out to the settlers as needed. Almost from the first a few commodities, such as lumber, dyestuffs, and sassafras, were sent back to England in the company's ships to help pay expenses; but it was not until tobacco culture became the chief business of the colony that much was produced worth shipping away. Towards the end of the company's rule several

[1] This subject is well covered in such general accounts as T. J. Wertenbaker, *The First Americans, 1607–1690* (1927); L. G. Tyler, *England in America* (1904); Edward Eggleston, *The Beginners of a Nation* (1896); and C. M. Andrews, *The Colonial Period* (1912).

innovations, designed in part to keep the colonists contented and in part to attract new settlers, were introduced. (1) The right to private ownership of land was conceded, and liberal grants were made to indentured servants whose period of service had expired, and to all freemen. (2) The harsh laws deemed necessary during the first hard years of the colony were abrogated, and (3) a representative assembly "freely elected by the inhabitants," to consist of two representatives from each "plantation," was authorized to share in the making of the laws.[1]

For a time the affairs of the infant colony aroused much interest in England, and many prominent men bought stock in the venture. In
Charter revisions order to increase the power of the company and to enlarge its territory, the original charter of 1606 was twice revised, once in 1609 and again in 1612. The new land grant was especially generous, for it gave the company a frontage along the coast of two hundred miles north and two hundred miles south of Old Point Comfort, while inland the company's rights were to extend "west and northwest" from sea to sea. Unfortunately King James I regretted the liberal powers of government he had permitted the company to exercise, and he especially disliked the concessions to popular rule that it had made. He accordingly obtained in 1624 from a subservient court an annulment of the charter. All governmental rights now devolved upon the King, and Virginia became a royal colony. By this change the Virginians lost the help they had been accustomed to receive from the London Company, but they were permitted to retain their land titles, and, after some hesitation on the part of the King, their representative assembly. As for the investments made by stockholders in the company, they were a total loss.

The success of tobacco culture was what enabled the Virginia colony to survive. When the Jamestown settlement was made, the use of to-
Tobacco culture bacco was already known in Europe, but the tobacco Europeans first learned to like came from the Spanish colonies in America. Virginia tobacco was regarded as inferior and undesirable until about 1616, when a new method of curing it was discovered. From this time on the Jamestown colonists had a product that would yield them a profit, and the colony soon began to prosper. Land was easy to obtain under the so-called "head-right" system, by which each immigrant and each person who paid for an immigrant's passage received fifty acres. The more prosperous planters came to own many

[1] The early history of Virginia has been elaborately set forth in a number of books by P. A. Bruce. Among them are *The Economic History of Virginia in the Seventeenth Century* (2 vols., 1896); *Social Life of Virginia in the Seventeenth Century* (1907); *The Institutional History of Virginia in the Seventeenth Century* (2 vols., 1910).

head-rights, and even in the seventeenth century the tendency toward large plantations was already marked.

The prosperity of the colony was reflected in the rapid increase of its population during the middle decades of the seventeenth century. Many newcomers came in response to an insistent demand *The labor* for more labor. Tobacco planters who could afford to do *problem in* so imported indentured servants, of whom some had crim- *Virginia* inal records, but most were merely poor or unfortunate. English children of the lower classes were sometimes kidnapped and sold into servitude, and frequently political prisoners were sold under indenture. The indentured servants in due time became free, obtained plots of land along the western fringe of settlement, and shared with other citizens whatever prosperity the New World had to offer. Beginning in 1619, Negroes were brought into the colony as slaves, although the number of such persons in early Virginia was very small. Unlike the indentured servants, the slaves could never be assimilated into the white population, and their presence ultimately produced a problem that led to the American Civil War. During the middle decades of the seventeenth century war broke out in England between the adherents of the King, or "Cavaliers," and the supporters of Parliament, or "Roundheads." When in 1649 the "Roundheads" triumphed and executed the King, many "Cavaliers" sought safety in Virginia. By 1652 the population of the colony was estimated at twenty thousand.[1]

The next successful English experiment in colony planting was at Plymouth, on the coast of what later became Massachusetts. Here the religious motive undoubtedly assumed commanding im- *The English* portance. The church establishment which had been *dissenters* worked out in England under Queen Elizabeth occupied a place midway between extreme Catholicism and extreme Protestantism. All connections with Rome were severed, the sacraments were reduced in number, services in Latin were discontinued, and the head of the state became the head of the church; but many of the old forms of Catholicism, such as the vestments of the clergy, the elaborate ritual of worship, and the hierarchy of priests, bishops, and archbishops, were retained. Inevitably many Englishmen were dissatisfied with these halfway measures and wished to go further in the direction of Protestantism. Of these "dissenters," some, known as "Puritans," desired only to reform the existing English church in such a way as to bring it into closer harmony with the teachings of John Calvin; others, less numerous and

[1] More readable than scholarly is John Fiske, *Old Virginia and her Neighbours* (2 vols., 1897). For a later edition see *The Historical Writings of John Fiske* (12 vols., 1902), IV, V.

influential, were called "Separatists" because they were ready to sever all connections with the established church. Neither group was seriously persecuted during the reign of James I, but there was enough threat of persecution to make all dissenters uneasy. A little band of Separatists from Scrooby, England, furnished the nucleus for the Plymouth settlement. They went first from England to Holland and later, in 1620, some of them, after returning to England, set sail in the *Mayflower* for America. Not all who went to Holland came to America, and not all of those who came to America had been in Holland. Indeed, when the *Mayflower* set sail from England, about half its passengers had never been outside their country before.[1]

If the religious motive was the dominant thing in inducing these "Pilgrims," as they have always been called, to emigrate to America, *The Pilgrims* it is equally true that their journey to the New World was made possible by capitalists who hoped for profits from the enterprise. An unincorporated joint-stock company was formed, in which both emigrants and investors held stock. Each person over sixteen who emigrated was the recipient of one share of stock valued at ten pounds, and he might buy additional stock if he chose. The greater part of the capital, however, was furnished by some London merchants. In the interest of the investors it was stipulated that the emigrants must work for a period of seven years as the servants of the company. During this time whatever they produced was to go into a common warehouse, and their needs likewise were to be met out of supplies held in common. A complete settlement was to be made at the end of the seven years, by which time, it was hoped, the colonists would be able to discharge their debts with interest.

On December 21, 1620, the *Mayflower* landed her hundred passengers at Plymouth harbor. Anticipating difficulty in controlling the action *The "Mayflower Compact"* of some of the more turbulent members of the group, the Pilgrim "Fathers," or at least forty-one of them, affixed their signatures while still on shipboard to the famous "Mayflower Compact," by which they bound themselves together into a "civil body politic" for their "better ordering and preservation." They chose John Carver as their first governor, and as a pure democracy faced the unknown trials of the New World. The first winter took a toll in dead of over half the company, but the survivors stayed on, and

[1] J. G. Palfrey, *History of New England* (5 vols., 1858–90), continues to be useful although written long ago. C. M. Andrews, *The Fathers of New England* (1921), is an excellent short account. J. T. Adams, *The Founding of New England* (1921), is brilliant, but definitely anti-Puritan in point of view. John Fiske, *The Beginnings of New England* (1889), is, like the rest of his historical works, extremely readable but not always dependable.

with the help of a few more immigrants they were able to found an enduring settlement. Farming, fur-trading, fishing, and lumbering furnished their chief occupations. In 1627 the heavy debt still owing to the London merchants was taken over by a few of the Pilgrim leaders, and was ultimately paid off from the profits of the fur trade. In 1628, with the London merchants now entirely excluded from the enterprise, the Pilgrims divided up their moveable property and voted to each colonist for private ownership twenty acres of land.

The title of the Plymouth colony to the land it had occupied was for some time clouded. The Pilgrims had permission from the London (or Virginia) Company to settle within the borders of its grant, *The Plymouth colony* but the *Mayflower* was blown out of its course and the location at Plymouth Bay was accepted almost of necessity. This site lay within the territory granted to the original Plymouth Company, which, after an unsuccessful effort in 1607 to plant a colony on the coast of Maine, had practically ceased to function. Reorganized in 1620 as the New England Council, with a sea-to-sea grant, the Plymouth Company stood ready to hand over to the Pilgrims the land they coveted. In 1630 William Bradford, who had succeeded Carver as governor of Plymouth, obtained title as trustee for the colony to the land about Plymouth Bay, and when finally in 1641 the debts owing to the London merchants were fully paid, the governor formally transferred to the people the rights he had acquired.

The government of the Plymouth colony was extremely simple. At first all the men who signed the Mayflower Compact, meeting together as an assembly, chose the governor, made the laws, and admitted such newcomers as they saw fit (in practice nearly *Democracy at Plymouth* all) to the full privileges of citizenship. Later, as the number of separate settlements grew, a representative assembly, or "General Court," was instituted to take care of matters pertaining to the whole colony, while local affairs were left to "town meetings." All efforts to secure royal approval of these governmental privileges through a charter failed, so the Pilgrims and their successors were left to govern themselves as a self-constituted commonwealth until 1691, when William III arbitrarily joined their colony to that of Massachusetts Bay. The Plymouth colony was never large — at the time it was annexed to Massachusetts its population numbered only about seven thousand — but it played a significant rôle in pointing for other dissenters the way to the New World.

Chief among those to follow the example of the Pilgrims were the founders of the colony of Massachusetts Bay. These were Puritans

rather than Separatists, but under King Charles I, who in 1625 succeeded
The English James I on the throne of England, they had reason to believe
Puritans that the "purification" of the English church was a vain
hope. With the King's consent Archbishop Laud prosecuted dissenters
vigorously, deprived Puritan pastors of their parishes, and showed himself in complete sympathy with the "high-church" party. The Puritans
fought back with spirit. They knew that the issue between them and
the King went deeper than religion. Their leaders were well-to-do
members of the middle class, men who aspired to places of influence in
the government, and who were unwilling to submit any longer to the
unfair taxes and other discriminations that the King, supported by the
landed gentry, was accustomed to place upon their class. When the
Puritans succeeded in winning a majority of the House of Commons, it
appeared for the moment that they, and not the King, would have their
way. But the King boldly dissolved Parliament, arrested the Puritan
leaders, and entered upon a period of personal rule that lasted from 1629
to 1640. During these years he levied taxes arbitrarily, and encouraged
Laud to deal more harshly than ever with the dissenters, for whom now
the situation became intolerable.

Persecution stirred many of the Puritans to armed revolt, and at
length under the leadership of Oliver Cromwell the "Roundheads" de-
The Com- feated the King; but in the meantime many others, de-
pany for spairing of England as a fit home for freemen, turned their
Massachu- eyes to America. It chanced that the way for a great mi-
setts-Bay gration had already been prepared. A group of English
merchants, some of whom were Puritans, had been attracted by the
possibilities of the New England fisheries, and in 1628 had obtained
from the New England Council title to all land lying between the Charles
and the Merrimac Rivers. Next year this "Company for Massachusetts-Bay" obtained a charter from the King which confirmed the grant
of land, and authorized the company to exercise the usual governmental
privileges over settlers. Two expeditions, one in 1628 and another in
1629, established Salem as a village of several hundred settlers with
John Endicott, a well-known Puritan, as the civil head of the community, and Francis Higginson, a Puritan minister, as the chief religious
leader. Here was the nucleus for a Puritan commonwealth in the
New World. If Plymouth could succeed under the Separatists, why
could not Salem, and perhaps many other villages also, under the
Puritans?

The Puritan leaders laid their plans carefully. They wished to establish in the New World an ideal Puritan commonwealth where a

really "purified" church might thrive. The government of the new colony must, therefore, be wholly in their hands. If they could secure complete control of the "Company for Massachusetts-Bay," *The "Great* and could take its charter with them to America, what better *Migration"* means could they ask for the accomplishment of their purpose? The scheme worked out as planned. A majority of the stockholders in the company voted to send its charter to America, and those who wished to stay at home sold out to those who wished to go. In October, 1629, the able and prominent John Winthrop was elected governor of the company, and next year, taking the charter with him, he led the vanguard of the migration. Before the summer of 1630 was done, seventeen ships had landed two thousand settlers in Massachusetts, and several villages, among them Boston, Dorchester, Watertown, and Roxbury, had been founded. Thereafter, as the troublous times continued in England, other emigrants came also, until by the year 1640 no less than twenty-five thousand refugees had found their way to Massachusetts. With that year the tide of battle began to turn against the King in England, and the "Great Migration" came to a close.[1]

In spite of the steady flow of immigrants, it was no easy matter for the Puritans to make their colony a success. As in Virginia and Plymouth, the percentage of deaths among the newcomers, es- *Suffering of* pecially during the early years of the migration, was alarm- *the colonists* ingly high. Life on the New England frontier turned out to be a bitter struggle against unyielding soils, cruel winters, ever-recurring disease, and constant privation. Hundreds of the faint-hearted returned to England at the first opportunity. And in spite of the Puritan saying that "God hath sifted a nation, that he might send choice grain into this wilderness," not all of those who stayed comported themselves well. In general, however, the seed was good. Most of the immigrants were uneducated farmers or humble artisans, but they were ready to make the best of their new environment, and they were ably led.

Soon the evidences of a less primitive society could be observed. Livestock was imported and bred; mills to grind the grain, brick kilns and sawmills to produce better building materials, and even ironworks to turn out a few household necessities began to appear. Trade with England came about naturally, for the colonists were quick to discover that with such articles as fish, furs, lumber, and potash to exchange,

---

[1] S. E. Morison, *Builders of the Bay Colony* (1930), describes the leading men of the colony with rare skill.

they could obtain from the mother country some of the many things for which they stood in need.[1]

As for government, the Puritan leaders had little difficulty in making over the charter of the Company for Massachusetts-Bay into the kind *Puritan* of constitution they wanted. All power, according to the *government* charter, rested with the stockholders, or "freemen," who were authorized to elect as a kind of board of directors a governor, a deputy governor, and eighteen "assistants"; also to meet four times each year to admit new freemen, elect new officers, and pass such regulations for the government of the company as they saw fit. Only twelve freemen had come to America, and every one of them, as governor, deputy governor, or assistant, was an officer of the company. This group, by neglecting to choose new freemen, at first kept all authority in its hands, but such arbitrary procedure did not long escape criticism. In the fall of 1630 one hundred and nine of the settlers asked to be made freemen of the corporation, and the ruling officers did not dare to refuse so reasonable a request. They maintained, however, that the sole privilege of the freemen was to vote for new assistants whenever vacancies should occur, and that all real authority lay with the assistants, who might hold office during good behavior, choose the governor and deputy governor, and make all the laws. Such an interpretation of the charter was wholly unwarranted, but the deception was not discovered for several years. Thus the Puritan leaders still kept in their own hands the direction of the colony's affairs.

Their avowed purpose was "to build a City of God on earth." What such a city should be like they determined from the teachings of John *Church and* Calvin, from much reading of the Bible, and from their *state* experience in the New World. On leaving England they had regarded themselves as members of the English church, the doctrines and practices of which they had merely sought to purify. But on establishing themselves in America they were content to become as definitely Separatists as the Pilgrims in Plymouth. They soon refused to recognize Church of England ministers as duly ordained, and they referred theological disputes to their own ministers sitting together as synods. They held that the church must set up standards of conduct as well as principles of theology, and they branded anything that savored of lightness or frivolity as a sin. Moreover, they had no intention whatever of tolerating views and practices in conflict with their own ideas. As they saw it, one of the first responsibilities of government was

---

[1] W. B. Weeden, *Economic and Social History of New England* (2 vols., 1890), is a work of enduring merit. See also C. M. Andrews, *Colonial Folkways* (1921).

to punish all departures from orthodoxy in theology or from propriety in behavior. Laws were passed to make the way of the transgressor hard, and the worst offenders were punished by expulsion from the colony. Church and state worked together, each to uphold the other, the state sustaining the decisions of the church, and the church proclaiming through its ministers the supremacy of the state. Early Massachusetts was not a democracy; it was an aristocratic theocracy.[1]

The attempt of the governing few to ignore the great majority of the settlers in matters of state was not wholly successful. In 1632 the freemen of the corporation boldly took into their own hands *Democratic* the election of the governor and assistants, and voted that *reforms* each town should choose two representatives to act with the assistants in the levying of taxes. In 1634, just before the spring meeting of the General Court, a committee consisting of two men from each of the eight towns in the colony demanded of Governor Winthrop that they be permitted to see the charter. Winthrop reluctantly consented, and the committee discovered that the law-making power was in reality vested in the freemen and not in the assistants. Thereafter each town chose delegates to meet with the assistants and to participate, not only in the levying of taxes, but in the making of all the laws. Moreover, at the first opportunity the newly constituted General Court ousted Winthrop from the governorship, fined some of the assistants for abuse of power, and in other ways showed its determination to play an important part in the government. But the colony was still far less than a democracy. The number of freemen admitted to the corporation was cautiously restrained, only church members being deemed eligible, and not all of them being chosen. Since the deference of the common people for ministers and magistrates was so strong, the will of the leaders was rarely contested. Even Winthrop was soon recalled to the governorship by the very freemen whose rights in the government he had once curtailed. Ultimately, following the precedent of the English Parliament, the Massachusetts General Court divided into two houses, one composed of representatives from the various towns, and the other composed of the assistants, who together with the governor were chosen annually by the votes of the freemen.

The intolerance of the Massachusetts government in all matters of belief and conduct provoked some irritation. Deportations for religious offenses were numerous, and harsh punishments were laid upon those who failed by ever so slight a margin to conform to the strict Puritan

---

[1] V. L. Parrington, *The Colonial Mind, 1620-1800* (*Main Currents in American Thought*, I, 1927), opens with a brilliant account of the Puritan heritage.

standards. The careers of Roger Williams and Anne Hutchinson, both of whom challenged the accepted order, serve to illustrate two facts, first, that dissent in Massachusetts Bay did exist, and secondly, that the dissenters usually lost in their conflicts with the ruling caste.[1]

Roger Williams was a godly but disputatious minister who came from England in 1631, and after short stays at Boston and Plymouth became *Roger* the pastor at Salem. He soon startled the authorities by *Williams* declaring that the state had no right to punish an individual for his personal habits and opinions. If a man did wrong to his fellow-men, then, according to Williams, the state should punish him; but if a man merely held uncommon religious views, or departed from the customary practice in a small matter like Sabbath-breaking, then his offense was no affair of the state. Williams's doctrine was really revolutionary, for if carried to its logical conclusion it would have withdrawn the power of the state from the support of the church and would have wrecked the whole Puritan experiment. Accordingly the General Court voted in 1635 to expel him from the colony. The sentence required his return to England, but he escaped to the Narragansett Indians, with whom he spent the winter, and next spring with the help of a few adherents he began the settlement on Narragansett Bay that developed into Providence, Rhode Island.

Anne Hutchinson, according to John Winthrop, was "a woman of a ready wit and a bold spirit" who "brought over with her two dangerous *Anne* errors." Just what these errors were, or the "many *Hutchinson* branches" that grew from them, would mean little to a non-theological age, but among other things she was free in her criticism of ministers, and she believed that good works as well as divine grace had a part in the plan of salvation. Roger Williams had comparatively few followers, but Anne Hutchinson attracted by her eloquent and logical arguments many adherents, among them young Henry Vane, at that time governor of the colony, John Wheelwright, a prominent minister, and a large majority of the Boston congregation. Soon the colony was in an uproar over her teachings, although, except in Boston, her doctrines were far more opposed than favored. Faced by this critical situation, the conservatives acted promptly and drastically. They removed Vane from the governorship and replaced him with the more dependable Winthrop; then they brought Mrs. Hutchinson and Wheelwright to trial before the General Court. The verdict of the Court stated succinctly the Puritan theory of intolerance, that "two so opposite parties could not contain in the same body without hazard of ruin to the whole," and

[1] E. J. Carpenter, *Roger Williams* (1909); Edith Curtis, *Anne Hutchinson* (1930).

banished the offenders from the colony. Some of those who believed in Mrs. Hutchinson's teachings recanted, but many others were compelled to leave. Mrs. Hutchinson, accompanied by a group of her sympathizers, founded a settlement at Portsmouth (1638), near Roger Williams's town of Providence, and also within the borders of what later became Rhode Island.

These are by no means the only instances of persecution within the Massachusetts Bay colony. The air was full of intolerance. The attitude of the Puritan leaders toward heretics was not un- *Religious* like the attitude of present-day health officers toward the *intolerance* carriers of contagious diseases. For the safety of the state the contaminated must be placed where they would have no power to do harm. Two Quaker women who came to Boston in 1656 were promptly deported. When other offenders of the same sect insisted on entering the colony and even on returning to it after having once been sent away, four offenders were actually executed. The harshness of this penalty gave some offense, however, and in 1661 the General Court, in a spirit of moderation, provided that unwelcome Quakers should merely be tied to a cart and whipped from town to town until they had passed the borders of the colony.

Just as religious intolerance in England had a part in bringing settlers to Massachusetts, so religious intolerance in Massachusetts helped along the formation of colonies elsewhere in New England. *Beginnings* Rhode Island is the most striking case in point. At Provi- *of Rhode* dence Roger Williams and his followers, after purchasing *Island* land from the Indians, instituted a secular government which left the individual free in religious matters to follow the dictates of his conscience. At Portsmouth Anne Hutchinson's adherents took the Bible as their guide of life and conduct, but disagreed on so many minor matters that a group of "come-outers" soon established themselves at Newport (1639). A fourth Rhode Island settlement at Warwick (1643) was the work of Samuel Gorton, a refugee from Massachusetts whose views were so heretical that even the liberal-minded Williams refused to permit him to settle permanently at Providence.

The four Rhode Island communities wasted little love on one another, but their common fear of Massachusetts, whose leaders deeply resented such near-by nests of heretics, drew them together. In 1644 Roger Williams secured from the English Parliament a "patent" which permitted the settlers on Narragansett Bay to govern themselves so long as their laws were in harmony with the laws of England; and in 1647 representatives from the various Rhode Island towns organized a political system not unlike that of Massachusetts. Church membership was not a qualification for voting, however, and the right of religious liberty was definitely safeguarded, "notwithstanding our different consciences touching the truth as it is in Jesus." In 1663 a formal charter was secured from King Charles II in which the Rhode Island system of representative government was accorded full approval, and the Rhode Island principle of "liberty in religious concernments" was definitely accepted.[1]

The "soul liberty" for which Rhode Island stood was not without its disadvantages. The colony soon came to be known as a paradise *"Soul* for "cranks," and a "dumping ground for the disorderly *liberty"* and eccentric elements" of all New England. Roger Williams admitted that if heretics disturbed the peace they might be punished for it, but he maintained steadfastly that the state had no right to "punish any for declaring by words their minds concerning the ways and things of God." Many protests came from Massachusetts against the way in which heretics from Rhode Island passed the borders of their own colony to preach heresy in orthodox lands, but in spite of all such obstacles Williams and his associates held out tenaciously for tolerance.

Meanwhile, out in the lower Connecticut Valley, another offshoot from the Massachusetts Bay colony had appeared. Fertile lands had more to do with the founding of Connecticut than religious *Beginnings of* dissensions. The soil around Massachusetts Bay was hard *Connecticut* to work and the harvests were not copious; hence, tales of better lands to the southwest made a strong appeal. Thomas Hooker, minister at Newtown (later Cambridge), and John Haynes, a former governor, were the chief promoters of the Connecticut project. Neither could be branded as a heretic, although Hooker was mildly liberal in his views and somewhat disgruntled with the aristocratic character of the Massachusetts government. But he was not forced to leave. Indeed, the Massachusetts authorities considered forbidding the migration to Connecticut, and in the end they consented to it only with great reluctance.

In the years 1635 and 1636 about eight hundred settlers from Newtown, Watertown, and Dorchester pushed through the forests to the Connecticut Valley. They knew that the Dutch claimed this region, and that they themselves had no legal title whatever to it, but they unhesitatingly took possession of the land they wanted and founded three towns, Hartford, Wethersfield, and Windsor. Some settlers from Plymouth had already established a trading-post not far from the site of

[1] I. B. Richman, *Rhode Island: Its Making and its Meaning* (2 vols., 1902).

Hartford, and some Puritans from England, acting under a grant of land from the Council of New England, had sent over a small force under John Winthrop, Jr., son of the Massachusetts governor, to found a colony at the mouth of the Connecticut River. Here Winthrop, in spite of threats from the Dutch, erected Fort Saybrook. Another settlement in the Connecticut Valley was made at Springfield by a Roxbury congregation, but the site was discovered later to be within the jurisdiction of Massachusetts.[1]

Progress towards the establishment of an orderly government for the Connecticut River towns was rapid. In 1639 representatives from Hartford, Wethersfield, and Windsor met at Hartford to *The "Fundamental Orders"* draw up a plan of union. The result was the Fundamental Orders of Connecticut, a document usually regarded as the first constitution to be written in America. The Fundamental Orders copied the governmental practices of Massachusetts, although the prerogatives of officials were somewhat more limited. The governor, for example, had no veto, he was ineligible for re-election, and he might not arbitrarily dissolve the General Court or prevent it from meeting when it so desired. As far as the relations between church and state were concerned, the Massachusetts system was deemed satisfactory. The Orders stated plainly that "the discipline of the Churches, which according to the truth of the said gospel is now practiced amongst us" must be maintained.

Meanwhile on Long Island Sound another Puritan colony, New Haven, was in process of evolution.[2] Its founders were John Davenport, an English Puritan minister, and Theophilus Eaton, a well-to- *The New Haven colony* do English Puritan merchant. These men visited Massachusetts in 1637, but decided to found an ideal Bible commonwealth and trading center outside the confines of any existing colony. At New Haven their dreams of commercial success failed to materialize, but with their small settlement as a beginning several other towns, Guilford, Milford, and Stamford, were soon founded. In government and religion the New Haven colony, like Connecticut, repeated with slight variations the Massachusetts experiment; indeed, no other colony was more circumspect in its Puritanism than early New Haven. Its separate existence came to an end in 1662 when the English King, Charles II, was induced, mainly through the efforts of John Winthrop, Jr., to unite the Con-

---

[1] G. L. Clark, *A History of Connecticut* (1914); C. M. Andrews, *Connecticut's Place in Colonial History* (1924).

[2] C. H. Levermore, *The Republic of New Haven* (1886); Isabel M. Calder, *The New Haven Colony* (1934).

necticut River towns and New Haven into the one colony of Connecticut under a liberal charter. Probably the ease with which both Rhode Island and Connecticut obtained their charters of self-government was due to the dislike Charles II felt for the Puritans of Massachusetts, whose whole-hearted opposition to his father, Charles I, was almost equaled in intensity by their distaste for other colonial establishments in New England. Charles II wasted little sympathy on the people of Rhode Island or Connecticut, but he enjoyed the discomfiture that his recognition of their rights gave the Massachusetts Puritans.

The secessions from Massachusetts to the southwest, which furnished the main impetus for the founding of Rhode Island and Connecticut, *New Hampshire and Maine* were matched by similar movements toward the north into the regions known as New Hampshire and Maine.[1] Here, however, settlers from Massachusetts were by no means the first on the ground. In 1623 two English gentlemen, Sir Ferdinando Gorges and Captain John Mason, had obtained from the New England Council a patent to all the land lying between the Kennebec and the Merrimac Rivers. They first called their grant Laconia, but presently, on determining to divide it between them, Mason took the western half and called it New Hampshire, while Gorges took the territory along the coast and called it Maine. Both men tried to establish settlements within the confines of their grants, but their successes were slight. Some trading-posts were founded, such as Portsmouth, Kittery, Dover, Exeter, and York, which eventually developed into towns, but most of these settlements owed nothing to the efforts of either Mason or Gorges; nor were these proprietors, as they styled themselves, able to maintain their control in the face of the steady influx of settlers from Massachusetts. These newcomers were exceedingly reluctant to acknowledge any other authority than that of the Puritan commonwealth in which they had lived, and finally the Massachusetts government, on the pretext that its land grant really entitled it to do so, extended its authority first over the New Hampshire towns, and finally over those in Maine. New Hampshire remained a part of Massachusetts until 1679, when Charles II made it a separate royal colony, but Maine was not accorded a separate existence until by the well-known Compromise of 1820 it became a state in the Union.

The advance of the New England frontier brought on at an early date trouble with the Indians, particularly the Pequots, whose holdings were seriously jeopardized by the founding of Connecticut. Attacks on iso-

[1] W. H. Fry, *New Hampshire as a Royal Province* (1908); H. S. Burrage, *The Beginnings of Colonial Maine, 1602-1658* (1914).

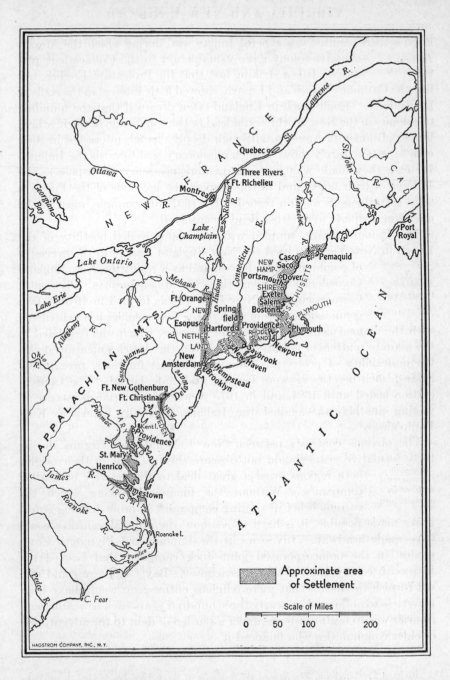

EARLY SETTLEMENTS ON THE CONTINENT OF NORTH AMERICA

lated settlers resulted in a general Indian war, during which the Massa-
Indian chusetts colony gave valuable aid to the Connecticut pio-
difficulties neers. It is a striking fact that the Protestant English, unlike the Catholic Spanish and French, showed little interest in the souls of
the Indians. Englishmen in England often dreamed that the founding
of colonies in the New World would lead to the conversion of the heathen,
but Englishmen in America, although deeply enough interested in their
own salvation, rarely showed much missionary zeal towards the Indians.
Instead, they made whatever efforts were necessary to dispossess the
Indians of their lands, and in this respect the methods of the Puritans
were as ruthless as any on record. By 1637, for example, most of the
offending Pequots were either dead or enslaved.

The Indian menace, coupled with the thinly veiled hostility of the
Dutch in New York, aroused the New England leaders to the necessity
The New of combining their forces, and as a result the New England
England Confederation, consisting of Massachusetts, Plymouth,
Confedera- Connecticut, and New Haven, was formed in 1643. Two
tion commissioners from each of the four colonies were entrusted
with the management of the common business, which was restricted in
the main to matters of military defense; but the Articles mentioned also
the desirability of protecting common religious interests, presumably
against such heretics as were located in Rhode Island. The Confederation lasted until 1684, and in 1675 it was of material assistance in
waging another war against the Indians, generally known as King
Philip's war.[1]

The obvious contrasts between New England and Virginia during
these formative years should not obscure the fact that in their origins
Commercial both regions owed a great deal to the activity of trading
motives in companies. Without the financial backing which the
colonization current belief in trading companies as profit-making enterprises made possible, it is hard to see how the original ventures could
have made headway. Investors in the London and Plymouth Companies, in the unincorporated joint-stock company that backed the
Plymouth colony, and in the Massachusetts-Bay Company could and
did furnish the means that mere religious enthusiasm would have been
powerless to obtain. For nearly three hundred years each new American
frontier was to begin existence under a burden of debt to the adventurers
of older communities who financed it.

On the other hand, it is clear that the religious motive was cogent in

---

[1] Richard Frothingham, *The Rise of the Republic of the United States* (1872), contains
lengthy discussions of the New England Confederation and the Indian troubles.

producing emigration, particularly to New England. Men did come
to America in order to establish colonies where they might   *The religious*
have freedom to worship as they pleased, and for this same   *motive*
reason they sometimes left the original settlements to found others.   In
general, the colonies as commercial ventures were failures, but as new
homes for emigrants they were successes. The men who came to
Virginia or New England found, if they searched far enough, a religious
environment that suited them; and they found also, if they survived
and could work, a certain degree of economic prosperity. As havens of
refuge in an intolerant age the colonies were important; as experiment
stations in the art of self-government they were extremely interesting;
but as places where ordinary men could acquire property, especially in
land, and could make a decent living they had their greatest significance.

CHAPTER III

THE PROPRIETARY AND ISLAND COLONIES

THOSE English colonies that did not spring, directly or indirectly, from the activities of trading companies were usually the work of individuals, *Proprietors* commonly called proprietors. Sir Humphrey Gilbert and *as colony* Sir Walter Raleigh were the forerunners of this type of *founders* colony founder, but neither their unhappy experiences nor the profitless aspect of the trading company ventures in America sufficed to deter other individuals from making similar experiments, particularly after the restoration of the Stuarts to the English throne. During the restoration period the favor of the royal family was ordinarily all that was needed to enable one to obtain a proprietary grant of land from the King, together with the right to rule its inhabitants. Some of these proprietors were impecunious nobles who merely aimed to sell or let out their lands on advantageous terms, and if possible to exact from their subjects the feudal dues common to an earlier age in England. A few coveted political power such as the Old World lords were no longer permitted to possess, and others, while by no means indifferent to the prospects of financial and political rewards, sincerely desired to found havens of refuge for the oppressed.[1]

The earliest of the successful proprietary provinces was Maryland. The launching of this colony was the work of George Calvert and his son *The Balti-* Cecilius, more commonly known as the first and second *mores in* Lords Baltimore. George Calvert was a man of means *Maryland* who had long been interested in colonial projects. He was a member of the London Company and of the Council for New England; and under a charter granted by James I in 1623 he had also made an independent but unsuccessful effort to establish a colony in Newfoundland. Convinced by a visit to this region in 1627 that its intolerable climate would always be an insuperable obstacle to colonization, he asked and received from King Charles I the promise of a grant of land farther to the south. Calvert, meantime, by embracing the Catholic

[1] H. E. Egerton, *A Short History of British Colonial Policy* (1905).

faith, had cut himself off from all chance of political preferment in England, although the King, whose religious leanings were also in the Catholic direction, bore him no grudge and even made him an Irish peer with the title Lord Baltimore. The first Lord Baltimore died before the King's promise of a new charter had been redeemed, but in 1632 the grant was made to his son, Cecilius, who was also a Catholic. By its terms the territory from the south bank of the Potomac northward to the fortieth parallel and inland to the source of the river was handed over to the Baltimore family as an hereditary estate. Two arrows and one fifth of all the gold and silver mined in the province must be paid each year to the King, but otherwise the proprietor was left as free to govern in America as the king in England. This meant, however, an important limitation on the proprietor's power, for he could make laws and raise taxes only with the advice and consent of the freemen, or landowners, in his colony, or of their representatives.[1]

The second Lord Baltimore greatly desired to make of Maryland a place where his Catholic co-religionists might worship without fear of oppression, and, perhaps because of an unrecorded under- *A Catholic* standing with the King, the royal charter offered no opposi- *refuge* tion to such a course. But the number of prospective emigrants among English Catholics was limited, and Baltimore was too good a business man to propose the exclusion of Protestants, who were cordially welcomed and from the first seem to have outnumbered Catholics. The *Ark* and the *Dove*, two small ships which Baltimore sent to Maryland in the fall of 1633, carried about twenty gentlemen and two hundred laborers to the new colony. Most of the gentlemen were Catholics, but most of the laborers were Protestants. Three Jesuit priests accompanied the expedition and labored with great earnestness but little success to convert the Protestant settlers and the Indians to Catholicism.

The beginnings of Maryland reveal no such suffering and hardship as accompanied the founding of the earlier colonies. The passage of the *Ark* and the *Dove* was long and trying, and it was not until *Early* February, 1634, that the Potomac was entered, but St. *settlements* Mary's, the site selected for the first settlement, turned out to be healthful, and the usual depredations from disease were not recorded. Lands which had already been cleared were peacefully acquired from the Indians, and the economic life of Virginia was closely copied. Baltimore's land system contained one unique feature. He proposed to grant

---

[1] W. H. Browne, *George and Cecilius Calvert* (1890); and, by the same author, *Maryland, The History of a Palatinate* (1884). For a very readable general account of the southern colonies, see Mary Johnston, *Pioneers of the Old South* (1918).

a manorial estate of a thousand acres to any adventurer who would transport five men to Maryland. But such "lords of the manor" were never numerous, although large estates mainly given over to the cultivation of tobacco did develop. All land was granted by the proprietor, who charged a small quit-rent. This feature of the land system, while producing for the proprietor a fair revenue when it could be collected, was by no means popular, and it accounts in part for the relatively small population which Maryland acquired in the seventeenth century. Elsewhere in the colonies lands were obtainable on easier terms.

Cecilius Calvert did not himself come to America, but sent instead as lieutenant governor his brother, Leonard Calvert. While recognizing *Popular* the right of the people to a voice in the making of the laws, *government* the proprietor and his lieutenant sought at first to hold popular participation in the government to a minimum. This was not long possible, and in Maryland as elsewhere a representative assembly soon developed. One of the most significant of its early acts, passed in the face of the rising power of Puritanism in England, was the Toleration Act of 1649. While this act threatened with death all non-Christians, including Jews and Unitarians, it guaranteed that no person "professing to believe in Jesus Christ, shall be in any wise molested or discountenanced for his or her religion." Persecution of Catholics, however, did break out in Maryland during the later years of the seventeenth century, and the Church of England, in spite of the Catholic origin of the colony, became the established church.[1]

Several other proprietary colonies of the Maryland type were founded shortly after the restoration of the Stuarts in 1660. The successes of the Baltimores, such as they were, inspired emulation on the part of the courtiers of the new king, Charles II, in whom they found a sympathetic and helpful friend. The national interest in colonization, which had died down somewhat during the period of the Civil War, now revived.

Among the regions in America that were still at the disposal of the King was the territory south of Virginia and north of Florida. For this *The Caro-* land, called first Carolana, then Carolina, eight prominent *lina grant* nobles now successfully petitioned the King. Their plan was to make of Carolina an ideal feudal state, and they induced John Locke, the most prominent political theorist of his time, to prepare an elaborate set of fundamental laws through which this purpose should be carried out. The scheme of government which Locke devised contemplated among other things several ranks of nobility above the ordinary freemen, while the latter were to be virtually stripped of political

[1] N. D. Mereness, *Maryland as a Proprietary Province* (1901).

power. Agents of the proprietors, sent to America for the purpose, formally proclaimed the new government in operation, but they made little headway in their attempt to apply the medieval features of Locke's carefully drawn scheme. The idea of a colonial nobility proved to be particularly inapplicable.[1]

As early as 1654, well before the Carolina proprietors received their grant, settlers from Virginia had found their way to the vicinity of Albemarle Sound. These pioneers and others who soon *North* followed them were for the most part men of small means *Carolina* who had found life in proximity with the more prosperous Virginia planters far from pleasant. Albemarle democracy was of the unqualified sort, and the unsolicited efforts of the Carolina proprietors to assert authority in this region were ignored, or even resisted. Towards the end of the seventeenth century the Albemarle settlements came to be known as North Carolina. Here, as in Virginia, the colonists raised tobacco and foodstuffs, and they traded a little with New England and the West Indies.

The Carolina proprietors were decidedly more interested in the southern part of their holding, where they had expected to establish a tropical colony similar in its economic life to the islands of the West *South* Indies. In 1670 they sent out an expedition under William *Carolina* Sayle which founded Charleston, or Charles-Town, as it was first called. Other immigrants soon came in, most of them, however, without any help from the proprietors, and within ten years Charleston had about twelve hundred inhabitants. The new settlements, soon called South Carolina, took on rapidly a cosmopolitan tinge. French Huguenots began to arrive about 1680, and emigrants from Ireland, New England, and the West Indies, especially Barbados, were numerous. The planters used indentured servants for labor when they could, but, as in Virginia and Maryland, they bought Negro slaves when the supply of white servants was deemed inadequate. They raised foodstuffs as well as tobacco, and beginning about 1693 they introduced the culture of rice. The excellent harbor at Charleston greatly facilitated trade with the outside world. In government both South Carolina and North Carolina tended to develop along the lines already marked out in Maryland.[2]

The Carolina settlements were designed, in part, to act as buffers against the Spanish in Florida. But the Dutch colony of New Nether-

[1] C. L. Raper, *North Carolina, A Study in English Colonial Government* (1904); J. S. Bassett, *Constitutional Beginnings of North Carolina* (1894); S. A. Ashe, *History of North Carolina* (1908).

[2] Edward McCrady, *The History of South Carolina under the Proprietary Government, 1670–1719* (1897); A. H. Hirsch, *The Huguenots of Colonial South Carolina* (1928).

land, on the Hudson, was an even greater menace to the English than
New Spanish Florida. New Netherland actually antedated
Netherland most of the English settlements, for Dutch merchants had
planted a trading post on Manhattan Island as early as 1612, while the
Dutch West India Company, which in 1621 had taken over the exploitation of the region, actively promoted settlement from that time forward.
Most of the wealth of New Netherland came from the fur trade, but the
company offered small tracts of land to freemen who would agree to
settle on it as farmers, and large estates to "patroons," or landlords,
who as a condition of their grant must bring over fifty tenants. The
semi-feudal powers accorded to the patroons were not popular in a region
where land was abundant, and most of the patroonships did not last
long; but the promoters of the Dutch colony induced so many of their
countrymen to come to America that a sparse Dutch population was
soon settled in the Hudson Valley all the way from New Amsterdam on
Manhattan Island to Fort Orange, the present site of Albany. Many
settlers from the English colonies also entered the Dutch territory.
Some of them were refugees from religious persecution, others were
pioneer farmers eager to accept the generous land terms offered by the
Dutch, and still others were former indentured servants in full flight
from the scene of their servitude. Thanks to these accessions, and to
the absorption in 1655 of a small colony that the Swedes had founded in
1638 on the Delaware, the population of New Netherland had risen before
the English conquest to about ten thousand.[1]

The presence of this Dutch colony in America was naturally distasteful to the English, whose holdings it cut squarely in two. Furthermore,
Dutch and the success of the Dutch as traders, not only in America
English but also in Europe, Asia, and Africa, led to a period of
rivalry intense commercial rivalry between the two nations, during
which the same sort of antagonism that English sailors had once concentrated on the Spanish was turned against the Dutch. The last half
of the seventeenth century was marked by three wars between England
and the Netherlands, and in 1664, on the eve of one of them, the English
King, Charles II, sent an expedition across the Atlantic to take possession of New Netherland. To his brother, the Duke of York, he granted
proprietary rights over the whole province.

In spite of the evident superiority of the English force, the Dutch
governor of New Netherland, Peter Stuyvesant, would have offered

---

[1] John Fiske, *The Dutch and Quaker Colonies in America* (2 vols., 1899); Maud W. Goodwin, *Dutch and English on the Hudson* (1919); Amandus Johnson, *The Swedish Settlements
on the Delaware, 1638–1664* (2 vols., 1911).

resistance, but the burgomasters of New Amsterdam, who recognized the futility of such a course, restrained him.   Colonel *'Conquest'* Richard Nicolls, whom the Duke of York had sent over as *of New* his agent, was allowed to take peaceable possession of the *Netherland* town of New Amsterdam and the colony of New Netherland, both of which were renamed New York.   The Duke of York's power, according to the terms of his grant, was almost absolute, and the "Duke's Laws," which Nicolls soon proclaimed, accorded to the inhabitants only an insignificant part in the government.   Not until 1683 was an elective assembly authorized, and then it was quickly suppressed.   Throughout the seventeenth century progress toward popular rule in New York lagged perceptibly behind that of every other English colony in America.

The Duke of York disposed of a part of his holdings to two nobles, Lord John Berkeley and Sir George Carteret, who were interested in the Carolina project also and who still hoped for riches *New Jersey* from the sale of their lands in America.   These gentlemen were given proprietary rights to the territory lying between the lower Hudson and the Delaware, a region which they called New Jersey, after Carteret's home in England.   Here a few Dutch settlements had already been established, and the new proprietors, by offering land to new-comers on easy terms, succeeded in attracting many emigrants from New England and from all parts of the British Isles.

It is probable that the grant to Berkeley and Carteret was not intended to carry with it the full governmental authority that the proprietors promptly assumed.   In 1665, however, they sent out as governor Philip Carteret, a relative of Sir George, the proprietor.   Governor Carteret was instructed to establish a completely separate government for New Jersey, and to call a legislative assembly; and in spite of repeated objections from the authorities in New York, he carried out his instructions to the letter.   The proprietors found out, however, that their subjects were hard to satisfy.   The New England Puritans, whose ideals of government were already well formed before they reached New Jersey, were particularly bothersome.   When an attempt was made in 1670 to collect a halfpenny quit-rent for each acre of land granted, the authorities were openly defied, and two years later the New Jersey citizens actually expelled their legal governor in order to choose one of their own.   The proprietors soon regained control, but the collection of quit-rents had to be indefinitely postponed.

Down to 1674 the two proprietors held New Jersey jointly, but in that year Berkeley, now thoroughly discouraged, sold his holding to two Quakers, John Fenwick and Edward Byllinge.   A division of the colony into two parts was then effected. Carteret retained as his portion the settlements in the northeast adjacent to New York, or East New *Division of* Jersey, while the Quakers took the region to the south and *the colony* along the Delaware, or West New Jersey. Byllinge and Fenwick had acquired their title with the intention of establishing a Quaker colony in America, but they were unable to agree upon the details of its management, and they soon sold out to a group of Quakers, among whom the most influential was William Penn.[1] The new proprietors promptly promulgated a liberal constitution, and they promoted settlement with marked success. Within a few years several new towns had been founded and the population of the colony had increased by about fourteen hundred.

East New Jersey also fell into Quaker hands. In 1679 Carteret died, and shortly afterwards his trustees sold his grant in America to William Penn and eleven other Quakers. New partners were soon admitted to the enterprise who were not Quakers, among them some Scotch Presbyterians who worked with energy and success to persuade a number of their countrymen to emigrate to New Jersey. Quakers came from England and Scotland, Puritans from New England, and somewhat later Scotch-Irish Presbyterians from the north of Ireland. Under the beneficent rule of Robert Barclay, a Quaker preacher who in 1682 became governor for life, the colony prospered greatly. The population of East New Jersey was probably twice that of West New Jersey, and in its economic character it closely resembled New England, whence so many of its settlers had come. West New Jersey, on the other hand, tended to copy the manner of life adopted by the settlers along the Chesapeake. Small holdings were the rule, but large plantations, worked in part by Negro slaves, were not unknown. By the end of the seventeenth century the two Jerseys together had a population of about fifteen thousand.

The name of William Penn, which appeared prominently in the early history of New Jersey, is associated even more conspicuously with the *William* founding of Pennsylvania. Penn came naturally by his *Penn* interest in colonization. By birth and training he was associated with the nobles and courtiers who in the last half of the seventeenth century were so often engaged in colonial projects, while by religion he was affiliated with a persecuted sect for which the New World seemed to offer the only secure refuge. Penn's father, Sir William, had been a high-ranking officer in the navy under Cromwell, but he somehow

---

[1] S. G. Fisher, *The True William Penn* (1899) and *The Quaker Colonies* (1921), furnish both good reading and good history. On the beginnings of New Jersey, see E. P. Tanner, *The Province of New Jersey, 1664–1738* (1908).

managed to retain and even to improve his status under the restored Stuarts. He was on friendly terms with King Charles II, with his brother the Duke of York, and with many of the nobles who had received proprietary grants of land in America. Young Penn, while still a student at Oxford, was impressed by the teachings of a Quaker preacher, and he soon became a member of the Society of Friends, as the Quakers called themselves. Penn's father was deeply distressed at his son's action, for the Quakers adhered to doctrines that were immensely at variance with the prevailing views of the time. They rejected all the sacraments, refused to pay tithes towards the support of the established church, denounced war unstintedly, declined to do military service, and in a great variety of ways put themselves entirely outside the pale of seventeenth-century respectability. Persecution under such circumstances was inevitable, and Penn, as one of the most prominent members of the sect, advanced the idea of founding as a retreat for the oppressed members of his faith a Quaker commonwealth in America.[1]

Penn's experience with West New Jersey led him to conclude that, in order to establish the kind of colony he desired, he must have a charter direct from the crown. It chanced that part of the estate *Pennsylvania* which the elder Penn had bequeathed to his son was a debt owed by the King, amounting to sixteen thousand pounds. The Quaker leader now asked that, in return for the cancellation of this debt, he be granted full proprietary rights to the lands along the Delaware north of Maryland; and on March 4, 1681, his request received the sanction of the King. Unfortunately the description of Penn's holding was stated so vaguely that boundary disputes with both New York and Maryland long marred the relations between Pennsylvania and her neighbors.

The early history of Pennsylvania centers about the efforts of its conscientious proprietor to establish a liberal government, to guarantee religious freedom to all settlers, and to induce emigrants to *Representative govern-* leave the Old World for his colony in the New. Penn's *ment* charter left to the proprietor much liberty of action with regard to the form of government to be established, but it did require him to obtain the advice and consent of the freemen in making laws. Penn was in full accord with this idea, and his liberal intentions were revealed in the "Frame of Government" which he promulgated for the colony in 1682. This system proved to be too complicated to work well, and it was quickly succeeded by another of simpler nature. Penn visited

[1] George Hodges, *William Penn* (1901), is an excellent short biography. For the Quaker doctrines, see R. M. Jones, *The Faith and Practices of the Quakers* (1927); and, for the Quaker contribution to early American history, by the same author, *The Quakers in the American Colonies* (1911).

America in 1682 and again in 1701. On these occasions he observed at first hand the conditions of life in Pennsylvania, conferred directly with the leading colonists on governmental problems, and finally after his second visit issued a "Charter of Privileges" that proved to be generally satisfactory. The government of Pennsylvania retained until the time of the American Revolution a few unique features. It had an appointive council, for example, which was never recognized as a co-ordinate branch of the government, but was distinctly inferior in power to the elective assembly.

Penn was a devout Quaker, but he had no notion of limiting in any way the privileges of Pennsylvania colonists who were not Quakers. *Freedom of worship*   One of his first measures was to guarantee full freedom of worship for such law-abiding persons as "acknowledged one Almighty and Eternal God to be the Creator, Upholder, and Ruler of the World." This guaranty went much further than the famous Toleration Act of 1649 in Maryland, for the latter discriminated against Jews and Unitarians, whereas the former did not. And yet, even in Pennsylvania, the ideal of religious freedom was not for a long time fully attained. Neither Jews nor Catholics were in practice accorded the full freedom to worship in their own way that was freely given to Protestants. Offices were limited from the first to professing Christians, while later, at the insistence of the English government, all Catholics were disqualified. Happily the great bulk of the people who came to Pennsylvania were less interested in holding offices than in escaping persecution. Not only Quakers, but members of various other oppressed sects also, looked upon the Quaker colony as an ideal retreat.

The adoption of religious toleration in Pennsylvania had an advertising value which Penn did not hesitate to exploit. In Germany, particularly, *Non-English immigrants* where many radical denominations lived under the constant shadow of persecution, Penn's agents pointed out the advantages of emigration to the Quaker colony. The terms upon which land could be obtained were made easy, both for speculators and land companies who desired large tracts, and for immigrant farmers who desired small tracts. Penn's advertising campaigns, which featured his generous land terms, his policy of religious toleration, and his liberal government, got a ready response. Bad economic conditions in Germany also helped him, and led to the emigration to Pennsylvania of German Lutherans and Catholics as well as members of the minor sects. A few Dutch and a few French Huguenots came also, and many English, Welsh, and Irish settlers, most of whom were Quakers. Some of the English settlers adhered steadfastly to the Church of England, and objected

[46]

strenuously, although for the most part ineffectively, to Penn's "holy experiment" in toleration.

The growth of Pennsylvania was remarkable. Its population, which had reached about twelve thousand by 1689, was in a short time larger than that of any other English colony in North America. *Rapid* Its capital, Philadelphia, which Penn himself laid out in *growth* squares, soon became the largest and busiest city in the English overseas possessions.[1] Part of this success was due to the fact that Penn and his settlers could profit from the experiences of the earlier colonists. The heavy mortality that had characterized the settlement of Virginia and New England was not repeated in Pennsylvania, nor were there such costly mistakes as the first American pioneers made in dealing with the Indians. Penn did not profit as much financially from his colonial venture as the prosperity of his colony seemed to warrant. Quit-rents were hard to collect, and the cost of promoting emigration was great. Nor was the Pennsylvania proprietor more rewarded in the devotion of his subjects than was the rule elsewhere. They heaped criticisms upon him that would have embittered a less religious spirit. Penn's heirs and successors were even less popular, although they retained their pro-prietary rights, except for a brief interlude, until the time of the American Revolution.[2]

Delaware was at first a part of New York, then later for a long time a part of Pennsylvania. Penn was determined to have for his colony free access to the sea, and in order to effect this purpose he *Delaware* obtained from the Duke of York in 1682 the territory lying immediately to the west of the Delaware River. When the "Charter of Privileges" was issued in 1701, these "lower counties" were accorded the right to select an assembly of their own. This they soon did, but the Penns continued as proprietors, and the relations between Delaware and Pennsylvania remained close.[3]

Georgia was the last of the English colonies to be established on the mainland of North America. Its founder, James Oglethorpe, who had been for thirty years a member of the House of Commons, *James* shared the current jealousy of French and Spanish colonial *Oglethorpe* expansion. One unappropriated region that might conceivably be claimed by any one of those three nations lay south of Carolina, north of Florida, and east of Louisiana. Here Oglethorpe wished to plant a

[1] J. T. Faris, *The Romance of Old Philadelphia* (1918).

[2] S. G. Fisher, *The Making of Pennsylvania* (1896); and, by the same author, *Pennsylvania; Colony and Commonwealth* (1897). On the vexing problem of quit-rents, see B. W. Bond, Jr., *The Quit Rent System in the American Colonies* (1919).

[3] Francis Vincent, *A History of the State of Delaware* (1870).

[47]

colony that would pre-empt for the English the territory in question, and would act as a buffer state against French or Spanish aggression. He had also a humanitarian desire to found a haven of refuge for the large number of Englishmen who, under the existing laws, would ordinarily be sent to prison because of inability to pay their debts. Many of these people, Oglethorpe believed, would prove to be ideal colonists. Apparently, too, he and his associates hoped that the colony might furnish a similar retreat for persecuted Protestants from continental Europe.

Governments by proprietors were by this time out of favor in England, but the advantages of founding such a colony as Oglethorpe planned were so appealing that in 1732 a group of trustees, of whom *Georgia* Oglethorpe was the most active, secured from George II title to the land lying between the Savannah and Altamaha Rivers, and westward from their headwaters to the Pacific. The grant, however, was subject to unusual limitations. The trustees, as individuals, were expressly forbidden to acquire any lands in the colony, or to make any profits from their connection with it, and at the end of twenty-one years their governmental privileges were to revert to the crown. In the meantime the officials they appointed, and the laws they made, had to receive the approval of the King.[1]

In January, 1733, Oglethorpe brought over about a hundred settlers and founded Savannah. Other immigrants soon came, Salzburgers, *Slow* Scotch Highlanders, Scotch-Irish, and Welsh, as well as *development* English. At first the terms on which land could be obtained were unusual. Not more than five hundred acres could be taken by any one person, and all such grants were entailed to male heirs. The proprietors also prohibited slavery, on the assumption that the near-by Spaniards might incite the slaves to revolt, and forbade the importation of rum. These provisions were extremely unpopular, and they checked somewhat the growth of the colony, although they were not long retained. English debtors were not sent to Georgia in as great numbers as Oglethorpe had hoped, and by 1760 the total population of the colony was not more than nine thousand. Of this number about one third were Negro slaves whose presence was demanded when the economic interests of Georgia began to approximate those of the other southern colonies.

Because the history of the English colonies in North America is ordinarily written as a prelude to the history of the United States, the attention of American historians has naturally centered upon the "continental colonies," and particularly upon the thirteen which event-

---

[1] V. W. Crane, *The Southern Frontier, 1670–1732* (1929); Henry Bruce, *Life of General Oglethorpe* (1890); J. R. McCain, *Georgia as a Proprietary Province* (1917).

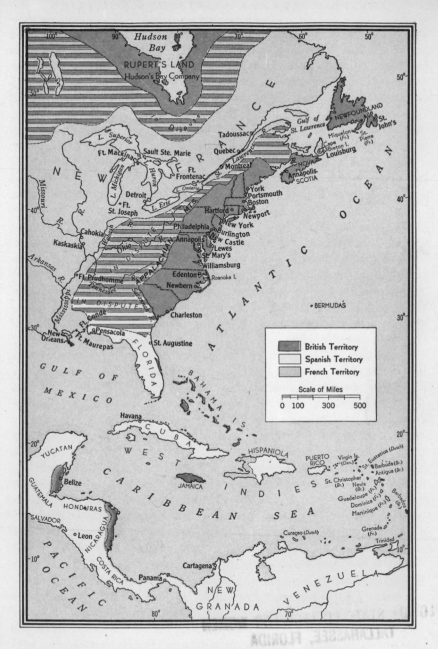

British Territory
Spanish Territory
French Territory

Scale of Miles

0   100   300   500

**EASTERN NORTH AMERICA AND THE CARIBBEAN
AFTER THE TREATY OF UTRECHT, 1713**

LIBRARY
FLORIDA STATE COLLEGE FOR WOMEN
TALLAHASSEE, FLORIDA

ually won their independence. But Englishmen of the seventeenth and eighteenth centuries, when they thought of the English settlements in America, included also the "island colonies," which seemed in many ways even more important than those on the mainland.[1]

Among the island colonies were the Bermudas, which at first were regarded as a part of Virginia. English interest in the Bermudas began in 1609, when a Virginia supply ship was wrecked on one of *The* the islands, and its commander, Sir George Somers, observed *Bermudas* their possibilities as a field of colonization. Somers, on returning to England, formed a company known as the Somers Islands Company, which in 1612 began to send out settlers, and in 1614 received a charter with full governmental rights. At this latter date the population of the colony was already about six hundred, and since tobacco growing soon proved to be even more profitable than in Virginia, other settlers came in rapidly. The rule of the company was never popular, even though representative government was early conceded, and in 1679 the Bermudas were taken over by the crown as a royal colony. By this time they possessed a population of about three thousand.

The British also had possessions in the West Indies, centering for the most part about St. Christopher, which was colonized in 1623, and Barbados, which was occupied in 1625. These two islands, *British West* together with others of the Lesser Antilles, were granted *Indies* to the Earl of Carlisle as proprietor in 1627. Tobacco-raising was at first the chief concern of the settlers, but presently the production of sugar-cane proved more profitable and became the leading industry. For nearly a hundred years Great Britain obtained most of her sugar from these islands, a circumstance that contributed immeasurably to their prosperity. By 1639, when the population of Virginia was only about seven thousand, there were twenty thousand people in Barbados alone. In 1661 the proprietor lost his rights, and ten years later the colony was divided, Barbados and the Windward Islands constituting one colony, and the rest, under the name of the Leeward Islands, another.

Jamaica was conquered by the British in 1655 during a war with Spain. Its possibilities as a "sugar island" had by no means been fully exploited under Spanish rule, but once the British assumed *Jamaica* control business-minded settlers flocked to the island. The sugar plantations were worked mainly by slave labor, and the importa-

[1] Howard Robinson, *The Development of the British Empire* (1922; revised and enlarged edition, 1936), gives an adequate account of the island as well as the continental colonies. On the later history of the island colonies see L. J. Ragatz, *The Fall of the Planter Class in the British Caribbean* (1928).

[49]

tion of Negroes went on so rapidly that soon the blacks outnumbered the whites many times over. Slave insurrections were common until well into the eighteenth century, and sometimes interfered considerably with the prosperity of the island. The government of Jamaica was such as existed in any royal colony, and the constitutional problems that arose were not unlike those which led the colonies on the mainland to revolt.

These island colonies contributed far more to the economic prosperity of the British Empire than did the continental colonies. They offered extraordinary opportunities for the investment of British capital. Their constant demand for slaves helped along the British slave trade to a pleasing prosperity. Moreover, because they stood ready to exchange their sugar and molasses for foodstuffs and other supplies from the continental colonies, they played an important part in making the colonies on the mainland a success.

Less important were the feeble British outposts in the Bahamas, Guiana, and Honduras; but far to the north the stations of the famous *Other Eng-* Hudson's Bay Company, chartered in 1670, tapped another *lish outposts* important source of the fur trade. By the peace of Utrecht in 1713 the British acquired clear titles to the Hudson's Bay region, to Acadia, which they renamed Nova Scotia, and to the island of Newfoundland, but the interests of English fishermen in the waters adjacent to some of these regions dated as far back as the first half of the sixteenth century.

The British possessions in America were thus at the outset of the eighteenth century a far-flung empire, stretching from the northern coast of South America to the Arctic Circle. Meantime the British had acquired still other possessions in Asia, Africa, and elsewhere. A great variety of peoples, a wide diversity of economic interests, a hopeless expanse of geography confronted the British statesman who turned his attention to colonial affairs. It is not surprising that the task of integrating such an empire proved to be too great for eighteenth-century British statesmanship, and that the relatively homogeneous continental colonies of North America chose presently to work out their destiny apart from the rest.

CHAPTER IV

COLONIAL AMERICA

WHILE each of the thirteen colonies has an important separate history, parallel conditions often existed in several colonies, and sometimes in all the colonies. It is possible, therefore, to ignore colonial boundaries to some extent, and to treat the development of the colonies more or less collectively. Until recent years, particularly in textbooks, this method of treatment was rare, and the reader who wished to gain a knowledge of colonial America was compelled to follow through at least thirteen separate narratives.[1]

But it is quite impossible to overlook the fact that the colonies were divided into three or four well-defined sections. The British settlements in North America extended from a region of long winters and short summers to a region of short winters and long summers. They comprehended within their boundaries extensive areas of mountains and high hills, and other extensive areas of broad valleys and fertile plains. Moreover, there were differences in the types of settlers who came to possess the various parts of English America. The plantation area, which included Maryland and Virginia and the colonies to the south of them, came early to be recognized as a section apart. The colonies of New England, also, had an identity of characteristics that drew them together, and at the same time separated them from the rest. The Middle Colonies — New York, New Jersey, Pennsylvania — had much in common with the sections to the northeast and to the south of them, but were yet different. Finally to the west of the more thickly settled areas, with boundaries less clearly defined than the other sections, lay the frontier, a region in which new settlements were constantly being made, and in which the conditions of life were apt not to vary greatly even from north to south.[2]

Sectionalism in the colonies

[1] Compare, for example, R. G. Thwaites, *The Colonies* (1891), one of the volumes of the original *Epochs of American History*, edited by A. B. Hart, with M. W. Jernegan, *The American Colonies* (1929), which the publishers of the *Epochs* series now offer.

[2] A good historical atlas is indispensable to the study of American history. Unfortunately the best work of this kind, C. O. Paullin, *Atlas of the Historical Geography of the United States* (1932), is too expensive to be generally available. A good cheap atlas is A. B. Hart and H. E. Bolton, *American History Atlas* (1930).

[51]

LIBRARY
FLORIDA STATE COLLEGE FOR WOMEN
TALLAHASSEE, FLORIDA

The type of civilization which developed in the plantation area was due in considerable part to the existence there of a wide coastal plain,

The Plantation Area indented frequently with spacious bays, unnumbered harbors, and wide-mouthed navigable rivers. Near the banks of the rivers a rich alluvial soil made for successful agriculture, although a little distance in from the waterline the soil was not so good. Owing to the fact that the tides swept far up the rivers, the coastal plain was frequently spoken of as the Tidewater. At varying distances into the interior waterfalls blocked navigation, and the Falls Line — that is, an imaginary line drawn from north to south through these waterfalls — marked approximately the end of the Tidewater. Between the falls and the mountains lay a rough, hilly country, known as the Piedmont.

Tobacco became the staple crop in most of the tidewater area, although in the Carolinas rice and indigo were also important products.

Tobacco Experience proved that the easiest road to prosperity was to raise these crops, particularly tobacco, for an outside market. In exchange for them the planter could obtain from Europe the articles he desired to make life agreeable in the New World. Of necessity the plantation owner maintained lively commercial relations with the Old World, most especially with the mother country. The Virginians and their neighbors raised all the tobacco they could raise, loaded it at their own or near-by wharves for shipment usually to England, and in return brought in all the goods they could buy.

As it turned out, tobacco culture led naturally to the development of large plantations. With no thought of rotation of crops, it was soon discovered that however fertile the soil might be, the constant

Large plantations the rule growing of tobacco exhausted it.[1] More and more acres must therefore be acquired if the yield was to be kept up. It was observed, too, that if lands were allowed to lie fallow for a time, they could again be put in cultivation. This the large landowner could manage much more easily than the small landowner. Moreover, the fall in the price of tobacco that followed inexorably as the supply increased did its share to promote the expansion in size of the plantations. With the decline in the price of tobacco, the prosperous tobacco-raiser who had built himself a fine house and had established himself on a somewhat lavish scale of living found his income decidedly inadequate. The only way to make good this loss was to acquire more acres and raise more tobacco, and this he promptly did if he could. If he could not, he sold out

[1] A. O. Craven, *Soil Exhaustion as a Factor in the Agricultural History of Virginia and Maryland, 1606–1860* (1926).

LIBRARY
FLORIDA STATE COLLEGE FOR WOMEN
TALLAHASSEE, FLORIDA

to those who could afford to buy his land and possibly dropped into the small farmer class, where his disadvantages were numerous. The great planter could own his own wharf, from it ship tobacco to England, upon it receive goods in return. The small planter, on the other hand, had to use the great planter's wharf — substantially, he had to buy and sell through the great planter on whatever terms the latter chose to exact. Nor could the small planter compete with the great planter in the ownership of indentured servants and slaves. As the price of tobacco went down, the price of servants and slaves went up. Only the prosperous could afford to own them in sufficient numbers to make their possession profitable. The British rule of primogeniture in the inheritance of land, which was applied in Virginia and elsewhere, did much toward keeping together large estates, once they were created.

The successful southern planter was apt to have frontage on some winding stream such as the James, York, Rappahannock, or Potomac. If he were fortunate he might own a whole neck of land jut- *Plantation* ting out into the river. The size of the ordinary great plant- *life* er's holding was about three thousand acres, but many planters — for example William Byrd of Westover, Virginia, who bequeathed to his son an estate of twenty-six thousand acres — held more. The headquarters of each plantation made a little village. The planter and his family lived in a large and usually well-appointed house, near which were clustered the workhouses in which the cooking, weaving, carpenter work, blacksmithing, and so forth of the plantation were done. Still other houses served as dwellings for the servants and slaves, or furnished shelter to the livestock. In so far as it was possible each plantation was a self-sufficing economic unit. Most of the food consumed on the plantation was produced upon it, and much of the wearing apparel and other necessities also. Such articles as tools, which could not easily be manufactured locally, and luxuries — fine clothes for the master and his family, expensive wines, furniture, and even building materials — were imported in return for the tobacco shipped abroad. Once a year these exchanges were made, ships bringing from England the orders sent over by the planters the year previously, and taking back with them the annual salable output of the plantation. Nearly always the planter overestimated the value of his crop, and in consequence over-ordered. Debts to British merchants began therefore to accumulate almost everywhere in the plantation area, and on the eve of the Revolution the irritation that the existence of these debts aroused helped materially to sever the ties that had bound the colonies and the mother country together.

During the eighteenth century slavery came to play a more important rôle in the life of the southern plantation than had been the case in the *Slavery and servitude* seventeenth century.[1] Adequate numbers of indentured servants were hard to get, and with an inviting wilderness to the West were harder still to keep, whereas Negro slaves were fairly cheap and endured the work of the plantations with fair contentment. In the rice-growing regions of South Carolina, where the climatic conditions were bad and white laborers quickly succumbed, Negro laborers were able to survive and to make good profits for their masters. By the close of the colonial period there were about four hundred thousand Negro slaves in the colonies. Three fourths of this number lived in the South, where they constituted two fifths of the entire population. In South Carolina they outnumbered the white population two to one. In the early years slaves were treated with extreme harshness, even cruelty; but as time went on the relations between masters and slaves greatly improved.

The plantation system left little chance for the development of towns and cities in the South. Annapolis, Williamsburg, and Wilmington, the capitals respectively of Maryland, Virginia, and North Carolina, were hardly more than villages except when a legislature met, or a court convened. Norfolk and Baltimore attained some importance as ports, and Charleston became a thriving little city, but these were exceptional instances. The life of the South was decidedly rural rather than urban in character.[2]

In consequence, when it came to the establishment of local political units in the South the example offered by rural England rather than urban England was followed. In the plantation area the parish was the smallest political division. Its boundaries included the residences of all the communicants of the parish church. A vestry, in practice consisting of the more important planters, governed the local church, cared for the poor, levied taxes to obtain necessary funds, and looked after the affairs of the parish generally. In theory, members of the vestry were supposed to be chosen by the parishioners, but in fact the vestrymen themselves filled vacancies in their membership, and became thus a "close corporation." A county usually consisted of several parishes, although sometimes the boundaries of a county and a parish were coterminous. In each county from eight to twenty justices of the peace were appointed by the governor from among

Local government in the South

[1] This subject is well treated in P. A. Bruce, *The Colonial Period, 1607–1763* (*History of Virginia*, I, 1924).

[2] *The Pageant of America*, edited by R. H. Gabriel and others (15 vols., 1929), is a successful effort to produce a pictorial history of the United States. The first volume is devoted to the colonial period.

the planters, and these justices held county court, usually monthly, but not less than four times a year. At such times they administered justice, chose constables and highway surveyors for the various precincts, ordered the building of roads and bridges, and assessed taxes. Orders of the county court were executed by the sheriff and the county lieutenant, the latter being the commander of the local militia. These officers, as well as new justices of the peace, were appointed by the governor, but usually only on nomination of the county court. The county seat at which sessions of the court were held was often of hardly enough consequence to be spoken of as a village. Sometimes it was only a "court-house" at a county crossroads.[1]

Once in two years, ordinarily, the voters of the county assembled to choose members of the colonial legislature. In Virginia each county was entitled to two representatives in the House of Burgesses. Property tests for voting were universal, but they did not exclude the small farmer from the suffrage. The elections were boisterous affairs, and by way of electioneering the opposing candidates usually treated the voters liberally to liquor. While the small farmers probably outnumbered the great planters nine or ten to one, the representatives were almost invariably chosen from the great planter class.

In religion as in government the plantation area of the South was not unlike rural England, where the strength of the Established Church was always great. In every southern colony, from Maryland to *Religion* South Carolina, the Church of England was by law established, and its ministers were held to be as much entitled to their pay as any other officers of the state. They were appointed, sometimes by the governor, sometimes by the proprietor, and sometimes, as missionaries, by an English organization known as the Society for Propagating the Gospel in Foreign Parts. These ministers were usually good men who took their duties seriously, but an occasional rake appeared among them whose conduct was injurious to the reputation of the Episcopal clergy as a whole. Unfortunately there was no bishop of the English Church resident in America, and the Bishop of London, under whose spiritual guidance the American Church was placed, never visited America. In consequence matters of discipline were extremely difficult to handle; moreover, the only way Americans could enjoy the rites of ordination and confirmation was by either themselves or the bishop making a trip across the Atlantic. The lack of an American bishop was an unending source of complaint, and contributed its share toward the general

[1] C. M. Andrews, *Colonial Self-Government* (1904), and E. B. Greene, *Provincial America* (1905), cover well the development of colonial institutions.

discontent with British control that lay back of the Revolution.[1] Dissenters existed in every southern colony, and well before the end of the colonial period their practices, if not always officially licensed, were at least generally ignored. But the bulk of the population in the tidewater area remained loyal adherents of the Established Church.

Schools were a rarity in the South, and only the children of planters were adequately educated. Very frequently these children were taught *Education* at home by tutors, although "pay schools" were not unknown; then later, if the means were at hand, the boys were sent to England for further education. One of the leading colonial colleges, William and Mary, founded in 1693, was located in the South and was liberally supported by the ruling class. But even so important a center as Charleston lacked both colleges and public schools.

With virtually a monopoly on education, and "to the manner born," the great planters of the South, while actually a small minority in the population, played the principal rôle in southern history. They managed the affairs of their great estates with considerable ability, and they used the talents thus sharpened in discharging the political duties that fell to their lot. They were naturally averse to governmental interference in their private affairs, and were quick to resent injustices, especially when the source of trouble lay as far away as England. They fancied themselves extremely democratic because in reality the first families were very democratic among themselves, given to much visiting back and forth, and fond of showing hospitality. They possessed a charm of manner and a distinction of bearing that distinguished them clearly, even from the élite of the northern colonies. They took a paternalist interest in the affairs of the lower classes — the yeomen and the slaves — that was for the most part beneficial to all.

In New England, as in the South, physiographic conditions had much to do with shaping the course of development. The early settlers of New *New* England found the topography exceedingly irregular, with *England* high hills or mountains, rising in clusters rather than ranges, not far from the sea. In an earlier age the whole region had been glacier-swept, and the surface, even in the level places, was apt to be covered with boulders. The soil, where it could be found, was good, but required infinite patience and endurance to work. Rapidly flowing rivers plunged at frequent intervals into the sea, and waterfalls furnished the power that one day would turn factory wheels, but for the moment merely made penetration into the interior more difficult. Natural har-

[1] A. L. Cross, *The Anglican Episcopate and the American Colonies* (1902); E. L. Goodwin, *The Colonial Church in Virginia* (1927).

bors dotted the coast-line, and foretold commerce, while heavy forests were everywhere available to furnish naval stores, masts, spars, and timbers for the builders of ships. The inhabitants of this "stern and rock-bound coast" were a fairly homogeneous group. Probably ninety-five per cent of the emigrants to colonial New England had come from England, and furthermore, in spite of their distinguished middle-class leaders, most of them had come from little peasant villages where they had worked as artisans or from which they had gone out each day to till their land. If they were not always Puritans on coming to America, as a rule they or their children soon fell in with the dominant religious faith.

Emigration to New England proceeded usually in groups. A congregation, led by its minister and financed by some wealthy Puritan, would come to America as a unit, establish a new town, sometimes *Group* named after the town in England from which the group had *migration* come, and continue to live thereafter in much the same fashion as in old England. This procedure was closely approximated, also, in the extension of the coast settlements into the interior. Actuated perhaps by some minor religious difference, and interested at the same time in seeking out new economic opportunities, a large number of families would put out together to found another town or another site. In the formative period New-Englanders showed little disposition to settle as individuals upon separate farms. Long-established custom, aided by the great desirability of having a church easily accessible and the necessity of protecting themselves against hostile Indians, kept the settlers together in villages. The New England town thus came to be the social and economic unit around which all New England life tended to center.

Furthermore, the town was also a natural, almost inevitable, political unit, and, as it turned out, a self-governing unit. The practice among the Puritans with respect to church government was to al- *The New* low to each congregation the complete right to choose its *England* minister, its deacons and elders, its tithing men. Even with *town* respect to matters of doctrine the decision of the congregation was final. In the government of the town, these same ideas of democracy prevailed. All matters of importance related to local government were at first brought before the town meeting, to which usually all the church members, or perhaps even all the citizens, were entitled to come. The levying of taxes, the distribution of land, the establishment of schools, the passing of local ordinances of government, all were brought before this meeting. Between meetings "selectmen," duly elected for the purpose, carried on the government, and as time went on the unwieldy nature of the town meeting made it necessary to hand over to this smaller group many of the duties first performed by the meeting itself. The town was also the unit from which members were chosen to the lower house of the colonial legislature, and for this purpose, ordinarily once each year, the voters convened.[1]

Agriculture was a necessity in colonial New England, for the people had to live. Fields were cleared of timber and of stones, the latter being *Agriculture* used extensively for the construction of stone walls to serve as fences, and crops of many sorts were planted. Individual land holdings were early introduced, and generally each farmer tilled his own land. Labor was scarce, for virtually anyone might acquire land of his own, hence the holdings, in contrast to the southern plantations, tended to be no larger than one man and his family could work. Lacking money with which to buy, farmers fell back upon their own ingenuity, and fashioned for themselves the tools they used, the shoes they and their families wore, the furniture that they needed, the very houses in which they lived. The women spun wool or flax into threads, wove cloth, and made the clothes that the family wore. Habits of thrift and frugality were established which persisted down through many generations.

Agriculture was supplemented by fishing and commerce. The New England coasts were themselves rich in fish, and the banks of New-*Fishing and* foundland, which had long been famed as fishing grounds, *commerce* were not far away. Fishing led directly to commerce, for far more fish could be taken than could be consumed locally. According to reliable estimates not less than three hundred thousand cod were exported by New England fishermen in 1641, and by the year 1675 no less than six hundred vessels and four thousand men were engaged in the cod fisheries alone. New England fishermen found ready markets for their wares in the West Indies and in the Catholic countries of Europe.

Commerce, once opened up, diversified rapidly. Foodstuffs of various kinds were carried to the West Indies, not only from New England, *The West* but also from ports farther down the coast where the Yan-*Indian trade* kee traders stopped to complete their cargoes. In return for these commodities molasses, sugar, ginger, and other insular products were obtained, and in addition bills of exchange which could be used in the purchase of manufactured articles in England. At first the West Indian trade was confined mainly to the British islands, but by the eighteenth century trade with the Dutch, French, and Spanish islands was

---

[1] Anne B. MacLear, *Early New England Towns* (1908); Melville Egleston, *The Land System of the New England Colonies* (1880).

A NEW ENGLAND CHURCH

also common.   From these sources came a good share of the money that found its way to the colonies.   In 1697 the slave trade, which had for some time before been monopolized by a few English trading companies, was opened to all British subjects, and an interesting "triangular trade" developed.   Molasses, brought from the West Indies to New England, was manufactured into rum, which was shipped to the African coast, where it was used in the purchase of slaves.   The slaves were then brought to the West Indies and there exchanged for more molasses, which was then brought back to New England to make more rum, to acquire more slaves, to exchange for more molasses, and so on.   Not all of the rum, however, was exported.   The New England fishermen themselves used it liberally, and other New-Englanders, even some of the very "elect," developed a keen taste for it.   Rum was useful also in the prosecution of the fur trade, which furnished yet another item for export.[1]

Shipbuilding went hand in hand with fishing and commerce.   Skillful craftsmen early contrived to build fleet and sturdy ships which not *Shipbuilding* only withstood well the battering of the elements, but frequently outran revenue vessels, and made an art of smuggling.   Especially was this the case after the British began to collect duties under the Navigation Acts.   Indeed, on the eve of the American Revolution smuggling became an industry in itself, comparable in some ways to the bootlegging industry of the Prohibition era.   Timbers for shipbuilding were obtained in plenty from the easily accessible forests, and such items as barrel-staves, clapboards, and naval stores were early added to the list of exportable commodities.   Yankee ships and Yankee seamen came to be seen and known all over the world, while the superiority of Yankee seamanship and the shrewdness of Yankee salesmen also received general recognition.   Many New England merchants, the owners of ships and dealers in foreign wares, made comfortable fortunes; and the active business life that centered in the principal posts caused the villages so located to grow into sizeable cities.   Before the Revolution, Boston, with less than thirty thousand inhabitants, was the largest city in New England and the second largest in America, but many other towns, such as Salem, Newport, and New Haven, had passed well out of the village class.

Religion played a far greater part in the life of New England than in the life of the plantation South, and the theology of Calvin made a profound impression upon the New England character.   The *Calvinism* cardinal doctrine of Calvinism was predestination. As Calvin conceived it, God had created man in his own likeness and image,

[1] S. E. Forman. *The Rise of American Commerce and Industry* (1927).

and had given him all the blessings of life in the Garden of Eden on condition that he must never eat of the fruit of a certain tree. But man, tempted by woman, broke the contract thus implied, and thereby lost not only all title to the joys of Eden, but also all hope of happiness in the world to come. Nor did the punishment stop here, for not only the original parents but also their children, and their descendants forever, being conceived in iniquity and born with the taint of original sin upon them, were in justice outside the pale of God's forgiveness. But God, in his infinite mercy, sent his Son into the world to suffer in the place of those who had been chosen to be saved. By the sacrifice of Christ on the Cross all those whom God had predestined and foreordained to be saved were freed of the punishment that rightfully should have fallen upon them. Only such persons as God had "elected" to be saved, however, could benefit from the sacrifice of the Son. All the rest of mankind, including even unborn infants, were "elected" to be damned.

This hard doctrine, morbidly dwelt upon by the long-winded Puritan divines, was driven deeply into the marrow of the thoughtful New-Englander. Was he of the elect whom God had chosen to be saved? One might never know, and yet the behavior of a man should show to some degree at least whether or not he had been deemed by God worthy to be saved. Those who were religiously inclined watched their conduct and searched their souls for evidences of the divine will towards them. They displayed also a not unnatural interest in the spiritual welfare of their neighbors. Who of those they knew were to be saved, who were to be damned? Village life with its intimate associations gave ample opportunity for observation to those who wished to scrutinize closely the details of their neighbor's lives. The injunction to be one's brother's keeper was cheerfully obeyed, and buttresses against temptation were erected in the shape of "blue laws" that regulated closely the behavior of the individual. Church attendance in some of the New England colonies was long required by law, and on Sundays, according to one chronicle, "no one ... could make mince pies, dance, play cards, or play any instrument of music, except the drum, trumpet, and Jew's harp." [1]

The "New England conscience" that was born of these austere doctrines and practices endured long after some of the Calvinistic tenets that produced it had lost their binding force. Scrupulous observance

[1] J. T. Adams, *Revolutionary New England* (1923), continues the anti-Puritan bias of his *Founding of New England*, and should be tempered by comparison with the more orthodox K. B. Murdock, *Increase Mather, the Foremost American Puritan* (1926). In lighter vein is Alice Morse Earle, *The Sabbath in Puritan New England* (1891). The witchcraft delusion that overtook Puritan New England late in the seventeenth century has been much overemphasized, although, before the frenzy was over, nearly a score of victims had lost their lives.

of the moral law, rigid self-control carried even to the length of self-denial, earnestness of purpose, and firm belief in the righteousness of *The New England conscience* God's way with man set the conscientious New-Englander somewhat apart from other Americans. His conscience was apt to carry over into business and politics, both of which he took with great seriousness. In these realms, however, the contract idea, so firmly embedded in Calvinistic theology, was not without its helpful side. A bargain was a bargain, and a contract once signed had to be obeyed. It behooved the maker of business contracts to watch carefully the terms laid down, and mercy was not always vouchsafed to the careless. Governmental charters and constitutions were likewise held to be sacred covenants, and the principals, whether kings, lords, or commoners, might justly be held to the last letter of their plighted word. Nor was the law of the land, duly made and recorded, to be lightly ignored.

Education was taken much more seriously in New England than elsewhere in the colonies. This was due in part to the religious interest *Education* which made it seem worth while for every individual to be able to search the Scriptures on his own account, and in part to the existence of towns where schools and the means of education could be easily maintained. Five years after Boston was founded, it had a school, and in 1642 the General Court of Massachusetts passed a law requiring that all parents should see that their children learned how to read and how to ply some trade. Another Massachusetts law, passed in 1647, proposed the establishment of free public schools throughout the colony, an ideal that was not soon attained. But schools of one kind or another, sometimes private and sometimes public, were the rule rather than the exception throughout New England. The common schools taught reading, writing, and arithmetic; Latin or grammar schools prepared boys for college; and academies, which admitted both boys and girls, offered a somewhat wider course of study. Religion received much attention in all the schools. Pupils were taught the catechism at an early age, they read selections from the Bible as exercises in reading, and such textbooks as came into use were strongly impregnated with the Scriptures and Calvinistic theology. Discipline was extremely severe, and any wanton tendencies toward self-expression on the part of the pupils were promptly and thoroughly suppressed. Colleges, designed primarily for the purpose of training ministers, presently put in their appearance. Harvard College was founded in 1636, Yale in 1701, Brown in 1764, and Dartmouth in 1769.[1]

---

[1] Edward Eggleston, *The Transit of Civilization from England to America in the Seventeenth Century* (1901), is extremely suggestive. See also Alice Morse Earle, *Child Life in*

New-Englanders believed genuinely in their own ways, and carried them along wherever they went. Into New York, New Jersey, Maryland, and other neighboring colonies streamed New England emigrants carrying with them the New England conscience and the institutions New-Englanders held dear. *New England propagandism* Indeed, in the settlement of the whole of the American West, New-Englanders were invariably present to reproduce as best they could in their new homes the civilization they had left.[1] The typical New-Englander was exceedingly intolerant of customs that diverged to any great extent from his own. Advocates of innovations were apt to be frowned upon heavily, although in eighteenth-century New England the narrowness in religious matters that had been so characteristic of the formative period was much less in evidence. Even Episcopalians and Catholics were treated with consideration, and many such communicants were to be found, particularly Episcopalians, in all the urban centers.

The Middle Colonies rested upon a geographic foundation that combined the chief characteristics of New England and the South. Here there was a coastal plain and a piedmont, but the plain was *The Middle Colonies* narrower than in the plantation area, and the piedmont was wider. Toward New England, in New York, the mountains were in great glacial-ground clusters, but toward the South, in Pennsylvania, the long parallel ridges of the Alleghanies began to rise. The rivers of the central area were fewer in number, comparatively, than in the other sections, but they were longer and furnished more convenient highways into the interior than could be found elsewhere along the Atlantic seaboard. Indeed, three great river systems, the Hudson, the Delaware, and the Susquehanna, furnished the chief key to the development of the region. Each of these rivers flowed, generally speaking, from north to south, each was entered through a spacious harbor, and each was navigable even by ocean-going vessels for a considerable distance into the interior. In each river valley a distinctive civilization developed, and in due time a great city marked the point where each river reached the sea. New York commanded the trade of the Hudson Valley, Philadelphia of the Delaware, and Baltimore of the Susquehanna. Even in colonial times the spirit of rivalry between these growing towns was much in evidence.

The Dutch influence left a lasting impression upon the people of the Hudson Valley. The hopes of those who invented the patroon system were never fully realized, but the pretensions of the system did tend to

---

Colonial Days (1899). On the early history of Harvard, S. E. Morison, *The Founding of Harvard College* (1935), is the definitive work.
[1] Lois Kimball Mathews [Rosenberry], *The Expansion of New England* (1909).

mark off from the other elements of society an aristocratic caste of great *Dutch* landowners. One patroonship, Rensselaerswyck, which *influence* was founded near Albany by Kiliaen van Rensselaer and came to embrace many thousands of acres, worked out much as the original plans had contemplated; and a number of other estates, while by no means so closely approximating the feudal pattern, at least reached large dimensions. On some of the great estates of the lower Hudson tobacco was raised much as in Virginia. In a country where free land was so plentiful, however, and where even in the days of Dutch control emigrants were practically given all the land they could improve, it was difficult to maintain a tenant class. The great estates might exist, but many of their acres remained unworked. Nevertheless their owners came to constitute a distinguished upper class of "Vans" and "velts," who, in spite of being overwhelmingly outnumbered by small free farmers, exerted a preponderant influence in the affairs of the colony.

Dutch governmental practices also left some traces upon the subsequent English colony of New York. During the period of Dutch control *Absence of* very little was permitted the colonists by way of a voice in *democracy* their government. New England emigrants protested vigorously against being thus deprived of rights to which they had long been accustomed, and on the eve of the British conquest Peter Stuyvesant, the Dutch governor, actually called together a representative assembly, which failed, however, to reach any important agreements. Thus, except for a limited amount of local self-government permitted in the Dutch villages, the English conquest found the colony wholly lacking in democratic political institutions. After the conquest, with the colony now under the rule of the reactionary Duke of York (later King James II), the introduction of democracy was still delayed. Richard Nicolls, the first British governor, was an astute diplomatist, and managed to keep discontent with such a system at a minimum, but his successor, Edmund Andros, had little such skill.

In 1683 the proprietor felt obliged to yield to the pressure for a representative assembly, but the Assembly adopted a charter of Liberties and Privileges which nettled him, and when he became king a year later he went back on his bargain. New-Yorkers ultimately won the right to participate in the control of their colony, although only a privileged few were granted the right to vote, and the government of the colony was distinctly less democratic than that of any other. New York politics, down to the American Revolution, tended to be little more than a series of factional fights among the important families to see whose influence would be strongest.

With respect to religion some Dutch survivals may also be noted. The Dutch adhered generally to the Dutch Reformed Church, which was as definitely Calvinistic in its teachings as even the *Religion in* Puritan congregations of New England could have asked. *New York* The Dutch, however, fed their souls less upon the doctrine of predestination than did the Puritans, and they were a little more content to rely upon God's abounding grace. With them religion played no such dominant rôle as in New England. Religious toleration, moreover, was a Dutch tradition, and the emigrant who came to New Netherland was rarely bothered about his faith. Peter Stuyvesant made some trouble for the Quakers, he once expelled a Baptist minister from the colony, and perhaps he discriminated unfairly against the Lutherans, but these acts were not so much an expression of Dutch policy as an expression of the personal predilections of Peter Stuyvesant. When New Netherland became New York, the Church of England supplanted the Dutch Reformed Church as the official church of the colony. But the number of Anglican communicants remained small for a long time, whereas, besides the members of the Dutch Reformed Church, there were on Long Island and elsewhere many Puritans from New England. Inasmuch as the proprietor, the Duke of York, was known to be a Catholic, it seemed expedient to carry over the Dutch spirit of toleration into the new régime, and this was done, although later some harsh anti-Catholic legislation was enacted.[1]

The Delaware Valley became the seat of a civilization quite as distinctive as was to be found along the Hudson, for it was here that the Quaker influence was preponderant. But democracy was inherent *Quakers on* in the Quaker teaching. Quakers believed that God spoke *the Delaware* to men directly by a voice that reached their hearts, and this "inner light" was denied to no man or woman. Since anyone might thus be in direct contact with the divine will, there was no room for ministers, or bishops, or ecclesiastical foundations. Even the Bible as a guide of faith and conduct suffered somewhat, for the "inner light" furnished quite as convincing an authority. All men were equal before God, so why should there be the distinctions in dress and manners that marked the aristocracy apart from the common run of men? Good Quakers called no man master, and used simply the word "Friend" by way of address. They objected to the use of the formal "you" when speaking to an individual, and employed instead the democratic "thee." They kept their hats on their heads even in the presence of kings, and they wore

[1] S. H. Cobb, *The Rise of Religious Liberty in America* (1902); W. W. Sweet, *The Story of Religions in America* (1930).

a plain, standardized garb that was designed to deny all social distinctions. Since the "inner light" came to women as well as to men, women were accorded the same privileges, at least in a religious way, that men enjoyed. Women spoke their minds freely "in meeting," notwithstanding the injunction of Saint Paul to "let the women keep silence in the church." Slavery the Quakers deeply deplored.

Faith in such democratic principles as these could not but affect markedly the development of the Quaker colonies. Their tolerance of many *Religious* varieties of religion, their unwillingness to propagandize in *toleration* the Puritan fashion, and their generous land terms attracted great numbers of settlers. The valley of the Susquehanna, however, quite as much as the Delaware, was to profit from these inviting practices. To the Susquehanna came a mixed population, including many colonials from other regions, but in far greater numbers emigrants from Europe, in particular the so-called "Pennsylvania Dutch" and the Scotch-Irish.

The "Pennsylvania Dutch" were not Dutch at all, but Germans who had left their homes for many good reasons. For one thing, the wars *The "Penn-* that Louis XIV of France prosecuted in his attempt to at- *sylvania* tain for his country its "natural boundaries" not only drew *Dutch"* the adjacent German states into the struggles, but made of them a periodic battle-field. For emigrants from this region, who sought relief from the brutalities of war, the Quaker doctrine of pacifism had a peculiar charm. Economic pressure furnished another motive. Petty feudal lords exacted heavy dues, required annoying services, and collected burdensome tithes for the support of state churches. Even in German Switzerland, where the ravages of war seldom touched, such exactions as these made many of the lower classes look with favor upon emigration to America. Religious persecution also played a part, for each prince of the Holy Roman Empire was left free to determine as he might choose the religious faith of his people — *cuius regio eius religio.* Catholics were in consequence subject to persecution in Lutheran states; Lutherans in Catholic states; and the minor religious sects, which came to have a great vogue in Germany, in all the states. Particularly oppressed were the sects, such as the Mennonites, who objected to military service. Penn's agents advertised persistently the advantages of America among the distressed Germans, and in 1709 the British Parliament, glad enough of the opportunity to stimulate outside immigration into the British Empire, passed a law for the naturalization of foreign Protestants.

Some German immigration reached the colonies late in the seventeenth century — Germantown, Pennsylvania, was founded in 1683 — but the great bulk of the German invasion came toward the middle *German* of the eighteenth century. A few settled at Newbern, *settlements* North Carolina; others settled in New York, acquiring lands as far inland as the Mohawk Valley; New Jersey, Maryland, and Virginia each were chosen by a few; but the main stream of German immigrants found their way to Pennsylvania, where they picked for themselves choice lands usually well up the valley of the Susquehanna, for the English colonists already had the Delaware. They came in such numbers that the provincials began to be alarmed, and the Pennsylvania legislature even passed laws restricting immigration. But these laws were invariably vetoed by the governors, and the Germans continued to come. It is estimated that, at the time the American Revolution broke out, about one third of the inhabitants of Pennsylvania were German. Living together as they did, they retained their own language, established their own schools, printing presses, and newspapers, and continued for many years to be a race apart. Indeed, many of their descendants in central Pennsylvania still speak and write a patois known as "Pennsylvania Dutch." [1]

The Pennsylvania Germans were not the only immigrants from Europe to enter the Susquehanna Valley, for they were soon followed by the Scotch-Irish, with somewhat similar reasons for migration. *The Scotch-* These Scotch-Irish newcomers were from the north of Ire- *Irish* land, but they were really not Irish at all. Their ancestors had been Scotch lowlanders, some of whom had been colonized on lands taken from the Irish during the reigns of Queen Elizabeth and King James I, and others on the Irish lands confiscated by Oliver Cromwell during the Protectorate. The Scotch-Irish troubles in Ireland were numerous. They could not get on well with the native Irish to whom they seemed to be mere trespassers. Also, being Presbyterians of the most unbending variety, they scorned the Catholicism of their Irish neighbors, who in turn had little pleasant to say about Scotch Presbyterianism. As dissenters, they resented stoutly the legal requirement that they pay tithes to the Anglican Church. They suffered also many economic grievances. The tenant system was peculiarly harsh upon them, since most of their landlords were absentees, and were not only unconcerned about the oppressive rentals, but were also often unaware of the still

---

[1] A. B. Faust, *The German Element in the United States* (2 vols., 1909), is scholarly and comprehensive. Less formidable are Lucy Bittinger, *The Germans in Colonial Times* (1901), and J. L. Rosenberger, *The Pennsylvania Germans* (1923). Attention is called to the significance of immigration in American history by A. M. Schlesinger, *New Viewpoints in American History* (1922).

more oppressive methods of collecting them. The English government, moreover, in its efforts to protect the interests of English citizens, passed laws against the importation of important Irish products, such as dairy cattle and woolen goods, and placed discouraging regulations upon the production of linen. Bad harvests and frequent famines added to the Irish discontent.

As was the case with the Pennsylvania Germans, some Scotch-Irish colonists reached America before seventeen hundred, but the great *Scotch-Irish* majority did not arrive until towards the middle of the next *settlements* century. Some of the Scotch-Irish settled in New England, New York, and New Jersey, but most of them penetrated into the back country of Pennsylvania by way of the Susquehanna and its tributaries. Coming a little later than the Germans, the Scotch-Irish went a little farther into the interior to find lands. They spoke English, and hence were not bothered in their relations with the native Americans by the language barrier that so often perplexed the Germans, but they were harder to deal with than the Germans. When some of them were accused of holding lands without legal title they replied that it was "against the laws of God and Nature, that so much land should be idle while so many Christians wanted it to labor on." There were fully as many Scotch-Irish as German emigrants to America, and probably more. At the time the American Revolution broke out, Pennsylvania was no less than one third Scotch-Irish.[1]

Diversity of population elements was thus an important characteristic of the Middle Colonies. In addition to the Hudson Valley Dutch, *Other* the English Quakers, the Pennsylvania Germans, and the *nationalities* Scotch-Irish, although in no such numbers, there were here French Huguenots, Irish from the south of Ireland, Scotch from Scotland, a few Welshmen, and a few Jews. The Jews were most numerous in New York, whither they had come from South America, Holland, Germany, and Poland during the Dutch occupation.[2] Coupled with variety in population elements was a variety of religious denominations. The Middle Colonies were thus a hodgepodge of races and creeds, and a natural hotbed for factional politics. It should occasion no surprise that this region gave rise to a group of astute politicians, quick to compromise and ready to shift their ground as each new emergency appeared.

Local government in the Middle Colonies borrowed a little from the New England colonies and a little from the colonies to the south. Coun-

---

[1] C. A. Hanna, *The Scotch-Irish* (1902); H. J. Ford, *The Scotch-Irish in America* (1915).

[2] S. P. Orth, *Our Foreigners* (1920), covers sketchily the various immigrant elements that went into the making of the original "American stock."

ties appeared after the fashion of the plantation area, but they were usually subdivided into townships that were reminiscent of *Local* New England. In New York the influence of New England *government* was more marked than elsewhere in the Middle Colonies, but well before the end of the seventeenth century a county board of supervisors, composed of representatives from the various towns, had absorbed many of the important functions of local administration. In Pennsylvania the townships were even less important than in New York. The combination of town and county government in the Middle Colonies proved to be of greater than local significance, for it was this example that most of the states of the West were to follow later on.

Public schools existed in the Middle Colonies from an early date, but the chief responsibility for educational establishments was here generally left with the various religious denominations. Colleges *Education* were relatively numerous by the time of the Revolution. The Anglicans founded Kings' College (later Columbia) in New York under a charter obtained in 1754; the Presbyterians established the College of New Jersey at Princeton as early as 1747; and Rutgers, opened in 1766, ministered to the educational needs of the Dutch Reformed faith. Benjamin Franklin led the way for the opening at Philadelphia in 1751 of an "Academy," free from sectarian influences, which later (1791) became the University of Pennsylvania.

Farming furnished occupations to most of the inhabitants of the Middle Colonies, where the production and exportation of foodstuffs gave rise to the name of "bread colonies." Indian corn, or maize, *The "bread* and other grains, livestock, particularly among the Ger- *colonies"* mans who understood the necessity of caring for domestic animals in winter, and vegetables, most of which were native to America and did not need to be acclimated, were produced in ever-increasing quantities. Nuts, fruits, and berries were abundant, and required little or no cultivation. Hemp and flax were also grown.

Manufacturing quickly sprang up, especially in Pennsylvania and New Jersey after the coming of the Germans, among whom there were many skilled workmen.[1] Iron, textiles, glass, and paper were *Manufac-* among the articles commonly made in these regions. Ac- *turing* cording to one observer, the inhabitants of Germantown were mostly manufacturers who were able to "make everything in such quantity and perfection, that, in a short time, this province will lack very little from England, its mother country." Weavers, tanners, metal workers, and printers plied their respective trades with good success. Sawmills fur-

[1] R. M. Tryon, *Household Manufactures in the United States, 1640–1860* (1917).

nished excellent lumber for building purposes, but good bricks were also made and in Philadelphia and New York brick houses abounded. Mills were numerous, and the flour they produced was as good as could be made anywhere in the world.

In commerce the Middle Colonies were not far behind New England, and the merchants of Philadelphia and New York prospered no less than

Commerce

those of Boston. Philadelphia, indeed, toward the close of the colonial period came to rival Boston in size. Grain, flour, and other provisions were exported in great profusion, mostly to the West Indies. New York by the middle of the eighteenth century numbered among its items of export no less than eighty thousand barrels of flour a year. Here the fur trade, which had been greatly fostered by the Dutch during their control of New Amsterdam, continued under the English as an important industry and an incentive to commerce. Shipbuilding was a natural accompaniment of overseas trade.

Interior from the seacoast, cutting across the boundaries of every other section and of most of the colonies, lay the colonial "West" — the front-

The frontier

ier.[1] Its limits were necessarily shifting; indeed, at some time every settled area in America had been frontier. But by the end of the colonial period the "back country," as the western settlements were then generally called, could be marked off fairly distinctly from the rest. In the South the piedmont and mountain valleys, in the Middle Colonies the upper reaches of the Susquehanna, the Delaware, the Mohawk, and their tributaries, in New England much of what is now Vermont, and except for settlements near the coast, of New Hampshire and Maine also, belonged to the frontier. Fur-traders, who almost invariably led the English advance upon the West, cattle-growers, who especially in the South were attracted by the free grazing lands of the interior, and soldiers, who in one or another of the wars against the Indians had seen the western country, revealed the possibilities of the regions they had visited, and presently settlement followed.

Various conditions worked together to promote the rapid expansion of the frontier. Colonial families were large, and the natural increase in

Why people went West

population provided many pioneers. The exhaustion of the eastern lands by poor methods of farming, particularly in the tobacco-growing areas, provided others. Still others came from the ranks of the indentured servants, who, once they were free, did not often linger long near the scene of their servitude. Frequently dissenters from the locally approved or established churches of their communities sought

[1] F. L. Paxson, *A History of the American Frontier, 1763–1893* (1924), traces chronologically the successive American frontiers.

homes in the West where they would not be looked down upon because of their religious faith. Immigrants from the Old World, who found themselves unpopular when they tried to settle in the older American communities, turned quickly to the more hospitable frontier. To all who would listen, the call of cheap western lands had an inviting sound. Speculators there were in plenty who acquired for almost nothing great holdings in the West and searched eagerly for settlers to whom they might sell them. But so abundant was the land that those who were too poor or were not too particular need pay little attention to the acquisition of land titles.

The conditions of life along the frontier were hard. Practically all the lands were heavily timbered, and the "clearings" upon which crops could be planted were made possible only through infinite *Frontier* labor. Luxuries were unknown. The pioneer had no *conditions of life* money with which to buy them, but even if he had, the difficulty of transporting goods from east to west held down such trade to the barest necessities. Along the "cutting edge" of the frontier, Indians were ever in evidence, and almost never wholly peaceful. Here pioneer families were accustomed to select some well-located farmhouse for a "station," and to build about it a stockade, duly equipped with shelters and storehouses, to which they could flee when an Indian attack seemed imminent. All good frontiersmen were adept with the axe and the rifle. With the former they cut the trees, fashioned the logs of which they built their houses, and smoothed down the planks from which they made benches, tables, and other household necessities. With their rifles they not only fought off the Indians, but also kept the family larder filled, and provided the skins from which many of their garments were made. Each pioneer cabin was apt to be on the farm that the pioneer owned, or hoped to own, and at a considerable distance from any other dwelling. Pioneer life was therefore lonely, particularly for the pioneer housewife, and the opportunities for such privileges as churches and schools were decidedly limited.[1]

The society which was thus established in the back country differed markedly from that to be found in the older and more settled areas along the coast. For one thing, it was extremely cosmopolitan in *Differences* character. Here English emigrants from the colonial East *between* met Pennsylvania Germans, Scotch-Irish, and a variety of *frontier and coast* other foreigners, and not merely met them, but mingled freely with them. The frontier thus became a great "melting-pot"

[1] Archibald Henderson, *Conquest of the Old Southwest, 1740-1800* (1920); Constance Lindsay Skinner, *Pioneers of the Old Southwest* (1921).

out of which a new and distinctively American race was to come. Furthermore, the frontier settlements, cutting across colonial lines as they did, tended to break down local peculiarities and to lay the foundations of a truly national point of view. Geographic considerations greatly favored this process, for the mountain valleys from Pennsylvania down lay parallel to the coast, and access to them was difficult except at favored points. In North Carolina not only mountains, but eighty miles of pine barrens also, separated the frontier outposts from the settled areas. Population entered the mountains mainly from Pennsylvania, and, spreading slowly southward, presented everywhere the same characteristics, often in striking contrast with the institutions and the traditions that bound the colonists who lived closer in toward the coast.

The genuine equality of conditions that existed among the frontiersmen bred a vigorous spirit of democracy. One man could not by the very nature of pioneer life be particularly above his neighbors. *Frontier democracy* He owned about the same amount of land, lived in the same kind of house, worked with the same primitive tools, dressed in the same crude fashion as his fellows. If he possessed education it was not important in the West. If he had illustrious ancestors he might as well forget them, for his neighbors surely would. If on the other hand his ancestors were unpleasant to remember, or if he himself had a past, those were things, too, that could easily be put out of mind.

This emphasis upon democracy in the West was paralleled by an equally marked emphasis upon individual freedom. Each pioneer was *Individual-ism* practically a law unto himself, and he came to set high store by the privilege which the wilderness gave him of managing his own affairs in any way he chose. The interference by government in anything that seemed to him his own business was apt to be met by wrathful opposition. He objected to hampering regulations with regard to the acquisition of land, and he resented bitterly every attempt to impose upon him a religious establishment to which he did not subscribe. The Scotch-Irish, so many of whom found their way to the West, added a contentious note to frontier individualism. They or their ancestors had argued as well as fought for their rights both in Scotland and in Ireland, and the habit of mind so developed was not lost by migration to America.

The contrasts between the people of the back country and the people of the coast led inevitably to some antagonisms.[1] Men of the East still

[1] An early example of antagonism between the frontier and the coast is "Bacon's Rebellion" (1676) in Virginia, which was instigated by the indifference of the eastern-controlled colonial legislature to the Indian problem of the back country. On Virginia biography see P. A. Bruce, *The Virginia Plutarch* (2 vols., 1929).

valued class distinctions and were careful to safeguard the rights of property. Men of the West had foresworn aristocracy, and to them the rights of the debtor were no less a matter of concern than the rights of the creditor. The strong foreign infusion in the western blood was another source of difficulty. *Antagonism between back country and coast*
The older elements of society feared that the institutions they held dear would not be safe in the hands of such people. The Westerners, on the other hand, saw little significance in racial differences, and resented the suspicions of the East. Differences of opinion developed also on such matters as religious freedom, the right to hold slaves, the assessment of taxes, the control of the Indians. Skeptical of the political wisdom of the backwoodsmen, colonial legislatures under eastern control rarely accorded to the frontier counties their proportionate share of representatives. The echoes of these conflicts could sometimes be heard as the American Revolution ran its course.

The lives which American colonials lived seem slow and humdrum in comparison with the lives of Americans today.[1] Transportation was difficult. The colonies were at least six weeks from Europe, and often, with contrary winds, the passage was longer. The coast towns communicated with one another most easily by sea; indeed, the Atlantic Ocean and the navigable rivers which emptied into it furnished perhaps the strongest of the ties that bound the colonies together. Even so, coastwise travel was far from speedy and sometimes it was far from safe. Roads existed between the principal cities, but elsewhere they were rare, and usually they were incredibly bad. Not a single hard-surfaced turnpike could be found anywhere in the colonies. By the middle of the eighteenth century horse-drawn carriages and stage-coaches were in common use, although travel by horseback was still very popular. At convenient distances taverns and inns of a sort could be found where the travelers found lodging and where local patrons found diversion. These inns were in a sense the social clubs of the time. Here, often amidst much drinking and gambling, but unhampered by the hurry and bustle of modern life and the noise of traffic and factories, public opinion took form. *Everyday life in the colonies*

The houses in which colonial citizens lived had progressed from the crude thatch-roofed affairs of wattle or planks stood on end, used by the earliest settlers, to roomy dwellings usually of Georgian design. In the seventeenth century the imprint *Colonial houses*

[1] For entertaining reading on this subject the books by Alice Morse Earle are unsurpassed. See, for example, her *Colonial Dames and Goodwives* (1895); *Customs and Fashions in Old New England* (1896); *Colonial Days in Old New York* (1896); *Stage-Coach and Tavern Days* (1901); *Home Life in Colonial Days* (1898).

THE HOUSE OF SEVEN GABLES, SALEM, MASS.

A COLONIAL FIREPLACE.
Courtesy of the Essex Institute, Salem.

of Dutch, Swedish, and German as well as English architectural ideas could be discerned in various parts of America, but after about 1720 the Georgian, or as it is now generally termed "colonial," style won its way into every section, except perhaps, the frontier, where log houses were well-nigh universal. Glass windows replaced oiled paper at about the same time, and among the well-to-do merchants of the North and the great planters of the South there was much striving after good architectural effects. The houses were mostly rectangular two-storied affairs, built usually of wood, painted white, with green shutters. Sometimes, especially in New England, where the snows were deep in winter, outbuildings were attached to the main house one after another in a long procession. A little before the time of the American Revolution tall-columned porticoes, such as Washington's home at Mount Vernon possessed, became very popular. Houses of stone and brick were also common, and numerous chimneys, made necessary because of the many fireplaces, broke the roof-lines. Churches, in much the same style as the houses except for their tall spires, were everywhere abundant.

Within the most sumptuous of the houses, however, there were few conveniences, judged by present-day standards. The fireplaces rarely provided enough heat for comfort in severe winter *Lack of* weather, adequate screening against flies and insects in *conveniences* summer was impossible, and such items as cookstoves, refrigerators, bathtubs, and plumbing were totally unknown. Water was obtained from springs or surface wells that were easily contaminated, and this accounted for much of the disease common in colonial times. Candles usually furnished light at night, although whale-oil lamps were not uncommon in fashionable circles. Food was obtainable everywhere in great abundance and even in the cities at low prices, but often the fare was severely plain. Corn bread, hominy, and salt pork furnished the chief items of subsistence for the poorer classes, particularly in the South. Whiskey, beer, hard cider, and rum were manufactured locally and were available in great profusion, but only the upper classes could afford the finer wines and brandies that had to be imported.

The colonial cities compared fairly favorably with cities of similar size in Europe. Philadelphia was built on a plan worked out by William Penn, with wide paved streets, crossing one another at *Colonial* right angles. Here the houses were mostly of brick, and *cities* sometimes they were as many as three stories in height. Sidewalks were plentiful, and street lamps made the lot of the night traveler easy. Both Boston and New York were noted for their general planlessness and their narrow crooked streets, but some of the more important streets in both cities were paved, and they were usually kept clean. Charleston, as the favorite resort of the South Carolina planters, enjoyed a lively social life not found elsewhere; but its method of garbage disposal was primitive, for buzzards were here protected by law as necessary scavengers. In all the cities ashes and garbage were dumped into alleys and on vacant lots, and in most of them hogs running at large in the streets served the purpose expected of the buzzards of Charleston. Sanitary conditions were bad, and the resultant prevalence of disease was little checked by the physicians that the times afforded. Bleeding was still in common use, and the herbs and drugs prescribed were of dubious value. Shortly before the outbreak of the American Revolution medical colleges were opened, one in New York and one in Philadelphia. These were the first of their kind in the colonies. Since commerce was the chief concern of all the colonial cities, the noise attendant upon modern industrial life was wholly lacking. Creaking carts loaded with merchandise were perhaps the chief offenders against the ear.

Attendance on church, public meetings, "Thursday lectures" (mostly theological) in New England, and in the less strait-laced communities *Amusements* dances and theaters furnished a large share of the amusement the people were permitted to enjoy. Lavish hospitality was a point of honor with the southern planters, and the constant visiting back and forth made life for the younger generation a succession of what today might be called house-parties. Dancing was a favorite amusement with all classes in the South, and despite the frowns of the godly was a common pastime nearly everywhere. Theaters existed in the larger cities only, but by the time of the Revolution the American stage was definitely established. Gambling, horse-racing, cock-fighting, and fox-hunting were major activities with the young bloods, especially in the South, but lotteries to raise money for churches, public works, and even college endowments were conducted without censure in Puritan New England, and were in especial favor with the clergy. Out in the rural districts, particularly along the frontier, "log-rollings," house-raisings, husking bees, weddings, and funerals furnished relief from the ordinary tedium of life. Courtship was officially surrounded with many hampering conventions that have since been wholly eliminated, but the habit of marriage was strong with the colonials, and ways seem to have been found. Bachelors and widowers were under great social pressure to marry, and sometimes laws which discriminated against the unmarried were added to the incentive of public opinion.

There was no such thing as a colonial nobility — even among the Cavaliers who came to America there were very few of noble birth — but throughout the colonial period there was a well-recog- *The colonial* nized aristocracy which held itself definitely above the *aristocracy* common run of men. To this class belonged most of the English officials resident in America, the ministers and magistrates, the well-to-do merchants, the owners of great estates in the central colonies, and the great planters of the South. Members of the aristocracy sought to distinguish themselves from the lower classes by their manners, their superior education, and particularly their mode of dress. Indeed, during early colonial times laws were actually passed in some colonies forbidding "men and women of mean condition" to "take upon them the garb of gentlemen." Wealthy men wore silk stockings, breeches of velvet, silk, or other expensive goods, and frock coats made of imported broadcloth and richly trimmed. Wigs were also quite generally affected during the eighteenth century. The colonial dames were likewise gorgeous with dresses of costly silks, duly amplified by the use of hoopskirts. The garb of the lower classes more closely resembled the garments universally worn today. Homespun fabrics were in general use, although on the frontier the men preferred leather jackets and breeches. The slow breakdown of class distinctions reflects the essential conservatism of the people who emigrated to America. They were accustomed to caste lines in Europe, and they naturally brought to the New World what they had known in the Old. Ultimately the equality of opportunity in America, duly emphasized by the existence of cheap lands along the frontier, tended to wipe out artificial class barriers. But even the aristocratic mode of dress lasted for many years after the Revolution.

Intellectual interests were for the most part confined to the upper classes. Newspapers, however, had come into vogue during the eighteenth century, and on the eve of the American Revolution *Intellectual* they were widely read. Books were far from numerous, *interests* although among the great planters of the South it was quite the fashion to have a library. Libraries of a semi-public nature also existed, strangely enough more in the South than in the North. Benjamin Franklin was instrumental in establishing in 1731 the first public library of Philadelphia, an example that was quickly followed in other northern towns and cities. Light literature was virtually unknown, and books on theology and law such as Calvin's *Institutes*, Blackstone's *Commentaries*, Locke's *Treatises on Government*, and Montesquieu's *Spirit of the Laws* had a wider appeal than would seem reasonable today. The Bible was everywhere read with much diligence.

Although literary achievement was not yet within the reach of most Americans, the intense theological interest of New England had not *Jonathan* failed to produce visible results. Probably most able *Edwards* of the theological writers was Jonathan Edwards (1703–1758), whose expositions of Calvinistic doctrines rivaled in logic and lucidity the works of Calvin himself. Edwards was the only son of a learned Connecticut clergyman, who himself prepared his boy for college. Jonathan turned out to be unusually precocious, and at fourteen read Locke's *Essay on Human Understanding* with unfeigned delight. He was among the first to attend Yale College, where Newtonian science also made a profound impression upon him. Graduated from Yale in 1720, he was soon hard at work as a Congregational minister, proclaiming and expounding the Calvinistic doctrines that his soul had learned to love. Predestination, which once had appeared to him a "horrible doctrine," quickly won his intense admiration. As Edwards saw it, the right to bestow salvation wherever He chose was an essential attribute of divine sovereignty. No man could paint more clearly the dire vengeance that was to overtake the damned, or make less promising the prospect of being saved, yet he set greater store than the earlier theologians on the importance of the individual, and became the foremost American preacher of the "Great Awakening," a religious movement that spread from Europe to America in the middle of the eighteenth century.[1] He was a successful revivalist, and counted his converts by the scores.

Edwards lived a life of great austerity. He rose at four o'clock each morning, studied and wrote thirteen hours each day, and even when he sought recreation by walks through the woods carried with him a notebook in which he jotted down his thoughts. He wrote many books, most of which had long theological titles. In 1754 he published *A Careful and Strict Enquiry into the Modern Prevailing Notions of that Freedom of Will which is Supposed to be Essential to Moral Agency, Vertue and Vice, Reward and Punishment, Praise and Blame.* On this work rests much of his fame as a philosopher. Shortly before his death he accepted the presidency of the Presbyterian College at Princeton, New Jersey, but his period of office was too short for him to make a profound impression upon that institution.

[1] George Whitefield, an English Methodist, who visited America about this time, helped spread the revival throughout the colonies. An excellent sketch of Edwards's life, by Arthur Elson, is in the *Dictionary of American Biography*, VI. This work, edited by Allen Johnson and Dumas Malone (1928–1936), now complete in twenty volumes, provides short biographies of practically every American of consequence. See also A. V. G. Allen, *Jonathan Edwards* (1889).

JONATHAN EDWARDS

The Works of the late Dʳ Benjamin Franklin Consisting of HIS LIFE Written by himself Together with ESSAYS Humorous, Moral, & Literary, chiefly in the manner of the Spectator.

NEW-YORK Printed by Tiebout & Obrian for H. Gain, P. Nutter, R. M'Gill, T. Allen, T. Reed, E. Duyckinck, & C° and Edward C. Mitchell, N° 9, Maiden Lane.

Dʳ BENJAMIN FRANKLIN.

FRONTISPIECE AND TITLE-PAGE OF BENJAMIN FRANKLIN'S "WORKS," NEW YORK, 1794

More palatable to present-day readers are the writings of Benjamin Franklin (1706–90),[1] who, in the opinion of many historians, ranks *Benjamin Franklin* as the first American of his time. Franklin's span of life, like Edwards's, lay entirely within the eighteenth century, and his keen zest for living contrasts markedly with the other-worldliness of the great Puritan theologian. Franklin was a Bostonian by birth, and for several years attended a Boston grammar school. His father was a tallow chandler, but since Benjamin had no liking for that trade he was apprenticed when twelve years of age to his half-brother James, a printer. Before long the apprentice was mainly responsible for the publication by his brother of a newspaper known as the *New England Courant*, which was so indiscreet in what it printed that in 1722 James was jailed for a month. Shortly afterward Benjamin left his brother's employ and went to Philadelphia. Here he established himself as a printer of merit, and in due time began to pub-

[1] S. G. Fisher, *The True Benjamin Franklin* (1899); J. T. Morse, *Benjamin Franklin* (1889); P. L. Ford, *The Many-Sided Franklin* (1899).

[80]

lish much that he himself had written. His *Poor Richard's Almanack*, which appeared from 1732 to 1757, presented in homely garb the wise sayings of all the ages, and won almost universal acclaim in America as well as wide recognition in Europe. The *Pennsylvania Gazette*, with which Franklin was long associated, furnished another outlet for his pen, and it was here that some of his earliest scientific observations were set down. He was interested in a great variety of natural phenomena, but won recognition as a scientist chiefly through his experiments with electricity.

Franklin wrote only one book, his *Autobiography*, and it was never finished, but his numerous occasional articles, written in a severely plain, yet remarkably effective style, made him easily the literary leader of America. Franklin was not merely a writer, but lived an exceedingly full life. He was interested in business, he had a remarkable flair for inaugurating or helping along such projects as appeared likely to improve the lot of his fellow men, he was many times called upon for political service, and he spent years together on various errands abroad. He wrote only when he had some definite purpose to serve by his writing, but perhaps this is one of the reasons why he wrote so well.

CHAPTER V

COLONIAL SELF-GOVERNMENT AND IMPERIAL CONTROL

CONTRARY to a common conception, not many of the colonists came to the New World with unique political ideas and a burning desire to set up new forms of government. They came, for the most part, from the British Isles; they were familiar, or at least their leaders were familiar, with the British type of government; and in their various attempts to solve the problems that soon confronted them they sought merely to adapt to new world conditions the institutions which they already knew.

At the head of the English government stood the King, who at the time the American colonies were founded could still claim that he ruled *The English* by divine right.[1] This was the more plausible inasmuch *government* as the King's title to the throne rested in no way upon popular consent, but exclusively upon the fact that he was the nearest living relative to his predecessor. He had powers of no mean sort; indeed, under the Tudors and the early Stuarts his authority tended to dwarf almost to insignificance the power of Parliament. For advice the King relied mainly upon his Privy Council, a group which varied in number from twenty to forty, and included many of the high officials of state. The "King in Council" kept an eye on all the affairs of the realm, and sometimes issued orders that were as much legislative as executive in character.

The English Parliament was a bicameral body, and consisted then, as now, of the House of Lords and the House of Commons. The House *Parliament* of Lords was a comparatively small body, with perhaps fifty "Lords Spiritual" and "Lords Temporal," the former entitled to their seats by virtue of the high ecclesiastical offices they held, the latter by the right of birth. The House of Commons was a much larger body than the Lords, with a total membership of no less

[1] On the English constitution see F. W. Maitland, *Constitutional History of England* (1908), and A. F. Pollard, *The Evolution of Parliament* (1920).

[82]

than five hundred. Each shire, or county, was entitled to two members in the Commons, and some three hundred towns were entitled to one or two members each. This distribution of seats was historic merely, and not at all in proportion to population. Great cities were wholly without representation, and "rotten boroughs," which for centuries had been without inhabitants, sometimes returned two members. The suffrage was rigorously limited, more so in some boroughs than in others, but practically always by property qualification. The whole system was well designed to throw the control of Parliament into the hands of the upper and middle classes. In theory, however, Parliament represented "all the men of England," and while there was a wide difference of opinion among seventeenth-century Englishmen as to exactly how far its powers went, the right of Parliament to a voice in the levying of taxes and in the making of all important laws was generally conceded.

The national courts of justice also occupied an important place in the English plan of government. All judicial officers, from the justices of the peace to the judges who sat on the highest courts of *The English* the realm, were appointed directly by the King and were *judiciary* directly removable by him. In medieval times the King's judges had formed the habit of traveling about the country on circuit duty, and had gradually supplanted the feudal and ecclesiastical courts, whose powers had once been great. The King's judges developed for both civil and criminal cases precedents and principles that came to be known as the "common law." For example, a defendant had the right of trial by jury, and no man might be deprived of life, liberty, or property without due process of law. Such rights as these the courts stoutly defended, and in general the judiciary was independent of interference either by the King or by Parliament. There were, however, numerous exceptions to this rule.

Such was the government with which the colonists were familiar when they established themselves in America; and such was the model after which their governments were patterned. The *The colonial* colonial governments, however, were not all alike.[1] Some *governments* of the colonies operated under charters of incorporation that were little constitutions in themselves, and were therefore often spoken of as "corporate" colonies; others had proprietors into whose hands governmental authority had been placed, and were usually called "propri-

[1] The constitutional aspects of colonial development receive elaborate treatment in the volumes by H. L. Osgood, *The American Colonies in the Seventeenth Century* (3 vols., 1904–07), and *The American Colonies in the Eighteenth Century* (4 vols., 1924–25). Channing, I, II, are also excellent.

etary" colonies; still others were under the direct supervision of the English government, and were called "royal" colonies. But the influence of the English pattern was strong in each case; furthermore, the types of government instituted in America did not differ as much from one another as the names used to describe them would seem to indicate. This can be made more apparent by the examination of a typical colony from each of the three forms of American colonial government.

The corporate colonies enjoyed the greatest degree of self-government and departed most from the English precedents. Of these Massa-

Massachu-setts, a cor-porate colony
chusetts, in spite of the fact that her charter was drastically altered in 1691, is the natural example; for during the formative years Massachusetts led the way in working out a plan of self-government that could be applied successfully in the New World. Although the original Massachusetts charter was designed to fit the needs of a joint-stock company rather than a self-governing commonwealth, it served, with certain adaptations, not only as a satisfactory constitution for Massachusetts, but also as a model after which the other self-governing colonies could pattern.

The Massachusetts governor was elected by the freemen, or voters, at first in primary assembly, but later, when the size of the colony had

The governor
made this impracticable, by ballots taken in all the towns. The governor thus obtained his office by the vote of the people, and not by divine right as was the case of the King of England, but the voters in selecting him were limited nevertheless by the prevailing opinion that only men of the highest rank should ever be considered for this office. The governor had no veto power, and since elections were held annually he might be retired after a single year. In practice, however, he possessed tremendous influence, and compared favorably with the English King in power.

The General Court, or legislature, of Massachusetts was a two-house body after 1644, and laws could be passed only by the consent of both

The General Court
houses. Assistants, who constituted the upper house, were elected in the same fashion as the governor, but here again the weight of custom restrained the voters to a limited choice. The number of assistants was small, and in practice they were chosen from among the leading citizens, men of wealth and high standing in the colony. Furthermore, it was customary to re-elect assistants year after year, so that once having attained that office the incumbent was likely to hold it for life. Two members of the House of Deputies were chosen by each town entitled to representation. While there was a rule that a man might not serve as deputy who was not orthodox in religion,

there was no such high standard of qualification for the Deputy as for the assistant. The governor was the presiding officer for the assistants, while the deputies elected a speaker of their own. Obviously the General Court of Massachusetts was closely analogous to the English Parliament.

The judicial system of the colony was slow to develop, but it followed, at least vaguely, the English model. The governor and assistants, to begin with, exercised full judicial authority, but as the *The judicial* population increased provision was made for a system of *system* county courts. For this purpose a number of towns were joined together into counties, and court was held for each county by the local assistants and such other assistants as they could get to sit with them. Or sometimes citizens nominated by the freemen of the county and approved by the General Court sat with the assistants. Appeals could be taken to the Court of Assistants and then to the General Court. These magistrates were by no means always learned in the law, and they were guided as often by their own judgment or by the precepts of the Bible as by the English common law. The uncertainty of decisions so arrived at led in 1641 to the preparation and adoption by the General Court of a code of laws known as the "Body of Liberties." Some of the provisions of this code would seem harsh today, but in general the "Liberties" marked a distinct advance on the prevailing practice of the time. Magistrates were no longer permitted to inflict punishment at their discretion, but only on the basis of specific law; jury trial with the right of "challenge" was provided; while the "Liberties of Women" and the "Liberties of Children" were safeguarded in varying degrees. A married woman, for example, was to be free from bodily correction by her husband, "unless it be in his own defense upon her assault."

Maryland was the first continental colony in the government of which a proprietor figured, and is fairly typical of the rest. Lord Baltimore, by the grant of power received from the King, *Maryland,* was authorized to govern his province as he chose, except *a proprietary* that in raising taxes and making laws he must obtain the *colony* advice and consent of the freemen or their representatives. This was exactly the situation in which the English King found himself, and no doubt it was intended that the proprietor should rule in Maryland just as the King ruled in England. The proprietor, however, chose not to come to America, but instead to assert his authority through a governor, whom he appointed to represent him, and a council, whom he appointed to advise the governor.

The development of the legislature in Maryland came slowly, with the proprietor contesting every step. Baltimore assumed that he had *The legisla-* the sole right to propose laws, and that the "advice and *ture* consent" of the freemen meant only what the words implied. Accordingly, when an assembly of the freemen, which he had authorized his governor to call together, took a different view, and passed laws on its own initiative, the proprietor promptly vetoed all of them. Ultimately, however, the proprietor had to give way, and permit the assembly approximately the same right in the making of the laws of Maryland as the English Parliament had in the making of the laws of England. At first all the freemen, which in Maryland meant the landowners, met together as the assembly, but in due time, as the colony grew, the representative principle was adopted. Division into two houses came in 1650, when the members of the council began to sit separately as an upper house, and the elected representatives sat as the lower house. Both the governor and the proprietor maintained a veto over all legislation, and the governor was authorized to dissolve the assembly at will. But the proprietor and his agents learned to exercise their prerogatives sparingly, and the assembly insured its frequent meeting by voting supplies for only a year at a time.

The administration of justice in early Maryland lay in the hands of the governor and his council, but in due time county courts were in-*Courts of* stituted to care for minor cases, and the governor and *justice* council sat as a provincial court with appellate jurisdiction and original jurisdiction in the more important cases only. As time went on the personnel of the provincial court came to consist largely of judges who were not also members of the council. Circuit courts were also presently instituted, with the judges of the provincial court doing circuit duty in the various counties. There was much shifting of jurisdiction among these courts and the circuit courts were for a long time abandoned, but the pattern eventually became clear. All judges were commissioned directly by the governor and held office during his pleasure. In civil cases the "rules by which right and justice used and ought to be determined in England" were followed, but in criminal cases much was left to the discretion of the judges. The following penalties, all of which were prescribed by the Maryland assembly during the eighteenth century, illustrate the state of public opinion in the matter of punishment for crime:

> A person convicted of embezzling, impairing, razing, or altering any will or record within the province . . . was to forfeit all his goods, chattels, lands, and tenements, be set in the pillory for two hours, and have both of his ears nailed thereto and cut from off his head; a person convicted of stealing that

which was valued at less than one thousand pounds of tobacco was to pay fourfold, be put in the pillory, and given not to exceed forty lashes; a person convicted of fornication was to be fined 30 s. or six hundred pounds of tobacco; a person convicted of wilfully burning a courthouse was to suffer death without benefit of clergy; a person convicted of blasphemy was for the first offense to be bored through the tongue and fined 20 pounds sterling, or, if unable to pay the fine, be imprisoned for six months; for the second offence to be stigmatized by burning in the forehead with the letter B and fined 40 pounds, or, if unable to pay the fine, be imprisoned for one year; and for the third offence to suffer death without benefit of clergy.[1]

In Virginia, after 1624 when it became a royal colony, the colonial form of government most closely approximated its English prototype. The governor was now appointed directly by the King and *Virginia, a* held office at the King's pleasure. He was charged with *royal colony* the duty of carrying out such instructions as might be sent to him by the English authorities, and he must also execute the laws passed by the colonial assembly. He commanded the local military and naval establishments, supervised religious affairs, presided over the council, and with its consent appointed justices of the peace and other court officials. He could call the assembly together, could propose measures for its considerations, could prorogue or dissolve it at will, and could disallow any or all of the laws it passed. He could remit fines and pardon criminals. He was, indeed, a little king in America.

When the Virginia Company lost its charter, there was some doubt as to whether or not the representative assembly would be continued, but perhaps because of the earnest insistence of the Vir- *Representa-* ginians themselves the assembly was presently recognized *tive govern-* by the King. At first governor, councillors, and burgesses *ment* all sat together, but as in the other colonies division into two houses was soon agreed upon. The council was chosen by the King on nomination of the governor from among the leading men of the colony — only the richest and most prominent were considered eligible. Councillors held office indefinitely, and usually received new commissions whenever there was a new king in England or a new governor in the colony. Two burgesses were chosen from each county, and one from each of several towns, by the qualified property-holders. A miniature parliament was thus produced, with the council equivalent to the Lords, and the burgesses to the Commons.

As in Maryland, the governor and council were charged also with certain judicial duties, and when sitting together in their judicial ca-

[1] N. D. Mereness, *Maryland as a Proprietary Province* (1901), pp. 277–78. By permission of The Macmillan Company.

pacity were known as the General Court. Before them came all major *The judicial* criminal cases and all civil cases involving above sixteen *system* pounds sterling. The county courts had jurisdiction in criminal cases not involving "peril of life or limb," and in civil cases of as much as twenty-five shillings. Lesser suits came before single justices. Appeals were allowed to the General Court, and during most of the eighteenth century a further appeal might be taken to the assembly itself. This practice was discontinued, however, about 1680. Another practice that fell into disuse was the custom of councillors' sitting, when they chose, as judicial members of county courts.

Government in the colonies, it thus appears, followed closely after the English model. A single executive, corresponding to the King, a *The colonial* two-house legislature, corresponding to Parliament, and a *pattern of* judicial system, less pretentious and less complicated than *government* the courts of England but roughly on the same plan, appeared in every colony. It follows also that the government in one colony did not differ markedly from the government in any other colony, whether the colony had a charter of self-government, or shared the powers of government with a proprietor or with the King. The citizens of every colony, moreover, enjoyed the same personal rights as Englishmen that would have been their privilege in the mother country — jury trial, freedom of speech, freedom from arbitrary imprisonment. These were privileges, moreover, that were not enjoyed in like measure by the colonists of any other nation.[1]

It was natural that many Americans should come to think of the colonies as practically separate and independent units of the British. *British view* Empire, but English officials generally looked upon the *of colonial* colonial foundations as mere dependencies of the English *governments* government which were entitled to the privileges they enjoyed only by its sufferance. It was quite in harmony with the English view, therefore, to suppose that the colonies should be subject to such regulations on the part of the mother country as the home government chose to establish. But for many reasons a definite policy of colonial control was slow to develop. The English government lacked experience in dealing with colonies; indeed, the American colonies were practically the first of the kind it had ever had. Moreover, during much of the seventeenth century English governmental machinery was itself in bad order. The attempts of the early Stuarts to expand the royal prerogative were bitterly resisted by Parliament, and for many years the boundaries between the rights of the King and the rights of Parlia-

[1] G. P. Gooch, *English Democratic Ideas in the Seventeenth Century* (1927).

ment in respect to colonial affairs were in heated dispute. The existence of Civil War in England during much of this period also paralyzed such feeble efforts at control as the English authorities attempted. The colonies were thus left free during the formative period to work out their destinies in their own way with a minimum of outside interference.

With the restoration of the Stuarts to the throne of England in 1660 it was possible to give more definite attention to the colonial problem.[1] A committee of the Privy Council was created, known at *Efforts to* first as the Council for Foreign Plantations, but later, with *establish* its membership somewhat altered, as the Lords of Trade *control* or the Board of Trade and Plantations. This committee was authorized to inquire into colonial affairs and to recommend to Parliament and to the Privy Council such legislation and such administrative policies as it saw fit. The committee took its duties seriously, for a time at least, and soon began to make suggestions. It accepted the prevailing theory that the colonies were to be regarded as primarily foreign plantations established for the purpose of giving to England a national source of supply in staples that she might otherwise have to obtain outside the Empire. The colonies should be encouraged, therefore, to produce those commodities in which England stood in greatest need. They should plant vines to relieve the English of dependence upon the French vineyards. They should produce spices and tropical fruits to replace the business now done with the English in those commodities by the Dutch and the Portuguese; they should supplement the English fisheries; they should destroy the Scandinavian monopoly on the production of naval stores. The colonies should also be encouraged to buy English goods; if possible, to be better buyers than sellers, so that a steady flow of gold to redress the trade balance might find its way from the colonies to the mother country. Gold and silver mines, it was long hoped, would be abundant in the colonies, and of use toward this end.

The Committee on Trade and Plantations was never able to carry its theories into full effect, but it sincerely wished to make England the hub and center of a self-sufficient Empire. It recom- *The imperial* mended that the colonists should preferably sell all their *system* products to England; they should, if they could, buy from England or through England only; they must not devote themselves to manufacturing, since that was England's interest; they must be required to seek, not merely their own individual good, but rather the common imperial good.

[1] The leading authority on this subject is G. L. Beer, whose *Commercial Policy of England towards the Colonies* (1893), and *The Old Colonial System, 1660–1754* (1912), should be consulted.

Legislation looking in this direction actually anticipated the recommendations of the Committee on Trade and Plantations, for during the *First Navigation Act* Protectorate period Parliament had passed a law, aimed primarily at the Dutch carrying trade, which forbade the products of Asia, Africa, and America to be carried to British ports except in English-owned and English-manned vessels, and forbade European goods to be brought to colonial ports except in English ships or in ships belonging to the country in which the goods were produced. The colonies were thus left free to buy wherever they pleased, but they might not legally make free use of foreign shipping. This act was restated and expanded in 1660 as the First Navigation Act, and its purpose, no less than that of its predecessor, was to encourage English shipping rather than to vex the colonists. England needed a large navy, and in time of war trading ships could easily be converted into warships. Hence the wisdom of building up a strong merchant fleet and of preventing the Dutch, whose ships it was believed carried altogether too much of the colonial trade, from building up their navy at the expense of the English. Specifically the First Navigation Act required that only English or colonial-owned ships with English captains and crews three fourths English might engage in the colonial trade. A little later it was further stipulated that the ships must also be built in England or the colonies (not including Ireland). These provisions were not seriously damaging to the colonists. Temporarily there was some shortage of ships, and freight rates rose, but there was compensation in the fact that the law tended to stimulate the shipping interests in the colonies quite as much as in the mother country; furthermore, Parliament remained deaf to all English pleas that this colonial competition be eliminated.

The First Navigation Act also contained a list of "enumerated articles" — sugar, tobacco, cotton-wool, indigo, ginger, dye-woods — *Enumerated articles* that might be sold only to England or to another colony. This list was later expanded, but for the time being it contained only one item, tobacco, that seriously affected the continental colonies. Moreover, the intent of the English government to benefit the colonies as well as the mother country was indicated by the fact that the growing of tobacco in England, and the purchase of tobacco from foreign colonies for use in England, were forbidden.

The Second Navigation Act, passed in 1663, affected the continental *Second Navigation Act* colonies decidedly more than did the earlier law. It provided that all imports from Europe to the colonies must pass through England. This was designed to prevent the trade and the products of the colonies from passing to other countries, although by smuggling freely the colonists managed to avoid any serious restrictions. It was supposed, too, that the profits of English merchants would be somewhat enhanced by the routing of foreign goods through England. Duties, both import and export, were charged by the English government, but an elaborate system of rebates, or drawbacks, enabled the colonists to buy foreign goods through England about as cheaply as Englishmen themselves could buy them. Some items, for example Dutch and German linens, the colonists, thanks to the rebates, could buy even more cheaply than could Englishmen.

The Third Navigation Act, otherwise known as the Plantation Duty Act, was passed in 1672 (effective 1673), and was meant to bear directly upon the colonists. There had been much evasion of the *Third Navigation Act* law requiring the "enumerated articles" to be shipped only to England or to another colony. Colonial shipmasters carried such goods from one colony to another, perhaps across the Potomac from Virginia to Maryland, then, deeming the law fulfilled, shipped the goods where they chose. The Third Navigation Act required that a duty equal to the English import duty should be collected *in the colonies* unless the ship captain would bind himself to carry the cargo to England. This law meant the appointment of a considerable number of colonial collectors who were directly responsible to the English commissioner of customs. These officials soon made themselves obnoxious to the colonists not only because of their efforts, usually unsuccessful, to enforce the law, but also because of the constant complaints they registered with their English superiors on the unwillingness of the Americans to co-operate with them. Perhaps the most unpopular of the English collectors was Edward Randolph, who headed the imperial customs service in New England. At all events, the law was more honored in the breach than in the observance.

This tendency on the part of the colonists to pay attention to the British regulations only when they chose to do so was in large part responsible for a very determined effort on the part of *Efforts to* James II and his advisers to reform the colonial govern- *discipline* ments. The attitude of New England towards the Acts *the colonies* of Trade was regarded as particularly reprehensible. Most of the New England governors were elected officials who made little or no effort themselves to enforce the disagreeable laws of Parliament, and refused to give adequate support to the tax-collectors appointed from England for this purpose. Finally the Committee on Trade and Plantations brought suit for the annullment of the Massachusetts charter, and in

1684 won its case. The way now lay open for a series of radical reforms. In the interest of efficient imperial control royal colonies were to supplement corporate or proprietary colonies, small colonies were to be consolidated with their larger neighbors, and royal officials — governors and councillors — were to have their duties enlarged and their powers strengthened. These changes, it was supposed, would be of material assistance, also, in solving the problem of colonial defense.

Between 1684 and 1688 the policy of colonial consolidation went on so rapidly that by the last-mentioned year the eight northernmost colonies had been thrown together into one, the "Territory and Dominion of New England," with Sir Edmund Andros at its head. All the New England colonies — Massachusetts, New Hampshire, Plymouth, Rhode Island, and Connecticut — were included in the combination, and in addition New York, East New Jersey, and West New Jersey. New Hampshire and New York were already royal colonies, and the Plymouth colony had no embarrassing legal rights to be overthrown; but legal proceedings had to be brought against the governments of the remaining colonies. Andros, however, asserted his authority over them all, regardless of charters and grants of authority. Colonial assemblies were abolished, quit-rents were demanded of the owners of land, taxes were levied without the consent of any representative body, and religious worship according to the rites of the Anglican Church was given official encouragement.

Dominion of New England

These drastic changes, enforced as they were by a stubborn and tactless governor, would doubtless have led to revolt in the colonies had there been no "Glorious Revolution" in England. But the efforts of James II to free himself from the control of Parliament had aroused as deep resentment in the mother country as the arbitrary acts of Andros had aroused in America. The King, moreover, was at heart a loyal Catholic, and he had married for his second wife a Catholic Italian princess, Mary of Modena. In 1688 the birth of a son, who presumably would be brought up as a Catholic and would succeed to the throne, was announced. This was a serious blow to English Protestants, Anglicans and dissenters alike, for they had counted on a Protestant daughter of James II, Mary, the wife of William, Stadholder of the Netherlands, as the next in line of succession. Without bloodshed and almost by common consent James was therefore deprived of his royal rights, and by act of Parliament William and Mary were invited to mount the throne of England as joint sovereigns. The "divine right of kings" was thus summarily disposed of. James II fled with his family to France, and the kings of England thereafter owed

The Glorious Revolution

their title to the throne solely to the will of the English people as expressed in Parliament. To leave no doubt in the matter this doctrine was presently recorded in the famous Bill of Rights and also in the Act of Settlement, passed in 1701.

The Glorious Revolution in England was followed promptly in America by the imprisonment of Andros and the collapse of the pretentious "Dominion of New England."[1] The once self-governing *The reaction* colonies of New England now resumed their former bound- *in the* aries and privileges, except that Massachusetts temporarily *colonies* held on to New Hampshire; New-Yorkers submitted with what grace they could to the dictatorship of a popular leader named Leisler, who had frightened Andros's lieutenant, Nicholson, into leaving the colony; and the proprietors in the Jerseys re-established their control. In the colonies where the rule of Andros had never been felt there was much less excitement, except in Maryland. There the occasion was seized upon to overthrow the rule of the proprietor, who, it was claimed, had refused unfairly to permit an increase in the membership of the assembly, had filled the appointive offices with his relatives, and had been overgenerous in his treatment of Catholics.

When the English government was free to turn its attention once more to America, it abandoned the principle of consolidation, which James II had so strongly favored, but it did not hesitate *Governmen-* to establish royal colonies in preference to any other type *tal changes* wherever that could conveniently be done. New Hampshire was again cut off from Massachusetts, and given a royal governor. Massachusetts was given a new charter (1691), according to which the governor was appointed by the crown instead of being elected by the people as formerly. Connecticut and Rhode Island were allowed to keep their old charters, but the Plymouth Bay Colony and the settlements in Maine were now joined to Massachusetts. In New York a royal governor backed by English troops soon took charge, and Leisler and two of his chief adherents were hanged. Maryland became a royal colony with a Protestant governor, and the rights of the proprietor were not restored until 1715. Penn's friendship with the fallen Stuarts was held against him, and in 1692 Pennsylvania became a royal colony with the governor of New York at its head. Two years later, however, Penn got back the rights he had lost. For the time being the Jerseys, since they were regarded as of small consequence anyway, were left to their proprietors, but in 1702 they were united as the royal colony of New Jersey, although until 1728 they had the same governor as New York.

[1] Viola F. Barnes, *The Dominion of New England* (1923), covers this subject admirably.

[93]

These changes in America were somewhat less significant than the Glorious Revolution in England. The pretentions of Andros were *Significance* eliminated, but by the multiplication of royal colonies *of the* the way was paved for closer control by the mother country *changes* than had been possible before Andros's rule began. In England, on the other hand, not only was "divine right" given a shattering blow, but the power of Parliament began to rise. William III was an important factor in the English government, but his successors were weaklings who allowed the royal power to fall into disuse. Before many years the English King reigned, but ministers, responsible to Parliament rather than to the King, really ruled. For America, however, no such transformation was in sight. It made little difference whether royal governors were appointed on the recommendation of the English ministers or at the whim of the English monarch. In either event the source of authority lay entirely outside the colony, and the right of the people to control their executive, a right which, as the power of Parliament grew, was coming more and more to be recognized in England, was largely denied in America. Colonial assemblies could, and sometimes did, sway royal governors by refusing to grant funds unless specific grievances were abated, but the power of these English officials was still great. The following diagram will perhaps make clearer the contrast between the English and the American results of the Revolution of 1688:

THE ENGLISH AND THE AMERICAN GOVERNMENTS

Before 1688		After 1688	
ENGLAND	AMERICA	ENGLAND	AMERICA
God	King or Proprietor	King	English Government
↓	↓	↑	↓
King	Governor	Ministers	Governor
		↑	
Parliament	Assembly	Parliament	Assembly
↑	↑	↑	↑
People	People	People	People

Neither did the Glorious Revolution mean any abatement of the English determination to control the trade of the colonies in the in *Another* terest of the mother country and of the Empire as a whole.[1] *Navigation* Indeed, the Navigation Act of 1696 was designed to make *Act* more effective than ever before the enforcement of the three Navigation Acts passed during the reign of Charles II. According

[1] O. M. Dickerson, *American Colonial Government, 1696–1765: a Study of the Board of Trade in its Relation to the American Colonies* (1912). See also the excellent study by W. T. Root, *The Relations of Pennsylvania with the British Government, 1696–1765* (1912).

to the law of 1696 all colonial governors, whether royal governors or not, must take a strong oath to enforce the English regulations, and in case they failed to do so, or failed to live up to their oaths, they were made liable to heavy fine and removal from office. Governors not directly appointed by the crown had to receive the King's approval — a difficult requirement for the self-governing colonies to meet. Provisions were also made for tightening up the colonial customs service, and colonial laws out of harmony with the acts of trade were declared null and void. Furthermore, after the passage of this act admiralty courts were established in the colonies to enforce the English regulations. Inasmuch as these courts were patterned after the Roman law, they were not embarrassed by the necessity of holding jury trials; hence colonial juries, ever a source of difficulty in the enforcement of English law in America, could be avoided.

The determination to enforce commercial regulations upon the colonies continued unabated during the early years of the eighteenth century. The list of enumerated articles was lengthened *New regula-* by the addition of rice, molasses, naval stores, ship timbers, *tions for co-* copper, and beaver skins. Even non-enumerated articles *lonial trade* might not be sent to Ireland or Scotland except after payment of the regular import duties in England. Colonists were forbidden to carry wool, or articles manufactured of wool, from one colony to another. But the most unpalatable of all such measures, however, was the Molasses Act of 1733, which was aimed at the profitable trade carried on between the continental colonies and the non-English colonies of the West Indies. In order to ensure that the former should buy West Indian produce from the English islands exclusively, practically prohibitive duties were placed on all sugar, molasses, rum, and spirits imported from foreign plantations. This was a stupid piece of legislation, for the continental colonies had more to sell than the markets of the English West Indies could absorb, and would have suffered acutely had the law been enforced. Furthermore, much of the hard money that found its way to the continent and ultimately went to England to redress an unfavorable balance of trade came from the foreign West Indies, and thus English traders and manufacturers stood a good chance to lose should the law be enforced. But as a matter of fact the Molasses Act did little harm, for from the date of its passage it was cheerfully ignored.

In various other ways, also, the English government undertook to control the behavior of the colonies. Manufacturing, it was assumed, could best be done in England, and colonial manufactures were therefore

discouraged. A law of 1732, for example, placed a limit upon the num-
Other efforts at control ber of apprentices that colonial hat makers might employ, and a law of 1750 restricted rigorously the right of the colonists to manufacture iron goods. Paper-money issues by colonial legislatures were severely frowned upon, and excesses along this line were prohibited either by law of Parliament or by disallowance of the colonial laws involved.[1] For the latter purpose royal governors were instructed to veto or to suspend such colonial enactments as might run counter to English policy, and the Privy Council reserved for itself a further veto, which was exercised usually only on recommendation of the Board of Trade. Appeals were also taken from colonial courts to the Privy Council, and many colonial laws as a result of this process were finally set aside. Since royal governors were more easily controlled than those chosen by proprietors or by the people there was a marked tendency to eliminate as many proprietary and self-governing colonies as possible. Misgovernment in the Carolinas gave an excuse to withdraw the privileges of the proprietors there in 1728, whereupon both colonies received royal governors. When Georgia became a royal colony in 1751, there were left of the corporate colonies only Connecticut and Rhode Island, and of the proprietorships only the holdings of the Penns in Pennsylvania and Delaware, and of the current Lord Baltimore in Maryland.

It must not be supposed, however, that English interference in American affairs was unduly burdensome. Sometimes, as in the case *Privileges accorded the colonies* of tobacco, the legal restriction actually ran against the mother country and in favor of the colonies. When naval stores and ship timbers were placed on the enumerated list, bounties were made available to encourage their production. Colonial agents, among whom the most notable was Benjamin Franklin, appeared in England to lobby against proposed Parliamentary measures that might be damaging to American interests, and to argue the American case when a dispute came before the Board of Trade. Colonial governors, even when they were appointed from England, tended to place a high valuation upon American public opinion, and to interpret unpopular obligations as narrowly as possible. The fact that in most cases they were paid out of money appropriated by a colonial assembly also kept them fairly respectful of the will of the people they governed. Even the English revenue-collectors sometimes absorbed the American point of view. Many Americans could see, too, that the protection

---

[1] C. P. Nettels, *The Money Supply of the American Colonies before 1720* (1934), is a work of great merit.

given to colonial trade by the English navy and by English treaties far more than outweighed the damage suffered by commercial restrictions; and for this protection the Americans were taxed not a cent.

Finally, it should not be forgotten that the English will to maintain restrictions on the colonies often lagged seriously. Sir Robert Walpole, who was the virtual head of the English government for *"Salutary* more than two decades (1721-42), believed that more was *neglect"* to be gained for England by encouraging colonial trade than by restricting it, since trade of any sort would make the colonies prosperous and better able to buy English goods. This opinion was shared also by the Duke of Newcastle, who had much to do with colonial affairs during Walpole's supremacy, and continued powerful even after Walpole's fall. Indeed, Newcastle's frankly admitted policy of "salutary neglect" was not seriously amended until the close of the French and Indian War.

CHAPTER VI

THE WINNING OF THE WEST

As THE English settlements expanded farther and farther into the West, it presently became apparent that in the course of time a struggle with the French must ensue to determine definitely which nation, England or France, should control the interior of the continent. Should the English colonies end at the crests of the Appalachians, with France in possession of the lands beyond? Or should the great Mississippi Basin become the next swarming-place of the English? Clearly it was a case in which the fittest would survive, and the answer to the question might easily have been read in a comparison of the existing French and English foundations.[1]

The French settlements in North America dated back to 1608, when Samuel de Champlain founded Quebec on the St. Lawrence River. In *New France* due time other French settlements appeared at Three Rivers and Montreal. The location of the colony was not a happy one. The soil was poor and the climate was hard. The seacoast was far away, and for fully half a year ice floes in the St. Lawrence River blocked communication with the mother country. Moreover, the way to the West was temptingly easy. No such formidable barrier existed as the mountains that lay back of the English settlements, and the pathways of the lakes and rivers invited explorations. Such Catholic missionaries as Father Marquette, and such intrepid traders and explorers as Joliet and La Salle, soon penetrated far into the Mississippi Valley. La Salle's imagination took fire, and he dreamed of a magnificent French dominion that would extend from Canada to the Gulf of Mexico; in 1699 an adventurer named d'Iberville actually established a French outpost at Biloxi, near the mouth of the Mississippi. Somewhat

---

[1] New France was fortunate in having as its historian one of America's most brilliant writers, Francis Parkman, whose *Count Frontenac and New France under Louis XIV* (1877), *Half-Century of Conflict* (2 vols., 1892), and *Montcalm and Wolfe* (2 vols., 1884) cover the period of rivalry with the English. These and other volumes by Parkman have been many times republished, most conveniently as *The Works of Francis Parkman* (20 vols., 1897–98).

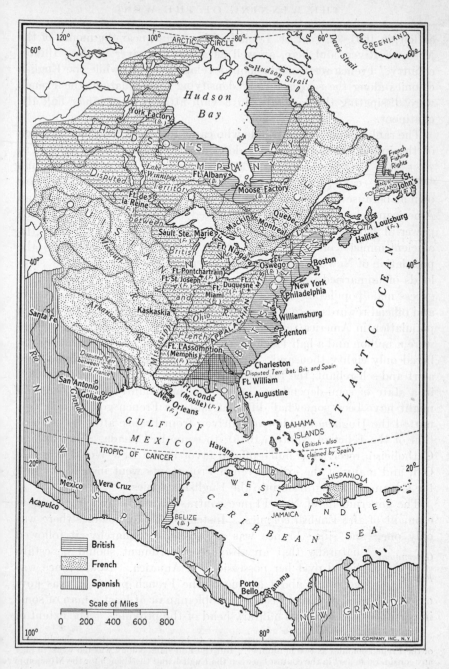

EUROPEAN CLAIMS IN NORTH AMERICA, 1754

earlier, in 1691–92, Fort St. Louis had been built near the mouth of the Missouri River, and here, as well as across the river in the "Illinois country," French settlements soon developed. Thus while the English colonies along the seacoast were densifying in population, the French were dissipating their energies in a vain attempt to conquer half the continent.

The rank and file of the people who came to New France lacked much of the individual initiative and determination to succeed that was so *The habit-* marked among the English colonists. The French habitants *ants* came, for the most part, not so much for reasons of their own as because the national government was determined to build up an American colony. This project enlisted the support in turn of such powerful figures as Henry IV, Cardinal Richelieu, and Colbert, the efficient minister of Louis XIV. Every effort was made to increase the population of New France. Bounties were offered for immigrants; shiploads of unmarried women were sent over to become the wives of the excess male population; unmarried individuals were ostracized socially; and official rewards were offered for large families. But still the French population in America refused to grow rapidly. By 1750, when there were a million and a half English colonists in America, the French numbered only eighty thousand. The English Americans as a whole were alert and self-reliant; the French were relatively unprogressive, and still in a state of semi-dependence on the mother country. The situation might have been somewhat different had the French government permitted the Huguenots, who were driven from France after the revocation of the Edict of Nantes (1685), to come to Canada. But Roman Catholicism received as much official favor in the New World as in the Old, and many of the exiled French Protestants went instead to swell the stream of immigration into the English colonies.

The government of New France contrasted markedly with the government of the English colonies. Instead of many colonies there was only one,[1] and since France was an absolute monarchy, it followed *Government* naturally that an absolute government should be estab-*of New* lished over her possessions in America. New France was *France* governed about as one of the French provinces was governed. A royal governor, usually a nobleman or at least a man of some importance, was civil and military head of the province. The extent of

[1] Louisiana had a separate government; hence to be entirely accurate one should speak of the French colonies as two in number. But the Louisiana colony was too weak to play any considerable part in the contest between the English and the French for the Mississippi Valley. On the beginnings of Louisiana, see Parkman, *La Salle and the Discovery of the Great West* (2 vols., 1879), and *Pioneers of France in the New World* (1865).

his power depended in part upon his personality, and in part upon the nature of the times in which he ruled. During periods of active warfare the governor's power tended to increase, while in times of peace his power waned. Count Frontenac, who was sent to America in 1672, was doubtless the most influential of all the French governors. The legal and financial ruler of the province was the intendant, an official of lesser rank but often greater power than the governor. The intendant, a lawyer, was at the head of the judicial system of the colony; he was entrusted with public expenditures; and he reported directly to the King, thus acting as a sort of check on the governor. The spiritual head of the province was the bishop, but his temporal power as the ruler of the church made him one of the triumvirate by which the colony was governed. In theory a "superior council," consisting of the three officers named and a number of resident councillors appointed on recommendation of the governor and the intendant, was the chief governing body of the colony; but in practice the governor, the intendant, and the bishop were able to control the rest. Local self-government was unknown, and many of the personal rights cherished by Englishmen everywhere were freely denied. "It is of the greatest importance," one official declared, "that the people should not be at liberty to speak their minds." There was, moreover, continual interference in colonial affairs from Versailles, "where a fickle-minded monarch and a corrupt court played fast and loose with their often misguided colony." [1]

With the possible exception of the patroonships in New York, the land system of New France differed from anything to be found in the English colonies, where every man was permitted to own *The seigno-* his own land, with at worst a nominal quit-rent. In the *rial system* French colony an attempt was made to maintain the old feudal system of land tenure. Nobles held large estates or seigneuries with a wide expanse of river front; and the peasants who worked the land were supposed to pay to the nobles such dues and fees as contemporary French practice required. The maintenance of such a system of land tenure in the face of the plenty of lands in America was foredoomed to failure, but the effort was made. In general French peasants, or habitants, paid their dues only when they felt like it; and if the exactions of agriculture proved too burdensome they took to the fur trade, where they might live more as they chose.[2]

[1] R. G. Thwaites, *France in America* (1905), p. 128. Quoted by permission of Harper and Brothers, publishers. Among the many useful books on New France this volume of the *American Nation* series takes high rank.

[2] W. B. Munro, *The Seigneurs of Old Canada* (1914), describes the effort to transplant feudalism from the Old World to the New.

LIBRARY
FLORIDA STATE COLLEGE FOR WOMEN
TALLAHASSEE, FLORIDA

French industries compared most unfavorably with those of their English neighbors. Agriculture was sickly, and fishing, although en-

Economic conditions couraged in various ways by the government, was not notably successful. Fishing villages did spring up, however, especially those on the coasts of Newfoundland and about Port Royal in Acadia. But for the bulk of its prosperity New France relied upon the fur trade. The French Canadians, it turned out, got along well with the Indians, intermarried freely with Indian women, and in the quest of pelts scattered willingly over the whole interior. They competed on even terms for the northern fur trade with the enterprising agents of the English Hudson's Bay Company. They generally outdistanced the English traders on both sides of the Great Lakes and in the Valley of the St. Lawrence; and they took their share of furs from the upper Mississippi Valley in spite of both Spanish and English opposition. Supplementing the work of the traders regularly licensed by the government, independent or illegal traders known as *coureurs de bois* roamed the wilderness without much fear of punishment, so long, at least, as their catch went to New France and not to the rival English.

In one matter the French in America possessed a decided advantage over the English. When it came to the problem of defense they were

Military efficiency not embarrassed by a multiplicity of authorities; instead, there was unity of command and unity of action. Furthermore, the French government expected little military assistance from the colonists themselves, but kept French ships and soldiers available for their protection. The English government, on the other hand, assumed that the English colonies in America would take care of the defense problem themselves except in cases of great emergency. When attacked by the Indians or the French, the English colonies ordinarily had recourse only to their own raw militia levies. Moreover, there was not only much conflict of authority but also not a little evasion of responsibility, especially on the part of those colonies whose borders were not directly threatened. To be sure, the English fleet stood ready to guard the high seas, and no colonial navy was required, but the English army was reserved for use only when the colonists had already exerted themselves to the limit and stood a chance to fail without help. But events proved that the greater immediate effectiveness of the French military power was not sufficient to outweigh the other notable advantages possessed by the English.

The rivalry between the French and the English, first for European hegemony and then for world empire, lasted many years and involved the two countries in numerous wars. The earlier of these struggles,

LIBRARY
FLORIDA STATE COLLEGE FOR WOMEN
TALLAHASSEE, FLORIDA

"King William's War" (1689–97), "Queen Anne's War" (1701–13), and "King George's War" (1744–48), to use the American names *Rivalry* for these conflicts, involved no serious test of strength be- *with the* tween the French and English in America. In each of them *English* Indian raids promoted by the French disturbed the peace of the New England and New York frontiers, and in some of them privateering was a source of much annoyance on both sides. During King George's War an expedition under the command of Governor Shirley of Massachusetts and supported by British ships took the French fortress of Louisburg on Cape Breton Island; but the conquest was restored by the treaty of peace. These three wars left the status of French and English rivalry in America relatively unchanged. The final contest, the French and Indian War, actually began in America two years before its European counterpart got under way, and it was fought primarily to determine whether the French or the English were to have the right of way in North America.[1]

The struggle for the continent was precipitated by the ambition of some Virginia gentlemen, with whom a few Englishmen were associated. to establish a colony west of the Appalachian mountains. *The Ohio* For this purpose, an Ohio Land Company was formed, and *Land* in 1749, royal consent to a grant of two hundred thou- *Company* sand acres of land below the "forks" of the Ohio was obtained. Next year Christopher Gist, a well-known surveyor and land prospector, was sent out to prepare the way for the coming of settlers, upon whose purchases of lands the company hoped to realize a handsome profit.

This project immediately alarmed the French, who recognized at once the peril to their Ohio Valley fur-trade interests in case English settlers were allowed to come in; hence, in 1749 the governor of *French* New France dispatched Céloron de Bienville to the con- *alarm* tested area to plant leaden plates on which was inscribed the claim of the King of France to the region the English now sought to possess. Céloron buried a plate near the source of the Allegheny River on July 29, 1749; and then as he progressed down the Allegheny and down the Ohio planted others. He turned back only after having passed the mouth of the Miami River. The leaden plates did little to deter the English advance, but three years later, when the Marquis Duquesne de Menneville became governor of Canada, a more vigorous policy was

[1] G. M. Wrong, *The Rise and Fall of New France* (2 vols., 1928), and *The Conquest of New France* (1918), summarize entertainingly the results of recent scholarship. John Fiske, *New France and New England* (1902), also makes delightful reading. A good short account is Carl Wittke, *History of Canada* (1928).

inaugurated. Indians friendly to the French were induced to attack Indians friendly to the English, and French forts made their appearance in the disputed area, one on the southern shore of Lake Erie, and two on French Creek, a tributary of the Allegheny.

Warned of the new developments, the British Secretary of State for Colonial Affairs sent word to the colonial governors in America that *Washington and Gist* while they must not take the offensive against the French, they were at liberty to "repel force by force." [1] Armed with this authority Governor Robert Dinwiddie of Virginia determined to warn the French that they must withdraw from the Ohio Valley. George

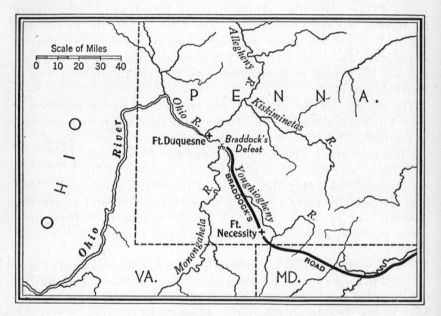

THE FORKS OF THE OHIO

Washington, an enterprising youth of twenty-one years, whose elder brother Lawrence had been one of the founders of the Ohio Land Company, was selected to carry the message, and in the fall of 1753, accompanied on the latter part of the journey by Gist, he pushed through to the nearest French post and delivered Dinwiddie's ultimatum. The French commandant, however, had only defiance for an answer, and with this reply Washington returned to Virginia.

[1] C. W. Alvord, *The Mississippi Valley in British Politics* (2 vols., 1917), and *The Illinois Country, 1673–1818* (*Centennial History of Illinois*, I, 1920), presents the British point of view with regard to the West.

Meantime, some Virginians had begun work on a fort near the junction of the Allegheny and Monongahela Rivers, the "forks" of the Ohio; and a small detachment of troops under Washington *The forks of* and a certain Colonel Fry were sent out to their aid. But *the Ohio* the French ousted the English from the forks before Washington's force arrived, and completed the fort themselves, naming it Fort Duquesne, in honor of their new governor. Presently a French reconnoitering party met Washington's advancing troops, and in the first clash, at Great Meadows, the English won. Washington, understanding well the difficulties that lay before him, now halted to build a stockade, Fort Necessity, for the better protection of his men. A large body of troops from Fort Duquesne soon attacked him and forced him to capitulate. On July 4, 1754, he was allowed to abandon his post with honors of war, and the French and Indian War had begun.[1]

When the news of this frontier fighting reached Europe the governments concerned decided to regard it as a strictly local affair, and to postpone a general war as long as possible. But the gravity of *Braddock's* the situation was fully recognized, for the French promptly *expedition* sent reinforcements to America, which the English navy tried in vain to intercept, while the English sent fifteen hundred regulars under General Braddock to co-operate with the Virginians in the capture of Fort Duquesne. Braddock's column, supported by about four hundred and fifty Virginia militia under Washington, advanced toward Fort Duquesne from Fort Cumberland on the upper Potomac, along the same route Washington had taken previously. The colonials complained that Braddock, unaccustomed to the ways of the wilderness, had to "level every mole-hill, and build a bridge over every brook." Nevertheless, he worked his way to within seven or eight miles of Fort Duquesne, where, unfortunately, his troops were surprised and defeated by the French and he himself slain. A later historian has claimed that "Braddock's defeat" might better be termed "Braddock's victory," for the road he built became a highway later on for the English migration that conquered the Ohio Valley;[2] but at the time the defeat was keenly felt. Indians under French influence harassed the frontier, and Washington, with a little army of not more than fifteen hundred men, found himself almost powerless to beat them off.

By the year 1756 England and France were in an open state of war, and for some time the advantage in America seemed to lie with the

---

[1] Rupert Hughes, *George Washington, the Human Being and the Hero, 1732–1762* (1926), gives a complete account of Washington's part in the French and Indian War.
[2] A. B. Hulbert, *Braddock's Road (Historic Highways of America, iv, 1903).*

French.   One reason for this was to be found in the personality of the French commander, the Marquis de Montcalm, who took charge of the *Open* Canadian forces the year war was declared.   Montcalm not *warfare* only possessed great ability as a general, but he was able also to communicate to the Canadians much of his enthusiasm for the task before them and his optimism as to the ultimate outcome.   The English in America, on the other hand, lacked nothing else so conspicuously as competent leadership.   British officers sent to America were too often, like Braddock, unacquainted with colonial traditions, unversed in frontier methods of warfare, and unwilling to accept advice.   Colonial officers were deficient in training, and whenever projects were undertaken that required the co-operation of troops from two or more colonies, they were much given to quarreling with respect to priority of rank.

For this latter situation the lack of any intercolonial organization was in large part responsible.   But all efforts to unite the colonies, even in the *The Albany* face of the French menace, seemed doomed to failure.   In *conference* 1754, the British government called a conference at Albany to discuss the Indian problem, particularly with reference to the near-by Iroquois.   Representatives from seven colonies attended, and, realizing that the problem before them involved the larger problem of colonial unity, they sought earnestly to devise some scheme which would ensure colonial co-operation, particularly essential in view of the impending war with France.   Benjamin Franklin was a member of the Congress, and the "Albany Plan" which it presented was largely his work.   Had this plan gone through there would have been established an intercolonial council composed of forty-eight representatives, apportioned among the colonies with regard to their wealth and population, and elected by the several colonial legislatures.   Also there would have been a president-general for all the colonies, appointed and paid by the crown. Subject to veto by the president-general, the council was to have had the right to control Indian affairs, raise and pay armies, build forts, and levy the taxes necessary for these purposes.   But this plan was promptly rejected by the colonial assemblies, who objected to any such curtailment of their own prerogatives, and who possibly feared also that such an intercolonial organization would transfer too much responsibility for the winning of the war from England to the colonies.   A counter-proposition submitted by the English Board of Trade met a similar fate.   The English plan contemplated the establishment of a council composed of one commissioner from each colony; these commissioners might then agree by majority vote upon the necessary military forces and their apportionment among the colonies. A commander-in-chief for all the colonial forces would have been appointed by the crown.

The failure of these plans left each colony free to support the war as much or as little as it chose. The colonies that were in greatest danger from the French did most; those that were far removed *Colonial* from the scene of conflict did least; and in general there was *support of* much waiting to see what the other planned to do. Sug-*the war* gestions from England that taxation of the colonies for their own defense might be undertaken by the authority of Parliament met a chilly reception in America, and were never acted upon.[1]

William Pitt, who was called to the English ministry in the fall of 1756 and next year virtually took charge of the war, worked out a requisition system which secured perhaps as much colonial assistance as *Pitt's* was possible under existing circumstances. Pitt's plan left *requisition* with the colonies the responsibility of levying, clothing, and *system* paying provincial soldiers. The English government, however, undertook to furnish the colonial troops with arms, ammunition, and provisions, and promised further to compensate the colonies later for their outlays in accordance with the vigor of their actions. The amount of the compensation actually paid by England to the colonies was equal to about two fifths of the expenditures the colonies made. Spurred on by this appeal, as well as by the real menace of the French and Indian attacks, the New England colonies supported the war with becoming zeal; in New York and Pennsylvania, however, quarrels between governor and legislature prevented anything like adequate support of the war; Virginia did only fairly well, considering how great she assumed her stake to be in the outcome; and most of the other colonies scarcely participated in the war at all.

Pitt's plans, so far as America was concerned, did not stop at debarring the French from occupying territory claimed by the English; he would expel the French entirely from North America. But in *French* carrying through such an undertaking he had to reckon with *successes* no mean adversary in the person of Montcalm, the French commander-in-chief. Soon after his arrival in America Montcalm had blocked one English approach to Canada by the capture of Fort Oswego on the southern shore of Lake Ontario. The next year (1757) he blocked another approach by the capture of Fort William Henry at the lower end of Lake George. And in view of the fact that the English efforts to dislodge the French from their fortress at Louisbourg on Cape Breton

[1] G. L. Beer, *British Colonial Policy, 1754–1763* (1907), is an excellent discussion of British policy towards the colonies during the French and Indian War.

Island had so far failed, a British expedition up the St. Lawrence seemed out of the question. The year 1758 opened with the advantage all on the side of the French.

But the tide soon turned. Pitt replaced incompetent officers ruthlessly, and elevated promising young men to positions of great respon-

Turn of the tide sibility. By this means the task of capturing Louisbourg was taken away from Lord Louden, whose ineptitude had been adequately demonstrated, and handed over to two younger officers, Jeffrey Amherst and James Wolfe. With the assistance of Admiral Boscawen, a naval commander of genuine ability, the siege of Louisbourg was finally brought to a successful termination. In the Lake Champlain region the British under Abercrombie attacked the French outpost at Ticonderoga, only to be beaten off; but farther to the west a small British force composed mostly of colonial troops took Fort Frontenac on Lake Ontario, and thus cut the French communications with the West. Thereupon the French abandoned Fort Duquesne, and the British under General Forbes quickly occupied it. The crowning event of the war came next year when Admiral Saunders and General Wolfe successfully advanced up the St. Lawrence, and forced Montcalm to fight a decisive battle (September 13, 1759) on the Plains of Abraham overlooking Quebec. Both Wolfe and Montcalm lost their lives in the struggle, but the English victory was complete. Next year Montreal surrendered to Amherst, and the conquest of Canada was at an end.

Other British victories took place in America in spite of tardy support to the French from the Spanish, who entered the war in 1761. Guada-

British conquests loupe and Martinique in the West Indies were taken from the French, and Cuba from the Spanish. On the other side of the world a British fleet captured Manila. On the Continent the armies of Frederick the Great, the chief ally of the British, had won decisive victories. Everywhere the British flag was supreme on the high seas.[1]

By 1763 the French gave up the struggle, and at Paris, on February 10, signed a humiliating peace. Canada and all the French possessions east of the Mississippi River, most of the French stations in India, and some of the French West Indies were ceded to England. Some of the English leaders would have been willing to return Canada to France in return for a cleaner sweep of the French West Indies, but, won over perhaps by the arguments of Benjamin Franklin, the conquest of Canada was allowed to stand. The Philippines and Cuba were returned to

[1] A book of epoch-making significance is A. T. Mahan, *The Influence of Sea Power upon History, 1660–1783* (1890).

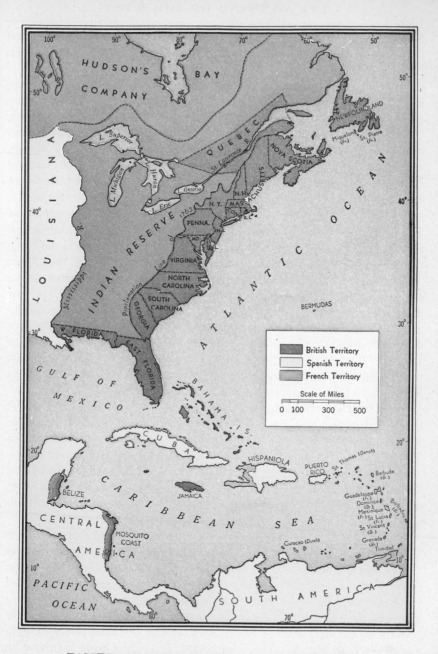

EASTERN NORTH AMERICA AND THE CARIBBEAN
AFTER THE PEACE OF 1763

LIBRARY
FLORIDA STATE COLLEGE FOR WOMEN
TALLAHASSEE, FLORIDA

Spain; but the English demanded and received Florida. This somewhat unwarranted Spanish loss was made good by the cession of Louisiana and the Isle of Orleans from France to Spain; and thus the French possessions on the continent of North America were entirely wiped out.

In bringing about this happy solution of their difficulties with New France the colonies had played a considerable part; and yet to most Englishmen conversant with the situation it seemed that *Colonial* the Americans had done far less than their full duty. They *indifference* had depended upon British regulars when colonial levies might well have been materially increased; they had refused to unite under the Albany Plan, or any other plan, for their common defense; and they had been guilty of almost wholesale trade with the French in utter defiance of the will of the imperial government. British orders to stop all commerce with the enemy had been met in the colonies by the smuggling of great quantities of colonial stores, particularly foodstuffs, both to Canada and to the French West Indies, and because of this illicit trade the war had been appreciably prolonged.

One unforeseen result of the conflict was to drive England and her colonies farther apart than they had ever been before. The disloyalty and disobedience of the colonists embittered many Englishmen against the Americans, and led to an agitation in favor of closer control of the colonies by the mother country. On the other hand, the removal of the French menace in America removed also the necessity of British assistance to confront it, and on this account left the colonies less disposed than ever to submit to British control. The disruption of the expanded empire lay only a short distance ahead.

The French and Indian War, so far as the colonists were concerned, had been fought primarily to insure that the region west of the mountains should be opened to settlement, and the terms of the treaty of Paris seemed to indicate that this object had been attained. The war was hardly over, however, when grave obstacles to the expansionist program began to appear.

In the first place, the British government itself seemed disposed to hold in check, at least temporarily, the ambitions of those who wished to push farther into the West. The Indians of the *The Procla-* trans-Appalachian region were soon engaged in a danger- *mation Line* ous uprising against the English, known as Pontiac's Conspiracy. It was plain to be seen that the colonies, working independently of each other, would never be able to devise a consistent Indian policy, and since all admonitions looking in the direction of a colonial union had proved futile, the imperial government now decided to take the whole matter of Indian relations under its direct control. On the assumption that a little delay in western expansion could do no harm, and that assurance against the invasion of their land might induce the Indians to give up their warlike behavior, the British government ordered that the Allegheny watershed should mark for the present the farthest west that settlement might be permitted to go. Beyond the sources of the rivers flowing into the Atlantic, grants of land were not to be made; and even the settlers who had already entered the forbidden region were ordered to return. The Proclamation of 1763, which announced this policy, thus closed the very door which the war had been fought to open. Further, it ignored utterly the western land claims of those seaboard colonies whose original charters had contained "sea to sea" grants.

Secondly, the seriousness of the Indian outbreak soon became a most effective check on pioneer ambitions. Inevitably there were *Pontiac's* differences between the rule of the English and the rule *conspiracy* of the French, and these differences from the Indian point of view all appeared to be to the discredit of the new régime. The English garrisons in the captured French posts were not given to fraternization; the English traders drove hard bargains; and the interest of the English colonists in settlement rather than trade was all too evident. French renegades held out hopes that the time would soon come when the French would send an expedition to reconquer their former possessions, and, spurred on perhaps by vague promises of this sort, Pontiac, an Ottawa chief with far more organizing ability than was common among the Indians, induced most of the western tribes to join him in a great "conspiracy." A concerted attack upon the British military outposts began in May, 1763, each Indian tribe attacking the nearest fortified post, and within a few weeks only four out of twelve were left in British hands. At Detroit, where the whites retained control, a siege was instituted which lasted for five months before the Indians gave up. Attacks were also made upon the outlying settlements, and the whole frontier was thrown into a panic. But the Indian victories had been won chiefly through the element of surprise, and the war which resulted could end in only one way. In 1764 two strong expeditions were dispatched into the Indian country. As a result Pontiac and his allies were defeated, and finally in July, 1766, at Oswego Pontiac agreed with Sir William Johnson to a treaty of peace and amity.[1]

[1] Francis Parkman, *The Conspiracy of Pontiac* (2 vols., 1851); W. L. Stone, *Life and Times of Sir William Johnson* (2 vols., 1865).

That the British government had no intention of forever withholding the region west of the Proclamation Line from settlement was soon fairly apparent. Two treaties were negotiated in 1768, *British plans* one with the Iroquois at Fort Stanwix, and the other *for the West* with the Cherokees at Hard Labor. These and subsequent treaties gave the English a title, defective, perhaps, since all the tribes who asserted claims to the region concerned were not consulted, to a large strip of land extending west of the mountains into the upper Ohio Valley. Probably the government hoped to establish a neutral zone from which as a precaution against future troubles both whites and Indians should be excluded. But that some of the lands so acquired would be opened to new settlement was clear from the support given by the Board of Trade to a project which contemplated the creation of a new colony in the West to be known as Vandalia. For this purpose a British-American syndicate was formed which numbered among its membership such prominent men as Benjamin Franklin and Sir William Johnson, and much pressure was brought upon the Board of Trade to agree to the necessary land grant. After considerable dissension a patent was made out in favor of the petitioners which would have handed over to them most of what is now West Virginia and eastern Kentucky. But by the time consent to this grant had been fully won, the American Revolution was on, and the project lapsed.

Nevertheless, the settlement of the Vandalia region had already begun. Even before the French and Indian War thousands of pioneers had found their way into the eastern part of this district, *The upper* and while most of them had been compelled to get out *Ohio frontier* during the war, many promptly returned as it came to an end. After the war was over, with the help of Braddock's road from Fort Cumberland to the Ohio, and the road Forbes had cut through Pennsylvania to Fort Pitt (the British name for Fort Duquesne), migration into the upper Ohio region was made relatively easy. Regardless of the Proclamation of 1763 and the absence of regular land titles, settlers pushed out along the mountain trails, and as early as 1767 permanent settlements on the upper Ohio and its tributaries were beginning to appear. , Before the Revolution broke out both Pittsburgh and Wheeling were sizeable villages.[1]

During these years other irregular settlements west of the crest of the mountains were being made farther to the south. In 1769 pioneers from the back country of Virginia pushed southwestward across

[1] C. E. Carter, *Great Britain and the Illinois Country, 1763–1774* (1910); A. T. Volwiler, *George Croghan and the Westward Movement, 1741–1782* (1926).

the watershed into the Watauga Valley, which they supposed to be
The within the limits of Virginia, although actually it was a part
Watauga of North Carolina. Two years later they were joined by
settlements a number of "Regulators" from the back country of
North Carolina, who were compelled to seek safety in flight because
of an unsuccessful revolt they had waged against the domination
of the colony by the eastern propertied class. James Robertson,
who led this latter migration into the West, and John Sevier, a Virginian of French Huguenot descent who came to Watauga in 1772,
furnished the little settlement with unusually effective leadership.

A survey of the boundary line, made in 1771, between Virginia and
North Carolina revealed to the Watauga pioneers that their settlement lay in North Carolina rather than in Virginia. With the nearest
North Carolina settlements almost a hundred miles distant, and with
the Regulators indisposed to acknowledge the supremacy of the North
Carolinian government in any case, the Wataugans found themselves
practically outside any colony. They set to work, therefore, to form
a government of their own. With Robertson and Sevier as leaders
they held a mass meeting at Robertson's station, and adopted Articles
of Association by which in the future they agreed to be governed. A
convention of thirteen delegates — one from each of the thirteen
stations — was elected by manhood suffrage, and the convention in
turn chose a court of five members to rule the community. As an independent and totally unauthorized government the Watauga Association lasted on until 1778, when Watauga became Washington County
of the revolutionary state of North Carolina.[1]

The rapid advance of the white frontier, particularly in the valley
of the upper Ohio, led to the outbreak of another Indian war in 1774.
Lord Dun- The failure of Pontiac's conspiracy had left the north-
more's War western Indians with a deep-seated grudge against the
whites, and the further penetration of country which until recently
the Indians had regarded as exclusively their own added fuel to the
smouldering fire. The Shawnees first took the warpath along the
Virginia frontier, but their example was soon followed by many neighboring tribes. Lord Dunmore, the last royal governor of Virginia,
was not slow to act. Two expeditions were organized at once for the
relief of the frontier, one under the governor himself, which advanced
to Fort Pitt and thence down the Ohio, the other under General Andrew
Lewis, which marched through the wilderness to the mouth of the

---

[1] Theodore Roosevelt, *The Winning of the West* (4 vols., 1894–96), begins with the
advance of the frontier after the French and Indian War.

Kanawha River. It had been intended that the two columns should meet, but Dunmore changed his plans, and it fell to Lewis with a band of valiant but none too well-disciplined frontiersmen to do the bulk of the fighting. In the battle of Point Pleasant, fought near the mouth of the Kanawha, Lewis's men won a bloody victory, and Cornstalk, the Shawnee chief, was forced to give up. Lord Dunmore's War, as the Virginians called this struggle, was of great significance, for from it the Indians learned that they might not hope to stay the white man's advance across the mountains.[1]

The whites were quick to follow up their victory. The treaty which Cornstalk signed with Dunmore gave up the Shawnee title to all lands south as well as east of the Ohio River, and the former region had already aroused great interest among the whites. As *Kentucky* early as 1769 Daniel Boone, a frontier hunter who regarded himself as "ordained of God to settle the wilderness," had been impressed by the possibilities of Kentucky, and in a few years the whole frontier was aware of the existence in central Kentucky of a blue-grass region where game abounded and natural clearings made easy the task of the pioneer. The cupidity of the speculator was also aroused, and Judge Richard Henderson of North Carolina dreamed the not unusual dream of another colony to the west with himself as chief financial beneficiary. Accordingly in 1774 he formed a partnership known as the Transylvania Company, and next year purchased from the Cherokees whatever title they claimed to the region between the Kentucky and the Cumberland Rivers. To promote settlement Daniel Boone was set to work with a party of thirty men to cut a road through from the back country of North Carolina to the blue-grass region in Kentucky. By the first of April, 1775, Boone and his men, having cleared their "Wilderness Road" from the Holston River through Cumberland Gap to the Kentucky River, began the settlement of Boonesborough. Near-by at Harrodsburg other settlers, led by James Harrod of Pennsylvania, were already on hand, and the Kentucky pioneers were soon numbered by the hundreds.[2]

Henderson tried to organize a government for Transylvania, and for the purpose held an open-air convention of delegates from the various settlements, May 23, 1775. The convention met under a giant elm, and adopted a simple plan of government not unlike that devised for Watauga. But Henderson's land title was obviously defective, his hope of

[1] R. G. Thwaites and L. P. Kellogg have edited from the Draper Manuscripts of the State Historical Society of Wisconsin a valuable *Documentary History of Dunmore's War, 1774* (1905).

[2] H. A. Bruce, *Daniel Boone and the Wilderness Road* (1910); R. G. Thwaites, *Daniel Boone* (1902); W. S. Lester, *The Transylvania Colony* (1935).

securing royal support for his project was ended by the outbreak of the Revolution, and the petition which he sent to the Continental Congress that Transylvania be recognized as one of the united colonies was denied. In December, 1776, the Virginia legislature, acting at the request of the Harrodsburg settlers, acknowledged Kentucky as a county of Virginia, and the Transylvania project broke down. But the settlers stayed on and prepared to defend themselves against the Indians, whose ruthlessness, when they heard the news of war in the East, was abundantly apparent.

CHAPTER VII

A DECADE OF CONTROVERSY

The French and Indian War had brought to the attention of the British government a variety of problems with reference to America that might otherwise have escaped serious notice. British officers *British* reported with considerable feeling that the customs service *opinion on* in the colonies was hopelessly defective. Smuggling was *the colonies* rife, and trade with the enemy existed during the war in spite of stringent British regulations against it. Moreover, the cost of collecting the customs was out of all proportion to the amount of revenue taken in. It seemed apparent also that the Navigation Acts, most of which dated back to the seventeenth century, were in many ways obsolete. They permitted, according to some critics, altogether too free trade with the foreign West Indies, they failed to take into consideration the numerous additions that had been made to the Empire since the time of their passage, whatever the letter of the law might have been, and they did not in practice restrict the markets of North America wholly to English merchants. Most obvious of all was the laxity of the colonists in dealing with the problem of defense. Unity of colonial action had proved to be utterly unattainable, and only by the flattering promises of Pitt's requisition system were any of the colonies induced to do their duty in the raising of troops.[1]

Nearly two years before the close of the French and Indian War William Pitt had resigned from office because he wished to pursue a more aggressive policy against Spain than the Cabinet was willing *Grenville* to approve. Pitt understood American affairs better than *succeeds Pitt* most Englishmen, and his absence from the government at this juncture was extremely unfortunate. When the war ended it fell to the lot of George Grenville, Pitt's brother-in-law, but the leader of a faction far less friendly to America, to deal with the colonies. Grenville had long been a member of the Cabinet, but in April, 1763, as Chancellor of the

[1] E. I. McCormac, *Colonial Opposition to Imperial Authority during the French and Indian War* (1911); W. S. McClellan, *Smuggling in the American Colonies at the Outbreak of the Revolution* (1912).

[115]

Exchequer and First Lord of the Treasury, h...
a man of great obstinacy, but little talent, wh...
Not well versed in American affairs, he was n...
reforms in colonial administration were necess...
them through at once. He began the work by...
service. Commissioners of customs for Amer...
should proceed at once to the colonies, instead...
as was customary, and hiring substitutes to...
important, relentless war was declared upon...
authorizing the commanders of British men-of...
waters to act as customs officials and seize offe...
ing the jurisdiction of the admiralty courts, w...
pend upon the whims of local juries, and thirdl...
to colonial governors that they must enforce th...

Grenville also pushed through Parliament t...
1764, by which he proposed not only to regulat...

| The Sugar Act | tinental colonies and the foreign V...
raise a revenue. This measure
Molasses Act of 1733, the provisions of which h...
enforced. Ostensibly the new law was milder...
duced from 6d to 3d a gallon the duty charged ag...
from the foreign islands. But the old duty, had...
have been prohibitive, whereas the new duty was...
ment would mean only a curtailment of the West I...
raise a revenue. The act also provided for new a...
duties on refined sugar, coffee, pimento, indigo, a...
commodities, while the importation from these isl...
was strictly prohibited. A curiously phrased sta...
quired that all the duties paid under it must be pa...
His Majesty's Exchequer." Many Americans...
correctly, that this statement meant that for these...
silver would be received, and that the colonies acco...
drained of all their hard money.

As if to leave no stone unturned to vex the colo...
that the Sugar Act was passed saw the enactment of...
use in the colonies of paper money as legal tende...
colonial issues of paper be payable in a reasona...

[1] C. H. Van Tyne, *The Causes of the War of Independence* (1922)...
by an American writer on the background of the Revolution.
the subject are C. M. Andrews, *The Colonial Background of the Am*...
G. E. Howard, *Preliminaries of the Revolution* (1905); H. E. Egert...
acter of the American Revolution (1923); Carl L. Becker, *The Eve*...

American colonies did not have and never had had an adequate supply
of metallic currency, and since the inevitable tendency was for such hard
money as they did obtain to be drawn to England by an *Paper money
regulation* unfavorable balance of trade, the Americans regarded this
measure as extremely ungracious. It was designed, of course, to check
the normal tendency of a debtor community to resort to money inflation
as a means of scaling down debts. And for this very reason the law
was especially unpopular among the people who found the most difficulty in meeting their financial obligations. The Sugar Act particularly
angered the rich merchants; the limitations placed upon paper money
issues angered the ordinary citizen.

Grenville was nothing if not thorough, and the problem of colonial
defense remained to be solved. Pontiac's conspiracy had shown that
this problem was not brought to an end by the happy out- *Colonial
defense* come of the French and Indian War; it would recur at intervals as long as whites and Indians were in contact. It was with a
view to lessening the amount of such contact that the Proclamation of
1763 had been issued; but if the Proclamation Line or any other line was
to be defended, more adequate provision for the purpose must be made
than the colonists had so far shown themselves willing to undertake.
According to the British version, colonial troops had been found undependable during the French and Indian War, colonial levies could be
secured only after much wheedling, and colonial unity of action was
utterly out of the question. Grenville proposed, therefore, that the
imperial government, as the only central and effective agency, should
take over completely the problem of defense and that a permanent
garrison of ten thousand British soldiers should be stationed in America.
Incidentally, the presence of these troops might strengthen the hands of
British officials charged with the duty of putting an end to smuggling.

But Grenville had no notion that the entire cost of defending the
American frontier should be borne by the British government. Part of
the burden, he insisted, should fall upon the colonies. The *The Stamp
Act* cost of maintaining the requisite number of British troops
in America was estimated at about £360,000 per year, and according to
Grenville's plan one third of this sum should be raised by taxing the
colonists. Assuming that the revenue to be collected under the Sugar
Act would amount to about £45,000, Grenville saw the need of raising
£75,000 more by the imposition of a new tax. This tax, he decided,
might best be a stamp tax levied upon newspapers and upon the various
official and legal documents through which colonial business, both of a
private and public nature, had to be transacted. Knowing full well that

[117]

the colonists would raise objections to any such tax, Grenville gave notice of his intention a full year in advance, and even suggested that if the colonial assemblies should present a better plan he would consider it. But the colonists seemingly could think of nothing better than the requisition system used during the recent war, and Grenville, recalling how unsatisfactory that system had been, put his Stamp Act through Parliament early in 1765 by a good majority in the House of Commons and without opposition from the Lords.

It took some time for American sentiment on the question of the stamp tax to crystallize. Franklin, who, while the act was under consideration, *American reaction* was in London representing the colony of Pennsylvania on another matter, opposed such a tax in principle, but assumed that if the act were passed the colonists would have to obey it. James Otis, in a pamphlet entitled *The Rights of the British Colonies Asserted and Proved*, argued that the taxation of the Americans without the consent of their own representatives was contrary to the English constitution and irreconcilable with the rights of the colonists as "British subjects and men." But he, too, assumed that if Parliament chose to act in this high-handed and illegal fashion, there was nothing that the Americans could do about it. As time went on, however, and the full import of the various policies initiated by Grenville began to be realized, American resentment grew. Grenville's program seemed admirably designed to cripple in the most effective manner the economic life of the colonies. The Proclamation of 1763, granted that it could be enforced, would stop migration to the West just as hard times in the East, following close on the heels of the French and Indian War, had made the search for new homes in the West all the more essential. The Sugar Act would not only hamper trade with the foreign West Indies; but since those colonies were better buyers than sellers, it would interfere also with the normal flow of hard money from the islands to the continental colonies, and would make increasingly difficult the payment of balances owed by New England merchants to London. As if this were not sufficiently embarrassing, colonial paper issues were outlawed by the Currency Act, and the Stamp Act demanded more money when money was harder than ever to obtain. The colonies were poor, and the debts that they had incurred, or that some of them at least had incurred, during the French and Indian War seemed heavy; yet this was the time the English government selected to restrict their trade, remodel their monetary system, and tax them for a kind of protection that they did not want and thought that they did not need.

The most vulnerable point in the Grenville program, and the one which therefore drew the heaviest fire, was the Stamp Act. This, from the colonial point of view, was a clear case of taxation without representation. Patrick Henry,[1] the leader of a group of insurgents in the Virginia House of Burgesses, forced through that body a set of res- *"Taxation* olutions that denounced the act in language so extrava- *without rep-* gant that the more conservative members were deeply con- *resentation"* cerned; and in the heat of debate Henry uttered his famous defiance of the British King: "Caesar," he said, "had his Brutus, Charles the First his Cromwell, and George the Third ——" Here cries of "Treason! Treason!" arose from the House, while Henry continued; "may profit by their example. If this be treason, make the most of it."

The Virginia resolutions, one of which asserted "that the general assembly of this colony have the only and sole exclusive right and power to lay taxes and impositions upon the inhabitants of this colony," were given wide currency throughout the colonies, and served as topics of much discussion. There was a fair consensus of opinion that Parliament had definitely exceeded its authority. Most Americans were willing to admit that external taxes in the shape of duties on imports might be levied on the colonies by Parliament in the course of regulating imperial trade. But internal taxation without the direct sanction of popular representatives was "taxation without representation." [2] Some of the northern merchants agreed among themselves that they would cease importations from England as long as the law held, and the general court of Massachusetts sent out a circular letter inviting all the colonies to participate in a conference at New York on the first Tuesday in October through which an appeal for relief might be made to the English government.

The date set for this conference made it impossible for some of the colonial assemblies to select delegates, but with nine colonies represented the Stamp Act Congress, as it was generally called, presently *The Stamp* convened. This Congress repeated the argument of the *Act Congress* Virginia resolutions, and held that since the only persons who might legally represent the colonies were those "chosen therein by themselves," the British Parliament, in which not one American sat, was wholly without authority to enact such a measure as the Stamp Act. Moreover, the resolutions that it adopted not only denounced the Stamp Act but objected also to the use of admiralty courts as a device to circumvent the

---

[1] M. C. Tyler, *Patrick Henry* (1887); W. W. Henry, *Patrick Henry* (3 vols., 1891).

[2] The constitutional aspects of the Revolution have naturally attracted much attention. An excellent summary is to be found in A. M. Schlesinger, *New Viewpoints in American History* (1922), but this should be compared with C. H. McIlwain, *The American Revolution; a Constitutional Interpretation* (1923). C. E. Merriam, *History of American Political Theories* (1903), gives a good brief statement of the American contentions.

traditional right of trial by jury, and described the restrictions on American commerce as unduly "burthensome and grievous."

Opposition to the Stamp Act, however, went much further than the adoption of resolutions. An organization known as the Sons of Liberty directed an active campaign of intimidation against the stamp agents which made their lives so miserable that nearly all of them resigned. At first refusal to buy the stamps required to be affixed upon clearance papers kept many ships in port, and the same attitude toward stamps on legal papers caused court sessions to be suspended in every colony but Rhode Island. But open defiance soon reigned. Newspapers refused to buy the stamps, official business was transacted without them, and legal papers that showed no evidence of having paid the tax were issued freely. Many deeds of violence occurred, the worst of which probably was the burning of Chief Justice Thomas Hutchinson's house by a Boston mob. Extremely effective upon English public opinion was the decline in American importations from England. Non-importation agreements multiplied, and English merchants began to complain bitterly of their loss of trade.[1]

Faced by this situation, there seemed nothing for the British government to do but back down. Fortunately for the American cause the *Repeal of the Stamp Act* course of factional politics in England had thrown Grenville out of office in June, 1765, and a new ministry had been formed under the Marquis of Rockingham which could yield on the Stamp Act with less loss of face. "I rejoice that America has resisted," said William Pitt, and many other Englishmen agreed with him that the colonists had the better of the argument. They had before them, also, the testimony of Benjamin Franklin, who appeared before the House of Commons and stated the colonial case with great lucidity, that the colonists would never submit to any internal taxes levied by Parliament. The repeal did not come without a struggle, however, and the American theory of taxation came in for unsparing denunciation. To the argument that the colonists were unrepresented in Parliament because they had no direct representation there, the theory of "virtual representation" was advanced. "There can be no doubt, my lords," said Chief Justice Mansfield, "but that the inhabitants of the colonies are as much represented in parliament, as the greatest part of the people of England are represented; among nine millions of whom there are eight which have no votes in electing members of parliament." As for the distinction the

---

[1] A. M. Schlesinger, *The Colonial Merchants and the American Revolution, 1763–1776* (1917), brings out clearly the motives that actuated the merchant class. See also Channing, III.

colonists sought to draw between internal and external taxes, the Chief Justice found it equally invalid. A tax laid upon tobacco "in the ports of Virginia or London," he argued, "is a duty laid upon the inland plantations of Virginia, a hundred miles from the sea, wheresoever the tobacco may be grown." When the repeal was finally accomplished (March 17, 1766) Parliament did not surrender to the American arguments, but to expediency. To make this perfectly clear a Declaratory Act was also passed which stated that the King and Parliament had "full power and authority" to legislate for the colonies "in all cases whatsoever."

The repeal of the Stamp Act was received in America with much enthusiasm, and the menacing gesture of the Declaratory Act was scarcely noticed. According to John Adams the decision of the British government to abandon the stamp tax had "hushed into silence almost every popular clamor, and composed every wave of popular disorder into a smooth and peaceful calm." Popular protestations of loyalty towards the mother country were common, and such a spirit of good-will existed that only a little tact seemed necessary to avoid for the future all such outbreaks as had just occurred.

The good relations thus happily restored might possibly have been maintained but for three unfortunate circumstances. In the first place, George III, the English King, cherished fond hopes of ac- *George III* quiring great personal power in the direction of national affairs. In order to accomplish this end without undue violence to the British constitution, however, he proposed to control Parliament rather than to overthrow it. Members were induced by the gift of honors, pensions, or offices and by every other means of corruption then current to become the "King's friends," and to vote as he chose to have them vote. On the subject of American affairs, unfortunately, the King was both ignorant and prejudiced. He was opposed to the repeal of the Stamp Act, and was ready at any time to see Parliament defy American opinion. Accordingly, as his followers grew in number the chances of good relations with the colonies correspondingly declined.[1]

Another unfortunate circumstance was the illness of William Pitt (now the Earl of Chatham), who was the real, although not the nominal, head of a new British ministry which was formed in the *Illness of* summer of 1766 and lasted on until 1770. The new min- *Pitt* istry did not represent any particular party. Indeed, it included members chosen from a great variety of factions, both Whig and Tory,

[1] L. B. Namier, *England in the Age of the American Revolution* (1930); Reginald Coupland, *The American Revolution and the British Empire* (1930); R. L. Schuyler, *Parliament and the British Empire* (1929).

among them several of the "King's friends." Party government was never at lower ebb in England, and the talents of Pitt might well have been insufficient to hold so composite a group to an even reasonably consistent course. As it turned out, Pitt because of illness practically retired from the Ministry; and left thus without a leader each minister tended to do as he pleased within his own domain. The result, at least so far as it related to American affairs, was one colossal blunder after another.

The third unfortunate circumstance was that the Chancellor of the Exchequer, Charles Townshend, to whom fell the task of finding an *Charles* adequate revenue, was distinctly hostile to the colonies, and *Townshend* did not hesitate to take advantage of his position to translate his feelings into deeds. He speedily got into an unnecessary quarrel with New York. British troops were still kept in America, and as was customary requisitions for their supplies were made to the colonies in which they were stationed. The New York legislature, however, scaled down one such requisition on the ground that more was being asked than would be provided for the same troops in England. In answer, Townshend pushed through Parliament a law suspending the New York legislature until it should show itself ready to yield. He proposed, also, to continue the war which Grenville had begun against smugglers. A Board of Commissioners of the Customs with headquarters at Boston was created, and was given ample authority to enforce the Navigation Acts. Also writs of assistance, that is, general search warrants in which the premises to be searched need not be specifically mentioned, were formally authorized. Such writs had been issued during the French and Indian War, and in 1761 they had been declared legal in spite of the efforts of James Otis as counsel for some Massachusetts merchants to prove that they were a violation of the constitutional rights of English subjects. Townshend's reopening of the subject was therefore as unnecessary as it was provocative.

Furthermore, Townshend was determined to revive the contest with the colonies over taxation. Without so much as consulting his colleagues, most of whom, like Pitt, appear to have been *The Town-* leagues, most of whom, like Pitt, appear to have been *shend duties* friendly to the Americans, he gave out that he intended to raise a revenue from the colonies, and soon presented in fulfillment of his promise an act imposing duties upon all tea, paper, glass, and painters' lead to enter American ports. The Townshend Duty Act, as this measure was called, did mock deference to the American distinction between internal and external taxes, for it was a strictly external tax; but the preamble definitely stated that the law was designed to raise a

[122]

revenue rather than to regulate trade, and that the revenue so obtained might be used at the discretion of the government to pay the salaries of colonial governors and colonial judges. The law was in fact, and was meant to be, a challenge to the Americans — a challenge to them to defend if they could their theory of taxation and their practice of disciplining governors and judges by withholding salaries. But probably neither Townshend nor the members of Parliament who voted to support him realized fully the serious nature of the challenge they had made. Townshend died soon after the acts that bore his name were passed, but his successor, Lord North, one of the King's friends, attempted for three years to enforce them.

The Townshend Acts aroused in America the resentment that might have been expected. The suspension of the New York legislature struck at the very roots of colonial self-government, for if *Opposition* the lawmaking body of a colony had to make appropriations *in America* whenever the British government told it to do so, or else lose its life, there could be no such thing as legislative independence in America. Indeed, all the colonial legislatures might be suspended permanently on one pretext or another. Townshend's reorganized customs service likewise led to bad feeling, particularly in Boston, where lax enforcement of the Navigation Acts had been treated as a sort of vested right, and rigorous enforcement might prove ruinous to business. The Duty Act was denounced generally as an unwarranted and unconstitutional measure. Some said that an external tax that was designed primarily to raise a revenue was no less an instance of taxation without representation than an internal tax, such as the Stamp Act had been. Others held not merely that taxation without representation was tyranny, but that all legislation by the British Parliament for America was unconstitutional. For the slogan, "No taxation without representation," these extremists would substitute the slogan, "No legislation without representation."

The most widely read of the arguments against the Townshend Acts was a series of pamphlets entitled *Letters from a Farmer* published by John Dickinson of Pennsylvania.[1] Dickinson did not *"Letters* deny the legislative supremacy of Parliament, nor did he *from a* object strenuously to reasonable measures in regulation of *Farmer"* colonial trade and manufacture. But he did argue in simple and convincing language that the new acts were unfair to the Americans, contrary to the best interests of Englishmen, and fit only to be repealed. While opposed, except as a last resort, to the use of violence in attempt-

[1] C. J. Stillé, *The Life and Times of John Dickinson* (1891).

SAMUEL ADAMS
From the portrait by John Singleton Copley in the Museum of Fine Arts, Boston

ing to put an end to the Townshend system, he suggested that the Americans, as a means of making their power felt, might well proceed with a boycott on British goods.

In Massachusetts opposition to the Townshend Acts was particularly determined, for there an unsettled state of the public mind already existed which made easy the work of agitators. The aristocratic clique which ran the affairs of the colony had long been in bad odor with the common people — the farmers and the artisans — who believed that their interests had often been betrayed by their rulers. Orthodox Puritans, already fearful because of the growing influence of Anglicans in colonial affairs, took added fright at the talk of establishing an Anglican bishopric in America. The royal governor had quarreled tactlessly and needlessly with the legislature about many things. The merchant class, which because of its wealth might under ordinary circumstances have been counted upon to be conservative, was on edge lest too rigorous enforcement of the Navigation Acts might bring it to grief. Small wonder that Samuel Adams (1722–1803), the astute leader of the popular party in the Massachusetts legislature, became at once the man of the hour.[1]

Adams was of such good family that when as a boy he had attended Harvard College he had ranked fifth, socially, in a class of twenty-two. His father was a man of some means who tried to establish *Samuel* his son in business and left him one third of the family *Adams* estate. It soon became apparent, however, that Samuel Adams was not designed for a successful business career. He ran through his property and remained forever after impecunious. But however unfit he may have been in the management of his own affairs, he early demonstrated a remarkable talent for managing the affairs of the public. By the time the controversy over the Townshend Acts broke, Adams had risen from the level of town-meeting politics to be the chief radical leader in the colonial House of Representatives. He was not a merchant and never could have been one for long, but he united all classes of malcontents in opposition to the vexatious Duty Act. He displayed rare skill as a writer, and not a little aptitude as a thinker. He maintained that the British constitution, like the constitutions of all free peoples, was "fixed in the law of Nature and of God," and that "neither the supreme legislature nor the supreme executive" could alter it. In various documents adopted by the Massachusetts House, Adams's views were set forth, and finally in a *Circular Letter*, which he drafted, all the colonial assemblies

[1] R. V. Harlow, *Samuel Adams Promoter of the American Revolution* (1923); J. K. Hosmer, *Samuel Adams* (1884).

were invited to join with Massachusetts in resisting the policies of the English government. This act deeply offended Lord Hillsborough, Secretary of State for the Colonies in the English Ministry, and he promptly ordered the Massachusetts House to rescind it; when this order was defied the governor of the colony, acting according to instructions from England, dissolved the assembly. In spite of the threat that the same fate would befall any assembly which dared discuss the *Circular Letter*, legislative halls throughout the colonies rang out repeatedly with resolutions supporting the position of Massachusetts and deploring the act of the British government. The Virginia Resolves of 1769 are famous, not only for their statement of the American case, but also because they were introduced by George Washington himself.

The weapon by which the colonies might defend their rights had already been forged during the controversy over the Stamp Act. Once *Non-importation agreements* more non-importation agreements were entered into by the merchants of the leading cities, a program which many southern planters also chose to adopt. British trade began to fall off; British merchants began to protest; the British government had little choice but to back down once again. Moreover, time had demonstrated that it cost more to collect the Townshend duties than the amount of revenue they brought in. Accordingly, Lord North, the King's friend who became in 1770 the head of the British Ministry, moved the repeal of the duties except the tax on tea "to keep up the right."

Meantime two regiments of British soldiers had been transferred from Halifax to Boston to overawe the radicals in that port. The *"The Boston Massacre"* presence of the troops was deeply resented, and they received scant courtesy from the townsmen. On the same day that Lord North asked Parliament to repeal the Townshend duties (March 5, 1770) seven British soldiers under the command of Captain Preston were so irritated by a mob of fifty or sixty jeering men and boys that the soldiers fired into the crowd. Four citizens were killed, and news of the "Boston Massacre," duly exaggerated, spread like wildfire through the colonies. Captain Preston, on the ground that he had ordered the men to fire, was indicted for murder, and demands from Samuel Adams and his friends forced the governor to quarter the troops outside the city. But saner heads saw that the mob was quite as much to blame for the outrage as the soldiers, and John Adams, a rising young lawyer distantly related to Samuel Adams, in spite of his many misgivings as to the effect of such a course upon his future, defended Preston and his men in the trial that followed. Preston was acquitted, but two of the soldiers were given slight punishment for manslaughter.

The BLOODY MASSACRE perpetrated in King — Street BOSTON on March 5.ᵗʰ 1770 by a party of the 29.ᵗʰ REG.ᵗ

Engrav'd Printed & Sold by PAUL REVERE BOSTON

Unhappy BOSTON! see thy Sons deplore,
Thy hallow'd Walks besmear'd with guiltless Gore.
While faithless P—n and his savage Bands,
With murd'rous Rancour stretch their bloody Hands,
Like fierce Barbarians grinning o'er their Prey,
Approve the Carnage and enjoy the Day.

If scalding drops from Rage from Anguish Wrung,
If speechless Sorrows lab'ring for a Tongue,
Or if a weeping World can ought appease
The plaintive Ghosts of Victims such as these;
The Patriot's copious Tears for each are shed,
A glorious Tribute which embalms the Dead.

But know, Fate summons to that awful Goal,
Where Justice strips the Murd'rer of his Soul:
Should venal C—ts the scandal of the Land,
Snatch the relentless Villain from her Hand,
Keen Execrations on this Plate inscrib'd,
Shall reach a JUDGE who never can be brib'd.

The unhappy Sufferers were Mess.ʳˢ SAMᴸ GRAY SAMᴸ MAVERICK, JAMˢ CALDWELL, CRISPUS ATTUCKS & PATᴷ CARR
Killed. Six wounded two of them (CHRISTᵉ MONK & JOHN CLARK) Mortally

THE BOSTON MASSACRE
From an engraving by Paul Revere

The news that the Townshend duties had been repealed tended once more to restore good relations between the colonies and the mother *Good rela-* country. Non-importation agreements were generally *tions restored* rescinded or were reduced in scope to oppose merely the importation from England of tea, which, it was well understood, could be smuggled in from Holland without much difficulty, and even the boycott on tea was not well observed. The fact that the British government had not backed down on the right of Parliament to tax the colonies troubled very few, for most Americans cared less about the theory of taxation than about the practice, and in practice the British attempt to tax the colonies had failed.

It would not be correct to say, however, that the fires of discontent had gone out; they were merely burning low. Evidence that they might flame up again at any time was not difficult to find. The enforcement of British trade regulations was a never-ending source of irritation, and sometimes led to violence. When, for example, a revenue schooner, the *Gaspee*, ran aground on the Rhode Island coast, her captain and crew were overpowered by a mob of colonists and the vessel burned (June, 1772). Efforts on the part of the British to bring the culprits to trial proved futile, for no one could be found who would give evidence against them; and British talk that suspects might be taken to England for trial made a bad situation worse.

In Massachusetts Samuel Adams continued with strong backing his attacks upon the aristocratic control of the colony, now admirably *Committees* personified in the new governor, Thomas Hutchinson,[1] who *of corre-* was appointed in 1770. With some asperity the two set *spondence* forth in detail their conflicting notions on the sovereignty of Parliament. In 1772 Adams, who had heard that the King intended to pay Massachusetts judges out of money collected from the colonial customs, organized the radical elements of the colony through "committees of correspondence," which were charged with the duty of informing one another of the current state of affairs. Next year some of the back-country radicals in the Virginia House of Burgesses, led by Patrick Henry, Richard Henry Lee, and Thomas Jefferson, decided that intercolonial committees of correspondence would be a good thing, and induced the House to appoint such a committee for Virginia. Radicals elsewhere soon took up with the idea, and presently a network of radical committees came into existence through which, when occasion should demand, revolutionary sentiment might easily be fomented and revolutionary action taken.

[1] J. K. Hosmer, *The Life of Thomas Hutchinson* (1896).

At a time when the British government might well have been exerting itself to maintain good relations with the colonies, it blundered most unfortunately by passing a Tea Act which was well designed *The tax on* to revive once more the old controversy over taxation. *tea* The East India Company, it chanced, was in sore straits financially and a fitting object for governmental solicitude. It had on hand in English warehouses a large quantity of tea which it had found difficulty in marketing, partly, no doubt, because too many Americans drank tea smuggled in from Holland. To help save the company from bankruptcy by finding a market for its tea, the British government now agreed to remit the twelvepence a pound duty charged in England on all tea imported, and to allow the tea to be reshipped to America, where it would pay only threepence duty (May, 1773). Since the cost of transportation would not be great, it seemed evident that tea could thus be landed and sold in the colonies for less than it could be sold in England, where the twelvepence duty still held, and probably for less even than the Americans would have to pay for smuggled tea. For the most part the measure was designed merely for the relief of the East India Company, but the hope that cheap tea might induce the Americans to forget their scruples on taxation was by no means absent. As Lord North said, "the king meant to try the case in America."

The Tea Act was extremely annoying to colonial merchants who had grown rich from smuggling, and it furnished Adams and his radical following with a new and attractive grievance. It proved *Colonial* easy to organize resistance to the landing of the tea, and a *resistance* variety of unpleasant receptions were arranged for the tea ships now dispatched for all the more important colonial ports. So much opposition to the sale of the tea developed that many of the agents appointed to receive it were afraid to carry out their commissions, and resigned. The ships sent to New York and Philadelphia returned to England with their cargoes intact. Tea was landed at Charleston, but since no one was on hand to pay the duty it was stored in government warehouses and left there until after the Declaration of Independence, when it was sold at auction for the benefit of the patriot cause. At Annapolis a mass meeting decided that the tea ship should not be permitted to land its cargo, and to insure that result a mob set fire to the ship.

Boston was thus not alone in refusing entry to British tea; but the Boston Tea Party attracted more attention than all the other colonial acts of insubordination put together. The Boston agents, *The Boston* close relatives of the governor, Thomas Hutchinson, re- *Tea Party* fused to resign, and Hutchinson refused to permit the tea ships to return to England. On November 29, 1773, a mass meeting of citizens held in the Old South Church voted that the tea should not be landed, and a few weeks later (December 16), following another mass meeting, fifty or sixty men, faintly disguised as Indians, boarded the ships and threw the tea into the harbor. In Boston a large crowd looked on approvingly while the tea was destroyed, and elsewhere in the colonies, when the news was known, there were many to commend the act. Some Americans, among them Benjamin Franklin, regretted what had been done, and nearly all Englishmen, including as consistent a friend of America as William Pitt, regarded the Tea Party as an outrage. Why Americans should refuse to buy tea for even less than Englishmen could buy it seemed to many of the latter almost beyond comprehension.

The British government under the circumstances could hardly fail to attempt retaliation. Early in 1774 five measures, usually called by the *The "Intol-* Americans the "Intolerable Acts," were passed by Parlia- *erable Acts"* ment.[1] The Boston Port Act ordered that the port of Boston should be closed to all commerce except the barest essentials until the tea destroyed had been paid for. The Massachusetts Government Act re-formed the government of that colony by increasing the power of the governor, by making the council, or upper house of the assembly, appointive instead of elective, and by suppressing town meetings — "hotbeds of sedition" — except as the governor might permit. An Act for the Impartial Administration of Justice enabled royal officials who were accused of capital offenses in Massachusetts to be sent for trial to England or to another colony whenever, in the opinion of the governor, a fair trial in the local courts would be difficult to secure. The Quartering Act, which applied to other colonies as well as Massachusetts, authorized colonial governors to requisition such buildings as might be needed for the use of royal troops stationed within the boundaries of a given colony.

The Quebec Act, which to the Americans seemed quite as "intolerable" as any of the rest, was not designed by the British government as *The Quebec* a punitive measure. It was based upon several years' *Act* experience in attempting to govern the territory in America recently acquired from France, and showed a spirit of accommodation towards the French subjects of Great Britain that was all too rarely in evidence when the British government dealt with its English colonists.

[1] W. E. H. Lecky, *The American Revolution, 1763–1783* (1898), is a selection from the author's eight volume *History of England in the Eighteenth Century* of all "chapters and passages relating to America." Edited by J. A. Woodburn.

The French, unaccustomed to participation in the affairs of government, were given once more an autocratic régime. French rather than English legal traditions were permitted to govern in the trial of civil suits, thus eliminating the use of juries in such cases; and the religion of the French, Roman Catholicism, including the right of priests to collect tithes, received full legal recognition. Less defensible was the extension of the boundaries of the province to include the territory north of the Ohio River and east of the Mississippi, although Canadian fur-traders operated throughout this region and several French villages were located in the Illinois country. The passage of this act suggests that England did not consider the western land claims of the seaboard colonies to be worthy of much respect.

These five measures could scarcely have been better calculated to arouse to the highest pitch the spirit of resistance in America. General Gage, who now replaced Hutchinson as governor of Massa- *American* chusetts, appeared in Boston with four regiments of troops *resentment* to enforce the acts designed for special application there; and he discharged his duty with such thoroughness as to leave no doubt about the seriousness of the British intentions. What was happening to Boston and Massachusetts might at any time happen to other ports and other colonies. Colonial charters might be altered or abolished at the whim of the British Parliament. The expansion westward of such of the colonies as had claims to western lands was definitely blocked by the Quebec Act. That ill-timed measure seemed, indeed, to threaten American liberties in more ways than one. Did the British government intend that the autocratic government established in Canada should be the pattern to which all the American colonies must conform? Were such fundamental rights of Englishmen as trial by jury on the wane in America? Was Roman Catholicism to be encouraged as a counterweight to New England Puritanism? It was true enough that the Intolerable Acts were denounced by some outstanding English liberals such as Burke and Chatham (William Pitt), but they pleased the King, and the King's power was on the rise.

The network of committees of correspondence that Samuel Adams had inaugurated now began to function, and Massachusetts was soon assured that she had the sympathy and support of the *The First* radical element throughout the colonies. A plan for con- *Continental* certed action was soon devised. When the Virginia House *Congress* of Burgesses adopted a resolution naming June 1, the day Boston harbor was to be closed, as a day of fasting and prayer, the royal governor dissolved the House for its impudence; but the members, meeting un-

[131]

officially afterwards, adopted a resolution calling upon all the colonies to send delegates to a Continental Congress, to meet in Philadelphia the following September. This resolution, which was industriously circulated by the committees of correspondence, received a hearty response, and delegates to the proposed Congress were speedily selected. Sometimes they were chosen by the committees of correspondence themselves, sometimes by self-appointed committees of safety, sometimes by provincial mass meetings, and in a few cases only by colonial legislatures. In the main the more radical opponents of British policy controlled the selection of these delegates. Conservatives were not interested or were not consulted.

The years of controversy with Great Britain had divided colonial society more or less definitely into two schools of thought. There was *Radicals vs.* general agreement that the British government had dealt *conservatives* unfairly with the colonies, but there was a wide divergence of opinion as to how best to meet the situation. The radicals were determined never to yield to the British pretentions. They meant to stand firmly by the rights Americans had always enjoyed and to gain new rights if they could. But the conservatives, who saw more clearly the great benefits of British trade and British protection, favored conciliation. The colonies, they thought, could even afford to give up some of their cherished rights rather than lose the advantages that their status within the British Empire gave them. In general the lower and middle classes inclined more toward the radical point of view, while the well-to-do upper classes were conservative. There were, however, many interesting deviations from this division. Many rich colonial merchants were so greatly outraged by the course of the British government that they were willing to make common cause with the radicals. So also were the bulk of the planter aristocrats of the South, intense individualists almost to the last man, who regarded with extreme disfavor both the regulations of the British government and their own embarrassing indebtedness to British merchants. Class lines were still further shifted by the fact that to many Americans, particularly those of the interior and the "back country," "home rule" was of rather less consequence than "who should rule at home." [1] In New England and some of the Middle Colonies, revolt against English control and revolt against the local governing aristocracy was practically one and the same, for an end to British domination would be the surest means of undermining the power of the local aristocrats. In Virginia, back-country farmers

[1] On the attitude of the back country toward the East, see C. H. Lincoln, *The Revolutionary Movement in Pennsylvania, 1760–1776* (1901).

[132]

and tidewater planters postponed their local differences to make common cause against the more pressing dangers of British misrule; but in the Carolinas the pioneer farmers generally took the British side, for they found it difficult to understand how there could be any good in a cause which won the support of so many tidewater aristocrats.

The First Continental Congress, which began its sessions in Philadelphia September 5, 1774, was attended by fifty-five delegates representing every colony except Georgia. It was soon apparent *Galloway's* that the radicals were in the majority; indeed, considering *plan* the methods used in selecting the delegates, there could have been no other result. Nevertheless a plan of compromise that was proposed by Joseph Galloway of Pennsylvania came within one vote of adoption. Galloway's plan suggested that a grand council should be constituted which would consist of delegates chosen by the various colonial assemblies and would have authority to deal with such matters as might concern both Great Britain and the colonies or more than one colony. A president-general, appointed by the crown, was to possess an absolute veto on all measures passed by the council; and the consent of both the British Parliament and the colonial council was to be required to give validity to imperial regulations touching America. In time of war the council might levy taxes independently.

But the radicals were eager to avoid any appearance of yielding to the British contentions, and succeeded presently in pushing through a far less conciliatory program. A Declaration of Rights and *Declaration* Grievances was adopted which stated the American case *of Rights and* against taxation without representation as clearly as the *Grievances* somewhat conflicting opinions of the delegates on that subject would permit, branded the "Intolerable Acts" as "unpolitic, unjust, cruel and unconstitutional," and demanded their repeal. The language of the Declaration was deferential enough, but the statement of the American case was thoroughly unyielding. To ensure that words would be backed by deeds, the Congress went on to frame a "Continental Association," by which the delegates bound themselves and, so far as they could, those whom they represented not to import or use British goods against which duties were levied. Also, the slave trade was to be discontinued, and if the British government failed to come to terms with the Americans inside of a year, American exports to the British Isles and to the West Indies were to be stopped. The enforcement of this measure was to be turned over to popularly elected local committees, who should make it their business to publish violations of the agreement, seize goods imported in defiance of its terms, and maintain a united front against the

British. And after the lapse of a year a second Continental Congress should meet to observe the progress of events.

The actions of the First Continental Congress were essentially revolutionary. Without any constitutional authority whatever the Congress *Work of the* had to all intents and purposes passed a law and provided *Association* the means for its enforcement. For the Association proved to be singularly effective. In nearly every colony radical committees were organized which resorted, when it was deemed necessary, to such acts of violence as tarring and feathering to secure obedience to the regulations of the revolutionary Congress. Radical spokesmen urged also with some success that such home industries as might serve to diminish dependence on Great Britain be patronized, and that as a fit precaution against further British injustices militia companies be formed and munitions of war collected.

These measures had much the same effect upon British opinion as Americans had learned by previous experience to expect. Burke and *English* other English liberals urged that the various repressive acts *opinion* be repealed, and that the status which the colonists had enjoyed at the close of the French and Indian War be restored. Pitt believed that a bargain could be struck with the colonists by which they would agree to acknowledge the legislative supremacy of Parliament in return for the promise that Parliament would not construe its power to include the right to tax the colonies. Merchants in London and elsewhere, who were losing heavily from the American boycott, petitioned Parliament to conciliate the Americans and reopen trade. But this time the ministry, strongly supported by the King and by a majority in the Parliament just elected, refused to yield to the clamor. Instead it placed closer limits on New England trade and voted to send more troops to America. Lord North's "Conciliatory Proposition," which offered immunity from parliamentary taxes to any colony which would agree to assume of its own accord its fair share of imperial expense, was generally regarded in America as merely a device to promote dissension among the Americans, and probably was so intended.

Meantime party lines in America became more and more definite. The day of temporizing was soon over, and wavering citizens were *Growth of* gradually forced to decide what course they meant to sup- *radicalism* port. For some time even the radicals were not precisely *in America* of one mind. All were agreed that no concessions should be made to the British point of view, but the more moderate, who hoped to avert the use of force unless in case of extreme necessity, viewed with some misgivings the military preparations under way. Similarly the conservatives disagreed among themselves. Some thought that resistance, so long as it was strictly peaceful, might well be continued in the hope of ultimate success; others were eager for conciliation and compromise. Ultimately the conservatives parted company. The extremists, preferring the British connection to anything that resistance to the mother country had to offer, became the "Tories" or "Loyalists" of the American Revolution. The moderates, on the other hand, gradually drifted over to the radicals, and ultimately joined with them as "Whigs" or "Patriots" to take up arms and to win independence. Doubtless a minority in the beginning, the radical extremists through their effective organization and aggressive tactics ultimately won over a majority to their way of thinking. But probably as many as a third of the colonists were openly or secretly loyal to the mother country throughout the Revolution.

CHAPTER VIII

REVOLUTION

EVENTS were now moving rapidly in the direction of that appeal to arms which many observers on both sides of the Atlantic had long foreseen.[1] In Massachusetts the authority of Governor Gage was openly defied; "minute men" were being drilled upon the village commons, and stores of munitions were being collected at strategic spots. Neither side wished to precipitate hostilities, but as a necessary measure of self-defense Gage finally felt obliged to seize the military supplies that the radical leaders had accumulated at Concord, and to arrest, if possible, the arch-conspirators, Samuel Adams and John Hancock.

With these ends in view a small detachment of troops left Boston on the night of April 18, 1775. The governor had counted on surprise,
Lexington and Concord but his opponents had been on the lookout, and thanks to the activities of Paul Revere and others the whole country-side was soon aware of the coming of the "redcoats." When, early on the morning of the nineteenth, the troops entered Lexington, they found a company of armed militia drawn up on the meeting-house green, presumably with intent to oppose the British advance. Thereupon Major Pitcairn, in command of the British, rode forward and ordered the Americans to disperse. Captain John Parker, who led the colonial militia, observing that his men were badly outnumbered, also ordered them to withdraw. But from some quarter, whether British or American will never be known, a shot was fired, after which the firing became general.[2] Resistance to the British troops proved futile, as Parker had

---

[1] Most of the books cited in the preceding chapter are useful also on the period of actual warfare. S. G. Fisher, *The Struggle for American Independence* (2 vols., 1908), is in many respects the most satisfactory general account of the period. Strongly sympathetic with the American cause is Sir George Otto Trevelyan, *The American Revolution* (3 vols., 1905). John Fiske, *The American Revolution* (2 vols., 1891), has not stood the test at every point of recent critical scholarship, but is extremely interesting. One of the best single volumes on the war is C. H. Van Tyne, *The American Revolution, 1776–1783* (1905). On the strictly military side of the struggle F. V. Greene, *The Revolutionary War* (1911), is excellent.

[2] The documents needed to study the controversial phases of this battle are set forth in A. C. McLaughlin and others, *Source Problems in United States History* (1918).

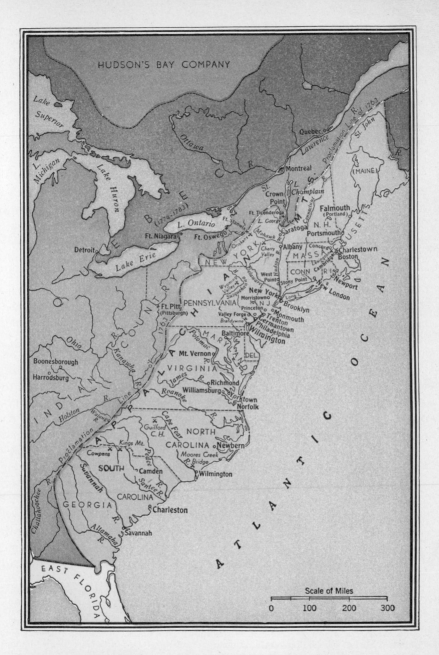

THE UNITED STATES DURING THE REVOLUTION

LIBRARY
FLORIDA STATE COLLEGE FOR WOMEN
TALLAHASSEE, FLORIDA

foreseen, and leaving the Americans to care for a number of dead and wounded, Pitcairn marched on to Concord. There he found and destroyed the American supplies, but he scored no further triumphs. On the return to Boston his troops were the target for farmers and militiamen who lined the roads, and from behind stone walls, rocks, and trees picked off so many of the redcoats that the retreat to Boston ended in a humiliating rout. The news of this long-awaited clash soon penetrated to every village and hamlet throughout the colonies. From all New England armed militiamen collected around Boston to lay siege to the city, and patriotic resolves from far and near assured the Massachusetts radicals that in the course they had chosen they would not lack for support.

On the tenth of May following the affairs at Lexington and Concord the second Continental Congress began its sessions at Philadelphia. The new Congress was a far more radical body than its *The second* predecessor, partly because the colonial governors had re- *Continental* ceived instructions from England to prevent the election *Congress* of delegates to another Congress, and the choices had therefore to be made by strictly revolutionary groups. There were moderates present, however, such as John Dickinson of Pennsylvania, and they not only prevented an immediate declaration of independence, but they also succeeded in inducing the delegates to appeal once more to the King for redress of grievances. But the tide of revolution could not be stemmed for long. On June 15 Congress took over the troops gathered near Boston as the Continental Army, and assumed authority to direct the course of the war. At the suggestion of John Adams, it gave the command of these troops to George Washington, the well-known Virginia aristocrat. While this selection was designed in part to flatter the South and in part to placate the upper classes of every section, probably no wiser choice could have been made.

Washington was present in uniform as a delegate to the Continental Congress from Virginia when he was chosen to head the army. He set out at once to join his command, but before he could com- *Bunker Hill* plete his journey another battle had been fought. Reinforcements had brought the number of British soldiers in Boston to about ten thousand men, and General Gage, fearful lest the Americans should gain possession of the hills that surrounded the city and open on him with cannon fire, planned to occupy some of the hills himself. But the Americans anticipated him, and sent twelve hundred men under Colonel William Prescott to occupy Bunker Hill in Charlestown, although Prescott's command went beyond Bunker Hill to Breed's Hill, and began fortifications there. It would have been easy for the British to entrap the Americans, since the heights in Charlestown were connected with the mainland by only a narrow neck of land. But Gage, instead of attempting to cut off Prescott's chance of retreat, ordered a direct assault up the hill from the bay. Twice the colonial lines held, and twice the British after heavy losses retreated to re-form their lines. On the third assault, the Americans gave way, for they had run short of ammunition. But the battle of Bunker Hill, as it has always been called, fought June 17, 1775, proved alike to the British and to the colonists that as soldiers the raw American militia were not wholly to be despised.

Nevertheless the colonial troops about Boston, numbering perhaps twenty thousand, that Washington now undertook to command were *Washington in command* less an army than a mob. Organization was lacking, bickering over precedence in military rank was rife, supplies were woefully inadequate, desertions were dangerously numerous. Washington's ability to draw order out of chaos never showed itself to better advantage. The troops were drilled and taught to obey, desertions were checked, and a better plan for the siege of Boston was evolved. All summer and fall and far into the winter, the American army watched and waited, while the British within the city, now under the command of General Howe, hesitated to attack. At length, on the fourth of March, 1776, Washington occupied Dorchester Heights, to the south of Boston, and trained his cannon on the city. Faced by this dire threat, Howe hastily embarked his troops for Nova Scotia, taking with him also nearly a thousand Loyalists who feared to face the American occupation.

The cannon that Washington used to make Boston untenable for the British had been dragged overland from Ticonderoga, a captured British *The attack on Canada* fort at the southern end of the Lake George–Lake Champlain approach to Canada. This post and Crown Point, which lay farther to the north, were made the objectives of two expeditions, one led by Ethan Allen, who held a Connecticut commission, and another led by Benedict Arnold, under the authority of Massachusetts. The two expeditions combined, and on the very day that the second Continental Congress opened, Ticonderoga surrendered without the firing of a gun. With Crown Point also taken, the pathway to Canada seemed open, and Congress, hoping that the French there might be induced to join in the revolt, authorized Richard Montgomery and Benedict Arnold, with separate commands, to continue the northward advance. In November, 1775, Montgomery took Montreal and then co-operated with Arnold, who had made an heroic march through the

Maine woods, in the attack on Quebec. But an assault made December 31, 1775, which cost Montgomery his life, was unsuccessful, and the winter siege that followed proved equally futile. With the French showing no desire to help the Americans, and the British ably commanded by Sir Guy Carleton, Montreal was abandoned and Arnold's troops were soon forced back to Crown Point.[1]

The only other military activity of consequence during the first year of the war occurred in the Carolinas, where the British made a bid for the support of the back-country Loyalists. An ex- *The* pedition was dispatched by sea to attack Wilmington and *Carolinas* Charleston, but before the fleet reached Wilmington a clash at Moore's Creek Bridge, February 27, 1776, between North Carolina Patriots and Loyalists gave a complete victory to the former. General Clinton, in command of the British expedition, then gave up hope of taking Wilmington, and went on to Charleston, where he met such stiff resistance that he abandoned the entire project and retired (June, 1776).

The first year's fighting thus ended in a kind of stalemate, with the Americans repulsed in their effort to conquer Canada, and the British equally unable to secure a foothold anywhere in the col- *Sentiment* onies. But American opinion during this period had not *for inde-* remained stationary. At the outbreak of hostilities, only *pendence* a few extremists were ready to go the whole length of separation from Great Britain; the great majority thought of the conflict as merely a civil war conducted to maintain American rights within the British Empire. Indeed, such was their sentimental attachment for the mother country that many colonials took up arms against her with extreme reluctance. They counted on the aid of powerful English liberals, such as Burke and Pitt, to bring the British government to a more conciliatory point of view, and they hoped devoutly that the fighting would not last long. But the events of the year seemed to belie their hopes. George III had turned down the American petition for the redress of grievances, had branded the Americans as rebels, apparently with the full support of Parliament, and had even begun to hire German troops — "Hessians" — to assist in the vigorous prosecution of the war. Furthermore, there were changes in America. The old colonial governments had crumbled away, and to forestall anarchy new political foundations had had to be laid. Revolution had thus taken place in fact if not yet in name. Also, American trade was suffering acutely, and since seemingly trade with Great Britain could not be reopened — was now forbidden by an act of

[1] This campaign is entertainingly described by Justin H. Smith, *Our Struggle for the Fourteenth Colony — Canada and the American Revolution* (1907).

Parliament — other outlets for American trade must be found. Such outlets only an avowedly independent nation, fully competent to make treaties for itself, would be able to obtain. And, since the war must needs continue, expediency demanded that help be sought from the traditional enemies of Great Britain, particularly from France. But what foreign nation would care to exert itself merely to secure a redress of grievances for Americans within the British Empire? On the other hand, if the disruption of the Empire was the American goal there was plenty of outside interest in that.

At precisely the right moment there appeared a pamphlet by Thomas Paine, entitled *Common Sense*, which stated simply and effectively the American case for independence. Paine had only lately come from England to America, but he was a lover of liberty, and the opportunity to strike a blow in its behalf appealed to him strongly. He ridiculed the idea of personal loyalty to the King, of which so much had been made in American protests against the tyranny of Parliament, and called George III a "royal brute." He saw "something absurd in supposing a continent to be perpetually governed by an island," since "in no instance hath nature made the satellite larger than the primary planet." He branded reconciliation as "a fallacious dream," and found a potent argument for separation "in the blood of the slain." The pamphlet sold by the hundreds of thousands, and in the early months of the year 1776 was read and quoted everywhere in America. Neither its logic nor its language was above reproach, but the common man liked both, and the sentiment in favor of independence grew accordingly.[1]

Paine's "Common Sense"

That Congress was in a mood to respond to the shift in public opinion soon seemed evident. As early as April, 1776, the North Carolina delegates received instructions to work for independence, and next month Virginia openly proclaimed her own secession from the British Empire. On the seventh of June, Richard Henry Lee, seconded by John Adams, offered a resolution "that these United Colonies, are, and of right ought to be, free and independent states." Doubtless this resolution expressed the sentiments of an overwhelming majority of the delegates, but to satisfy a small minority it was agreed, June 10, that the vote should be delayed three weeks. Not until July 1, however, was the debate resumed, and at this time a vote in committee of the whole showed only nine states favorable. But when the formal vote was taken next day, every state save New York, whose provincial convention gave its assent a week later, was for independence.

[1] M. C. Tyler, *Literary History of the American Revolution, 1763–1783* (2 vols., 1897).

Meantime a committee headed by Jefferson had been at work upon an appropriate declaration through which to convey to the world the decision that it was confidently believed Congress would reach. On July 2, the same day that Congress voted for independence, this committee presented its report. After striking from this document a passage which censured the British people as well as their rulers, and another which severely arraigned the King for forcing the slave trade upon the colonies, the remainder of the Declaration of Independence that the committee had formulated was adopted, July 4, 1776. Two weeks later Congress decided that the document should be engrossed on parchment and signed by all the delegates; and this was done. On August 2 the members of Congress who were present affixed their signatures, and later as occasion offered those who had been absent were given an opportunity to sign their names.

The Declaration of Independence

The Declaration of Independence, which was written almost entirely by Jefferson, borrowed heavily from Locke's *Second Essay of Government*, and asserted in language already familiar the natural rights of men, including the right of revolution. It differed markedly from earlier American protests in that it directed its attack primarily against the King rather than against Parliament. Hitherto the Americans, while they had denounced Parliament unsparingly for assuming powers unwarranted by the British Constitution, had been content to acknowledge the King as a common sovereign. Now they blamed him even for some of the offensive acts of Parliament, and held that the long list of grievances they were able to recite constituted a kind of breach of contract on the part of the monarch which gave the colonies the right, if they chose, to become free and independent states.[1]

The appearance of unanimity which accompanied the Declaration quite belied the facts. Not less than a third of the Americans would have preferred that the colonies retain their membership in the British Empire, and in the course of the next few years probably as many as fifty thousand of these "Loyalists" proved their sentiments by fighting with the British forces and against the "Patriots." So numerous were the pro-British Americans in some localities that Washington's forces, rather than his adversaries, sometimes suffered the disadvantage of fighting in enemy territory. Natur-

Loyalists vs. Patriots

[1] Naturally this document has been subjected to the closest scrutiny. The best such study is Carl L. Becker, *The Declaration of Independence; a Study in the History of Political Ideas* (1922). See also Herbert Friedenwald, *The Declaration of Independence, an Interpretation and an Analysis* (1904); and J. H. Hazleton, *The Declaration of Independence; its History* (1906).

ally the Loyalists, unless they were fortunate enough to live where they could receive the protection of British troops, came in for as severe persecution as the Patriots could inflict. Many Loyalists saw their property destroyed or confiscated, they often suffered great personal violence, and they were driven by the thousands to take refuge in Canada, the West Indies, or England.[1]

Nor had complete political unification been achieved in America. When the thirteen separate colonies became thirteen separate and independent states, the difficulties of union that had been so overwhelming before the Revolution were by no means eradicated. The new states did indeed co-operate through Congress in a way that they had been unable to agree upon before; but the Articles of Confederation which were presently presented and adopted as a codification of the existing practice merely provided for a loose alliance that only the necessities of war could hold together. Congress was sadly lacking in authority, and often proved to be a debating society when what was needed was a powerful and efficient central war office.

Over against these political dissensions in America, however, the English were unable to present a united front. The King's party, *English opinion on the war* which strongly favored the war, was supported by the upper classes generally — the ministers, the nobility, the majority in Parliament, the leading lawyers, the clergy of the established church, and even a few of the dissenting clergy such as John Wesley, the founder of Methodism. But the opposition party was far from enthusiastic at taking up arms against the Americans. Liberal leaders, long convinced that such a step was as unnecessary as it was unwise, reflected that failure to win the war would serve their ends well by discrediting the personal power of the King and causing the downfall of his satellites in the ministry; merchants desirous of retaining American trade longed for normal times and were not too particular about how they should be restored; dissenting ministers very generally lined up against the King and the established church; the common people, who were practically without a voice in politics, showed their resentment against being required to fight far from home and against Englishmen by refusing to enlist; and there was the customary trouble in Ireland.

The inefficiency of the British government as a war-making machine was also a handicap. The King's friends in the ministry were often of little merit as administrators. Lord George Germain, Secretary of

[1] C. H. Van Tyne, *The Loyalists of the American Revolution* (1902), clears the "Tories" of many of the charges made against them by the "Whigs" and believed by later generations. *The War of Independence* (1929), by the same author, brings events only to the year 1778.

State for the Colonies, had himself been cashiered from the army, and was sorely lacking in talent. Lord Sandwich, in charge of the Admiralty, was a notorious corruptionist. The American Congress with its defective organization and its lack of experience was at times not more inept in the direction of affairs than the British government under these incompetent leaders.

In the comparison of armed forces, the odds told more heavily against the Americans. The number of enlistments in the Continental Army was great, reaching perhaps ninety thousand in the year *The Patriot* 1776, but this was due to the fact that short-term enlist- *army* ments, often for only three months, were permitted. Washington rarely had as many as sixteen thousand men under his command at any one time, and at Valley Forge his forces had dwindled to a paltry two thousand. As the war wore on the difficulty of obtaining enlistments increased, for the soldier's wages, low enough in any event, were always in arrears, while work was plentiful and brought a much higher and surer reward. Moreover, the American troops were never adequately supplied with munitions, and they were often clothed only in rags. Supplementing the Continental Army which Congress created was the state militia. These troops sometimes fought well when defending their own homes and firesides, but otherwise they were exceedingly undependable. Practically none of the American volunteers had had anything like adequate training in military tactics, thanks to the short-term enlistments, and the American officers were forced to whip a new army into shape for practically every battle. For all their shortcomings the American soldiers were as individuals hardy and resourceful; some of them had profited from military service during the French and Indian War, or other Indian wars; and at least a small nucleus were deeply enough devoted to the cause for which they fought that they stood together regardless of all difficulties.[1]

To oppose the Americans the British had a well-drilled regular army of perhaps sixty thousand men, most of whom were needed on garrison duty somewhere in the far-flung British Empire. What *The* might have amounted otherwise to an embarrassing short- *redcoats* age of troops was made up for by the use of "Hessians," of Loyalists, or "Tories," and of Indians. The British commanders in America were, on the whole, adequately supplied with troops. Clinton's army in 1781 reached a total of thirty-four thousand men. While Howe was at Philadelphia he had under his command about seventeen thousand

---

[1] L. C. Hatch, *The Administration of the American Revolutionary Army* (1904); C. K. Bolton, *The Private Soldier under Washington* (1902).

men. The British redcoats, moreover, were not "summer soldiers and sunshine patriots," but were enlisted for long terms, were rigorously disciplined, and were adequately supplied with the materials of war. They were backed also by almost unlimited naval power, for Great Britain was the clearly acknowledged mistress of the ocean. Even with the assistance of the French, the efforts of the Americans to challenge British sea-power were painfully inadequate. And yet all this superiority was not enough to enable the British to win. Their armies were three thousand miles away from home; their attack had to be delivered along a thousand miles of seacoast; and they were confronted, once they had penetrated into the interior, with a trackless wilderness where conquest was virtually impossible as long as the will to resist endured.[1]

In point of military leadership, thanks mainly to the solid qualities of Washington, the Americans were superior to the British. It cannot be *Washington the general* demonstrated that as a commanding officer Washington was a genius. He was not thoroughly versed in military tactics, and he might have had great difficulty in commanding large armies. But whatever the limits of his ability, he proved equal to the existing emergency. His obvious integrity, his unflinching courage, and his dogged determination inspired his men with confidence and paved the way to ultimate victory. He was a master of the strategy of retreat, and understood thoroughly that while he had an army in the field the Patriot cause was not lost.[2]

Unfortunately most of Washington's immediate subordinates were of mediocre or even inferior abilities. Charles Lee, with perhaps more military experience than Washington himself, proved to be untrustworthy and insubordinate. Benedict Arnold, with all his dash and brilliance, lacked something of fundamental importance in the way of character. Horatio Gates, a favorite of the politicians, disappointed even their expectations. Possibly Nathanael Greene, who had had virtually no military experience prior to the war, was the ablest of Washington's lieutenants. The contribution of a number of European officers who joined the American army was highly creditable. Chief among these were the two Germans, Steuben and Kalb, whose up-to-date knowledge of military tactics was an invaluable asset to the Americans; the two Poles, Kosciusko and Pulaski, who brought enthusiasm as well as ability to the defense of the American cause; and the young

[1] E. E. Curtis, *The Organization of the British Army in the American Revolution* (1926).

[2] G. M. Wrong, *Washington and his Comrades at Arms* (1921), gives a satisfactory estimate of Washington's military achievements. More detailed are the volumes by Rupert Hughes, *George Washington, the Rebel and the Patriot, 1762–1777* (1927), and *The Savior of the States, 1777–1781* (1930).

WASHINGTON AS A SOLDIER
From a painting by Charles Wilson Peale

Frenchman, Lafayette, who so spectacularly displayed the interest that many of his countrymen felt in the success of the Americans.

The British commanders were not well chosen. Neither Howe, who was placed in command at the outset of the war, nor Clinton, who suc-*The British commanders* ceeded him, were first-rate men, and both of them for reasons that are more or less unaccountable failed to do even the best that might have been expected of them. There is some truth in the assertion, frequently made, that Howe should share equally with Washington the credit for the final American victory. Probably his lack of vigor at the outset was due in part to his hope that a reconciliation between the mother country and the colonies could be obtained, but with respect to the later period of his command there was much more than humor in Franklin's remark, "Philadelphia has taken Howe." [1] Clinton's task was more difficult than his predecessor's, but he too was dilatory, and by his failure to take full advantage of his opportunities more than once seemed to give the game away. The British commanders, and their subordinates also, far outmatched the Americans in the matter of technical knowledge, but the unusual character of the fighting in America sometimes turned this seeming advantage, as for Braddock before them, into a liability.

From the outset the financial situation in America was well-nigh hopeless. The colonies were not rich in taxable resources, and such opportunities *American finances* for taxation as existed could not be fully exploited. The unpopularity of taxes in general had not a little to do with the American revolt, and the new revolutionary governments dare not risk their permanence by demanding heavy levies. Nor did they find it either easy or expedient to borrow great sums. As for Congress, it lacked any power of taxation whatever, and it had little credit upon which to rely for loans. Very early, therefore, it resorted to paper money issues. By the end of 1778 one hundred million dollars in "continental currency" had been placed in circulation, and within the next year Congress issued one hundred and forty-three million dollars more. In consequence, by 1780 continental currency had fallen in value to two cents on the dollar. Jefferson had to pay one hundred and twenty-five dollars for a quart of brandy; Washington complained that it took a wagonload of currency to buy a wagonload of provisions; and an enterprising Philadelphia barber used the continental issues to paper the walls of his shop. Once just before the battle of Princeton, Washington, in order to keep his army from disintegrating, had to pledge the soldiers his private fortune

[1] T. S. Anderson, *The Command of the Howe Brothers During the American Revolution* (1936), weighs the evidence carefully and adjudges Howe incompetent.

to convince them that the money due them would be paid: and Robert Morris, upon whom Congress placed the chief burden of financing the war, was also compelled to borrow upon his own personal credit.[1]

The English government was in none too comfortable a financial state, but it represented at least three times the total American wealth and population, and it had the double advantage of good credit and a well-established system of taxation. British gold was available at all times in America to purchase needed supplies for the British forces — often to make difficult also the purchase of supplies for the American army, for Washington usually had only paper and promises with which to pay. Indeed, the presence of the British soldiers, while menacing to American liberty, did much for American prosperity. Farm prices kept at a high figure, labor brought good returns, and manufacturers throve as never before.

When General Howe abandoned Boston it was with the intention of striking a blow later on at some more strategic point. For several reasons, the logical place for the delivery of this blow seemed to be New York. That city was located midway between the northern and southern colonies, it possessed the best harbor on the coast, and its inhabitants were notoriously Tory in sympathy. Furthermore, by controlling the Hudson Valley, to which New York City was the gateway, the British hoped to separate the New England colonies from the rest. Also, by the Lake Champlain route, land connections with Canada might possibly be established.

Accordingly, after a short stay at Halifax, General Howe embarked a formidable army — twenty-five thousand British and eight thousand Hessians — for New York. Anticipating his move, Washington had abandoned Boston, and with perhaps eighteen thousand men under his command had prepared to defend New York. *Howe takes New York* Probably his decision to oppose Howe's effort to take the city was unwise, for the Americans suffered several discouraging defeats, and in the end the British succeeded in their attempt. Most of Washington's troops were stationed on Long Island, and after the battle of Brooklyn Heights, August 27, 1776, in which the Americans were badly defeated, only the dilatory tactics of Howe and the aid of a friendly fog which enabled Washington to ferry his troops across to New York prevented an overwhelming disaster.

Perhaps Howe might have been more aggressive had it not been a part of the British policy to make peace with the Americans if possible.

[1] E. P. Oberholtzer, *Robert Morris* (1903); W. G. Sumner, *The Financier and the Finances of the Revolution* (1891).

Indeed, Lord Howe, the general's brother, who commanded the British fleet at New York, had definite instructions to offer liberal terms if the Americans would only lay down their arms. After the battle of Brooklyn Heights he conferred with a committee of three appointed by Congress, Adams, Franklin, and Rutledge, but nothing could be accomplished because the Americans insisted on independence, and Howe was not authorized to go that far. Washington found himself unable to prevent the landing of Howe's troops on Manhattan Island, and presently retreated across the Hudson to New Jersey. New York was held by the British until the close of the war, and furnished a haven of refuge for Loyalists from every part of America. Here the tables were turned, and the Patriots were the sufferers from persecution.

During the winter of 1776–77 Washington's army dwindled down to as few as three thousand men, and had Howe been more aggressive he *Trenton and* would certainly have had a fair chance to bring the war to *Princeton* an end. But he twice, at Trenton (December 26, 1776) and at Princeton (January 3, 1777), permitted Washington to inflict stinging defeats upon isolated British detachments, after which, with amazing indolence, he allowed the American army to remain unmolested at Morristown for the rest of the winter.

The year 1777 saw two major movements on the part of the British, one a shift of base on the part of Howe from New York to Philadelphia, *The British* the other an advance down the Lake Champlain–Hudson *occupy* Valley route by troops under the command of General Bur- *Philadelphia* goyne. Howe chose not to proceed directly overland against the rebel capital, but sent his troops most of the way by sea. To avoid the American defenses on the Delaware, the ships sailed up Chesapeake Bay as far as possible, and then marched the remaining distance. Before Philadelphia as before New York, Washington attempted against overwhelming odds to make a defense, and at Brandywine he suffered a severe defeat. Thereupon (September, 1777) Howe entered Philadelphia, and shortly afterward won another victory when Washington attacked an outlying detachment of British troops at Germantown. The occupation of Philadelphia was a great blow to American pride and caused much rejoicing among the British and Loyalists, but its military significance was slight.

Historians are still at a loss to explain adequately why Howe did not, instead of taking Philadelphia, send help to Burgoyne, who was at the *Surrender of* very time advancing toward New York from Canada with *Burgoyne* reinforcements intended for Howe's use in the campaign against Washington. Howe seems to have been well advised as to Burgoyne's plans, and had he so desired, he might have rendered that luck-

less commander invaluable assistance.   Without it Burgoyne's position
soon became desperate.   He had counted on aid from some Mohawk
Valley Loyalists and Indians under the command of Colonel St. Leger,
but the back-country Patriots, many of them Germans, furnished such
effective resistance that St. Leger's troops never got through to Burgoyne
at all, and St. Leger himself went back to Canada.   Moreover, the small
detachment of regulars with which the Americans hoped to block Burgoyne's advance was swollen by accretions of local militia until the American force numbered twenty thousand men — several times as many men
as Burgoyne commanded.   In the second of two battles, both fought at
Freeman's Farm, near Saratoga, the British suffered a disastrous defeat,
and on October 17, 1777, with his army entirely surrounded, Burgoyne
surrendered his force of fifty-eight hundred men to General Gates.   This
was the most notable victory that the Americans — or for that matter,
either side — had yet won.   It gave the Patriots good reason to hope that
in spite of their difficulties they might eventually win the war.

The surrender of Burgoyne made possible also the consummation of the
greatly desired alliance with France.[1]   Early in 1776, Congress had sent
Silas Deane to Paris with instructions to obtain whatever *The French*
aid he could from France.   A little later he was joined by *alliance*
Arthur Lee and Benjamin Franklin.   Deane was presently recalled and,
smarting under what he deemed to be unjust treatment, ultimately went
over to the British.   Lee proved to be of even less value, but in Franklin
the Americans had an ideal representative.   His venerability — he was
now seventy years old — his achievements in the realms of literature
and science, his simplicity of manner and of speech made him a natural
social lion, and he soon captivated the French.   Louis XVI's minister of
foreign affairs, Vergennes, was fortunately favorable to the idea of assisting the Americans.   He wished to get even with the British for the
losses they had inflicted on France at the close of the French and Indian
War; and he was possessed of an unreasonable fear that unless France intervened with aid for the revolting American colonies, she and her ally
Spain might lose their possessions in the West Indies to whichever power
won the war, England or America.   So even before Franklin appeared,
there was a secret but very helpful flow of arms and other supplies from
France to the Revolutionists.

With the news of Burgoyne's defeat to support his argument that
with a little help the Americans could win, Franklin pressed successfully

[1] E. S. Corwin, *French Policy and the American Alliance* (1916); J. B. Perkins, *France in
the American Revolution* (1911); Bernard Faÿ, *The Revolutionary Spirit in France and
America* (1927).

for an alliance, and on February 6, 1778, two treaties were signed between France and the United States. By one of these treaties the two nations opened their ports freely to each other's commerce; by the other they united in a military alliance to effect the independence of the United States. France agreed, when peace with England should be made, not to ask for additional territory on the mainland of North America, and the United States in turn promised to guarantee to France indefinitely the French West Indies. Neither party was to make peace without the full consent of the other.

There was much that was anomalous about this alliance between an absolute monarch and a people fighting for freedom from aristocracy; but there was also much that was natural about it. France and England were traditional enemies; each could be counted on to take every advantage of the other's distress. Then, too, there was already popular sympathy in France for the same ideals that motivated the Americans. The French Revolution was not far away, and the doctrines that lay back of it were as well known and in certain circles were as well received in France as anywhere on earth.

The value of the alliance to the American cause can hardly be over-estimated. The loans obtained from the French government supplied *French aid to America* the funds which enabled Washington to keep his army intact and in some degree prepared to fight. French officers helped in the training of American troops, and on some occasions, particularly at Yorktown, French soldiers co-operated with the Patriot army. Most significant of all was the aid of the French navy. Before France entered the war the Americans had encouraged privateering, with results that were often extremely annoying to the British; but in spite of some praiseworthy efforts on the part of Congress and the various state governments it could hardly be said that an American navy existed. French sea-power supplied this fundamental lack, and the freedom to use French ports greatly expanded the opportunities of American sea-captains. The exploits of John Paul Jones, for example, whose *Bonhomme Richard* took the *Serapis* (September, 1779) in a naval battle justly famous, would have been impossible but for the backing of the French. Even though British superiority on the high seas was at no time fully overcome during the war, French fleets hampered the British movements of troops along the American coast, threatened an attack on England that drew attention from America at a critical time, and held the British fleet at bay during the later phases of the war.[1]

[1] C. O. Paullin, *The Navy of the American Revolution* (1906); A. T. Mahan, *The Major Operations of the Navies in the War of American Independence* (1913).

Since Spain was bound firmly by the "family compact" in an alliance with France, the entrance of France into the war practically insured the entrance of Spain also. The Spanish government refused, *Spain enters* however, to make a formal alliance with the United States. *the war* Possessed of an extensive colonial empire of its own, Spain was naturally loath to encourage the idea of colonial revolts, and she viewed with some misgivings the American successes. But in England, Spain, like France, had a traditional enemy; England's possession of Gibraltar was a standing national insult. Secretly some financial aid was given the Americans before the outbreak of war between Spain and England; and after that event, which occurred in 1779, the Spanish navy co-operated constantly with the French.

Late in the war (1781), Holland, whose merchants hoped to succeed the English in the exploitation of American trade and were adepts at smuggling war materials into America, irritated the English *Holland* government into a declaration of war. The increase of naval strength which resulted from the addition of Holland to the list of England's enemies had much to do with the outcome of the war. John Adams, who was dispatched to Holland to represent America there, succeeded also in obtaining helpful loans from the Dutch bankers, and in 1782 a treaty of commerce. England had also to deal with the "Armed Neutrality," a combination of neutral nations, effected by Catherine II of Russia in 1780, which objected strenuously to the regulations which the British navy imposed upon neutral trade. Holland had been a member of the Armed Neutrality before her entrance into the war, and just how soon Russia and her allies — which included Denmark, Sweden, Portugal, and Prussia — might also exchange the status of neutrality for the status of war was a matter of conjecture. It is important to remember that in the later years of the Revolutionary War the British were fighting not only against the United States, but also against a powerful European combination which might at any time become even more powerful by the addition of new members.

Unaware of these bright prospects, Washington held his army in winter quarters at Valley Forge, near Philadelphia, during the winter of 1777–78, and wondered how long resistance could be main- *Valley* tained. During these dark days the Patriot army almost *Forge* vanished, and thanks to the inefficiency of Congress, which listened to intrigues against Washington when it should have been at work supplying his men with the necessities of life, the handful of soldiers who remained true to the cause suffered incredible privations. Howe in Philadelphia, meantime, was faring sumptuously. British gold brought in supplies from the outlying country which Washington, with only worthless promises-to-pay as currency, found himself unable to command. But fortunately for the Patriot cause Howe took his ease, and Washington's little army, in spite of its suffering, was allowed to come through the winter still an army.

Next spring the British government, visibly shaken by the news of the French alliance, was ready to offer the Americans all that they had originally taken up arms to obtain. Independence was not yet to be thought of, but a royal commission was sent to Philadelphia with terms of peace that included amnesty for those who had fought against England, the cessation of parliamentary taxation, the restoration of the Massachusetts charter, and perhaps, if the Americans wanted it, actual colonial representation in Parliament. But Congress was as much cheered by the news of the French alliance as the English government was depressed; hence terms of peace that would have been regarded as highly satisfactory two years before were now refused consideration.

With a close eye to what the French navy might be able to do, the British government now ordered General Clinton, who succeeded Howe *Clinton succeeds Howe* as commander of the British army in America, to abandon Philadelphia and concentrate his forces at New York. This movement was accomplished by a march across New Jersey, with Washington's army, infused with new life by the turn which events had taken, in close pursuit. At Monmouth, June 28, 1778, the Americans attacked the British and should have won, but the cowardly disobedience of General Charles Lee, who ordered his troops to retreat when he had been commanded by Washington to attack, cost the Americans all hope of success. Clinton got safely into New York, and Washington's army once more stood guard about that city. The British also held Newport, Rhode Island, which the Americans, counting on the assistance of a French squadron, now attempted unsuccessfully to capture. But the next year (1779) Newport also was abandoned by the British. From this time on to the close of the war no major military movements took place in the North. The British conducted many raids along the coast adjacent to New York, but these raids had little significance except, perhaps, that they diminished the prosperity of the region and intensified the opposition of its inhabitants to British rule.

Meantime the feeble American settlements along the frontier had been suffering acutely from marauding bands of Tories and Indians. Sentiment *Frontier fighting* among the traders was definitely anti-American, for the success of the revolutionary forces was sure to mean an advance of the agricultural frontier and a consequent curtailment of

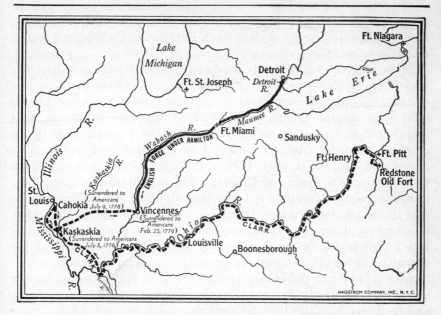

GEORGE ROGERS CLARK EXPEDITION IN THE WEST

their opportunities. The Indians, too, were well aware of the bearing of this situation on their future; they listened willingly to Colonel Henry Hamilton, in command of the British post at Detroit, and to other British officers who encouraged them to make war upon the frontier settlements. In 1778 the Wyoming Valley of Pennsylvania and the Cherry Valley of New York were the scenes of terrible massacres; and well before that date constant fighting had brought the pioneer outposts in Kentucky to the very verge of extinction.

It was at this point that George Rogers Clark, a young Kentucky land speculator who realized fully the gravity of the situation, obtained leave from Patrick Henry, the governor of Virginia, to or- *George Rogers Clark* ganize a retaliatory expedition. Clark realized that the old French towns in the Illinois country, Kaskaskia, Cahokia, and Vincennes, although seemingly indifferent to the outcome of the war, were actually havens of refuge for hostile Indians and breeding-places for conspiracies. He planned, therefore, to capture them, and if possible also the British post at Detroit. With much difficulty he succeeded in organizing a few hundred frontier militia, with which in the summer of 1778 he set out down the Ohio for the Illinois towns. From the mouth of the Cumberland he marched overland, and taking the inhabitants by

[153]

surprise captured Kaskaskia, then Cahokia, without a blow. Vincennes, also, with the connivance of the French residents in the captured towns, readily accepted Clark's control.[1]

News of these events greatly exercised Colonel Hamilton at Detroit, who determined at once to repossess Vincennes, and from that vantage-
The War in the West
point the next year to advance against the other French towns. He succeeded without difficulty in retaking Vincennes, but he was again surprised by Clark, who marched his troops overland through midwinter cold and ice to attack and capture Vincennes once again (February, 1779). Hamilton himself was sent, none too tenderly, as a prisoner to Virginia. This exploit greatly cheered the frontiersmen, for Hamilton, it was commonly reported, had made presents to the Indians in return for scalps, and the downfall of the "hair-buying general" was no small comfort. Clark never succeeded in capturing Detroit, but his activities greatly diminished the frontier difficulties with British and Indians, and probably saved the Kentucky settlements. In order to punish the Indians for their part in the Wyoming and Cherry Valley massacres of 1778, the following year Washington sent an expedition into the Iroquois country, which succeeded fairly well. Frontier fighting did not cease, but the menace from this quarter was distinctly lessened.

From 1778 to the close of the war practically all of the important fighting took place in the South. In this region there were many Loyal-
The War in the South
ists whose services the British leaders, hard-pressed for troops to face an ever-expanding list of enemies, wished to enlist. Moreover, with sentiment so badly divided in the South, victories in that quarter presumably would come easily, and the successful conquest of a number of states might serve as a wholesome warning to the rest. Accordingly Clinton dispatched an expedition by sea late in 1778 which captured Savannah, and with the aid of troops brought up from British Florida soon brought the whole of Georgia under British control.

Events now moved slowly, for the war in Europe occupied the major attention of the British; but next year an American effort to recapture Savannah with the aid of a French fleet was thwarted, and in May, 1780, the British took Charleston, making prisoners an entire Patriot army of five thousand men whom General Lincoln, the American commander, found it impossible to extricate. A small army under General Gates, sent by Congress to the assistance of the beleaguered southern Pa-

---

[1] J. A. James, *The Life of George Rogers Clark* (1928), is the best of the many biographies of the "Washington of the West." Less detailed is R. G. Thwaites, *How George Rogers Clark Won the Northwest* (1903).

triots, was poorly led, and was badly defeated by Cornwallis at Camden (August 16, 1780). South Carolina, like Georgia, now seemed lost to the Patriot cause, although irregular bands of Patriots under such leaders as Sumter, Marion, and Pickens kept close watch on the British, and seriously impeded their every movement of troops.

North Carolina was the next British goal, and Cornwallis began preparations for its conquest by sending Major Patrick Ferguson through the back country to recruit Loyalists. This action was somehow interpreted by the Watauga pioneers from across the mountains, most of whom were Patriots, as a threat against their settlements, and possibly Ferguson had *King's Mountain and the Cowpens* it in mind to teach them a lesson; in any event, they crossed the mountains in force and in October, 1780, with the assistance of such other Patriots as cared to join them, won a barbarous victory over Ferguson at King's Mountain. As a result the British advance into North Carolina was delayed until 1781, and by that time the Patriots were able to offer strenuous resistance. General Gates had been succeeded by General Nathanael Greene, a far abler leader; and Greene's chief subordinate, Daniel Morgan, soon proved his mettle by defeating a British and Loyalist force under Tarleton at the Cowpens (January, 1781). Greene himself, however, was defeated at Guilford Court House (March 15, 1781) by Cornwallis, but the British victory was so hardly won that Cornwallis temporarily gave up his advance and retired to Wilmington.

All this time Washington's main army had been kept in the vicinity of New York to prevent Clinton from expanding his lines. An atmosphere of deep gloom, which affected even Washington himself, pervaded the American camp. In addition to the dispiriting news that came from the South, there were troubles from a worthless currency, from an insufficient supply of food and clothing, from backbiting and incompetent members of Congress, and, hardest of all to bear, from the treason of Benedict Arnold.

Arnold, far more than Gates, had deserved the honor of bringing about Burgoyne's surrender, but after that time a serious wound, acquired near Saratoga, had kept him out of active fighting. He joined Washington at Valley Forge, however, and he was *Benedict Arnold* stationed at Philadelphia when Howe abandoned that city. Here he married a social favorite, lived far beyond his means, and even fraternized with British sympathizers. Naturally such conduct provoked criticism, and to clear himself of numerous petty charges Arnold demanded and received a court martial. On some of the charges, however, the court found him guilty and sentenced him to receive a reprimand.

But Washington, in delivering this reprimand, did not fail to call attention to Arnold's great services in the American army, and later, at Arnold's request, did not hesitate to give him the command of West Point, a position of great strategic importance on the Hudson.

In the meantime Arnold, deeply involved in debt, and unable to collect from Congress for expenditures he had made during the campaign against Quebec, had turned informer. Through him, from the early summer of 1779 on, Clinton had been fully apprised of the American plans and movements of troops, and Arnold had asked for West Point only because he wished to betray it to the British. Fortunately, however, Major André, through whom negotiations for the surrender of West Point were being conducted, was captured within the American lines, bearing papers that revealed the plot (September, 1780). Arnold promptly fled to the British, and André was executed as a spy.[1] The loss of West Point, which would have cost the Americans control of the whole Hudson Valley, was avoided, but the whole episode was a sad blow to American morale.

Clinton believed that a policy of ruthless raids would bring the war home to noncombatant Americans and lead to a demand for peace and *British raids* he found work for Arnold to do in laying waste the Virginia plantations. Early in 1781 Cornwallis, leaving Greene to the South, joined Arnold in Virginia and gave chase to a small force of Americans under the "boy" Lafayette.[2] But the "boy" successfully eluded his pursuers. Arnold returned to New York in June, 1781, to lead another marauding expedition, this time against New London, Connecticut; and Cornwallis, at Clinton's suggestion, fortified himself in the village of Yorktown on the tip of the peninsula made by the York and the James Rivers.

Washington now saw an opportunity to strike the British a telling blow. His own resources had recently been supplemented by the landing of several thousand French regulars under Rochambeau, and he felt justified in detaching a strong enough force to march into Virginia and

[1] Arnold claimed that he was genuinely converted to the British point of view, and possibly he was. But there is good reason to doubt the story, commonly repeated, that this end was accomplished through the influence of his wife and her Loyalist relatives. Arnold's father-in-law seems to have favored the Americans. Probably Arnold was influenced somewhat by his disgust at the alliance with the French, whom he hated and had fought; but his hurt pride and his great need of the sixty-three hundred pounds he received from Clinton as the price of treason must suffice in the main to account for his change of heart. R. G. Adams, "Benedict Arnold," in *Dictionary of American Biography*, I (1928); Malcolm Decker, *Benedict Arnold, Son of the Havens* (1932).

[2] Lafayette's part in the American revolution has attracted much attention. Most useful of the books on this subject are Charlemagne Tower, *Marquis de La Fayette in the American Revolution* (2 vols., 1895); and Brand Whitlock, *La Fayette* (2 vols., 1929).

trap Cornwallis. This plan would require the co-operation of the French navy, however, and both Rochambeau and Washington urged the French naval commander, de Grasse, whose fleet was in the West Indies, to bring his ships north to the mouth of the Chesapeake. With some reluctance de Grasse consented, whereupon Washington, taking care to make Clinton believe that an attack on New York was imminent, started southward to join Lafayette in Virginia.

The allied plan worked out perfectly. On August 30 the French fleet under de Grasse anchored within the capes that guard the mouth of Chesapeake Bay, and a week later the French beat off the *Surrender of* attack of a British fleet under Admiral Graves. A few days *Cornwallis* more and Cornwallis found himself not only cut off from retreat by sea, but hemmed in also by an allied army of sixteen thousand men, more than twice the number of British in Yorktown. He held out for several weeks, but on October 19, 1781, surrendered his entire command. Only two days later Admiral Graves reappeared, this time bringing reinforcements from Clinton, but the damage had already been done. Admiral de Grasse, in spite of Washington's urgent request that he attack New York or Charleston, sailed back to the West Indies, where next spring, after a terrible battle, he was defeated by the British fleet under Admiral Rodney (April 12, 1782). The war ended with England still in command of the seas.

But the French and American victory at Yorktown practically assured the independence of the United States. Lord North took the news of this setback, according to an eye-witness, "as he would have taken a ball in the breast, for he opened his arms, exclaiming wildly, as he paced up and down the apartment during a few minutes, 'Oh, God! it is all over,' words which he repeated many times under emotions of deepest agitation and distress." The charges of wholesale corruption and inefficiency in the prosecution of the war that had continually been brought against the King's Ministers could now be pressed with good effect, and in March, 1782, Lord North bowed to the inevitable and resigned. His downfall ended the personal rule of George III, and brought into power a ministry under Lord Rockingham (succeeded presently by Shelburne) that included several of the ablest of the men who had defended the colonies during the long-drawn-out contest over taxation. The British public was by this time weary of war, and Rockingham's ministry favored peace with all the enemies of England. Indeed, after Rodney's victory in the West Indies the English could look forward to reasonably good terms as far as their European adversaries were concerned. As for America, the colonies would be welcomed back within the British Empire on their own terms if they would come; but if they would not come, they might have their independence.

There were many anxious months for the Patriot leaders after Yorktown, for the British with thirty thousand troops in America continued to hold New York, Charleston, and Savannah; and the war-weariness of the Americans was no less marked than that of the British. Congress seemed less effective than ever, the unpaid army was sadly depleted and almost mutinous, and irregular fighting between bands of men who called themselves Loyalists or Patriots, but were often in reality mere adventurers, caused a needless loss of life and property.

Peace commissioners had been selected even before Yorktown: John Adams, Benjamin Franklin, Thomas Jefferson, John Jay, and Henry *The Peace* Laurens; but only three of them served. Jefferson de-*Commission* clined the appointment, and Laurens, whom the British held captive in the Tower at London, was released too late to play any important part in the proceedings.[1] With needless timidity Congress instructed the commissioners to work for the Mississippi River boundary rather than to demand it, and to take no step of any consequence without the knowledge and concurrence of the French, by whose advice and opinion they should ultimately be governed.

The negotiations began at Paris in the spring of 1782, when Franklin was the only American delegate present. Jay, who had been the American agent to Spain, arrived in June, and several months later Adams came over from Holland. At the insistence of Jay, the British envoy, Richard Oswald, was authorized to treat with the "Thirteen United States of North America"; hence independence was conceded at the outset. But the ambitions of the United States and of Spain for territory west of the Appalachian Mountains were in sharp conflict, and Vergennes, the French foreign minister, was somewhat put to it to satisfy both his country's allies. Vergennes's private secretary, Rayneval, actually proposed that the trans-Appalachian West be divided at the Ohio River, and that the northern half be assigned to England, while the southern half should be left to the Indians under the protection in part of Spain and in part of the United States. Probably Vergennes feared also that the United States might become too powerful if it were given

---

[1] Laurens was finally exchanged for Cornwallis. The story of his interesting career is given by D. D. Wallace, *The Life of Henry Laurens* (1915). Of more value on the treaty of peace are George Pellew, *John Jay* (1890), and J. T. Morse, *John Adams* (1884). Franklin's mission to France is entertainingly presented by Bernard Faÿ, *Franklin, the Apostle of Modern Times* (1929). The literature of American diplomatic history is abundant. Among the many general accounts, the following may be cited: C. R. Fish, *American Diplomacy* (1915); J. H. Latané, *A History of American Foreign Policy* (1927); R. L. Jones, *History of the Foreign Policy of the United States* (1933).

the Mississippi for its western boundary. The English, on the other hand, who wished to make friends with the new nation and hoped to avoid the Spanish as near neighbors, seemed entirely willing to give up to the United States the region north of the Ohio that Reyneval would have joined to Canada.

Jay strongly suspected that Vergennes was planning to sacrifice the interests of the United States to Spain, and he proposed, therefore, that the American delegation should ignore the instructions of *The Treaty* Congress in order to deal directly with England. To this *of Paris* policy Adams willingly consented, and with some difficulty the two won Franklin over also. The English government was delighted to contribute all it could to discord among its opponents, and on November 30, 1782, agreed to a preliminary treaty between Great Britain and the United States which should be incorporated in the final treaty of peace. This preliminary treaty gave to the United States the boundaries of the Great Lakes and the Mississippi. It was not clear at the time, however, whether the British would retain Florida or re-cede it to Spain; hence a secret provision was adopted whereby the boundary between the United States and Florida should be drawn at the thirty-first parallel in case Spain received Florida, but at a line nearly a degree and a half farther north in case Great Britain retained it. The final treaty, signed September 3, 1783, accepted the terms of the preliminary treaty, and since later on Spain received Florida, the United States regarded its southern boundary as thirty-one degrees. Since the English ceded Florida to Spain without definition of boundaries, however, the setting was arranged for a boundary dispute that was to last for many years. Vergennes was much annoyed at the success of the American diplomats, and was amazed at the generosity of the British terms. "The English," he wrote to Rayneval, "buy peace rather than make it. Their concessions ... exceed all that I could have thought possible."

Several other provisions were included in the treaties. Citizens of the United States retained the same rights to fish off the coast of Newfoundland and in the Gulf of St. Lawrence that they had enjoyed as British subjects; the navigation of the Mississippi River was to be open alike to the commerce of Great Britain and of the United States; suits might be instituted for the collection of unpaid debts contracted by Americans of British subjects before the outbreak of the war; and the restitution of confiscated Loyalist property was to be recommended by Congress to the several states. The last two provisions were in the nature of compromises. At first the British insisted that the payment of private debts owing to British subjects and the indemnification of the

Tories should be guaranteed by the United States; but the Americans pointed out that the states rather than the nation had jurisdiction in such matters, and after long discussions the provisions as stated were accepted by both sides. Since many of the debts had actually been confiscated and the money had been collected into various state treasuries, the provision governing this subject proved virtually unenforceable; and ultimately, under the terms of the Jay Treaty of 1795, the central government agreed to pay them off. As for the misused Loyalists, confiscations continued even after the treaty of peace was signed, and laws which discriminated against them remained on the statute-books of some of the states until after the close of the War of 1812.

The treaty of peace was a magnificent victory for American diplomacy, but the terms were not free from criticism in America. An enduring hatred for the Loyalists made the clauses on that subject unpopular as well as unenforceable; the lack of an adequate commercial treaty, particularly to reopen the important West Indian trade, was keenly felt; and the failure of the commissioners to obey their instructions was unduly lamented. But with barely a quorum on hand for the purpose, Congress ratified the treaty, January 14, 1784.

CHAPTER IX

POLITICAL AND SOCIAL REORGANIZATION

WHETHER the American Revolution was merely one revolution or thirteen separate revolutions will probably never be settled to the complete satisfaction of even the closest students of the period. Certain it is, however, that the outbreak of war not only brought into existence a new and revolutionary central government, but also resulted in the establishment of new and equally revolutionary governments within the several colonies — or, as they were soon more properly called, states.[1] The first serious hostilities caused most British officials, including governors and judges, to make "sudden and abrupt departures," while the numerous members of the colonial councils, whose sympathies usually lay with England, were often not far behind. Tory members of the lower legislative chambers were also soon eliminated, and the whole business of maintaining government thus devolved upon the remaining Patriot members, who either carried on directly, or helped in the organization of provincial conventions or committees of safety to take over the reins of authority. In only two instances, Rhode Island and Connecticut, where liberal charters of self-government existed that needed only to be renamed to become constitutions, were the old forms of government retained. Elsewhere drastic changes were necessary, although in Massachusetts an effort was made for a time, in spite of the absence of a royal governor, to adhere to the terms of the colonial charter.

The colonies become states

These transformations, which began well before the Declaration of Independence, put an end to the operation of the British bureaucracy in America, and left the colonists, or at least such of them as had joined in the revolt, in control of their own governments. Irregular bodies of one kind or another made laws, levied taxes, and raised troops. There was much about the situation, however, to cause grave concern

[1] The best work on this subject is Allan Nevins, *The American States during and after the Revolution, 1775–1789* (1924).

[161]

to the more conservative opponents of British rule. Legally constituted courts could not be convened, and the more turbulent members
of society took advantage of the situation to indulge in deeds of violence. In order to safeguard personal and property rights, local committees sometimes assumed authority that they did not legally possess,
but conditions at best were far from satisfactory, and several
states applied to Congress for advice on how to deal with the
problem.

In response to such a request from the provincial convention of New
Hampshire, Congress recommended that representatives of the people
New should be chosen to "establish such a form of government as
constitutions in their judgment will best produce the happiness of the
people and most effectually secure peace and good order in that province,
during the present dispute between Great Britain and the colonies."
New Hampshire and South Carolina promptly acted on this advice
and formed provisional constitutions. A little later, May 15, 1776, in
a general recommendation Congress again urged the formation of
constitutions, but this time omitted all reference to the temporary
nature of such governments, a change of front, which, according to
John Adams, bespoke "absolute independence." In Virginia, the decision to form a permanent constitution for an independent state was
reached before the action of Congress was known, and by the end of
June, 1776, the new frame of government was duly adopted. In the
course of the next few years all the other states, save only Rhode Island
and Connecticut, followed the advice of Congress and the example of
Virginia.

The methods by which the new constitutions were framed and
adopted followed no definite pattern, although in many instances the
procedure was precisely the same as might have been used in the passing
of an ordinary law. This was the case in Virginia, although Jefferson
pointed out that the state constitution, if it was to be distinguished
from an ordinary law that any legislature might repeal at will, ought
to be submitted to the people for their ratification. In Delaware the
procedure was somewhat more modern. There a convention was
chosen for the specific duty of drawing up a constitution; but once its
work was done, the convention put the constitution into effect without
delay. In Massachusetts the will of the people was carefully ascertained. The Assembly first sought permission of the towns to authorize it in going forward with the work of framing a constitution; but
when that request had been twice denied, it asked and received permission to call a convention for that purpose. Accordingly in 1779

a constitutional convention, directly chosen by the people, formulated a constitution and submitted it to the towns for approval. Not until June, 1780, after more than two thirds of the towns had voted to approve, was the Massachusetts constitution put into effect. In New Hampshire much the same procedure was followed as in Massachusetts.[1]

It was natural enough that the Americans should wish to have written constitutions. In the past most of the colonies had been able to point to some specific document according to which their government had been carried on, and the new states were merely following precedent when they replaced the old document with a new one. Moreover, the contract theory of government was then generally accepted, and in setting up such a relationship, between the people on the one hand and those who were to be placed in authority over them on the other, there was an obvious advantage about a plainly worded written statement. There seems to have been no disposition whatever to follow the English example and permit an accumulation of precedents to grow into an unwritten constitution.

Not only did every new state feel obliged in some fashion or another to acquire a written constitution, but the constitutions so acquired were also remarkably alike. This was due in the main to the fact that in the establishment of the new governments colonial traditions were followed as far as possible. *Similarity of state governments* Indeed the question has sometimes been raised whether or not the name "revolution" should be applied to what happened in America during these years, since the changes made were so conservative. What the colonists really desired, according to this argument, was not revolution but the prevention of revolution. It was England with her innovations in the way of taxation who was threatening to overthrow long-established American rights, and the colonists fought merely to preserve and maintain the institutions they had always had. Certain it is that the men who drew the new constitutions showed no considerable interest in experimentation, and since the colonial governments had been remarkably alike, whether classified as royal, proprietary, or corporate, it followed that the new state governments were also remarkably alike.

By means of bills of rights, many of the new constitutions ordinarily paid their respects to the same political theories that were maintained in the Declaration of Independence. These bills of rights re-empha-

---

[1] H. A. Cushing, *History of the Transition from Provincial to Commonwealth Government in Massachusetts* (1896); W. C. Abbott, *New York in the American Revolution* (1929); J. T. Adams, *New England in the Republic, 1776–1850* (1926).

sized the doctrine then commonly accepted in America that the powers of government were limited, and that there were certain in-
Bills of rights   alienable rights of men upon which government might not trespass. Such notions came not merely from the teachings of political philosophers like Richard Hooker and John Locke, who argued strongly in favor of the "natural rights" of men, and were well known in America; they owed something also to colonial experience. Colonial governments had always been limited in scope and authority, and by colonial charters the rights of Englishmen had often been specifically guaranteed to Americans. The new constitutions therefore followed both theory and practice when they listed those individual rights that government must leave inviolate. Such matters as freedom of speech and of religious belief, freedom from arbitrary arrest, the right of an accused person to trial by a jury of his peers, immunity from cruel and unusual punishments and from excessive bails and fines appeared to Americans not merely as privileges that a good government wisely extended to the people over whom it ruled, but rather as items that lay entirely beyond the limits of governmental interference. The theory that the powers of government were unlimited, or, as specifically applied to England, where Parliament was fast becoming supreme, that the powers of Parliament were unlimited, was thoroughly distasteful to Americans, as much before as after the Revolution. With respect to religious liberty the declarations in the various constitutions sometimes went further than actual practice. In many states discriminations were still made against Catholics, religious qualifications for office-holding were not wholly eliminated, and state-supported churches continued to exist.[1]

The framers of the first constitutions assumed that there should be three branches of government, executive, legislative, and judicial,
The separation of powers   and that each should be kept as distinct as possible from the others. Here again their opinions were based upon both theory and practice. Many of them knew well the writings of Montesquieu, who eulogized the principle of the separation of powers; and they all knew that in the colonial governments precisely this situation had existed. The English government, which Montesquieu thought so fine an example of the separation of powers, was actually in process of evolution towards an all-powerful Parliament, but the American governments, thanks mainly to the control of the mother country over governors and to some extent over judges also,

[1] J. B. McMaster, *The Acquisition of Political, Social, and Industrial Rights of Man in America* (1903).

had made little progress in this direction. The new constitutions merely codified colonial experience when they provided for a single executive, to be known as the governor, a two-house legislature, and an independent judiciary.

Late unpleasant relations with royal governors, however, tended to keep the powers of that official at a minimum. In ten states he was elected for a year only, and in eleven states he had no veto power. Only in New England was he chosen by popular *Governors* vote; elsewhere he was elected by one or both houses of the legislature. Pennsylvania at first had no governor, but tried out a plural executive in the form of a council of five, one of whose members was termed president. But this innovation worked badly, and was soon abandoned in favor of the traditional single executive. As British governors receded farther into the background, the lack of confidence in the executive disappeared, and the powers he had normally exercised were restored.

Since confidence in the legislature had not been impaired by the events leading up to the American Revolution, the tendency was to expand the powers of this branch of the government. *Legislatures* In most of the states, for example, the appointive power ordinarily vested in the governor was transferred to the legislature. Frequent elections, however, were deemed a necessity. In six states new legislatures were chosen every year; in two states they were chosen twice a year. Four states adopted the plan now in common use of selecting the upper house for a longer term than the lower house, but in only one instance was the lower house chosen for as long a period as two years. Pennsylvania and Georgia experimented for a time with single-chamber legislatures, but soon gave their adherence to the usual plan.

The courts were complicated and varied. The judges were usually chosen by the legislatures, and were bound by the precedents already set during colonial times. The right of a court to declare *Courts* unconstitutional an act of the legislature was neither asserted nor denied, but in colonial times judges had frequently refused to enforce laws which they found to be out of harmony with the colonial charter or contrary to the laws of Parliament. Probably the doctrine of judicial review was not yet foreseen, but the case of *Trevett vs. Weeden*, in which a Rhode Island court declared a law duly passed by the legislature to be null and void because it was out of harmony with the state constitution, came during the confederation period.

In spite of their revolutionary surroundings, the men who framed

[165]

these constitutions were fairly timid when it came to entrusting full authority to the people. The upper house of the legislature was invariably constituted in such a way as to ensure that it would represent the well-to-do upper classes rather than the common people. *Limitations on democracy* Outside of New England, ordinary voters were in no case entrusted with the selection of high officials, such as governors and judges. Oftentimes the upper house of the legislature was chosen by the lower house instead of directly by the voters. Property qualifications for those who were to exercise the suffrage were maintained in every state, and in a few instances a man had to be a landholder to be eligible to vote. The property qualifications were sometimes graded, so that the man who was entitled to vote for a member of the lower house of the legislature might not be entitled to vote for higher officials. In North Carolina, for example, any taxpayer might vote in elections to the lower house, but only the owners of at least fifty acres of land might vote in elections to the upper house. The same state also prescribed far higher property qualifications for office-holders than for voters, and required of some office-holders higher property qualifications than of others. It is abundantly clear that the framers of these constitutions did not include within the natural rights of men the right to vote or the right to hold office. Probably the adoption of universal manhood suffrage would have expanded the electorate fourfold.

That the future might hold something of the sort in store, however, might have been judged from the constitution adopted by the more or less irregular state of Vermont. In colonial times the region north *Vermont* of the Massachusetts border and west of the Connecticut River had been claimed by both New Hampshire and New York. When the Revolution broke out the frontier inhabitants of the disputed territory took advantage of the unsettled situation to organize a government of their own. At first they relied upon "the laws of God and Connecticut," but in 1777 they adopted a constitution that, unlike those of the thirteen states, granted the right of suffrage to all men over twenty-one years of age. But Vermont was not accorded official recognition for many years.

The constitution-makers of the Revolutionary epoch must have thought well of their work, for they made quite inadequate provisions for future changes. As often as not they overlooked the matter of amendments altogether; and when they did include a clause on the subject it was rarely well thought out. In Delaware and Pennsylvania the process of amendment was too difficult to be workable, while in some of the other states an amendment to the constitution could be made in about the same way that a new law could be passed. Massachusetts and Georgia alone made adequate provision for the calling of subsequent constitutional conventions.

The various states assumed for themselves without question all rights of sovereignty, and paid scant attention to the Continental Congress, through the work of which a central government *State* was being evolved. Loyalty to state, indeed, was probably *sovereignty* far stronger than loyalty to nation, and it is not surprising that the idea of state sovereignty died hard. Nevertheless the exigencies of war required that there be unity of action, and the problem of union, always evaded in colonial times, now had to be faced.

The Continental Congress, which in 1775 had taken over the direction of the war, was quick to recognize that it had little if any legal authority for the powers it was forced by the logic of *Plans for a* events to exercise; and in June, 1776, with independence *national* imminent, it appointed a committee, headed by John Dick- *government* inson, to draft a plan of confederation. Dickinson's committee, in undertaking this task, was not without precedents for its guidance. Most important, of course, was the Continental Congress itself, and the work it was actually doing, with or without authority; but there had been much talk of union before, and fully matured plans were available, particularly the one Franklin had presented at Albany in 1754, and with suitable modifications had brought to the attention of Congress in 1775. There seems to have been no thought, either on the part of Franklin or on the part of Dickinson's committee, of replacing the existing *de facto* government with something decidedly different. The sufficiency of this type of central government seems rather to have been taken for granted; all that was deemed necessary was to write in the details and obtain the necessary grant of powers from the states. Franklin would have preferred that the states be given voting strength in Congress according to their population, but this innovation was easily blocked by delegates from the small states who insisted on preserving the principle of complete equality. Dickinson's committee undertook merely to ascertain what problems were common to all the states, and to clothe Congress with authority to deal with them.

Shortly after the Declaration of Independence, Dickinson's committee made its first report, but Congress, faced by the more pressing problems of the war, acted slowly, and it was not until November 15, 1777, that the Articles of Confederation were recommended to the states for adoption.[1]   They provided for just such a Congress as already existed.   It was to be composed of delegates, not less than *The Articles of Confederation*   two nor more than seven, from each of the thirteen states.   These delegates were more like diplomatic agents than representatives, for they were paid by the states that sent them, and, while they were chosen annually, were subject to recall at any time.   Regardless of the number of delegates it sent to Congress, each state had only one vote.   A curious, and as it proved a most unfortunate, provision required that any delegate might serve only three years out of each six.   Another provision, even more unfortunate, required the consent of two thirds of the states to pass any measure of importance.   To cast the vote of a state at least two delegates must be present and in agreement.   If a state delegation divided equally on any matter, then the state lost its vote.   Otherwise, a majority of the delegation determined the vote of the state.

The listed powers of Congress gave it complete control over foreign affairs and some control over interstate relations.   Congress might *Powers of Congress*   make peace or war, send and receive ambassadors, make treaties and alliances, govern trade relations with the Indians, determine the standards of coinage (the states might still coin money) and of weights and measures, and organize a postal service. These were powers which in colonial times had been exercised to a large extent by the imperial government, and in assigning them to Congress the states in reality denied themselves few privileges that they had ever held as colonies.   The Articles specifically stated, however, that a state might not, without the consent of Congress, make treaties with foreign powers, send or receive ambassadors, or engage in war.   It was intended that within these spheres the Congress should be unhampered by state interference.

Congress had only such powers as were definitely assigned to it; the states had all the rest.   It was natural enough that in making *Reserved powers of the states*   such a division the new states should wish to retain as their own the prerogatives for which they had made war rather than yield them to the mother country.   The right of taxation was one of these; hence only the states might levy taxes. If Congress wanted money, it might requisition funds from the states. This the English Parliament in its day might also have done without raising the question of constitutionality, for the colonies would have

[1] A. C. McLaughlin, *The Confederation and the Constitution* (1905), is particularly good on the problems of union.   On the work of the Continental Congress, see A. W. Small, *The Beginnings of American Nationality* (1890).   John Fiske, *The Critical Period of American History* (1888), is generally accounted the best of Fiske's books.

THE UNITED STATES DURING THE CONFEDERATION PERIOD

LIBRARY
FLORIDA STATE UNIVERSITY
TALLAHASSEE, FLORIDA

been left free to meet requisitions or not just as they chose. So, too, under the new system there was no way to compel the states to pay. The regulation of commerce was another power fully reserved to the states. Indeed, the Articles in this respect withheld from the central governing body some privileges that the English Parliament had been accustomed to exercise; the states alone might levy tariffs and tonnage taxes, and Congress was denied the right of laying down even the most general sort of regulations. Only through the incidental provisions of treaties could Congress control commerce in any way, and while it was given full permission to make commercial treaties, only the states might retaliate against a foreign country which discriminated against American trade. Nor did the states concede to Congress any authority whatever over interstate commerce.

There was no room for doubt as to where sovereignty lay under the Articles of Confederation, for they pointedly declared that each state retained its "sovereignty, freedom, and independence." Congress in a sense was merely an assembly of diplomats to whom had been entrusted the control of certain common problems. It derived its authority wholly from the states, as whose agent it acted. It was in no sense responsible to the people of the United States, nor could any of its actions bear directly upon them. Changes in the Articles could be made only after the approval of Congress and ratification by every state legislature.

It seems surprising that a document so conservative, and so in line with experience, as the Articles of Confederation should have been delayed in adoption. And yet such was the case. One by one, the various states gave their consent until only Maryland remained. Her objections, shared by some of the other "small states," had to do with the ownership of western lands. Were these the property of the individual states who claimed them, or were they the property of all the states collectively? The Articles of Confederation seemed to favor the former assumption, for according to that document no state might be deprived of territory for the benefit of the United States. Six states — Massachusetts, Connecticut, Virginia, North Carolina, South Carolina, and Georgia — had claims to western lands based upon early grants from the crown. New York had a shadowy title, based on an Indian treaty, to some lands in the upper Ohio Valley. The other six states had no western claims of any kind. Maryland, always fearful of her powerful neighbor, Virginia, had urged upon Congress, even before the Articles were adopted by that body, that "the back lands, claimed by the British

Maryland and the western land claims

[169]

crown, if secured by the blood and treasure of all, ought, in reason, justice, and policy, to be considered a common stock, to be parcelled out by Congress into free, convenient, and independent Governments, as the wisdom of that body shall hereafter direct." When Congress refused to accept this advice, Maryland refused to accept the Articles, and, with both justice and expediency favoring her contention, she finally won out. Thomas Paine wrote an article entitled "The Public Good" supporting the Maryland contention, Congress reversed itself and urged such a policy "for the common good of the United States," and public opinion gradually veered around. There was no better claim than that of Virginia, which was now based not only upon the original grant, but also upon the military exploits of George Rogers Clark, so when Virginia agreed to relinquish her claim to Congress, Maryland was content. On March 1, 1781, more than two years after every other state had agreed to the Articles, Maryland also ratified, and at last they went into effect.[1]

In some respects the Articles registered a definite step in advance. The various states agreed, for example, to permit to the citizens of all the other states the same privileges that their own citizens enjoyed. National citizenship was thus brought a step nearer. Also the extradition of fugitives from justice who had fled from one state to another was made possible, and the public records and judicial proceedings of each state were given full faith and credit in every other. As an experiment in federation the Articles are not to be despised. They were weak enough, to be sure, but they were destined at least soon to demonstrate their shortcomings and thus to speed the way to a closer union.

The Articles left Congress free to work out as best it could a plan for the discharge of its executive duties. The committee system was *The executive authority* first given a trial, but by the close of the Revolution three executive departments had been created, with individuals at the head of each: Robert Livingston as Secretary of Foreign Affairs, Robert Morris as Superintendent of Finance, and General Lincoln as Secretary of War. A naval department was also provided for, but remained unorganized. It is interesting to speculate on how far this course of development might have gone, had the Confederation continued, in the direction of evolving for the United States the cabinet system of government already fairly well defined in England.

The Articles failed, also, to establish a well-rounded national system of courts. Congress, however, was authorized to act as a court of appeal in cases of disputes between the several states, and it was given author-

[1] H. B. Adams, *Maryland's Influence in Founding a National Commonwealth* (1877).

ity to provide, on request, for the creation of special committees to try such cases. It might also select certain state courts in which piracies and felonies on the high seas might be brought to trial, and it might establish appellate courts for the rehearing of prize cases. Had the Confederation lasted longer, it is not beyond belief that these grants of authority might have been so interpreted as to make possible an adequate system for the handling of such business as could not readily be disposed of by the state courts.

Congress was most seriously handicapped by its lack of power to tax, its absence of authority to control commerce, and its inability to act directly upon the people of the states rather than merely upon the states themselves. Even so, had the process of amendment been less difficult these defects might have been remedied. It is by no means certain that, given better times and a longer term of life, the Confederation might not have developed into a fairly satisfactory form of government.

While the leaders of the American Revolution were no doubt chiefly interested in bringing about political changes, the transformation that actually took place in American life during this eventful *The Revolution, socially considered* period was by no means confined to politics. As one distinguished historian observes, "Who shall say to the waves of revolution: thus far shall we go and no farther?" It is a fact that "many economic desires, many social aspirations were set free by the political struggle, many aspects of colonial society profoundly altered by the forces thus let loose." Nor was this social revolution ended with the conclusion of the war, for the forces making for change merely gathered momentum with each successful assault upon the older order.[1]

The downfall of the colonial aristocracy was far more than a political phenomenon. Making due allowance for exceptions — and there were many — the Patriots represented in the main the common people, and the Loyalists the upper strata of society. The victory of the former, together with their studied persecution of the latter, made it possible for men who in colonial times had been regarded as of low degree to hold high office and enjoy important privileges. Common men came naturally to hold themselves in higher esteem, and their superiors in lower. Many, indeed, read into the Declaration of Independence, with its emphasis upon the equality of men, a demand for the emancipation of the slaves, and in all the northern colonies the abolition of slavery fol-

[1] On non-political aspects of the Revolution the reader should consult J. F. Jameson, *The American Revolution Considered as a Social Movement* (1926). See also the entertaining essays by Dixon Ryan Fox, *Ideas in Motion* (1935).

lowed fairly promptly upon the attainment of independence. Even in the South emancipation societies were common, and the gradual disappearance of slavery was generally expected.

The trend towards small independent holdings of land, which was marked even in colonial times, was greatly accelerated by the Revolu-

Land-ownership   tion. Many of the largest estates, the property of Loyalists, were confiscated and sold out in small tracts to free farmers. The old feudal rules of primogeniture, which provided that property in land should descend to the eldest son, and of entail, which held such property in the family by prohibiting its owner either to sell it or to give it away, were quickly abolished. Quit-rents, always regarded as a nuisance and rarely paid without protest, became a thing of the past. Moreover, such British restrictions upon the advance of the agricultural frontier as the Proclamation of 1763 and the Quebec Act lost their meaning, and cheap lands to the West were available for all who wished them, particularly for those veterans of the war who had been granted land bounties as a part of the inducement to enlist. Landownership no longer served as a test of gentility, and, even as a qualification for voting, it extended the suffrage, so one conservative asserted, "to every biped of the forest."

Changes with respect to landownership were closely paralleled by changes in industry and commerce. American manufactures, always

Industry and commerce   hampered to some extent by British restrictions and still more by the habit of buying manufactured articles from England, were immensely stimulated by the war. Far more attention was given than formerly to the making of such necessary articles as firearms, gunpowder, nails, salt, paper, and cloth, and the occupations of the people shifted accordingly. Commerce, on the other hand, suffered acutely from the war, although much successful privateering kept the sailors' art alive, as the speedy return of American ships to the seas at the close of the war abundantly attested. Freedom from the British restrictions on colonial trade opened up some new opportunities to American skippers, but this advantage was probably more than offset by the loss of trade privileges that the colonies had once enjoyed as a part of the British Empire.

Independence served also to force a series of readjustments with respect to the religious life of the Americans. The union of church and

Religious adjustments   state that existed in nine out of thirteen of the colonies was promptly attacked, although with varying results. In the South, where the state church was the Church of England, disestablishment was naturally associated with revolution, and was early accomplished. Here the demand for religious freedom met its most vigorous resistance in Virginia, but in 1786 the legislature of the Old Dominion asserted, in words penned by Jefferson, that "no man shall be compelled to frequent or support any religious worship, place, or ministry whatsoever, nor shall be enforced, restrained, molested or burthened in his body or goods, nor shall otherwise suffer on account of his religious opinions or belief; but that all men shall be free to profess, and by argument to maintain, their opinion in matters of religion, and that the same shall in no wise diminish, enlarge, or affect their civil capacities." In New England, where, except for Rhode Island, the Congregational Church was supported by the state, patriotism could not so easily be invoked on the side of religious freedom, and the struggle lasted far into the nineteenth century. In Massachusetts, the strongest citadel of Puritanism, disestablishment was not voted until 1833.

After the Revolution most of the American denominations undertook to reorganize their systems of church government. With this in mind, the American Anglicans, when they failed to obtain the co-operation of English church officials, persuaded the non-juring bishops of Scotland to consecrate in 1784 an American bishop, Samuel Seabury. With an American episcopate thus assured, the Protestant Episcopal Church of the United States was organized. About the same time the separate status of the American Catholic Church was recognized by a decree from Rome, and in 1790 Father John Carroll was made Bishop of Baltimore. At the close of the Revolution John Wesley, the English founder of the Methodist Church (who himself never left the Church of England), sent Thomas Coke, another Englishman, to the United States as general superintendent of the American Methodists. On arriving in America, Coke promptly associated himself with Francis Asbury, the leading spirit among the American Methodists, and in December, 1784, at a conference of the church held in Baltimore, the two were designated joint superintendents. Asbury and his successors, contrary to Wesley's wishes, assumed the title of bishop, and the denomination over which they presided was officially known as the Methodist Episcopal Church. Other denominations, although freer from overseas connections than these three, generally redefined and elaborated their systems of government.

Of still greater significance was the revolution in thought and feeling that came over the American people during the period of the war. Religion, in the more formal sense, suffered disastrously, for churches were destroyed, religious ties loosened, standards of morality lowered, and traditional beliefs swept away. On the other hand, the revolu-

[173]

tionary ideals of liberty and equality were deeply impressed upon the minds of the people. The inhuman penal codes of the eighteenth *The* century were more frequently denounced, and imprison- *revolution* ment as a means of punishment for debt sometimes received *in thought* the ridicule it deserved. A change could be noted, *and feeling* also, in the popular concept of education. The colonial schools, such as they were, had been virtually destroyed by the years of Revolution, and new systems had to be devised. In an age that exalted the rights of the common man, pressure upon the state to accept the obligation of popular education steadily increased. Prophetic of the future was the provision in the first constitution of the unrecognized state of Vermont that a school system, beginning with the towns and including a state university, should be established. Systems of this sort were slow to develop, and seven of the original state constitutions made no mention whatever of education; but when, in the nineteenth century, the American school system did take form, it was under secular, not religious, control, and its right to public support was still defended on the grounds Jefferson had stated years before. "Above all things," he had written, "I hope the education of the common people will be attended to; convinced that on their good sense we may rely with the most security for the preservation of a due degree of liberty."

CHAPTER X

THE CONFEDERATION AND THE WEST

OF ALL the problems with which it was required to deal, the Congress under the Confederation did best with the problem of the West. That this section would play a part of great importance in the *The problem* history of the nation seemed evident enough in the light *of the West* of recent events. The French and Indian War had been fought primarily to determine whether the English or the French should have the opportunity to expand into the Ohio Valley. The Revolutionary War itself had been brought on in no small part because of western problems. It was the determination that the colonies must help pay for the defense of their western frontier that had led to the passage of the ill-fated Stamp Act. It was the fear that England wished to cut off expansion into the West that had made so many Americans resent deeply the Proclamation Line of 1763 and the Quebec Act. It was discontent with the rule of the East that made many back-country settlers support the war against England, for out of the Revolution against English tyranny they hoped also to achieve freedom from the tyranny of eastern aristocrats.

The cessions of western lands to Congress by the states claiming them were not completed until 1802, when Georgia at last surrendered her claim, but after the adoption of the Articles of Confederation in 1781 it was apparent that the nation rather than the states must deal with the West. Here a number of permanent settlements had already been made. Farthest in the interior lay the French villages that George Rogers Clark had conquered, which together with Detroit and other centers of fur trade had a population numbering several thousands. On the upper Ohio around Pittsburgh, in the valleys of the Holston and Watauga Rivers, in the blue-grass region of Kentucky, and now also along the Cumberland in central Tennessee were other settlements of varying sizes, all of which were growing rapidly.[1]

That attention must be given to the needs of these western communi-

[1] F. J. Turner, *The Significance of Sections in American History* (1932), has a chapter on "Western State-Making in the Revolutionary Era."

ties by the central government was soon made evident. In the region
Western south of the Ohio River, where new settlers were entering more
independence rapidly than anywhere else in the West, there was a marked
tendency to disregard the authority of the present states to the east.
New western states that might willingly acknowledge the supremacy of
a national government, but would not forever remain content to be
merely western divisions of eastern states, were in the making. As for
the region northwest of the Ohio River, Congress, thanks to the insistence of Maryland, had full control there, and full responsibility.

Among the states that followed the lead of Virginia in the cession of
western lands was North Carolina, which in 1784 passed an act to hand
over its transmontane territory to the United States, provided that Congress accept the gift within twelve months' time. The region ceded
included the Watauga settlements, which had been made first into one
and then into several counties of North Carolina only a short time before,
and now contained probably more than ten thousand settlers. There
was reason to believe that the North Carolina legislature felt that it was
exhibiting considerable shrewdness in getting rid of these western counties. Their inhabitants paid very little into the state treasury, and yet
on western insistence the state had made expensive treaties with the
Indians to acquire more lands. With the cession of the territory in
question to Congress it was assumed that the state of North Carolina
would be under no obligation to continue the payments to the Indians
that the treaties provided; and much to the dissatisfaction of the
Indians, who promptly threatened to take the warpath, these payments
were discontinued.

Already the Wataugans had known what it was to govern themselves
without the aid of North Carolina, and they now promptly took steps to
State of set up once more a wholly independent government. Pos-
Franklin sibly they might become a new state in the United States,
or failing that, at least they would be in a better position to meet the
Indian menace. Following a series of conventions, the state of Franklin
was created, with John Sevier as governor and the laws of North Carolina
as a legal guide of conduct.[1] For some time the new state charted its
own course; but the North Carolina legislature was quick to repent its
action and to repeal the cession act, and by 1788 the western counties
had returned, with some reluctance, to their former allegiance. Meantime Congress had taken no action whatever on the manner.

[1] J. R. Gilmore, *John Sevier as a Commonwealth-Builder* (1887); F. M. Turner, *Life of
General John Sevier* (1910). For a general account of the advance into the West, see Justin
Winsor, *The Westward Movement* (1897).

By this time still another settlement had been made in the western land claimed by North Carolina. For this venture, Richard Henderson, the same that had attempted the Transylvania project in *Cumberland* Kentucky, was chiefly responsible. When his rights in *settlements* Kentucky were taken over by Virginia, Henderson sent James Robertson with a few companions into central Tennessee to found a colony along the Cumberland. Willing pioneers came in from Watauga and from the Virginia frontier, and under the guidance of experienced leaders they soon provided themselves with a temporary form of government. In May, 1780, at Nashborough (or Nashville) all adult male settlers, two hundred and fifty-six in all, affixed their signatures to an agreement that amounted to a constitution. Following the Watauga precedent a court of twelve judges was to be chosen by manhood suffrage to represent the several stations; but it was expressly stipulated that whenever North Carolina should be ready to take over the government of the "Cumberland settlements," no impediment should be placed in the way. For a few years this temporary government functioned smoothly, but in 1782 the Assembly of North Carolina recognized the new region by the creation of Davidson County.

The most populous of the western areas of settlement, however, was Kentucky.[1] Here thousands of pioneers came in during the closing years of the Revolution, so that by the end of that struggle *Kentucky* the total population of the blue-grass region was probably not less than twenty-five thousand. All of the western communities showed signs of restiveness under the rule of the eastern states, but the size of the Kentucky settlements, which continued to grow rapidly during the entire Confederation period, made their protests seem the most important. Kentuckians objected strenuously to the inaccessibility of courts, which in some cases could not be reached without crossing the mountains, and to the lack of local authority to call out the militia and otherwise deal with the Indian problem. Numerous conventions were therefore held — ten of them in all — in the interest of separate statehood for Kentucky. Virginia proved generous, and three times voted to give the Kentuckians what they desired. But during the Confederation period Congress failed to take the necessary steps to make Kentucky a state.

Nevertheless, the strong sentiment in the Southwest for separate statehood and the willingness of its residents to rely upon *The North-* the national government for protection and support seem not *west* to have been wholly lost upon Congress. In the territory northwest

[1] R. M. McElroy, *Kentucky in the Nation's History* (1909).

of the Ohio River, where the title of the national government to the land was already clear, some provision for the future had to be made, and with this end in view Congress passed a series of "Northwest Ordinances" which showed a sympathetic appreciation of the problems of the West. Whether the attitude of Congress was directly affected by the situation in the Southwest is not entirely clear, but the Ordinances safeguarded in a most satisfactory way the right of settlers to adventure into the West and to establish states with the same privileges as were enjoyed by the old.

The initiative in this matter was taken by Thomas Jefferson, who was a close student of the problems of the West, and realized more fully than *Ordinance* most men of his time that provision must be made for the *of 1784* development of a great country. In 1784 he introduced into Congress a plan for the organization of the West. He proposed, first, that certain fundamental guarantees should be made for the guidance of future legislators. The new states to be created in the West should remain forever a part of the United States. They should remain subject to the central government as the original states were subject; they should be liable for their portion of the federal debt; they should have a government republican in form; within their borders slavery should not exist after the year 1800. Jefferson also worked out a mechanical division of the West, marking it by lines of latitude and longitude into prospective states, ten of which he named, somewhat fantastically, Sylvania, Michigania, Cherronesus, Assenisippia, Metropotamia, Illinoia, Saratoga, Washington, Polypotamia, and Pelisipia. As for the plan of government, he suggested three stages. First, the settlers should meet together to establish a temporary government by the adoption of the constitution and laws of any one of the original states; secondly, whenever a given division could show that it had twenty thousand free male inhabitants it might establish a permanent constitution and send a delegate to Congress; thirdly, whenever its population should equal that of the smallest of the original thirteen it should be admitted to full statehood. Jefferson's ordinance, shorn of the pedantic names and the anti-slavery clause, passed Congress, but it was purely preliminary and tentative. In most of the territory under consideration the Indian titles had not yet been extinguished, and north of the Ohio River, except in the French villages, white population had not yet begun to come in.

Jefferson also believed that the lands of the West should be made to yield a revenue for the sorely depleted treasury of the Confederation, and to pay off obligations owing to soldiers who had fought in the American Revolution.   Treaties with the Indians which would make these ends possible were speedily signed, one at Fort Stanwix in *Ordinance* 1784, and one at Fort McIntosh in 1785.   These treaties *of* 1785 opened up to sale and settlement a tract of land immediately to the west of the upper Ohio.   Before the land should be finally disposed of, however, Congress, again accepting Jefferson's leadership, passed the famous Ordinance of 1785, which set forth the system of survey and sale to be followed.   Instead of permitting the location of tracts as the whims of purchasers might direct, the Ordinance of 1785 provided for the "rectangular" or "rectilinear" system of survey, so familiar to western Americans of later generations.   Parallel lines were to be drawn at six-mile intervals, both north and south, and east and west, as nearly as the sphericity of the earth would permit.   Each of the squares so described was to be called a township, and each north and south tier of townships was to be called a range.   Further subdivisions of the townships were to be made by east and west as well as north and south lines surveyed at intervals of one mile, so that each township would be marked off into thirty-six "sections."   The sections, each of which was thus a mile square and contained approximately six hundred and forty acres, might then be divided into "halves" and "quarters," the "quarters" into "half-quarters" and "quarter-quarters," and so on indefinitely.   Jefferson would have preferred a township ten miles square rather than six miles square, but Congress thought the lesser unit more practicable.

This elaborate and systematic method of survey came as the result of many unhappy experiences with colonial land surveys, in which, as a rule, there was no orderly system of survey whatever.   A grant of land, or deed, would ordinarily describe the plot under consideration by reference to trees, streams, rocks, or other natural markers, many of which might vary in location from time to time, and some of which were nearly sure to disappear altogether.   Under such circumstances boundary disputes between the owners of adjacent property inevitably clogged the colonial courts.   Moreover, there was a tendency for individuals to acquire titles to only the more choice lands in a given area, leaving in the hands of the state quantities of irregular, unsalable bits of "waste land."   Under the system adopted in the Ordinance of 1785 the purchaser would have to take all the land of a section, or subdivision thereof, regardless of the fact that some of the land almost certainly would not be as desirable as the rest; but he would be insured against the annoyance of uncertain boundaries and the expense and irritation of boundary disputes.

The Ordinance of 1785 also made provision for the sale of the lands

[179]

to be surveyed. ⌐In accordance with a New England precedent, section sixteen of each township was to be reserved as a bounty to public schools, but the rest of the land was to be offered for sale to the highest bidder in lots of a section or more.⌐ The minimum price was fixed at one dollar per acre, but it was hoped that by holding auctions in each state competitive bidding would result in a considerably higher average price being paid.

Congress, faced by dire calamity because of its lack of an adequate income, may well be pardoned for seeking to obtain a revenue from the

Revenue from public lands

public lands, although in a sense such a policy was a reversal of colonial precedent. Throughout the colonial period the lands of most of the colonies had been so administered that the pioneer farmer obtained his holding practically as a reward for his venture. The fees charged against him were usually nominal, and they were not always collected. It was assumed that in advancing the frontier and in contributing his share to its defense against the Indians, he was rendering a service of sufficient value to the colony that he was entitled to the lands he needed. To be sure, land speculators did acquire large tracts of land, and they sometimes disposed of them at a profit; but such a grant was usually made on the theory that it would promote the rapid colonization of the West, and the colony itself rarely made any money out of the project. Under the terms of the Ordinance of 1785, however, the poor man was virtually deprived of the opportunity to buy lands of the United States, for he could rarely amass as large a sum as six hundred and forty dollars; and the chief purchases were to be made by speculators who would buy in order to resell their land to actual settlers for a profit.

Congress authorized in 1785 the survey of seven ranges of townships west of the western boundary of Pennsylvania, and named General Rufus

The Ohio Company of Associates

Putnam of Massachusetts as United States Geographer to have charge of the work. Putnam declined, and the appointment went instead to his friend General Benjamin Tupper, also of Massachusetts, who was eager to see the West, and promptly took up his residence at Pittsburgh. Tupper employed General Samuel Parsons, another citizen of Massachusetts, to proceed down the Ohio and start the work, and Parsons went as far west as Louisville. Both Tupper and Parsons saw the boundless possibilities of the West, particularly the opportunity for speculation that the almost certain rise in land values would permit. Already some Massachusetts officers who had served in the Revolutionary Army had considered a plan for accepting western lands from Congress in lieu of the debts the nation owed them, and now, spurred on by the glowing reports of Tupper and Parsons, the project was revived. At a meeting held in Boston, March 1, 1786, at the Bunch of Grapes Tavern, the Ohio Company of Associates was formed for the purchase of a tract of land in the region being surveyed. The purchase price was to be subscribed by Massachusetts veterans of the Revolution in the certificates of indebtedness — now considered worthless — with which they had been paid. It was hoped that a total of one million dollars might be subscribed in this way, of which no individual might contribute more than five thousand dollars. The scheme had its good points. Congress might in this way discharge an obligation which otherwise would probably never be met; and for virtually nothing at all the Ohio Associates could obtain title to a large tract of valuable land.

Congress had yet to be persuaded as to the feasibility of the proposition, and with this object in view General Parsons made a trip to New York, where Congress was then holding its sessions. His efforts were unavailing, and the company next selected *Manasseh Cutler* the Reverend Manasseh Cutler, minister at Ipswich, Massachusetts, to try his hand. Cutler proved to be an admirable choice. He found Congress unable to function for lack of a quorum, but used his persuasiveness on individual congressmen with good effect. He pointed out that the settlement of the company's lands would stimulate interest in the West, would lead to other settlement, and eventually would lead to the sale of more of the lands which Congress held. Finally, as a last resort, he agreed that a group of congressmen and their friends, to be known as the Scioto Company, should be let in on the deal. To the Ohio Company Congress would sell a million and a half acres of land at two thirds of a dollar an acre; to the Scioto Company it would give an option on the purchase of an additional three and a half million acres adjacent to the Ohio Company tract. Cutler also suggested that General Arthur St. Clair, whose duties as President of Congress would soon be brought to an end if the Constitution, already pending, was adopted, would be wholly acceptable to the Ohio Company as the first governor of the new territory. When a quorum could be assembled Congress promptly chartered both companies; and Cutler, still making himself useful, succeeded in inducing the Scioto Associates to advance some $143,000 to further the work of settling up the Ohio Company's lands.[1]

Meantime Congress was at work on the famous Ordinance of 1787 for

[1] Amelia C. Ford, *Colonial Precedents of Our National Land System as it Existed in 1800* (1910); P. J. Treat, *The National Land System, 1785–1820* (1910); B. H. Hibbard, *A History of the Public Land Policies* (1924). The last-mentioned book is valuable for every phase of national land policy down to very recent times.

the government of the territory northwest of the Ohio River. On July
Ordinance 13 the Ordinance was adopted. Like the Ordinance of
of 1787 1784, which it supplanted, it provided for three stages in
the evolution of government. During the first stage a governor, a
secretary, and three judges, all appointed by Congress, were to adopt and
enforce such laws of the older states as might seem appropriate to the
new territory. Whenever the district could show five thousand free
male inhabitants, however, the freeholders might choose a representative
assembly, which on coming together would nominate ten persons, from
whom Congress would choose five to be a legislative council, or upper
house. The two-house legislature thus established might then enact
whatever laws it chose, subject to the governor's veto. Furthermore,
a delegate to Congress might be chosen, who might speak and introduce
bills, but might not vote. The Ordinance presumed that ultimately the
territory northwest of the Ohio River would be divided into not less than
three nor more than five states, and whenever a given district had attained a population of sixty thousand free inhabitants it should be
admitted "on an equal footing with the original states in all respects
whatsoever," and with full "liberty to form a permanent constitution
and state government." [1]

The promise of ultimate statehood and a number of other declarations
were set apart from the rest of the Ordinance as "articles of compact
between the original states and the people and states in the said territory" which were to remain forever "unalterable, unless by common
consent." Freedom of religious worship, freedom from arbitrary imprisonment, and the right of trial by jury were thus solemnly guaranteed;
schools and the means of public education were to be forever encouraged;
the utmost good faith was always to be observed toward the Indians; the
settlers in the new territory were to be required to pay their share of
the federal debts and the expense of federal government; the prospective
territorial or state legislatures were never to interfere with the administration of the public lands by the United States; the navigable waters of
the West were to remain forever free for use without tax or duty by all
citizens of the United States from whatever state; and there should be
"neither slavery nor involuntary servitude in the said territory, otherwise than in punishment of crimes whereof the party shall have been
duly convicted." By this last clause Jefferson's plan to exclude slavery
from the Northwest, which had barely failed of adoption in the Ordinance
of 1784, was now revived and accepted.

[1] J. A. Barrett, *Evolution of the Ordinance of 1787* (1891), is a useful study that, unfortunately, is available in only a few libraries.

The Ohio Company lost little time in beginning the work of colonization it had planned. The tract of land it selected lay along the Ohio River just west of the Seven Ranges, and at the mouth of *Marietta* the Muskingum River. In the spring of 1788 the first settlement, Marietta, was begun. Forty-seven colonists had been sent out from New England the preceding fall, had spent the winter at the forks of the Ohio, had constructed there a flatboat which they named appropriately the *May-Flower*, and in April, 1788, had floated down the Ohio in five days' time to the site selected. Other settlers, attracted by the low price of the land and the offer of free transportation, soon followed. Before many months Marietta was a village of many log cabins, surrounded by numerous clearings, and possessed of the customary "block-house" for defense against the Indians. In due time churches, schools, and even a college — Marietta College, the first institution of higher learning in the region west of the mountains — also made their appearance. The Ohio Company did not prove to be the money-making project that its founders had hoped, and it was able to redeem only a fraction of the land to which it was entitled according to its original contract with Congress.

The Scioto Company, in spite of the fact that it owned no land whatever, attempted to obtain settlers for the region upon which it held an option. Fearful, perhaps, lest Americans might examine *Gallipolis* into its land titles too closely, it sought to interest foreigners, and for this purpose sent Joel Barlow, the poet, to France. Barlow associated himself with an enterprising and none too scrupulous Englishman by the name of Playfair, and between the two many thousands of purchasers of Scioto Company lands were found. In 1790 some six hundred French settlers actually reached the Ohio and founded the village Gallipolis some distance down the river from Marietta. It turned out, however, that the settlement had been made on Ohio Company land, and to make matters worse for the French immigrants, the Scioto Company was never able to take up its option. The sufferings of the residents of Gallipolis, who were at best unaccustomed to American pioneering, ultimately led Congress to donate them a tract of land sufficient for their needs.

Another early settlement in the Ohio country was made by a well-to-do citizen of New Jersey, John Cleves Symmes, who in 1788 was granted permission to purchase a million acres of land between the *Symmes* Great and the Little Miami Rivers. Symmes advertised for settlers with some success, and within a short time the villages of Cincinnati, Columbia, and South Bend were founded in what came to be called the "Symmes tract." Like the Ohio Associates, Symmes was never able to buy all the land that he had contracted for, and the size of his tract had to be cut down materially.

By 1790 the Northwest Territory had nearly forty-three hundred inhabitants — perhaps thirteen hundred in the vicinity of Cincinnati, *Governor* a thousand at Marietta, and two thousand in the old French *St. Clair* villages. There was need, therefore, of the government which, under the terms of the Ordinance of 1787, had accompanied the settlement. When Marietta was about three months old Arthur St. Clair had appeared as governor, and had instituted the type of autocratic rule that the Ordinance had made provision for during the period of sparse settlement. St. Clair's difficulties, however, were many and great. The inhabitants tended increasingly to resent his assumption of arbitrary powers, and the Indians, many of whom refused to concede that the land being settled was ever legally ceded to the whites, indulged freely in scalping parties and in other ways showed their hostility. To meet the Indian menace and to keep a watchful eye on the French in the Illinois country, St. Clair soon moved his capital to Cincinnati. The confederation period had ended, however, and the new government under the constitution was in effect before the Indian problem in the Northwest came to a head.[1]

[1] The Old Northwest has attracted many historians. Among the best general accounts are B. A. Hinsdale, *The Old Northwest* (1899); F. A. Ogg, *The Old Northwest* (1919); and B. W. Bond, Jr., *The Civilization of the Old Northwest* (1934).

CHAPTER XI

FAILURE OF THE CONFEDERATION

THE Confederation Period coincided closely with a period of economic depression that came in the wake of the Revolutionary War. The waste and over-expenditure of those eight years had been a serious *A period of* drain on the resources of a country which at best was far *depression* from rich, and the war was not long over before the new nation was made fully aware of the heavy price it had paid for freedom. Also, separation from the British Empire made necessary a set of painful readjustments. If American commerce suffered somewhat in the colonial period from British regulations, it had also the advantage of British trade treaties and British protection. As a new and independent nation, the United States now had to make its own way in such matters. Being outside the British Empire was in itself a serious handicap, for, contrary to a common impression, the British government did not, as a result of the American war, give up immediately its efforts to promote imperial self-sufficiency; and the United States found itself deprived of trade privileges which the colonies as members of the imperial family had freely enjoyed. Then, too, the removal of the British troops from America, while a source of much satisfaction to good patriots, eliminated also the gold supply from British payments to Americans for foodstuffs and other necessities. With commerce at low ebb, and with an inadequate market for farm produce, unemployment became common, radical doctrines found a ready hearing, and criticism of the government grew by leaps and bounds.[1]

It was apparent that the re-establishment of normal commercial relations with Great Britain, and particularly with the *Trade with* British West Indies, was greatly to be desired. American *the British* trade had always flowed naturally to Great Britain, and *Empire* once the interruption of war was at an end probably half of the

[1] The Confederation Period is taken as the beginning point for two monumental works on American history: J. B. McMaster, *A History of the People of the United States from the Revolution to the Civil War* (8 vols., 1883–1913); and James Schouler, *History of the United States of America under the Constitution* (7 vols., 1880–1913). McMaster makes an especial effort to include social history, but he leaves few subjects of consequence untouched. Schouler's chief interest lies in political history.

American exports went once more to the mother country, while at least three fourths of the American imports were from British sources. But the treaty of 1783, generous as it was with respect to political matters, was not a treaty of commerce, and American shippers soon found that they could not always count on the same privileges in English ports that they had once been accorded. Particularly trying was the exclusion from English ports of American fish-oil and whale products. Americans found, too, that the British commercial policy which restrained the West Indies from purchasing outside the Empire, except in case of necessity, cut off a large share of what had been in colonial times a most lucrative trade. For example, citizens of the United States were no longer permitted to share in the West Indian carrying trade, or even to send their surplus salt-meat and fish to the West Indies even in English vessels. The loss of these markets disrupted the famous "triangle" trade, and deprived the Americans of a traditional source of supply for the bills of exchange with which in colonial times they had been accustomed to redress their balances in London. It seemed essential, therefore, to secure a trade treaty with Great Britain which would put an end to discriminations against American commerce in British ports, and would reopen the West Indian markets to American products.

Another problem of Anglo-American relations arose out of the fact that many of the British posts in the Northwest, despite the treaty of *The North-* peace which gave the region south of the Great Lakes to the *west posts* United States, were still held by British troops. The reason for this lay in the fact that the fur trade, upon the profits of which Canada depended so largely for its prosperity, desired to retain as long as possible the advantages it enjoyed in American territory. The military posts south of the lakes at Oswego, Niagara, Detroit, and elsewhere were sources of comfort and security to the fur-traders, as well as centers of anti-American influence among the Indians. It was important to the fur trade that the settlement of the Northwest be held back, for wherever settlers came in fur-bearing animals did not long survive. Every encouragement therefore was given to the Indians to resist the encroachments of the whites, and the presence of British soldiers, whom the Indians could regard as potential allies in their attacks upon the American pioneers, seemed to the fur-traders highly desirable. Among the Americans the retention of the Northwest posts by British garrisons, with an unmistakable tendency to give moral support to the Indians, was regarded as an inexcusable breach of faith.

To deal with these problems of commerce and of the frontier, John Adams was dispatched to England in 1785, but his mission failed miserably. As for the commercial treaty, it was apparent that the English could count on whatever American trade they wanted with- *Adams's* out it. Congress lacked the power to make or enforce any *mission to* such trade discriminations as might have brought the English *England* to terms, and Adams was taunted by the query, Did he represent one nation or thirteen? Indeed, many Englishmen believed that the new United States might yet see the error of their way and beg to be restored to their former status as British colonies. With reference to their retention of the Northwest posts the British had good excuses to offer. The treaty of peace had promised that no legal obstacles should stand in the way of the collection of private debts owing by Americans to British subjects before the war, but the debts nevertheless could not be collected. Furthermore, the persecution of Loyalists outlasted the war and the treaty, and the promised restoration of confiscated Loyalist property was virtually a dead letter. If the Americans themselves disregarded important clauses in the treaty of peace, how could they expect the British to do otherwise? In 1788 Adams returned to the United States with the objects of his mission wholly unobtained.[1]

Scarcely less important than the difficulties with Great Britain were those that existed between the United States and Spain. There was the same problem of trade discrimination in Spanish ports that *Spanish-* confronted the Americans when they sought entrance to *American* British ports, and there was the same special need of a free *relations* interchange of commodities with the Spanish possessions of the West Indies as with the British. There was difficulty, too, about the Florida boundary, which in the British cession to Spain had been left undefined, and there was a complete difference of opinion with regard to the rights of American citizens to the free navigation of the Mississippi River. In this latter dispute, the American contention was based on a clause in the Treaty of 1783 between the United States and Great Britain which gave to the citizens of both nations full freedom of navigation of the Mississippi River to its mouth. The Spanish contested the right of the English to grant any such privilege, for the lower Mississippi, by any interpretation of the international boundaries, lay wholly within Spanish territory.

The free navigation of the Mississippi River was a matter of great consequence to the growing settlements of the American West, for almost the sole outlet for western produce was by means of flatboats down the

[1] Adams's account of his mission is given in *The Works of John Adams*, edited by C. F. Adams (10 vols., 1850–56), III. For brief summaries see L. M. Sears, *A History of American Foreign Relations* (1927); and J. W. Foster, *A Century of American Diplomacy* (1900).

river to New Orleans. To cut off this trade, as the Spanish claimed they *The* had a perfect right to do, was to strike a body blow at the *Mississippi* growth of the West. This power the Spanish hoped to use in such a way as to give them control of the greater portion of the trans-Appalachian West. They let it be known through their agents, chief among whom was James Wilkinson, a former officer in the Revolutionary Army, that the western communities could find an easy solution for their difficulties by seceding from the United States and joining forces with the Spanish; and they negotiated directly with the United States government to secure its admission that the American claim to the navigation of the Mississippi was invalid. They also sought to restrain the too rapid growth of the American population by encouraging the southwestern Indians to resist the advance of the American frontier.

The first Spanish minister to the United States, Don Diego de Gardoqui, arrived during the summer of 1785. John Jay, who in 1784 had *The Jay-* been charged by Congress with the conduct of American *Gardoqui* foreign affairs, soon entered into negotiations with Gardoqui *negotiations* for a settlement of the outstanding difficulties between the two countries, and for the formulation of the trade treaty so much desired by the United States. It speedily became apparent to Jay that his country had very little with which to bargain. Threats of commercial discrimination or of war were of no avail; for in the one case Congress lacked the necessary power, and in the other the people lacked the will to fight. Jay therefore was tempted to secure what he could from a bargain that Gardoqui proposed whereby the United States should receive a favorable trade treaty in return for giving up for a period of twenty-five or thirty years its claim to the right of navigation of the lower Mississippi. Such an agreement would be of great value to the northeastern states, and, as Jay reasoned it out, would hardly damage the West, for that region, he supposed, was destined at best to grow very little in population during the next quarter-century.

Jay was able to secure the support of seven states in Congress for this compromise, but he needed nine, and so the negotiations came to nothing. The northern states, which would have profited most by the trade treaty, supported him; but the southern states, whose representatives knew better the problem of the West than the Northerners, voted the proposition down. Virginia was still in possession of Kentucky, so her western boundary reached the Mississippi; while North Carolina, South Carolina, and Georgia had not yet surrendered their claims to western lands. These states were thus vitally interested in the welfare of the West, and were opposed to a measure which might hamper its growth. They knew,

[188]

too, that the independent spirit of the West would never brook such restraint as the treaty proposed, and would find a means to use the Mississippi even at the cost of secession from the United States.[1]

The Confederation thus failed miserably in its dealings with England and Spain, and it showed an equal lack of ability in negotiating with other foreign powers. A few trade treaties were signed, notably those with Sweden and Prussia, but they turned out to be relatively unimportant to American commerce. The treaties with France and Holland, signed during the war, were maintained and renewed, but they too failed to attact American trade away from its normal pre-revolutionary channels, while the good relations between the United States and her former allies in the war with England were continually imperiled by the inability of the American government to pay its foreign debt.

The financial embarrassment of the Confederation government was always acute.[2] To meet its ordinary expenditures it required an income of about a half million dollars a year, and this sum made no provision for payments, either of interest or principal, on the public debt. Altogether the United States had incurred an indebtedness of well over forty million dollars during the prosecution of the war. About six million dollars had been borrowed from France, and perhaps another two millions from other foreign sources. The remainder, mostly in the shape of back pay for soldiers and certificates of indebtedness to those who had furnished supplies for the army, was owing to the citizens of the United States. *Confederation finance*

The means by which the government could raise money to discharge its financial obligations were strictly limited. It might resort to paper-money issues, but during the war this source of revenue had been dried up by overuse. It might also indulge in further borrowing provided creditors could be found to lend, and some funds were actually obtained in Holland for use in paying the interest on the foreign debt. A small sum was realized from the sales of public lands, and the post-office brought in ten or fifteen thousand dollars a year. In the main, however, Congress had to rely upon requisitions levied upon the states for money it needed to meet obligations of every sort and kind. The requisition system proved to be entirely inadequate. Requests for funds were honored by the states only in so far as they chose to honor them, and

[1] On Spanish-American relations during this period consult A. P. Whitaker, *The Spanish American Frontier, 1783–1795* (1927); and F. A. Ogg, *The Opening of the Mississippi* (1904).

[2] D. R. Dewey, *Financial History of the United States* (1903), has gone through many editions, and is still the most useful general work on the subject. Somewhat broader in scope, and closer to the present in its point of view, is H. J. Carman, *Social and Economic History of the United States* (2 vols., 1930–34). A third volume from Professor Carman's pen is expected.

probably not to exceed one tenth of the sums asked for by Congress were ever paid in. Much of the money that was obtained, moreover, was of uncertain value, for the states also had their financial difficulties, and many of them had resorted to overissues of paper currency. Plans for the compulsory collection of the sums levied upon the states were considered, but none seemed practicable enough to warrant giving it a trial.

On two occasions Congress made an earnest effort to obtain alterations in the Articles of Confederation that would make possible an independent *Efforts to* source of revenue for the central government. The first *amend the* request (1781) was for a five per cent ad-valorem duty on *Articles* imports, from the proceeds of which the interest on the national debt might be paid and a beginning made toward the payment of the principal. This modest proposal, while agreeable to most of the states, met with serious objections, and was defeated. The Revolution had been fought in part as a protest against taxation by an outside agency, and to many citizens Congress seemed quite as much beyond the control of the individual state as the British Parliament itself. Moreover, with unpleasant memories of the activities of British tax-gatherers still fresh in mind, there was much skepticism as to the widsom of allowing the agents of Congress to enter a state for the purpose of collecting taxes within it. Rhode Island refused outright to consent to such a tax, and Virginia withdrew her consent after it had been given; and since the Articles of Confederation could not be amended without a unanimous vote the proposal came to naught. Congress then modified its request (1783), and sought the power to levy duties on imports for twenty-five years only, the states themselves to appoint the revenue officers. But again Rhode Island refused, New York gave only a qualified consent, and several other states failed to take action in the matter. It seemed evident, therefore, that while the Articles of Confederation endured the central government must depend for its financial support upon the unsatisfactory requisition system.

The financial impotence with which it was cursed soon made the Congress of the Confederation a joke. The men best qualified to serve as *Impotence* delegates refused to risk their reputations or waste their *of Congress* time in such futile labor, and the states were compelled to send second-rate men to represent them. Some states preferred to send no delegates at all. Moreover, the delegates chosen often neglected to attend the sessions of Congress. Only twenty-three members were present to ratify the treaty of peace by which the Revolution was brought to an end — the opposition of a single state could have defeated ratification. Washington's resignation as head of the army was presented to Congress when only twenty delegates were present. The Northwest Ordinance of 1787, doubtless the most notable of the acts of Congress under the Confederation, was passed with but eighteen delegates present.

The state governments were confronted by problems almost as difficult as those which embarrassed Congress. They possessed the power to levy tariffs which Congress so much coveted, but its exercise *State* by so many different agencies resulted in serious complica- *tariffs* tions. Promptly at the close of the Revolution, British merchants began to unload their excess goods upon the American market, almost regardless of price. American manufactures were ruined, and retaliatory tariffs were demanded. But to secure genuine retaliation, thirteen different sets of tariff regulations would have had to be brought into general agreement, and nothing of the sort could be done. Imports tended to arrive at the ports of low-tariff states rather than high-tariff states, with smuggling as an inevitable concomitant. Rhode Island, for example, profited greatly from the fact that her tariff was relatively low, whereas the tariffs of some of her neighboring states, especially New York, were relatively high. Endless confusion and much bad feeling was added by the states' levying duties against each other. New York taxed farm produce from New Jersey at a very high rate, and New Jersey in retaliation taxed a lighthouse built by the New-Yorkers on Sandy Hook. Connecticut taxed goods from Massachusetts more than she would have taxed the same goods if imported from England.

Then, too, the financial difficulties of the states actually rivaled those of the central government. Much of this trouble came from the almost inevitable tendency to resort to paper-money issues. This *Paper* was nothing new to America, for before the Revolution the *money* colonies had frequently yielded to a similar temptation, and had resented deeply the efforts of the British government to restrict their activities along this line; one might almost say that the Revolution was caused in part by a difference of opinion between the mother country and the colonies on the paper-money question. During the Confederation period the lack of gold in the United States, always a chronic complaint of the continental colonies, became an acute menace. Neither gold nor silver was mined anywhere within the United States; hard money was difficult to obtain from the Spanish colonies in the West Indies because of the existing restrictions on commerce; the reward of privateering that had brought some precious metals into the country during the Revolution could no longer be reaped; and the gold left by the British army was soon drained off to meet an unfavorable balance of trade. Furthermore, the debtor classes within each state, more articulate than ever as a result of the Revolution, urged paper money because of the blessings that an inflated currency would bring to them; and in many states the more conservative propertied classes, who opposed inflation, were outvoted.

The records of Rhode Island and Massachusetts on the paper-money question give a fair understanding of the situation. In Rhode Island *Trevett vs.* the paper-money faction got the upper hand in the legisla- *Weeden* ture, and multiplied issues until the currency was almost valueless; then, when "legal-tender" paper money was refused, passed a law making its refusal a punishable offense without so much as requiring a trial by jury for the offender. The attempt to enforce this law led to one of the most important judicial decisions in American legal history, for in the case of *Trevett vs. Weeden* the state supreme court held that the law just cited was out of harmony with the Rhode Island charter and therefore unconstitutional. This decision was attacked by the legislature, which summoned the judges before it and voted unsatisfactory the defense of their action that they made. Furthermore, at the next election three out of the four judges concerned were retired. But the precedent set was not overthrown, and the later power of the courts over legislation which they deemed unconstitutional owed much to this decision.

In Massachusetts the contest over paper money took the form of a test of strength between the coast towns, which were relatively prosperous *Shays's·* from what commerce still endured, and the small farmers of *Rebellion* the interior, who found it difficult during the prevailing hard times to pay their debts and taxes. As a measure of debt relief the rural classes demanded liberal paper-money issues, but the legislature was under the control of the coast towns and refused to comply with the farmers' demands. Instead, heavy taxes were levied to pay off the war debt, and sheriffs' sales were multiplied. In the summer of 1786 open rebellion broke out. Bands of insurgents, composed of farmers, artisans, and laborers, marched on the courts in several districts and prevented them from sitting. Daniel Shays, a veteran of Bunker Hill, with an insurgent army of about two thousand men forced an adjournment of the court at Springfield and made wild threats. "My boys," he told his followers, "you are going to fight for liberty. If you wish to know what liberty is, I will tell you. It is for every man to do what he pleases, to make other people do as you please to have them, and to keep folks from serving the devil." Shays's Rebellion, as this outbreak was called, was put down by militia led by General Lincoln and paid by means of a loan to which well-to-do citizens, fearful that a wholesale attack upon property rights was imminent, subscribed generously. But the enduring power of the debtor classes was demonstrated in the next state election when Governor Bowdoin, under whom the "Rebellion" had been suppressed, was defeated for re-election by John Hancock, who was still the idol of the radicals.[1]

Not only in Rhode Island and Massachusetts, but in practically all the states the conservative property owners were genuinely frightened by the growing power of the agrarian and unpropertied *Growth of* classes. The new state constitutions, while by no means *radicalism* radical documents, had added much to the power of the masses, and the Revolution itself had unsettled traditional habits of deference to those in authority. Extremists reasoned that if it had been right and proper to revolt against England because of one type of tyranny, it was now equally right and proper to revolt against local governments or practices that seemed equally tyrannical. If debts owing to British merchants could be legislated out of existence, why not also debts owing to American merchants? Grievances that might ordinarily be overlooked were magnified because of the existing hard times and unemployment, and a spirit of discontent bordering faintly on anarchy was abroad in the land. Acts of violence, such as boycotts, tea-parties, the terrorizing of tax-collectors, had characterized the outbreak of the Revolution; Shays's Rebellion indicated that more of the same thing, this time directed against the upper classes in America, might be in store.

Confronted by this menacing situation, conservative men of property began to cast about for some means of checking the democratic tendencies that were so painfully in evidence. What seemed to be *Demands* needed was a government strong enough to maintain order *for a* at home and if possible also to protect American rights *stronger* abroad. Clearly the state governments could not be trusted *government* to do these things; their authority was limited, and in some cases the lower classes already had control. As for the central government, its impotence under the Articles of Confederation was abundantly demonstrated. It was without an effective executive, and its feeble gropings in that direction had so far proved unavailing; it had no judiciary whatever; it could not regulate commerce; it had no taxing power; and it was at best a mere creature of the states utterly incapable of acting directly upon individuals. Worst of all, amendments to the Articles of Confederation required a unanimous vote, and experience seemed to prove that on this account any strictly legal change would be impossible.

[1] A contemporary view is given by George R. Minot, *History of the Insurrection in Massachusetts in the Year 1786* (1788).

Clearly a stronger central government was needed, and toward that end the propertied classes began to direct their efforts. Such men as Alexander Hamilton, Peletiah Webster, and Governor Bowdoin openly proclaimed their belief in the necessity of a closer and more powerful union.

Nor was this agitation confined merely to words. In the spring of 1785 a joint commission composed of delegates from Virginia and Mary-
The confer- land met at Alexandria, Virginia, to find a way out of the
ence at perplexing difficulties that had arisen between the two states
Alexandria because of conflicting regulations with regard to navigation
of Chesapeake Bay and the Potomac River. This proposition greatly interested George Washington, who as the owner of perhaps thirty thousand acres of western lands hoped especially for improvements in the navigation of the Potomac that would make it a better highway to the West, and at Washington's invitation the convention adjourned to Mount Vernon. On the particular points at issue the two states reached an agreement, but the legislature of Maryland suggested that a conference on commercial matters that would include the neighboring states of Pennsylvania and Delaware might achieve even greater results. This idea found support from the Virginia legislature, which promptly issued a call for such a convention to meet at Annapolis the first Monday in September, 1786. The Virginia call, however, was not restricted to the four states suggested by Maryland; instead every one of the thirteen states was invited to send delegates.

Nine states named representatives to attend the Annapolis Convention, but from only five, Virginia, Delaware, Pennsylvania, New Jersey,
The and New York, did the delegates chosen actually attend.
Annapolis With the representation so inadequate it soon became ap-
Convention parent that the convention could make little progress with
the matter it had in hand, but it nevertheless managed to do something very much more important. It adopted a report from the able pen of Alexander Hamilton which pointed out some of the conspicuous defects in the Articles of Confederation and called upon the states to send delegates to a new convention through which a remedy for these defects should be sought. The date set for the new convention was the second Monday in May, 1787, and the place of meeting suggested was Philadelphia. Hamilton represented the extreme conservative opinion of the country and sincerely hoped for a strong central government that would represent the propertied classes, but he dare not in this document openly advocate the overthrow of the Confederation. His report merely suggested that the convention confine its efforts to such provisions as

seemed necessary "to render the constitution of the federal government adequate to the exigencies of the union." He also pointed out, by way of assuring the radical element, that whatever amendments to the articles were adopted at Philadelphia would have to be submitted to all the states for their approval.

Hamilton's proposal was transmitted not only to the various state legislatures, but also to Congress, and on February 21, 1787, the latter body joined in the call for the Philadelphia Convention. *Another* In doing so, however, Congress stated that the purpose of *convention* the convention was merely to propose amendments to the *called* existing Articles of Confederation. The clear inference was that only by the subsequent ratification of all the thirteen states could any such amendments be adopted. It is interesting to note that ultimately the convention disregarded this interpretation of its mission, and submitted a new constitution which, instead of awaiting the unanimous consent that the Articles of Confederation would have required, was to take effect when ratified by only nine of the thirteen states. It is also interesting to note that there is no way of demonstrating that the complete abandonment of the Articles of Confederation was necessary to the attainment of a vigorous national government. Could the existing Congress have been assured more power over commerce and an adequate revenue, it is possible that the other defects would have been remedied with the passage of time. The heads of the executive departments, already established or to be established, might eventually have become a responsible cabinet, and the development in the United States of the same type of parliamentary government that was already beginning to operate in England and was later to become so common elsewhere might not have been so effectively and perhaps unfortunately forestalled. Indeed, the old government under the Articles of Confederation, with all its defects, might not have been so unsuccessful had the times been prosperous. But with the country in the depths of an economic depression all through the period of its existence, the Confederation government had no chance to show what it could do under normal circumstances.

Many of those who were most interested in making the Philadelphia Convention a success were yet skeptical of its outcome. Forces had long been at work, however, to ensure that ultimately the *Forces* hope of a stronger union would be realized. The very *making for* isolation from the rest of the world that the thirteen Amer- *union* ican states shared with one another tended to force them together. Their inhabitants were for the most part of a common racial stock, spoke a common language, read much the same books, and had inherited practically the same traditions. Every part of the new nation had, at some time not far removed, gone through the frontier process — a process which did not differ markedly from place to place or from time to time, and tended therefore to supply a common mold for the formation of American traits. The frontier of the 1780's itself acted as a binding tie. In the mountain valleys of the Appalachians and in the new communities still farther to the west there was a continual mingling of settlers from many different states and even from the Old World. Here state boundaries were freely passed, and old loyalties were soon forgotten. Democratic frontiersmen might fear for the moment the attempt of an aristocratic group in the East to form and dominate a strong central government, but potentially at least the West was inescapably nationalistic.

Moreover, the problems that faced the American states were increasingly national in character. The conflicting interests of debtors and creditors cut across state lines. In the back country the debtor point of view dominated; along the coast the creditors tended to maintain their control. Commerce vied with agriculture, but most of the states were neither strictly commercial nor strictly agricultural; the commercial classes everywhere tended to present a solid front against an almost equally united agricultural interest. Even in matters pertaining to religion there was a tendency to divide along national rather than along state or local lines. In the East adherents of the old settled faiths, Congregationalists in New England, Quakers in Pennsylvania, Dutch Calvinists in New York, and Episcopalians in the South, found themselves drawn together in defense of the old ways against hordes of upstart Presbyterians, Methodists, and Baptists, who challenged church establishments wherever they found them, overturned timeworn customs, and demanded complete religious freedom as the right of every man. Such common problems as these revealed lines of cleavage within the nation as a whole rather than within the individual states. Efforts to solve these problems nationally tended to draw together radicals from every state and section no less than conservatives, and to prophesy the speedy formation of a closer union.

CHAPTER XII

THE CONSTITUTION

By the end of the Confederation Period the line of cleavage in the new nation between the possessors of considerable property and the common people was clearly drawn. The merchants and importers, *Classes in* the shipbuilders and shipowners, the possessors of landed *America* estates, the speculators and money-lenders were set apart by their economic interests from the small farmers, the artisans, and the non-propertied classes generally. Among men of property the fear had grown almost to the proportions of panic that the lower classes would eventually secure control of all the state governments (as they already seemed to have done in Rhode Island), and that as a result property interests everywhere would suffer perhaps even to the point of confiscation. Out of this state of mind came the agitation in favor of a strong central government — a government which would be independent of state control, and would possess the will and the power to protect the rights of property. The movement for the Philadelphia Convention was thus primarily an upper-class affair, and when the time came for the choice of delegates it was the interested upper class that determined the selections.[1]

Fortunately for the well-to-do, the call for the Philadelphia Convention did not designate the method by which delegates should be chosen, and the selections were made, therefore, by the various state *Conserva-* legislatures, in most of which the men of property still had *tism of the* comfortable majorities. Rhode Island refused to choose *delegates* delegates, but from the other states a total of seventy-three men were elected, of whom only fifty-five ever put in their appearance at the convention. These men were typical representatives of the conservative upper class. They were almost without exception men of financial and social standing, well prepared for their labors by education and by

---

[1] C. A. Beard, *An Economic Interpretation of the Constitution of the United States* (1913), is a work that has profoundly affected the thinking of most students of American history. Beard's flair for brilliant interpretation is also given free rein in Charles A. and Mary R. Beard, *The Rise of American Civilization* (2 vols., 1927).

previous governmental experience. One may fairly say that the small-farmer-artisan class was not represented in the convention at all.

When May 14, 1787, the day for opening the convention arrived, there were too few present to organize, but on May 25 twenty-nine delegates *Philadelphia* met in Independence Hall and chose George Washington to *Convention* be their presiding officer. For three and a half months the sessions continued, usually with not many more in attendance than appeared the first day. The convention at once decided that, to promote freedom of discussion and to avoid outside interference, its sessions must be held behind closed doors and all proceedings carefully guarded from the public. This decision was adhered to with great consistency. Indeed, only the barest details of business were recorded in the official journal kept by the convention, and for a more intimate account of what went on the historian must turn to the notes kept by individual members, particularly to James Madison's *Journal* in which the Virginia delegate recorded a careful summary of every important speech he heard.[1]

The seriousness of the situation in which the conservative men of property felt themselves to be probably had much to do with the care *Leaders in* they exercised in their choice of delegates. Undoubtedly, *the conven-* the best men they could send to the convention were actually *tion* chosen to go. The presiding officer, George Washington, was even then probably the most respected and revered of Americans. Benjamin Franklin had for many years been known as America's most distinguished scientist and literary light. Alexander Hamilton, in spite of his youth, had already exhibited genius of high order in the realm of finance. Of nearly every delegate who sat in the convention something similar could be said. The list included George Mason and Edmund Randolph of Virginia, Robert Morris and Gouverneur Morris of Pennsylvania, Charles Pinckney and Charles Cotesworth Pinckney of South Carolina, Roger Sherman and Oliver Ellsworth of Connecticut, John Dickinson of Delaware, Luther Martin of Maryland, and William Paterson of New Jersey.

These men had little faith in democracy; indeed, one might almost say that it was their fear of democracy that had brought them together. *Fear of* Their problem was how to make a government democratic *democracy* enough to be adopted but not so democratic as to constitute any menace to upper-class control. Again and again during the conven-

---

[1] Two admirable collections of the documents relating to the formation of the Constitution have been made: *Records of the Federal Convention of 1787*, edited by Max Farrand (3 vols., 1911); and *Documents Illustrative of the Formation of the Union of the American States*, edited by C. C. Tansill (1927).

tion this attitude on the part of the delegates found forceful expression. Once when Roger Sherman was protesting against the election of members of the House of Representatives by direct vote of the people he remarked that "the people immediately should have as little to do as may be about the government." Elbridge Gerry held that the evils from which the country suffered were due mainly to an "excess of democracy." Edmund Randolph, the brilliant young governor of Virginia, took occasion to deplore the turbulence and follies of democracy. John Dickinson felt that a limited monarchy was "one of the best governments of the world," and hoped that the Senate might be made "as nearly as may be like the House of Lords of England." Such statements could be multiplied almost at will.[1]

The convention was quick to decide that the mere strengthening of the Articles of Confederation would never produce the kind of government desired by men of property. It voted, therefore, without much hesitation, to form an entirely new constitution. Some writers tend to feature the differences of opinion that developed in the convention and to emphasize chiefly the difficulty with which decisions were reached. It is true enough that many conflicting views had to be reconciled, and that innumerable compromises had to be made. But an even more striking fact is that on so many of the essentials the delegates were in almost complete accord. They agreed perfectly as to the fundamental ends that the new government was to accomplish; they accepted with little debate many of the precedents set by the English Constitution and by the constitutions of the new states; and they evinced a remarkable willingness to arrange compromises on all matters of minor detail.

It was not easy, however, to adjust the relative weight of states and nation in the new government. The extreme nationalistic point of view was embodied in the so-called Virginia Plan, which had re- *The Virginia Plan* sulted from the daily meetings of the Virginia delegation. The plan proposed a two-house legislature, the lower house to be chosen by the people of the several states in such a manner as to give small states like Delaware and Rhode Island only one representative and large states like Massachusetts and Virginia sixteen or seventeen representatives, and the upper house to be chosen by the lower house. Separate executive and judicial departments were to be established, but the holders of both executive and judicial offices were to be selected by the legislature, which would also be given authority to veto state laws out of harmony with its

[1] From the many excellent books on the framing of the Constitution, the following are selected: Max Farrand, *The Framing of the Constitution of the United States* (1913), and *The Fathers of the Constitution* (1921); Charles Warren, *The Making of the Constitution* (1928); R. L. Schuyler, *The Constitution of the United States* (1923).

own. The two obvious defects in this plan from the small-state point of view were the absence of any provisions guaranteeing the equality of states, and the uncertainty that the small states would secure any representation whatever in the upper house of the legislature. Moreover, the Virginia Plan really implied the formation of a consolidated national government which could and probably would relegate the states to the position of mere administrative units. The Virginia Plan was presented to the convention May 29 in a brilliant speech by Edmund Randolph, and for two weeks clause by clause was earnestly debated.

This debate served to bring out the most important line of cleavage that the convention developed. The Virginia Plan satisfied the large *Large states vs. small* states, Virginia, Pennsylvania, and Massachusetts, fairly well, and was supported also by North Carolina, South Carolina, and Georgia, states in which the possibilities of growth were great. But the small states, New Jersey, Delaware, Maryland, Connecticut, and New York (which then meant little more than the Hudson Valley), were profoundly agitated at the prospect of large-state tyranny, and feared even that the small states might ultimately lose their separate identity. Thanks to the system of voting by states in the convention, the small states had great weight in the deliberations; indeed, but for the failure of Rhode Island to send delegates and the tardy participation of New Hampshire, whose representatives did not arrive until July 23, the small states would have been in the majority. It was natural enough, therefore, that they should present a plan of their own as a substitute for the plan suggested by the Virginians.

The small-state point of view finally found expression in a report by William Paterson of New Jersey, commonly called the New Jersey Plan. *The New Jersey Plan* It proposed to retain the states as equal, and perhaps sovereign, units. There would be no change in the organization of Congress, although a genuine executive and an independent judiciary were contemplated; but the powers of Congress were to be expanded to include the right to levy tariffs, to regulate commerce, and to force a state to pay requisitions made upon it by the central government. The New Jersey Plan was debated for a week, and then, to the great chagrin of its defenders, was voted down. The small-state men did not leave the convention, however, but sought instead to modify the Virginia Plan, to which the convention now recurred, in such a way as to emphasize the federal rather than the strictly national idea.

Ultimately a solution was found which in a measure, at least, satisfied both parties. In accordance with the Virginia Plan the convention voted to establish a two-house legislature, with the membership of the

lower house to be apportioned according to population. It then left
to a committee on compromise the composition of the upper   *The "Great
chamber.* This committee, upon which sat some of the   *Compro-
ablest men of the convention, including Franklin, finally rec-   *mise"*
ommended that the national character of the lower house, whose membership was to be apportioned among the various states according to population, should be offset by an upper house in which the states should be
equally represented, two members to be chosen by each state. On July
16 this report was accepted by the convention, and the "Great Compromise," so called, became a fact. Thereafter the suspicions that had
kept the large states and the small states so far apart tended to disappear.
Ultimately it was decided that representatives of the lower house should
be elected by the people for a period of two years, and that two senators
were to be chosen for six-year terms by the state legislatures in every
state.

There remained, however, many adjustments to be made, and one may
say that almost every line of the constitution that was written came as
the result of some compromise. Even on the matter of rep-   *The "Three-
resentation in the lower house a serious dispute arose.   *Fifths"
Should the slaves, so numerous in some of the southern   *Compromise*
states, be counted in apportioning the number of representatives to which
the states were entitled? Or should these slaves be regarded as property
rather than persons? These questions were the more perplexing in view
of the fact that the convention had already agreed to assess direct taxes
upon the states in accordance with the population. The northern states
were unwilling to allow the South to count its slaves in determining the
representation a state should have in the lower house of Congress, but
desired to count them when direct taxes were to be assessed; the South,
on the other hand, wished to count its slaves when the question of representation in Congress was up, but not when taxes were to be levied.
A reasonable, if utterly illogical, solution was found in the decision to
count five slaves as equal to three whites both in the apportionment of
representatives and in the assessing of direct taxes.

During the debate that led to the "Three-Fifths" Compromise the
question of the part that new western states were to be allowed to play
in the new government also came to the fore. Gouverneur   *Provision
Morris argued earnestly that the rule of representation ought   *for new
to be so fixed as to secure to the Atlantic states a prevalence   *states*
for all time in the national councils. The new frontier states, he said,
would know less of the public interest than the old, and in particular
might involve the nation in wars with the Indians and with neighboring

nations that would have to be paid for by the maritime states. Representing as he did the conservative property-holding classes of the East, Morris maintained that if the untutored and irresponsible small farmers of the West got the power into their hands, they would ruin the Atlantic interests. Even Elbridge Gerry of Massachusetts, one of the least conservative members of the convention, feared that the Westerners, if they were given the opportunity, might use it to "oppress commerce and drain out wealth into the Western Country." He suggested that the number of representatives to be chosen from the West should never exceed the number chosen by the Atlantic states.

Fortunately for the good of the country and for the permanence of the constitution, the narrow view expressed by Morris and Gerry did not prevail. Instead, the convention took the advice of Wilson of Pennsylvania, who insisted that "the majority of people, wherever found, ought in all questions to govern the minority. If the interior Country should acquire this majority, it will not only have the right, but will avail itself of it whether we will or no. This jealously misled the policy of Great Britain with regard to America." Probably, however, many members of the convention comforted themselves with the thought to which Roger Sherman gave expression, that the number of future states would probably never exceed that of the existing states anyway.

The sectional character of the dispute over representation came out again when the convention discussed the extent to which Congress *Commerce* should have authority over commerce. The northern states, in which commerce was a dominant interest, were ready to clothe Congress with ample regulatory power, but some of the southern states feared that this power might be used to revive the tyranny that England had been guilty of in passing the Acts of Trade. If, for example, Congress should require that all American products should be carried in American-built and American-manned ships, it would greatly stimulate the shipbuilding and commercial interests of the northern states, but it would almost certainly increase the expense and the difficulty of the agricultural South's getting its produce to market. Some of the southern states, particularly Georgia and South Carolina, were also concerned lest Congress might tax heavily or even forbid the importation of slaves, and thus strike at what in their section was still believed to be an essential labor supply; consequently they insisted that there should be no tax on exports or upon "such persons" as the several states should "think proper to admit," and they demanded that navigation acts should be passed only by a two-thirds vote of both houses of Congress. To resolve these differences, the northern states yielded to the South on the prohibition of export duties, and agreed also that the importation of slaves should not be forbidden before the year 1808, although Congress might levy a tax of ten dollars per head for each person imported. The southern states, thus reassured, gave up their insistence on a two-thirds vote in Congress for the passage of navigation acts.

The convention early decided that the national government should have only "enumerated powers"; hence one of the most important sections of the Constitution was that which listed the powers *The powers* of Congress. In this enumeration many provisions of the *of Congress* old Articles of Confederation were taken over almost intact. Such, for example, were those which authorized Congress to borrow money on the credit of the United States, to declare war, to maintain an army and navy, and to establish post-offices and post-roads. Extremely significant, however, were the new powers, especially those which gave Congress authority to lay and collect taxes, duties, imposts, and excises, to regulate commerce with foreign nations and among the several states, to coin money and regulate the value thereof, and "to make all laws which shall be necessary and proper for carrying into execution the foregoing powers." The last-mentioned provision, spoken of later as the "elastic clause" of the Constitution, made it possible to stretch the grants of power specifically enumerated to lengths that the members of the constitutional convention would scarcely have deemed possible. To ensure obedience to the central government, Congress was also authorized to provide for the calling forth of the militia to execute the laws of the Union and to suppress insurrections and repel invasions.

Hardly less important than the delegation of powers to the national government was the withdrawal of certain powers from the states. States were forbidden to coin money, to emit bills of credit, *Limitations* to make anything but gold and silver legal tender in pay- *on the states* ment of debts, to have direct relations with foreign countries, to levy duties on imports or exports (without the consent of Congress), "to pass any bill of attainder, ex post facto law, or law impairing the obligation of contracts, or grant any title of nobility." Most of these provisions were designed to prevent the radical non-propertied classes, in case they should win control in any of the states, from passing legislation hostile to the interests of the propertied classes. For example, while the national government was left free to print paper money, and even to declare it legal tender, the states were expressly forbidden to exercise these powers.

Following closely Montesquieu's interpretation of the English Constitution and the actual practice of government in the American colonies and states, the delegates to the Philadelphia Convention agreed without

hesitation to the principle that the legislative, executive, and judicial
The   powers of government ought to be separated as completely
separation as possible. Bent as they were upon establishing a power-
of powers   ful central government, they therefore assigned to the
executive and to the judiciary powers that compared well with the
powers of the legislature. Indeed, it was an old theory that each of the
three branches of government should be strong enough to act as an
effective check or balance to the others, and that in this fashion the
danger of tyranny or error on the part of any one could be measurably
cut down.

The creation of an executive department caused the convention a great
deal of trouble. Extreme conservatives were in favor of a single execu-
The   tive chosen by Congress for life, or at least for a very long
executive   term. Some, however, felt that such a plan was too closely
akin to monarchy, and argued for a plural executive, or at least for short
terms and frequent elections. The idea of a plural executive was quite
out of harmony with British and American experience, and was quickly
voted down; but many delegates held that the possibility of re-election
might stimulate an executive to faithful performance of his duties. The
objection to frequent elections was that in case Congress thus held the
right to continue the executive in office or to dismiss him, his independence would vanish. Obviously the method of escape from this dilemma
was to find some way to elect the executive other than by vote of Congress. Popular election seemed the natural alternative, but the judgment of the people was sorely distrusted by the great majority of the
delegates, and this idea was hastily thrust aside. Election by popularly
chosen electors suffered from the objection that such a system would give
undue power to the large states, and was also voted down.

For a time it seemed as if the long-term system with election by Congress would have to be adopted, but toward the close of the convention a
The elec-   way out was discovered. A committee appointed to solve
toral college the problem reported in favor of a modified electoral system,
and the committee report, somewhat amended, went into the Constitution. The President was to be chosen for a term of four years, and was
to be eligible for re-election. As many electors were to be named in each
state as the state had senators and representatives, and the method of
choosing the electors was to be left for each state to determine for itself.
The electors were to vote for two candidates for President, and if anyone should receive the votes of a majority of the electors he was to be declared elected, while the candidate receiving the next highest number of
votes, whether a majority or not, was to become Vice-President. It was

assumed, however, that unless there were some outstanding candidate, such as in the first election General Washington was sure to be, an election by a majority of the electoral college would be impossible, and each state delegation would merely cast its vote for some favorite son. To meet this contingency it was provided that in case the electoral college failed to choose a President, the duty should devolve upon the House of Representatives, where for this purpose each delegation might have only one vote. This arrangement involved a subtle compromise. Since the House could choose only from the five highest names on the list voted for by the electors, it appeared that the large states would ordinarily nominate the candidates, while the more numerous small states would hold the balance of power in the election to follow. The committee report left this choice to the Senate, but because so many powers had already been conferred upon that body it was decided that the election of the President should be the prerogative of the House, voting by states. Needless to say, the delegates failed completely to foresee the subsequent practice of presidential elections.

There was little hesitation about granting extensive powers to the President. He was made the commander-in-chief of the army and navy and also of the state militia whenever it was called into *Powers* national service; he had the power to make treaties with *of the* foreign nations "by and with the advice and consent of the *President* Senate . . . provided two-thirds of the Senators present concur"; he could with the consent of the majority in the Senate name ambassadors, ministers, consuls, judges of the federal courts, and all the other officers of the United States not otherwise provided for; he might call Congress into extraordinary session when he believed such a session necessary; he must "take care that the laws be faithfully executed"; and he had the right to veto bills passed by Congress, with the qualification that a two-thirds vote of both houses might make the bill a law without the President's signature.[1] As a safeguard against executive usurpation or other misbehavior a method of impeachment was devised, with the House bringing the indictment and the Senate sitting as a court. A two-thirds majority of the Senate was required to convict and remove from office.

The importance of a federal judiciary was not underestimated, but there was surprisingly little debate on the subject during the convention, and the section on the judiciary that was finally written is *The* very brief. That there should be a supreme court was *judiciary* generally agreed, but many believed that the existence of state courts made inferior federal courts unnecessary. This difference of opinion was

[1] E. C. Mason, *The Veto Power* (1890).

compromised by providing merely that Congress might establish inferior courts if it chose to do so, but nothing was put into the Constitution to require their establishment. The appointment of judges occasioned some debate, and at first was made the duty of the Senate; later it was decided that the President should have the right to appoint them, subject to confirmation by the Senate. The judicial power of the federal courts was so defined as to extend to all cases arising under the Constitution, the laws of Congress, and the treaties to which the United States was a party; to all cases affecting ambassadors, other public ministers, and consuls; to all cases of admiralty and maritime jurisdiction; to controversies to which the United States was a party; and to controversies between two or more states, between a state and citizens of another state, and between citizens of different states. The supreme court was given original jurisdiction over cases affecting foreign ministers and cases to which a state was party; otherwise its jurisdiction was appellate only.

Curiously, the Constitution itself says nothing with regard to the power which the judiciary soon assumed of declaring invalid such laws as *Judicial* in its opinion were contrary to the Constitution — a power *review* which ultimately was to become the most characteristic feature of the American judiciary, as well as its most effective weapon. It was plainly stated, however, that "the constitution, and the laws of the United States which shall be made in pursuance thereof; and all treaties, made or which shall be made, under the authority of the United States, shall be the supreme law of the land; and the judges in every state shall be bound thereby, anything in the constitution or laws of any state to the contrary notwithstanding." Many leading members of the Philadelphia Convention felt that the federal judges would as a matter of course have the right of declaring null and void laws out of harmony with the Constitution, and so expressed themselves time and time again during the debates. To James Madison, for example, it seemed perfectly obvious that "a law violating a Constitution established by the people themselves, would be considered by the judges as null and void." Indeed, a proposition to give the supreme court a qualified veto over laws of Congress was voted down partly because the federal judges would probably exert some such authority anyway. Thus the doctrine of judicial review can hardly be regarded as the usurpation of a power that the framers of the Constitution never intended the courts to exercise.[1]

The three-headed system of government, with its separate legislature, executive, and judiciary, provided numerous opportunities for preventing

[1] E. S. Corwin, *The Doctrine of Judicial Review* (1914); H. L. McBain, *The Living Constitution* (1927); C. A. Beard, *The Supreme Court and the Constitution* (1912).

those excesses of democracy which were so much feared by the framers of the Constitution. The powerful judiciary was designed *Checks on* to act as a check on the President and Congress, while the *democracy* executive would also check the legislature, and the legislature the executive. A number of provisions for the direct operation of this principle were written in; such, for example, as the power given the Senate to reject treaties and appointments made by the President, and the right of the President to exercise a qualified veto over the acts of Congress.

Democracy was still further qualified by the insistent emphasis upon the representative principle in the new government. As little as might be was left to the people themselves to do; and the powers of *The repre-* government were handed over instead to representatives re- *sentative* moved once or twice from the popular will. The judges *principle* were appointed by the President for life, the President was elected by electors who might be chosen directly by the people, but if the legislature of a state so determined might be chosen indirectly; the Senate was chosen by the legislatures of the various states; the only officers of the central government chosen directly by the people were the members of the House of Representatives. Probably some qualifications on the right of citizens to vote would also have been set up had it not seemed necessary to leave this matter to the states themselves. Because of the great variety of election laws in the several states, it was finally decided that in choosing representatives to seats in the national House the qualifications for voters should be the same as were set up by a given state for the election of the most numerous branch of its legislature. In time this particular clause came to have a decidedly leavening influence, for as the suffrage was widened in the states the qualifications of those who could vote for members of the national House of Representatives were correspondingly scaled down. Nevertheless the national government was designed to be, and to this day remains, a representative system. The people have the right to vote; but their representatives make and execute the laws. In theory, at least, and probably also in fact these representatives of the people were supposed to be even more conservative than the voters who chose them, and thus, according to the framers of the Constitution, more trustworthy and dependable.

While from the American point of view the Constitution was, and was meant to be, an eminently conservative document, when compared with the forms of government that existed in the rest of the *Radical* world it fell little short of radicalism. It continued the *features* doctrine of popular sovereignty that had formed the philosophic background of the American Revolution, and was yet to find support from the results of the French Revolution. Thus in a day when nearly every other government adhered to the principle of monarchy, with its implied belief in the divine right of kings, the American government was strictly republican in form. Unique also was the effort to establish a dual or federal type of government. Undoubtedly the framers of the Constitution believed in the divisibility of sovereignty, and they sought to hand over certain sovereign powers to the federal government while retaining for the states certain other sovereign powers. Time proved that either the nation or the states must be supreme, and ultimately a civil war had to be fought to decide the issue. But the attempt to establish two entirely separate agencies of government, each operating upon the same individuals, turned out to be as successful as it was unusual. Furthermore, the federal Constitution, like the state constitutions, took cognizance of the reserved rights of individuals upon which government might not tread. Since the central government was designed to be one of strictly specified powers, it was not deemed necessary to include an extensive bill of rights such as had characterized the early state constitutions. But such specifications as that the privilege of the writ of habeas corpus should not ordinarily be suspended, and that bills of attainder and ex post facto laws should not be passed, showed the same determination to set limits beyond which in its dealing with individuals the government might not go. Early amendments to the Constitution went much further in the direction of stating definitely the "rights of man" upon which government was forbidden to transgress.

Forewarned by the difficulties they had experienced in their efforts to amend the Articles of Confederation, the framers of the Constitution did

Amendments made possible not omit to provide for a means of amendment. Probably they felt that many changes would surely be necessary, and that in a relatively short time the whole document would have to be supplanted. Accordingly Congress was given authority, whenever two thirds of both houses should deem it necessary, to propose amendments to the Constitution; or in case the legislatures of two thirds of the states should demand it, Congress was required to call a special convention for proposing amendments. All amendments, however proposed, must be submitted for ratification or rejection either to the various state legislatures or to conventions in each state called for the purpose, and the approval of three fourths of the states was necessary to complete the process. The convention system of proposing amendments has never been used, and ratifying conventions were called for the first time when the eighteenth (or prohibition) amendment was repealed.

The last article of the original Constitution provided that the ratification of the conventions of nine states should be regarded as sufficient for the establishment of the Constitution among the states so *Method of* ratifying. This was completely out of harmony with the *ratification* original call for the convention, which took for granted that anything done by that body would be submitted as an amendment to the existing Articles of Confederation, and hence would require for adoption the ratification of all the states. To this extent the Constitution actually proposed, and the formation of the government under its terms before unanimous ratification had been achieved actually constituted, a revolution. So weak, however, was the sanction under which the Articles of Confederation still operated that this procedure drew no protest from Congress. The Constitution, indeed, was first submitted to that body, and by it was formally submitted to the states.

Ratification was not accomplished, however, without a struggle.[1] The men who had framed the Constitution and those who now favored its adoption were representatives of the propertied classes, and *The contest* the strong central government which they proposed to set up *over ratifi-* would presumably be in their hands. Such popular leaders *cation* as Patrick Henry, Richard Henry Lee, and Samuel Adams expressed their emphatic disapproval of the way in which the new Constitution proposed to curtail the power of the states, and the whole debtor class looked with particular disapproval upon the clause which forbade the states to issue paper money. Westerners feared that their freedom to use the Mississippi outlet might be bargained away to Spain, just as Jay had attempted to do a few years before. Philosophic liberals, most of whom were earnest champions of the doctrine that all men were possessed of certain inalienable rights, deplored the absence of a formal bill of rights to guarantee individuals as well as states against undue oppression on the part of the central government.

The defenders of the Constitution, fearful of the offense they might give by calling themselves Nationalists, chose to be known instead as Federalists. They made an admirable case for adoption. The Constitution, they argued, was the only alternative to anarchy. Its provisions might leave much to be desired, indeed few if any of its defenders could say truthfully that they liked it all, but if this Constitution, made as it was by the best talent the country could produce, could not be adopted,

[1] Some of the arguments advanced against the Constitution are given in P. L. Ford, *Pamphlets on the Constitution of the United States* (1888). For the struggle over ratification see *The Debates on the Federal Constitution*, edited by Jonathan Elliot (5 vols., 1827–45). Two useful monographs are C. E. Miner, *The Ratification of the Federal Constitution by the State of New York* (1920); and S. B. Harding, *The Contest over the Ratification of the Federal Constitution in the State of Massachusetts* (1896).

what hope, they asked, could there be for relief from the chaos of the Confederation? The Federalists had an advantage over their opponents in that many of their leaders had been members of the Philadelphia Convention and already knew well the arguments which had resulted in the adoption of the various provisions of the Constitution. The anti-Federalists, as opponents of the Constitution came to be called, had on the other hand to begin their study of the Constitution after the document was made public.

Both sides filled the press with propaganda, and numberless pamphlets upholding or attacking the Constitution found their way to the news-*"The Federalist"* stands. Among the most illuminating of these writings were the arguments in defense of the Constitution made by Hamilton, Madison, and Jay, and signed anonymously *The Federalist*. These articles, collected together and published as a book, still constitute the best commentary available on the Constitution as its framers intended it to be interpreted. One of the strongest of the Federalist arguments was that the new Constitution would pave the way for a return of prosperity. Its provisions for dealing with foreign nations, together with the new powers over commerce to be given the central government, were cited as evidence that a more vigorous trade between the United States and foreign countries could be expected once the Constitution went into effect. Possibly some wise heads foresaw that the prevailing hard times would not last forever, and that the adoption of the Constitution on the eve of a revival of prosperity would be a shrewd stroke of policy.

The Federalists did not have to depend wholly upon their arguments to secure results. In every state restrictions on the suffrage existed *Ratifying conventions* which made the conventions chosen to pass on the Constitution far more favorable to adoption than the attitude of the general public would seem to have justified. In some states, Pennsylvania for example, the back country, which was especially hostile to the Constitution, was given far less representation in the ratifying convention than it should have received in view of its population. Some of the elections were held with undue haste so that anti-Federalists would have insufficient time to organize their forces and distribute their propaganda. Nearly everywhere the Federalists included within their numbers the more astute and experienced politicians who knew how to make the most of the opportunities that came their way.

By the end of the year ratifications were being recorded. Equality of representation in the Senate seemed to satisfy most of the small states, for several of them were among the first to ratify. The ratification of

Delaware came December 7, 1787, by a unanimous vote. Five days later Pennsylvania ratified by a vote of 46 to 23. Pennsylvania was one of the large states, but her central location and her composite population both pointed in the direction of nationalism. The ratifications of New Jersey on December 18, 1787, and of Georgia on January 2, 1788, were both unanimous. Connecticut voted to ratify, 128 to 40, on January 9. In Massachusetts there was a determined fight, which the Federalists won only by promising to favor amendments to the Constitution that would guarantee the rights of individuals. John Hancock, who was a power in the convention and for a time none too friendly to ratification, may also have received the impression that he was slated to be chosen Vice-President at the first election. Even so the victory for the Federalists was achieved, February 6, 1788, by the narrow margin of 187 to 168. The ratification of Maryland came April 28, 1788, by a vote of 63 to 11; that of South Carolina, May 23, 1788, by a vote of 149 to 73. In New Hampshire the first session of the convention failed to reach a decision, but the second session ratified, June 21, 1788, by a close vote, 57 to 46.

Since New Hampshire was the ninth state to ratify, the Constitution could now be put into effect, but it was conceded on all sides that the new government could not hope to succeed without the support *Virginia* of Virginia and New York. In both states the opposition *and New* was strong. The back-country farmers of Virginia, led by *York* Patrick Henry, fought valiantly to prevent ratification, and almost succeeded. The landowners of the Hudson Valley, fearing heavier taxation in case the United States rather than the state of New York should collect the duties on imports at New York City, made an equally hard fight. In the end, the arguments of Madison and John Marshall persuaded the Virginia convention to ratify, June 25, 1788, by a vote of 89 to 79; while Alexander Hamilton, aided by the fact that the Constitution would surely be given a trial anyway, brought the New York convention to a half-hearted ratification, July 26, 1788. The New York victory was won by a vote of 30 to 27, the narrowest margin thus far accorded in any state. The North Carolina convention postponed ratification until steps should actually be taken to amend the Constitution by the inclusion of a bill of rights. The state of Rhode Island showed as little interest in the adoption as in the framing of the Constitution, and for the time being failed even to hold a ratifying convention.

The success of the Federalists in securing the ratification of the Constitution by enough states to give it a trial does not prove that there was any great popular mandate in its favor. Five states, Pennsylvania, Virginia, Massachusetts, New York, and South Carolina, had ratified only with

[211]

(reservations,) most of which demanded the adoption of an adequate
Ratification bill of rights. This much the Federalists were willing to
with reserva- concede, but even so, according to as prominent a Federalist
tions as John Marshall, there was good reason to believe that
"in some of the adopting states, a majority of the people were in the opposition. In all of them," he added, "the numerous amendments which
were proposed, demonstrate the reluctance with which the new government was accepted; and that a dread of dismemberment, not an approbation of the particular system under consideration, had induced an ac-
quiescence in it." There was great relief, however, that the long dispute
over the government was at an end, and among the bitter opponents of
ratification there were many who were ready, now that the Constitution
was actually adopted, to give it a fair trial. The old Congress of the
Confederation, even before the ratification of New York had been received, in acknowledgment of the fact that its authority had been supplanted, ordered the states to choose presidential electors, senators, and
representatives, and set the first Wednesday in March, 1789, as the date
for the new Congress to convene.

CHAPTER XIII

LAUNCHING THE NEW GOVERNMENT

ONE of the arguments in favor of the Constitution that carried conviction to many minds was the undoubted fact that George Washington would be the first President. No other American leader has so captured the confidence of his contemporaries as did Washington, and the certainty that his solid judgment and rugged honesty would be at the command of his countrymen during the experimental period allayed many misgivings. In the first presidential election every electoral vote was cast for Washington, and there is every reason to suppose that, had the Constitution permitted it, the people would gladly have elected him President for life.[1]

Washington's hold on the public imagination was somewhat dimmed during the later years of his term of office, but the criticisms that had then assailed him were mostly forgotten once he retired to private life. Upon his death the Washington legend began to take form. *The first President* Weems's *Life of Washington,* an early and popular biography, yielded to every temptation of the hero-worshiper, and in glowing words of praise pictured such a boy and man as never could have lived. The portraits painted by Gilbert Stuart, likewise, which were obviously designed to make Washington look as godlike as the father of his country should look, were accepted by later generations at face value. The popular estimate of Washington thus set was long continued, and only recently have biographers sought to skim off the fancy from the fact in order to present the first President more nearly as he was.

[1] Many biographies of Washington have been written. H. C. Lodge, *George Washington* (2 vols., 1889), rivals Weems in the impossible perfection it attributes to Washington, but contains nevertheless much good history. Rupert Hughes, *George Washington* (3 vols., 1926–30), emphasizes the human qualities of Washington, and conducts a not very successful search for his weaknesses. W. E. Woodward, *George Washington, the Image and the Man* (1926), denounces everything that Washington did with great indiscrimination. J. H. Morgan and M. Fielding, *Life Portraits of George Washington* (1931), reproduces elaborately every known portrait of Washington. The following biographies also deserve mention: P. L. Ford, *The True George Washington* (1896); W. R. Thayer, *George Washington* (1922); L. M. Sears, *George Washington* (1932).

In their efforts to destroy what was merely legend, however, some recent writers have overreached the mark, and have unfairly denied to Washington the greatness that was really his.

Washington was born, February 22, 1732, in tidewater Virginia, the son of a moderately well-to-do planter who owned several estates. *The youth of* Washington's father had gone to school in England, but *Washington* this privilege was denied George, whose education was somewhat limited. He took an interest in mathematics, and at an early age knew the rudiments of surveying. When he was only sixteen years old he accompanied a surveying party into the Shenandoah Valley, and after his return became surveyor-general for Fairfax County. His frequent surveying trips into the back country gave him a glimpse into the possibilities of the West that he was never to forget. His career as surveyor was cut short when his elder brother Lawrence died in 1752, and left to George the management of the estate at Mount Vernon. A few years later Washington married Martha Custis, the widow of a wealthy planter, and her property, added to his own, made him for the times a very rich man. For many years he lived the usual life of the prosperous southern planter, entertained lavishly, participated actively in parish affairs, and sat for his county as a member of the House of Burgesses.

Washington's trip to the West in 1753 to warn the French from the forks of the Ohio, and his subsequent exploits in the French and In-*His military* dian War, drew him into the limelight as a military leader. *career* If a southern aristocrat was to be chosen to lead the American forces in the Revolutionary War, Washington, as John Adams so wisely observed, was the natural choice. The events of the war proved that no mistake had been made. Washington's knowledge of military tactics was no doubt defective, but it was sufficient to meet the needs of the situation. He never commanded a large army, and perhaps he could never have commanded a large army well, but with the limited supply of troops he was able to obtain he did effective fighting. He understood clearly the necessity of preserving at all costs the little army he had, and he invoked frequently the strategy of retreat. He was fertile in new ideas, and always ready to take a promising chance. Unlike most commanders, he often had to help raise his own army, and he nearly always had to struggle against odds to keep it together. By the end of the war his military exploits had won the admiration, not only of Americans, but also of his British opponents, and of such a master-strategist as Frederick the Great.

Washington's success as a soldier was no guaranty that he would not fail as a political leader, but in this respect also the people trusted him.

GEORGE WASHINGTON

From a portrait by Gilbert Stuart. Courtesy of the Museum of Fine Arts, Boston

Time proved that they were right. As an administrator he possessed the *His states-* ability, so strikingly absent in some men, to make up his *manlike* mind, and to make it up before the time for acting had passed. *qualities* He was an unusually keen judge of men, and surrounded himself with an able group of subordinates. He knew how to ask and to take advice, and he rarely made any important decisions without consulting others. His judgment as to what the future held in store was right a surprisingly large number of times. He saw clearly the important part that the West was to play in the history of the nation, he recognized the dangers involved in a growing sectionalism, he understood better than most men of his time the menace of slavery, and he realized fully the wisdom of diplomatic isolation from Europe until the nation he had helped to create could get securely upon its feet. Few statesmen have a clearer record on so many important matters. Washington could hardly be called brilliant, but his character was unassailable, he possessed much sound common sense, and he could do many things well.

On the fourth of March, 1789, the day designated by the old Congress of the Confederation for the new government to go into operation, only *The first* eight senators out of twenty-two and thirteen represent- *inauguration* atives out of fifty-nine had arrived at New York, the temporary capital. This was not wholly due to indifference; roads were bad, streams were swollen by the spring rains, and for those who came by sea the winds were not always favorable. It was the sixth of April before a majority of the members in each house required by the Constitution for a quorum were on hand. The electoral votes were then counted, and the election of Washington to the Presidency, and of John Adams, who had the next highest number of votes, to the Vice-Presidency, was announced. Word was then sent to Washington of what had transpired, after which the President-elect journeyed on horseback to New York. The trip was an ovation all the way, and so consumed twelve days. It was April 30 before the inauguration actually took place.[1]

Nor was the new government then fully launched. The Constitution was a relatively short document, and much legislation had to be passed in order to make it effective. Laws had to be enacted, for example, to create departments of state, of war, and of the treasury, to establish a judiciary, and most important of all to provide for the levying and collection of taxes. Once the essential laws were enacted the President still had to select the officials to carry them into effect, and the

---

[1] Channing, IV, begins with the constitutional period. Other useful general accounts are J. S. Bassett, *The Federalist System* (1906); and H. J. Ford, *Washington and his Colleagues* (1918).

Senate had to pass on the President's appointees. It was months, even years, before the actual machinery of government was fully constituted.

In many matters important precedents had to be set. Among the most vexing of these, at least to certain members of Congress, was the question of titles. Should not the President be decorated *The establishment of* with some resounding title such as His Excellency, or His *lishment of* Elective Majesty? Should not senators, and possibly even *precedents* representatives, be styled Honorable? Ultimately democratic simplicity won out, but the failure of important officials to obtain high-sounding titles rankled in some breasts for a long time. Nor did the Constitution make fully clear the powers of the Vice-President as presiding officer in the Senate, and the Speaker as presiding officer in the House. Very largely because of the personalities involved the Vice-President came to be a mere moderator, whereas the Speaker soon came to play such an important rôle in the affairs of the House that for over a century he was regarded as second only to the President himself in power. Out of the clause in the Constitution which provided that the President might ask for the opinions of heads of departments in writing, grew the Cabinet as the official board of advisers upon whom the President was to lean. The free use of the veto power by the President, negotiation of treaties in advance of asking the "advice and consent" of the Senate, and many other modes of procedure came about as mere customs based on precedent rather than upon any requirement of the Constitution.

Extreme democrats, such as William Maclay, one of the senators from Pennsylvania, were alarmed almost at the start at some of the undemocratic tendencies they witnessed.[1] The President to *Democratic* some extent, and the Vice-President to a great extent, *misgivings* seemed concerned about the matter of titles. The behavior of the English House of Lords and House of Commons was much cited. The President, instead of receiving callers in true democratic fashion, held levees like a king. How long would it be at this rate before a monarchy would exist in fact? Conservatives were almost equally worried at the openings which the new Constitution gave to democracy. There was not much to be hoped for at best. Probably Fisher Ames expressed the mingled feelings of many observers, as they saw the new government take form, when he said: "A monarchy is like a merchantman. You get on board and ride the wind and tide in safety and elation but, by and by, you strike a reef and go down. But democracy is like a raft. You never sink, but, damn it, your feet are always in the water."

[1] The *Journal of William Maclay*, edited by E. S. Maclay (1890), is a delightful bit of American literature that throws much light on the organization of the new government.

The Confederation had failed largely because it was unable to solve the problem of finance. If the new government was not also to go on the rocks, clearly its financial policy must be wisely conceived. Washington recognized this fact when he chose as his Secretary of the Treasury Alexander Hamilton, a young man only thirty-two years of age who had already displayed remarkable talent along financial lines.[1]

Hamilton (1757–1804) was a West Indian by birth, the son of a Scotch father and a French Huguenot mother. He was a promising lad, no less *Alexander* liberally endowed with the shrewdness of his father's race *Hamilton* than with the charm of manner and impetuosity of his mother's. He was sent to school in Boston when he was only fifteen years of age, and later attended Kings College in New York. Here, although New York was a Loyalist center, he absorbed the American point of view on the quarrel with England, and when war broke out joined the army. Washington made use of him for staff duty so that he had little opportunity to distinguish himself in the field, but he emerged from the war a lieutenant-colonel, and the husband of a daughter of General Philip Schuyler, whose influence in New York politics was great.

Hamilton was early interested in financial matters. During the war he wrote Robert Morris a letter on the state of the nation's finances that described fully the evils of an inflated currency and urged that a halt be called on such a policy. Later he advocated the contraction of the currency, and the negotiation of a foreign loan to be used in starting a bank. During the Confederation period his interests were varied. He studied law and was admitted to the bar, served for a time as a member of Congress, tried hard as receiver of taxes for New York to obtain money for the central government, served in the Philadelphia Convention which framed the Constitution, and also in the New York state convention which so reluctantly ratified it. He was, in spite of his youth, an ultra-conservative. He believed that the rights of property must be protected at all costs, and he never doubted that government, to be really effective, must be the monopoly of the upper classes. "The people," he once said in a moment of anger, "is a great beast."

As Secretary of the Treasury, Hamilton concerned himself first and foremost with the establishment of the nation's credit. To make sure that there could be no doubt about the determination of the United States to pay its just debts, he proposed that all outstanding loans be

[1] Biographers of Hamilton, like those of Washington, find it difficult to write without a bias. H. C. Lodge, *Alexander Hamilton* (1882), finds little fault in the man. Claude Bowers, *Jefferson and Hamilton* (1925), tips the scales heavily in favor of Jefferson and against Hamilton.

ALEXANDER HAMILTON
From a painting by John Trumbull.   Courtesy of the Museum of Fine Arts, Boston

funded at their face value. The United States had borrowed from abroad *Funding the national debt* about twelve million dollars, and against the meeting of this obligation in full there could be no valid complaint. But the domestic debt, which amounted to nearly forty-two million dollars, seemed to many honest men a totally different matter. Probably the original obligations incurred far exceeded the returns in services, supplies, and depreciated paper currency that the government had realized on them; moreover, they were now as a rule no longer in the hands of the original owners, but had fallen to speculators who had purchased them for a fraction of their face value. Since these securities were worth on the market about twenty-five cents on the dollar, there were many who thought that for the government to purchase them back at that price, or a little above, with a new and valid issue would be an entirely respectable procedure. But Hamilton was determined to win the enthusiastic approval of the moneyed class, and he ultimately succeeded in having his own way. The entire debt was funded at par, and the speculators, including some members of Congress, who as they voted for the funding bill were not unaware of the opportunity it gave them to profit, reaped a rich harvest.

Hamilton's plan did not end, however, merely with the funding of the debts owed by the United States. He wished also to take over such *Assumption of state debts* of the debts incurred by the states themselves for the cause of independence as they had not yet paid. His object, again, was to place the creditor class under deep obligation to the central government, and thus to win its hearty support. But the assumption of state debts by the central government was not accomplished without a struggle. It was all very well to argue that these debts were incurred for a common cause and should be paid out of the common treasury, but the fact remained that some states had large obligations to pass over and some did not. Virginia, for example, had financed the war to a great extent with paper-money issues that had either been redeemed in western lands or had ceased to have any value. The South in general opposed the scheme, and it was finally put through Congress only after Hamilton, working through Jefferson, the Secretary of State, had struck a notable bargain. The South was exceedingly desirous of securing the capital, and Hamilton now offered to use his influence in favor of a southern site if Jefferson would help find the votes to pass the assumption bill. The bargain worked, Congress agreed that the new capital should be located at Philadelphia for a period of ten years, and thereafter on the Potomac; and it voted also the assumption

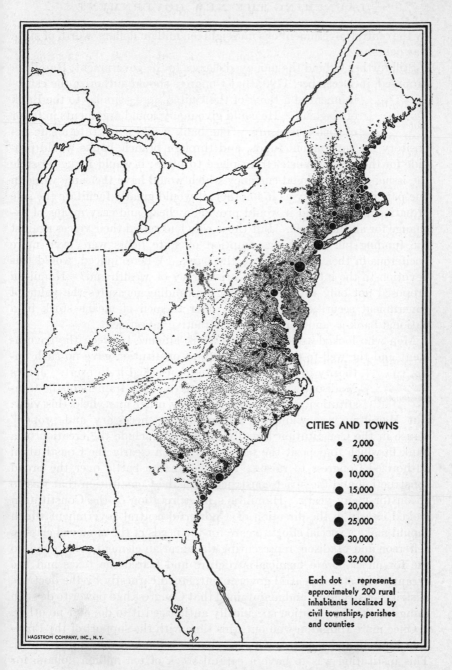

CITIES AND TOWNS

- • 2,000
- • 5,000
- • 10,000
- • 15,000
- • 20,000
- • 25,000
- • 30,000
- • 32,000

Each dot • represents approximately 200 rural inhabitants localized by civil townships, parishes and counties

HAGSTROM COMPANY, INC., N.Y.

DISTRIBUTION OF POPULATION IN 1790

by the central government of some eighteen million dollars' worth of state war debts.

Still further to bind the moneyed classes to the government, Hamilton proposed, in December, 1790, that Congress should authorize the estab-

Bank of the United States

lishment of a Bank of the United States similar to the Bank of England. He could give many sound arguments in favor of such a measure. The bank would constitute a safe depository for government funds, and through branch banks would provide for their easy transfer from place to place; it would make possible the issuance of a national currency which would have the same value in one part of the country as in another; it would greatly facilitate the sale of national bonds; and it would provide a cheap and easy means of exchange for all the people. But those who had raised their voices against the funding bill and the assumption of state debts were even more vociferous in their opposition to the bank. Where, indeed, would this devotion to the interests of the aristocracy of wealth end? Hamilton proposed not only to quadruple by his funding measures the value of government securities, but also to offer to men of means stock in a national bank as another safe and attractive investment.

Men who looked askance at this frank alliance between the government and the well-to-do urged that the Constitution gave no such au-

"Broad" vs. "strict" construction

thority to Congress as Hamilton asked it to exert. James Madison, who knew the motives of the framers of the Constitution at least as well as any other man, held this view. But Hamilton was willing to interpret the "necessary and proper" clause in the Constitution broadly enough to include the creation of a bank in which to deposit the tax money which clearly the Constitution authorized Congress to raise. Thus began the battle over the broad construction and the strict construction of the Constitution that was to go on for many years. Hamilton's interpretation of the Constitution looked clearly in the direction of a powerful central government which should make a special effort to care for the needs of the moneyed classes. Jefferson and Madison, representing the agrarian element, which had no use for an elaborate financial structure and feared the taxes and the tyranny of a strong central government, stood earnestly by the doctrine of strict construction, and maintained that Congress had power to do such things as the Constitution specifically authorized it to do, and no other.

Once more Hamilton won out, this time with the support of the President himself, and Congress voted to charter a Bank of the United States. This institution was to have a capital stock of ten million dollars, for the time a very large sum. Of this amount one fifth was to be subscribed by the United States, and the other four fifths by private individuals. Into the bank went all the deposits of the United States, and this fact, coupled with the fact that the national government also owned a large part of the bank stock, tended to win for the institution the confidence of the public. The bank had the right to issue paper money, and these notes were made receivable for public dues. Investors were quick to take advantage of the opportunity offered them, and the bank was soon doing business. For twenty years it prospered to such an extent that those who held bank stock realized on an average about eight and one half per cent annually on their investment.

Hamilton's plan for funding the debt cost money, and the modest tariff that Congress had levied as one of its first measures was unequal to the emergency. In consequence, the Secretary of the *The whiskey excise* Treasury offered yet another suggestion. The Constitution clearly authorized Congress to levy an excise tax, and this power, Hamilton felt, should be used. Not only was money needed, but in addition the people should become accustomed to the taxing power of the central government. When it came to choosing the item upon which to place the tax, however, Hamilton took care not to offend the moneyed men whose good-will toward the government he deemed so essential to its success. Instead, he suggested a tax on whiskey which would hit the small farmers of the back country who had opposed the adoption of the Constitution, and who were still doubtful as to whether the new government merited their support. There was then no odium attached to the manufacture and sale of whiskey. Thrifty farmers who lived far from market turned their surplus grain into whiskey in order to solve easily the problem of transportation, and the sale of this commodity brought them almost the only ready cash they knew. An excise tax on whiskey was as sure a way to arouse their wrath as could possibly have been devised. Hamilton knew this full well, but he considered it right and proper to levy the tax, if for no other reason than to show that he could collect it by force, if necessary, and thus prove to those who were least friendly toward the central government that they had to obey it whether they wished to or not. Congress, with a comfortable majority now completely under Hamilton's influence, passed the bill.

Washington had hoped that the new government might be carried on without the development of political parties, and he had not hesitated to place men of such divergent views as Jefferson and Hamil- *Opposition to Hamilton's policies* ton side by side in his Cabinet. But the financial program that Hamilton carried through Congress was so clearly designed to benefit a favored class that those who were not of that class were certain to be in opposition. The creation of a powerful central government which at all times could be counted on to serve the interests of the well-to-do aroused the deep resentment of the agricultural classes generally. The merchant, the manufacturer, the shipbuilder, and their dependents might profit much, directly and indirectly, by Hamilton's policies; but the small farmer and landowner would not. For them the Hamiltonian system meant the multiplication of taxes and the curtailment of liberty no less than the British government had once planned. The agrarian interests tended, therefore, to join hands under the leadership of Jefferson and Madison. Hamilton's friends called themselves Federalists, so their opponents were often called anti-Federalists. But before long the opposition took for its party label the more significant term, Republican.[1]

The attempt to enforce the excise tax soon brought on the trouble that Hamilton had foreseen. Wherever it was collected, the tax was resented, but the chief center of opposition developed in western Pennsylvania in the Pittsburgh area. The tax was offensive, not merely for the money it took, but also because of its prying nature. The pioneer farmer set high store by his personal freedom, and he felt outraged at the behavior of tax-collectors who pried into his private business, and told him what he must and must not do. As early as 1791 popular meetings of protest were held at which speakers urged the farmers to resist the excise. During the next two or three years bands of "Whiskey Boys" raided stills that paid the tax, handled roughly the tax-collectors, and ultimately succeeded in setting the law completely at nought in a number of western counties. Albert Gallatin, a highly respected resident of western Pennsylvania, tried to counsel moderation, but the people showed more interest in the writings of one "Tom the Tinker," who urged uncompromising resistance. Particularly burdensome was the system of enforcement, which required for the accused an expensive trip across the mountains to Philadelphia, where the delays of justice might detain the victim of the law for months.

At length smouldering resistance broke into open revolt. On August 14, 1794, a convention was held to remonstrate, and even before that *The* date two thousand armed militia threatened to attack a *"Whiskey* small detachment of regulars stationed at Pittsburgh. *Rebellion"* Washington had already warned the law-breakers to change their ways, and now he prepared to use force. Again testing a power

[1] C. A. Beard, *Economic Origins of the Jeffersonian Democracy* (1915), continues the argument begun in his *Economic Interpretation of the Constitution*, already mentioned. On party history J. P. Gordy, *Political History of the United States with Special Reference to the Growth of Political Parties* (2 vols., 1903), is still an excellent guide.

derived from the Constitution, he called out fifteen thousand militia from the states of Virginia, Maryland, and Pennsylvania, and ordered them to march to the scene of trouble. The troops were forthcoming, and the overwhelming strength of the army sent against the revolters made them more willing to listen to Gallatin's admonitions than they had been before. When the troops reached their destination late in 1794, all resistance had vanished. A number of men who had been leaders in the "Whiskey Rebellion," as the episode was called, were arrested, and eighteen were sent to Philadelphia for trial. Of these only two were convicted, and they were pardoned by the President. But the power of the government had been amply demonstrated, and thereafter distillers of whiskey generally paid the tax. Politically this strong show of force was probably a mistake. Not only the residents of western Pennsylvania but many others also were aghast at the ruthless power that the Federalists in control of the government chose to wield. In consequence they gave their support the more willingly to Thomas Jefferson and the Republicans.[1]

The revolt in western Pennsylvania was not the only western problem that the new government was called upon to solve. Still farther to the west were other pioneers whose troubles with the Spanish in the Southwest, with the English in the Northwest, and with the Indians in both regions were even more perplexing than they had been in the time of the Confederation. As the West grew in population, the uncertainty of trade down the Mississippi became constantly more serious. The Spanish remained sullenly unwilling to open the river freely to trade from the United States, they continued to urge their claim to a boundary for Florida much farther north than the United States was willing to concede, and they placed no obstacles in the way of Indians under their control who moved to attack the southwestern frontier. In the Northwest the English continued to hold on to their posts south of the Great Lakes, and Canadian fur-traders gave aid and encouragement to the Indian tribes of the Northwest who had already gone on the warpath against the pioneers in Ohio. Washington realized fully that the loyalty of the West to the central government would be sorely tried if the frontier was not relieved. Moreover, the prestige of the nation was at stake.

The southwestern frontier

Realizing that he was sure to become involved in war with the northwestern Indians, Washington resolved to try diplomacy with the Indians

---

[1] Gallatin's part in this affair is given in Henry Adams, *The Life of Albert Gallatin* (1879). Two contemporary accounts are available in many libraries: H. H. Brackenridge, *Incidents of the Insurrection in the Western Parts of Pennsylvania* (1795); and W. Findley, *History of the Insurrection in the Four Western Counties of Pennsylvania* (1796).

of the Southwest. The leading Indian chief of this region was a half-breed Creek named Alexander McGillivray, who had fought with the English during the American Revolution, and still cherished a deep hatred for the United States. Washington succeeded in persuading McGillivray to pay a visit to New York, where he was received with every courtesy. An agreement was reached whereby McGillivray received one hundred thousand dollars for damages he claimed to have sustained at the hands of the Patriots during the Revolution, in return for which he promised to use his influence to keep the Indians at peace. McGillivray's word proved to be of little worth, and the attacks on the southwestern frontier continued. At length the Tennesseans took matters into their own hands, and extensive raids conducted in 1793–94 by local militia under Sevier and Robertson brought better results than came from Washington's negotiations with McGillivray.

McGillivray

The Indian troubles of the Northwest resulted ultimately in no less than three extensive campaigns. The United States during the Confederation period had made two treaties with the north-western tribes, Fort Stanwix (1784), and Fort McIntosh (1785), by which a large section of land west of the western boundary of Pennsylvania and north of the Ohio River was supposedly to be cleared of Indians in preparation for the coming of white settlers. But the Indians, while they had signed the treaties, had little understanding of what they meant. The white man's concept of private land-ownership was quite beyond the Indian's comprehension, for the only kind of ownership he understood was tribal ownership. In consequence serious friction developed between roving groups of Indians and white settlers, who viewed all such visitors with alarm and looked upon them as trespassers. Indian democracy constituted another barrier to good relations between the races, for Indians who had not been present when the treaties were signed held that they were not bound by anything other Indians had done for them. The Indian memory of treaty terms, moreover, was short, while the presence of white men drove away their game and interfered seriously with the trapping of fur-bearing animals. It seemed evident to the red men that the white advance at all costs must be turned back.

The north-west Indians

Indian resistance was immensely strengthened by the existence of the British forts and fur-trading posts south of the Great Lakes. Here the talk was all against the further invasion of the West by American settlers. Canadian fur-traders saw in the expansion of the American frontier a corresponding decrease in their business,

Harmar's expedition

and they did not hesitate to provide the Indians in the course of trade with the weapons and ammunition they needed to drive back the whites. The Indians, emboldened by this support, committed so many depredations that by the time Washington took office drastic retaliatory measures had to be taken. In 1790, therefore, Washington dispatched General Harmar in command of about fifteen hundred militia to destroy the Indian villages on the Maumee. This task Harmar accomplished, but on his return from the Indian country his troops were ambushed and he was forced to make a humiliating retreat.

Next year Governor St. Clair took the field himself in command of about two thousand militia. He sought to profit by the mistakes of his predecessor, and advanced deliberately, building as he went *St. Clair's* retaining posts about a day's journey apart. But this *failure* procedure proved too slow and uninteresting for the frontier militia he commanded, which preferred action to work, and resented any pretense at discipline. Wholesale desertions depleted his ranks, and on November 4, 1791, his expedition was ambushed by the Indians and utterly overwhelmed. The uncertain frontier militia fled precipitately from the scene of the action, only to be pursued by the Indians so successfully that not more than one third of the whites escaped uninjured.[1]

It is said that when Washington received the news of St. Clair's defeat his rage knew no bounds. It was necessary now at all costs to redeem the reputation of the government. Who next to *"Mad" An-* send against the Indians was a matter of grave concern, and *thony Wayne* the choice finally fell upon "Mad" Anthony Wayne, the hero of Stony Point. Wayne demanded as the terms of his acceptance that he be permitted to enlist twenty-five hundred volunteers for a period of two years, and there was nothing for Washington to do but to accept. Wayne took his time, drilled his troops carefully, hired Indian scouts, and when at length he began his advance had a force that he could depend upon. Wayne followed St. Clair's plan of building forts as he advanced, and at one of these stations, Fort Greenville, far in the Indian country, spent the winter of 1793–94. In the spring he was joined by sixteen hundred mounted troops from Kentucky, and began a relentless campaign. The Indians counted heavily on British support and retreated toward an outpost on the Maumee that British soldiers were erecting. But, confident that they would defeat Wayne as they had defeated Harmar and St. Clair, they attacked the Americans south of the British post at a place known as Fallen Timbers, only to be disastrously defeated. Real-

---

[1] *The St. Clair Papers*, edited by W. H. Smith (1882), reveal the reasons for St. Clair's troubles.

izing Wayne's strength, the British now refused to give the Indians further succor, their villages and winter supplies were destroyed by Wayne's soldiers, and they were left no choice but to treat for peace. In the summer of 1795 at Fort Greenville a treaty was signed. The Indians now ceded vast stretches of land in central Ohio to the whites, and agreed to bury the hatchet. So stinging was the defeat they had been dealt that they gave the United States no further trouble for many years to come.

No less gratifying to the people of the West was the willingness of the new government to admit frontier states into the Union. Vermont had *Admission of new states* carried on a state government since the beginning of the Revolutionary War, but was left outside the Confederation. In 1791, however, Congress agreed to accept Vermont as a fourteenth state. The pleas of Kentuckians also were given favorable consideration. In 1789 Virginia gave full consent to the separation from the Old Dominion of the Kentucky counties, and in 1792 Congress allowed Kentucky to become a state. In Tennessee matters moved more slowly toward the same end. The state of North Carolina finally ceded her western lands to Congress in 1790, whereupon a territory was set up similar to the territory established northwest of the Ohio River by the Confederation. In 1796 this territory gave way to the state of Tennessee. The constitutions of these new western states all showed a tendency toward greater democracy than was yet the rule in the original thirteen states. Especially were they willing to expand the right of suffrage. Vermont and Kentucky went the whole length of universal manhood suffrage, and Tennessee closely approximated it.

Meantime the outbreak of the French Revolution had started a train of events in Europe that was to prove of tremendous interest to citizens *The French Revolution* of the new republic across the Atlantic. A week after Washington's inauguration, the French Estates-General that Louis XVI had found it necessary to call had begun its sessions. In a short time the evolution of a more democratic government for France had begun. Most Americans sympathized whole-heartedly with this development, and the country took pardonable pride in seeing the principles of the American Revolution accepted by one of the greatest, if not the very greatest, of European powers. Superficially the two revolutions had many things in common. Both were fought to redress long-standing grievances against an autocratic king; both maintained steadfastly the right of any people to a voice in levying the taxes they were called upon to pay; both attacked privilege and proclaimed lustily the doctrine of the rights of man. Moreover, Lafayette, a hero of the American Revolution, was no less a hero of the new régime in France.

Even European nations were for quite different reasons constrained to look at first with some satisfaction upon what was happening in France. Rival European monarchs were not altogether unhappy to see Louis XVI in trouble at home. The English nation rejoiced to see the decline of its hereditary foe. Austria, Russia, and Prussia, busy for the moment with the final partition of Poland, were glad to be rid of the danger of French interference. This smug satisfaction gave way to alarm, however, when the French Revolution grew definitely more radical and more propagandist. If the outbreak of democracy in France was to become in fact "a war of all peoples against all kings," something would have to be done about it. By the Declaration of Pillnitz (1791), Emperor Leopold II of the Holy Roman Empire and King Frederick William of Prussia agreed to act together in case either should be attacked by France. In April, 1792, France declared war on Austria, and the French Revolution was no longer an internal affair.

In the conflict which followed, French arms by a miracle began to win. American opinion tended still to be overwhelmingly pro-French, and the victory of the revolutionary army at Valmy (September 20, *Sympathy* 1792) was celebrated in Boston by a great civic feast in *for France* which all parties joined. But when a short time later the French actually put their king to death, and issued declarations of war against both England and Spain, the more conservative Americans began to have grave doubts as to the course France was pursuing. The United States was bound by a treaty of alliance to France. Would another war with England have to be fought, and perhaps also a war with Spain? Any such development might mean the death of American commerce, which ran mostly with England and Spain, and it might mean the loss of American independence as well. Hamilton did not disguise his disgust for the French Revolution, and to most of the Federalists it now seemed that England was fighting for the preservation of civilization while France had become a public enemy. But Jefferson and the Republicans took a very different view of the situation. Representing as they did mainly the agrarian interests, the safety of American commerce gave them little concern. England was the traditional enemy of American democracy, and she still unlawfully held on to the northwest posts. Spain was an even older antagonist, and was now planted at the mouth of the Mississippi to dispute the right of western farmers to the use of that river. Republican clubs, many of which had already been formed out of sympathy for France, multiplied amazingly, particularly in the South and

West. Many of the Republicans were ready to make common cause with France in a war against the English in Canada and the Spanish on the Gulf of Mexico. To Jefferson the French Revolution was still "the most sacred cause that man was ever engaged in."

With public opinion thus divided, Washington received with many misgivings the news that the revolutionary government had dispatched *"Citizen"* a minister, "Citizen" Edmond Charles Genêt, to the United *Genêt* States. The President at once put certain questions that perplexed him to his Cabinet. Should Genêt be recognized as the rightful minister from France to the United States? Were the French treaties, made before the outbreak of the French Revolution, still binding on the United States? If so, could the United States, in spite of them, maintain an attitude of neutrality? The last question was particularly perplexing, for the United States had guaranteed to France her West India possessions, and had agreed that French prizes captured at sea might be brought into American ports for adjudication. Privateers, also, were to be reciprocally admitted into French and American ports. On the question of the French treaties Hamilton and Jefferson divided sharply. Hamilton took the ground that the treaties were with the King of France, and the King's government being done away with, they were no longer binding. Jefferson took the more correct view that treaties were between nations, and that the existing French government had the same claims upon the United States that the King's government had had. All agreed that for the present, at least, neutrality was the only possible course. Washington decided to issue a proclamation of neutrality before Genêt should arrive at the American capital, and to live up to the treaties as well as he could without involving the United States in war. He would recognize Genêt as the rightful minister of France, but make clear to him that the United States did not intend to participate in the war.

Genêt was a young man of great enthusiasm, a fair representative of the visionary Girondin faction for the moment in control of the French *Genêt's* government. On April 8, 1793, he landed at Charleston, *projects* South Carolina, a center of pro-French sentiment, and was given a great ovation. Without thought of being hampered by American neutrality, he planned to begin hostilities from the United States as a base against the Spanish in Florida and Louisiana, and also to make use of American ports in a campaign of privateering against British commerce. In South Carolina these projects were popular, and Genêt found no difficulty in finding plenty of volunteers to serve in a campaign against the Spanish, and plenty of sea-captains to accept his commissions as

"CITIZEN" EDMOND CHARLES GENÊT

privateers.   In due time he progressed by land to Philadelphia, now the seat of government.   The route he chose led through the interior, where the sentiment was strongly pro-French.   Genêt passed from triumph to triumph, and when at last he reached Philadelphia he had no doubt that the whole of the American people were with him.   Had he landed at Boston, and gone overland from that port to Philadelphia, he might have gained a far different impression.

Genêt was duly received by Washington, although without much cordiality, and was given to understand that the proclamation of neu-
American *neutrality* trality meant what it said.   The young Frenchman had no notion, however, of giving up his plans.   Already he had not only taken the initial steps toward organizing an expedition from South Carolina and Georgia against Florida, but had also accepted an offer made by George Rogers Clark, who proposed to organize another expedition from Kentucky to float down the Ohio and the Mississippi and attack New Orleans.   Both these projects required financial assistance, and this Genêt meant to get from the United States government by discounting the debts it owed France in return for immediate payments. Washington held, however, that any other plan of payment than the one already agreed upon would constitute a breach of neutrality, and so Genêt found himself totally without funds.   The expedition against Florida was given up, but George Rogers Clark took his commission as an officer in the "French Revolutionary Army of America" seriously, and found a few Westerners who were sufficiently eager to dislodge the Spanish from the mouth of the Mississippi to be willing to serve as his "Revolutionary Legion of Kentuckians" regardless of financial reward. Had they known that Genêt also hoped to separate the back country from the rest of the United States in order to make it over into a republic under French influence, their attitude might have been different.[1]

Meantime Genêt got into trouble with Washington over his plans for privateering.   The President was willing to live up to the letter of the
The Little *Democrat* treaties of alliance as he interpreted them, but he insisted that they did not authorize the use of American ports as bases of operation for privateers, and he would not countenance the sending into American ports for sale of the prizes that the French privateers took at sea.   Genêt was much disappointed at this attitude, and in spite of it proposed to convert a prize, the *Little Sarah*, into an armed ship, and send her out to sea.   He was warned that this must not

[1] F. J. Turner, *The Significance of Sections in American History* (1932), contains two excellent essays on the diplomatic relations between the United States and France during this period.

happen, and promised not to allow the *Little Democrat*, as he had rechristened the ship, to sail without notice. Within a few days Genêt broke his word. After discussing the matter with his Cabinet, Washington asked the French government to recall Genêt, and announced that thereafter all French prizes and privateers would be denied access to American ports. By this time the French Revolution had progressed another step in the direction of radicalism, and Genêt was already out of favor at home. A new minister, Fauchet, was appointed, who was instructed to send his predecessor home under arrest. Genêt realized that his return to France might cost him his life, so he asked permission of Washington to stay on in the United States. Washington mercifully consented.

After Genêt's retirement the President learned of the activities of George Rogers Clark, and ordered the governor of Kentucky to put an end to them. The governor took his time about it, but Fauchet, anxious to redeem the reputation of his nation with Washington, also denounced the project, and nothing more came of it.

It soon became apparent that neutrality was not altogether without its rewards. The export trade, particularly in provisions bound for the warring nations, grew by leaps and bounds. The American *The profits* carrying trade also prospered, for neutral vessels were safer *of neutrality* than the merchant ships of nations flying enemy flags. Particularly lucrative was the trade between the French West Indies and France, which had hitherto been a monopoly of French traders, but was now opened to vessels from the United States. Prices responded to the increased demand for American produce, sailors' wages rose, and shipbuilders as well as shipowners reaped a rich harvest. Congress under these circumstances backed the President strongly in his policy of neutrality. It established by a law of 1794 definite rules of neutrality, emphasizing particularly the duties of neutrals, and it appropriated seventy-five thousand dollars to be used if needed in enforcing the law. With the public, the policy of neutrality came to be better appreciated, and for the time being there were not many who would have preferred war.

Prosperity, indeed, seemed to be an accompaniment of the new government. Probably the period of depression that had coincided with the years in which the Articles of Confederation were in effect *Election* had by 1789 about run its course, and doubtless better times *of 1792* would have come regardless of the form of government. But to a great share of the public it seemed that the adoption of the Constitution had brought about the change, and by the end of Washington's first administration there were comparatively few who regretted the establishment of the new government. There were many, however, who felt that the Federalists had gone too far in the direction of centralization and had granted unreasonable favors to the propertied interests. To remedy this defect they were already considering the wisdom of placing the government in other hands. Had Washington retired at the end of his first term, as he had wished to do, undoubtedly there would have been a hard fight between the Hamiltonian and Jeffersonian factions over the choice of his successor. But Washington was persuaded to stand for re-election, and there was none who would oppose him. When it came to the Vice-Presidency, which John Adams held, the Republicans had fewer scruples, and gave their votes to George Clinton. In the election of 1792, Washington again received a unanimous vote, but Clinton, who carried New York, Virginia, North Carolina, and Georgia, and took one vote in Pennsylvania, received a total of 50 votes to 77 for Adams. It was clear that in the course of time a real party struggle for the control of the national government would be staged.[1]

[1] Edward Stanwood, *A History of the Presidency* (2 vols., 1898, new ed., 1916), is in reality a history of presidential elections, and as such is indispensable.

CHAPTER XIV

THE FREEDOM OF THE SEAS

WITH the establishment of the government under the Constitution, American shipping interests took a new lease of life. In 1789 a navigation act was passed which placed a duty of fifty cents per ton upon ships built and owned by foreigners, and thirty cents per ton upon ships built by Americans but owned by foreigners. Ships that were both American-built and American-owned paid only six cents per ton. The result of this legislation was to stimulate greatly the carrying of American imports and exports in American ships. During the Confederation period it was the exception when an American ship carried goods either to or from America, but a few years after the adoption of the Constitution it was the rule.

An overwhelming proportion of American overseas trade was still with Great Britain, although the British government as yet gave no evidence of willingness to sign a trade treaty with the United States, *Trade discriminations* or to relax any of the discriminations against American trade that had been laid down at the close of the Revolutionary War. American ships entering British ports were faced by heavy port duties, and such American trade with the British West Indies as was permitted had to go in British ships. To remedy this situation, Madison proposed in 1789 that discriminatory tonnage duties should be levied against the ships of any nation with which the United States did not have a commercial treaty. Madison's proposal was not adopted, but the threat worried the British, and an unofficial agent, Major Beckwith, was sent to the United States from Canada to find out what the new government proposed to do. Instead of dealing with Jefferson, the Secretary of State,[1] Beckwith made contact with Hamilton, the Secretary of the Treasury. In 1791 the British for the first time sent a minister to the United States, George Hammond, and the United States sent Thomas Pinckney in the

---

[1] *The American Secretaries of State and their Diplomacy* (10 vols., 1927–29), edited by S. F. Bemis, is a co-operative work that covers in detail the history of American foreign relations.

same capacity to England. But Beckwith stayed on in America to keep the ear of Hamilton, and to act as a go-between for him and Hammond. The Secretary of the Treasury was deeply solicitous about the maintenance of good relations with England, and from him Beckwith soon gained the impression that the Federalists would never allow a war to break out between the two countries. Hamilton believed sincerely that war with England would mean the destruction of American commerce, and that in preference to such a blow peace should be maintained at any price.

The outbreak of war between England and France precipitated a situation that put a serious strain upon American neutrality.[1] One of the *War in Europe* first war measures of the French government was to open to neutral nations the trade between the French West Indies and France. Ordinarily this trade was a French monopoly, but the possibility that the British navy might cut the communications between the French islands and the mother country was great, and so in time of war the French government stood ready to countenance trade which in time of peace it strictly forbade. The French officials fully expected that Americans would assume the trade thrown open, and they doubtless hoped that such a development would mean trouble between Great Britain and the United States.

As foreseen, American ships soon flocked to the French islands, and the prospect of splendid wartime profits seemed great. But in June, *The "rule of 1756"* 1793, the British government announced that it would adhere to the so-called "rule of the War of 1756," according to which trade not open to a nation in time of peace could not be opened to that nation in time of war. All vessels and cargoes found to be engaged in any such trade were ordered to be seized. The news of this regulation, and the ruthless way in which it was enforced, filled Americans with dismay. Hundreds of American ships were taken, and American seamen and passengers were subjected to the grossest indignities. To make matters worse, the British government soon announced that all ships engaged in carrying the private property of French subjects would be confiscated when captured, but the American protests against this order were so sharp and so well justified that it was soon modified. Ships carrying French produce to Europe remained liable to capture, but the normal trade between the French islands and the United States was allowed to go on.

At best the rights of neutrals were subject to much dispute. Eng-

---

[1] C. M. Thomas, *American Neutrality in 1793* (1931); J. B. Moore, *The Principles of American Diplomacy* (1918).

land, accustomed for centuries to naval pre-eminence, tended to multiply the privileges that a belligerent power might exercise, *Neutral* while the Continental nations, with their less formidable *rights* navies, were disposed to challenge the British point of view and to defend the rights of neutrals. The United States, naturally enough, preferred the Continental way of thinking, and saw in the British practices indefensible violations of international law.

As time went on the disagreements multiplied. The United States held that neutral ships made neutral goods; hence, French goods on American ships should have been free from molestation. But the British orders flouted this doctrine. The United States held that foodstuffs were not to be regarded as contraband of war. The British argued that, inasmuch as imported provisions were essential to the French in their prosecution of the war, such cargoes might lawfully be taken over by the British and paid for. The United States adhered emphatically to the principle that a blockade to be legally binding must be effectively maintained by a blockading squadron off port, but the British did not hesitate to establish paper blockades of many French ports, or to capture neutral ships, bound for a forbidden destination, anywhere on the high seas. The United States held that the British had no international sanction whatever for their "rule of 1756." The British contended that it was unfair for France to monopolize trade with her colonies in time of peace, when her ships ran no risk, and then to expect that the same trade in time of war could enjoy immunity under a neutral flag.

The difficulties attendant upon enforcing the British regulations brought out still other differences. It was agreed on all sides that a belligerent ship might in certain cases visit and search a *Visit and* neutral merchantman. On the extent to which the search *search* might go there was complete disagreement. The United States contended that the boarding party had no right to do more than examine the ship's papers. The British insisted that such a search was no search at all in view of the ease with which fraudulent papers could be obtained. British boarding parties, therefore, examined the cargoes of suspected ships to see what was really carried.

Another difficulty was the disposition shown by these boarding parties to impress seamen into the British service. In the eighteenth century impressment from British merchant vessels was a per- *Impress-* fectly normal and legal method of recruiting the royal navy; *ment* hence, when British sailors were found on American ships, it seemed reasonable enough that they should be taken off and made to serve under the British colors. Sometimes the men so impressed were actually

British subjects, and sometimes they were American-born. In the latter event they were usually returned, after suffering much hardship and inconvenience. But impressed sailors who were British-born, whether naturalized by the United States or not, were never returned, for the British government still held to the doctrine, "Once an Englishman, always an Englishman." The United States never conceded the right of impressment, and later on this abuse caused much friction between the two countries. For the moment the American government seemed less concerned about the rights of men than about the rights of property.

The British attack on American commerce gave to the pro-French Republicans an opportunity to urge drastic measures of retaliation. *Embargo of 1794* They pointed out that commercial reprisals had brought the mother country to terms in the years preceding the Revolution, and that England was in as great need of retaining the American trade now as then. Madison, speaking for Jefferson, advocated that whenever a foreign nation restricted American commerce, whether by duties, by tonnage taxes, or by the exclusion of our ships from her ports, the President should be empowered to return discrimination for discrimination. While this particular plan was not adopted, the illegal acts of the British so aroused public opinion in the United States that something spectacular had to be done. An embargo on foreign trade for one month (later extended to two months) was therefore authorized. For this space of time American ships were excluded from the high seas, and all foreign ships were excluded from American ports.

The embargo was a mere stop-gap, designed to call attention to the seriousness of the problem, and to give the government time to decide on a better plan. Nevertheless, many Republicans favored its continuance and argued that to abandon it would be to give the appearance of yielding to England. Subsequently they brought forward a non-importation bill, directed specifically at English commerce, but it failed of adoption by the casting vote of the Vice-President. Extremists even suggested that debts owing to British creditors by Americans be seized — an act that could hardly have failed to provoke war. The strengthening of the military forces of the country was voted enthusiastically.

The Federalists, meantime, guided by the reasoning of Hamilton, had decided that a far safer policy than any that the Republicans proposed would be to seek concessions from England by treaty, and they finally persuaded Washington to send the Chief Justice, John Jay, to London for this purpose. Jay's instructions explicitly required him to obtain (1) evacuation by the British of the military posts they held south of the Great Lakes, (2) compensation for their illegal seizures of American ships, (3) a satisfactory commercial treaty, which must embody, among other things, the American position on disputed points of international law. If such a treaty seemed unattainable, Jay was told to seek the co-operation of the northern nations of Europe in a joint effort to maintain neutral rights. He was then to report to his government for further instructions.[1]

Jay should have been able to obtain a good treaty. His mission to England was a plain avowal that the United States would not be drawn into the war against England if such a course could be honor- *Jay's nego-* ably avoided, and that friendly treatment by the English *tiations* might ultimately array the Americans on the English side against the French. Also, the threat that the United States might join with the northern neutrals of Europe in an armed neutrality ought to have had some weight in the negotiations. But Hamilton did much to undermine Jay's strength. He gave Hammond to understand that the United States could neither be provoked into war nor into co-operation with any armed neutrality that the northern neutrals might propose. Jay was thus handicapped more than he knew, and perhaps under the circumstances he did as well as could have been expected. His decision to ignore his instructions is hard to defend, but, as one writer has pointed out, the treaty he negotiated should really have been called "Hamilton's treaty."

Jay succeeded in arranging in a fairly satisfactory way the disputes that had arisen out of the settlement of the Revolutionary War. The news of the battle of Fallen Timbers had made a deep im- *Jay's* pression in England, and the British now agreed to with- *treaty* draw their military posts from south of the Great Lakes. Plans were also made for the establishment of two joint commissions, one to settle the non-payment by Americans of their pre-Revolutionary War debts to British subjects, and the other to straighten out the disputed boundary line between Canada and Maine. This time the British lived up to their agreement with regard to the northwestern posts, and in 1796 their troops were withdrawn. In due time, also, a settlement of the debts controversy required the United States to pay British claims amounting to $2,664,000, and a compromise boundary line was recommended.

On commercial matters the treaty left much to be desired. A commission on spoliations was established to determine what payments the British should make for their recent illegal seizures of American ships and

---

[1] S. F. Bemis, *Jay's Treaty: A Study in Commerce and Diplomacy* (1923), covers the problems that led to Jay's mission, as well as the formation of the treaty. It is invaluable on this episode of American diplomacy. See also Frank Monaghan, *John Jay, Defender of Liberty* (1935).

cargoes, and *vice versa*. Ultimately a balance of $5,705,654 was awarded to the United States. A trade treaty, to remain in force for a period of twelve years, was also agreed upon. It recognized at last the "most favored nation" principle in all trade relations between the United States and the "dominions of his majesty in Europe."

Colonial trade was separately considered. It was agreed that both nations should be permitted to use freely for trade purposes the "rivers, lakes, and waters" of the American continent, except within the limits of the Hudson's Bay Company's monopoly. The United States was also given generous trade privileges in the British East Indies. But the provisions that applied to the British West Indies fell far short of what Americans expected Jay to obtain. Article XII stipulated that American small sailing-vessels (not over seventy tons) might trade without discrimination in West Indian ports *on condition that* the United States would forbid American ships to carry molasses, sugar, coffee, cocoa, and cotton from the West Indies to any other country than the United States, *or from the United States to any part of the world except the United States*. British vessels, however, might freely enjoy the West Indian trade with the United States, and discriminations against them were expressly forbidden. These extraordinary provisions were designed to remain in force until two years after the close of the war between England and France, when they might or might not be renewed.

On the subject of neutral rights Jay gained very nearly nothing at all. He promised that the enemies of England should not be permitted to fit out privateers in American waters, as Genêt had once attempted, and that Americans who accepted commissions to serve against England might be treated as pirates. On such important matters as visit and search and impressment, the treaty was ominously silent.

Although deeply displeased with Jay's failure to carry out his instructions, Washington, after some hesitation, decided to submit the treaty to *Ratification* the Senate. There the terms that Jay had made, particularly with reference to the West Indian trade, almost defeated ratification; only by voting to strike out the obnoxious Article XII was a two-thirds majority obtained. Also, the President himself, because England had issued a new order for the seizure of provisions bound for France, seriously considered the advisability of halting the progress of the treaty. Finally, however, he decided to accept it if England would withdraw her provisions order, and would agree to the elimination of Article XII. On this basis ratifications were ultimately exchanged. From the moment its terms were known, the public heartily denounced the treaty. Jay was excoriated at every turn, and Washington himself shared in the general disapproval. When Congress met in December, 1795, the House of Representatives almost refused to appropriate the funds necessary to carry the treaty into effect, but capitulated ultimately to the argument that, bad as it was, the treaty was preferable to its alternative, war.

Time seemed to show that the acceptance of the treaty was no mistake. It eased somewhat the obstacles confronted by American trade, and in conjunction with the treaty of Fort Greenville it opened the way for a new advance of settlement into the Northwest. Most important of all, its adoption greatly facilitated negotiations between the United States and Spain for the settlement of their long-standing difficulties over the southwestern frontier.

By 1795 Spain had withdrawn from her alliance with England, and had revived her normal friendship with France. The news that the United States had just signed an agreement with England disturbed the usual serenity of Count Manuel Godoy, then the most powerful statesman in Spain, who feared that Jay's treaty might be only the prelude to an alliance between the two English-speaking nations. Should such an alliance be formed, Spain stood a chance, in case of war, to lose Florida, and perhaps even more of her American possessions. As an offset to Jay's treaty, Godoy determined, therefore, to sign an even more generous treaty with the United States. Suddenly Thomas Pinckney, in charge of the American negotiations at Madrid, found his difficulties at an end.

In the resulting Treaty of San Lorenzo, or "Pinckney's treaty," [1] as it is sometimes called, the Spanish King consented to the thirty-first parallel as the northern boundary of Florida, conceded to Ameri- *Pinckney's* cans the navigation of the Mississippi "in its whole breadth *treaty* from its source to the ocean," and agreed to allow citizens of the United States the right to deposit at New Orleans, duty-free, such merchandise as they planned to export. This "right of deposit" at New Orleans was to run for three years; thereafter the Spanish monarch promised renewal, but, if he chose, at some suitable site other than New Orleans. Thus, within a few months' time the most critical problems of the Northwest and the Southwest seemed to be solved. With trade freely opened down the Mississippi, the rapid growth of the West was assured.

So far as the relations between the United States and France were concerned, the signing of Jay's treaty had most unfortunate results. The treaty specifically denied that any of its provisions were meant to violate the French treaties, but the French government assumed, not without some reason, that the closer relationship established with England was in

[1] S. F. Bemis, *Pinckney's Treaty* (1926).

reality designed as a blow at France. Early in 1796 the French foreign minister taunted the American minister to France, James Monroe, with the statement that the agreement with England had nullified the French treaties.

Already the French had developed what was known as the doctrine of retaliation. They held that a neutral nation was obliged to defend its *French* rights. If it failed to do so, then it was actually aiding the *retaliations* belligerent power from which it permitted mistreatment. Accordingly, the opposing belligerent had the right to retaliate on the erring neutral by doing the same things that the other belligerent did. In accordance with this doctrine, French seizures of American ships had taken place for a long time, but after the adoption of Jay's treaty French sea-captains were definitely ordered to treat American ships in the same way that American ships were being treated by the British. If, for example, the Americans permitted the British to seize provisions as contraband, the French might also seize provisions as contraband. The interpretation of this order naturally varied somewhat according to the whims of the individual French commanders, but before long French violations of American neutral rights began to be about as offensive as anything the British had ever done.

In spite of these depredations, the French government felt that it could count on the friendship of the Republican Party in the United *Monroe's* States. Republicans were usually bitter in their denuncia- *indiscretion* tion of Jay's treaty, and firm in their devotion to the French treaties. Moreover, the Republican minister from the United States, James Monroe, showed plainly that his sympathy lay with the French.[1] Inadequately informed as to the real purpose of Jay's mission to England, he had done nothing to prepare the French for the treaty, which shocked him as deeply as it shocked them. In this frame of mind, he neglected to present the official explanation of the treaty that he had belatedly received, and he may have dropped the hint that after the next presidential election things would be different in the United States. For his indiscreet conduct he was promptly recalled, but the French government truculently refused to receive the reliable Federalist, C. C. Pinckney, whom Washington sent to replace him.

By the time the election year of 1796 had arrived, Washington had made up his mind not to accept another term. This meant that a clear- *Jeffersonian* cut party conflict could no longer be forestalled. Jefferson, *Republicans* out of the Cabinet since 1793, had built up a strong following among the common people, with which he meant to wrest control of

[1] B. W. Bond, Jr., *The Monroe Mission to France, 1794–1796* (1907).

[242]

THOMAS JEFFERSON

the government from the Federalists. The small farmers, deeply offended by every item of Hamilton's financial program and by the forceful suppression of the Whiskey Rebellion, were readily induced to follow his lead. The states'-rights element was also with him, for the Supreme Court, in one of its first important decisions, *Chisholm vs. Georgia* (1793), had held that a state might be sued by a citizen of another state. No more complete denial of the doctrine of state sovereignty could have been devised, and the decision was promptly recalled by the submission and ratification of the Eleventh Amendment. Federalists as well as Republicans favored the amendment, but Republicans blamed the Federalists for the decision, and maintained that they repudiated it only because they dared not do otherwise.

The whole anti-English element in the population tended to favor Jefferson. Such persons denounced the truckling attitude of the Federalists toward England and the humiliating treaty that it had brought forth. They professed still to admire the French Revolution, and to believe that in the war with England France was battling against autocracy on behalf of "liberty, fraternity, and equality." Supported by a bitingly sarcastic press, and surrounded by a group of efficient lieutenants, Jefferson was ready to make his bid for the Presidency. For strategic reasons his choice for Vice-President fell on Aaron Burr, a leader in the New York democracy.

The Federalists, meantime, had lost ground. Their concern for the commercial classes and the well-to-do, however much it might make for *Federalist losses* the prosperity of the country, was totally lacking in popular appeal. They had been long enough in office for numerous grievances against them to accumulate, and for dangerous internal dissensions to appear. They were unable to nominate their ablest leader, Hamilton, who, notwithstanding the fact that in 1795 he had followed Jefferson's example in leaving the Cabinet, had retained a powerful voice in the administration. A caucus of the Federalist members of Congress, fearful that Hamilton's ultra-conservatism might cost the party votes, chose John Adams to be the Federalist candidate for the Presidency, and Thomas Pinckney for the Vice-Presidency. Thereupon Hamilton, knowing well that his influence over Adams would be slight, intrigued to throw the election to Pinckney. Hamilton's plan came out during the campaign, and revealed a rift in the party that almost cost the Federalists the election. Also, it left Adams with an abiding distrust of Hamilton.

The French government, quite unintentionally, came to the aid of the Federalists. Its attack on American commerce, although undoubtedly designed to heighten dissatisfaction with the Jay treaty and thus to help the Republicans, merely added to the anti-French feeling *Election* in the United States, and strengthened the Federalists. *of 1796* The French government also, in protest against the Jay treaty, ordered Adet, the French minister to the United States, to give up his office; but it unwisely permitted him to remain in America to work for the election of Jefferson. Adet tried to induce American voters to support the Republican candidates by the threat of a war with France in case the Federalists were not turned out. Undoubtedly the chief result of the French efforts to interfere in the election was to turn many voters to Adams who might otherwise have supported Jefferson. The American people were then, and still are, deeply resentful of any attempt on the part of a foreign nation to influence their internal political decisions. By a narrow majority, 71 to 68, Adams was chosen over Jefferson. Hamilton's scheme to elect Pinckney to the Presidency was foiled by the action of many New England electors who voted for Adams, but refused to support Pinckney. The curious outcome of this procedure was that Pinckney received fewer votes than Jefferson, and the Vice-Presidency fell to the leader of the defeated party.

Washington left office with far less popularity than when he assumed it. His dream of avoiding the formation of political parties in the United States had been shattered, and he had been forced, alike by his temperament and by his convictions, to ally himself with the Federalists. This display of partisanship exposed him to many bitter attacks. Even his Farewell Address, which later generations came to revere so much, was published on the eve of the election of 1796, and was construed by the Republicans as a campaign document. He urged loyalty to the Union, cautioned against an "irregular opposition" to government, and warned against the entanglements that might result from a too active participation by the new nation in European politics. From the Republican press there was little but rejoicing when the first President laid down the reins of office. After March 4, 1797, he retired to Mount Vernon in order to take up again the life of a Virginia planter. For the most part he kept carefully away from the stir of politics, and even before his death, in 1799, he had regained much of his former popularity.

The new President, John Adams (1735–1826), looked the part of greatness less than his predecessor. During the debate on titles in the Senate his short, stout figure caused some wit to suggest that a *John Adams* suitable title for the first Vice-President would be "His Rotundity." But Adams was one of the ablest men ever to occupy the presidential chair. He had been a lawyer of more than local fame before

JOHN ADAMS

the Revolution, and his rôle during that eventful struggle was always an important one. He served as minister to England during the Confederation period, and it was no fault of his that his mission did not succeed. He assumed the duties of Vice-President with some pride, only to write a little later in disillusionment to his wife: "My country has in its wisdom contrived for me the most insignificant office that ever the invention of man contrived or his imagination conceived." Subsequent Vice-Presidents have usually agreed that Adams was right, and with better reason than he; for the early Senate was often evenly divided, and the casting vote of the Vice-President gave Adams real power. In spite of the radicalism of his Revolutionary War utterances, Adams was a thoroughgoing aristocrat, and supported willingly the policies of Washington and Hamilton. But he was never anybody's man but his own. Vain of his own ability, and often irritable to the point of anger when crossed, he was nevertheless, in the words of Jefferson, "as disinterested as the being who made him." His decisions with regard to national policy were invariably the result of his best judgment, and were wholly disregardful of the political fortunes of John Adams. Few men have ever served their country so well.[1]

He was soon called upon to show his mettle. The result of the election of 1796 still further alienated the French, whose spoliation of American commerce in no wise abated. As a crowning insult James Monroe, the Republican, was shown exceptional courtesies in France, while Pinckney, the Federalist, was not only refused recognition as minister but was also pointedly informed that a French law forbade aliens to remain in the country longer than two months without permission. When news of this outrage reached the United States, many Federalists were ready to sever all relations with France, even at the risk of war. But Adams, for the time being supported by Hamilton, knew that the United States was in no position to take such a stand. Public opinion was badly divided, with many of the southern states still overwhelmingly pro-French, and the nation was utterly unprepared for war. Adams urged instead that a mission to consist of three envoys be sent to France to treat for the restoration of good relations. *Anti-French sentiment*

With the help of the more moderate Federalists, Adams got his mission. Two Federalists, C. C. Pinckney and John Marshall, and one Republican, Elbridge Gerry, were appointed, and in the fall of 1797 they appeared in Paris. The French Directorate was then *A mission to France*

[1] J. T. Adams, *The Adams Family* (1930), contains a discriminating appraisal of the second President and his work. See also J. T. Morse, *John Adams* (1884).

at the height of its glory, with the unsavory Talleyrand as its foreign minister. Corruption ruled the day. Talleyrand probably meant to treat with the Americans, but seeing no harm in obtaining a bribe as the price of opening negotiations, he instructed three of his subordinates, later known as X, Y, and Z, to call upon the American envoys and so inform them. When the Americans explained that they were not authorized to offer a bribe, and tried to talk of other things, one of the agents exclaimed: "Gentlemen, you do not speak to the point. It is money; it is expected that you will offer money." To which Pinckney, who was a little deaf and was loath to believe his ears, at length replied, "No, no; not a sixpence." The envoys then drew up a full statement of the American case and delivered it to Talleyrand. Two months later the French minister stated the French contentions, and insulted the American delegation by expressing his desire to continue conversations with the Republican, Gerry, but not with the Federalists. Thereupon Pinckney and Marshall left the country. Gerry had the bad judgment to stay on, although in a private capacity only, until Adams peremptorily ordered him back to the United States.

The "X Y Z dispatches," as the report on the French negotiations came to be called, were not at once made public. Adams's Cabinet was *The "X Y Z* for war to avenge the insult, but Adams, still supported by *dispatches"* Hamilton, was determined to avoid war if he could. Ultimately Congress asked to see the correspondence and Adams released it, reserving only the names of the French agents, X, Y, and Z. Members of Congress were as shocked as Pinckney had been and voted for the publication of the dispatches in full. The result was great excitement throughout the country, and Pinckney's refusal to consider a bribe, liberally translated, yielded a brilliant slogan: "Millions for defense, but not one cent for tribute." Adams himself declared that he would "never send another minister to France without assurances that he will be received, respected, and honored as the representative of a free, powerful, and independent nation." Congress voted liberal appropriations to strengthen the national defense, but following Adams's sensible leadership it kept cool and made no declaration of war. The treaties with France were repealed, however, and the alliance with France was thus brought formally to an end.

The defense program included the establishment of a separate navy department, and the addition to the navy of twelve armed ships and ten *Prepared-* galleys. Three powerful frigates which had already been *ness* authorized, the *United States* and the *Constitution*, of forty-four guns each, and the *Constellation*, of thirty-six guns, were now made ready for battle. Merchantmen were permitted to carry guns for use in their own defense, and over four hundred privateers were released. The ships of the national navy, as fast as they could be commissioned, were ordered to seize French privateers wherever found, and to take whatever measures were necessary for the protection of American commerce.

The new navy gave a good account of itself. The *Constellation* attacked, outfought, and captured *L'Insurgente*, a French frigate that had seized many American merchantmen, and stood off the superior French ship, *La Vengeance*. The *Boston* took the *Berceau*. Many minor engagements occurred, and altogether the Americans captured eighty-four French ships, most of them privateers. American losses were also heavy. For over two years this period of "armed neutrality" continued, but the existence of a state of war went unrecognized by either nation.[1]   *Naval war of 1798*

Meantime there was much wrangling about the establishment of an army. France was far away, and was unlikely to send an invading force across the Atlantic, so that the use to which this weapon could be placed was problematic. Nevertheless Congress authorized the enlistment of a new regiment of artillery and gave the President authority to raise ten thousand volunteers. The command of this army became immediately a matter of public discussion. All agreed that Washington should be commander-in-chief, but the age of the ex-President precluded his taking an active part in campaigns. Who, then, should be second in command? Hamilton, it soon developed, burned with a great desire for the place, and intrigued to get it. Unfortunately Adams had kept Washington's Cabinet, most of whom were still under the influence of Hamilton, and in the end Hamilton had his way. Probably he dreamed of active service against the Spanish in America. He was in close touch with Don Francisco de Miranda, a Spanish-American who wished to enlist the aid of the United States in the cause of independence for the Spanish colonies, and he still had means of private communication with the English government. With English naval assistance and a small American army, dazzling possibilities lay open, among them the conquest of Florida and Louisiana for the United States, and the formation of a great Spanish-American republic, whose trade relations with the United States would be intimate.

But the army was slow to materialize, for Adams did not much believe in it. "Regiments cost money," he told his Secretary of War, when the latter complained of the slowness of the President in exercising the power Congress had given him. And money was   *The army*

[1] G. W. Allen, *Our Naval War with France* (1909).

hard to raise. Tariff receipts, owing to the troublous times on the high seas, were going down. Congress therefore levied new excises, and attempted with as little success as under the Confederation to collect a direct tax from the states. In the end heavy loans had to be floated. It was the spring of 1799 before recruiting actually began, and by that time the war fever had cooled off. "The army is progressing like a wounded snake," said one observer.

All the while Adams was eager for peace, although Hamilton, with high hopes of glory and combat for himself, now wished for war. Un-
A second mission to France
official information that the French government did not really desire war came to the President from several sources, and finally Talleyrand opened communications through the French representative at The Hague with our minister to Holland, William Vans Murray. In due time Murray informed Adams that Talleyrand was ready to receive a minister from the United States should one be sent. Adams's cabinet, in close harmony with Hamilton, was against any such action, for clearly it might lead to peace. But in February, 1799, when Hamilton was bending every effort to recruit an army, Adams sent to the Senate the nomination of William Vans Murray as minister to France. The more warlike Federalists were shocked beyond measure, but with the country less and less inclined toward war they dared not oppose the President. They urged a commission, however, instead of a minister, and on that the President gave in. Adams appointed Oliver Ellsworth, W. R. Davie, and Murray as the commission, but before he would send them he asked and obtained from Talleyrand a direct promise that they would be properly received.

By the time the envoys reached Paris, the star of Bonaparte was in the ascendancy. Under his leadership the new French government was
Peace restored
eager to make peace, not only with the United States, but also as nearly as possible with all nations. With Bonaparte posing in the rôle of peacemaker, the task of the Americans was easy. By a convention ratified on July 31, 1801, France agreed to the abrogation of the earlier treaties, and accepted the principle that neutral ships make neutral goods. The United States, on the other hand, waived indemnities for illegal seizures by the French of American shipping. When the treaty reached America, the country was entirely over its war mood, and however much some of the Federalists disliked the prospect of peace, the treaty could not be turned down. The Federalist Senate accorded it only a conditional ratification, but once the Federalists were out of power the new Republican Senate, on December 19, 1801, ratified it without reservation.

John Adams was much criticized by some members of his party for keeping the country out of war, but there are few now who would not concede that he was right. By his course those embarrassing entanglements with European nations that Washington had advised against were avoided, and the policy of permanent American neutrality with regard to European wars was given an added impetus. What the schemes of Hamilton might have brought forth had he actually commanded an army in time of war, one can only surmise. Adams at length revolted against the Hamiltonian influence in his Cabinet, and reorganized that body with John Marshall, a moderate Federalist, as Secretary of State.[1] A less conscientious man would have taken such action years before. Adams was never forgiven by the extreme Federalists for his unwillingness to lead the country into war, but years later he said that as his epitaph he could ask nothing better than "Here lies John Adams, who took upon himself the responsibility of peace with France in the year 1800."

[1] A. J. Beveridge, *The Life of John Marshall* (4 vols., 1916–19), is not only a biography of Marshall, but is also a brilliant history of the period from a conservative point of view.

CHAPTER XV

THE REVOLUTION OF 1800

THE victory of the Federalists over the Republicans in 1796 was won by an extremely narrow margin, and Adams was always sensitive to the
Pro-Federalist sentiment taunt that he was "President by three votes"; but the threat of war with France tended both to strengthen his hands and to give courage to the diminished Federalist majority in Congress. In part to guard against the danger of anti-war activities within the United States, and in part to ensure against the calamity of a Republican victory at the polls, the Federalist leaders pushed through Congress during the summer of 1798 an extensive program of legislation known as the Alien and Sedition Acts.

Unhappily for the Federalists, most of the foreigners who came to the United States during this period joined the Republican Party. Many of them were refugee Frenchmen who had been thoroughly indoctrinated with the theories of the French Revolution. Others were Irishmen or Englishmen whose radicalism had made it expedient for them to emigrate. Among the newcomers were many highly educated men who, as pamphleteers or editors of newspapers, gave no quarter to Adams and the party he represented.

Three of the Federalist measures dealt with the problem presented by these aliens. A naturalization law extended the period of residence in
The Alien Acts the United States preliminary to citizenship from five to fourteen years. Another law, the Alien Friends Act, which dealt with aliens in time of peace, authorized the President to order any alien whose presence he regarded as dangerous to leave the country. Should the alien refuse to obey, he might be imprisoned for three years; or should he return after having left, he might be imprisoned for as long a term as the President saw fit. A third act, the Alien Enemy Act, designed to apply to aliens in time of war, gave the President the right to order such persons out of the country, or to imprison them at will. The Alien Acts were never applied. Their purpose was probably to frighten

[252]

pro-Republican Frenchmen out of the country, and undoubtedly they served their purpose well.

Another thorn in the flesh to the Federalists was the intemperate criticism to which the President, Federalist members of Congress, and all other Federalist leaders were subjected by the Republican "rabble." Such criticism was often libelous, and it nearly always passed the bounds of truth. Scurrilous editors delighted in multiplying epithets, and pamphleteers stopped at nothing. Federalists as well as Republicans could call their adversaries names, but the leading office-holders were Federalists, not Republicans. Furthermore, Federalist measures as well as men were assailed, and the drift toward war with France was bitterly denounced.

A fourth repressive measure, the Sedition Act, was designed to subdue all such criticism of the administration. It defined as a high misdemeanor, punishable by a fine of not more than five thousand *The Sedition* dollars and imprisonment for not more than five years, any *Act* combination or conspiracy to oppose the legal measures of the government, or to interfere with their execution. The publication of any false or malicious writing directed against the President or Congress, and designed to stir up hatred against them, was made a misdemeanor, conviction of which carried a fine of not more than two thousand dollars and imprisonment for not more than two years.

The Sedition Act, like the Alien Acts, accomplished more by the threat it made than by any actual enforcement. A large number of indictments were returned, but only a few persons, most of them prominent Republican editors, were brought to trial. When trials were held, however, the methods of the prosecution were as ruthless as the law under which the charge was made, and Federalist judges sometimes laid themselves open to the charge of partisanship. In general, the law proved to be a boomerang to the Federalists. Republicans who were convicted were regarded by their fellows as martyrs to the cause of free speech, and the process of enforcement was held continually before the people as an example of what might be expected if Federalist rule were to continue.

To offset the Alien and Sedition Acts, which the Republicans regarded as unconstitutional, Jefferson and Madison soon put forward their famous Kentucky and Virginia Resolutions. These meas- *The Kentucky and* ures proposed that the states should assume the right to de- *tucky and* cide when Congress had exceeded its powers under the Con- *Virginia* stitution. Some pointed to the Supreme Court as the logi- *Resolutions* cal place for this authority to reside, but the case of *Marbury vs. Madison*, by which the Court first clearly declared itself on this question, was several years in the future. The resolutions of the Virginia legislature, which Madison had drafted, stopped with an assertion that the states might properly "interpose" their authority against such "palpable and alarming infractions of the constitution" as were contained in the Alien and Sedition Acts, but those which the Kentucky legislature adopted, and which had secretly come from the pen of Jefferson, went much further. They called upon the other states to join Kentucky in declaring the Alien and Sedition Acts "void and of no force, and . . . in requesting their repeal at the next session of Congress." [1]

The Kentucky and Virginia Resolutions were not echoed by the legislatures of other states, and probably their authors had no such expectation. The chief purpose of the resolutions was to furnish Jefferson a platform on which to make his race for the Presidency in 1800. He meant to drive home to the electorate the dangers of Federalist rule. If the Federalists chose to violate the Constitution in one way, why not in another? And if a halt were not called soon, how long would it be before some Federalist administration, supported by a strong army and a strong navy, would choose to obliterate the rights of the states themselves as well as the rights of individuals? But the remedy that Jefferson had in mind was not really nullification. It was the election of Thomas Jefferson to the Presidency.

When Adams kept his country out of war he did so at the expense of his own chance of re-election. In 1798, with war seemingly imminent, *Federalist* the determination of the voters to stand by the President *dissension* was so strong that the Federalists made almost a clean sweep of the mid-term congressional elections. Had Adams then made war rather than peace, it seems reasonable to suppose that he might have retained the support of the people until after the election of 1800 was over. Furthermore, the Alien and Sedition Acts would have aroused less resentment in time of war, and could have been used far more successfully to silence the opposition. But the Federalists, instead of being united in the support of a popular war, again found themselves handicapped by factional strife. Hamilton, thoroughly disgruntled by Adams's peace policy, denounced the President vigorously in a pamphlet intended for private distribution among selected Federalist leaders. The pamphlet naturally fell into the hands of the Republicans, who used it to good advantage in the campaign. Hamilton also revived his scheme of four years before to defeat Adams by throwing the election to C. C. Pinckney,

[1] E. D. Warfield, *The Kentucky Resolutions of 1798* (1894), is still the best book on this subject.

[254]

whom the Federalists intended to make Vice-President. But all such efforts, as in 1796, worked only in the interest of the Republicans.

The result of the election was a clean-cut victory for the Republican candidates, Jefferson and Burr. Seventy-three Republican electors were chosen, as against sixty-five Federalists. The strength of the Republicans lay mainly to the south of the Mason and Dixon line, where they lost only the votes of Delaware, one half the votes of Maryland, and one third the votes of North Carolina. The Republicans also carried New York, thanks mainly to the activities of Burr, who succeeded in uniting all factions opposed to the Federalists in that state; and they won eight votes out of fifteen in Pennsylvania. The only solidly Federalist territory was New England, New Jersey, and Delaware. Probably the trend of the masses toward the Republicans would have shown even more clearly had there been fewer restrictions upon the suffrage. It was particularly significant that the new western states, Kentucky and Tennessee, voted for Jefferson, and that nearly every state with a considerable frontier element either voted for Jefferson or gave him more votes than it gave Adams. Already the leavening influence of frontier democracy had begun to work.

Election of 1800

Unfortunately, the election was not decided when the electoral college had registered its will. The provision in the Constitution which permitted each elector to vote for two candidates for the Presidency had made Jefferson Vice-President in 1796 when a majority of the electors were against him, and it now almost cost him the Presidency. A thoughtful New England Federalist threw away a vote on Jay, so that Pinckney got one less vote than Adams, but the Republican electors with greater zeal than foresight voted unanimously for Jefferson and Burr. These two having, therefore, an equal number of votes, it fell to the strongly Federalist House of Representatives, elected in 1798, to choose between them. A Federalist caucus decided to support Burr rather than Jefferson, but this decision was disobeyed by enough southern Federalists to deadlock the House. For thirty-five ballots there was no choice. At last, acting on the advice of Hamilton, who disliked Jefferson but knew Burr to be a rogue, the Federalists relented sufficiently to give the Presidency to Jefferson. Once the Republicans were in power they lost no time in amending the Constitution so that each elector should thereafter vote separately for President and for Vice-President.

The sullen unwillingness of the Federalists to bow to the popular will was shown again in the passage after the election of a new Judiciary Act. To make sure that the Supreme Court would not pass from Federalist control for a long time, the law provided that the

Judiciary Act of 1801

next vacancy on the Court should not be filled, so that thereafter the number of Supreme Court justices would be one less than formerly. Also, the old practice whereby Supreme Court justices on circuit duty sat with district judges as courts of appeal was discontinued, and a whole new panel of circuit judges was authorized. Then, in spite of the fact that the duties of the district judges were thus reduced, their number was increased from thirteen to twenty-three. The evident and expressed intent of the law was not so much to reform the judiciary as to give the outgoing President the chance to pack it with Federalist judges who could be trusted to thwart the Republicans in the years to come. Adams, who on internal matters was as narrowly partisan as anyone, had already bequeathed to the Jefferson administration his Secretary of State, John Marshall, as Chief Justice, and he carried out the terms of the law in the spirit of its framers.

It is not surprising that the Federalists went down to defeat. They failed to recognize that in a democracy the opinions of the masses must *Why the* be considered. They persisted too long in their assumption *Federalists* that government could be monopolized by the well-educated *lost* and the well-to-do. They proceeded too rapidly in their endeavor to build up a powerful centralized government, and they paid far too little attention to the strong state loyalties that had grown so naturally out of the separate status of the various colonies. Moreover, they were led by men who were for the most part commercially minded, and ignored the fact that the vast majority of the American people got their living from the soil.

Nevertheless, the Federalists in many important ways had served their country well. They had succeeded in making the new government work; the Constitution, and many of the precedents they had set, were destined to endure. They had successfully avoided entanglements in European affairs when a contrary policy might well have been fatal to the new nation. They had established the credit of the United States at home and abroad, and had given a praiseworthy example of honest and frugal administration.

Thomas Jefferson (1743–1826),[1] whose election to the Presidency ushered in what he was pleased to term the "Revolution of 1800," was, like Washington, a Virginia planter, but with that the similarity ends.

---

[1] Among the numerous lives of Jefferson the following merit citation: D. S. Muzzey, *Thomas Jefferson* (1918); A. J. Nock, *Jefferson* (1926); Gilbert Chinard, *Thomas Jefferson* (1929); J. T. Morse, *Thomas Jefferson* (1883). Edward Channing, *The Jeffersonian System* (1906), is one of the best of the volumes of the *American Nation* series. Allen Johnson, *Jefferson and his Colleagues* (1921), covers the same period for the *Chronicles of America*. Claude Bowers, *Jefferson in Power* (1936), brilliantly defends Jefferson at every turn.

Jefferson's father was from Albemarle County, which at the time Thomas was born was properly regarded as "back country." Jeffer- *Jefferson* son's mother was a Randolph, and hence from one of the first families of Virginia, but this aristocratic connection did not in the least undermine the sturdy, frontier democracy of her husband, nor prevent the development of her son into perhaps the outstanding theoretical democrat of all time.

Jefferson's formal education was much better than Washington's. The former attended William and Mary College, where he learned Latin, Greek, and French, and acquired such facility with languages that he soon added to his accomplishments Spanish, Italian, and Anglo-Saxon. He had also a good familiarity with mathematics, especially the calculus, and his knowledge of natural sciences was unusual for his day. His whole life long Jefferson maintained his thirst for learning. He was interested also in music and the arts, played the violin well, and knew enough about architecture to design his house at Monticello. After leaving college he studied law, and for a number of years he practiced that profession. The death of his father, however, gave him an estate to manage, and its management interested him more than the law. So also did the fascinating game of politics.

On the eve of the American Revolution, Jefferson's liberalism was beginning to assert itself. In 1774 he wrote *A Summary View of the Rights of America* which was widely read both in England and in America, and the philosophy of this pamphlet was later given classic expression in the Declaration of Independence. He was ill when the First Continental Congress met, but sat in the Second until after his work on the Declaration of Independence was done. He then resigned in order to accept a seat in the Virginia legislature while the new state constitution was being written, and the laws revised. Jefferson did not need to read Rousseau and Montesquieu to become a thoroughgoing believer in the doctrine of the rights of man. He read them, but he was less influenced by the writings of Europeans than by his own experience in the democratic West. On the strength of his own observations he urged his fellow Virginians to do away with such medieval relics as entail and primogeniture, to guarantee every one complete freedom of conscience, to abolish state support of an established church, to set up a system of public education, and to substitute for the existing cruelties of the penal code more reasonable and humane punishments. He even championed, well before the Revolution, the emancipation of the slaves. Some of his reforms were deemed too radical for even a revolutionary generation to adopt, but eventually practically all of them were accepted.

His public service continued through the closing years of the Revolution, when he succeeded Patrick Henry as governor of Virginia, and into the Confederation and Constitutional period. His influence upon the famous Northwest Ordinance has already been noted. As Secretary of State he respected Washington, and sometimes influenced him, but he came to look with increasing alarm upon the ascendancy of Hamilton, whose disdain of popular rights and determination to centralize the government were so out of harmony with the democratic principles for which Jefferson had come to stand. He left Washington's Cabinet to organize the opposition to Hamilton's policies, and even as Vice-President he kept at his work, although sometimes under the cloak of secrecy. Jefferson understood the popular whims and fancies better than most politicians, and possessed great talent as an organizer. He was not an orator, but he wrote with exceptional skill, and most of the documents he produced had an irresistibly popular appeal. If Hamilton's sympathies were with the commercial classes, Jefferson's were as definitely agrarian. A society consisting exclusively of small free farmers would, from Jefferson's point of view, have very closely approximated the ideal.

This was the man who became President on the Fourth of March, 1801. He deplored the sham of pomp and ceremony, so the inauguration *The new* of Republican rule took place in a setting of extreme sim- *capital city* plicity. The new President even walked from his boarding-house to the Capitol to deliver his inaugural address. Elaborate ceremonies might have been difficult to stage, however, if they had been desired, for Jefferson was the first President to take the oath of office in the new capital city on the Potomac, appropriately named Washington. An admirable plan for the city had been devised by a Frenchman named L'Enfant; but the streets were unpaved and most of them unopened, the public buildings were as yet unfinished, and only the distances between them were magnificent. The wisdom of laying out a new city to serve primarily as the political capital of the nation has since been amply justified, but many of those who surveyed the scene for the first time at Jefferson's inauguration undoubtedly thought otherwise.

And yet the capital city, in which great possibilities were only faintly realized, was not unlike the nation as a whole.[1] The United States, with *Census* a population of only 5,308,473, according to the census of *of 1800* 1800, was still a small nation. Nine tenths of these people lived to the east of the mountains; the other tenth, as far removed rela-

---

[1] Henry Adams, *History of the United States of America during the Administrations of Jefferson and Madison* (9 vols., 1890–91), is a work of enduring merit. The first volume contains an admirable survey of American society in 1800.

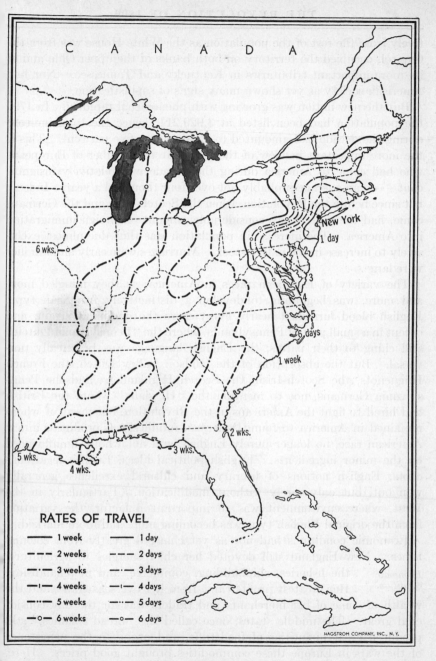

RATIO BETWEEN TIME AND DISTANCE OF TRAVEL IN THE UNITED
STATES FROM NEW YORK IN 1800

Courtesy of the Carnegie Institution of Washington and the American Geographical Society of New York.

tively from the rest of the population as the White House was from the Capitol, occupied the territory on both banks of the upper Ohio and of its more important tributaries in Kentucky and Tennessee. Nor had American society as yet shown many signs of sophistication.

But the new nation was growing with phenomenal rapidity. In 1790 the population had been listed at 3,929,214; hence the total increase during the decade had amounted to about thirty-five per cent. This is the more important in view of the fact that the number of Europeans who had come to America during the decade was relatively insignificant — on an average probably not over four thousand a year. Indeed, not since before the Revolution, when the Scotch-Irish and the Germans came, had there been any considerable amount of foreign immigration into America. The increase in population was thus due almost exclusively to increase in the native stock. Marriages were early and families were large.

The variety of European races in America, as they mingled more and more, was beginning to develop a distinctively American type. English blood furnished nearly everywhere the dominant strain, and except in a small part of Pennsylvania, where the "Pennsylvania Dutch" still clung to their patois, the English language was practically universal. But the absorption of the Hudson Valley Dutch, the French Huguenots, the Scotch-Irish, the Scotch Highlanders, and the Pennsylvania Germans, not to mention the "Hessians" whom the British had hired to fight the Americans in the Revolution, but many of whom remained in America to found American families, was producing a new American race, no longer purely English, and not wholly uninfluenced by the minor ingredients. English political ideas, English legal concepts, English notions of literary and cultural excellence generally won out, but only rarely without modification. Particularly in the West, where environment was so important a factor, the variation from the original English type was becoming more and more marked.

Economic conditions had not as yet changed greatly from colonial times. New England still devoted her chief energies to agriculture, *Economic* the fisheries, shipbuilding, commerce, and merchandising. *conditions* Her greatest profits came from her overseas trade, and the wealth of some of her merchants and traders was for the day considered great. The middle states, once called the "bread colonies," still produced great quantities of foodstuffs, and owing to the persistence of the wars in Europe these commodities brought good prices. Here, too, were carried on nearly all the activities upon which the prosperity of New England depended, and "infant industries," such as the manufacture of iron, grew increasingly numerous. In the South the large planters sometimes made money, but nobody else had a chance. The old colonial staples, tobacco, rice, and indigo, produced by the labor of over a million slaves, were still the chief sources of prosperity for those who had it. In 1793 Eli Whitney invented the cotton gin, and the resulting change in the status of cotton was already slightly in evidence. By 1800 the country exported twenty-five thousand bales of cotton, but the later significance of cotton-growing in southern economy was as yet hardly foreseen. Free farmers in the West made a living for themselves, and enjoyed sometimes a little prosperity from trade down the Mississippi in flatboats, or, in spite of Hamilton's tax, from the distilling of whiskey. Speculators in western lands were almost as numerous as the hills, and they sometimes took good profits. Many Easterners were interested in this business, and on account of their western holdings they often became the most ardent champions of western rights. The rôle of the land speculator in American history has not yet been given its just due.

Americans still lived in the country rather than in the city, and the danger that Jefferson most feared, a city proletariat, seemed too far away for any but theorists to worry about. Philadelphia with 70,000 people was the most populous of American cities. New York came next with 60,000; Baltimore had 26,000; Boston, 24,000; Charleston, 20,000. These "cities" still wanted what would today be called "all modern conveniences." Sewers were conspicuously absent, and as in colonial times, hogs ran loose in the streets to dispose of the city's garbage. The country was as primitive as the city. The farmers' tools were much the same type as in the days of Ruth and Boaz, and small children had no reason to inquire what was meant by such Bible verses as "his yoke is easy and his burden is light."

Education and culture had as yet made no rapid strides. One might easily argue that since colonial times much ground had been lost. The war, and in its wake the hard times of the *Education* Confederation period, had undermined the foundations *and culture* of the old educational systems, and had left the people with but little taste for the finer things of life. Nor did the relative prosperity of the last decade in the eighteenth century do much to improve such matters. New England still had some flourishing public academies, some short-term elementary schools, and colleges of a sort. But Harvard College in 1800 put its faith in a president, three professors, and four tutors. From New England to the South or the West educational opportunities grew progressively worse. In the whole country there was still comparatively little interest in literature; European books were read proportionately less than in colonial times; newspapers were relatively few, and in content hardly commendable; periodicals were almost non-existent. In an age when only the exceptional person could read and write, this is perhaps not surprising.

As in colonial times, religion still played an important part in the life of the people. Piety, or the pretense of piety, suffused New England,

Religion although the Congregational monopoly had long since been broken. In the cities the Episcopalians had a strong following, in Vermont there were many Quakers, and in Roger Williams's Rhode Island the Baptists were numerous. In the middle states there were many sects: Quakers, Presbyterians, Lutherans, Episcopalians, Dutch Reformed. In the South along the coast the Episcopalians were dominant, although in Maryland there were many Catholics and some Congregationalists. The back country and the frontier, during and for some time after the year 1800, was experiencing one of its chronic revivals. Here the Methodists, with their intense emotionalism and their democratic doctrine that salvation was equally open to all, set the pace; but the Baptists, the Presbyterians, and numerous minor sects were not far behind. The great revival swept like wildfire through the West, and the pioneer people, always sorely in need of an emotional outlet, attended the camp-meetings by the thousands and the tens of thousands:

> At first appearance, those meetings exhibited nothing to the spectator, but a scene or confusion that could scarce be put into human language. They were generally opened with a sermon; near the close of which, there would be an unusual outcry; some bursting forth into loud ejaculations of prayer, or thanksgiving for the truth; others breaking out in emphatical sentences of exhortation; others flying to their careless friends, with tears of compassion, beseeching them to turn to the Lord. Some struck with terror, and hastening through the crowd to make their escape, or pulling away their relations. . . . Others, trembling, weeping and crying out for the lord Jesus to have mercy upon them; fainting and swooning away, till every appearance of life was gone, and the extremities of the body assumed the coldness of a dead corpse. . . . Others surrounding them with melodious songs, or fervent prayers for their happy resurrection in the love of Christ. . . . Others collecting into circles around this variegated scene, contending with arguments for and against. And under such appearances, the work would continue for several days and nights together.[1]

The country stood in great need of better means of communication.

[1] Richard M'Nemar, *The Kentucky Revival* (1807), pp. 19–26. See also W. W. Sweet, *The Baptists* (1931); C. C. Cleveland, *The Great Revival in the West* (1916); and W. B. Posey, *The Development of Methodism in the Old Southwest, 1783–1824* (1933).

Sailboats plied slowly and without schedule from point to point along the coast, while stage-coaches, traveling at about four *Need of* miles an hour, connected the principal cities. In the *better com-* South the roads were frequently unsafe for vehicles, and *munications* overland travel was ordinarily on horseback. Inns were as primitive as in colonial times. The rivers of the interior, even above the falls line, were much used by all kinds of crude boats, and the "western waters" furnished alike the easiest means of expanding the frontier and the chief outlet of frontier trade.

The West was already "the most American part of America." Here the melting-pot had fused racial elements more completely than elsewhere; here the difference between American ways and *The West* European ways was most pronounced. Here cheap lands, almost literally, opened opportunity equally to all. Here democracy was practiced as well as preached, and here each citizen believed himself to be as good as anyone else. Here people looked out for themselves, and the ideal of individual freedom held universal sway. The society of the West was crude and rough, and the "men of the western waters" were mostly uncouth and illiterate, but they had begun the conquest of a continent, and they had little time for anything else. Out of their experiences were to come many of the guiding principles of American democracy. Jefferson understood these men, believed in them, and thought that, as President, he fully represented them.

Jefferson was a man of simple tastes who hated affectation of every sort, and he made short work of the pretentiousness with which the Federalist Presidents had surrounded themselves. Partly because he lacked fluency in speech, he substituted a written message to Congress for the formal address that preceding Presidents had felt obliged to deliver. He refused in social matters to recognize any rank whatever, and he persuaded his Cabinet to agree that "when brought together in society all are perfectly equal, whether foreign or domestic, titled or untitled, in or out of office." This rule confounded the diplomatic agents, who set great store by precedence, and almost led to international complications. The weekly levees, which Washington had instituted as a kind of imitation of the British court, were discontinued, and the President lived as nearly as possible in the same manner as if he were a private citizen.

Neither Jefferson's simplicity nor his devotion to the rights of the ordinary man could disguise the fact that he was himself as much a member of the upper stratum of society as any Federalist. Nor did

Jefferson choose to surround himself with men from the lower walks of life.
Jefferson's He believed in the good sense and the solid judgment of
appointees the people, and depended on these qualities in them to
ensure that the offices would go to able men. For his Secretary of State
Jefferson chose James Madison, the "father of the Constitution," and
like himself a Virginian of good position. For Secretary of the Treasury
he chose Albert Gallatin of Pennsylvania, a Genevan by birth who had
excellent family connections in Europe and had taught at Harvard
College. Nathaniel Macon, Speaker of the House, was, like the President,
an able southern planter in politics. John Randolph, who, as
chairman of the powerful House Committee on Ways and Means, was
the chief financial spokesman of the administration, also represented
the southern planter class. In general, the "Revolution of 1800"
meant the transfer of leadership in government from men who were
principally interested in commerce and finance to men whose chief
concern was agriculture; and it was rare indeed when high office, even
under Republican rule, fell to a man of low estate.

Jefferson really wished to win over the rank and file of the Federalists
to his party. His inaugural address was designed primarily to reassure
them "that though the will of the majority is in all cases to prevail,
that will to be rightful must be reasonable." The two parties, he
contended, were "brethren of the same principle. We are all Republicans,
we are all Federalists." When it came to the removal of Federalist
office-holders, the new President acted with extreme caution. Under
Washington, who by 1795 had made up his mind that it was "political
suicide" to appoint his adversaries to office, and under Adams, whose
partisanship from the beginning had been thoroughgoing and complete,
the offices had gone to the Federalists. Jefferson made a few
removals on the ground of offensive partisanship, and a few others
for misconduct in office. Vacancies were filled as a rule by Republicans,
but vacancies were rare. "Those by death are few," the President
complained, "by resignation none." Some of Jefferson's followers
were much disappointed at his conservatism in the matter of removals,
but by the end of his first administration a majority of the office-holders
were Republicans.[1]

"A wise and frugal Government, which shall restrain men from
injuring one another, shall leave them otherwise free to regulate their
own pursuits of industry and improvement, and shall not take from
the mouth of labor the bread it has earned" — this was the ideal that

[1] C. R. Fish, *The Civil Service and the Patronage* (1905); H. C. Hockett, *Western Influences on Political Parties to 1825* (1917).

[264]

Jefferson set for himself and his party when he took office in 1801. To his way of thinking the national debt, which Hamilton *"The less* had gladly assumed and the Federalist régime had steadily *government* increased, ought to be paid, not perpetuated for the *the better"* benefit of wealthy investors. But such a policy presented difficulties, since the Republicans, to carry out their campaign promises, were compelled to repeal the excise tax at a cost of six hundred and fifty thousand dollars annually to the treasury. The Secretary of the Treasury, Albert Gallatin, was equal to the emergency. He recommended that drastic reductions be made in all public expenditures, and particularly in appropriations for the army and navy. This plan of retrenchment, while unpopular with many politicians of both parties, was pushed through Congress with Jefferson's hearty support. The President seemed wholly unconcerned about the national defense, and in place of a national navy suggested that small gunboats, to be manned when needed by naval militia, be supplied to the harbors along the coast — "mosquito fleets," his opponents called them.

Gallatin succeeded admirably with the reduction of the national debt, and had conditions remained normal it might have been eliminated, as he predicted, in sixteen years. Increased pur- *Case of* chases abroad, due to the growing wealth and population *the Polly* of the country, led to corresponding increases in the tariff revenues. Help came also from an unexpected quarter. In 1800 Sir William Scott, a British judge, held in the case of the *Polly* that American ships engaged in the French West Indian trade might proceed without molestation to France, provided that they had first landed their cargoes at an American port and paid the duty. Thereafter American ships engaged in this once forbidden trade not only made good profits for themselves, but also piled up revenues for the American government. Except for a brief interlude, from March, 1802, to May, 1803, the European war raged on, and before the end of Jefferson's administration Gallatin, aided by the advantages of American neutrality, had retired as much of the national debt as was due and payable. His achievement was the more remarkable in view of the unforeseen expense attendant upon the purchase of Louisiana and the Tripolitan War.

The Tripolitan War probably saved the American navy from extinction. It had long been the habit of European nations to pay tribute to the piratical rulers of the maritime states of northern Africa — Morocco, Algiers, Tunis, and Tripoli — *The Tripoli-* *tan War* sometimes known as the Barbary States. In this practice the new United States, whose trade relations in the Mediterranean were of some consequence, soon joined. Nevertheless, in May, 1801, the Pacha of Tripoli, claiming that he had not received his proper share of the tribute, dramatically declared war on the United States by cutting down the flagstaff at the American consulate in Tripoli. Six days later, Jefferson, quite unaware of the Pacha's insolence, ordered a naval squadron to Mediterranean waters. The new President and his Secretary of the Treasury resented the expenditures necessary to maintain a navy, but they resented even more the idea of paying tribute money to pirates.

For the next three years American squadrons fought with varying success in Tripolitan waters. Jefferson and Gallatin had even to consent to an increase in the size of the navy. But when an American ship, the *Philadelphia*, was lost, and Congress voted to have it replaced, Gallatin, ever jealous of his revenues, refused to pay out the money until Congress had levied a special duty, called the "Mediterranean Fund," for the purpose. The war was finally brought to an end, less perhaps by the exploits of the navy than by the Pacha's fear of a small overland expedition from Egypt, headed by a pretender to the Tripolitan throne. An American citizen, William Eaton, entirely on his own authority, had stirred the pretender to action. The Pacha, faced by enemies on land and on sea, agreed to require no further tribute from the United States. His submission had a good effect upon the other Barbary rulers, who thereafter were far more tractable, but for many years a strong American squadron had to be retained in the Mediterranean, and the practice of paying tribute did not wholly disappear until 1815.[1]

The Republicans made haste to rid the country of much Federalist legislation. The period of residence for naturalization was again set *Repeal of Federalist legislation* at five years. The Alien and Sedition Acts were by their own terms to last for two years only, and they were of course not renewed. The Bank of the United States, chartered in 1791 for twenty years, was performing a needed service well, and was left alone. The Judiciary Act of 1801, however, and the "midnight appointments" Adams had made under its terms, were attacked mercilessly. This measure, passed hurriedly in the closing days of a Congress that the people had already repudiated at the polls, is a classic example of what Americans came to call a "lame duck" bill. It was designed, according to one critic, to act as a "hospital for decayed politicians," or in the language of today for "lame ducks" who had been defeated for

[1] Gardner W. Allen, *Our Navy and the Barbary Corsairs* (1905); C. O. Paullin, *Commodore John Rodgers* (1910), and *Diplomatic Negotiations of American Naval Officers* (1912).

re-election. The rank partisanship of such a bill was easily attacked, but the Republicans claimed also that it called for needless extravagance, and replaced it with a measure of their own, which added a new justice to the Supreme Court, and restored circuit duty to Supreme Court justices. Circuit courts were to consist of one justice of the Supreme Court and one district judge; in case of disagreement an appeal was to be taken to the Supreme Court. For fifty years longer this system of courts, which the Federalists had repudiated in 1801 as out of date, continued to work fairly well. As for the new judges that Adams had just appointed, they were left without duties and without salaries.

The Federalists at once charged that the Republicans had violated the Constitution, for federal judges were supposed to hold office "during good behavior." They maintained further that the Supreme Court might take a hand in the matter by declaring the Republican changes in the judiciary null and void. No such action was taken, but Marshall soon let it be known that the Court under his leadership could, if it chose, declare a law of Congress unconstitutional and refuse to enforce it.[1]

Marshall selected with skill the case upon which to announce this doctrine. One of Adams's midnight appointments had gone to a certain William Marbury, who had been commissioned a *Marbury* justice of the peace in the District of Columbia. But *vs. Madison* Marbury's commission, owing to the press of time, was not delivered before the fourth of March, 1801, and after that date Madison, the Secretary of State, refused to deliver it. Marbury then asked the Supreme Court to issue a mandamus compelling Madison to deliver the commission. From the Federalist point of view such a victory over the new administration was not to be despised. But Marshall, after reading Madison a lecture on his dereliction of duty in failing to deliver the commission, held that the Court could do nothing about it, and denied Marbury's request. The reason assigned by the Chief Justice for this startling decision was that the Supreme Court lacked the authority to grant such an order, even though it might wish to do so. The law, to be sure, gave the Court abundant authority, for it specifically stated that the Supreme Court might issue precisely such writs as the one Marbury now desired; but in giving this authority to the Supreme Court, Marshall held, the law went beyond the power delegated to Congress, for according to the Constitution the only

[1] A. J. Beveridge, *The Life of John Marshall*, III (1919), is very complete at this point. See also E. S. Corwin, *John Marshall and the Constitution* (1919); and Charles Warren. *The Supreme Court in United States History* (2 vols., 1928).

JOHN MARSHALL

original jurisdiction the Supreme Court might enjoy was in "cases affecting ambassadors, other public ministers and consuls, and those in which a state shall be party." With the law and the Constitution thus in direct conflict, the Chief Justice maintained that the Constitution must be followed and the law disregarded.

The "doctrine of judicial review," as the rule of law laid down in *Marbury vs. Madison* (1803) has come to be called, placed a powerful weapon in the hands of the Federalist judiciary. It *The doctrine* might now, on the theory that the law and the Constitu- *of judicial* tion were in conflict, set aside when opportunity offered *review* such laws passed by the Republican Congress as the Court could construe to be unconstitutional. But Marshall's reasoning was logical and quite in line with precedent. In colonial times judges on both sides of the Atlantic had held invalid colonial laws out of harmony with colonial charters or with the laws of Parliament. Subsequently the state supreme courts had frequently done the same thing with state laws that contravened a given state constitution. Probably it was supposed by most of the framers of the Constitution that the Supreme Court would act ultimately in precisely the way Marshall had acted. But it is nevertheless true that this rule of law placed in the hands of the Supreme Court of the United States a degree of authority not then enjoyed by any similar body of men anywhere else on earth.

What use to partisan ends the Court might make of its power was a question, and the Republicans were at once in search of a weapon of defense. They might rid themselves of obnoxious inferior judges by abolishing the offices that these judges held, *Impeach-* but the Supreme Court was set up by the Constitution, *ment of* and its justices held office for life unless impeached by vote *federal* *judges* of the House and removed by a two-thirds vote of the Senate. Apparently, then, in impeachment lay the only hope of remedy. Some actions along this line by the Republicans of Pennsylvania, who had successfully impeached and removed from office Judge Alexander Addison, had already been taken; and in 1804 a federal district judge, John Pickering, was impeached and removed when it was clear that he had become insane. Could impeachment be used against a Supreme Court justice who was guilty of grossly partisan actions? The Republicans meant to find out, for the adoption of such a policy would mean that Federalists on the bench must either restrain their partisanship or else run the risk of removal from office. Associate Justice Samuel Chase, a Federalist and a hero of the Revolutionary War, gave the

Republicans the chance they craved to bring a trial case. In an address to a Baltimore grand jury, Justice Chase denounced the introduction of universal suffrage, and excoriated those who were ruining the nation by making the people think that all men were entitled to enjoy equal liberty and equal rights. His attack was obviously partisan, and since there was no other way to remove judges than by impeachment the Republicans should have rested their case on that ground alone. Instead, they added irrelevant and unprovable charges of misconduct. The Senate refused to convict (1805), and a precedent was established that a man could not be impeached for anything for which he could not also be indicted. As partisanship was no crime, the Federalist justices were now free to go as far as they liked; but in the face of the growing popularity of Republican rule they conducted themselves with greater discretion.

CHAPTER XVI

JEFFERSON AND THE WEST

WHEN Jefferson took office it appeared that most of the problems of the West had been solved. By Jay's treaty the English posts in the Northwest had been abandoned; by Pinckney's treaty the Mississippi outlet had been opened to western trade; by the treaty of Fort Greenville the Indian frontier had been thrown back; by the admission of new western states the right of the West to local self-government and to full participation in national affairs had been duly recognized; and, finally, by a law passed in 1800 the West had been given nearly everything it desired by way of land legislation.

In the attempt to develop a national land policy two points of view were early apparent.[1] Easterners, for the most part, wished to administer the lands in such a way as to obtain from them *National land policy* the maximum amount of revenue. Their point of view was well set forth by Hamilton, who, as Secretary of the Treasury, made a report on the public lands. Hamilton believed that the most money could be realized by persuading speculators to purchase the land in large tracts. He was therefore ready to give two years' credit to the large purchaser, but not to the small. Also, he wished to abandon the rectangular system of survey, so that the better lands might the more easily be separated from those less promising. While he recommended the survey of land in small tracts as well as in large, he obviously expected that the small purchaser would buy from the speculator rather than from the government. Westerners, on the other hand, tended to resent the idea that the public lands should be used to produce a revenue. They maintained that, instead, the real object of the government in disposing of its lands should be the development of the country. To this end the needy should be permitted to acquire farms on the easiest possible terms.

Hamilton's plan was ignored by Congress, and not until after the

[1] Thomas C. Donaldson, *The Public Domain, Its History* (1884) is a useful compilation of official data, although marred somewhat by omissions and inaccuracies.

treaty of Fort Greenville had opened to settlement much new territory in central Ohio was a land law passed. In 1796 Congress authorized the sale of single sections (six hundred and forty acres) at a minimum price of two dollars per acre, but provision was also made for "wholesale" disposals. Townships were first to be divided equally, after which one of the halves was to be further subdivided into sections, while the other half was left for the speculative purchaser to subdivide as he chose. Two western land offices were opened, one at Pittsburgh and one at Cincinnati, where purchasers were allowed to pay one twentieth of the purchase price down, nine twentieths at the end of six months, and the remaining half within a year. The law did not work well. It provided for too large minimum tracts, and it placed the price of land at what for the time was a prohibitive figure. Settlers preferred to buy state lands south of the Ohio, or to take possession of public lands without title. Under the terms of the law only forty-eight thousand acres of land were sold.

Under these circumstances Congress was willing to listen to the arguments of William Henry Harrison, who in 1799 became the first *Land Law of 1800* territorial delegate from the Northwest Territory; and the Harrison Land Law of 1800 made notable concessions to the western point of view. Four local land offices were established in the Northwest instead of two; tracts as small as three hundred and twenty acres were offered for sale; and credit was extended to all purchasers for a period of four years, one fourth of the purchase price to be paid down, and one fourth with interest each succeeding year. As a concession to those who wished to obtain the maximum revenue from the lands, the law provided that auctions should be held for a period of three weeks whenever a new tract was opened for sale, but after the auction was over unsold lands were to be equally open to all at the minimum price, two dollars per acre. Congress also refused to agree to the so-called "right of pre-emption," according to which the trespasser on government or Indian land claimed that he should have the first chance to purchase the land he had settled upon, but did not own. In 1804 Congress reduced the minimum unit of sale to one hundred and sixty acres, so that thereafter a man with eighty dollars in cash could make the first payment on a frontier farm.

Migration to the West was definitely stimulated by the Land Law of 1800, and the population of the Northwest Territory increased so *Admission of Ohio* rapidly that by 1802 Congress voted to admit the new state of Ohio. The "enabling act" by which this decision was made effective set two important precedents: (1) national aid to public education, and (2) national aid to road-building. The law redeemed the promise of the Ordinance of 1787 that each new state should be given one section of land out of every township in aid of education; and it provided also that five per cent of the proceeds of the sales of public lands within the state should be "applied to laying out and making public roads" in Ohio, and from Ohio to the "navigable waters emptying into the Atlantic." In return for these favors the state of Ohio agreed to leave untaxed for a period of five years all lands of the United States sold within its borders. Under a constitution that was typically western and democratic, the new state was formally admitted in 1803.[1]

When Jefferson became President the only state that still retained its western lands was Georgia. By its original charter the colony of Georgia had had the usual sea-to-sea grant, but this title was somewhat clouded by revisions in the Georgia boundaries that the British government had ordered after the Proclamation of 1763. The state of Georgia claimed, nevertheless, that its domain extended westward to the Mississippi River. The situation was further complicated by the secret agreement over the Florida boundary that the United States and Great Britain had made during the negotiations that led to the Treaty of 1783. According to this understanding, the international boundary would have been located much farther to the north than the thirty-first parallel had Great Britain retained Florida instead of ceding it to Spain. Thus the United States had a reasonable claim of its own to the lands in the disputed area.

But the state of Georgia not only refused to relinquish its claims to the United States; it also undertook in 1795 to sell over thirty million acres in the disputed area to the so-called Yazoo Land *The Yazoo* Companies. The price required was five hundred thousand *Land Companies* dollars, or approximately one and one half cents an acre. *panies* Among the stockholders in the companies were many prominent citizens, including, it developed, all but one of the members of the legislature that voted the Yazoo grants. The charge of fraud was promptly made, and the next legislature declared the Yazoo contracts null and void. In the meantime, however, many innocent purchasers had bought Yazoo stock, and they as well as the original holders were unwilling to concede that the land titles were invalid.

In 1798 Congress voted to set up a territory in the disputed region, and authorized the President to appoint three commissioners to treat

[1] Rufus King, *Ohio: First Fruits of the Ordinance of 1787* (1888); E. O. Randall and D. J. Ryan, *History of Ohio* (4 vols., 1912); R. C. Downes, *Frontier Ohio, 1788-1803* (1935).

with a like number from Georgia for a final settlement. Action was delayed until Jefferson became President, when an agreement was reached that Georgia should cede its lands to the United States on condition that the state be allowed $1,250,000 from the proceeds of the sale of the lands. Other conditions of the agreement provided that the northern and western boundaries of Georgia should be fixed as at present; that the United States should extinguish the existing Indian titles to land within the state of Georgia; that the ceded territory might be admitted as a slave state when its population reached sixty thousand; and that five million acres might be set aside to satisfy the Yazoo claimants. The agreement was duly ratified, and ultimately it went into effect.

The indemnification of the Yazoo claimants, however, was long delayed, for John Randolph of Roanoke set himself the task of blocking *John Randolph and the "Quids"* the necessary legislation in Congress.[1] In this stand he was opposed by the President, for many of the claimants were northern speculators, and Jefferson was eager to strengthen his party in the North by conciliating them. Over this and other differences with the administration Randolph led a small faction of the Republican Party into open revolt. The "Quids," as these insurgents were sometimes called, claimed that Jefferson had forgotten the states'-rights doctrines of 1798, and had in reality become a Federalist. In 1810 the Supreme Court held in the case of *Fletcher vs. Peck* that the state of Georgia had no right to invalidate its original contract with the Yazoo companies; and in 1814, with Randolph temporarily out of Congress, eight million dollars was voted for the settlement of the Yazoo claims.

Meantime the problem of the Mississippi had been unexpectedly revived. In 1800 Napoleon Bonaparte, temporarily dazzled by a scheme *Napoleon's American projects* of Talleyrand's for the revival of the French Empire in America, had required of Spain the retrocession of Louisiana. For some time the Treaty of San Ildefonso, by which this transfer of title had been arranged, was kept secret, and the Spanish officials in Louisiana were not dislodged. The reason for this delay seems to have been Napoleon's decision that the long-standing revolt against French authority in Santo Domingo must be crushed before the French occupation of Louisiana could begin. But General Leclerc, who was sent with ten thousand men to pacify Santo Domingo, found more opposition than Napoleon had counted on. The islanders fought val-

[1] Henry Adams, *John Randolph* (1882), is one of the best of the volumes in the *American Statesman* series, although quite unsympathetic toward Randolph. More recent, but no better, is G. W. Johnson, *Randolph of Roanoke, A Political Fantastic* (1929).

iantly under the leadership of the brilliant Toussaint L'Ouverture, and the yellow fever proved to be an even greater obstacle to French success. Repeatedly reinforcements had to be sent, and General Leclerc himself succumbed to the fever.

Less than a year after the Treaty of San Ildefonso was signed, Jefferson had learned of Napoleon's intentions toward Louisiana. In a letter dated April 18, 1802, he expressed his deep concern to Robert R. Livingston, the American minister to France:

> Of all nations of any consideration, France is the one which, hitherto, has offered the most points of a communion of interests. From these causes, we have ever looked to her as our natural friend, as one with which we never could have an occasion of difference. Her growth, therefore, we viewed as our own, her misfortunes ours. There is on the globe one single spot, the possessor of which is our natural and habitual enemy. It is New Orleans, through which the produce of $\frac{3}{8}$ of our territory must pass to market, and from its [the West's] fertility it will ere long yield more than one half of our whole produce, and contain more than half of our inhabitants. France, placing herself in that door, assumes to us the attitude of defiance. The day that France takes possession of New Orleans ... we must marry ourselves to the British fleet and nation.

Jefferson's worst fears seemed confirmed when he learned a few months later that the "right of deposit" at New Orleans had been suspended. The West, now also aware of the secret treaty, *Jefferson's* was immediately in a furor. Potentially the West was the *reactions* most nationalistic part of America, but western loyalty depended, as Jefferson knew full well, mainly upon the ability of the United States to serve western interests. Not many years before, the West had listened to the blandishments of Spanish agents; still more recently it had shown its sympathy for George Rogers Clark's expedition down the Mississippi; and only in 1798 a Kentucky legislature had willingly accepted Jefferson's own resolutions in defiance of the central government. Two possibilities, neither of them agreeable to a President who was by nature a pacifist, seemed open. The West might seek, with or without the aid of the central government, to dislodge the French from the mouth of the Mississippi; or it might leave the Union and join in the formation of another New France. The choice of either alternative meant war for the United States, a war in which Great Britain and the United States must be allies.

Faced by this situation, Jefferson was not slow to act. He ordered Livingston to suggest the purchase by the United States of the Isle of Orleans and West Florida, and he sent James Monroe to France as minister extraordinary, clothed with authority to offer as much as ten million dollars, if necessary, for the coveted territory.[1] Meantime Napoleon, irritated by the losses in Santo Domingo and weary of military inaction for himself, had decided to abandon expansion overseas in favor of expansion on the continent of Europe. Inevitably this meant a resumption of the war with England. Since, for the time being at least, England would have control of the seas, the French could not hope to take possession of Louisiana. Why not sell it to the United States for cash to be used in the war? Even before Monroe arrived, Talleyrand had startled Livingston by asking him what the United States would be willing to pay for the whole of Louisiana.

Once Monroe had arrived, the bargain was quickly struck. For eighty million francs, or about fifteen million dollars, the United States was to purchase the whole of Louisiana. Of this sum one fourth was to go to the payment of French debts to American citizens which had been recognized by the convention of 1800. Neither of the Floridas was included in the purchase, for the simple reason that Napoleon had not acquired title to them. The Americans secured a verbal promise, however, that France would never attempt to take over Florida from Spain. As to the boundaries of Louisiana, Napoleon agreed that they should be the same "that it now has in the hands of Spain and that it had when France possessed it." When Livingston tried to find out more definitely what this clause meant, Talleyrand refused to commit himself, saying merely, "You have made a noble bargain for yourselves, and I suppose you will make the most of it." As a matter of fact Talleyrand, in his instructions to the first French governor of Louisiana, had already defined the Louisiana boundaries as the river Iberville on the east and the Rio Grande on the west.

The purchase of Louisiana

Jefferson was greatly astonished when he learned what his ministers had done, but he had no disposition to renounce the bargain they had made. He did feel, however, that there was no constitutional authorization for any such act, and he hoped to see the Constitution so amended as to make the purchase legal. As a matter of fact, the right to acquire new territory could easily have been implied from the treaty-making power, or from the war-making power, or from the fact that the United States was a nation, just as other nations, and had a right to do what

---

[1] Besides the general histories and the biographies of Jefferson, all of which devote a generous amount of space to the Louisiana Purchase, the following special works should be consulted: Charles E. Hill, *Leading American Treaties* (1922); E. W. Lyon, *Louisiana in French Diplomacy, 1759–1804* (1934); T. L. Stoddard, *The French Revolution in San Domingo* (1914); A. P. Whitaker, *The Mississippi Question, 1795–1803* (1934); J. K. Hosmer, *The History of the Louisiana Purchase* (1902).

nations ordinarily did. But Jefferson was committed to the doctrine of strict construction, and wished to hold himself within the letter of the law. A suggestion from Livingston that Napoleon might change his mind seems to have resolved the President's doubts. He submitted the treaty to the Senate, where it was promptly ratified by a vote of 26 to 5. The sentiment in the House on the measure was shown when that body authorized the funds necessary to carry the treaty into effect by a vote of 90 to 25.

Seemingly Jefferson's conscience was not in the least troubled by what Napoleon had done. That unscrupulous ruler had sold Louisiana to the United States in direct contravention of a provision in the French constitution, and he had also violated his pledge to Spain never to sell Louisiana to a third power. The French had not so much as occupied Louisiana at the time the treaty was ratified, and the French agent of Napoleon, Laussat, handed the province over to the United States only seventeen days after he received it from the Spanish governor. In a sense the United States had acted as the receiver of stolen goods. Napoleon took Louisiana from Spain because he had the might to do it, and he sold Louisiana to the United States in order to get money for his impending war against England. Viewed from any angle it was not a pretty proceeding, but it proved to be of vast importance to the United States, whose territory was expanded by the purchase not less than one hundred and forty per cent.

The government of the new territory raised some interesting questions. Some of the Federalists, alarmed at the growing political power of the strictly agricultural sections of the country, favored *Government* keeping Louisiana in a perpetual state of dependency. This, *of Louisiana* however, was probably contrary to the treaty, which guaranteed to the inhabitants of the ceded area "the enjoyment of all the rights, advantages, and immunities of citizens of the United States"; and it was certainly out of harmony with Republican sentiments. It was decided instead to adapt the Northwest Ordinance to the Louisiana territory, and to permit the formation from its area of new western states. At the outset, however, even a limited extension of the American system of self-government seemed impossible. The French and Spanish inhabitants of Louisiana were unaccustomed to democratic institutions and were unready for them. As a temporary expedient, therefore, the President appointed all territorial officers, including the governor, secretary, judges, and thirteen members of a legislative council. French civil law was permitted to remain in force. This autocratic régime did not last long, and the process of breaking up Louisiana into territories and states was soon begun. In 1812 the state of Louisiana, with its present boundaries, was admitted to the Union.

With their appetites now whetted for expansion, the Republicans cast longing eyes on Florida.[1] Jefferson decided that the eastern bound-

Florida
ary of Louisiana was the Perdido River, a somewhat fantastic claim in which, however, Congress promptly backed him up. This boundary pushed American territory far over into West Florida, and Jefferson, both by intriguing through Talleyrand and by negotiating with Spain, tried to acquire more. Congress was induced to appropriate two million dollars for the purchase of the Floridas, but Spain, although helpless to defend her rights against either the United States or France, remained defiant, and Napoleon found no occasion to betray Spanish interests to the Americans again.

Except among the more conservative elements of the Northeast, the purchase of Louisiana aroused tremendous enthusiasm, and served to

Election of 1804
increase the good-will felt toward Jefferson's administration. Under the circumstances the result of the impending presidential election of 1804 was never in doubt. Some northeastern Federalists, rather than face the prospect of continued agricultural control of the government, were ready to break up the Union. In the Vice-President, Aaron Burr, they found a willing tool for their plots. Back in 1800, when the Federalist House was attempting to choose between Jefferson and Burr for the Presidency, Burr had seemed willing to accept the office if Congress should so decide. For this breach of loyalty Jefferson never forgave him, and as Vice-President, bereft of presidential patronage, his control over the Republican factions in New York gradually ebbed away. When a number of Federalists suggested that he become their candidate for governor of New York in 1804, he was not averse. Their plan was to elect Burr, and then under his leadership to take New York and New England out of the Union. Fortunately Hamilton learned of the plot, and by exposing it caused it to fail. Burr, now completely discredited, challenged Hamilton to a duel, and on July 11, 1804, mortally wounded him. In the election the Federalists, compelled now to defend themselves against the charge of treason, were overwhelmed. George Clinton, Burr's chief rival in New York politics, became the Republican vice-presidential candidate and helped, as Burr had done four years before, to carry that state for Jefferson. Even New England, with the exception of Connecticut, went Republican. The electoral vote stood 162 for Jefferson to 14 for C. C. Pinckney, the Federalist candidate.

[1] I. J. Cox, *The West Florida Controversy, 1798–1813* (1918).

The purchase of Louisiana insured the ultimate loyalty of the West to the Union, but there was no certainty that the purchase would bring peace. The boundaries of Louisiana were left vague, and Jefferson had promptly opened a dispute with Spain over West Florida. Already hostile Indians were using Florida as a base of operations against the American frontier, and as a haven of refuge. Many Westerners were ready, also, by force if necessary, to push the southwestern boundary of Louisiana far into Spanish territory. Moreover, the creole population of Louisiana was restive under the rule of William C. C. Claiborne, a frontier politician whom Jefferson had sent to New Orleans as governor. Actually a greater menace, however, was General James Wilkinson, in charge of American troops in Louisiana. Wilkinson was a spy and a turncoat who was at the time and had been before in the pay of Spain. How long trouble could be averted in Louisiana under such circumstances, no one knew.

The possibilities of the situation were not lost on Aaron Burr, whose career in the East seemed ruined.[1] What he really intended to do will never be known, for he told so many conflicting tales about *The Burr* his plans. His story to Merry, the English minister, was *conspiracy* that with one hundred and ten thousand pounds in British cash, and the assistance of a British fleet to take New Orleans, he would assemble a thousand men on the Ohio, float them down to the mouth of the Mississippi, get the Louisiana legislature to declare for independence, and form a new state under British control with himself at its head. He let the Spanish minister think that his purpose was merely to set up a buffer state midway between Louisiana and Mexico. He made a trip to the West and talked freely of his plans. To some he said merely that he was going out West to make a new start in politics. To others he spoke of carving a Mississippi Valley Confederacy out of the possessions of Spain, or of the United States, or both. With consummate skill he suited the degree of treason to the taste of each listener.

Burr's "conspiracy" was well received by many Westerners. The feeling that Spain might still be a menace to the West persisted, and Burr's brave words of an attack on Vera Cruz or even Mexico City won much support. Some were interested merely because of the excitement that the project promised. Wilkinson, a past master at intrigue, was easily attached to the scheme. Harmon Blennerhassett, a rich Irishman who lived in splendor on an island in the Ohio River near Parkers-

[1] The Burr conspiracy has attracted a host of writers, many of them fictionists. W. F. McCaleb, *The Aaron Burr Conspiracy* (1903), makes an able defense of Burr. Other accounts of merit are to be found in the works of McMaster, Adams, and Beveridge. See also S. H. Wandell and Meade Minnigerode, *Aaron Burr* (2 vols., 1925).

burg, West Virginia, was the most useful of Burr's converts, for on the assumption that he would one day become Burr's minister to England he allowed his island to be made the headquarters for a proposed river expedition to New Orleans, and he gave the "conspirators" money, boats, and supplies.

Whether or not Burr actually plotted treason is a question upon which historians cannot agree. Wilkinson said that he did, but Wilkinson's word was less trustworthy than Burr's. The fact that Burr's preparations were so open argues in his favor. At any rate, he collected boats at Blennerhassett's Island, and set a date, November 15, 1806, for his departure. His start was delayed, however, by an unsuccessful attempt to indict him for treason in Kentucky. Had he left at the time he originally planned, he would have found on his arrival in New Orleans that Wilkinson's troops, perhaps by prearrangement, were far to the west of the city, and that the first elective legislature of the territory had just convened. With good luck he might have started his new state. As it was, Wilkinson, for reasons best known to himself, supplied the President with the information necessary to charge Burr again with treason. Meantime the "expedition," consisting of only thirteen flat boats carrying sixty men, had started; but before he reached Natchez, Burr learned of Wilkinson's duplicity, and fled, only to be caught and sent to Richmond, Virginia, for trial.

The case was not decided strictly on its merits. Jefferson's eagerness to convict his former lieutenant gave grounds to the charge that the *Trial of Burr* defendant was being tried less for treason to his country than for treason to his party. On the other hand, Chief Justice Marshall, before whom on circuit duty the trial was set, was the bitter political foe of the President, and was ready to discredit him at every turn. In the course of the trial the Chief Justice ruled that to be guilty of treason a man must be present when the overt act is committed. Since the overt act was held to be the starting of the expedition from Blennerhassett's Island, and since Burr was not present at that time, but joined the expedition later, his acquittal followed as a matter of course.

The case is also interesting for its constitutional implications. By bringing about Burr's acquittal the Chief Justice successfully stopped all efforts on the part of the executive to use the courts as instruments of political persecution. On the other hand, when the Court summoned Jefferson to appear during the proceedings, and to bring certain papers with him, Jefferson ignored the summons. The President could not be at the command of the courts. It was a drawn battle in which each department of government stoutly and successfully maintained its independence of the other.

Jefferson's interest in Louisiana antedated many years its acquisition by the United States. As a dabbler in natural science he was deeply interested, long before he became President, in its geographic secrets, its fauna and flora, and its opportunities for trade. In January, 1803, while the news that the *The Lewis and Clark Expedition* Spanish had withdrawn the right of deposit at New Orleans was still fresh, he sent a message to Congress asking authority to send an exploring expedition into the far Northwest. At the time this authority was asked, all of the territory to be explored was outside the United States, but there is nothing to prove that Jefferson had any ulterior designs upon it. Congress granted the President's request, and in the winter of 1803–04 a small party of soldiers made ready, under the command of Meriwether Lewis, the President's private secretary, and William Clark, the brother of George Rogers Clark, to penetrate the Northwest. The expedition was commissioned to ascend the Missouri River to its source, to cross over the Continental Divide, and then to descend the Columbia to its mouth. The explorers were to make careful notes on the geography of the region, the native tribes they encountered, the animal and plant life of the West, and the evidence they found of valuable mineral deposits.

At St. Louis in the spring of 1804, Lewis received for his government the formal transfer of the upper part of Louisiana to the United States, and on May 14, with a party of forty-five, he began the ascent of the Missouri. It took six months for the expedition to reach the Mandan village where Bismarck, North Dakota, now stands. Five months more were spent in winter camp among the Mandan Indians, and another six months brought the expedition to the mouth of the Columbia, where the winter of 1805–06 was spent. Then by approximately the same route the explorers returned, arriving in St. Louis in September, 1806, after an absence of nearly two and one half years. The *Journals of Lewis and Clark*, published in many editions, record with meticulous detail the doings and discoveries of the party. They show Lewis and Clark to be resourceful leaders, but they also give great credit to Sacajawea, the Indian wife of a worthless French guide and interpreter.[1]

Lewis and Clark brought back much new information for the mapmakers, and themselves gave names to several rivers of the Northwest.

---

[1] While the sources in this instance make better reading than secondary accounts, the following books merit citation: R. G. Thwaites, *Brief History of Rocky Mountain Exploration* (1904); and O. D. Wheeler, *The Trail of Lewis and Clark, 1804–1904* (1904).

They reported also that the Indians of the regions visited were numerous and friendly. These savages, hungry and destitute, might and often did steal, but if well treated they were ordinarily peaceful. As for the future of the country, Lewis and Clark held that it was not fit for white men to live in. Traders might go there; indeed, the evidence was abundant that they had already been all over it; but white settlers, never. The expedition also gave the United States a claim by right of exploration to the region beyond the Rocky Mountains, a region which could not by any stretch of the imagination be regarded as a part of Louisiana.

In 1805 General Wilkinson sent Zebulon Montgomery Pike on a similar expedition to seek out the source of the Mississippi River. The *Pike's ex-* experiences of Pike and his party were in every essential *peditions* particular similar to those of Lewis and Clark. Pike thought that he had reached his goal, but later explorations proved that he had not. By April, 1806, he was back in St. Louis, but the following August he was off again under orders to penetrate far into the Southwest, as Lewis and Clark had penetrated into the Northwest. He reached the base of the Rocky Mountains at a point about where the city of Pueblo, Colorado, now stands, and then, with a part of his force, struck out into New Mexico. At length he was picked up by the Spanish, his papers were taken away from him and he and his men conducted back to the United States. One detachment of the men that Pike left behind when he entered Spanish territory was never heard from again, but another group, suffering every privation, descended the Arkansas River and returned to St. Louis. Pike published an account of his explorations soon after his return that rivaled in interest the *Journals of Lewis and Clark*. Over a hundred years later the documents the Spanish had taken from him were found in the Mexican archives by an American investigator, and published. Except in minor details they confirmed all that the young explorer had reported.[1]

No doubt Jefferson was responsible for the expeditions of Pike, although there is no direct evidence to prove it. Certainly his interest in the expansion of the United States struck a responsive chord in the hearts of most of his countrymen. When he left office he could at least count on the loyalty of the West, not only to the United States but also to the Republican Party.

[1] H. E. Bolton, "Papers of Z. M. Pike, 1806–1807" in the *American Historical Review*, vol. XIII, pp. 798–827.

CHAPTER XVII

THE STRUGGLE TO MAINTAIN NEUTRALITY

For all the growing interest in the West, the United States during Jefferson's administration was still bound by close commercial ties to Europe, and particularly to England. The era of American self-sufficiency had not yet arrived, and great quantities of manufactured articles still had to be imported. The United States as a producer of raw materials, particularly foodstuffs, was still heavily dependent on outside markets. During part of Jefferson's first administration, Europe was at peace, and this trade went on in normal fashion. But war between England and France was resumed in 1803, and from that time forward the two-fold task of American diplomacy was to keep the United States out of the war, and at the same time to defend her rights as a neutral.[1]

The customary difficulties with England were soon in evidence. By 1805 Napoleon's best-laid plans to secure the control of the seas had come to naught at Trafalgar, and thereafter the British *Case of the* fleets were free to tighten their control over commerce. *Essex* They now found inconvenient the decision that Sir William Scott had handed down in the case of the *Polly*, and the same judge that had issued it held in the case of the *Essex* (1805) that a French-owned West Indian cargo could not be shipped by way of the United States to Europe unless the owners could show that their original intent had been to leave the goods in the United States. This, of course, could almost never be shown; indeed, the American customs officials, to encourage the trade, had adopted the policy of granting drawbacks upon goods brought in with the obvious intent of reshipment, and in the case of the *Essex* such a drawback had been taken. Sir William's decision enabled the British to use their judgment as to what part of the West Indian trade in neutral ships to permit, and what part to restrain.

Unfortunately the commercial clauses of Jay's treaty were to expire

[1] The diplomacy of this period is best set forth in the volumes of Henry Adams, *History of the United States*, already mentioned. Other works of special value are A. T. Mahan, *Sea Power in its Relation to the War of 1812* (2 vols., 1905); and F. A. Updyke, *Diplomacy of the War of 1812* (1915).

in 1807; hence, after that date, the trade of the United States would be *Efforts to treat with England* completely at the mercy of the British squadrons. In the belief that a threat of commercial restrictions might bring the British to terms, the Republicans pushed through Congress in 1806 the so-called Nicholson Non-Importation Act, which prohibited the importation of such British goods as the United States was able to manufacture for herself, or could buy from other nations than Great Britain. Armed with this threat, William Pinkney of Maryland was sent to aid James Monroe, the regular minister from the United States to Great Britain, in obtaining a new and satisfactory trade treaty. Pinkney carried explicit instructions. The British must promise to abandon the practice of impressing sailors from American ships; they must restore West Indian trade to the favorable conditions laid down in the *Polly* decision; and they must pay an indemnity for the captures they had made under the *Essex* ruling. On other matters the envoys were free to use their own judgment. It was understood that, in case the British consented to a sufficiently favorable treaty, the Non-Importation Act would never go into effect.

The American envoys, according to well-established precedent, departed from their instructions, but they negotiated a treaty that might not have worked so badly had the British been willing to live up to the terms they had made. According to the treaty the British refused to give up the right of impressing British subjects from American ships, but they promised to take greater care in the future not to impress American seamen. They refused indemnity for captures made under the *Essex* decision, but they were willing to legalize much of the lucrative West Indian trade on condition that the goods carried must actually be American-owned, and must have paid a duty in American ports of one or two per cent. Unfortunately, before Monroe and Pinkney had affixed their signatures to the treaty they were told that the British would not consider themselves bound by it unless the United States agreed to resist the terms affecting neutral trade that were contained in Napoleon's recently issued Berlin Decree. The American envoys were foolish enough to sign anyway, but Jefferson refused under the circumstances to submit the treaty to the Senate, and recalled Monroe, who for the second time came home from a foreign mission in disgrace.

The struggle in Europe had now reached a degree of intensity in which *Napoleon's Continental System* neither side cared much what happened to neutral rights. Napoleon, hopelessly foiled in his efforts to control the high seas, had resolved to bring England to terms by other means. The English, he reasoned, were a nation of shopkeepers, whose livelihood depended upon their trade with the outside world. Europe was England's chief customer, and Napoleon could, or at least thought that he could, control most of Europe. His Continental System was devised to stop as nearly as might be all imports into European ports from England. He would rob England of her markets and by an unfavorable balance of trade drain her of her gold supply. He would also, in so far as he could accomplish it by threats or violence, prevent trade between England and her customers outside of Europe, particularly the United States.[1]

Indulging his taste for the dramatic, Napoleon issued from foreign capitals the decrees by which this policy was set forth. The Berlin Decree, November 21, 1806, laid a paper blockade about the British Isles, and forbade all trade in British merchandise. All private property of British subjects was declared good prize. Ships coming from England or from the British colonies were not to be received in any French-controlled port, and the falsification of a ship's papers in an effort to evade the decree was to result in the confiscation of the ship. A year later this drastic and unprecedented series of regulations was followed by the Milan Decree, which dealt more specifically with neutrals. All neutral ships that had permitted a British boarding party to visit them, or had paid the duty in a British port, or were bound to or from a British port, were to be confiscated. The Berlin and Milan Decrees were meant to forbid every known kind of trade between Great Britain and the rest of the nations of the world. Napoleon knew that he could not enforce his decrees fully, but he believed that he could stop much trade to the continent of Europe, and, even with the limited sea-power he possessed, he thought that he might interfere somewhat with trade between England and the neutral nations.

The English replied to Napoleon's decrees with a series of Orders in Council that were quite as careless of neutral rights as the decrees themselves. The first, dated January 7, 1807, forbade trade *British* from one port to another, "both which ports shall belong to *Orders in* or be in the possession of France or her allies." Neutral *Council* ships were to be warned of this order, and if they violated it were to be seized. A second Order in Council, dated November 11, 1807, established a blockade of "all the ports and places of France and her allies, or of any country at war with His Majesty." This meant that neutral trade with Europe, from Trieste to Copenhagen, was forbidden; although

[1] F. E. Melvin, *Napoleon's Navigation System* (1919); F. L. Nussbaum, *Commercial Policy in the French Revolution* (1923); W. F. Galpin, *The Grain Supply of England During the Napoleonic Period* (1925).

the English navy, strong as it was, obviously was unequal to the task. The blockade, therefore, was, like Napoleon's, a "paper" blockade. The British hoped by these orders to hamper the movement of foodstuffs to Europe to such an extent that Napoleon would withdraw his decrees.

The plight of American shipping was now a sorry one, indeed. Ships destined to France or to any of the nations controlled by France, which then meant most of Europe, were subject to seizure by the English. Ships sailing to any English port were subject to seizure by the French. The only trade with Europe left fully open to American ships was with Russia, Sweden, and Turkey; and for a time Napoleon even won the cooperation of the Czar. Nor did the British Orders in Council serve to deter Napoleon from his purpose. He was never able to prevent all trade between England and the Continent, and he had frequently even to license it himself, but the rest of his career was a sustained effort to make the Continental System work. To put down opposition to it he engaged in his costly expedition into Spain; to win back support for it from the apostate Czar he undertook the disastrous invasion of Russia.

Both the French and the British enforced their illegal blockades by captures on the American side of the Atlantic, where privateers and warships took what prizes they could. The French naturally took fewer, for their ships were less numerous and were themselves in danger of capture by the British. Admiralty courts in the West Indies, both French and British, decided against the captured American ship. British impressments of sailors from American ships occurred more and more frequently, and were sometimes carried out with unbecoming brutality. American resentment against this practice, particularly among the people along the coast whose friends and relatives had been victimized, grew steadily more intense.

The supreme outrage occurred in June, 1807, when a British man-of-war, the *Leopard*, attacked an American frigate, the *Chesapeake*, and *The Chesa-* took off four members of her crew.[1] This untoward in-*peake affair* cident followed shortly after the escape of a boatload of sailors from the sloop *Halifax*, which, together with several other British warships, had put in at Lynnhaven Bay, near the mouth of the Chesapeake. The commander of the British squadron had noted that an American warship, the *Chesapeake* was preparing to leave the harbor for a cruise in the Mediterranean, and he hastily concluded that the deserting British sailors must be upon it. Accordingly, while signifying at the

[1] R. D. Paine, *The Fight for a Free Sea* (1920); J. F. Zimmerman, *Impressment of American Seamen* (1925).

same time his willingness to grant a similar privilege to American captains in pursuit of deserters, he gave orders that the *Chesapeake* should be searched. Inasmuch as American sailors were not then deserting to the lower pay and stricter discipline of the British service, this offer was a mere gesture.

When the *Chesapeake* finally put out to sea, she was followed by the *Leopard*, which, on the pretense that she had dispatches to deliver, asked and received permission to send a boarding party to the *Chesapeake*. But the purported dispatches consisted merely of the British commander's order for the search of the *Chesapeake*, and a note from the captain of the *Leopard* demanding that he be accorded that privilege. On the approach of the *Leopard*, Captain Barron of the *Chesapeake* had failed to take the normal precaution of preparing his ship for action, but he refused nevertheless to permit the search. Thereupon the *Leopard* opened fire, and the unready *Chesapeake*, after firing one gun, hauled down her colors. For his carelessness Captain Barron was later court-martialed, and sentenced to five years suspension from the service without pay. Three Americans were killed during the fray, and eighteen wounded. The British then boarded the *Chesapeake* and took off four deserters, only one of whom, it transpired, was an Englishman. The others were Americans who had previously suffered impressment into the British service, and had then deserted. With their object accomplished, the British permitted the *Chesapeake* to put back to port.

The news of this outrage caused the most profound excitement throughout the United States. British depredations against American merchantmen had long been common, but in this instance it *Popular* was an American national ship that had been attacked. *reaction* The colossal effrontery of the British commander, who in spite of the incident did not hesitate to return to an American port, was even more galling. The country was in such a belligerent mood as the sinking of the *Maine* and the *Lusitania* aroused in later years, and had Jefferson wanted war undoubtedly he could have had it. But the President chose to keep the peace if he could. By proclamation he forbade British warships to take on supplies in American ports, and ordered them out of American waters. He also demanded reparations from the British government, including adequate punishment for the offending British commander; and he set a date, somewhat distant, to be sure, for a special session of Congress.

When Congress convened, Jefferson proposed an embargo on all commerce with the outside world as the most effective means of defending American rights. He genuinely believed that the warring nations of

Europe, rather than suffer long the loss of American trade, would with-
The Em- draw their obnoxious regulations. Naturally the commercial
bargo Act interests of the country were extremely skeptical of such a
policy, but resentment over the *Leopard-Chesapeake* affair was still
strong, and the President had his way. An Embargo Act, passed December 21, 1807, prohibited all ships, except foreign ships in ballast, to
depart from the United States for any foreign port. Ships engaged in
the coasting trade were required to give heavy bond that they would land
their cargoes in the United States.[1]

Time proved that Jefferson had greatly overestimated the results that
the embargo could obtain. The American flag did not disappear, as he
had hoped, from the high seas. Many of the American ships that were
at sea when the law went into effect kept out of American ports, and
plied between foreign ports. Moreover, in spite of repeated enforcement
acts, it was impossible to prevent ships from leaving port in defiance of
the law; and sometimes they were aided by the very officials that were
charged with its enforcement.

Nevertheless, the law was sufficiently effective to disrupt completely
the economic life of the country. Shipowners and importers took heavy
losses, while thousands of sailors, shipbuilders, sailmakers, and other
artisans were thrown out of employment. Commodities that the
United States had long been accustomed to import from abroad were
lacking, and the inferior substitutes that American manufacturers began
to produce cost high prices. Even agriculture soon began to feel the
effects of the embargo, for the crops of 1808 found the gateways to
market closed, and farm prices dropped precipitately. Under such circumstances the law became increasingly unpopular, and the Federalists,
who opposed it, gained ground.

The election of 1808 showed the changing temper of the country.
Jefferson was importuned to stand for re-election again, but he declined
Election with such emphasis as to set a precedent that has not been
of 1808 broken since. He did not hesitate, however, to throw the
"succession" to his Secretary of State, James Madison. The Federalists
supported C. C. Pinckney, and by emphasizing the unpleasant features
of the embargo, they won back many voters who had deserted them for
Jefferson four years before. In the electoral college Madison received
122 electoral votes to 47 for Pinckney. Six electors cast their ballots for
George Clinton, the Vice-President, whose claims to the succession
Jefferson had overlooked. Congress remained Republican, although by
a much-reduced majority. It is significant that New England, with the

[1] L. M. Sears, *Jefferson and the Embargo* (1927).

exception of Vermont, now returned to the Federalist fold, although this was the time that John Quincy Adams, senator from Massachusetts and son of the second President, chose to leave the Federalists and become a Republican.

The results of the election made it abundantly apparent that the Republicans must repeal their embargo or witness an even more embarrassing revival of Federalist strength. The endurance of the country was at an end. Probably the United States had not suffered much more from the embargo than Great Britain, *Repeal of the Embargo Act* where sales to the United States had dropped off one half, and manufacturers, already heavily handicapped by Napoleon's decrees, had suffered acutely from the loss of American customers. But the British had shown great energy in opening up new trade with Latin-American countries, and in picking up the carrying trade that formerly had gone in American ships. The British public, moreover, was inured to the sufferings of war; the embargo was merely one unpleasant thing among many. When two nations resort to commercial retaliations, the one that can stand the most punishment wins. England was distressed by the embargo, but she was willing to put up with it as a necessary accompaniment of her war against Napoleon. The United States was also distressed by the embargo, and having no great urge to continue this self-inflicted punishment, she repealed it. After the election, Jefferson left the determination of future policy to his successor, and with Madison's approval Jefferson signed a bill a few days before he left office bringing the embargo to an end. It was with some humiliation that he was thus compelled to confess his favorite project a failure.

James Madison (1751–1836),[1] the fourth President, was another representative of the Virginia planter class, although from his youth he was more the politician than the planter. Only a few years out of Princeton and still undecided as to his life work, the out- *James Madison* break of the American Revolution determined his course for him. Successively he served as a member of the local committee on public safety, of the convention that drew up the first Virginia constitution, of the Continental Congress, of the Virginia House of Delegates, of the Convention that framed the Constitution of the United States, and of the national House of Representatives. For eight years he was Jefferson's Secretary of State and close adviser. Certainly his political apprenticeship had been ample.

Unlike Washington and Jefferson, who possessed powerful physiques, Madison was small and of delicate health. He was a better scholar along

[1] S. H. Gay, *James Madison* (1884); Gaillard Hunt, *The Life of Madison* (1902).

some lines, particularly constitutional history, than Jefferson, but he was not so many-sided. In spite of his long political career, he had had less administrative experience than any of the Presidents who had preceded him, and he was less able than they to recognize and withstand the pressure of designing politicians. As Secretary of State, he had of necessity been dominated by the views and personality of Jefferson, and as President he had some difficulty in shaping a course of his own. His wife, "Dolly" Madison, a woman of great personal charm, brought needed grace and beauty to White House society.

For a time Madison had toyed with the idea of continuing the embargo for a few months longer, and then following it up with war; but the opposition to such a course was strong, and a far less dramatic *The Non-* policy was adopted. In the place of the embargo a Non-*Intercourse* Intercourse Act was substituted which closed American *Act* ports to the ships of England and France and forbade the importation of goods into the United States from either of those nations, or their colonies or dependencies. American ships were permitted to leave American ports, provided only that their destinations were not French or British. The act also carried with it an offer to the offending belligerents. In case England would withdraw her Orders in Council, the President was authorized to suspend non-intercourse with England; and in case Napoleon would withdraw his decrees, to suspend non-intercourse with France.

Meantime the British government had been making some half-hearted efforts to restore good relations with the United States. Shortly after *Rose's* the *Chesapeake* outrage, the British admiral who had author-*mission* ized the action was recalled from his command, and a special envoy, George Rose, was sent to Washington to arrange a settlement satisfactory to the United States. But the British showed no disposition to abate their policy of impressments from American merchant ships, and Rose's instructions demanded that Jefferson's order forbidding British warships the use of American ports be withdrawn. Rose also refused to return the seamen that the *Leopard* had impressed unless the United States would agree to condemn Captain Barron for encouraging desertions — something Barron had been very careful not to do. Diplomatically considered, the net result of Rose's mission was exactly nothing at all. He returned to England, however, with the impression that the Republican policy of commercial coercion was extremely unpopular in New England, and he even believed that under sufficient pressure that section of the United States might be brought back into the British Empire.

JAMES MADISON

The adoption of the Non-Intercourse Act led to another friendly gesture on the part of Great Britain. Canning, the British foreign minister, was at least willing to consider the withdrawal of the British Orders in Council in return for the opening of American trade and some other favors. Accordingly he instructed Erskine, the British minister to the United States, to prepare the way for a treaty that would settle all outstanding differences between the two countries. Erskine's sympathies, unfortunately as it turned out, were too whole-heartedly with the United States. He was a Whig, and as such he disapproved of the truculent attitude his government had taken in its handling of American affairs; and he was married to the daughter of a distinguished veteran of the American Revolution, General John Cadwalader of Philadelphia. Moreover, Erskine was a young man, comparatively new to the diplomatic service, while his antagonist, James Madison, had age and experience to guide him.

Erskine's instructions were explicit. He was told that the British government was ready to disavow the act of the *Leopard* and to offer *Erskine's* redress in case the United States would agree to the equal *"treaty"* treatment of French and British warships in American ports, and to the exclusion of foreign seamen from American ships. Also, the British Orders in Council might be withdrawn if the United States (1) would reopen trade with Great Britain while keeping up non-intercourse with France, (2) would agree to abide by the rule of 1756, and (3) would acknowledge the right of British ships to seize American merchant-vessels found to be disobeying the law forbidding intercourse with France. These instructions, literally interpreted, really precluded all possibility of settlement, but Erskine chose to believe that they indicated a great desire on the part of the British government to restore good relations with the United States, and interpreted them most liberally.

In this frame of mind he quickly reached an agreement with Madison. With regard to the *Chesapeake* affair the United States consented to withdraw its request for the punishment of the British admiral responsible, while the British promised full redress for the damage done. Restrictions on trade between the United States and Great Britain were to be mutually withdrawn, although trade between France and the United States was to remain closed only as long as Napoleon continued to enforce his decrees. Erskine failed also to secure acceptance by the United States of the rule of 1756, and he got no acknowledgment that British vessels might be permitted to enforce the American law against trade with France. It was little short of amazing, therefore, that he assumed the authority to declare, June 10, 1809, that the Orders in

Council would be withdrawn in so far as they applied to the United States. Nor did Madison show much foresight when he issued a proclamation restoring intercourse with Great Britain, and permitting American ships to sail for British ports.

As might have been expected, Canning repudiated the Erskine agreement at sight, and recalled Erskine for having violated his instructions. American ships that had left port were allowed to proceed unmolested to their destinations, but the Orders in Council were continued in force, and Madison had no choice but to issue a proclamation restoring non-intercourse with Great Britain. To make matters worse, Canning sent over in Erskine's place the notoriously ill-tempered Francis James Jackson, with the promise that he might stay in America for a full year. Jackson's behavior was so offensive that, after a few exchanges, Madison announced that no further communications from him would be received. When his year was up he was recalled.

Non-intercourse left the way open for a revival of American commerce. Doubtless some new avenues of trade were opened up, as the law intended, but the old connections were restored to a great extent in spite of the law. It was impossible to tell, *Macon's Bill Number 2* once a ship cleared from an American port, what her destination would be, and many ships, in defiance of all regulations, departed directly for England or France. Even Napoleon winked at his own prohibitions, and issued licenses for trade that his decrees pointedly forbade. Within a year after the adoption of non-intercourse the Republicans were willing to admit that this policy was as great a failure as the embargo. They would not concede, however, that the principle of commercial coercion was wrong, and they tried once more to apply it. Nathaniel Macon of North Carolina, chairman of the House Committee on Foreign Affairs, now reported out a bill that provided for the importation of French and British goods in American bottoms only. This measure had Madison's support and passed the House, but the Federalists, aided by a disgruntled minority of the Republicans, defeated it in the Senate. Whereupon Macon's committee presented a new bill that Macon himself disliked, but that was always known as Macon's Bill Number 2. It repealed the Non-Intercourse Act outright, and tried to bargain with the contending European powers for their favor. If England would repeal her obnoxious Orders in Council the United States would revive non-intercourse with France; if France would withdraw her offensive decrees, the United States would revive non-intercourse with England. On May 1, 1810, this bill became a law.

The embargo had fitted in well with Napoleon's policy of crippling

British trade, although he took advantage of it to issue his famous *New Napoleonic decrees* Bayonne Decree, April 17, 1808, which ordered the seizure of all American ships found in French ports. Such ships, Napoleon argued trickily, could not be truly American, for the embargo forbade American ships to leave American ports. Non-intercourse, however, was far less satisfactory to the Emperor than the embargo, for it opened the way to a far greater amount of illicit trade between the United States and Great Britain; besides, it ordered the confiscation of French ships found in American ports. Somewhat in the spirit of retaliation, and with an eye to the profits, Napoleon now issued the Rambouillet Decree, March 23, 1810, which ordered the seizure and sale of all American shipping that had entered French ports since the date set for the Non-Intercourse Act to go into effect. Napoleon knew full well that, after Canning's repudiation of the Erskine agreement, the United States could not be irritated into friendship with England, and he hoped for a restoration of the embargo.

When, instead, the American policy of commercial coercion was practically abandoned by the passage of Macon's Bill Number 2, *The Cadore letter* Napoleon had to change his tactics. He proposed to take advantage of the offer that the United States would resume non-intercourse with England in case France withdrew her decrees. Accordingly, his foreign minister, the Duke of Cadore, wrote a letter to General Armstrong, the American minister to France, which stated that the Berlin and Milan Decrees were revoked to take effect November 1, 1810, "it being understood that, in consequence of this declaration, the English shall revoke their Orders in Council ...; or that the United States, conformably to the act you have just communicated, shall cause their rights to be respected by the English." Madison should have paid more attention to these conditional clauses than he did. The law authorized him to restore non-intercourse with England if France withdrew her decrees, but it said nothing about the United States causing "their rights to be respected by the English." But the President, perhaps beguiled by honeyed phrases — "His Majesty loves the Americans," the Cadore letter had said, "their prosperity and their commerce are within the scope of his policy" — or more likely in sheer desperation, accepted Napoleon's repeal as valid, and reinstituted non-intercourse with England. Thereupon Napoleon, having accomplished his purpose, laid down new regulations against American shipping in French ports that were quite as distressing as the decrees he had repealed.

The relations between the United States and Great Britain went steadily from bad to worse. The English were not deceived by Napoleon's pretense that he had repealed his decrees, and William Pinkney, the American minister to England, could get no pledge that *Relations* the British Orders in Council would be withdrawn. More- *with* over, since Jackson's return to England, the British *England* government had sent no one to take his place. On this latter ground Pinkney, acting under instructions from his government, left England in 1811. Thus the two nations had reached a diplomatic *impasse*. Nevertheless, the British, feeling keenly the need of American goods and desirous of using their entire energy against Napoleon rather than against irrelevant neutrals, were now ready to adopt a more favorable attitude toward the United States. A new minister, Augustus J. Foster, hastened across the Atlantic to settle the *Chesapeake* affair, and to pave the way for more amicable relations.

By the time Foster arrived, the people of the United States had tasted battle and had found that they liked it. Because a British frigate, the *Guerrière*, operating off Sandy Hook, had repeatedly im- *The President* pressed American sailors, an American frigate, the *President*, *dent and the* was ordered to the vicinity to protect American commerce. *Little Belt* Some ten days later the *President* sighted a British man-of-war, and, thinking it was the *Guerrière*, determined to inquire about the impressed seamen   The British ship fled, however, and it was sundown before she was overtaken and hailed. Then a shot from the Britisher started a battle which lasted fifteen minutes and ended in a complete victory for the *President*. To his chagrin, the American captain found that he had beaten the *Little Belt*, a ship half the size of his own, instead of the *Guerrière*. But the country was not so particular, and the people rejoiced immoderately that the *Chesapeake* insult had at last been avenged. Foster, the British minister, found the American government likewise unconcerned about the *Chesapeake*. What the government demanded was the immediate withdrawal of the Orders in Council, and on that subject Foster had no authority to treat.

The British government was slow to realize the changed temper of the United States, and Foster, in closer touch with the Federalists than with the Republicans, was for a time no great help. Again and *Drifting* again the British refused to withdraw their Orders in *into war* Council unless assured that France had genuinely repealed her decrees, not for the United States alone, but for all nations. But at last the evidence began to compound that stubborn refusal to repeal the orders would mean an American war. For this the British, engaged in a life-and-death struggle with Napoleon, had no stomach. Moreover, British manufacturers had suffered about all they could stand from the loss of

American markets, and the British people stood in desperate need of American food. On June 16, Castlereagh, speaking for the British ministry, announced in the House of Commons that the Orders in Council had been withdrawn. Actually the American policy of commercial coercion, plus a little show of fight, had won; for when Castlereagh made this announcement he did not know that at the very moment the American government was pushing a declaration of war through Congress. On June 1, 1812, Madison sent in his war message; on June 4, the House by a vote of 79 to 49 declared for war; and on June 18, just two days after Castlereagh's announcement, the Senate, by a vote of 19 to 3, concurred.

But to understand fully the change in American sentiment that made war possible it is essential to take note of a series of developments in the American West.

CHAPTER XVIII

THE WAR OF 1812

For a long time after the Treaty of Fort Greenville was signed, the northwestern Indians fell back helplessly before the advance of the white frontier. By the year 1809 they had agreed to as *The frontier* many as nine separate treaties of cession, and, in addition *advance* to the territory of Indiana, which Congress had created in 1800, two other new territories, Michigan (1805) and Illinois (1809), had been marked out as goals for the ambition of restless pioneers. In the Southwest the Indians, also duly chastened, watched with apprehension but with little show of opposition the encircling of their lands by settlers on the Yazoo tracts and in the valley of the lower Mississippi. Whether to the north or to the south the natives were keenly aware of the disastrous consequences of the white pressure upon them. The Indian economy was hunting and trapping supplemented by agriculture; the white man's economy was agriculture supplemented by hunting and trapping. The two modes of life were hopelessly incompatible. The whites settled thickly, cut down the forests, destroyed the game, and made existence difficult for the adjacent Indians; and the Indians, debauched and depraved by contact with the white man's vices, degenerated into a perpetual nuisance to the frontiersmen. The power of the whites was great, and for a long time Indian resistance seemed out of the question.[1]

On only a few occasions has Indian leadership approached the level of statesmanship, and the eve of the War of 1812 was one such occasion. During these years the outstanding Indian chieftain was *Tecumseh* Tecumseh, in whose person, according to tradition, the blood of northern and southern tribes was united, for his father, this tradition held, was a Shawnee and his mother was a Creek. Whatever his ancestry, Tecumseh had not only the Indian's natural dignity

[1] The steady advance of the whites into the Northwest is admirably set forth by B. W. Bond, Jr., *The Civilization of the Old Northwest, 1788–1812* (1934). See also M. M. Quaife, *Chicago and the Old Northwest, 1673–1835* (1913).

and persuasive eloquence, but he had also a keen understanding of human nature, whether of red men or of whites, and unlike most Indians he could devise and execute far-flung plans. Tecumseh understood clearly the difficulties that confronted the Indians in their dealings with the whites, but he saw also that much of the strength of the whites lay in their unity, and he therefore preached the same doctrine among the Indians. Tribe by tribe they might never hope to stem the advance of the white frontier, but united into a great Indian confederacy, embracing possibly all the tribes of both North and South, their chances would be immeasurably improved. All Indian land, he argued, should be under the joint control of all the tribes; and only by the consent of a warrior's congress might it be alienated.) For Tecumseh challenged also the Indian tradition of following the lead of the old chiefs. The warriors were the men who must carry out the orders of the councils; let the warriors themselves decide.

Tecumseh did not wish for war against the whites, although he hated them, but he did hope to unite the Indians into a confederacy so strong that the cessions of land could be stopped. In 1808 he joined with his brother, a medicine man generally spoken of as the "Prophet," to found near the mouth of Tippecanoe Creek on the banks of the Wabash a headquarters soon known as "Prophet's Town." To and from this center came many young warriors whose great hope was the realization of Tecumseh's dream. Gradually Indian resistance stiffened, and when, in 1809, William Henry Harrison, the governor of Indiana Territory, exacted a cession of several million acres of land in the lower Wabash Valley, it was evident that a crisis was at hand. Tecumseh frankly repudiated this cession, but he was eager to avert war, and for some time he was able to restrain his followers.[1]

The "Prophet"

For two years the northwestern frontier lived under the shadow of impending war. In 1810 Tecumseh, with four hundred armed warriors to defend him, visited Harrison at Vincennes, the capital of Indiana, to deliver the Indian ultimatum. In a dramatic speech the Indian chief proclaimed that his people were "once a happy race, but now made miserable by the white people, who are never contented, but always encroaching. They have driven us from the great salt water, forced us over the mountains, and would shortly push us into the lakes — but we are determined to go no further."

The next year Tecumseh made a visit to the South to secure greater

[1] D. B. Goebel, *William Henry Harrison* (1926), contains a good analysis of the situation that produced the clash at Tippecanoe.

support from the tribes of that section for his program. He had notified Harrison of his departure, and had asked that all matters be left as they were pending his return. Harrison made no pledges, however, and as soon as Tecumseh was well out of the way set out with a strong force for Prophet's Town with the avowed intention of destroying it. His march met no resistance, and he was in sight of his goal when an Indian delegation appeared and asked for a parley. Harrison should have been wise enough to push on at once for the attack, but he agreed to a council set for the next day, and encamped his command on a knoll about a mile from the Indian village.

A careful sentry was set, and about four o'clock the next morning (November 7, 1811) the inevitable Indian attack was disclosed. The whites, who had slept on their arms, fought as well as they could in the darkness, and when day broke beat *Tippecanoe* off the Indians, but Harrison had lost sixty-one killed and one hundred and twenty-seven seriously injured, while the enemy losses had been slight. The battle of Tippecanoe was hailed, nevertheless, as a great victory for the whites. The Indians did not return to the attack, and Prophet's Town, which they had abandoned, was duly destroyed. With much difficulty because of his many wounded, Harrison returned to Vincennes, only to learn a few weeks later that Tecumseh, back from the South with the news that he had won much support in that region, had rebuilt Prophet's Town and revived the drooping spirits of his followers. The great Indian chieftain still counseled peace, but after Tippecanoe Indian depredations along the northwestern frontier occurred with ever-increasing frequency. An Indian war had in truth begun.

When Harrison reported the battle of Tippecanoe he complained bitterly that the Indians were well supplied with powder and guns obtained from the British in Canada. Possibly these supplies did not come from the King's stores as Harrison thought, but the fact that Tecumseh was in close touch with the British authorities was a matter of common knowledge. Almost the same situation existed in the Northwest that had confronted Washington when he entered the Presidency. To be sure, the British had removed their military posts to the Canadian side of the boundary, but these posts still existed, and their garrisons were as much concerned as ever with the protection of the fur trade south of the Great Lakes. Tecumseh's plan for organized Indian resistance to the advance of the farmer's frontier fitted in well with Canadian needs. Should the Indians make good their efforts, the northward flow of pelts from the unsettled western lands of the United States might still continue. To the Westerner it appeared that the Canadian fur-trader and the Indian, with identical interests, were merely preparing once more to join forces for the protection of those interests.

It was only natural under these circumstances that the people of the West should applaud vigorously each step taken by the national *Western clamor for war* government in the direction of war with England. They knew, certainly as early as 1811, that a war with the Indians was sure to come, and they believed implicitly that to make war against the Indians without fighting an accompanying war against the allies of the Indians in Canada was to leave the task half-done. Strong in their devotion to the doctrine of the rights of men, the Westerners resented undoubtedly such violations of this principle as the impressment of American sailors by the British, but there is room to question whether western resentment against these outrages would have been so great had there not been other and more local grievances against the British. The congenital appetite of the West for expansion was also easily whetted. If war with the British was to come, why not make it a war for the conquest and annexation of Canada? Upper Canada was as logically athwart the path of the American westward movement as the Michigan peninsula, and the need of the West for more lands was perpetual. With the English held at bay in Europe by Napoleon, what was more reasonable than that the United States should seize the opportunity to eliminate the British from North America and thus end for all time the menace of the English-Indian alliance? [1]

In the Southwest there was less certainty of immediate war than in the Northwest, but the preaching of Tecumseh had aroused the *The southwestern frontier* latent forebodings of the southern tribes and had bolstered up their will to resist. In this region, despite the cession of Louisiana to the United States, the Spanish were still the traditional enemies of the Americans and the natural allies of the Indians, for Florida remained in Spanish hands, and the boundary dispute was still alive. As the southwestern frontier expanded, its residents saw with increasing clarity the necessity of ousting the Spanish from the adjacent seacoast. Through the Florida panhandle ran many of the rivers by which the produce of the new Southwest could most easily find access to the sea. Along the coast of Florida were nests of dangerous pirates that the now enfeebled

---

[1] J. W. Pratt, *Expansionists of 1812* (1925), presents with great effectiveness the reasons why the West and the South desired war with Great Britain.

rule of Spain was powerless to destroy. Hostile Indians took refuge within the borders of Florida, and mingled with the runaway Negroes and renegade whites to produce bands of ruffians as unsavory as were to be found anywhere on the American continent. In 1810 Madison, carrying out Jefferson's policy of acquiring West Florida, ordered the governor of Louisiana to extend his territory peacefully over that portion of the Spanish province adjacent to the Mississippi River, but the southern expansionists wanted more. They were ready, if it were necessary, to fight another Indian war; they saw in a war against England the prospect of the greatly-to-be-desired war against Spain, now the ally of England; and they were willing to help the Northwest acquire Canada on the assumption that the Northwest in return would help the Southwest acquire Florida.

Thus from the interior, whether to the north or to the south, every strongly anti-British stand of the administration in Washington was received with unbounded enthusiasm, while every sign *The "War* of weakening was unsparingly denounced. In the elec- *Hawks"* tions of 1810 and 1811 the weak-kneed policy embodied in Macon's Bill Number 2 received a thoroughgoing rebuke. Nearly half the congressmen who had voted for that measure were left at home, and a new generation of politicians seized the reins of power. Among them were John Sevier and Felix Grundy from Tennessee, John C. Calhoun from the back country of South Carolina, and young Henry Clay from Kentucky, whom the newcomers banded together to make Speaker of the House. These young patriots and their followers were eager for war, and quickly won for themselves, from the erratic John Randolph of Roanoke, the designation, "War Hawks." They defended more stoutly than any Easterner the rights of American sailors and American commerce on the high seas; they denounced in unmeasured terms the assistance that the British in Canada were giving to marauding bands of Indians on the frontier; and they pointed out as the chief prize to be won from the war the easy acquisition of Canada. "I am not for stopping at Quebec," said Clay, "but I would take the whole continent." In vain were the efforts of conservatives who sought to restrain the clamor for war, and in vain also were the continued tongue-lashings of Randolph who denounced the "agrarian cupidity" of the War Hawks, and taunted them for the "whip-poor-will" monotony of their battle-cry, "Canada! Canada! Canada!" Even Madison himself, alive to the meaning of the recent elections, capitulated to the War Hawks.

Nevertheless, the vote for war that the administration obtained from Congress in 1812 was far from unanimous. The commercial

The vote for war

interests of the Northeast were desperately opposed to the measure, and their sentiments were reflected by a majority of the congressmen from that section. Nor were the opponents of the war all Federalists, for a large section of the Republican Party either voted against the declaration or refused to vote at all. Many thoughtful citizens of both parties felt especially humiliated to see the United States throw in its lot with the hypocritical Napoleon, whose fair words only faintly disguised quite as ruthless mistreatment of American commerce as ever the British had inflicted. Moreover, the ambition of Napoleon turned increasingly toward an ever-expanding military despotism, whereas England and her allies were fighting not only to preserve separate national independence, but also to maintain what little Europe then knew of constitutional government. There was actually as good reason for a declaration of war by the United States against France as against England, and so far as neutral rights were concerned, such a policy might have proved ideal. The English government, in belated negotiations conducted after the declaration of war, did definitely block the way to peace by refusing to give up the right of impressment, but it seems reasonable to suppose that even this knotty problem might have been solved as the price of American aid against France. With English assistance the United States might have fought against Napoleon a really successful war on behalf of neutral rights. But the frontier, ably seconded by the South, was far less interested in a war to avenge wrongdoing on the high seas than in a war against England to ensure a settlement of the Indian problem and the conquest of Canada. From the four frontier states, Vermont, Ohio, Kentucky, and Tennessee, every vote but one was cast for war. Most of the rest of the majority came from the South.[1]

In spite of its name, the "War of 1812" was barely begun in the year 1812, and the news that the British were willing to repeal their

Should the war be fought

decrees would have presented a valid excuse for withdrawing the declaration, had the country so desired. With the British Orders in Council repealed, the only technicality that lay in the way of peace was the British refusal to abandon impressments. Americans who had opposed the War Hawks while the country was at peace now turned their attention to the task

---

[1] K. C. Babcock, *The Rise of American Nationality* (1906), covers adequately the period of the War of 1812. For the Canadian point of view see William Wood, *War with the United States* (1915).

of preventing the war that had been declared from being fought. The presidential election of 1812 was made to hinge on this issue. Since Madison, now completely committed to the program of the War Hawks, sought re-election with the avowed intention of seeing the war through, peace men among the Republicans advanced as an opposing candidate DeWitt Clinton of New York, whom the Federalists were also induced to support. The issue was clean-cut: a vote for Madison meant a vote for war, and a vote for Clinton meant a vote for peace.

The results of the election made further manifest the responsibility of the West for the war. New England, with the exception of Vermont, cast 43 electoral votes for Clinton and peace, while the *The election* middle states (including Maryland and Delaware) pre- *of 1812* ferred Clinton over Madison by a vote of 46 to 31. The South voted solidly, 59 to 0, for Madison and war. Thus the seaboard states — the original thirteen — were as nearly equally divided as possible, with a vote of 90 for Madison to 89 for Clinton, certainly too narrow a margin upon which to wage a war. But the five states that had been admitted to the Union by act of Congress — Vermont, Kentucky, Tennessee, Ohio, and Louisiana (admitted in 1812) — broke the balance by casting their entire vote for Madison, who was thus elected, 128 to 89. It was another victory of the West, aided by the dominantly agricultural South, over the commercial Northeast.

Most of the War Hawks had little or no understanding of the serious financial problems that the fighting of a war entailed, and they actually allowed the Congress that had declared the war *End of* to adjourn without voting the war taxes for which Galla- *the Bank of* tin, still Secretary of the Treasury, had asked. They *the United* refused also to take cognizance of the crippled state of *States* the nation's banking and currency system. Hamilton's Bank of the United States had been chartered for twenty years in 1791, and had therefore to be rechartered in 1811 or allowed to die. Opposed alike by states'-rights Jeffersonians of the old school and by Westerners who preferred the easier credit facilities that state banks were sure to offer, the Bank of the United States was eliminated at the very moment that the nation needed more than ever before the stable currency and the machinery for floating loans that it alone could provide.

Moreover, the taxation system of the country was already in bad repair, and Gallatin had predicted a deficit for the year 1812, even without the abnormal expenditures of war. Nearly all *Taxation* of the revenue upon which the national government depended for its support came from the tariff, and receipts from this quarter had been seriously impaired by the unstable state of commerce during the preceding months and years. Congress voted to double the tariff rates, and enough importations continued in spite of the war to make this measure a fairly fruitful source of revenue. Internal taxes were at first indignantly spurned as "unrepublican," and Gallatin was heartily denounced for recommending them; but before the war was over both an excise tax and a stamp duty had been laid. Inasmuch as a completely new system for the collection of these taxes had to be worked out, the war was nearly over before they began to yield an appreciable revenue. In 1813 Congress also tried to levy a direct tax upon the states in spite of the fact that a similar effort, made during the war scare of 1798, had brought highly unsatisfactory results. Since no power existed on the part of the nation to coerce the states, payments of such a tax were made, or were not made, quite as each state saw fit.

From all tax sources together not more than one third enough income was realized to pay the expenses of the war, and the remaining *War loans* expenditures had to be met by loans. This proved to be an exceedingly difficult matter, for the moneyed classes of the country, with a few exceptions, did not favor the war. Gallatin succeeded in raising about one hundred thousand dollars from loans, but in order to attract investors he was compelled to sell government securities at a serious discount, and to pay interest rates sometimes as high as seven and one half per cent. New England capital practically refused to support the war; altogether only three million dollars' worth of war bonds were sold in that section. By the end of the war the government was virtually bankrupt.

From the angle of military preparedness the United States was likewise little justified in assuming the burdens of war. The regular *Lack of pre-* army consisted of not more than seven thousand men, *paredness* all of whom were needed for garrison duty. An increase in this number was ordered, but in spite of such inducements as better pay and land bounties, recruits were hard to obtain. For the most part the administration had to rely upon state militia to do the fighting. Presumably there were about seven hundred thousand enrolled militia, and a nation of nearly eight million people should surely have found little difficulty in putting an army of two or three hundred thousand men in the field. But the requisitions on the states for troops were half-heartedly filled, and sometimes flatly refused. At no time during the war did the government have in actual service more than thirty or thirty-five thousand men; and on occasion whole

Culver Service

"THE NATION'S BULWARK A WELL-DISCIPLINED MILITIA"
From an old cartoon.

detachments of the militia refused to fight outside the boundaries of their state. Nevertheless, this slight show of strength should have been sufficient for the conquest of Canada, for the armies that the Canadians could muster were even less formidable. But unfortunately the United States was woefully lacking in capable military leaders. The old officers were, as Winfield Scott said, "decayed gentlemen" who were "utterly unfit for any military purpose whatever," and the West Point Academy, although authorized in 1802, had not yet begun to bear fruit. Madison thus had a meager field from which to pick, but even so he could hardly have done worse than he did. All the high ranking officers were in their late fifties or sixties, and only one or two of them had ever commanded a regiment in battle.

In an administrative way also the war found the government unfit for duty. The President, James Madison, was built for peaceful and harmonious times. His Cabinet was probably the weakest that the nation had yet known, and the one really strong man in it, Albert Gallatin, was crippled in effectiveness because of the bitter opposition he had incurred from members of his own party. The Secretary of War, William Eustis, and the Secretary of the Navy, Paul Hamilton, were weak-kneed politicians whom Madison, had he been himself a man of action, would have dismissed at once. Robert Smith, Madison's notoriously incapable Secretary of State, had been replaced in 1811 by James Monroe, whose talents were considerable, in spite of his previous diplomatic blunders; but generally speaking the direction of the war lay in the hands of men who had not the wit to plan nor the energy to act.

In spite of the sparseness of Canada's population, the military strength of the province was not to be despised. At the time the war broke out, four British regiments were stationed in Canada, and the Canadian authorities had, on the whole, better luck in enlisting troops to resist an invasion than the Americans had to make one. The Canadians, moreoover, were far more ably commanded than the Americans, and they could count on the assistance of Tecumseh's adherents in the Northwest. It is not surprising that, from the American point of view, the war got off to a poor start.

The American plan for the conquest of Canada, to which all other considerations were subordinated, was to attack the border defense *The American plan of campaign* in three concerted movements. Henry Dearborn, the senior major-general, was to advance northward by the Lake Champlain route toward Montreal; Stephen Van Rensselaer, relying mainly upon New York militia, was to attack the British at Niagara; and William Hull, the governor of Michigan Territory, was to launch from Detroit an invasion of Upper Canada. Unfortunately not one of the three officers mentioned was in the least fitted to cope with the situation that confronted him.

A week before the American declaration of war, Hull received orders to march, and with fifteen hundred men he succeeded in reaching Detroit, although his attempt to send his baggage from Toledo Bay by boat resulted in its capture by the enemy. For this misfortune the American commander was not wholly to blame. By the time it happened war had been officially declared, but Hull was left in complete ignorance of the fact, whereas his British opponents knew all about it. Hull pointed out to the government the difficulties involved in trying to conduct an invasion of Canada without first securing control of Lake Erie, but he was compelled nevertheless to begin his campaign without naval support. On July 12 he crossed the Detroit River and marched timidly toward the British post at Malden. His doubts and fears multiplied as he observed the hostility of the inhabitants, the poverty of their country, and the evidence that a strong force was concentrating at Malden to oppose him. When finally the news came that Tecumseh and a band of Indian warriors had joined the British, Hull's courage completely evaporated, and he fell back to Detroit. Had he followed his own judgment he would have retreated even farther, for he believed, probably correctly, that with the British in control of Lake Erie Detroit was untenable; but his men objected to any further retreat, and he awaited with much anxiety the British attack.

General Isaac Brock, the British commander, was a man of great energy and resourcefulness who soon had Detroit surrounded. Hinting broadly that he could not be sure what the Indians would *Surrender* do, once the fighting had begun, Brock demanded that Hull *of Detroit* surrender without a struggle. Paralyzed with fear and foreseeing only a horrible massacre if he refused to comply, Hull acceded to the British demands, August 16, 1812. A month earlier the American garrison at Michilimackinac had been forced to surrender, and the day before Hull gave in the garrison at Fort Dearborn had been massacred by the Indians. Thus the two months' time that, according to many of the War Hawks, was to have been more than ample for the conquest of all Canada ended with the Americans on the defensive, and the northwestern military frontier forced back to the line of the Wabash and Maumee Valleys. For his conduct at Detroit Hull was later court-martialed and sentenced to be shot, but because of his creditable record in the American Revolution the President pardoned him.

The attacks on Canada from the Niagara frontier similarly miscarried. With Detroit safely in British hands, Brock quickly transferred his activities to Niagara, and made ready once more to receive an American invasion. In a preliminary skirmish led by Captain John E. Wool, a few American regulars crossed the Niagara River on October 13, 1812, and attacked Queenstown Heights, at first with marked success. In this engagement Brock himself was killed, and a notable victory might have been won had the New York militia been willing to co-operate. But when reinforcements were ordered up from the American side of the river, the militiamen were filled with terror and refused to move. They had been called into service to defend their state, they maintained, and not for an attack on Canada. The British forces were soon strengthened, however, and the attacking Americans were driven back to the river, where, within sight of a thousand armed militiamen on the other side, they were surrounded and compelled to surrender. After this Van Rensselaer in disgust resigned his command. He was succeeded by General Alexander Smyth of Virginia, who issued many bombastic proclamations, but after a few feeble feints lost his nerve entirely and

ordered his men into winter quarters. By the time he could be superseded, it was too late in the season to continue the campaign.

Meantime Dearborn, the senior major-general, charged with the duty
of advancing on Montreal, had collected at Plattsburg on Lake Cham-
Dearborn's plain a stronger force than either Hull or Smyth had
failure commanded. But he, too, lacked most of the qualities
needed to make an efficient officer, and he delayed his forward movement
until late in November. Finally, on the nineteenth of the month, he
marched his command twenty miles to the Canadian border, only to
discover that his militia also was unwilling to leave the country. Still
further disheartened by the news of an advancing British column and
by a minor military reverse, he gave up his plans entirely and marched
his troops back to Plattsburg. Dearborn should have been removed
at once for his incompetence, but Madison weakly allowed him to hold
his post for several months longer.

Had the American officers possessed sufficient ability to make careful
plans for the co-ordination of their movements, and had the American
militia stood ready to obey orders, it seems reasonable to suppose that
the invasion of Canada in 1812 might not have ended so disastrously.
All three movements should have been in progress at the same time, not
in slow succession, and a workable plan for the union of the whole
American army before Montreal should have been devised. Moreover,
the necessity of American naval preponderance on the Great Lakes should
not have been overlooked. As matters stood, the year ended with the
Americans balked in New York, and defeated in the Northwest.

Fortunately on the high seas American captains and crews were giving
excellent accounts of themselves.[1] The navy that the Federalists had
The high begun during the last years of the preceding century had
seas been strengthened during the Tripolitan War and numbered
now some sixteen ships-of-war, together with a fair number of smaller
craft. This was an insignificant force to oppose the two thousand or more
ships that composed the British navy, nearly a hundred of which were
assigned to trans-Atlantic duty, and the scorn of a London journalist for
the "fir-built" American frigates "manned by a handful of bastards and
outlaws" was a fair sample of British opinion. As a matter of fact the
men who manned the American ships were well-paid and competent
volunteers, while the captains who commanded them were veterans of

[1] The exploits of the American navy during the War of 1812 have not been overlooked
by historians. Theodore Roosevelt, *The Naval War of 1812* (1882), is most detailed. Other
useful accounts are to be found in E. S. Maclay, *History of the United States Navy from 1775
to 1901* (3 vols., 1901–02); and J. R. Spears, *The History of Our Navy from its Origin to the
Present Day* (4 vols., 1897).

the Tripolitan War. The "fir-built frigates," moreover, were carefully constructed to carry more guns and sail than the corresponding units in European navies. Thus in ship-for-ship engagements the Americans stood a chance to win, although the ultimate outcome of a war in which the forces were so unevenly matched should have been as apparent to citizens of the United States as it was to Englishmen.

Before the end of the year 1812 a number of ship duels had been fought in which the American came off victor. On July 11, Captain David Porter of the *Essex* captured the *Minerva* and two days later in a ten-minute engagement forced the *Alert* to sur- *American sea victories* render. On August 19, Captain Isaac Hull of the *Constitution* atoned for his uncle's surrender of Detroit three days earlier by thoroughly outmaneuvering and outfighting a British frigate, the *Guerrière*, in what was probably the most brilliant American victory of the war. On October 18, an American sloop, the *Wasp*, took the evenly matched *Frolic* in a bloody conflict during which the British casualties exceeded those suffered by the Americans eight or nine to one. On October 25, Captain Stephen Decatur of the *United States* defeated the British frigate *Macedonian*, and in December brought her back to New London as a prize. The luck of the *Constitution* continued under a new captain, William Bainbridge, who on December 29 so shattered the *Java*, another British frigate, that she could not even be brought to port, and had to be blown up. It was this battle that won for the *Constitution* the name "Old Ironsides." On February 24, 1813, Captain James Lawrence of the *Hornet* sank the *Peacock* after a combat that lasted only fifteen minutes. Meantime American warships and privateers were also taking a frightful toll of British commerce.

The uninterrupted series of naval victories tremendously lightened the gloom that the military blunders along the northern frontier had cast over the American people, but the effect on the British public was even more marked. For centuries British sea- *English astonishment* captains had been accustomed to win against whatever odds confronted them, and the defeats by Americans seemed beyond comprehension. Commenting on the loss of the *Java* the London *Times* exclaimed:

> The public will learn with sentiments which we shall not presume to anticipate that a third British frigate has struck to an American.... This is an occurrence that calls for serious reflection; this, and the facts stated in our paper of yesterday, that Lloyd's list contains notices of upward of five hundred British vessels captured in seven months by the Americans: five hundred merchantmen and three frigates! Can these statements be true? And can the English people hear them unmoved? Anyone who had predicted such a result of an American war this time last year would have been

treated as a madman or a traitor. He would have been told, if his opponents had condescended to-argue with him, that long ere seven months had elapsed the American flag would have been swept from the seas, the contemptible navy of the United States annihilated, and their marine arsenals rendered a heap of ruins. Yet down to this moment not a single American frigate has struck her flag.

But the American luck on the high seas was not to last. With the spring of 1813 the British established a tight blockade of the American *The British* coast, and from that time forward American ships of war *blockade* scarcely dared to leave port. When the *Chesapeake*, now commanded by Captain Lawrence, accepted the challenge of the *Shannon* to come out of Boston Harbor and fight, the British ship won a notable victory (June 1, 1813), and Lawrence lost his life. On the same day a British squadron chased the *United States*, the *Macedonian*, and the *Hornet* into the port of New London, where they were compelled to remain until the end of the war. The *Essex* was destroyed the next year (March 28, 1814) by two British ships in a battle off the coast of Chile, and a few days after the peace treaty had been signed the *President* failed to make good her escape from a British squadron of four, and was captured. Four or five American warships, including the *Constitution*, managed to continue intermittently on the high seas until the war was over, and some of the American privateers took good prizes to the very end; but as a fighting weapon for either offensive or defensive purposes, the American navy had ceased to function. New England, which from New London northward was exempted by the British from the blockade because of its notorious opposition to the war and its readiness to sell to the enemy, could still carry on a fair export trade, but elsewhere shipments from American ports were held down to nearly nothing. In 1814 not more than $200,000 worth of goods left the ports of New York, and hardly $17,500 worth left the ports of Virginia.

In the spring of 1813 American war policy called for another attempt at the invasion of Canada. The disaster at Detroit, however, had convinced the administration that the control of the Great Lakes must no longer be left to the British, and during the winter of 1812–13 the Navy Department began the construction of a small fleet on Lake Erie. With great difficulty the youthful Captain Oliver Hazard Perry, who was placed in control of the half-built squadron in March, 1813, succeeded in equipping and navigating his ships; most of his ordnance, sail, and other supplies had to be hauled across the mountains by wagon, and his lack of adequate numbers of sailors had to be overcome by a detail of one hundred Kentucky militiamen. At Put-in-Bay, on

September 10, 1813, Perry found the British squadron, and mainly because the American ships threw a greater weight of metal than the British, won a most significant victory. Perry's terse report to Harrison, who commanded the adjacent American army, has lived deservedly: "We have met the enemy and they are ours: two ships, two brigs, one schooner, and one sloop."

To William Henry Harrison, the hero of Tippecanoe, fell the task of retrieving the defeats of 1812 in the Northwest. Under his leadership a winter campaign against Detroit was begun, only to be *The invasion* frustrated when a detachment of Harrison's army under *of Canada* General James Winchester was disastrously defeated, January 22, 1813, near Frenchtown, on the Raisin River. General Henry Proctor, in command of the British and Indian army that had won this victory, made no effort to protect the five hundred American prisoners he had taken, and the night after the battle they were massacred to the last man by the savages. Infuriated by this atrocity and by the numerous scalping parties that were let loose upon the frontier, the western states supported the war in the spring and summer of 1813 with a vigor they had not shown before. With a far larger army than Hull had commanded, Harrison made ready to attack Detroit and invade Ontario. Had Perry lost, doubtless Proctor would have attempted to force the fighting on the American side of the boundary, but the loss of Lake Erie convinced him that a British retreat was necessary. Accordingly he burned both Detroit and Malden, and attempted to withdraw his army from the dangerous western salient. But on October 5, 1813, Harrison overtook the retreating British, and on the banks of the Thames River won a signal victory. Tecumseh himself was slain, and Proctor had to flee for his life. The battle of the Thames not only recovered the ground lost by the surrender of Detroit the year before, but it definitely ended the menace of the northwestern Indian confederacy that Tecumseh had worked so hard to achieve. Harrison's invasion of Canada did not proceed much farther, but the war ended with the Americans definitely in control of the northwestern frontier.

Meantime, two other American campaigns, one on the Niagara front and the other before Montreal, had achieved far less gratifying results. In April, 1813, General Dearborn led a successful raid on York, the capital of Upper Canada, later known as Toronto. During this episode American soldiers wantonly set fire to the two houses of the provincial parliament, an act which their officers deplored, but which later gave the British an excuse to burn the government buildings at Washington in retaliation. York had to be abandoned by the Americans, for, although making strenuous efforts to wrest the control of Lake Ontario from the British, they had not yet succeeded in doing so. Other severe fighting, mostly of negligible military significance but destructive alike of life and property, occurred during the year on both sides of the Niagara frontier, and on December 30, 1813, the British took Fort Niagara. As for the second advance on Montreal, it was quite as feeble and futile as the first.

Up to the end of the year 1813 the American war had been, from the British point of view, a mere side issue; the main thing had been the *British plans for counter-invasion* defeat of Napoleon. But with the spring of 1814 the downfall of Napoleon's empire was an accomplished fact, and the British were free to turn the full strength of their victorious army and navy against the United States. British opinion strongly favored the thorough chastisement of the Americans for their attack upon England at a time when the English nation was standing almost alone against the tyranny of Napoleon, and there was much feeling, too, that the American naval successes must not be allowed to go unavenged. Accordingly, the British government decided to send over ships enough and troops enough to overwhelm the Americans. The military attack, adequately supported by the navy, was to be delivered from three points, Niagara, Lake Champlain, and New Orleans.

Had the British been able to attack in this fashion in the early stages of the war, the result might have been disastrous to the Americans; but by 1814 most of the incompetent among the American officers had been removed from high command, and the undependability of raw militia levies had been so fully demonstrated that chief reliance was placed on regulars. On the Niagara front General Jacob Brown got into action before the British reinforcements from Europe had arrived, and by the fourth of July had set a force of five or six hundred men across the Niagara River. On the same day he took Fort Erie, and on the next day the advance guard of his army under Winfield Scott won a hard-fought battle at Chippawa. The culmination of the campaign came about three weeks later (July 25) at Lundy's Lane, close to Niagara Falls, when two thousand American troops outfought a superior British force, but were compelled to fall back when news came that the British had received reinforcements. Although Brown was forced to retire to the American side of the river, he had demonstrated that an American army could and would fight well, even on Canadian soil.

The British plan was for their first serious blow to be delivered down the Lake Champlain route through New York, possibly with the idea of cutting off New England from the rest of the Union and reannexing

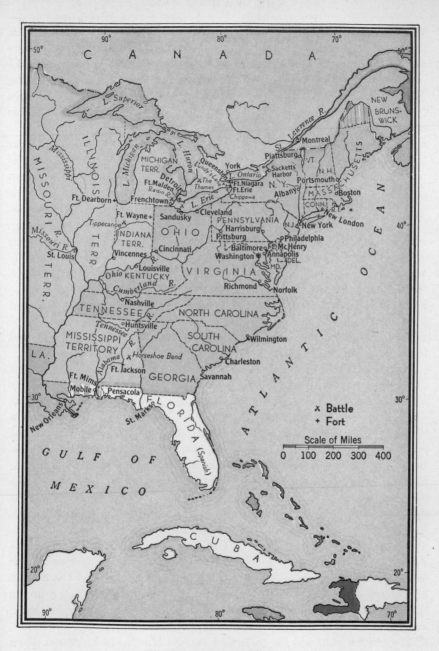

THE WAR OF 1812

LIBRARY
FLORIDA STATE UNIVERSITY
TALLAHASSEE. FLORIDA

it to the British Empire. For this purpose Sir George Prevost was given about eleven thousand soldiers, more than five times as many as General Alexander Macomb, his American opponent, had on hand at Plattsburg. The Prevost cam- *McDonough at Champlain* paign depended, however, upon the elimination from Lake Champlain of a small American flotilla under the command of Captain Thomas McDonough, and the British squadron that had been made ready for this purpose, although seemingly far superior to McDonough's in strength, proved utterly unequal to the task. The naval battle fought off Plattsburg Bay was a fight to the finish, in which the superior seamanship of the Americans won the day. The American losses were startling, but every British ship was either sunk or else was compelled to strike its colors. Prevost, in dismay, led his army back to Canada without risking a battle.

The British navy on the high seas, meantime, was able to terrorize the American cities and villages along the Atlantic coast at will. To ensure against adequate assistance being sent by the American government to the Lake Champlain front a particularly active demonstration was planned against Washington and Baltimore, and a detachment of four thousand British troops under General Robert Ross was sent over to co-operate with the navy. President Madison learned of this plan several weeks before it was put into execution, and made desperate efforts to assemble an army for the defense of the capital. He managed to find troops enough, so far as numbers went, but they were nearly all militia, and they were commanded by a totally incompetent officer, General William Henry Winder. The British were allowed to land unopposed on the west bank of the Patuxent River, which flows into the Chesapeake southeast of Washington, and to march their column to within five miles of the capital.

Here the Americans, adequately supported with artillery, were drawn up in a strong position to receive the enemy attack. Winder's superiority in numbers gave the American officials an undue sense of security, and the President, accompanied by some of his *Capture of Washington* Cabinet, came out from Washington prepared to witness a telling victory. Instead the American militia broke and ran after firing a few shots, and only a handful of marines and sailors under Captain Joshua Barney were left to dispute the field. Barney's men fought bravely, but were soon overpowered, and the British marched triumphantly into Washington (August 24, 1814). A dinner prepared at the White House for President and Mrs. Madison was eaten by British officers, and the President himself narrowly escaped capture. In retaliation for the vandalism of the American troops at York the preceding year, the British officers ordered their men to set fire to all the American public buildings, but they prevented a general looting of the city, and the amount of private property destroyed was slight. Their purpose accomplished, the invaders withdrew. The military significance of the episode was negligible, but the blow to American pride was great.[1]

The British attack on Baltimore did not fare so well, and the boast of Ross that he intended to spend the winter in the city even if it "rained militia" proved vain. The harbor was well defended by Fort McHenry and by sunken hulks, while the people of the city and state had collected about fourteen thousand men to resist the invaders. A naval demonstration against the city proved futile, and the first skirmish on land cost the life of General Ross himself. Thoroughly discouraged, the British gave up the attack, and soon sailed off to join in the campaign against New Orleans.

The final phase of the war was fought in the Southwest, where, as in the earlier phases, both Indians and British were involved. In spite of *The Fort* the preachings of Tecumseh, southern tribes had abstained *Mims* from war as long as they could. In 1813, however, some *massacre* hotbloods among the Creeks attacked a stockade known as Fort Mims, on the lower Alabama River not far from Mobile, and massacred several hundred pioneers who had gathered there for protection (August 30, 1813). Already Tennessee troops, commanded by Andrew Jackson, were making ready for an attack on Spanish Florida, but they now had a more satisfactory objective. With thirty-five hundred troops under his command, Jackson advanced southward in search of hostile Indians. No better commander of frontier militia had ever taken the field. Jackson somehow overcame the lack of discipline among his men, he found by one unusual means or another the supplies that they had to have, and on March 27, 1814, at Horseshoe Bend, he thoroughly avenged the Fort Mims massacre. A few months later at Fort Jackson (August 9, 1814) the chastened Creeks were compelled to sign a treaty which handed over to the whites thousands of acres of their choicest lands.

Jackson was now placed in command of all the American operations in the Southwest, and upon his shoulders fell the task of warding off the *Battle of* final British attack of the war. When the British sought *New Orleans* to use Pensacola in Spanish Florida as a base of operations, Jackson, with equal disregard of neutrality, occupied and burned the town. The British then sailed off to the attack of New Orleans, and

[1] *Memoirs and Letters of Dolly Madison*, edited by Lucia B. Cutts (1886).

Jackson soon learned that he must face there an army of ten thousand invaders. Undaunted, he hastened to the city with all the troops he could obtain, and made vigorous preparations for its defense. Sir Edward Pakenham, an experienced officer and a brother-in-law of the Duke of Wellington, was in command of the British expedition. Fortunately for the Americans he held militia soldiery in great contempt, and after his dependable regulars were landed he pursued a plan of battle that he would not have considered tenable had he respected his opponents. Jackson, however, was neither a Hull nor a Winder, and from behind hastily improvised defenses, consisting partly of cotton bales, he received the ill-advised attack. On January 8, 1815, the inexperienced frontier commander won the most notable victory of the war, and one of the most remarkable victories in history. General Pakenham himself was killed, and against British casualties of nearly two thousand the Americans could count losses of only thirteen. Thus defeated and humiliated, the British expedition withdrew.[1] Naturally Andrew Jackson was the hero of the hour, but curiously his great victory was won after the war was over. Had the means of communication been available in 1815 that were known less than half a century later, the battle of New Orleans would never have been fought, for on December 24, 1814, a treaty of peace had been signed by British and American plenipotentiaries at Ghent.

During the dark days of 1814 the loyalty of New England to the Union was put to the test, although in point of fact New England suffered far less from the war than some of her people seemed to think. *New England discontent* Until the last year of the war the British avoided blockading the coast of New England, and thus practically all American imports that entered the country had to pass through the hands of New England merchants. Moreover, the serious check that the embargo and the war had given to New England commerce was not unmixed with good. With British manufactures excluded, far-sighted men saw a great opportunity for Americans in this field, and the number of New England factories, textile mills in particular, increased during the war most amazingly. Nevertheless, the injured commercial interests pointed to the war as proof positive that agriculturalist control of the nation would ring the death-knell for northeastern prosperity. With new Indian territory opening up for settlement in the West, and with the Louisiana Purchase available to be carved up into new agricultural states, many New-Englanders held that for their section the Union had lost

---

[1] A critical study of the battle of New Orleans is contained in C. F. Adams, *Studies Military and Diplomatic, 1775–1865* (1911).

its attraction. Some talked freely of secession, and the British hope that New England might even return to its colonial allegiance was not without justification.

Curiously, raids made by the British in 1814 along the coast of New England aroused among New Englanders even greater resentment against *The Hartford Convention* the government at Washington than against the British themselves, and on October 5, 1814, the legislature of Massachusetts voted to call a convention to meet at Hartford, Connecticut, for the purpose of voicing the opinion of New England on the state of the Union. Rhode Island and Connecticut responded to the call, and on December 15, 1814, the Hartford Convention, representing these two states and Massachusetts, assembled. Two delegates chosen by popular meetings in New Hampshire, and one by the town of Windham, Vermont, were also admitted. Some of the extremists among the delegates would gladly have followed the advice of Timothy Pickering to prepare the way for "the separation of the northern section of the states" from the rest of the nation. But the more moderate wing of the Convention, led by Harrison Gray Otis, prevented any precipitate action being taken, and lodged instead a dignified protest against the "multiplied abuses of bad administrations" and the "acts of Congress in violation of the Constitution." In language definitely reminiscent of the Kentucky and Virginia Resolutions, the Convention maintained "the right and duty of a state to interpose its authority" in cases of "deliberate, dangerous, and palpable infractions of the Constitution," but insisted also that it would be unwise "to fly to open resistance" upon every offense.[1]

The report of the Hartford Convention favored neither nullification nor secession, but referred back to the states concerned, for proposal to Congress, a list of seven suggested amendments to the Constitution. These amendments, had they been adopted, would have limited the power of Congress to make war, to admit new states, to lay embargoes, and to restrict commerce. Also, as a blow against the "Virginia dynasty," they would have declared a President ineligible for re-election, and would have prevented the choice of successive Presidents from the same state. In order to limit the power of the agricultural South, one amendment proposed to set aside the "three-fifths" compromise of the Constitution, so that only the white population might be counted in the apportioning of representatives. In adjourning, the Convention voted

---

[1] On the Hartford Convention the following works will be found useful: S. E. Morison, *Life and Letters of Harrison Gray Otis* (2 vols., 1913); H. C. Lodge, *Life and Letters of George Cabot* (1877); Theodore Dwight, *History of the Hartford Convention* (1833).

to meet again at Boston on call of its president, presumably so that if, in the meantime, Congress failed to agree to its demands the adjourned session might advise a more radical course of action. The happy termination of the war and the subsequent prosperity of New England naturally ended all danger of a northeastern revolt; and it also made those who had preached such doctrine exceedingly regretful of their words. Since the Hartford Convention had been primarily the work of Federalists, it was possible, after the war was over, for the Republicans to charge the whole Federalist Party with treason — a charge which, duly pressed, had much to do with the elimination of the party of Washington and Hamilton from the American political scene.

Almost from the beginning of the War of 1812 there had been negotiations of one kind or another that looked in the direction of peace.[1] As previously stated, there was at the outset much feeling, *Peace* both in England and in America, that the war had been *negotiations* prematurely declared and need not be fought. It was hardly under way before the Russian government, seeking to take advantage of this sentiment, offered mediation. This action was easily understandable, for almost at the very moment that the United States decided to throw in its lot with Napoleon, the Czar of Russia went over to the English side. Still friendly to the United States and now an important ally of England, he hoped to iron out the difficulties that estranged the two English-speaking nations and weakened the alliance against Napoleon. Madison was quick to accept the Russian offer, and promptly dispatched James A. Bayard and Albert Gallatin to aid the American representative at St. Petersburg, John Quincy Adams, in the quest of peace. But the English government rejected the Czar's offer, although expressing a willingness to undertake direct negotiations with the United States. Unfortunately it was not until January, 1814, that Madison learned that this offer of direct negotiation had been made. Thereupon he dispatched Henry Clay and Jonathan Russell to join the three commissioners already in Europe, but it was not until August that the American and British commissioners finally met at Ghent.

The American peace delegation was as able as the country could command, and the commissioners themselves felt aggrieved when three British subordinates were detailed to meet them. The British government intended, however, to keep close watch on the proceedings at Ghent, and its best talent was required to effect the European settlement

[1] The peace negotiations are set forth fully in the works of Adams, McMaster, Channing, and Schouler. See also W. A. Dunning, *The British Empire and the United States* (1914); R. B. Mowat, *The Diplomatic Relations of Great Britain and the United States* (1925); *Cambridge History of British Foreign Policy*, edited by A. W. Ward (3 vols., 1922–23), i.

soon in progress at Vienna. As it turned out, the superior ability of the Americans was a great advantage to the United States, while the obligation felt by the British delegation to refer every important matter to London for decision was by no means helpful to Great Britain.

The British demands were set forth at the outset in the form of an extraordinary ultimatum: (1) the boundary between the United States *The British* must be "rectified" by the cession to England of a part of *ultimatum* Maine and strategic ports along the Great Lakes; (2) all Indian land cessions in the Northwest made since 1795 were to be annulled, and an Indian buffer state was to be created in that region into which the whites must never go; (3) the British interpretation of the rules of warfare on the high seas, against which the United States had for so many years protested, was to remain unaltered; (4) the United States must give up the rights it had acquired by the Treaty of 1783 in the Newfoundland fisheries, must relinquish to Great Britain the navigation of the Great Lakes, and must continue the British right of navigation of the Mississippi River. The American delegation received these demands with great dismay, and prepared to leave. "Such terms were prescribed," wrote Bayard, "as put an end to all hope of peace. . . . The terms will certainly be rejected and the negotiation will terminate in a few days."

The instructions which the American commissioners had received were by no means modest. They were told to secure if they could: *American* (1) recognition of the American position on maritime law, *demands* although on impressments the United States might be willing to forbid British-born sailors the right to serve on American ships; (2) indemnity for illegal prizes taken by the British; (3) the cession of "the upper parts and even the whole of Canada to the United States"; (4) the exclusion of the British from the Great Lakes. The American terms, however, were not presented as an ultimatum, and the American delegation had full authority to make whatever concessions it saw fit without referring to Washington for advice.

In spite of Bayard's fears, the negotiations at Ghent proved to be of long duration. The American commissioners were able to convince the British agents that the terms asked were out of the question, and modifications were sought and obtained from the British government in London. Undoubtedly the attitude of the Ministry was greatly influenced by the Duke of Wellington, whom Lord Liverpool, the British Premier, had asked to take command in America, "with full power to make peace, or to continue the war with renewed vigor." To this request Wellington replied:

I have already told you ... that I feel no objection to going to America, though I don't promise to myself much success there.... That which appears to me to be wanting in America is not a General, or General officers and troops, but a naval superiority on the Lakes.... I suspect that you will find that Prevost will justify his misfortunes ... by stating that the navy were defeated.... The question is, whether we can acquire this naval superiority on the Lakes. If we can't I can do you but little good in America; and I shall go there only to prove the truth of Prevost's defense, and to sign a peace which might as well be signed now.... In regard to your present negotiations I confess that I think you have no right from the state of the war to demand any concession of territory from America.... You have not been able to carry it into the enemy's territory, notwithstanding your military success, and now undoubted military superiority.

Wellington's arguments also fitted in with the temper of the British public. The wave of enthusiasm for the American war that had followed the defeat of Napoleon soon subsided. With war a thing *Treaty of* of the past in Europe, English merchants and traders were *Ghent* less interested in the punishment of America than in the complete restoration of normal peace-time trade. In consequence the British demands were gradually toned down until terms were offered that the Americans could accept. As finally signed, the Treaty of Ghent reflected well the state of the military situation. It provided, according to Adams, for "a truce rather than a peace. Neither party gave up anything; all the points of collision which had subsisted between them before the war were left open.... Nothing was adjusted, nothing was settled — nothing in substance but an indefinite suspension of hostilities was agreed to."

While the Peace of Ghent merely restored for the time being the *status quo ante bellum*, it did make provision for the future settlement of some of the outstanding differences between England and Amer- *Subsequent* ica. Stimulated in part by these clauses in the treaty and *agreements* in part by the mutual desire to clear up misunderstandings, there thus came about several important agreements between the two nations. On July 3, 1815, a commercial convention was signed by which trade discriminations, except for the exclusion of American trade from the British West Indies, were mutually withdrawn. Not until Jackson's administration did the United States obtain the West Indian trade privileges it so long had sought. On April 28, 1818, the justly famous Rush-Bagot Agreement provided for complete disarmament by both nations on the Great Lakes. A few gunboats were permitted for police purposes only. The agreement could be denounced by either party on six months' notice, but it still endures. The difficult question of the northeastern fisheries was treated in a convention signed October 20, 1818. The

English had claimed that all rights to the fisheries acquired by the United States under the Treaty of 1783 were annulled by the declaration of war in 1812, and following the war American fishermen had suffered considerable molestation from the British. The Convention of 1818 "acknowledged" the right of American citizens to fish along the coasts of Newfoundland and Labrador, and to dry and cure their fish on unsettled shores, but the meaning of the agreement was in some respects so obscure that trouble over the fisheries continued for many years to come.

The same convention that dealt with the fisheries question also attempted to draw a boundary line between the possessions of the United *The* States and of Great Britain in the Northwest. The Treaty *northwestern* of 1783 had determined the boundary as far west as the *boundary* Lake of the Woods, and from thence "on a due west course to the river Mississippi." Such a line could not be drawn inasmuch as the source of the Mississippi lay well to the south of the Lake of the Woods. Moreover, the undetermined boundaries of Louisiana had to be taken into consideration. The Convention of 1818 sensibly adopted the forty-ninth parallel as the dividing line between the United States and Canada as far west as the "Stony" mountains. Beyond the mountains neither side was willing to acknowledge the other's pretensions, and the dispute was left open by an agreement that the subjects of both nations might occupy the region jointly.

A precedent in favor of arbitration was set by reference to the Czar of Russia in 1818 of an American claim for the restitution of slaves captured by the British during the war. The Czar decided that the slaves need not be restored, but that they should be paid for, and by an agreement reached in 1822 the amount of compensation to be paid by Great Britain was set at well over a million dollars.

It is not surprising that the War of 1812, which was at best a drawn battle, settled into the American consciousness as a telling victory. *American* The news of Jackson's magnificent triumph at New Orleans *impression* was quickly followed by the news of peace, and the un- *of victory* thinking public naturally, though wholly mistakenly, assumed that between these two impressive events there was the relation of cause and effect. Furthermore, the defeat of the Indians, both in the Northwest and in the Southwest, together with the death of Tecumseh, opened the way for an unprecedented advance of the frontier. No real need had ever been felt for the lands of Canada, and the failure of the War Hawk program of conquest and annexation was quickly forgotten. With peace in Europe restored, American commerce on the high seas was no longer molested, and American patriots were not above imputing to the battle of New Orleans a happy situation that was in reality the result of Leipsig and Waterloo. Pride in the achievements of the American frigates during the early part of the war soon obscured their helplessness in the face of British superiority at its close. American manufacturers, moreover, had benefited greatly by the trade restrictions that preceded and accompanied the war, and their successes had promoted a degree of economic independence from England that the United States had never known before. From the political point of view it is absurd to speak of the War of 1812 as the "Second War for Independence," for political independence had been won in fact no less than in theory by the American Revolution; but from the economic point of view it is abundantly clear that the second war with England markedly accentuated the divorcement of the two countries. Possibly this situation served also to heighten materially the ill-feeling that the war had engendered between the English and the American peoples, and that was to last for so many years to come.

CHAPTER XIX

THE NEW NATIONALISM

THE War of 1812 marks a definite turning-point in the history of the United States. Prior to that conflict the American people, for all their political independence, were in their economic life still tributary to Europe, and most especially to England. The factory system was slow to take root in America, for it was cheaper to import goods from England, where manufacturing on a large scale was already well established, than to make them in America. Moreover, the commercial connections of colonial times had been promptly resumed at the close of the Revolution, and at the beginning of the nineteenth century there were no stronger vested interests in the country than those concerned with the importation and distribution of foreign goods. Planters and farmers, likewise, were accustomed to depend heavily upon foreign trade. Their excess produce was sent to Europe quite as consistently as during colonial times, while the continual wars of the French Revolution and the Napoleonic period forced the prices of American raw materials and foodstuffs to high figures. With a steady trade flowing both ways, there was little difficulty in making exports balance imports in value.

A new era

The embargo, non-intercourse, and the War of 1812 upset completely this scheme of things. American commerce was for the time being almost destroyed, and the opportunity to import foreign goods was reduced to a minimum. Naturally enough, much of the capital that had formerly been invested in commerce turned now to manufactures, for which the existing situation was equivalent to a heavy protective tariff. Manufacturing, moreover, became a patriotic duty which states, counties, municipalities, and societies sought to encourage by offering attractive bounties. As early as 1810 Gallatin reported to the House of Representatives a surprisingly long list of items in which American manufacturers were already able to supply the American demand. Throughout the period textile mills for the production of cotton, linen, and woolen cloth in-

Growth of manufactures

creased rapidly in number, and even more rapidly in the volume of their output. Facilities for the manufacture of such significant articles as paper, leather goods, woodenware, iron, and iron goods multiplied until the most urgent needs of the American market were fully met. By the end of the war American manufacturing was definitely established, and the shortage of European imports was no longer keenly felt.[1]

New England promptly took the lead among the sections in the shift toward manufacturing. Not only was there occasion here to offset with some other interest the decline in commerce; *New* in a variety of ways New England was ideally fitted to *England* assume the manufacturing rôle. Power to turn the wheels *factories* of the new machinery was abundantly supplied by the swift-flowing streams and their numerous waterfalls, shippers and shipping were available to send the products of the loom and factory down the coast to the other American states, and an abundant and intelligent labor supply was at hand. Workers in the New England factories consisted mainly of farmers and their families, who were only too willing to give up the unequal struggle with the hard climate and the unyielding soil to accept the more certain financial rewards of the mills. They brought with them a degree of dexterity and ingenuity, acquired through years of self-dependence on the farm, that placed them among the most capable, although possibly not among the most tractable, factory employees anywhere in the world.

But the interest in manufacturing was by no means confined to New England. As far south as the Chesapeake the new opportunity for American manufacturers was producing results. If New England led in the production of textiles, Pennsylvania, New York, and New Jersey excelled in the production of iron ore and the manufacture of iron goods. In this region coal could be obtained cheaply to supplement water-power, and by the end of the War of 1812 bituminous, and even anthracite, coal was being used by occasional manufacturers with good success. In the South there was talk of establishing factories and putting the slaves to work in them, but practically nothing of the sort was actually accomplished. Instead the South turned to cotton-growing, and became a heavy purchaser of northern goods. In 1814, according to one estimate, New England bankers received

---

[1] H. J. Carman, *Social and Economic History of the United States*, II (1934), covers admirably the rise of industrialism in the United States following the War of 1812. Other useful economic histories are H. U. Faulkner, *American Economic History* (1924); E. L. Bogart, *The Economic History of the United States* (1907); Katherine Coman, *The Industrial History of the United States* (1905); C. D. Wright, *Industrial Evolution of the United States* (1895); F. A. Shannon, *Economic History of the People of the United States* (1934).

SOME EARLY AMERICAN TEXTILE MILLS

on an average a half million dollars a month from the banks of the South, practically all of which was drawn northward in payment for factory products.

The period of enforced divorcement from Europe had witnessed many changes also in American agriculture. The growth of the woolen industry made sheep-raising profitable as never before. *American* In the back country of New England and in the middle *agriculture* states, where with the decline of the export trade foodstuffs had become a drug on the market, there was a noticeable trend in the direction of wool-growing. In the South the production of cotton took on ever-increasing significance. Before Eli Whitney's invention of the cotton gin in 1793, only the long-staple cotton grown in the lowlands could be profitably raised. But the cotton gin, by reducing immensely the cost of separating the seed from the cotton, made practicable the growing also of the short-staple cotton which throve well in the uplands. The results were revolutionary. The output of southern cotton, which in 1791 had amounted only to about two million pounds, had grown by 1801 to forty million, and by 1811 to eighty million pounds. Until the period of commercial restriction began, the bulk of this cotton had found its way to foreign markets, and only the establishment of the northern textile mills saved the southern cotton planters from deep disaster. Once the war was ended, both foreign and domestic manufacturers clamored for cotton, and the spread of cotton culture was more rapid than ever before. The increasing cultivation of sugar-cane in Louisiana, and to some extent elsewhere in the South, added another commodity to the list of articles that could be supplied within the borders of the United States.

Much was therefore achieved toward that national self-sufficiency which economists of the eighteenth century had regarded as so vital to the life of a nation. Accompanying this development the discerning observer might have noted also the rapid emergence of an American national type. When the Revolution ended, the typical American was still essentially an English colonial whose tastes and aptitudes were definitely reminiscent of the Old World. By the end of the eighteenth century some notable changes were already in evidence, but in the years following the War of 1812 a new nationality, with new and different characteristics, was clearly in the making. The decline of commerce, and the consequent lessening of contacts between Americans and Europeans, undoubtedly stimulated the divergence of American from European ways, but probably the unique opportunities of the New World, now better realized than ever before, account for most of the changes. America had become pre-eminently a land of "opportunity." To the resident of the Northeast the newly introduced factory system brought to employers and employees alike undreamed-of avenues to prosperity. To the southern planter, and to the southern small farmer who hoped to become a planter, the revolutionary possibilities of cotton culture seemed to point the way to sure success. To the restless of every section came with renewed vigor the call of the West. Almost for the first time the boundless possibilities of the new nation were fully realized. Now anyone could see that future generations of Americans had before them a task no less inviting than the conquest and exploitation of half a continent. The lure of rich rewards, whether in industry, in cotton culture, or in the development of the West, captured the imaginations of Americans and determined their characteristics. Small wonder that they saw little reason to imitate or esteem the ways of an Old World where opportunity was limited, but paid deference instead to whatever qualities in themselves seemed best calculated to insure success in the new undertakings.

Fortunately for the historian, there came to America during the years following the War of 1812 a procession of foreign travelers who *Foreign travelers in America* wrote down freely what they saw — or what they thought they saw. Some of these visitors, as the official or unofficial agents of European governments, were in search of an outlet for European emigration. The Napoleonic wars had left a train of economic distress in their wake, and most European nations were faced by an acute unemployment problem. Why not send their excess population to America? Those who visited the United States in search of a land of opportunity for emigrants found what they wanted to find, and wrote glowing reports. But there were many other travelers who came to America in a purely private capacity, not so much to chronicle the opportunities they saw as to criticize a nation that flaunted its "democracy." These travelers were drawn mostly from the classes of the well-to-do and the socially élite, who found much to confirm their long-established prejudices, but were nevertheless able to see clearly many things that an American observer would have overlooked. It is chiefly upon this travel literature that the historian must rely when he seeks to set forth the traits that were peculiar to Americans of this age.[1]

---

[1] Among the many travel books the following may be cited as samples: William Cobbett, *A Year's Residence in the United States of America* (1818); Henry B. Fearon, *Sketches of America* (1818); Morris Birbeck, *Letters from Illinois* (1818); Thomas Hulme, *Hulme's Journal of a Tour in the Western Countries of America, 1818–1819* (1828). *Early Western Travels, 1748–1846*, edited by R. G. Thwaites (32 vols., 1904–07), reprints nearly all of the important books of this nature for the period covered. A handy compilation is *American Social History as Recorded by British Travelers*, edited by Allan Nevins (1923).

All accounts agree that the typical American was very "provincial." To some extent this was only another way of saying that he differed from the typical Englishman, or Frenchman, or other *American* European. But it was also a fact that most Americans *traits* knew little or nothing about the world outside America, and oftentimes they cared even less. Somewhat on the defensive because of this ignorance, Americans were inclined to be boastful, both about themselves and about their country. They were particularly proud of the American experiment in democratic government, and they would neither admit that mistakes had been made, nor that any other form of government was half so good. Patriotism became almost a national obsession.

In one respect, at least, foreigners were quick to consent that American boastfulness was justified. The ordinary American was truly remarkable for his ingenuity. He could turn his hand with considerable skill to almost any problem that confronted him. He was not precisely inventive, but he was a natural-born jack-of-all-trades whose adaptability rarely left him baffled by a new situation or defeated because of an unanticipated need. The American practice of moving houses, for example, struck foreigners with peculiar force. Houses in Europe usually stayed where they were built; in America one might meet them coming down the street.

American ideas as to good manners did not always conform to European standards. Such crudities as normally accompanied the unrestrained use of chewing-tobacco excited the amazement of travelers, and sometimes for good reason their anxiety as well. The American's habit of bolting his meals in record time also induced comment, and to gouty Europeans who set much store by the leisurely disposal of food the popularity of the American "quick lunch" quite passed belief. The restlessness and nervousness of the Americans also annoyed the foreigners. Americans resented delay, and were forever in a hurry. This quality, incidentally, marks a pronounced change from the habits of colonial Americans — habits for which their descendants could have found no more appropriate adjective than "lazy." Some observers blamed this restlessness on the American climate, which, they avowed, exhibited a greater variety of conditions in a given space of time than could be found in any other country on earth. Others thought that the American diet was enough to account for it, and for the sallowness of the American complexion as well. But probably the real reason why Americans were such "hustlers" was that they were so keenly aware of the challenging opportunities that confronted them. With riches seemingly a sure reward for enterprise, the typical American felt that he had no time to waste.

Optimism was another by-product of opportunity. In America there was room for all to prosper. Unemployment for the physically fit *Optimism* was a matter of disposition, not of necessity, for the supply of labor was rarely up to the demand. America had neither slums nor poor in the European sense of those terms, and the most worthless sort of person could at least make a living. Faith in the future sometimes overshot the mark and tempted to speculation. "Stock-watering" was often not so much a matter of fraud as of great expectations — the profits of the company were sure to grow. The misrepresentations of land speculators were more frequently than not a fair statement of what they genuinely believed: that land values would assuredly go up. Overissues of bank currency were not all made with dishonest intent — more money was needed to care for the natural demands of a growing country.

Equality of opportunity had much to do with the turn that democracy was taking in America. The equalitarian doctrine of the Declaration of Independence was in its day merely the statement *Equality of* *opportunity* of an ideal; fifty years later it was not far from a correct description of American society. To be sure, an aristocracy still existed in every part of the country, except possibly in the West, but the new aristocracy, whether of industrial New England or of the cotton-planting South, was an aristocracy to which now even the lowliest might aspire. Caste lines were ever more loosely drawn, and family trees counted for less and less. Not by birth, but by material success, was one marked as a member of the upper class, and the road to success was equally open to all. As if in deference to this new definition of aristocracy, the old distinction between the dress of the aristocrat and of the common man disappeared, but it was the aristocrat who gave up his furbelows, not the common man who put them on. The status of women in the new democracy seemed also to be rising toward a frank admission of equality with men. In the place of the obsequious and condescending chivalry which Europeans of the better class were accustomed to exhibit toward their own class only, all Americans, to the consternation of some foreign observers, tended to treat women of whatever class with marked respect and courtesy.

For a people that set great store by its government, this democratic trend was sure to be reflected in politics. The new western states on admission to the Union unhesitatingly established universal manhood suffrage, and the older states of the East soon followed their example.

In the latter it did not follow at once that the common people held the offices, for the old colonial tradition that candidates should be chosen from the better classes only died hard. In the *Democracy* West, however, there was no authentic aristocracy from which to choose, and the common people themselves held the offices. It was not to be long before this excess of democracy should be in evidence throughout the land. Travelers could observe even then a growing intolerance of superiority which in time would turn into a kind of worship of mediocrity. To elect one's betters to office was to admit that one had betters. To throw one's betters out of office was to rebuke for their pretensions those who thought themselves superior, and to prove that the people really ruled.

The abundance of opportunity in America opened the way to an almost unrestrained individualism. With the chances for success everywhere so great, anyone with an ambition to fulfill *Individual-* rushed forward to achieve his goal by whatever means *ism* seemed good to him. He asked only to be let alone. Fortunately there was room enough for all. The New England manufacturer who expanded his mills need not necessarily destroy his competitor; with abundant markets the two might expand and prosper side by side. If new machinery threw employees out of work, more likely than not other jobs, equally good, soon appeared. As for the increasing number of farmers and farm laborers, cheap lands and a fertile soil beckoned them to the West, where as pioneers they might achieve a greater success and a greater degree of independence than they could ever have known anywhere else. Throughout the West individual freedom was a frontier heritage much prized by all. Pioneers made their way in the world by their own efforts, and they took pride in the work they had done. They made a fetish of their freedom, and would brook few restraints, whether of government or of society. All this was possible, however, only because of the abundance of opportunity in America. Three quarters of a century later, when lands and markets had become more limited, individual freedom ceased to be an unmixed blessing.

Ever since colonial times religious freedom, as a natural corollary of individual freedom, had made steady gains. During the American Revolution the number of church establishments in the *Religious* United States had been greatly reduced; in 1786 Thomas *freedom* Jefferson had won his notable victory for the complete divorcement of church and state in Virginia; and in the first amendment to the Constitution of the United States Congress had been forbidden to pass a law "respecting the establishment of religion or prohibiting the free exercise thereof." Nevertheless, the feeling that religion must somehow be supported by the state was slow to die. The new western states would have nothing to do with church establishments, but in New England, where the Congregationalists were strongly intrenched, the last citadels of conservatism were not broken down until after the War of 1812. In New Hampshire the reform was delayed until 1817, in Connecticut until 1818, and in Massachusetts until 1833. But by this time the complete separation of church and state in the United States had become a fixed principle. This was one of the evidences of American superiority that the typical American could point out to travelers from abroad with confidence and pride.

With the great multiplicity of religious sects, mutual toleration for all and special privileges for none were well-nigh inevitable developments. To the Congregationalist, Dutch Reformed, Quaker, Catholic, and Episcopalian denominations of the seaboard were added the Presbyterian, Lutheran, Baptist, and Methodist churches of the back country, not to mention literally scores of minor religious units. Each denomination was now organized on a national basis, usually with a type of church government strongly reflecting the political institutions of the United States, and with as complete separation from Old World churches as was consistent with its theology. The western denominations, such as the Methodists and the Baptists, were growing with far greater rapidity than those of the East. This was due in large part to the democratic appeal that the frontier churches were willing to make. They did not insist upon an educated ministry, but were generally willing to accept as preachers all those who felt that they had received the divine "call." They were democratic in church government, they rekindled at every opportunity the revival fervor that had swept the country in the early years of the century and in their camp-meetings they preached a gospel of salvation for the many rather than merely for the few. Even in conservative New England, where the Unitarian revolt was still in full swing, the leaven of democracy was taking hold. Calvinistic theology, with its emphasis upon the unworthiness of man, a creature "conceived in sin and born in inquity," was losing steadily before the attacks of the Unitarians, who held after all man was the noblest work of God, born in his Maker's image, and endowed with no less spiritual possibilities than were given to the man Jesus himself. From the religious point of view there could be no greater exaltation of democracy than was implicit in the commonly made assertion that in every man there was a spark of the divine.

Afraid as they were to confess a shortcoming, Americans generally made light of their cultural deficiencies, and featured instead their great success in dealing with the practical problems that confronted a rapidly growing nation. But there is much reason to believe that they had a secret regard for the sophistication they associated with older civilizations, that they would have rejoiced to be less completely outdone in this respect. As a matter of fact, in such realms as education, art and architecture, and even literature the new nation already had something to its credit.

One reason for the lack of popular interest in education was the slowness of the schools to adapt themselves to the needs of a democracy. For the most part they still operated on the theory that *Education* it was their business to educate the leaders of society only, and to ignore the needs of the masses. This concept of education, however, was breaking down, and the popular prejudice against education was being correspondingly undermined. Free elementary schools were sometimes starved for lack of financial support, but the people were quick to acknowledge, especially in their new state constitutions, the duty of the state to provide such instruction at public expense. Private academies designed to meet the educational needs of children whose parents could afford to pay flourished in the East, and were available in surprisingly large numbers even in the West. Higher education was still left mainly to the churches, but between 1810 and 1820, while the number of American colleges was being doubled, evidence also accumulated that the strictly classical and theological training of an earlier age would not endure. Thanks mainly to the work of Jefferson, the curriculum of the College of William and Mary now included such subjects as law, history, political economy, and modern languages, while the University of Virginia, founded in 1825, not only adopted an unusually liberal course of study, but also made the entrance requirements easier, and allowed students great freedom in their choice of subjects. The democratic ideal of education for citizenship was clearly supplanting the older ideal of religious education.[1]

Americans cared relatively little for art, yet in an age which knew nothing of photography they could at least see point to the *Portrait* painting of portraits. Gilbert Stuart (1755–1828), whose *painters* skill would have won him recognition in any age, is best remembered

---

[1] Among the numerous manuals that recount the history of early American education are E. P. Cubberley, *Public Education in the United States* (1919); E. G. Dexter, *A History of Education in the United States* (1904); E. E. Slosson, *The American Spirit in Education* (1921). E. M. Coulter, *College Life in the Old South* (1928), is an entertaining history of the University of Georgia before the Civil War.

for the great number of Washington canvases he left. He painted portraits of many other well-known Americans also, among them most of the early Presidents. Charles Wilson Peale (1741–1827) portrayed famous Americans of the same generation with less technical excellence, perhaps, than Stuart, but with greater simplicity and fidelity to truth. Peale was also interested in cultivating an American interest in art, and furnished much of the inspiration which led to the founding of the Pennsylvania Academy of Fine Arts (1805) and the National Academy of Design (1826). John Trumbull (1756–1843) discovered that historical paintings had an appeal for Americans that was almost as hard to resist as that of portraits. He discreetly admitted that the occupation of painting as a rule was "frivolous, little useful to society, and unworthy of a man who has talents for more serious pursuits. But to preserve and diffuse the memory of the noblest series of actions which have ever presented themselves in the history of man, is sufficient warrant for it." And so, along with his portraits, he left many colorful representations of scenes in the American Revolution — paintings deeply esteemed by many subsequent generations of patriots. It is proper to point out, however, that all the early American artists owed most of their proficiency to European training. Some of them, like John Singleton Copley (1738–1815), lived as much of the time in Europe as in the United States.[1]

In architecture, too, there were some worthy American beginnings. The practicality and good taste of the old colonial and Georgian designs *The classical* were not forgotten, but shortly after the Revolution a classi- *revival* cal revival set in which had pronounced results. Thomas Jefferson, whose variety of interests had not failed to take in architecture, was the leading exponent of this new trend. He used classical traditions in designing a house for himself at Monticello, houses for his neighbors and friends, a new capitol for his state, and a building plan for the University of Virginia that has since been called "the finest example of classical architecture in America." Throughout the country, but especially in the South, the more pretentious private dwellings with their high column-supported porticos reflected clearly the classical influence, and many public buildings also, such as the White House, the Bank of the United States, and the Philadelphia Library, were similarly designed. New churches still adhered closely to colonial tradition.[2]

American writers who were interested in the exploitation of American themes found a ready outlet for their efforts in the rapidly increasing numbers of newspapers and magazines that were appearing. By 1810

[1] Samuel Isham, *The History of American Painting* (1905).
[2] Howard Major, *The Domestic Architecture of the Early American Republic* (1926).

there were no less than three hundred and fifty newspapers in the United States, as against only forty at the close of the American Revolution. The increasing popularity of magazines is shown by the fact that in 1800 there were not more than a dozen such publications in the whole country, whereas in 1825 there were nearly a hundred. *Magazines and newspapers* Newspapers still emphasized political news and political arguments, but the magazines, although by no means unconcerned with politics and actually at great pains to defend the new republic against foreign critics, presented more varied offerings. Both newspapers and magazines had as a rule only small and local circulations, but the *North American Review,* which was founded in 1815, soon gained a well-deserved notice even outside the United States.[1]

Although the first real flowering of American literature is usually associated with a somewhat later period, the names of at least two notable American writers, Washington Irving and William Cullen Bryant, were known even before the War of 1812. Curiously, both men opened their literary careers with attacks on Thomas Jefferson. Irving's *Knickerbocker History of New York* was less a satire on the Dutch in early New Netherland than on the policies of Jefferson's administration, while the *Embargo*, from the pen of the thirteen-year-old Bryant, disdained subtleties: *Literary lights*

> Go, wretch, resign the Presidential chair,
> Disclose thy secret measures, foul or fair;
> Go, search with curious eye for hornéd frogs
> 'Mid the wild wastes of Louisiana bogs,
> Or, where Ohio rolls his turbid stream,
> Dig for huge bones, thy glory and thy theme.

A little later the still youthful Bryant was penning his striking lines *To a Waterfowl*, and his immortal *Thanatopsis*. Another great name in American literature won prominence when James Fenimore Cooper published *The Spy* (1821), a story of American life during the Revolution.[2]

The multiplication of books and libraries during these years testifies eloquently to the growing literary interests of Americans. They might pretend that there was for such a race of practical men as they professed themselves to be no charm whatever in learning and culture, but six thousand tons of paper, according to estimates made for 1816, were required annually to make the books they bought. Many Americans took great pride in assembling libraries. The largest private libraries in the

[1] F. L. Mott, *A History of American Magazines, 1741–1850* (1930).

[2] V. L. Parrington, *The Romantic Revolution in America* (*Main Currents in American Thought*, II, 1927), covers the years 1800 to 1860.

country were probably those of John Quincy Adams and Thomas Jefferson, each of which ran to over five thousand volumes, but practically every prominent citizen aspired to own a library and busied himself with the collection of books. Public libraries also were becoming increasingly common, and the manufacture of books in America had reached the point where works on nearly every known subject were printed on this side of the Atlantic.

The ultranationalism of the United States after the War of 1812 is in no way more emphatically portrayed than in the program of legislation *Nationalism* which Congress, once the war was at an end, made haste to *in politics* adopt. President Madison in his annual message of December 5, 1815, showed plainly that as far as he was concerned the era of narrow particularism and states' rights was over. He urged upon Congress the necessity of a strong military establishment, a uniform national currency, a tariff to protect the new American industries, a national system of roads and canals, and a great national university. On every point save the last his recommendations were accepted. These facts are the more striking when it is remembered that the President had once been, next to Jefferson himself, the most prominent critic of Federalist centralization, while the Congress which now followed his lead had an overwhelmingly Republican majority in each house. The Republican Party, which during its fifteen years of power had gradually moved over to the positions once occupied by the Federalists, had discovered that with each move in the direction of nationalism its popularity with the voters had increased. Moreover, the new generation of Republicans had never known devotion to the doctrines of early Jeffersonianism. Madison, although somewhat changed by time, represented after all the earlier age and shifted ground with some reluctance, but such newcomers in national politics as Henry Clay of Kentucky and John C. Calhoun of South Carolina had little concern for party tradition, and felt free to follow current trends of thought.

The experiences of the war gave abundant point to Madison's plea for a strengthening of the national defense. In the place of the old feeling *The* ing that a standing army might endanger the liberties of *national* the people, and that an unscrupulous President might use *defense* it to make himself a dictator, there was frank recognition of the need of a dependable fighting weapon, and complete confidence that an American President would make no effort to overthrow the Constitution. A standing army of ten thousand men was authorized, and an appropriation of eight million dollars was voted for the construction of fifteen new naval units. The Military Academy at West Point, which had been established in 1802, was reorganized with a view to greater efficiency, and was given increased support. Thus the nation willingly embarked upon what was for the time a notable preparedness program.

An even more significant revelation of the nationalistic trend of the times is to be found in the act to establish a second Bank of the United States.[1] With the disappearance of the Hamiltonian bank in 1811 the banking business of the country had been turned over completely to the state banks, each of which operated under a private charter granted by a state legislature. *Second Bank of the United States* These banks had served an important purpose even while the first Bank of the United States was in existence, for the national bank issued notes only in large denominations, and the smaller currency of the country was mostly supplied by the state banks. They were able also to do a flourishing local business that was beyond the reach of the Bank of the United States, and accordingly their number and strength steadily increased. Whereas there were all told only four state banks in 1790, there were eighty-eight of them in 1811. The prerogatives of the state banks varied greatly, but they were universally banks of issue, and most of them printed as much paper money as they dared. In the Northeast, state banking was carried on along conservative lines, but in the South and West, particularly after 1811, the paper issues were excessive, the currency was inflated, and speculation, which ordinarily took the form of speculation in land, was dangerously stimulated. Moreover, except in New England specie payments were wholly suspended by the state banks during the War of 1812, and the purchasing power of their notes exhibited bewildering variations.

It was partly with a view to correcting these evils that a new national bank was proposed in 1816. Such a bank could put out a national currency, which, unlike the state bank currency, would have the same value anywhere in the nation. Also, the second Bank of the United States could use its power, as the first had done, to check the "wildcat" tendencies of the state banks, and to force them to do a more conservative business.

The committee of seven which framed the bank bill was headed by John C. Calhoun, and had only two members from the non-slave-holding states. Nevertheless, it decided in favor of establishing precisely the sort of bank that southern states'-rights Republicans had once opposed so vigorously. The new bank should have a capital stock of $35,000,000;

[1] Ralph C. H. Catterall, *The Second Bank of the United States* (1903), recounts the history of the bank in detail.

the United States government should subscribe one fifth of the stock, private individuals the other four fifths, and the directors should be similarly apportioned; the bank should have a monopoly on the business of the United States and the national banking business; it might establish branch banks throughout the several states; and it might continue in operation for a period of twenty years. For the valuable privileges the bank was to enjoy it was required to pay to the government of the United States a bonus of $1,500,000.

This measure received the ardent support of Calhoun, who dismissed all doubts as to its constitutionality by the argument that the Constitution had delegated to Congress full control of the monetary system of the country, and that for this purpose a national bank was essential. Henry Clay, who had argued in 1811 against the constitutionality of a national bank, had greater difficulties to surmount, but he was equal to the occasion. Congress, he maintained, had power to make such laws as were "necessary and proper" to carry out the powers set down for it in the Constitution, and whereas a national bank was by no means "necessary and proper" in 1811 it had become so by 1816. In general the views of Calhoun and Clay represented fairly their respective sections, but from New England there came opposition. Daniel Webster was against the measure. He made no attempt to oppose it on constitutional grounds, but he argued that the state banks, if properly managed, could take care of the nation's business. The banks of his section were safe and sound, and he reflected their fear that a national bank under western and southern management might become a source of danger rather than of strength. The opposition which Webster voiced was insufficient to block passage of the bill, and the second Bank of the United States was chartered. To insure a return on the part of the state banks to specie payments, Congress also resolved that dues payable to the United States should be received only in specie or in the notes of banks which, like the Bank of the United States, stood ready to redeem their currency issues in specie.

Further evidence of the national spirit that characterized the times is to be found in the Tariff Act of 1816.[1] The first tariff law, passed at the beginning of Washington's administration, had been amended upward by 1812 to a level of approximately twelve and one half per cent. These duties were doubled during the War, but with the understanding that they should be dropped to the normal

Tariff of 1816

---

[1] F. W. Taussig, *Tariff History of the United States* (1888), is a standard work that has gone through many editions. See also Edward Stanwood, *American Tariff Controversies in the Nineteenth Century* (2 vols., 1903–04).

peace-time level a year after its close. It became clear soon after the War was over that the peace-time duties would not be high enough to keep out foreign goods; indeed, English manufacturers, long cut off from their accustomed markets, soon began to "dump" their accumulated surpluses upon American importers at such ridiculously low prices that American manufacturers were greatly perturbed. If the degree of self-sufficiency that the country had lately attained was not to be lost, high enough tariffs to shut out the cheap foreign goods must be levied. To most Americans continued industrial independence was well worth this price. Calhoun pointed out also that the tariff would serve to bind the various sections of the country together more closely, for they would henceforth be dependent for necessities upon other parts of the United States instead of upon other parts of the world.

A tariff bill which maintained or increased the wartime duties was carried by a two-to-one majority in the House and by a four-to-one majority in the Senate. From the point of view of the commercial interests, whose hope of profits lay in the complete resumption of overseas trade, this tariff measure was a sad mistake. In defense of their interests Daniel Webster and a small group of Federalists opposed the tariff, although within a few years these same men were to become the chief champions of protection. Nor could even a majority of the southern Republicans be brought in line for the bill; only twenty-three votes were obtained from the South for protection, while thirty-four Southerners voted against it. For this latter group John Randolph of Roanoke was the most effective spokesman. "No," he said, "I will buy where I can get manufactures cheapest, I will not agree to lay a duty on the cultivator of the soil to encourage exotic manufactures; because, after all, we should only get much worse things at a higher price." The tariff bill was intended, even by its friends, to remain on the statute books only temporarily; as soon as the infant industries could stand alone protection should be withdrawn. But to manufacturers who profited from high duties the time for their repeal was never to seem ripe.

Madison's recommendation of a national program of internal improvements was somewhat guarded. No man knew better than he what the framers of the federal Constitution had meant when they listed the powers which Congress was to exercise, and the power to build a national system of roads and canals had been deliberately omitted. Madison suggested, therefore, that Congress should take steps to enlarge its powers by proposing an amendment to the Constitution definitely permitting it to undertake works of internal improvement. In the meantime he saw no objection to its making use of its "existing powers," whatever they might be. The subject was touched upon first in his message of 1815, and when Congress failed to act upon his suggestion at that session, he renewed his recommendation a year later.

Congress was as ready to go ahead with internal improvements as with the bank or the tariff, and the younger Republicans were unaware

The Cumberland Road

of any constitutional obstacles. The Cumberland Road, designed to connect the East and the West along the route Braddock had taken in the French and Indian War, was already in process of construction at national expense, and its completion was a matter of good faith. When Ohio was admitted to the Union in 1803, Congress had promised that such a road would be built in return for assurance that the new state would not attempt to tax federal lands within its borders, and five per cent of the receipts from Ohio land sales had been definitely allocated to this purpose. Contracts were let in 1811 for the beginning of construction, and in spite of the war other contracts were let in 1812, 1813, and 1814; but with only twenty miles actually finished by the end of the war there remained much to be done. Neither Madison nor his successor, Monroe, made any effort to prevent appropriations being made for the continuation of this road, and Congress regularly supplied whatever funds were needed. By 1818 the road was completed.[1]

Congress was willing to stretch the Constitution further than the President could follow, however, in the adoption of a program of internal

The Bonus Bill

improvements. Calhoun, the leader of the nationalists, introduced in December, 1816, a bill to pledge to the promotion of internal improvements the bonus of a million and a half dollars that the newly chartered Bank of the United States was to pay into the treasury. The constitutionality of the Bonus Bill, as this measure was called, was stoutly defended by Calhoun, who held that the Constitution "was not intended as a thesis for the logician to exercise his ingenuity on; that it ought to be construed with plain good sense; and that when so construed nothing could be more express than the Constitution upon this very point." Opponents of the Bonus Bill in Congress questioned, nevertheless, whether money might properly be raised and spent for internal improvements under the "general welfare" clause, and some of those who hailed from New England or the lower South thought that, regardless of constitutionality, the states through which the roads were to

---

[1] T. B. Searight, *The Old Pike, A History of the National Road with Incidents, Accidents and Anecdotes Thereon* (1894), is all that its title implies. The story of the road is also told in A. B. Hulbert, *The Paths of Inland Commerce* (1920).

be built should bear the expense. The strongest demand for internal improvements came from the middle and western states, and since these states would profit most from the building of the roads why should they not pay for them? As for Madison, he had no objection to national expenditures for internal improvements, but he believed that on this subject the Constitution granted no such latitude to Congress as Calhoun and his followers seemed to think. The Bonus Bill passed Congress, but was vetoed by the President. The young Republicans tried in vain to pass the measure over the President's veto, but they were not discouraged. They meant to continue the policy of national improvements that the building of the Cumberland Road had begun, and they were unwilling to risk the delay and uncertainty of a constitutional amendment to give Congress the power which in their opinion it already possessed.

The election of 1816 found the Federalists out of touch with the nationalistic spirit that pervaded the country as a whole, and still further handicapped by their bad war record. The Republicans, on the other hand, were assured of victory, although by no *Election of 1816* means certain as to whom they should nominate. This matter was decided, according to custom, by a caucus of the party delegation in Congress, but the caucus system of making nominations had begun to arouse criticism. Some felt that it gave Congress too great power over the choice of the chief executive; others that the sitting President could wield too much influence over the caucus. Much to the dissatisfaction of those who held these views, Madison made no secret of his wish that James Monroe, his Secretary of State, should succeed to the Presidency. When the customary caucus was held, Monroe won the nomination over W. H. Crawford of Georgia by the narrow vote of 65 to 54. The Federalists did not even trouble themselves to name candidates, and in the election which followed they carried only three states, Massachusetts, Connecticut, and Delaware, whose electors cast 34 votes for Rufus King of New York. Monroe's vote from the other states reached 183.

Like three out of four of his predecessors, James Monroe (1758–1831) was a Virginia planter.[1] His family, however, was by no means of the first families of Virginia; it was rather of the western, small-planter class, and included in its family tree many Scotch and Welsh ancestors. Monroe was just beginning his college work at William and Mary when the Revolutionary War broke out, and although he was only sixteen

---

[1] D. C. Gilman, *James Monroe* (1883), is one of the relatively few biographies of Monroe, who, as an individual, has been somewhat neglected by the writers of American history.

years of age he promptly joined the Patriot army. He had an honorable record in the war, and emerged from it, in spite of his youth, with the rank of lieutenant-colonel. Later he studied law under Jefferson, and inevitably absorbed the political principles of the older man. Monroe never became the scholar that Jefferson was, or for that matter, Madison, and to many of his contemporaries it seemed that he was hardly of presidential calibre. But his political experience was more than ample. By the time he reached the Presidency he had served in the Virginia Assembly, in the Congress of the Confederation, and in the United States Senate; he had represented his country on important missions to France, Spain, and England; he had been governor of Virginia for several terms; and he had been at one time both Secretary of State and Secretary of War.

Firmly grounded in the states'-rights principles of early Jeffersonianism, Monroe found it somewhat difficult to keep abreast of the nationalistic trend his party had taken. He and Jefferson were openly at odds over this subject when the latter left office, and Monroe was no more able than Madison to accept as constitutional the ambitious program of internal improvements at national expense that the young Republicans were beginning to preach. He allowed the Cumberland Road to be finished, but in 1822, when a bill passed Congress to provide funds for its repair by establishing toll gates and collecting tolls, he interposed a veto. The exercise of such power by Congress, he claimed, implied a "power to adopt and execute a complete system of internal improvements," and for this he found no constitutional warrant. He believed, however, that a change in the Constitution to permit the United States to build "great national works" would be desirable, provided that "all minor improvements" should be left to the states.

The Cumberland tolls veto

While Madison and Monroe were struggling to adjust their consciences to the new nationalism, the Supreme Court under the leadership of another Virginian, John Marshall, was doing all it could to help them. "The judiciary of the United States," wrote Thomas Jefferson in 1820, "is the subtle corps of sappers and miners constantly working underground to undermine the foundations of our confederate fabric. They are constantly construing our constitution from a co-ordination of a general and special government, to a general and supreme one alone. They will lay all things at their feet, and they are too well versed in the English law to forget the maxim, '*boni judicis est ampliare jurisdictionem.*'" Thomas Jefferson had done his part as President toward exaggerating the power of the central government, but

The Supreme Court

there can be but little doubt that the Supreme Court under Marshall had done far more.[1]

John Marshall (1755–1835) was born far out on the Virginia frontier in what became a few years later Fauquier County. His father, Thomas Marshall, was a man of good education who did what he *John* could to communicate to his son his own love of history and *Marshall* literature. Young Marshall early determined upon a legal career, but when the Revolution broke out he left off the study of law to enter the army, where for a time he fought against the British as a member of his father's regiment. Toward the end of the war, when the fighting had died down, he attended some lectures on law at William and Mary College, and in 1781 he began to practice in Fauquier County. When presently he won an important land title case for the tenants of Lord Fairfax, his reputation was made, and he was soon recognized as the leader of the Virginia bar. His legal labors, however, did not prevent him from playing an important part in politics. He was chosen eight times to the Virginia legislature, sat in the Virginia convention called to ratify the Constitution, served as one of the three commissioners whom Adams sent to make peace with France in 1797, represented his state in Congress for one term, and became Secretary of State during the last year of the Adams administration.

Marshall, like Adams, was identified with the more moderate wing of the Federalist Party, but he had a deep distrust of the radical democracy preached by Thomas Jefferson and the Republicans. After the election of 1800, when Adams thought it his patriotic duty to save the judiciary, if possible, from the menace of Jeffersonian control, he made the young and energetic Marshall Chief Justice of the United States. Marshall served only thirty days under a Federalist president, but for thirty-four years after the Federalists lost control of Congress and the Presidency he guided the Supreme Court in a thoroughly Federalist interpretation of the Constitution.[2] So great was the power of his personality and so convincing his logic that, to the despair of Republican Presidents, the

[1] In addition to the lives of Marshall, already cited, the following will be found useful: John P. Kennedy, *Memoirs of the Life of William Wirt* (2 vols., 1849); W. W. Story, *Life and Letters of Joseph Story* (2 vols., 1851); G. T. Curtis, *Life of Daniel Webster* (2 vols., 1870). A. C. McLaughlin, *A Constitutional History of the United States* (1935), covers the work of the Court under Marshall in great detail. Excellent short accounts are contained in J. W. Burgess, *The Middle Period* (1897); and Allen Johnson, *Union and Democracy* (1915).

[2] The post was first offered by Adams to John Jay, who declined it; Marshall's name was sent to the Senate January 20, 1801, the nomination was confirmed on January 27, and on February 4 the new Chief Justice took office. Curiously, he continued also as Secretary of State until the end of the Adams administration, although he accepted a salary only as Chief Justice.

new judges they appointed were soon following Marshall's lead. The growth of the national spirit during and after the War of 1812, however, served to bring the Court and the dominant political party more closely together than they had ever been before. The nationalistic decisions of Marshall and his colleagues now aroused respect and approval, particularly among the young Republicans, rather than condemnation.

The foundations of American constitutional law were carefully laid. Many important opinions were written by Marshall himself. They were ably reasoned and forcefully stated, and, since precedents were being made rather than followed, were unencumbered by tedious citations. They became, as Marshall intended, a guide to public opinion as well as to lawyers. As the importance of the Court came to be fully recognized, the best lawyers in the country were retained to appear before it. Such men as Luther Martin and William Pinkney of Maryland, William Wirt of Virginia, and Daniel Webster of Massachusetts contributed from their wisdom and research many of the arguments upon which the Court drew in formulating its opinions.

Marshall's decision in the case of *Marbury vs. Madison*, already noted, and the utter failure of the Republicans to undo it, added greatly to the *Marshall's* prestige of the Court. Its power to declare null and void an *opinions* act of Congress out of harmony with the Constitution was repeatedly reasserted, and, in spite of the fact that the actual exercise of such authority was not again attempted in an important case until the Dred Scott decision, the doctrine of judicial review soon won general acceptance. A few years later in the case of the *United States vs. Judge Peters* (1809), the Court found opportunity to show that its power, in case of conflict, transcended that of a state legislature. It happened that a federal district court in Pennsylvania had awarded some prize money obtained from the sale of a British sloop, the *Active*, captured during the American Revolution, to a certain Gideon Olmstead and others. Locally this decision was extremely unpopular, and the legislature of Pennsylvania passed a law to prevent the payment that the federal judge had ordered. Finally the Attorney-General, when all other means had failed, asked the United States Supreme Court for a writ of *mandamus* directing Judge Peters to enforce his decision. Marshall not only issued the writ, but in so doing he also stated plainly the importance of the issue that had been raised. "If the legislatures of the several states," he said, "may at will annul the judgment of the courts of the United States, and destroy the rights acquired under those judgments, the Constitution becomes a solemn mockery, and the nation is deprived of the means of enforcing its laws by the instrumentality of its own tribunals." The Pennsylvania

[342]

authorities did not yield gracefully, and made use of the state militia to defy the federal decision, but force was met with force, and when the state militia were confronted with a federal *posse comitatus* of two thousand men, plans for resistance were abandoned. Olmstead was allowed to collect his prize money, and the immunity of the federal courts from state interference was singularly vindicated.

The Supreme Court presently took occasion to demonstrate in two notable decisions, *Martin vs. Hunter's Lessee* (1816) and *Cohens vs. Virginia* (1821), that its power was also superior to that of the state courts whenever federal rights were involved. In Virginia, where these cases originated, the idea that a decision by the highest tribunal of the state could be reviewed and reversed by an outside authority was deeply resented. John Taylor of Caroline, in a series of pamphlets, *Construction Construed* (1820), *Tyranny Unmasked* (1822), and *New Views of the Constitution* (1823), came powerfully to the defense of the state courts, and public opinion in Virginia was with him. But his efforts, and all others like them, were unavailing. Litigants began to make use of federal rather than state courts whenever the former would accept jurisdiction, since the finality of a state decision was so frequently open to question. This influx of new business into the federal courts added greatly to their prestige, and particularly to that of the Supreme Court of the United States, which now in so large a number of instances became the court of last resort.

Superiority of federal courts

In the two Virginia decisions and in others also the Court was at pains to defend not only its own prerogatives as a court, but also the supremacy of the national government over the states. The classic expression of this point of view came in the case of *McCulloch vs. Maryland* (1819). The state of Maryland had attempted to tax out of existence the Baltimore branch of the Bank of the United States, and the bank had refused to pay the tax. The state courts naturally found against the bank and ordered it to pay, but an appeal was taken to the Supreme Court of the United States. Here was a clear-cut issue between state and nation, and Marshall made the most of it. He upheld the constitutionality of the act of Congress by which the bank was created, and in so doing gave the approval of the Court to Hamilton's doctrine of implied powers. "Let the end be legitimate, let it be within the scope of the Constitution, and all means which are appropriate, which are plainly adapted to that end, which are not prohibited, but consist with the letter and spirit of the Constitution, are constitutional." He held also that the state of Maryland had exceeded its authority in attempting to tax the notes of the Baltimore branch. "The power to tax" he reasoned, involved the "power to destroy," which, if conceded in this case, would leave the states free to undo such strictly constitutional laws of Congress as they disliked. In the course of his argument Marshall took occasion to speak out plainly against the theory that the Constitution emanated from the states, and that the government established by it was therefore merely a creature of the states. "The government of the Union," he maintained, "is emphatically, and truly, a government of the people. In form and in substance it emanates from them. Its powers are granted by them, and are to be exercised on them, and for their benefit. . . . If any one proposition could command the universal consent of mankind, we might expect it would be this — that the government of the Union, though limited in its powers, is supreme within its sphere of action. . . ." No better statement of the supremacy of the nation over the states has ever been made.

The Court made an honest attempt, nevertheless, to draw a line between the powers that were granted exclusively to the national government and those that were reserved wholly or in part to the states. In the case of *Gibbon vs. Ogden* (1824), it held that a law of the state of New York which granted to one company a monopoly upon the use of the waters of the state was unconstitutional, because it interfered with the complete control which Congress had been given over interstate commerce. Obviously, commerce among the states could not be construed as stopping at the borders of any one state. On the other hand, in the case of *Ogden vs. Saunders* (1827), the Court conceded that it was within the province of a state to pass a bankruptcy law, although Congress had similar authority. It is significant, however, that this decision drew from Marshall the only dissenting opinion that he ever wrote on a constitutional case. The Chief Justice was willing to protect the states in the exercise of their rightful powers, but he made no secret of his intention to exalt the power of the nation whenever he could find warrant for it in the Constitution.

States' rights

The framers of the Constitution, fearful lest the states might lack either the power or the disposition to defend adequately the rights of private property, had consciously endeavored to make of the national government in this particular a great bulwark of strength. They specifically prohibited the states from passing any law "impairing the obligation of contracts," and in this clause Marshall found opportunity to range the Court as definitely as the framers of the Constitution could have wished on the side of property rights. In the case of *Fletcher vs. Peck* (1810), already noted, the Court had held that even so dishonest an act as that by which the state of Georgia had granted lands to the Yazoo companies could not be repealed without "impairing the obligation of contract." In the case of *Dartmouth College vs. Woodward* (1819), it maintained that a charter of incorporation was also a contract within the meaning of the Constitution. The state of New Hampshire had attempted to revise by law the old colonial charter under which Dartmouth College had been founded. The change was resented by the trustees of the college, who brought suit to retain their powers. When the case came to the United States Supreme Court, Daniel Webster, a Dartmouth alumnus, represented his *alma mater*, and won the Court not only to his reasoning, but even to the very wording of his argument. In vain did counsel for the state of New Hampshire plead that the framers of the Constitution had never intended the word "contract" to be so broadly construed. Marshall held that it was "necessary to go farther, and to say that, had this particular case been suggested, the language would have been so varied as to exclude it, or it would have been a special exception." Marshall's Dartmouth College decision was used later on to secure for business corporations an immunity from state control that he could hardly have foreseen. Thanks to the precedents he set, special privileges, obtained sometimes by wholesale corruption, were held inviolate long after public opinion demanded their limitation or repeal. In recent years, as a means of self-protection, states ordinarily reserve in all charters they grant the right to modify the terms of the charter at will.

Marshall's decisions, with their tremendous emphasis upon the power and importance of the national government, fitted in well with the temper of the American people in the years immediately following the War of 1812. The country was young and growing, conscious of its strength, confident of the future. Even the decisions with respect to property rights were not so out of harmony with the democratic trend of the times as they now seem. The opportunities for the acquisition of private property were not then limited to a few, but were the prerogative of the many, Marshall's decisions, while later used to build up a specially favored propertied class, were in their time meant to protect the small property-holder no less than the great.

CHAPTER XX

THE RISE OF THE NEW WEST

"THE rise of the new west," according to Frederick Jackson Turner, "was the most significant fact in American history in the years immediately following the War of 1812." [1] Applied to a period in which so many important developments were taking place, this is a broad statement, yet only a few critics appear to have questioned it. Certainly the rapidity with which the frontier was advanced during these years set a new record. During the thirty-six years that elapsed between the signing of the Declaration of Independence and the outbreak of the War of 1812, only five new states were added to the original thirteen: Vermont, Kentucky, Tennessee, Ohio, and Louisiana. But during the half-dozen years following the War of 1812, six new states, all of them frontier and five of them definitely western, were added to the Union: Indiana (1816), Mississippi (1817), Illinois (1818), Alabama (1819), Maine (1820), and Missouri (1821).

The opening up of new western states was undoubtedly promoted by the war itself. Both in the Northwest and in the Southwest the *Why people went west* war made an end to the Indian menace, so that now, wholly without risk, new western lands could be acquired as rapidly as the advance of settlement demanded. Moreover, the war served greatly to advertise the West. Throughout the nation the western campaigns were followed with intense interest, an interest which often carried over from the fighting to the region in which the fighting was taking place. Soldiers who participated in the western campaigns observed, as frontier soldiers had always done, the fertility of the lands over which they fought, and when the war was over they frequently returned to the West as emigrants, bringing their friends and neighbors with them. The business dislocations produced by the conflict also stimulated westward migration. In the Northeast unemployment crises

[1] F. J. Turner, *Rise of the New West* (1906), p. 67. Quoted by permission of Harper and Brothers, Publishers. This book, covering the decade 1819 to 1829, treats not only of the West, but of the various other sections also, and of the nation as a whole. It takes high rank in the literature of American history.

developed, first as a result of the commercial restrictions that preceded and accompanied the war, and secondly, as a result of the British policy of "dumping" their surplus manufactured goods in America to compete with the expensive products of American infant industries. These crises materially increased the volume of migration to the West. So also did the destruction of the Bank of the United States in 1811, and the outbreaks of wildcat banking which recurred from that time until 1817 — developments which unsettled business generally, inflated the currency, and promoted a reckless speculation in western lands.

Long-distance emigration to the West was made easier by the completion of the Cumberland Road, and by the increasing success with which steamboats were able to conquer the "western *The river* waters." The first river steamboat to be launched in the *steamboats* West, the *New Orleans*, was the work of Nicholas J. Roosevelt, a Pittsburgh agent of the famous firm of Fulton and Livingston, which had sponsored in 1807 the epochal trip of the steam-driven *Clermont* up the Hudson from New York to Albany and back again in sixty-two hours. The *New Orleans* was launched at Pittsburgh in 1811, and next spring it reached the city after which it was named. It lacked the power to return against the current, but in 1816 the *Enterprise* steamed from New Orleans to Louisville in twenty-five days. By the end of the decade not less than sixty steamboats were in operation on the Mississippi and its tributaries. Most of the early boats harbored defects that brought them to untimely ends, but the reports of such disasters did less to discourage the use of the boats than to make the rest of the nation better aware of the West.[1]

To such unconscious advertising as the blowing up of steamboats, and the earthquake which shook the Mississippi Valley in 1811, were added the reports of the European travelers in America, whose books were read with much greater interest on this side of the Atlantic than on the other. Comparatively few Europeans responded to the call of opportunity in the American West which the travelers almost invariably made clear, for during the years 1812 to 1821 the annual immigration into the United States averaged only about eight thousand. But that many Americans were quickened to action by the tales of European travelers can hardly be questioned. Many others, no doubt, were set in motion by the reports of such explorers as Zebulon M. Pike, whose memoirs were published just before the War of 1812, and Lewis and

[1] Seymour Dunbar, *A History of Travel in America* (4 vols., 1915), is particularly valuable because of its excellent illustrations. Channing, v, which begins with the close of the War of 1812, gives much attention to transportation. to the westward movement, and to social and economic conditions generally.

Clark, whose *Journals* appeared just after it. These accounts, to be sure, described a farther West than that which was now open to settlement. But they bespoke a new field of activity for the trapper and the fur-trader, and they were probably more influential than seems reasonable in inducing undecided Americans to make up their minds to join the advance of the agricultural frontier.

The phenomenal growth of cotton culture in the years following the War of 1812 added a strong southern element to the stream of westward *Southern migration* migration. The lands of the new Southwest were in large part ideally fitted for the production of cotton, whereas the cotton lands of the Southeast soon showed signs of wearing out. Sometimes well-established planters sold their eastern lands in order to purchase more fertile acres in Mississippi, or Alabama, or Louisiana, and by transferring themselves and their slaves to the West they contributed directly to the westward movement. Frequently, however, eastern planters sought to enlarge their holdings in accordance as their yield per acre declined. In the latter event they contributed indirectly to the westward movement by buying out neighboring planters and farmers, whose best recourse was to re-establish themselves somewhere in the West. Members of the non-slaveholding class often displayed great eagerness to escape from an environment dominated by the great planters. In such a society only the planters made money; the free laborer barely made a living. Moreover, wherever slaves were employed in large numbers it was natural to assume that manual labor was beneath the dignity of free men. Some of the poorer southern whites in their retreat from the slavery system went directly West, felled the timber, grubbed the stumps, tilled the fields until the cotton-grower's frontier caught up with them, and then sold out to move farther West and repeat the process. Others, unwilling to live where slavery existed, crossed the Ohio River into the Northwest to swell the populations of such frontier states as Illinois and Indiana. Still others crossed the Mississippi River into Missouri, where slavery was legalized but for climatic reasons could never flourish.

This rapid assault upon the West was not without its unfortunate aspects. The great majority of those who went West, whether they came *Western banking* from the South or from the North, were men of very slender means. More often than otherwise they were compelled to go into debt for the cost of their migration, for the price of the land they settled on, and for the expense of making their new land over into productive farms. Western farmers had developed the habit of borrowing a large part of the funds they needed from banks, a practice which

NINETEENTH-CENTURY IMPROVEMENTS IN WATER TRANSPORTATION

GROWTH OF THE WEST, 1810–1830

	1810	1820	1830
Kentucky	406,511	564,317	687,917
Tennessee	261,727	422,823	681,904
Ohio	230,760	581,434	937,903
Louisiana	76,556	153,407	215,739
Indiana	24,520	147,178	343,031
Illinois	12,282	55,211	157,445
Mississippi	{40,352}	75,448	136,621
Alabama		127,901	157,445
Missouri	20,845	66,586	140,455

was greatly facilitated by the multiplication of state banks after the year 1811, when the first Bank of the United States ceased to exist. Between 1811 and 1815 the number of state banks throughout the country rose from eighty-eight to two hundred and eight, and by 1820 to three hundred and seven. The new banks, particularly those in the West, operated under few legal restraints, and their officers were apt to be grossly ignorant of good banking practice. They tried to meet the heavy demand upon them for loans by issuing paper money, often far in excess of their resources. They lent for long terms on land and other securities for which a ready sale could not always be found. They failed to discriminate carefully among would-be borrowers, and rarely kept an adequate supply of cash on hand. With specie payments generally suspended during and after the War of 1812, their reckless inflation of the currency brought on for business in general an unhealthy "boom," and for the West an orgy of land speculation. By 1815 the government was selling as much as a million acres of new land each year; by 1817, nearly two million acres; and by 1819, over five million acres. Rapid as was the migration of population into the West, the opening up of new lands was even more rapid, and the dangers in the situation were not difficult to see.

The second Bank of the United States, which began to operate in 1817, unfortunately sought at first to outdo the state banks in the quest of *Panic of 1819* speculative profits, and its Baltimore branch failed in 1818 because of mismanagement. Furthermore, the bank began an attack on the state banks, not so much because of the type of business they did as because of its desire to take their business away from them. To this end it used its power ruthlessly to force all competitors to an immediate resumption of specie payments. Notes of a given bank would be accumulated by the Bank of the United States and then

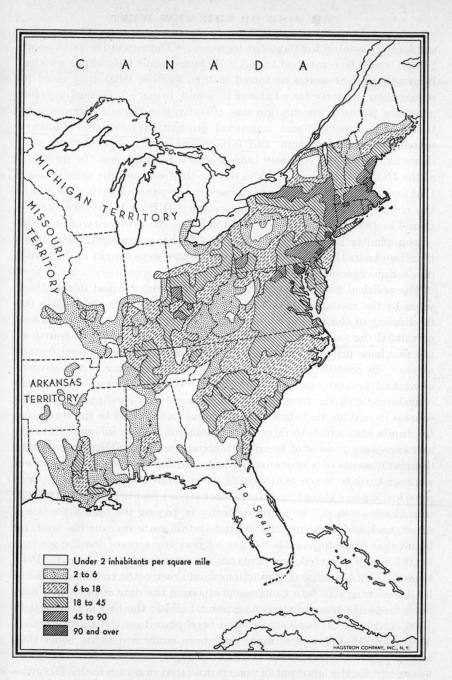

DENSITY OF POPULATION IN 1820

Under 2 inhabitants per square mile
2 to 6
6 to 18
18 to 45
45 to 90
90 and over

CANADA

MICHIGAN TERRITORY

MISSOURI TERRITORY

ARKANSAS TERRITORY

To Spain

HAGSTROM COMPANY, INC., N.Y.

suddenly presented for payment in specie. Thereupon the bank so attacked would be compelled to call in its loans, while individuals who had borrowed from it would be forced in turn to raise what they owed by selling their property for whatever it would bring. With such a policy generally pursued, speculation was effectively, although perhaps unintentionally, arrested, and a general liquidation followed. Bankers, merchants, manufacturers, and farmers, as well as speculators, went down in the general collapse; indeed, a new management for the Bank of the United States barely saved that institution from the same disaster that overtook so many other businesses in the panic of 1819. To add to the country's distress the price of cotton fell from thirty-two cents a pound in 1818 to eighteen cents in 1820, and the prosperity of even the cotton planter seemed for the moment to have vanished. For more than two years the people of the United States were caught in the throes of a serious economic depression.

The political power of the new West was made manifest during these years by the success which attended its efforts to secure a change in the land policy of the United States. The Harrison Land Law of 1800 had permitted the purchaser of government land to pay only one fourth of the purchase price in cash, and the remainder in three annual installments. In practice the collection of these debts owing to the government had proved exceedingly difficult. With that over-optimism so characteristic of the frontier, land purchasers had used up all their resources in making their first payment, and had trusted to the future for the funds with which to meet later payments. Then followed the slow and expensive process of clearing the land, the inevitable accidents and disappointments of a new environment, and the discovery that markets were so hard to reach that profits, even when crops were good, were practically non-existent. If the pioneer farmer had borrowed the money to make his "start," he found difficulty in paying the high interest exacted, and as for paying the annual installments due on his land, he found that quite impossible. Year by year the arrears due the government for land mounted, and demands for relief began to be heard. Politicians, quick to realize that evictions would cost votes, readily responded by introducing bills into Congress postponing the date of payments due. Such measures became almost an annual affair; the first was passed in 1806, and by 1820 twelve more had been placed on the statute books. Meanwhile the West was more and more confirmed in its belief that money payments should not be required at all; that the land was valueless except for the labor put in upon it; and that in return for his labor the pioneer farmer was entitled to the land without price.

The panic of 1819 called serious attention to this situation. Overbuying had been particularly in evidence during the preceding years, and the customary relief bill was at hand. But Congress was *Land Law* now easily persuaded to put an end to the unworkable credit *of 1820* system. In 1820 a law was passed which reduced the size of the tract that an individual might buy to eighty acres, and fixed the price per acre at $1.25 in cash. Thus for one hundred dollars a man could become the owner of a farm. This was not quite the free gift of land to which the Westerners felt they were entitled, but it approximated that goal closely. To supplement the new land law a Relief Act was passed in 1821, according to the terms of which the man who had bought more land on credit than he could pay for was permitted to turn back to the government a part of his land in lieu of further payments. If, for example, he had purchased three hundred and twenty acres of land and had made only the first of the four payments due, he might keep whichever eighty acres he chose and return the other two hundred and forty to the government. If, however, he chose to keep all of his land, he was permitted one of two alternatives, either a cash payment with a discount of thirty-seven and one half per cent, or eight annual installments instead of four, with all interest remitted. The Land Law of 1820 and the Relief Act of 1821 gave much satisfaction to the people of the West, and facilitated materially the transition of that region from depression to normal conditions.

The rapid expansion of the West soon made the country acutely aware of an impending conflict, hitherto hardly suspected, between the North and the South. Fundamentally the issue upon which these *Slavery and* sections came to divide was whether slavery in the United *sectionalism* States was to be a temporary or a permanent institution, but for the moment the difference of opinion was restricted to the question of what limits, if any, should be set for the expansion of slavery in the territory west of the Mississippi River. Under French and Spanish rule slavery had been legal in the whole of Louisiana, a situation which the American occupation did not at first disturb. Most of the pioneers who crossed the Mississippi came from the southern states, and while the newcomers, particularly in the St. Louis area, were rarely slaveholders, they were accustomed to slavery and showed no disposition whatever to interfere with it. Once northerners fully realized, however, that the entire trans-Mississippi West was in danger of being appropriated for slavery, they were ready to call a halt.

When Jefferson purchased Louisiana from France, he acquired for the United States not only a vast area of land but about fifteen thousand new citizens as well, most of whom were of French or Spanish descent. The chief center of Louisiana settlement was along the lower Mississippi in the vicinity of New Orleans, but a somewhat smaller population was located near the confluence of the Missouri and the Mississippi, with St. Louis as its principal city. Soon after the purchase had taken place, American settlers began to enter the lower Mississippi region in numbers, and by the time of the War of 1812 thousands of them each year were crossing also in the vicinity of St. Louis to thrust a firm wedge of settlement up the valley of the Missouri.

The size of the Louisiana Purchase insured that, once its settlement was actively begun, numerous subdivisions would have to be made. Accordingly, in 1804, Congress created the Territory of Orleans out of the region adjacent to New Orleans, and the District of Louisiana out of all the rest. In 1812 the Territory of Orleans became the state of Louisiana, but meantime the District of Louisiana had been repeatedly reorganized. Temporarily it was attached to Indiana Territory; in 1805 it became an entirely separate territory with a government of its own; in 1812 its name was changed to Missouri; and in 1819 it was materially reduced in size by the creation of the Territory of Arkansas. At this time the population of Missouri closely approximated the sixty thousand which, according to precedents set in the Old Northwest, made a territory eligible to statehood. Successive Missouri legislatures petitioned Congress on the subject, and in 1819 the House Committee on Territories reported favorably a bill enabling Missouri, with its boundaries still further restricted, to draw up a constitution and make ready for statehood.[1]

Missouri Territory

It was at this juncture that Representative James Tallmadge of New York raised the question of setting limits to the expansion of slavery in the Louisiana Purchase. He proposed to amend the bill reported from committee by providing that the further introduction of slavery into Missouri should be forbidden, and that all children born of slave parents after the admission of the state should be free upon reaching the age of twenty-five years.

The Tallmadge amendment

Until the introduction of the Tallmadge amendment, the slavery question had played little part in national politics. The problem of how slaves should be counted when apportioning representatives in Congress or assessing direct taxes on the states had been satisfactorily settled in the federal convention by the three-fifths compromise. Also, an early Congress had exercised its constitutional authority to pass a fugitive slave act, and the administration of this measure had so far provoked

---

[1] All the general histories treat the Missouri Compromise elaborately. An excellent special study is F. C. Shoemaker, *Missouri's Struggle for Statehood, 1804–1821* (1916).

little criticism. Moreover, slavery had long been regarded as a dying institution. The founders of the American nation had almost unanimously so considered it, Southerners no less than Northerners. Many of them were eager to speed the day when slavery should cease to exist throughout the whole country. Washington emancipated his slaves by his will; Alexander Hamilton and Benjamin Franklin were prominent in the work of emancipation societies; Thomas Jefferson wrote his anti-slavery views into the Northwest Ordinance of 1787. Almost by common consent the slave trade was forbidden in 1808, the earliest date possible under the Constitution. Indeed, this act was mistakenly supposed by many contemporaries to ensure the decline and ultimate disappearance of the institution of slavery itself.

Hostility to slavery during these early years of the republic was firmly grounded on the fact that the institution had ceased to be economically profitable. For this reason, even before the American Revolution, many of the colonies would have taken some anti-slavery action had not the British government been so insistent on protecting the profits of British merchants engaged in the slave trade. Jefferson's original draft of the Declaration of Independence actually listed British disallowance of colonial acts aimed at the slave trade as one of the chief grievances from which the colonies suffered, but out of deference to the pro-slavery views of South Carolina and Georgia this clause was suppressed. As soon as independence became a fact, one state after another took action against slavery, and after 1804, the date when New Jersey voted to do away with it, not a slave state remained north of the Mason and Dixon line. The chief obstacle to abolition in the South, where the slaves were far more numerous than in the North, was the perplexity felt about what to do with the freed slaves, but southern emancipation societies were deeply concerned with this problem and were hopeful of finding a solution.[1]

The discovery that cotton could be grown profitably by means of slave labor served to revive the institution of slavery just at the time when it had seemed destined to disappear. Cotton-growing *Cotton and* was a simple process that the minds of illiterate blacks could *slavery* comprehend, and yet it was a long-continued process that kept workers busy from early in the spring until late in the fall. Furthermore, cotton-growing furnished adequate employment for women and children as well as men, and it lent itself so easily to supervision that one overseer could be entrusted with as many as forty slaves. The profits that could be

[1] Mary S. Locke, *Anti-Slavery in America, 1619–1808* (1901); Alice D. Adams, *The Neglected Period of Anti-Slavery in America, 1808–1831* (1908); W. E. B. Du Bois, *Suppression of the African Slave Trade to the United States of America, 1638–1870* (1896).

made from slave labor were revealed in the rapidly mounting price of slaves; whereas two hundred and fifty dollars would buy a good field hand in 1815, twenty years later an equally good man would cost no less than six hundred dollars. Free labor was correspondingly debased, for the small farmer who had few slaves or no slaves at all soon found that he could not raise cotton profitably in competition with the great planters. As already pointed out, it was in part this situation that led so many of the poorer whites to leave the Old South and move on into the West.

When the question of admitting Missouri came up, it happened that, more or less by accident, the number of free states and of slave states *Balance of* was the same. Of the original thirteen states, seven had *the sections* abolished slavery and six had retained it, while of the nine new states four had been admitted without slavery and five with it. Thus there were in the Union eleven free states and eleven slave states. Also, thanks to the fact that each state, regardless of the size of its population, was entitled to two members in the United States Senate, there were twenty-two free state senators and twenty-two slave state senators.

SLAVE STATES AND FREE STATES, 1820

Original Thirteen		New States	
Slave	Free	Slave	Free
Delaware	New Hampshire	Kentucky (1792)	Vermont (1791)
Maryland	Massachusetts	Tennessee (1796)	Ohio (1803)
Virginia	Rhode Island	Louisiana (1812)	Indiana (1816)
North Carolina	Connecticut	Mississippi (1817)	Illinois (1818)
South Carolina	New York	Alabama (1819)	
Georgia	New Jersey		
	Pennsylvania		

But here the equality between the sections stopped. In population the South had grown more slowly than the North; in fact, the Northwest had been peopled in large part by emigrants from the South. Whereas in 1790 the two sections had been almost equal in population (1,968,000 for the North to 1,925,000 for the South), by 1820 the North had forged far ahead (5,144,000 to 4,372,000). This difference was reflected in the number of representatives which the free and the slave states sent to the lower house of Congress, a difference made even more marked by the fact that five slaves counted only as three free men in making the apportionment of seats. Thus in 1790 there had been fifty-seven representatives from the states north of the Mason and Dixon line to forty-eight south of it, but by 1820 there were one hundred and twenty-three representatives from the free states to only eighty-nine from the slave states.

And now the Tallmadge amendment proposed further to curtail the weight of the slaveholding South in the Union. When, only a few years before, a government for the Louisiana Purchase was under consideration, probably little objection would have been raised to the adoption for the whole new region of just such a measure as Tallmadge now proposed, but by 1820 the cotton planters of the South were alive to the need of protecting slavery from any further assaults. Should Missouri and other states from the Louisiana Purchase be admitted as free states, then the balance of the sections in the Senate would be lost, and future Congresses might act, not only to exclude the slave-owner from the West in favor of the free farmer, but even to interfere with the now profitable institution of slavery where it had long existed. Actuated by these motives, southern members of Congress maintained that the Tallmadge amendment was unconstitutional because it put restrictions on a state as a condition of its admission to the Union; that it was contrary to the treaty of purchase from France, inasmuch as that document inferred that the states created out of Louisiana should be admitted to the Union on an equal footing with the other states; that it was unfair, since it would open settlement in Missouri to all free state men while closing it to such Southerners as owned slaves; and that it was unwise, because the people of Missouri wanted to legalize slavery within the borders of the proposed state, and the question was one for them, and not for Congress to decide.

Not for years had there been so heated a debate in Congress, nor one that had so aroused the interest of the country at large. To the pro-slavery arguments those who favored the Tallmadge amendment retorted that the measure was no more unconstitutional than the Northwest Ordinance, under the terms of which slavery had been excluded from the Old Northwest; that the treaty with France required the United States to accord only the same treatment to the states west of the Mississippi River that was accorded to the states east of it, many of which had been compelled to enter the Union as free states; that slavery itself was a moral and political evil contrary to the spirit of the Declaration of Independence; that it had been tolerated in the Constitution only by necessity and ought now to be restricted. With these arguments the free state majority in the House of Representatives showed itself in accord when by a close vote it adopted the Tallmadge amendment (February 16, 1819). But before further action was taken Congress adjourned.

In the next Congress, which met in December, 1819, the situation was

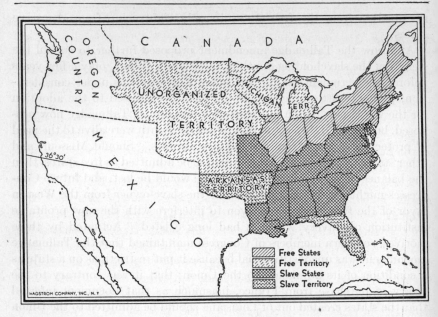

FREE AND SLAVE AREAS AFTER THE MISSOURI COMPROMISE

somewhat altered when Maine, with the approval of Massachusetts,
The Missouri Compromise applied for admission to the Union as a free state. Sensing
the possibilities of compromise, the Senate combined into
one measure the bill to admit Maine as a free state and the
bill to admit Missouri as a slave state, and listened with much interest to
an amendment introduced by Senator J. B. Thomas of Illinois which proposed that for the rest of the Louisiana Purchase, exclusive of Missouri,
the line of 36° 30′ should serve to divide free territory from slave territory. A solution of the vexatious problem seemed to have been found,
and a joint committee of the two houses was appointed to work out the
details. This committee recommended that the Senate abandon its
plan for combining in one bill the fortunes of Maine and Missouri; that
the House give up its attempt to exclude slavery from Missouri; and
that both houses agree to the dividing line between slave states and free
states advocated by Senator Thomas. These measures suited the
South better than the North, but enough northern votes were won over
to obtain the requisite majorities in both houses. The President seriously questioned the constitutionality of the exclusion of slavery from
states not yet created, but on this point his Cabinet unanimously reassured him, and he gave his approval (March 6, 1820). Strictly speak-

ing, the "Missouri Compromise" has usually been regarded as that portion of the Missouri Enabling Act which provided "that in all territory ceded by France to the United States ... which lies north of thirty-six degrees and thirty minutes north latitude, not included within the limits of the state [of Missouri], ... slavery ... shall be, and is hereby, forever prohibited."

The Missouri Compromise offered a natural solution to the problem of slavery expansion. East of the Mississippi River, the Mason and Dixon line and the Ohio River had long been accepted as the *The second* proper dividing line between slave and free states, and the *Missouri* idea of continuing such a line west of the Mississippi could *Compromise* readily be accepted. The Missourians, however, were somewhat irritated at the efforts which had been made in Congress to limit their control over slavery within the borders of their state. Hence, in spite of the fact that slavery seemed destined never to prosper so far north, they drew up a constitution which was as aggressively pro-slavery as possible. One of its provisions forbade the state legislature ever to pass a law emancipating slaves without the consent of their masters, and another forbade the entrance of free Negroes into the state on any pretext whatever. Obviously, since the latter clause was out of harmony with Article IV, Section 2, of the national Constitution, which required that the citizens of each state should "be entitled to all privileges and immunities of citizens of the several states," it could not be operative, but the very presence of such a statement in the proposed constitution caused the debate to break out in Congress anew. For a time it seemed that the admission of Missouri would have to be postponed, but through the efforts of Henry Clay a second Missouri Compromise was arranged. By its terms the state was admitted under the constitution it had written, but the Missouri legislature was required to pledge itself never to construe the offensive clause in such a way as to deny any citizen of any state the privileges which he enjoyed under the Constitution of the United States.

Once more the dispute died down, and for a generation the two Missouri Compromises served to hold the slavery question in abeyance. Far-seeing men were deeply disturbed, however, at the acute difference of opinion between North and South that the discussions over the admission of Missouri had revealed. They knew full well that some day the nation must face squarely the problem it had just evaded, and that out of the ensuing conflict might come civil war or even the dissolution of the Union.

Meantime the advance of population in the Southwest had brought

[359]

forcibly to the attention of the government the long-standing menace
Florida   of Spanish impotence in Florida, and the great desirability
of acquiring this territory from Spain for the use of American settlers. Spanish occupation had dwindled down to little more than the maintenance of garrisons at St. Marks, Pensacola, and St. Augustine, while the greater part of Florida was a kind of "no man's land" in which Indians, runaway Negroes, and ruffians of every description held sway. In July, 1816, a "Negro fort" on the Apalachicola, which had been established by a renegade Englishman known as Colonel Edward Nicolls, was blown up by some American troops, and shortly afterward war broke out between the United States and the unruly Seminole Indians. The task of restoring order was entrusted to General Andrew Jackson, who was authorized, in case he deemed it expedient, to pursue the Seminoles into their Florida retreats. Jackson, fully convinced that the administration had at last made up its mind to seize Florida, considered it his duty to prepare the way for the American occupation. By the spring of 1818 he had won an easy victory over the Indians, had taken St. Marks and Pensacola, had executed two white men whom he blamed in part for the Seminole outbreak, and had sent the Spanish governor and all his soldiers to Havana.

Jackson's exploits were immensely popular with the American people, but they embarrassed the administration, which in reality was working for the acquisition of Florida by peaceful means.[1] Angry protests were registered at Washington by the Spanish government against the gross insults Jackson had offered Spanish sovereignty. Also, the two white men Jackson had put to death turned out to be British, and British complaints had to be reckoned with. The Secretary of War, John C. Calhoun, was in favor of censuring Jackson openly for exceeding his instructions, but the Secretary of State, John Quincy Adams, defended Jackson's course as incidental to his main duty of crushing the Seminoles. The discussions of the Cabinet were kept secret, and Jackson did not learn of Calhoun's hostile attitude for years, but resolutions of censure were introduced into both houses of Congress, and although not adopted by either, their proposal gave Jackson great offense. Adams finally straightened matters out with the foreign powers by offering to restore St. Marks and Pensacola to Spain whenever the Spanish government stood ready to occupy the posts with adequate garrisons, and by convincing the British government that the two subjects in question were unworthy of British protection.

[1] Hubert B. Fuller, *The Purchase of Florida* (1906).

Moreover, negotiations for the acquisition of Florida were soon pushed to a successful conclusion. Adams insisted that Spain must either police Florida adequately or turn the province *Purchase of* over to the United States, and he drove home his point *Florida* so successfully that in 1819 the Spanish agreed to the cession on condition that claims of American citizens against Spain, amounting in all to five million dollars, should be met by the United States. On July 17, 1821, Jackson himself, acting now as the duly appointed governor of the territory of Florida, received for a second time the surrender of the Spanish province to the United States.

The same treaty that transferred Florida from Spain to the United States marked off also the boundary line between the United States and Spanish-American possessions west of the Mississippi *The south-* River. Adams believed that the boundary line should *western* have been placed at the Rio Grande, but the administra- *boundary* tion was eager to make sure of the Florida cession, and forced him to make an offer more favorable to Spain. As a result, all of what later became Texas was left in Spanish hands, and the western boundary of the United States was placed at the Sabine River, "up that river along the western bank to the thirty-second parallel, thence due north to the Red River, up that river to the one-hundredth meridian, thence due north to the Arkansas, up that river along its southern bank to its source, thence due north to the forty-second parallel, and then along that parallel to the 'South Sea.'" This article clearly gave over to the United States whatever claim Spain had previously held to the Oregon country, and it furnished for the first time since the purchase of Louisiana an authentic southwestern boundary.

Curiosity with respect to the unsettled portions of the trans-Mississippi West, to which American title was again confirmed, led to another exploring expedition similar to the expeditions *Long's* under Lewis and Clark, and Pike, that Jefferson had *expedition* authorized earlier in the century. Major Stephen H. Long, who had gained some experience in 1817 on a trip up the Mississippi in search of suitable sites for forts, was put in charge. For his use shipbuilders constructed at Pittsburgh a steamboat, the *Western Engineer*, which, in accordance with the latest designs, was a flat-bottomed stern-wheeler with a draught of only nineteen inches of water — too much, experience proved, for some portions of the Missouri. To impress the Indians the prow of the boat was shaped into a dragon's head through which steam might be exhausted. Major Long was instructed to explore the sources of the Platte River, after which he was to turn southward

[361]

and follow along the mountains to the valleys of the Arkansas and the Red. The *Western Engineer* left St. Louis in June, 1819, and arrived at Council Bluffs, near the mouth of the Platte, the following September. Here the expedition halted until the next spring, when, reinforced by a detachment which had marched overland from St. Louis, it advanced by land along the north bank of the Platte. When the forks were reached, Long led his men to the south bank of the south fork, and followed it out to the mountains. Long's Peak was sighted and named, but the sources of the Platte were not found. The expedition skirted the mountains to the Arkansas and a small party pushed on to what was mistaken for the Red River, but was actually the Canadian, a branch of the Arkansas. The return trip was attended by great hardship, and Long's report was full of pessimism. Beyond the Missouri he believed the country he had visited wholly unfit for cultivation, and thus uninhabitable by a people dependent upon agriculture. Probably Long's report did more than any other single document to fix in the American mind the legend of the "Great American Desert." [1]

Meantime the region north and west of the route taken by Long was being penetrated with singular completeness by fur-traders rather than *The north-* by official explorers. In 1808 William Clark, Manuel Lisa, *western* and others joined in the formation of the Missouri Fur Com- *fur trade* pany, through which they hoped to exploit the fur trade of the upper Missouri and its tributaries. After about a dozen years of bad management and inadequate capital the company collapsed, but the knowledge its agents had gained was not lost on its successor, the Rocky Mountain Fur Company, which in 1823 began a series of brilliant explorations by sending Jedediah S. Smith to the Green River Valley and the Great Salt Lake.

Other fur-trade activities of the period centered about the name of John Jacob Astor, a New York fur dealer who dreamed of bringing the whole American fur trade under one control, and even of connecting it up with the trade with China. His American Fur Company, organized a few years before the outbreak of the War of 1812, was designed to extend his interests in the Great Lakes region, while a subsidiary, the Pacific Fur Company, was to pioneer the way into the far Northwest. In 1810 Astor sent out two expeditions to the Oregon country, one by sea and the other by land. The seafarers arrived at the Columbia River early in 1811 and founded Astoria.[2] Next year they were joined

[1] Cardinal L. Goodwin, *The Trans-Mississippi West, 1803–1853* (1922), furnishes a convenient summary of western explorations and expansion during this period.

[2] The colorful events of this venture were first exploited in Washington Irving, *Astoria* (1836).

by the "Overlanders." Both parties encountered many harrowing experiences, but they would probably have succeeded in establishing the Pacific fur trade on a sound basis had the second war with England not intervened. This event frightened the Astorians into the sale of their outpost, including all the furs they had gathered, to the Canadian "Northwesters," who had also decided to enter the region. Astoria was rechristened Fort George, and under the powerful Hudson's Bay Company, which in 1821 took over the privileges of the Northwesters, it became the chief center of British influence in the Oregon country. In 1825, however, Fort George was abandoned in favor of the better-located Fort Vancouver.

Astor was never able to revive his Pacific interests, but after the War of 1812 was over he induced Congress to prohibit aliens from carrying on the fur trade within the United States. This law enabled him to purchase at his own price British trading-posts south of the international border. By the year 1830 he had virtually monopolized the fur trade within the United States, although the Rocky Mountain Fur Company long kept its separate identity, and its agents, rather than Astor's, were chiefly responsible for the exploration of the West. According to Frederick Jackson Turner, they " revealed the sources of the Platte, the Green, the Yellowstone, and the Snake Rivers, and the characteristics of the Great Salt Lake region; they pioneered the way to South Pass, descended Green River by boat, carried cannon into the interior basin; showed the practicability of a wagon route through the Rockies, reached California from Salt Lake, crossed the Sierras and the deserts of Utah and Nevada, and became intimately acquainted with the activity of the British traders of the northwest coast." [1]

The rapid settlement of the Mississippi Valley and the penetration of the farther West emphasized the feeling of aloofness from Europe that had come to characterize the United States during the American period of the War of 1812. The American people were now isolation content to concern themselves chiefly with the development of their own country, and they viewed with increasing pride their native manufactures, their expanding agriculture, and particularly the westward advance of their population. They were aware, almost for the first time, of the physical basis of greatness with which, thanks to the size of the West, their nation was endowed; and, reasonably enough, they wished to exploit as their interests might direct the magnificent opportunities that confronted them. Thus absorbed in their own affairs, they were less concerned than formerly with what was going on in Europe, but

[1] *Rise of the New West*, p. 122. By permission of Harper and Brothers, publishers.

they were willing to challenge instantly any tendency on the part of European nations to limit the natural course of development of the United States. Out of this attitude of mind came a significant statement of American foreign policy, the Monroe Doctrine.[1]

To understand this declaration of policy it is necessary to note briefly what had been happening in that portion of the New World which lay *Latin America* to the south of the United States. Here Spain had reared a mighty empire, with colonies more numerous and riches far greater than had fallen to the British in North America. The Spanish monopoly of South America and the southern parts of North America was not quite complete, for the Portuguese held Brazil, and both the Dutch and the English had small colonies bordering on the Caribbean and in the West Indies. But the leadership in colonial affairs, from the Sabine River to the southernmost tip of South America, lay definitely with Spain, whose colonial policy, like that of Great Britain, sought to benefit the mother country in every possible way, and sometimes worked to the serious detriment of the colonies. Particularly was the restriction of colonial trade to Spain a matter of great hardship, for Spain herself had little to exchange, and other European countries, notably Great Britain, not only coveted the raw produce of the Spanish colonies, but were prepared also to offer a wide variety of manufactured articles in return. Naturally the Spanish-Americans wished to establish direct trade relations with England, and they resented to the point of disobedience the roundabout system, required by law, of trading almost exclusively through Spain. In a general way the grievances of the Spanish colonies were duplicated in Brazil, with Portugal in the rôle of the offending mother country.

When, during the years 1807 and 1808, Napoleon Bonaparte, seeking to tighten up his unfortunate continental system, overran with his armies both Portugal and Spain and converted them into *Revolutions* satellite states of France, their American colonies, one after another, began to revolt. The situation in Brazil was unique, for the Portuguese ruler himself fled to America and reigned for the time being as a monarch of the New World. Eventually he returned to Portugal (1822), and his eldest son became the emperor of an independent Brazil.

[1] The literature of this subject is extensive. For the Latin-American situation F. L. Paxson, *The Independence of the South American Republics* (1903), is useful; and on the European background, W. P. Cresson, *The Holy Alliance* (1922). A brief but excellent account is given in J. H. Latané, *From Isolation to Leadership* (1918). Serviceable special works are W. F. Reddaway, *The Monroe Doctrine* (1898); Dexter Perkins, *The Monroe Doctrine, 1823–1826* (1927); and, by the same author, *The Monroe Doctrine, 1826–1867* (1933); F. F. Stephens, *The Monroe Doctrine, Its Origin, Development and Recent Interpretation* (1916); D. Y. Thomas, *One Hundred Years of the Monroe Doctrine, 1823–1923* (1923).

In the Spanish colonies revolutionary *juntas* took control, at first in the name of Ferdinand VII, whom Napoleon had deprived of the Spanish throne and held captive in France, but later, when the collapse of Napoleon's empire enabled Ferdinand to regain his throne, as the founders of independent republics. Invariably the revolting colonies established close and mutually lucrative trade relations with England, and in the wars of liberation through which, under the leadership of Simon Bolivar and José de San Martin, the Spanish-American republics maintained their independence, they received much unofficial British encouragement, and from individual Englishmen, direct aid. By the year 1822 the Spanish Empire in the New World had dwindled down to little more than the Caribbean islands of Cuba and Porto Rico, although Ferdinand VII consistently refused to acknowledge his defeat.

The successful revolt of the Spanish-American colonies was viewed with undisguised approval by the people of the United States, who saw in the actions of their neighbors to the south full vindication of the principles enunciated in their own Declaration of Independence. Moreover, the Spanish-American republics, while unable to combine into a single union, copied in other respects the form of government which had been developed in the United States. Duly flattered by this further evidence of esteem, public opinion in the United States called so strongly for recognition of the Spanish-American governments that John Quincy Adams, the Secretary of State, was able only with great difficulty to postpone such action until after his negotiations with Spain for the purchase of Florida were completed. By March, 1822, with Florida safely in hand, President Monroe was able to announce that the time for recognition had come. *Recognition by the United States*

European nations also were interested in the course of events in Spanish America, although with the exception of England they were far from pleased with what had happened. Following the defeat of Napoleon, the great powers of Europe had been closely associated in an effort to preserve the peace and prevent the return of Napoleon to power. At first the Quadruple Alliance, composed of the nations which had overthrown Napoleon — England, Austria, Russia, and Prussia — sought to direct the course of European affairs, but in 1818 France, whose conservatism was by that time no longer open to question, was admitted to full fellowship in the counsels of the powers. The leading statesman of Europe during this period was Metternich, the prime minister of Austria, whose hostility to democracy in government was extreme. In his opinion democracy was a kind of *The European system*

[365]

communicable disease that must be stamped out, wherever found, if the peace of the world was to be maintained. A conference held at Aix-la-Chapelle in 1818 considered seriously the request made by Ferdinand VII of Spain for aid in the recovery of his revolting American colonies, but England was able to block any such action. A year later Ferdinand, whose devotion to absolutist principles equaled that of Metternich him-self, was having trouble at home. A mutiny of some soldiers collected at Cadiz for service against the American revolutionists grew to the proportions of a revolt, and early in 1820 the King was compelled to ac-cept the liberal constitution of 1812 which, on his restoration to the Spanish throne in 1814, he had promptly abrogated. The Spanish rev-olution served also to stimulate sympathetic outbursts in two Italian kingdoms, Naples and Piedmont, where, since the overthrow of Na-poleon, reactionary monarchs had ruled with small regard for the wel-fare of their people.

Faced by this situation, Metternich persuaded Russia and Prussia to agree to the principle that revolution in any European state might *The doc-* properly be suppressed by the great powers. England *trine of* strongly dissented, and France at first held aloof, but at *intervention* Laibach in 1821 Austria was commissioned in the name of Austria, Russia, and Prussia (the three allies were sometimes called in-correctly the "Holy Alliance") to suppress the revolutions in Italy; and a year later at Verona France was authorized to do the same for Spain. England's opinion of this high-handed policy was stated clearly by George Canning, her foreign secretary, who sent word to Verona that "while England was no friend to revolution, she did emphatically insist on the right of nations to set up for themselves whatever form of government they thought best, and to be left free to manage their own affairs, so long as they left other nations to manage theirs." But Austrian troops in Italy, and French troops in Spain, stamped out the revolutions, and revived in each offending state the old system of au-tocracy.

While the doctrine of intervention stated at Laibach was confined specifically to European countries, the possibility of European inter-vention to suppress the revolts in Spanish America was a subject of much speculation. It was an open secret that Ferdinand VII would be deeply grateful for any such aid, and it was supposed that he might even be generous to any nation or nations from which aid might come. France at Verona actually proposed intervention in Spanish America as well as in Spain, and while the conference confined itself to the problem of suppressing European revolts, there was reasonable ground for fear that some future congress might not show such restraint. To England the possibility that the Spanish-American republics might be restored to Spain was alarming, for such a development would mean in all probability the revival of the old colonial trade-barriers and the consequent restriction of English trade. Moreover, if France should help subdue Spanish America, she could hardly be expected to do it for nothing. What pay could Ferdinand give other than an American colony for France? Could England stand idly by while France prepared to revive her empire in the New World?

All this diplomatic gossip in due time reached the United States, where it produced a reaction somewhat similar to that of England. Dare the United States permit Spain, presumably with the help of France, blot out the liberty of one American republic after another? Dare the United States risk the revival of a French empire in America, perhaps at her very doors? If it became the fashion for European absolutist governments to suppress democracy south of the United States, what guaranty was there that the same tactics would not presently be tried on the United States itself? Moreover, if European rivalries were once more let loose in America, could the United States hope to hold aloof from them? Would she not be drawn into the whirlpool of European diplomacy and war, and away from her strictly domestic program of internal development conditioned upon westward expansion? President Monroe was keenly aware of the dangers of the situation, and long before the publication of the famous doctrine which bears his name he was seeking to forestall intervention by urging Spain to recognize the independence of her revolted colonies.

The similarity of the views held in Great Britain and the United States on the Spanish-American question was not lost on the British foreign secretary, Canning. As the situation stood, his country *Canning's* was at odds with all the great powers of Europe, and in real *proposals* need of an ally to stand with her against a policy which *to Rush* might jeopardize her valuable Spanish-American trade. Why not enlist the aid of the United States? Canning decided to try. In a "private and confidential" communication to Richard Rush, the American minister to England, he suggested that it might be "expedient for ourselves, and beneficial for all the world" if the common principles held by the two nations "should be clearly settled and plainly avowed." Obviously Spain could not recover her lost colonies, hence recognition, which the United States had accorded but Great Britain had not, was only a matter of time and circumstance. As for Great Britain, she would not object to any amicable agreement reached by the mother country with her revolting colonies. On the other hand, while the British government did not itself aim at the possession of any Spanish-American territory, it could not look with indifference upon the transfer of such sovereignty to any other power. If these were also the sentiments of the United States, why should the two nations not unite in announcing their stand to the world?

Rush promptly referred this communication to President Monroe, who recognized its importance and gave it immediate attention. At *The Monroe* the outset he felt inclined to accept the British proposal, *Doctrine* although the departure involved from the policy set by Washington and Jefferson against entangling the United States in European affairs gave him much concern. On this matter, however, the counsel he received from the two Republican ex-Presidents, Jefferson and Madison, tended to reassure him. Jefferson, who regarded the question raised as the most momentous since independence, wrote to Monroe in part as follows:

> Our first and fundamental maxim should be, never to entangle ourselves in the broils of Europe. Our second, never to suffer Europe to intermeddle with cis-Atlantic affairs. America, North and South, has a set of interests distinct from those of Europe, and peculiarly her own. She should therefore have a system of her own, separate and apart from that of Europe. While the last is laboring to become the domicil of despotism, our endeavor should surely be, to make our hemisphere that of freedom. One nation, most of all, could disturb us in this pursuit; she now offers to lead, aid, and accompany us in it. By acceding to her proposition, we detach her from the bands, bring her mighty weight into the scale of free government, and emancipate a continent at one stroke, which otherwise might linger long in doubt and difficulty. Great Britain is the nation which can do us the most harm of any one, or all on earth; and with her on our side we need not fear the whole world.

Madison agreed with Jefferson, but was ready to go even further. He would protest also against the French invasion of Spain, and against any attempt to interfere with the progress toward independence of the Greeks, who had lately undertaken a revolt against Turkey.

In his Cabinet Monroe found a contrary opinion. John Quincy Adams, his Secretary of State, objected strenuously to the proposed *Opposition* joint declaration with Great Britain, and insisted instead *of Adams* that the United States issue a wholly independent statement. He had no desire to see the United States appear merely as a "cock-boat in the wake of a British man-of-war"; he had caught, perhaps from Henry Clay, the vision of a Pan-American system in which the United States would play a leading part; he was by no means certain that the United States should bind itself not to add more American territory to its boundaries; and he knew that Great Britain would do as much to prevent European intervention in Spanish America without an alliance with the United States as with it. "The ground that I wish to take," he said, "is that of earnest remonstrance against the interference on our part with Europe; to make an American cause and adhere inflexibly to that."

Monroe at length came around to the Adams point of view. In reaching this decision he was perhaps influenced by the fact that, although several months had elapsed, he had received no further word from Canning on the subject. Had Canning's ardor cooled? As a matter of fact, although Monroe could probably have had no definite information to this effect, Canning's interest in American co-operation had declined. He had hoped originally that Rush might join him, without referring the matter to President Monroe, in an immediate declaration, and when Rush refused had turned to other expedients. From the French ambassador to England Canning now sought and obtained assurance that the French government had no idea of using force against the revolting Spanish colonies, and this statement, privately communicated to the other European powers, completely eased his mind on the subject.

It must have occasioned the British foreign secretary, and many another European statesman, much surprise when the message which President Monroe sent Congress in December, 1823, reached Europe. Two widely separated statements in that document set forth clearly the position of the United States on the subject of European intervention in America. The first was aimed specifically at Russia, whose aggressions in the Pacific Northwest had already drawn protests from Secretary Adams, and asserted "as a principle in which the rights and interests of the United States are involved, that the American continents, by the free and independent condition which they have assumed and maintain, are henceforth not to be considered subjects for future colonization by any European powers." The second statement, much more elaborate, pointed out that the United States had taken no part in the wars of European powers relating to themselves, and did not intend to do so. But in matters relating to "this hemisphere we are of necessity more immediately connected."

> The political system of the allied powers is essentially different ... from that of America. This difference proceeds from that which exists in their respective Governments; and to the defense of our own, which has been achieved by the loss of so much blood and treasure, and matured by the wisdom of their most enlightened citizens, and under which we have enjoyed

unexampled felicity, this whole nation is devoted. We owe it, therefore, to candor and to the amicable relations existing between the United States and those powers to declare that we should consider any attempt on their part to extend their system to any portion of this hemisphere as dangerous to our peace and safety. With the existing colonies or dependencies of any European power we have not interfered and shall not interfere. But with the Governments who have declared their independence and maintained it, and whose independence we have, on great consideration and on just principles, acknowledged, we could not view any interposition for the purpose of oppressing them, or controlling in any other manner their destiny, by any European power in any other light than as the manifestation of an unfriendly disposition toward the United States.

Canning's subsequent claim to authorship of the Monroe Doctrine — "I called the New World into existence to redress the balance of the Old" — was somewhat absurd, in view of his failure to obtain the joint declaration he had sought and in view of his private negotiations with France. Probably no country was more annoyed at the Monroe Doctrine than Great Britain, whose own claim to pre-eminence in American affairs it summarily denied. Furthermore, Monroe's contention that Europe had one system of government and America another was somewhat far-fetched in view of the fact that constitutional governments existed in several European countries, notably England, while Brazil, the largest country in South America, was still a monarchy.

The Monroe Doctrine had no immediate consequences. Even before it was announced Russia had already called a halt in the Northwest and France had definitely given up all thought of intervention in Spanish America. Nor were the ambitions of Adams and Clay for the United States to assume hegemony in a great Pan-American system soon to be realized. But the statement did register once more the emphatic determination of the United States to maintain the doctrine of isolation. What the United States most needed, with its industries developing, its frontiers expanding, and its democratic government serving well the purpose for which it had been formed, was to be let alone. European interference anywhere on the western continent might endanger this cherished position and divert the new nation from its chosen course. Therefore Europe for the future must keep out of American affairs. It is obvious, of course, that in 1823, and for many years thereafter, the United States could not possibly have enforced against serious European attack the doctrine it had declared. But, thanks to the similarity of British and American interests, the British navy could be trusted to do what the United States could not do, and ultimately the United States would grow up to the doctrine she had declared.

CHAPTER XXI

SECTIONAL CROSS-CURRENTS

IN SPITE of the strongly nationalistic spirit that still pervaded the United States in the eighteen-twenties, the beginning of a three-cornered sectional struggle between Northeast, South, and West was plainly in evidence. Boundary lines between these three sections could not always be clearly drawn, but their points of view, determined respectively by the needs of the northern manufacturer, the southern cotton-planter, and the western free farmer, were fairly obvious. Intra-sectional conflicts, such as the struggle for mastery in New England between the commercial and the manufacturing classes, sometimes blurred the picture, but usually not for long. National politics became, in the main, a resultant of certain definite sectional forces acting upon it. Often, as in the case of the Monroe Doctrine, a community of interests made easy the task of charting the nation's course. But bitter strife between the sections also developed, and compromise solutions had to be found, such, for example, as those that made possible the admission of Missouri.[1]

Sectionalism in the United States

The Federalist Party, which in its day had ministered primarily to the needs of the commercial classes, was by the third decade of the century fast becoming only a memory. Manufacture now mattered more to the Northeast than commerce, and Republicans, not Federalists, had enacted the protective tariff law of 1816. In 1820 the Federalists made no effort to oppose the re-election of President Monroe, who won every vote but one in the electoral college; by 1824 the Federalist Party had virtually ceased to exist. The complete triumph of Republicanism during these years led contemporaries to characterize the period as an "era of good feelings," but the phrase is misleading. Within the dominant party factionalism was rife, and by the time of the election of 1824 no less than four candidates, each claiming to be a good Republican, contested for

---

[1] F. J. Turner, *The Significance of Sections in American History* (1932), strongly emphasizes this point of view.

the Presidency. Two of these candidates represented the rising West, one came from the Northeast, and one from the South.

Mention has already been made of the dissatisfaction generally felt with the system of nominating presidential candidates by means of a congressional caucus. In 1820 such a caucus was called, but fewer than fifty members of Congress attended, and they voted not to make nominations. Monroe, therefore, was re-elected without ever having been renominated. By 1822, however, the question of the "succession" was in hot debate, and the problem of how to nominate a candidate became acute. The President was known to favor the candidacy of William H. Crawford of Georgia, his Secretary of the Treasury, whose claim to preferment rested largely on the fact that he, more nearly than any other candidate, represented the old plantation aristocracy which, through the "Virginia dynasty," had controlled the Presidency every term but one since the Constitution went into effect. But there were other candidates. John Quincy Adams of Massachusetts, the Secretary of State, seemed to conservative New-Englanders the logical man to succeed Monroe; John C. Calhoun of South Carolina, the Secretary of War, was openly ambitious; Henry Clay of Kentucky, several times Speaker of the House, was actively interested; and Andrew Jackson of Tennessee, the hero of New Orleans and the conqueror of Florida, commanded loyal and enthusiastic support. Besides these there were many minor candidates, all of whom dropped out of the race. Calhoun, also, decided ultimately to bide his time, and in return for his withdrawal was very generally acclaimed as the proper person for the Vice-Presidency. But Crawford, Adams, Clay, and Jackson remained in the race to the end. Not often has the American electorate had the privilege of choosing a President from such a galaxy of stars.

With the congressional caucus discredited, state legislatures very generally usurped the privilege of making presidential nominations. Crawford's name was presented by the legislature of Virginia; Adams was nominated by the legislatures of Massachusetts and other New England states; Clay was first brought forward by the Kentucky legislature, then endorsed by many others; Jackson was supported by the lower house of the Tennessee legislature, and by mass conventions in various parts of the country. Crawford's candidacy won the approval of the customary congressional caucus, but on this occasion only sixty-nine members attended the meeting, and probably the support of the caucus did its nominee more harm than good. Prophetic of the future were some resolutions passed by a meeting of Republicans in Lancaster

Sectional candidates for the Presidency

County, Pennsylvania, which asserted that "the best and most unexceptionable method" of nominating a candidate would be by "a convention of delegates from all the States of the Union," a system, however, that was admittedly "impracticable, from the immense extent of the country, and from the great expense . . . "

William H. Crawford (1772–1834) [1] was a Virginian by birth and a lawyer by profession. He had long been a resident of Georgia, where as a member of the state legislature he had stoutly de- *William* fended the interests of the great planters against the back- *H. Crawford* country farmers, and had won for himself a seat in the United States Senate. In 1813 he was appointed by President Madison to be minister to France, a post which he gave up two years later to become Secretary of the Treasury. By discreet use of the patronage that went with his office he won a large following in Congress, and almost obtained the presidential nomination over Monroe in 1816. Like Albert Gallatin, Crawford stayed on at the treasury long after the President who originally appointed him had retired, but his political strength, unlike that of Gallatin, grew with his years of service. He was a man of his own mind, and had not hesitated to criticize party measures of which he did not approve; indeed, he was not always on the best of terms with Monroe. In his earlier career a strong nationalist, by the eighteen-twenties he seems to have felt that the pendulum had swung too far in the direction of nationalism, and must now swing back toward strict construction and states' rights. An able politician, and assured of the President's support, Crawford was far out in the lead until September, 1823, when he suffered a stroke of paralysis. His partial recovery permitted his candidacy to continue, but much of the early advantage he had gained was lost.

John Quincy Adams (1767–1848) [2] was the son of the second President, and in many respects an even abler man. In addition to his rare inheritance, no less from his mother, Abigail Adams, than *John Quincy* from his father, he had received a rigorous training for *Adams* public life. At eleven he was taken by his father to Europe, where under private tutors and in a variety of countries his education was carried on assiduously. He learned to speak French and Dutch fluently, and was once reprimanded by his father for writing better in a foreign language than in his own. At fourteen he went to Russia as private secretary to

---

[1] J. E. D. Shipp, *Giant Days; or, The Life and Times of William H. Crawford* (1909).

[2] John T. Morse, *John Quincy Adams* (1882), is an appreciative biography. The chapter on the sixth President in J. T. Adams, *The Adams Family* (1930), is an excellent attempt at character analysis. See also B. C. Clark, *John Quincy Adams: "Old Man Eloquent"* (1932).

the American minister, and at fifteen he returned alone from St. Petersburg to The Hague, a six months' winter journey by way of the Scandinavian countries. At twenty he was graduated from Harvard, and soon after began the practice of law; at twenty-seven he began a diplomatic career that took him on important missions to England, Holland, Russia, and Sweden. During all these years he read voluminously and wrote extensively. He had been trained by his father to keep a diary, and the information that he thus preserved from his early youth to the time of his death is of great value, not only because of the light it throws upon his character, but also because of his penetrating observations on public events. Indeed, this diary and other writings by members of the Adams family have been relied upon so extensively by historians that, according to some critics, American history needs to be "de-Adamsized."

When Jefferson became President, Adams returned to the United States, and after a short term in the Massachusetts state legislature was elected in 1803 to the United States Senate. This seat he resigned in 1808 because his conscience bade him approve the embargo, while the legislature of Massachusetts opposed it; and thereafter he became a member of the Republican Party, to which his diplomatic experience proved a valuable asset. In 1809 he was sent as minister to Russia; in 1814 he was chosen to be a member of the peace commission that drew up the treaty of Ghent; and when the war ended he was selected to represent the United States at London. When he took office as Monroe's Secretary of State, he was doubtless better fitted for that post by training and experience than any other American. He was almost painfully eager to crown his career by becoming President, but his demeanor was cold and forbidding, and the number of friends upon whom he could count was few. Moreover, he was belligerently incorruptible in all his dealings, and yet inclined to ascribe the worst motives to all who disagreed with him. New England accepted him as its candidate for the Presidency in 1824 with reluctance, but the obvious superiority of the man would have made any other candidacy from that part of the country seem ridiculous.

Henry Clay (1777–1852) [1] never attained the Presidency, but his name is far better known than that of many of the men who did. He *Henry Clay* was of no such distinguished lineage as Adams, for his father was only a Baptist preacher of back-country Virginia; and his education was as limited as Adams's was extensive. But Clay had a warm, magnetic personality, and won friends as easily as

[1] Carl Schurz, *Henry Clay* (2 vols., 1887).

HENRY CLAY

Adams lost them. He made the most of his meager opportunities, read law under a distinguished jurist, Chancellor Wythe, and when he was twenty years old opened a law office in Lexington, Kentucky. His legal career was successful from the start, not because he was learned in the law, but because of a native shrewdness that proved to be of greater value in the frontier courts than any amount of book learning. Within a few years he was a member of the state legislature, then for a short time, beginning even before he had attained the constitutional age of thirty years, of the United States Senate. On the eve of the War of 1812 he entered the House, where he was repeatedly chosen Speaker. He served with Adams on the commission that made peace with England after the war, and acquired from the experience an acquaintance with Europe that he sorely needed. Likeable, and desiring to be liked, Clay could usually be counted on to reflect his surroundings. In his youth he was a man of the West, tempersome and aggressive — a leading "War Hawk" when the West wanted war. As he grew older, contacts with the East and with Europe had a sobering influence upon him, and a discreet moderation took the place of his former recklessness. He saw intuitively the need of a political program that would satisfy all sections — a national program — and early set himself the task of finding one. He saw, too, the necessity of compromise when conflicting interests were involved, and his willingness to strike bargains that would satisfy all concerned won him the title, not undeservedly, of the "Great Compromiser." His persuasive oratory, once it was enlisted in any cause, was a potent influence in shaping public opinion. Few American statesmen have ever maintained, through victory and defeat, a larger or more devoted personal following.

Andrew Jackson (1767–1845),[1] like Henry Clay, was a product of the upland South, a North Carolinian whose parents had emigrated from *Andrew* the north of Ireland to the American frontier. In spite of *Jackson* his extreme youth he saw service during the later years of the American Revolution, and out of his wartime experiences emerged with a bitter hatred of England. With the faintest of qualifications he began the practice of law in western North Carolina when he was only twenty years of age, but within a year he followed the course of migration into Tennessee and settled at Nashville. Here he was soon public prosecutor, then for a brief time a member of the United States Senate,

---

[1] W. G. Sumner, *Andrew Jackson* (1924); James Parton, *Life of Andrew Jackson* (3 vols., 1860); J. S. Bassett, *Life of Andrew Jackson* (2 vols., 1911). Of these biographies Bassett's is best from the critical point of view, but Parton's contains the greatest amount of picturesque detail. Of importance in estimating the effect of environment on Jackson's character is T. P. Abernethy, *From Frontier to Plantation in Tennessee* (1932).

ANDREW JACKSON

From a painting by Charles Wilson Peale

then a judge of the Tennessee Supreme Court.   But it was as a warrior that he won his chief renown.   His successful campaign against the Creeks in 1814, his triumph next year over Pakenham at New Orleans, and his subsequent exploits against the Seminoles and the Spanish in Florida made him the outstanding military hero of the time.   As a fitting reward he was chosen in 1823 to represent the state of Tennessee once more in the United States Senate.   The pride of the West at having produced so great a man was unbounded, particularly when the great man had attained his eminence because he possessed in marked degree those qualities that the West most highly esteemed.   Jackson was a veritable personification of the western democratic ideal which held that common men were as good as aristocrats and deserved to play quite as important a part in the affairs of the nation.   He exhibited, too, the contentious individualism of the frontier, its unreasoning hatreds, its rashness, and its resourcefulness.   He was an ardent patriot, and identified with patriotism the Westerner's desire to obtain expanded boundaries for the nation and unlimited opportunities for its citizens.   He was not at first politically ambitious, but designing politicians saw the powerful appeal his candidacy would make to the masses, and pushed him into the race.

While the election of 1824 turned to a great extent upon the personalities of the candidates, it showed also the interplay of sectional forces. John Quincy Adams, the only candidate from a non-slaveholding state, and unmistakably associated with the Northeast, developed his greatest strength in New England and New York; Crawford, but for his physical condition, would probably have been a universal favorite in the older states of the South; Jackson and Clay divided the West.   Many of Crawford's adherents turned reluctantly to Jackson, who after all was a Southerner and a slaveholder as well as a Westerner; and the hero of New Orleans was aided also by the fact that he alone among the candidates was a newcomer to national politics.   The government of the United States ever since its inception had been in the hands of a relatively small group of aristocrats, and Jackson's managers argued cleverly that the time had come for the introduction of new blood.   This appeal won a hearty response from Westerners imbued with frontier ideals of democracy, from Easterners of the farmer and laborer classes who were just beginning to be conscious of their political power, and from backcountry Southerners who had long struggled within their respective states against the domination of an eastern planter aristocracy.   To a considerable degree Jackson thus became the candidate of the masses, while his opponents were the candidates of the classes.

[378]

All of the candidates professed to be members of the same political party, hence separate political platforms were hardly in order. The views of Henry Clay, however, were widely known, and *Clay's* they constituted an intelligible program which in a later *American* age would have been embodied in the customary resolu- *system* tions. Clay, more than any other candidate, was conscious of the divergent sectional interests of the nation, and was seeking eagerly for a solution that would benefit all sections equally. His "American system" — a "planned economy," a century ahead of "economic planning" — was the result. The War of 1812 had revealed the risk involved in the too great dependence of the United States upon the outside world, either for markets or for manufactures. Clay hoped, therefore, to build up home industries by a generous tariff policy, which would make the United States to a greater extent than ever before independent of the rest of the world, in time of peace no less than in time of war. Not only would the nation be encouraged to manufacture many articles that it had previously been forced to buy abroad, but the existence of a larger number of factory operatives would tend to ensure also a more satisfactory home market for the produce of the American farm. The industrial East could sell to the agricultural West and South; the agricultural West and South could sell to the industrial East. Nor need lack of transportation facilities constitute a drawback. With the heavy revenues that a tariff could be made to produce, the government would have the means to aid all worthy works of internal improvement and to ensure that a complete network of roads and canals would soon cover the nation. To carry through such a program much remained to be done. Those who favored increased tariffs, after a failure in 1820, won a modest victory in 1824, but Monroe's constitutional scruples still effectively blocked the efforts of Clay and his friends to turn any great part of the national revenue toward internal improvements.

The fact that Clay had a definite program forced the other candidates to declare themselves on the issues he raised. Crawford sought to appear as the only true heir to the Jeffersonian tradition, *Campaign* and won the approval of Jefferson himself, who regarded *of 1824* some of the other candidates as little better than Federalists. But Crawford dared not oppose too frankly a policy of tariff protection, for he hoped to win many votes in Pennsylvania and the other middle states where protection had its strongest appeal. On internal improvements he trimmed also, and like Monroe called for a constitutional amendment before the national government should proceed further along that line. Adams favored the tariff duties of 1824, although in some items he thought they might reasonably be lowered, and agreed with Clay heartily as to the desirability of internal improvements at national expense. Jackson as a member of the Senate had voted for the Tariff of 1824 and for internal improvements, but his managers sought to keep all such controversial matters in the background, and featured rather his opposition to the caucus system and the right of the common people to a larger share in governmental affairs.

The sectional character of the American nation was clearly apparent in the election results. Adams won the electoral votes of New England and most of the votes of New York. Crawford led only in Virginia and Georgia. Clay carried Kentucky, Ohio, and Missouri. Jackson alone had a large enough following to win electoral votes outside the section which he directly represented. He divided the West with Clay, obtained every electoral vote in North Carolina, South Carolina, Pennsylvania, and New Jersey, won seven out of the eleven votes of Maryland, and even received a single vote in New York. In the South he was helped materially by the support he received from Calhoun, who thought he had an understanding with Jackson that after four years the General would stand aside and allow Calhoun to capture the Presidency. The final vote stood: Jackson 99, Adams 84, Crawford 41, Clay 37. Statistics on the popular vote cast are misleading, for in some states the legislature still chose electors, while in only a few states were electoral tickets for every candidate in the field. Calhoun received more than two thirds of the electoral votes for Vice-President.

The failure of the electoral college to choose a President threw the election into the House of Representatives. Clay was now out of the *Election of* race, for the Constitution restricted the choice of the House *Adams* to the three highest on the list, but if he could not be President he could at least decide which one of his rivals should have the honor. His choice fell naturally upon Adams, who approved more fully than any of the others Clay's American system, and with the Speaker's influence powerfully at work in his behalf Adams won an easy victory. In addition to the votes of New England and New York he received the support of five western states and Maryland, 13 in all, as against Jackson's 7 and Crawford's 4.

Clay worked for Adams without much enthusiasm, and there is not the slightest evidence to show that a bargain had been struck between the two whereby Adams was to become President and Clay his Secretary of State. But the fact remains that Adams, also without enthusiasm, decided that Henry Clay was the right man for first place in the new Cabinet, and offered him the appointment. Already the cry of "bargain and corruption" had been raised, and when Clay accepted the proffered post all who so desired could believe the worst. Both Adams and Clay produced ample evidence to show that the accusation was false, and Clay even fought a duel with John Randolph of Roanoke about it, but the charge would not down. Andrew Jackson, who at the outset had taken his own defeat in good part, was at last convinced that this corrupt bargain had kept him out of the Presidency, and became an open enemy of the Adams administration. Before the year was out he had been renominated for the Presidency by the legislature of Tennessee, and had resigned his seat in the United States Senate in order to be free to carry on a three years' campaign.

Once more a two-party political division seemed in sight. Adams offered to retain Crawford as his Secretary of the Treasury, but the offer was declined and the Georgian passed out of public life. *A new party alignment* The followers of Adams and Clay, with some recruits from those who had once favored Crawford, combined to support the administration, while all others looked to Jackson as their leader. Such shrewd politicians as William B. Lewis of Tennessee, Martin Van Buren of New York, Thomas Hart Benton of Missouri, and the newly chosen Vice-President joined hands to oppose the administration and to advance the interests of their candidate. In 1826 a Missourian named Duff Green was brought to Washington to establish an anti-administration paper, the *Telegraph*, which repeatedly rang the changes on the "bargain and corruption" charge, and in a thousand petty ways criticized the conduct of the President and his supporters. Adams's title to the Presidency was even called into question on the ground that Jackson had received more electoral and popular votes than any other candidate, and should therefore have been chosen by the House in order to uphold the will of the people.

Faced by this kind of opposition, Adams might well have used the power he possessed as President to weld together a strong political machine that would uphold his administration, but his strict New England conscience would tolerate no such tactics. Instead, he consistently refused to remove his political opponents from appointive offices, and he sometimes even chose Jackson adherents to fill important vacancies. One such appointee was the Postmaster-General, John McLean of Ohio, who made it a point to dispense such patronage as he could command to Jackson men rather than to Adams men. The President's hope was to perpetuate the "era of good feelings" that was popularly supposed to have characterized the administration of James Monroe, but a better politician would have seen that such a course was impossible.

Adams's long experience with diplomacy made it seem reasonable that his administration should be distinguished for its record in dealing *The Panama* with foreign affairs. Such, however, could hardly have *Congress* been the case, for the problems that the country now faced were primarily domestic in nature. Clay understood, perhaps better than Adams, the determination with which the United States had turned its back upon Europe, but he had visions of an increasing pan-American co-operation, and he hoped to follow up the Monroe Doctrine by making the United States the acknowledged protector of all the lesser American nations. An opening soon appeared for the introduction of this policy. When, at the suggestion of Bolivar, the Spanish-American states decided to hold a congress at Panama to consider a union of forces by which they might compel Spain to recognize their independence, Mexico and Colombia inquired if the United States would care to send delegates. Clay was eager to accept the invitation, but Adams at first hesitated, for he feared that the war might be carried into Cuba and Porto Rico, and believed that the interests of the United States would be best served if those islands remained for the time being the colonies of Spain. One important consideration was that their separation from Spain would doubtless involve, as it had elsewhere in Spanish America, the abolition of slavery, and the turbulence of the black republic of Haiti aroused grave doubts as to the wisdom of such a course. But Adams was won over by Clay's representations, and sent to the Senate for confirmation the names of two delegates to attend the Panama Congress. Unfortunately the subject was not considered on its merits, either in the Senate or in the country at large. The opposition sought merely to discredit the administration, and while it did not succeed in preventing the mission from being sent, it did delay proceedings so long that the Panama Congress had adjourned before the delegates of the United States arrived. The results of the Congress were inconsequential, and perhaps the participation of the United States would not have altered its course, but the incident put the administration in a bad light before the country, quite as the Jackson leaders had intended.

Adams also aroused undeserved antagonism by his handling of Indian affairs. The expansion of the cotton South led to an insistent demand *Indian* from the Southwest that the lands held by the now semi-*affairs* civilized Creeks, Cherokees, Choctaws, and Chickasaws be made available for settlement. In response to this demand a treaty was signed at Indian Springs, just before Adams took office, by which the Creeks gave up all their holdings in Georgia. This treaty was duly ratified by the Senate, but it was promptly repudiated by the great

[382]

majority of the Creek nation, and one of its chief negotiators was put to death. Adams, on investigation, found that the treaty had been obtained by fraud, refused to proclaim it in effect, and ordered that new negotiations should be begun. This assumption that the Indians had rights which the national government was bound to respect profoundly irritated the frontier, where the doctrine that "there is no good Indian but a dead Indian" was in the ascendancy; and it also provoked the wrath of the southern cotton planters, who were delayed in their acquisition of the valuable Indian lands. The governor of Georgia claimed that the lands acquired by the treaty became immediately upon its ratification a part of the sovereign state of Georgia, and that the government of the United States had no right to reopen the question. Adams maintained with warmth that he was justified in defending the good faith of the nation towards the Indians by "all the means under his control." A glaring difference of opinion on the old question of states' rights versus national powers was thus revealed, a difference which the subsequent negotiation of a satisfactory treaty failed to obscure. Under Adams's administration the practice of obtaining from the Indians such lands as were coveted by the whites continued without abatement, but the scruples displayed by the President gave the states'-rights South and the nationalistic West a common grievance that they did not soon forget.

Sectional differences on the tariff question had become acutely apparent well before Adams entered the White House. The tariff of 1816 had received support from every section, although the *The tariff* commercial elements in the Northeast and a majority of the southern planters had opposed it. The depression of 1819–20 led to a movement, emanating chiefly from the middle Atlantic states, for increased duties as an aid to languishing manufacturing interests, and a bill to raise the duties on woolen and cotton manufactures, forged iron bars, and many other articles passed the House with a good majority. The West, particularly Kentucky, was favored by a high duty on hemp, and revenue duties on sugar, molasses, coffee, and salt were intended to relieve the embarrassment of the treasury. But the opposition of the South to protective duties had stiffened since 1816, and in the Senate the bill failed by a single vote. In 1824 the advocates of protection returned to the fray with a measure similar to that which had failed in 1820, but with a tariff on raw wool to win the support of the sheep-growing interests. The vote in the House was even closer than in 1820, but a slender majority was obtained in the Senate, and the measure carried. The representatives of the West, charmed by the arguments of Clay and by the agricultural duties, were almost solidly for the bill.

"The merchants and manufacturers of Massachusetts, New Hampshire, the province of Maine and Sagadahock," said John Randolph in fine irony, "repel this bill, whilst men in hunting shirts, with deer-skin leggings and moccasins on their feet, want protection for manufactures."

The woolen interests were not entirely satisfied with the Tariff of 1824, for the duties on raw wool cut deeply into the profits of manu-

Protectionist demands facturing. English competition was acute, for American laborers, with the leverage of cheap lands in the West to help them, demanded and received higher wages than the English operatives could obtain. Moreover, the English duty on raw wool had been reduced in 1824, and the English manufactures profited accordingly. The contradiction between a tariff on raw wool and a tariff on manufactured woolens was sufficiently apparent, but American wool-growers, who had found the duties levied in 1824 of great advantage, were determined to secure increased protection. A bill designed to satisfy both the wool-growers and the woolens manufacturers by increasing duties all around failed of adoption in 1827 only by the casting vote of the Vice-President, John C. Calhoun, who thus made clear his complete retreat from the protective principle he had so warmly espoused in 1816. It now seemed obvious that if the wool and woolens interests could get together with other interests desiring protection, a generally higher schedule of duties could be enacted. To promote this cause a hundred delegates from thirteen different states met at Harrisburg, Pennsylvania, in July, 1827, and strongly urged their combined wishes upon Congress.

The mid-term election of 1826, however, gave a majority in the lower house of Congress to the anti-administration forces, and when the tariff

The "Tariff of Abominations" question came up, a few of the Jacksonian leaders determined to make political capital of it. They knew that Jackson, in order to be elected in 1828, must win support from the South, which opposed a protective tariff, and from the Northeast and the West, where a strong majority favored it. Their plan, afterward fully revealed by John C. Calhoun himself, was to present a bill which placed such excessively high rates on raw materials that some of the manufacturers of the Northeast would join with the commercial interests and the South to defeat the measure. Amendments which would make the bill more satisfactory to the manufacturers were to be voted down, and thus the Jackson men could claim credit in the North for having introduced a high-tariff measure, and in the South for having defeated it. The bill, according to the sharp-tongued John Randolph, related "to manufactures of no sort or kind but the manufacture of a President of the United States." As it turned out, the ruse failed to work, for enough northern support for the bill was obtained to enact the "Tariff of Abominations," as it was generally called, into law. Among those who unexpectedly favored the measure was Daniel Webster of Massachusetts. In preceding tariff debates Webster had always led the fight against protection, and as late as 1824 he had held that it was "the true policy of government to suffer the different pursuits of society to take their own course and not to give excessive bounties or encouragements to one over another." His change of front reflected the growing importance of manufacturing in New England, just as Calhoun's change of front had indicated the complete conversion of the South to low-tariff principles. The Northwest, as in previous tariff debates, was still hypnotized by the arguments Clay presented for an American system, and particularly by the high duties proposed on such items as wool, flax, and hemp.

TARIFF VOTES IN THE HOUSE OF REPRESENTATIVES

	1816		1820		1824		1828	
	For	Against	For	Against	For	Against	For	Against
New England.......	17	10	18	17	15	23	16	23
Middle Atlantic*......	42	5	55	1	57	9	56	6
South Atlantic.......	16	35	5	49	4	56	4	47
Southwest.....	3	3	0	7	2	14	0	16
Northwest†....	10	1	12	3	29	0	29	1

* Includes Delaware.
† Includes Kentucky and Missouri.

Adams was an enthusiastic believer in internal improvements at national expense, and was unhandicapped by the constitutional scruples that had restrained Madison and Monroe in their dealings *Internal* with this subject. In 1824 Monroe had given his approval *improve-* to a General Survey Act which authorized the President to *ments* conduct such surveys of canal and turnpike routes as would serve an important national interest. Undoubtedly Adams hoped to use this power to lay out a great national system of transportation, and his efforts along this line were not entirely unavailing. During his term of office army engineers were detailed freely to survey prospective transportation routes, and the sums actually expended in aid of internal improvements grew by leaps and bounds. But almost the only strictly national project that the administration was able to carry on was the continuation westward of the Cumberland Road. Beginning in 1825 liberal appropriations were made for this purpose, and with Jefferson City, Missouri, as its intended western terminal the National Road, as it came to be called, progressed slowly across central Ohio, and then on through Indiana and Illinois. By 1838 construction reached Vandalia, Illinois, but was discontinued because of the hard times that followed the panic of 1837, and was not resumed because of the increasing evidence that railroads, not turnpikes, would soon carry the commerce of the country.

Adams's dream of a carefully planned national system of roads and canals had little chance to come true. At the close of the War of 1812 the national government might possibly have seized the leadership in developing such a system, but its failure to act quickly when the need was first keenly felt left the solution of the problem to the states and to private initiative. By the time Adams became President there was little left that the government could do except to aid enterprises already undertaken under other auspices. For such works Congress voted frequent subsidies, usually in the form of generous subscriptions of stock, but local rather than national interests determined the nature of the improvements made and the routes followed.

Undoubtedly the most spectacular development in transportation during this period was the building of the Erie Canal, a project which DeWitt

The Erie Canal Clinton had persuaded the state of New York to undertake.[1] Early in the nineteenth century Clinton served several terms as mayor of the city of New York, and he was among the first to catch the vision of what it would mean to that city if the Hudson River could only be connected by a canal with the Great Lakes. In 1812 he was the leading member of a commission that sought to interest the United States government in the idea, but neither at that time nor at any later time could Congress be persuaded to help. Finally Clinton decided that the state of New York must sponsor the work, and in 1816, with the canal as his ultimate objective, he won the governorship. So well were his efforts rewarded that the first excavation was made in 1817, soon after he took office, while only eight years later the canal was

---

[1] N. E. Whitford, *History of the Canal System of the State of New York* (2 vols., 1906). See also for this and other canals of the time A. F. Harlow, *Old Towpaths, The Story of the American Canal Era* (1926).

AN EARLY VIEW OF THE ERIE CANAL

open for business. This waterway, when completed, extended from Troy on the Hudson to Buffalo on Lake Erie, a distance of three hundred and sixty-three miles. It was forty feet wide at the top, twenty-eight feet at the bottom, and four feet deep. Eighty-one locks overcame a grade of about seven hundred feet. The cost ran to $7,602,000. Canals before this time were by no means uncommon, but Clinton's "big ditch" taxed the engineering resources of the period and the financial resources of New York to the limit. In revolt against the heavy expenditures, the people of the state turned Clinton out of office in 1822, but two years later he was triumphantly re-elected, and when the canal was opened he, as governor, took the leading part in an elaborate set of ceremonies. Accompanied by a number of distinguished guests, he boarded a canal boat, the *Seneca Chief*, at Buffalo, October 26, 1825, and ten days later, after witnessing enthusiastic celebrations all along the route, arrived at New York City. Thereupon he poured a keg of water taken from Lake Erie into the Atlantic Ocean, and the "marriage of the waters" was complete.

Clinton was not merely optimistic when he staged this celebration, for the canal, thanks to a lucrative local traffic that was making cities of such points along the route as Syracuse. Rochester, and Utica, was

already a financial success. A branch canal from Albany to Lake
Success of Champlain, completed in 1824 at a cost of two million
the canal dollars, was similarly successful, and the tolls produced by
the two canals were so heavy that by 1837 their original cost had been
entirely repaid. The Erie Canal was also of immense significance in
linking the East to the West. Before it was built the cost of transporting
a ton of freight from New York City to Buffalo had been about one
hundred dollars, and the time required, about twenty days. The canal
at once reduced the cost to ten dollars and the time to eight days, and
as the volume of business increased the cost of transportation went
steadily down. Steamboats on the Great Lakes made possible a cheap
all-water route to the shores of Lake Huron and Lake Michigan as well
as Lake Erie, and with the problem of transportation no longer a serious
barrier to settlement, pioneers by the tens of thousands took up vacant
lands in the northern parts of Ohio, Indiana, and Illinois. Michigan
Territory grew so rapidly in population that by 1836 the eastern half
was ready for statehood, while the western half, known later as Wisconsin, seemed likewise destined to an early maturity. Moreover, as
Clinton had foreseen, the tremendous volume of trade that flowed
through the Erie Canal–Great Lakes route to and from the West paid
a generous tribute to New York City. In population New York grew
from less than one hundred and twenty-five thousand in 1820 to over
two hundred thousand by 1830; during the same time the value of its
real and personal property rose sixty per cent; and the increasing volume of its import and export trade soon made it the leading American
city.

The success of New York in making connections with the West led
to quick emulation by her chief rivals, Philadelphia and Baltimore. The
The "Penn- prosperity of Philadelphia was based to a great extent upon
sylvania the growth of manufacturing and agriculture in eastern
System" Pennsylvania, but the city had long felt the need of better
communications with the West. Early in the century, when a system
of turnpikes was built across the mountains to Pittsburgh, she had enjoyed a temporary triumph, but the Cumberland Road and steamboats
on the Ohio had quickly diverted much of the trade of western Pennsylvania to Baltimore and New Orleans, respectively. In 1825, with the
superiority of canal communications to all others seemingly apparent,
the legislature authorized the construction of an elaborate system of
canals to unite the various sections of the state. Unfortunately the
route to the Ohio through Pennsylvania was far more difficult than the
Mohawk Valley route through New York, so that when the "Pennsyl-

vania System" finally reached its western goal in 1834 a portage railway thirty-six miles in length, for which the power was furnished by stationary engines on the inclines and horses on the leveler stretches, was necessary to carry the canal traffic across the mountains. The new route to the West did a flourishing business, but it never became a serious rival to the Erie Canal, and Philadelphia never seriously challenged the lead of New York in the race for the western markets.

Baltimore, meantime, saw all the advantages which the Cumberland Road had once given her slipping fast away. Engineers reported that a canal could not be built from Baltimore across the moun- *Chesapeake* tains, but incorrigible optimists began in 1828, with state *and Ohio* backing, the construction of the Chesapeake and Ohio *Canal* Canal, for which President John Quincy Adams at a Fourth-of-July celebration lifted the first shovelful of earth. On the same day, however, Charles Carroll of Carrollton, the sole surviving signer of the Declaration of Independence, broke ground for the building of the Baltimore and Ohio Railroad, a project upon which a few far-sighted men had set their hearts. Twenty years of labor and ten million dollars expenditure brought the canal no farther west than Fort Cumberland, but the railroad, in 1853, finally reached its destination.

The craze for canals in the twenties and thirties went to unreasonable lengths. In the East feeders to the main canals, and connecting links between arms of the Atlantic, were built with little regard *The Canal* to costs involved and possible earning power. In the new *Age* western states the task of connecting the Ohio–Mississippi River system with the Great Lakes was eagerly embraced. Ohio led the way in 1825 by authorizing the building of two such canals, the Ohio and Erie from Portsmouth to Cleveland, and the Miami and Erie from Cincinnati to Toledo. The former was completed in 1832, and for a little while did a thriving business; the latter was finished in considerable part by 1835, but by 1845, when it was opened the whole way through, railroads were rapidly making canals obsolete. Not to be outdone by Ohio, Indiana began in 1832 and completed in 1843 the Wabash and Erie Canal, while Illinois between 1832 and 1848 built the Illinois and Michigan Canal. In the fifties Wisconsin succeeded in opening a waterway from Green Bay to the Mississippi by way of the Fox and Wisconsin Rivers, and Michigan, by building a canal around St. Mary's Falls, greatly facilitated through traffic on the Great Lakes. Except for Maryland, there was little canal construction in the South, where the mountain barriers were obstinate and the highways of the rivers and the ocean still furnished fairly adequate means of transportation. Charleston, South Carolina, was eager for connections with the West that would give her a better chance to compete with her new western rival, New Orleans, but for topographical reasons she was compelled to turn to a railroad rather than to a canal. By 1850 the total canal mileage in the United States had reached thirty-two hundred miles.

The Canal Age continued for many years after John Quincy Adams left the Presidency, but it was during his term of office that this type of internal improvement won its first great popularity. Adams urged Congress to vote aid for many such works, and the total appropriations made for internal improvements during his administration reached many millions. On roads and harbors his administration spent more than twice as much as had been appropriated for such enterprises during the administrations of all his predecessors taken together. Ordinarily such benefactions by the national government won the hearty approval of the Northeast and the Northwest, but many Southerners saw little to applaud in a policy from which their section could profit so little. John Randolph as early as 1824, in the debate on the General Survey Bill, pointed out also the constitutional risk involved. He argued that if Congress could pass such a measure it could also emancipate every slave in the United States, "and with stronger color of reason than it can exercise the power now contended for." Moreover, Clay's linking of the obnoxious protective tariff with the program of internal improvements tended to make the two equally unpalatable to a section that was coming more and more to see in the high duties on manufactured articles a body blow at its prosperity.

CHAPTER XXII

THE REVOLUTION OF 1828

THE defeat of Adams and the election of Jackson to the Presidency in 1828 was long foreseen, even by Adams himself. The President and his chief advisers represented incontestably the old aristocracy of brains and wealth that had always, regardless of party, held most of the offices and governed the country. Jackson's candidacy was nothing else so much as a challenge to this type of governmental control. A new conception of democracy was abroad in the land. No longer were the people satisfied, as Jefferson had supposed they would be, to fill the offices from among their betters. Popular rule had come to mean that the common people should choose their rulers from among themselves, and by 1828 the extension of the suffrage had gone to such lengths that an aristocratic Adams in a contest with a democratic Jackson had not the remotest chance to win.[1]

Popular sovereignty, as set forth in the doctrines of the American Revolution and the French Revolution, logically demanded that every man should have the right to vote. This principle the *Suffrage extension* ruling classes in the United States had been slow to concede, but by 1828 the advocates of manhood suffrage had won battle after battle. In these contests the frontier states, now eleven in number, played an important part. Whereas, to begin with, not one of the original thirteen states had failed to place formidable restrictions upon the suffrage, the new states had with one accord either granted manhood suffrage outright, or else had put up such slight barriers against it as amounted to the same thing. Gradually the older states fell into step with this march of democracy. The example of the western states was before them, and the demands of their own disfranchised classes were insistent. The growth of the factory system increased the number of workmen who could scarcely hope to amass enough property to be able to

[1] K. H. Porter, *A History of Suffrage in the United States* (1918), gives a good account of the movement for suffrage extension. See also A. B. Darling, *Political Changes in Massachusetts, 1824–1848* (1925); and D. R. Fox, *The Decline of Aristocracy in the Politics of New York* (1918). The classic portrait of American democracy during this period is Alexis de Tocqueville, *Democracy in America* (2 vols., trans., 1862).

vote, and who yet stood more in need of the protection of the state than any other class. To obtain desired legislation they must have a voice on election day. Designing politicians, themselves often risen from the masses, saw in a widened electorate the chance for personal advancement that under the old régime they might have waited for in vain. Each potential party boss was a noisy and effective advocate of the principle that the people must have the right to rule. One after another the citadels of aristocracy fell before the attack, until by the time the election of 1828 was held three of the original states, New Hampshire, Maryland, and Connecticut, had abolished all property qualifications for voting, while two others, Massachusetts and New York, had made them only nominal. Thus by 1828 the masses in a good majority of the states had the ballot, and, what is even more significant, they had acquired the will to use it. In Pennsylvania, for example, only forty-seven thousand votes were cast in the election of 1824, whereas with no changes of consequence in the election laws one hundred and fifty thousand votes were cast in 1828.

After Jackson became President the suffrage movement continued to win victories, and ultimately the principle of manhood suffrage was *Constitu-* established in every state. The most exciting contest *tional* occurred in Rhode Island, where the popular forces won *changes* in 1843 only after they had staged a demonstration known as Dorr's Rebellion. Virginia and North Carolina were slowest to yield to the trend of the times. Not until the eighteen-fifties did they give up their requirement that only the owners of land might vote. The process by which these and other constitutional changes were made is in itself a remarkable revelation of the hold that democracy in government had taken upon the American people. Constitutional conventions, chosen by the people, were held during the years 1820 to 1850 in nearly every state. Ordinarily these conventions made the recommendations, and the changes were adopted by the people at the polls. In keeping also with the spirit of democracy was the tendency to make more and more officials elective rather than appointive. Even judges came to be numbered among the popularly elective officials. Experience led, however, to the substitution of biennial for annual elections, and to the placing of closer restrictions upon the power of the legislatures. Governors, on the other hand, seemed to have grown in popular estimation, and the narrow interpretation of their rights and duties, so common during the era of the American Revolution, was generally abandoned.[1]

[1] F. N. Thorpe, *A Constitutional History of the American People, 1776–1850* (1898), traces the course of state constitutional development during the period.

The movement for greater democratization in the state government was accompanied by a movement to put the Presidency more directly into the hands of the people. The constitution left to the various legislatures the right to decide how the presidential electors should be chosen, and the decision promptly made was in most cases that *Popular* the legislatures themselves should choose the electors. *choice of electors* But the advocates of more democracy in government were soon insisting that the choice should be made by popular vote. By 1824 only six states still permitted the legislatures to choose electors; by 1828, only two, Delaware and South Carolina. In most of the states the people voted for a general electoral ticket, so that ordinarily all the votes of a given state would be cast for one candidate; but in a few states the electors were chosen by districts, and the vote of the state might be split. Since the latter system was at best somewhat complicated, and served also to reduce the importance in the election of the state that adhered to it, the choice of electors on a state-wide ticket was ultimately adopted by all the states.

The campaign of 1828 gave a foretaste of what might be expected when an appeal had to be made to "King Numbers." Issues were lost sight of, and personalities held the center of the stage. *Campaign* Adams was portrayed by the opposition as a place-seeker *of 1828* who had lived almost his entire life at public expense, and had drawn hundreds of thousands of dollars from the national treasury. In spite of his well-known New England frugality, he was accused of unbridled extravagance, and even of purchasing from public funds "gaming tables and gambling furniture" for the White House. The old cry of "bargain and corruption" between Adams and Clay was relentlessly repeated, and other bargains and other corruptions were invented to suit the taste of Jacksonian orators and editors. Adams himself, while pouring out his spleen in his diary, maintained in public a correct aloofness, but his supporters did not hesitate to descend to the methods of their adversaries. Jackson's personal life was above reproach, but a mighty scandal was made of the fact that he had married a divorced woman, and indeed had married her, although quite innocently, before the divorce from her former husband had been granted. Much was made also of the crude frontier fights in which the General had participated, and of his abysmal ignorance of public affairs.

Jackson's election was not accomplished, however, without the assistance of many voters to whom an excess of democracy did not appeal. Calhoun, as the Jacksonian candidate for the Vice-Presidency, hoped to wield a great influence in the new administration and to succeed the

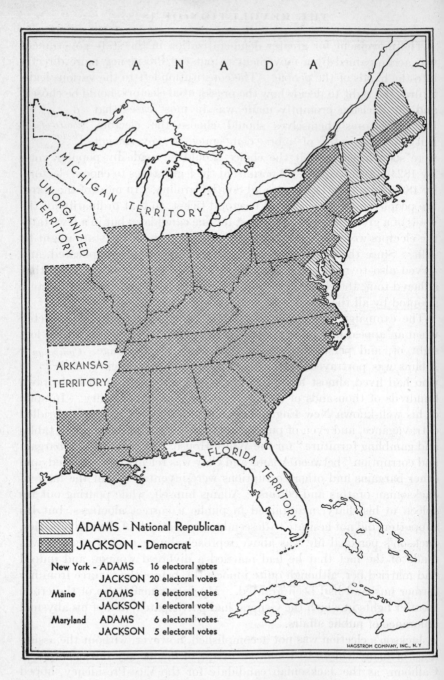

ADAMS - National Republican

JACKSON - Democrat

New York	ADAMS	16 electoral votes
	JACKSON	20 electoral votes
Maine	ADAMS	8 electoral votes
	JACKSON	1 electoral vote
Maryland	ADAMS	6 electoral votes
	JACKSON	5 electoral votes

HAGSTROM COMPANY, INC., N.Y

THE ELECTION OF 1828, BY STATES

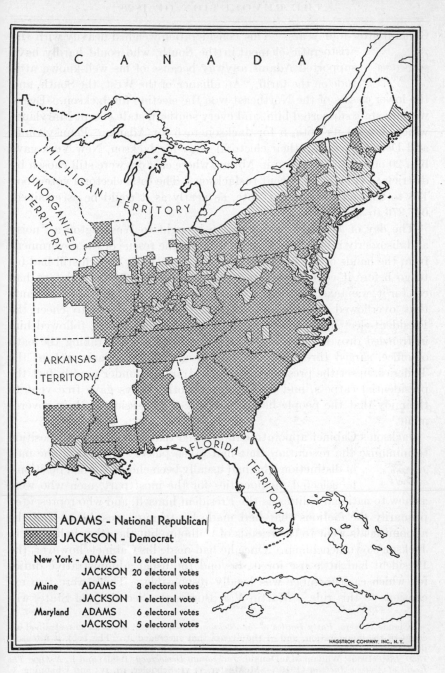

ADAMS - National Republican

JACKSON - Democrat

New York - ADAMS   16 electoral votes
           JACKSON 20 electoral votes
Maine   ADAMS   8 electoral votes
           JACKSON   1 electoral vote
Maryland   ADAMS   6 electoral votes
           JACKSON   5 electoral votes

HAGSTROM COMPANY, INC., N.Y.

THE ELECTION OF 1828, BY COUNTIES

General after four years. This consideration weighed heavily with the
Classes supporting Jackson aristocratic element in the South, who could hardly have supported Adams anyway because of his well-known attitude on the tariff. An alliance of the West, the South, and the lower classes of the Northeast won the election for Jackson. Every western state supported him, and every southern state except Maryland, which divided its vote, 5 for Jackson to 6 for Adams. Pennsylvania and Delaware cast all their electoral votes for Jackson, New York gave him 20 out of 36, and even in Maine, where electors were still chosen by districts, 1 vote out of 9 went to Jackson. The total electoral vote stood 178 to 83, and the popular vote, as nearly as it could be ascertained, 647,276 to 508,064.

The day of Jackson's inauguration brought to Washington a "noisy and disorderly rabble" bent on celebrating the rescue of the government from the hands of the aristocrats. The capital city, which still had far to go before it could grow up to the ambitious pattern L'Enfant had cut for it, was taxed to the limit to care for the huge crowd of celebrants that overflowed the boarding-houses, lined the streets to cheer the President-elect uproariously as he walked to the capital, followed him in frenzied droves as he rode down the Avenue after taking the oath of office, surged through the White House like the Paris mob at the Tuileries, upset the presidential punch, trampled under muddy feet the presidential carpets, and in a thousand other ways gave free vent to their joy that the people had at last taken possession of their government.[1]

Jackson's Cabinet appointments showed that he had little disposition to minimize the revolution that had taken place. Instead of the men
Jackson's cabinet of distinction who had usually been chosen to such positions, he selected mediocrities for the most part, men who were as new to national politics as the President himself, and who represented primarily the factions that had made his triumph possible. Half the appointments went to the friends of Calhoun, but the other half went to Jackson's own henchmen. Once he had made his Cabinet, however, the President had little use for it, beyond the usual administrative duties for which each member was legally responsible. There were two exceptions to this rule. Martin Van Buren, the Secretary of State, was

---

[1] Claude Bowers, *Party Battles of the Jackson Period* (1922), gives an unrestrained account of the inauguration, and of the events that succeeded it. The book is intensely pro-Jackson. More dependable accounts are contained in F. J. Turner, *The United States, 1830–1850* (1935); William MacDonald, *Jacksonian Democracy* (1906); and F. A. Ogg, *The Reign of Andrew Jackson* (1919). McMaster, v, vi; Schouler, iii, iv; and Channing, v, deal in whole or in part with this period.

close in the confidence of the President, and so also was John H. Eaton, the Secretary of War. Van Buren was the leader of the New York Democracy, a man of humble antecedents who had risen to power because he knew how to control the votes of the masses. Eaton was an old friend from Tennessee.

Jackson soon made it evident that a "kitchen cabinet" composed of men even less renowned than his official advisers would wield the chief influence in his administration. Ablest among these *The* men was Amos Kendall, a New-Englander who had re- *"kitchen* moved to Kentucky and had once been closely associated *cabinet"* with Henry Clay. Kendall was a graduate of Dartmouth, had edited a paper at Frankfort, Kentucky, and was possessed of considerable literary skill. His facile pen phrased many Jacksonian state papers, and provided besides a stream of pro-Jackson propaganda for the press. William B. Lewis of Tennessee was probably the President's closest friend. It was Lewis who had made Jackson a formidable candidate for the Presidency, who had directed his campaign, and who now lived at the White House to offer sagacious counsel on the petty ways of politics. Another of Jackson's intimates was Isaac Hill, a crippled, rebellious, vituperative editor from New Hampshire. The Senate refused to confirm Hill's appointment to a minor administrative office, but in 1830 a Jacksonian majority in the New Hampshire legislature, with fine irony, made Hill a member of the Senate itself. Others generally connected with the "kitchen cabinet" were Andrew Jackson Donelson of Tennessee, the President's nephew and private secretary, Duff Green, the vitriolic editor of the *United States Telegraph*, an administration paper published in Washington, and Francis P. Blair, who after 1830, when the *Telegraph* became too friendly to Calhoun, edited a new administration organ, the *Globe*. Undoubtedly this little coterie of friends, especially Kendall and Lewis, had great influence with the President, but he was himself the dominating figure of his administration, and was quite as capable of ignoring their advice as of taking it.

Jackson's decision to remove from office a large number of the men whom his predecessors had appointed was quite in keeping with the revolt against aristocracy in government that had brought *The "spoils* him to power. Appointments before his time had gone to *system"* needy members of the upper strata of society and only rarely to the common people. Moreover, once an individual obtained an office, he could usually count upon retaining it for life. This was not because earlier Presidents had been above partisan appointments, for Washington himself had been careful, after a few unhappy experiments, to appoint only Federalists to office, while Jefferson during his eight years in the White House had gradually replaced Federalists with Republicans. The next three Presidents after Jefferson were also Republicans, and they (with the exception of John Quincy Adams, whose conscience restrained him) lacked the incentive to remove office-holders for purely partisan reasons. When Jackson became President it was no doubt true that the efficiency of the public service was crippled by the presence within it of many aged and incompetent relics of an earlier day. Jackson held that the duties of all public officers were "so plain and simple that men of intelligence may readily qualify themselves for their performance." He professed also to believe that "more is lost by the long continuance of men in office than is generally to be gained by their experience." Furthermore, no one man had "any more intrinsic right to official station than another." Professing such views, the new President began immediately after his inauguration a proscription of office-holders that soon weeded out of the service hundreds of men who had supposed that they were to retain their positions indefinitely. Naturally the outcries from those who had been dispossessed and from their friends rent the skies, but Jackson's conduct was hardly as ruthless as they tried to pretend. During his first year and a half in office he made only about nine hundred removals from among civil servants numbering about ten thousand, and some of his removals could be accounted for on grounds that were not strictly partisan. Most of the men who lost office, however, were Adams men, and all of their successors were Jackson men.

Already the practice of rewarding the victors with the "spoils of office" had been tried out by local politicians in such states as New York and *The party "machine"* Pennsylvania with phenomenal results. The hope of obtaining office spurred party workers to far greater endeavor than could have been expected of them out of mere devotion to principle. The fear of losing an office, once obtained, proved likewise a powerful incentive to fighting the party's battles. On the basis of carefully distributed spoils, it was possible to build up a party "machine" which could raise money, wage campaigns, reward loyalty, punish disobedience, and perpetuate itself in power for long periods of time. Since such a machine could not function smoothly without a single directing genius to guide it, the party "boss" came into being. Sometimes he was honest; sometimes he was not. The opportunity for what a later generation called "graft" lay wide open.[1]

The kitchen cabinet which Jackson gathered around him knew well the advantages that accrued in the states from the use of offices as

[1] M. Ostrogorski, *Democracy and the Organization of Political Parties* (2 vols., 1902).

rewards for party service, and they insisted that Jackson should accept the same system in making appointments to national offices. The President was nothing loath, and his conviction that any intelligent American was capable of filling practically any office furnished a ready defense for appointing those most useful politically, regardless of other tests. When it became necessary to replace one party worker with another from the same party, the doctrine of "rotation in office" was devised. Politicians argued soberly that the valuable training in citizenship that went with office-holding ought to be widely diffused by passing the offices around. However specious these arguments may appear to a later generation, they were then accepted cheerfully by the great majority of the electorate, and for the next forty years the "spoils system" went practically unchallenged.

Jackson's interpretation of the Presidency also offered something new to American politics. The overwhelming majority by which he was ushered into office, coupled with the fact that the American *Jackson's* people themselves were responsible for the result, not a party *view of the* caucus nor a college of electors nor a series of favorable *Presidency* legislatures, gave rise to the theory that the executive was endowed with greater authority than any other branch of the government. Jackson as the chosen representative of the whole American people sought actively to secure the passage of the laws he favored, and he lectured Congress with regard to its duties in a fashion that Washington and Jefferson would have regarded as unbecoming, if not actually unconstitutional. Moreover, he made far more extensive use of the veto power than any other President had seen fit to do. All six of his predecessors in office together had vetoed only nine bills that Congress had passed, whereas Jackson during his two terms vetoed twelve measures, and used freely also the "pocket veto," a device which no previous President had dared to invoke. The pocket veto was made possible by a provision in the Constitution that unless the President vetoed a bill within ten days after it reached him, the bill would become a law anyway, "unless Congress by their adjournment prevent its return, in which case it shall not be a law." Since many important measures were passed in the closing days of a session, the President might, if he chose, defeat legislation by a mere failure to act, or in popular parlance "pocketing" the bill. Jackson's feeling of superiority extended even to his relations with the Supreme Court, and on one occasion he is reported to have said: "John Marshall has made his decision; now let him enforce it."

This clash with the Supreme Court arose out of Jackson's attitude on the Indian question. The quarrel between the state of Georgia and the Creeks, already alluded to, was paralleled by a somewhat simila *The Georgia* conflict between the same state and the Cherokees. Thi *Indians* tribe, like the Creeks, had attained a fairly high degree o civilization, and desired merely to be left alone in the possession of it land and customs. Treaties with the United States existed that seemec fully to guarantee these rights, and in 1827 the Cherokees went so fa as to adopt a constitution in which they declared pointedly that the were not subject to the jurisdiction of any other state or nation. Thi declaration the state of Georgia took as a direct affront, and the Georgi legislature promptly extended the authority of the state over all th inhabitants within its borders, both white and Indian. The position taken by Georgia was not without some legal basis, for the United State had promised in 1802 to extinguish all Indian titles within the state "a early as the same can be obtained on reasonable terms," and if th Indians were allowed to have their way it seemed likely that no more o their lands would be ceded. The matter was finally brought to the Supreme Court in the case of the *Cherokee Nation vs. the State of Georgia* but the Court, although complimenting the Indians on their successfu efforts at self-government, refused to take jurisdiction on the grounc that the Cherokees were a "domestic dependent nation" rather thar a "foreign state," as the suit contended. Later, however, in the case o *Worcester vs. Georgia*, the Court held that the laws of Georgia were of nc effect within the Cherokee borders. This decision was openly floutec by the Georgians, and the President, whatever the precise phrases tha may have sprung to his lips, made no effort to enforce it.[1]

As a matter of fact the Indian question had passed the bounds o a simple dispute between some Indians and a state. Who first caught th *The policy* vision it would be hard to determine, but for a long time th *of Indian* idea had been afloat that a kind Providence had arrangec *removal* for this vexing problem an easy solution. Explorers hac reported with great unanimity that the western half of the continen would never be useful to white men; on the other hand, because of it abundance of game, it was an ideal home for Indians. Why not accep this divinely ordained plan, and colonize the Indians in the West wher they need never fear the encroachments of the whites? As early as 1825 John C. Calhoun, then Secretary of War, had outlined this plan in ar able state paper, and had urged it upon President Monroe, who in turr had urged it upon Congress. Few objections could be raised to sc natural a solution, and from that time forward the removal of the Indian to the region west of the western borders of Missouri and Arkansas wa

[1] U. B. Phillips, *Georgia and State Rights* (1902), is the best work on this subject.

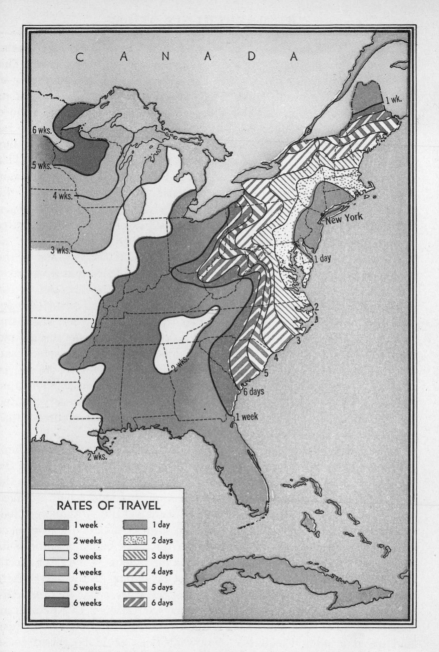

RATES OF TRAVEL

1 week	1 day
2 weeks	2 days
3 weeks	3 days
4 weeks	4 days
5 weeks	5 days
6 weeks	6 days

RATIO BETWEEN TIME AND DISTANCE, 1830

Courtesy of the Carnegie Institution of Washington and the American Geographical Society of New York.

LIBRARY
FLORIDA STATE COLLEGE FOR WOMEN
TALLAHASSEE, FLORIDA

regarded as settled policy. Thus Jackson did not inaugurate this policy, but he fell in line with it cheerfully, and under his administration it was successfully carried through. His irritation that the Supreme Court should dare to interfere with so benign a project is understandable, if not wholly defensible.

During Jackson's administration ninety-four Indian treaties were signed, most of which were treaties of cession; and under the steady pressure of the United States government even the Cherokees left sullenly for the West. Two disciplinary wars had to be fought in order to subject the Indians wholly to the white man's will. The Black Hawk War with the Sauk and Foxes, whose departure from northern Illinois was too slow to satisfy the frontiersmen, was fought in 1832; the Seminole War, which became necessary when most of that tribe refused to leave their homes, even after they had agreed to go, was an unhappy legacy that Jackson left to his successor, Van Buren, and that ended in the forties only when most of the Seminoles had been hunted down and killed. Jackson's Indian policy did not fail to arouse the sincere criticism of humanitarians like the Quakers, and the pretended criticism of many of his political adversaries, but the West as a whole approved it heartily, and the country in general was content to let events take their natural course. What is perhaps most remarkable is the restraint with which Jackson, himself a veteran of many Indian wars, dealt with the red men. For the most part the removals, although tragic enough, were carried out without bloodshed and with the consent of the tribes themselves.[1]

Perhaps many of those who supported Jackson in 1828 could have predicted the nature of his handling of the Indian question, but on most matters of public policy his views were at that time far from clear. One such issue was that of federal assistance to works of internal improvement. While he was a member of the United States Senate, he had cast his vote in favor of internal improvements, and yet he had written a letter of commendation to Monroe on the occasion of the latter's veto of the Cumberland Road Tolls Bill of 1822. As a Westerner he might be expected to favor internal improvements; as a Southerner, to oppose them. He gathered about him as his chief advisers men who held precisely opposite views on the subject, Calhoun, for example, who, in spite of his right-about-face on the tariff, still favored internal improvements, and Martin Van Buren, who opposed them. In his first inaugural

---

[1] Annie H. Abel, *The History of Events Resulting in Indian Consolidation West of the Mississippi* (1908), deals with this subject in great detail. A brief account is given in F. L. Paxson, *The Last American Frontier* (1910).

the President conceded that internal improvements, "so far as they can be promoted by the constitutional acts of the Federal Government, are of high importance," but so vague a statement left him free to take almost any stand he chose.

A shrewd observer might have guessed that Jackson's attitude toward internal improvements would be quite at variance from the views of *The Mays-* Adams and Clay. While Adams was President, Congress, *ville veto* with much encouragement from the executive, granted federal aid liberally for the building of roads and canals, the improvement of ports and harbors, and the clearing of obstructions from the channels of navigable streams. But Jackson, who in this matter seems to have leaned heavily upon the advice of Van Buren, was not long in concluding that many such expenditures were neither constitutional nor expedient. An opportunity to state his position came in May, 1830, when Congress sent him a bill which authorized federal assistance for the building of a road from Maysville, Kentucky, to Lexington, in the same state. Although this road was in reality a link in the famous route from Zanesville, Ohio, on the National Road, to the Tennessee River at the Muscle Shoals, and thence to Natchez on the lower Mississippi, the measure as it stood provided merely for a strictly intra-state road. Half the stock in the turnpike company that was to do the work was to be subscribed by the United States government, and the other half in equal parts by the state of Kentucky and by private individuals. Jackson refused his signature to the bill, and in an able veto message defended the position he had taken. He doubted its constitutionality and, like Madison and Monroe, believed that a constitutional amendment should be adopted if federal aid to roads and canals was to be continued; but his chief objection to the measure was the local character of the internal improvement it proposed to aid. The Maysville road, he declared, had "no connection with any established system of improvements; it is exclusively within the limits of a State, starting at a point on the Ohio river and running out sixty miles to an interior town, and even as far as the State is interested conferring partial instead of general advantages." He pointed also to the drain on the treasury entailed by lavish expenditures for internal improvements, and suggested that Congress might better reduce the revenue if it could spare the funds, or use its surplus to pay off the national debt.

The Maysville veto was the subject of acrimonious debate in Congress and in the country at large, but the veto was sustained, and Jackson clung tenaciously to the position he had taken. Other vetoes and pocket vetoes of similar measures soon followed. Convinced, as time went on, that the national revenues were likely to remain larger than the legitimate expenditures of the government would warrant, he urged that all surplus funds should be distributed to the states according to their ratio of representation in Congress. Should such a course be deemed unconstitutional, he suggested the adoption of an amendment to the Constitution that would grant to Congress the necessary authority. Then the states, provided with an adequate revenue and freed from the danger of national interference, might construct whatever works of internal improvement they saw fit. Jackson often pointed out that there was nothing necessarily final about his stand on internal improvements, and that the people, if they chose, might reverse it by a constitutional amendment. But their failure so to do convinced him that the weight of public opinion lay on his side of the argument, and he persisted in his course.

It should not be assumed, however, that Jackson's vetoes rang the death-knell of internal improvements at national expense. The President showed no disposition to interrupt work on the National Road, he signed many bills for federal assistance to road-building in the territories, and he offered no very effective opposition to federal grants in aid of river and harbor improvement. But the appropriation of national funds for the construction of roads and canals within and among the several states he did hold down to a minimum. The adoption of such a policy at such a time was of even greater significance than Jackson knew. Before his administration ended canals and turnpikes were giving place to railroads, and the enormous capacity of this new variety of internal improvements for absorbing federal funds was not hard to see. Jackson's policy, however, set a strong precedent against such expenditures, and for many years the railroads were unable to induce Congress to aid them, even by grants of land.

Scarcely less important than the problem of internal improvements was the enduring problem of the public lands.[1] Flushed with the vic-*The public lands* tories they had won by the Land Law of 1820, western representatives were soon demanding an even further liberalization of the public land policy. Many of them felt particularly aggrieved that the government insisted on collecting a minimum of $1.25 for each acre of the land it sold, regardless of quality. The best lands in a newly opened plot were quickly sold, although sometimes to specu-

[1] R. G. Wellington, *The Political and Sectional Influence of the Public Lands, 1828–1842* (1914), shows the great extent to which sectional interests and jealousies affected the course of events. Thomas Hart Benton, *Thirty Years' View; or, A History of the Working of the American Government, 1820–1850* (2 vols., 1854–56), presents the western view on the land question, and nearly every other.

lators who held them for a rise in value rather than to actual settlers. But the poorer lands were apt to remain vacant for many years. Why not, therefore, reduce the price of these left-over lands to a figure commensurate with their value? The low prices would in themselves attract new settlers to the West, and they would also serve to beat down the figure at which speculators held their lands. Senator Benton of Missouri, ever the mouthpiece of the West, repeatedly pressed "graduation" bills upon Congress. Let the price of vacant lands be reduced each year by twenty-five cents an acre. Any lands that remained unsold after their price had declined to fifty cents an acre might thereafter be donated outright to actual settlers. Any lands that fell to twenty-five cents an acre, but remained unsold or untaken, were to be donated to the states in which they were located for use as they saw fit. Some extremists went even further than Benton's proposition suggested. Why not, they argued, give the public lands outright to the states in which they lay? Only by such an act could the new states be placed on an equal footing with the old, who had originally owned their own lands. Needless to say, if the disposition of the public lands could thus be thrown into the hands of the western states, the terms for the settlers would lack nothing in liberality.

Another western demand was for a generous right of pre-emption. With increasing frequency pioneers, either because they lacked the means to pay for lands or because they were unwilling to await the slow process of extinguishing Indian titles and *Pre-emption* completing surveys, rushed far out into the West and selected for themselves the best lands they could find. Such foresight and energy the West was eager to reward, and it resented, sometimes to the point of armed resistance, the attempts of speculators and others to acquire for little or nothing the improvements that a "squatter" had made on his "claim." Westerners urged that the government should grant to the man who had braved the dangers of the far frontier first chance at the purchase of the land he had appropriated. One proposition, rejected in 1820 but by no means forgotten, was that the squatter should be given the chance, up to two weeks before land sales in any particular district began, to purchase at the ordinary minimum price one hundred and sixty acres adjacent to his house and improvements. The long-continued failure of Congress to recognize the right of pre-emption, or as it was more frequently called in the West, "squatters' rights," led to the formation in many frontier communities of "claims clubs," or "claims associations." Groups of settlers in a given community banded themselves together, elected a secretary or other official with whom they listed their

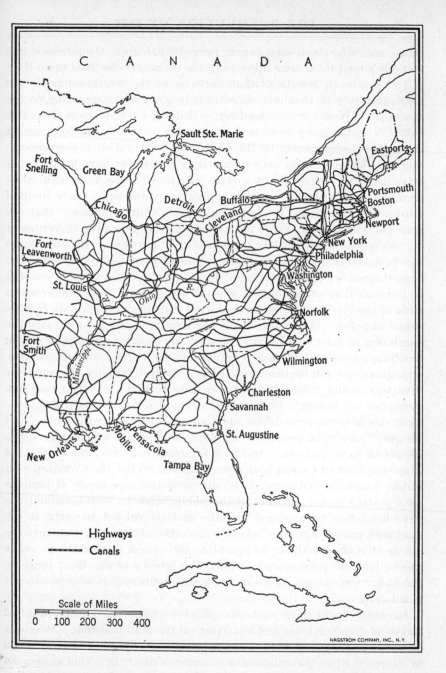

CANADA

Sault Ste. Marie

Eastport

Fort
Snelling   Green Bay   Portsmouth
                                                                            Boston
         Chicago   Detroit   Buffalo   Newport
                               Cleveland
                                                        New York
Fort   Philadelphia
Leavenworth
                                              Washington
St. Louis   *R.*
         Ohio   Norfolk

Fort
Smith   Wilmington

         Mississippi   Charleston
                                          Savannah
                    Pensacola
New Orleans   Mobile   St. Augustine

                               Tampa Bay

——— Highways
- - - Canals

Scale of Miles
0   100 200 300 400

HAGSTROM COMPANY, INC., N.Y.

PRINCIPAL CANALS AND HIGHWAYS IN THE UNITED STATES, 1834

claim, and, when land sales began, prevented by force the purchase of a member's land by anyone other than the squatter who lived upon it.

The continued growth of manufactures in the Northeast made the representatives of that section extremely wary about granting to the *The Foot* West the easy land terms it desired. Ever more favorable *Resolution* terms for western lands tended unmistakably to drain off the surplus population of the East into the West. Also, laborers could, and did, demand higher wages than they could ever have hoped to receive had they not had the alternative of a move to the West with which to threaten their employers. "It cannot be overlooked," wrote Richard Rush, Secretary of the Treasury under John Quincy Adams, "that the prices at which fertile bodies of land may be bought of the Government ... operate as a perpetual allurement of their purchase. It must, therefore be taken in the light of a bounty, indelibly written in the text of the laws themselves, in favor of agricultural pursuits." Far from desiring to increase this subsidy to the western agricultural states, representatives of the Northeast were by Jackson's time beginning to talk of a reversal of policy. They were ready, as Benton charged, to attempt the regulation of land sales in such a way "as to create and preserve, in certain quarters of the Union, a population suitable for conducting great manufacturing establishments." They spurned angrily the plan for squatters' rights. They refused to reduce the price of lands long surveyed but left unsold. They scoffed at the idea that the federal government should turn over public lands that had been won by the "blood and treasure" of all the people to the western states in which those lands happened to be located. And in a famous resolution Senator Samuel Augustus Foot of Connecticut even proposed "That the Committee on Public Lands be instructed to inquire into the expediency of limiting for a certain period the sales of the public lands to such lands only as have heretofore been offered for sale, and are subject to entry at the minimum price. And also, whether the office of Surveyor General may not be abolished without detriment to the public interest." In other words, had the time not come when the growth of the West must be checked, "for who would remove to a new country if it were not to get new lands?"

Inevitably politicians made the effort to reconcile the opposing interests of the Northeast and the West on the land question. Why not *"Distribu-* permit the sale of public lands to go on, and even encourage *tion"* it, but distribute the revenue derived therefrom among all the states? Probably this idea did not originate with Henry Clay, but he was quick to seize upon it and to fit it into his increasingly complicated American system. In April, 1832, he suggested that a small portion (later set at one eighth) of the revenue from the public lands be given to the states in which the sales were made, and that the remainder be divided among all the states "according to their federal representative population, to be applied to education, internal improvements, or colonization, or to the redemption of any existing debt contracted for internal improvements, as each state, judging for itself, shall deem most conformable with its own interests and policy." Early in 1833 a measure drawn along these lines passed both houses of Congress, but received a pocket veto from the President, who for the moment preferred, in common with many other Westerners, that the public lands should "cease as soon as practicable to be a source of revenue," and should be sold to actual settlers at a price barely sufficient to reimburse the United States for the cost of acquiring them from the Indians and conducting the necessary surveys.

During Jackson's administration the South consistently stood with the West to prevent the Northeast from placing new strictures on western land sales. Southerners, at least those who were moving into the Southwest, saw point to the expansion westward of the cotton-growing frontier, and they were not averse to the growth of an agricultural Northwest that might serve them well as a counterbalance to the industrial Northeast. "Distribution," as the scheme Clay favored was labeled, the South was also inclined to oppose, in part because it meant a too generous subsidy from the national government to the populous eastern states, and in part because what Clay really intended to do by distribution, as Benton took pains to point out, was to divert "the land revenue from the support of the Government," and thus "to create a vacuum in the treasury, which must be filled up by duties on imported goods." If distribution meant high tariffs, the South had little choice but to oppose it. On the other hand, Benton was unable to muster sufficient support to enact his "graduation" plans into law; and pre-emption, while foreshadowed by the passing of several special laws to meet the needs of particular groups of squatters, was delayed for a number of years.

Benton was not the only one to observe the close relation between public land policy and the tariff. The rapid growth of the West had led to steadily mounting receipts from the sales of public *The treasury* lands, and the treasury was by Jackson's time actually em- *surplus* barrassed by the surplus revenue it collected each year. Appropriations for internal improvements could readily take care of this surplus, but the Maysville veto had checked such expenditures, even if it had not completely stopped them. Both Jackson's plan for distributing the surplus among the states and Clay's plan for distributing the proceeds from the sales of public lands would have relieved the treasury, but the South, which had come to believe that its prosperity was imperiled by the high duties on imports, insisted upon tariff reduction as the only reasonable solution. But the Tariff of Abominations had apparently shown that any considerable lowering of the tariff schedules was politically impossible. The Northeast demanded high duties, not only to protect its manufacturers from European competition, but also as a fitting offset to the advantage which accrued to agriculture because of cheap lands in the West. And the West, except where cotton-planting throve, while deeply resentful of all eastern suggestions that one way to reduce the revenue was to throw no more new lands on the market, still agreed with the Northeast that a protective tariff was a good thing. The South thus found itself in a permanent minority whenever the question of the tariff was broached. However much it might try to rid itself of this handicap, it was sure to fail, for the Northwest and the Northeast by standing together were able, as they had repeatedly demonstrated, to command a comfortable majority in favor of the high duties.

South Carolina, of all the southern states, felt most aggrieved at this situation. The decline in her fortunes that had lately set in was unmis-
South takable. Like the rest of the lower South, she had devoted
Carolina herself to cotton culture almost to the exclusion of other pursuits. For a while the profits were good, but as the cotton-growing area spread farther and farther into the West the great quantities of cotton that were thrown on the market beat down the price. From one hundred and sixty million pounds produced by the South in 1820 the annual output had grown by 1830 to three hundred and fifty millon pounds. Naturally the price fell. The crop of 1820 brought $27,200,-000, whereas that of 1830, although more than twice as large, brought only $35,000,000. And South Carolina, whose lands could not compete in richness with the newly opened lands of the Southwest, saw her profits dwindle steadily away. In this respect the older states of the South were all alike. Western planters made money in spite of the drop in price of cotton, but eastern planters struggled in vain to keep their incomes up to the standard of living to which in more prosperous times they had become accustomed.

Other factors than the decline of cotton prices entered into the situation. Slavery as a labor system was in reality inefficient, and at best made only a few rich while leaving the bulk of the population permanently poor. Moreover, the existence of slavery practically forced upon the South the one-sided development to which it had succumbed. Manufacturing establishments, worked perhaps by slave labor, had been one of Calhoun's dreams, but as long as slavery existed the factories failed to appear. And no doubt the tariff did hurt the South. Three fourths or more of the cotton crop was exported, and from 1825 until the time of the Civil War the value of the cotton exported from the United States was greater than the combined value of all the other commodities that the country exported. Could the South have bought the manufactures it needed directly from Europe, the saving would have been considerable. Instead, it must pay high prices for northern goods, while the cotton it sent abroad was used to redress the balance of trade for the whole country. Southerners complained, not without some color of truth, that the tariff-protected profits of the northern manufacturers were paid out of the pockets of the southern planters. But the tendency to blame all the troubles of the South upon the tariff overlooked facts that were far more important. The Southwest was prosperous in spite of the tariff, while the Southeast suffered far more from its poor lands and the low price of cotton than from an unfair tariff policy.

Circumstances combined to make South Carolina take the lead in voicing protests against the tariff. The state possessed a unity that in many other southern states had not yet been achieved. Political differences between the seaboard and the back country had been adjusted by a compromise that gave control of one house of the legislature to each section. Moreover, Charleston, the only city of consequence in the old South, was to South Carolina, in a sense, what Paris was once supposed to be to France. At Charleston all the planters gathered for the social season, and here public opinion for the whole state was made. Nothing could be more apparent than that the fortunes of Charleston were, at least relative to other great cities, on the decline. The chief trouble, as thoughtful men must have known, was that New Orleans with its richer hinterland and better means of communication with the interior, was replacing Charleston as the metropolis of the South. But the fashion in Charleston was to blame everything on the tariff, and here the assembled planters, harassed by their mounting debts, railed against the tyranny of a government in which the prosperity of one section could be bought at the price of adversity for another.

Extremists flirted dangerously with the doctrine of secession, for in spite of Marshall's decisions there were many who still adhered to the theory that sovereignty resided wholly with the states. *The doctrine* The Constitution, they contended, provided merely for a *of secession* partnership of sovereign and independent states, joined together merely to accomplish certain specified ends; and therefore if any state chose for

[409]

any reason to withdraw at any time from the partnership, it had full power to do so. There was nothing necessarily sectional about the doctrine of secession, for many New England Federalists had once regarded it as their last defense against the tyranny of Jeffersonian democracy. The Hartford Convention, held during the War of 1812, had been restrained with difficulty from asserting secessionist views. Now the southern leaders, because their states were destined apparently to remain forever an oppressed minority section, boldly reasserted the right of a state to secede. Some of them, South Carolinians in particular, held that the time had about come when arguments should give way to deeds, and the oppressed states should leave the Union.

To the most distinguished statesman of the Old South, John C. Calhoun (1782–1850),[1] himself a South Carolinian, the disruption of the *John C. Calhoun* Union which secessionists had in mind was a disaster that must somehow be avoided. Calhoun had always been an ardent nationalist. He was a product of the back country, and his parents, like Jackson's, were of Scotch-Irish immigrant stock. He had been subjected in his youth to the nationalizing influence of the frontier, he had shared with Henry Clay the leadership of the expansionist "War Hawks" who had brought on the War of 1812, he had taken the lead when the war was over in demanding an extensive program of nationalistic legislation. A lawyer and, thanks in part to a marriage into the tidewater aristocracy, a rich planter, he had naturally made politics his career, but it was in the national arena that he had found his chief interest. From 1811 to 1817 he was a member of Congress, from 1817 to 1825 he was Secretary of War in Monroe's Cabinet, and after that he was Vice-President with a strong title to the "succession." If South Carolina should leave the Union, not only the nation but also the career of John C. Calhoun would be ruined. His every instinct and interest was therefore to preserve the existing Union, and not to destroy it. But a politician may not break away too far from his constituency. Calhoun could take the risk, perhaps, of supporting internal improvements at national expense, but he had no choice but to agree with the dominant sentiment of his state and section on the tariff. Nor could he disagree with the doctrine of secession now so stoutly held.

But he could, and did, take steps to prevent secession from being put

[1] Two excellent biographies of Calhoun exist: Gaillard Hunt, *John C. Calhoun* (1908); and W. M. Meigs, *The Life of John Caldwell Calhoun* (2 vols., 1917). The distinguished German historian, Hermann Eduard von Holst, showed a pronounced anti-southern bias, both in his *John C. Calhoun* (1882) and in his *Constitutional and Political History of the United States* (8 vols. 1876–92). Von Holst's opinions, however, gained currency, and they were long accepted.

JOHN C. CALHOUN

into practice.   A profound thinker and a clever dialectician, he had

The doctrine of nullification soon evolved the alternative doctrine of nullification.   He supported with irreproachable logic the contention that sovereignty is indivisible, and must reside either with the states or with the nation.   He saw eye to eye with those who held that the sovereignty of the states was unimpaired by the formulation of the Constitution and the establishment of a federal government.   He conceded that a state might withdraw from the Union in precisely the same manner it had entered the Union.   But he also maintained that a less drastic course of action was available which might make secession unnecessary.   Just as the states themselves, acting individually and separately through conventions especially called to ratify or reject the Constitution, had originally conferred certain powers on the federal government, so in the same fashion each state might at any later time through conventions of the same type decide whether and to what extent the federal government had exceeded the authority conferred upon it.   Should such a convention find the federal government guilty of an unconstitutional act "so deliberate, palpable, and dangerous, as to justify the interposition of the State to protect its rights," it might declare the act "null and void within the limits of the State; which solemn declaration, based on her rights as a member of the Union, would be obligatory, not only on her citizens, but on the General Government itself; and thus place the violated rights of the State under the shield of the Constitution." [1]

This doctrine was not wholly new, for it followed in the main the arguments of the Kentucky and Virginia Resolutions.   Calhoun, however, in advocating that each state alone might invoke the right of nullification, took a more radical stand than Jefferson and Madison had contemplated, for the resolutions of 1798 had presumed merely that there should be joint action by the several states.   The new doctrine of nullification, by which Calhoun hoped to avert secession and save the Union, was first authoritatively stated in a document known as the "South Carolina Exposition," which the legislature of South Carolina adopted in December, 1828, as part of a protest against the Tariff of Abominations.   Calhoun's connection with the "Exposition" was not known at the time, but later on he elaborated his arguments in various speeches and documents, particularly in an essay entitled *A Disquisition on Government*.   While undoubtedly he was concerned to preserve for himself a political future,

---

[1] Among the many illuminating studies of nullification the following merit special citation: E. P. Powell, *Nullification and Secession in the United States* (1897); D. F. Houston, *Critical Study of Nullification in South Carolina* (1896); and C. S. Boucher, *The Nullification Controversy in South Carolina* (1916).

DANIEL WEBSTER

he saw clearly and wrestled intelligently with the problem, still unsolved, of how in a democracy the rights of a minority are to be protected against the tyranny of a majority.

Calhoun's doctrine was readily accepted throughout the South, but the support, or at least the tolerance, of a majority of the states must be *Southern overtures to the West* obtained if nullification was to be anything more than an empty gesture or a prelude to secession. Nothing, certainly, was to be hoped from the industrial Northeast, to which the advantages of a strong central government were increasingly obvious. But the West, although it in part favored a protective tariff, had a well-developed grievance against the Northeast because some representatives from the latter section wished to bar settlers from the free and easy access to the public domain that they had come to look upon as their right. During the debate on the Foot resolution, which suggested that no further surveys of public lands be undertaken, Senator Robert Y. Hayne of South Carolina seized the opportunity to set forth to the irritated Westerners what advantages the doctrine of nullification might hold for them. He was promptly answered by Daniel Webster of Massachusetts, who upheld brilliantly the supremacy of the Union. The doctrine of nullification was on trial, and the West was to be the jury.

Daniel Webster (1782–1852),[1] like Jackson and Calhoun, was not far removed from the frontier. The son of a New Hampshire pioneer *Daniel Webster* farmer, he had surmounted many obstacles to obtain an education, and had won distinction as a lawyer no less because of the superb rhetoric in which his arguments were couched and the impassioned oratory with which they were presented than because of his able reasoning. For two terms, 1813–17, he served as a New Hampshire representative in the lower house of Congress, and devoted himself to the defense of the commercial interests with which his home city, Portsmouth, was then closely identified. He opposed the War of 1812 with all the vehemence at his command, and he charged Madison's wartime government with being "more tyrannical, more arbitrary, more dangerous, more allied to blood and murder, more full of every form of mischief, most productive of every sort and degree of misery than has been exercised by any civilized government, with a single exception, in modern times." He opposed, also, with similar vigor the nationalistic measures that followed the war, most of which were damaging to the commercial interests of New England. In 1817 he changed his residence to Boston, and did not reappear in Congress until 1823. By

[1] H. C. Lodge, *Daniel Webster* (1883); John B. McMaster, *Daniel Webster* (1902); F. A. Ogg, *Daniel Webster* (1914); C. M. Fuess, *Daniel Webster* (2 vols., 1930).

this time the particularistic sentiments that had satisfied commercial New England began to be supplanted by sentiments of extreme nationalism that pleased the manufacturing classes. First in the House, then after 1827 in the Senate, Webster led the friends of the nationalistic Adams administration, and when Calhoun's doctrine of nullification was proclaimed in the Senate, it was to Webster that all eyes turned for an answer.

The Webster-Hayne debate was not an affair of an afternoon or an evening, but of nearly two weeks' duration. The debate on the Foot resolution began on January 13, with Benton of Missouri *The Webster-Hayne debate* doing most of the talking. On January 19 Hayne made his first address, and from that time until the end of the month either Hayne or Webster had the floor the greater share of the time. Calhoun, as Vice-President and presiding officer of the Senate, could take no part in the debate, but he heard his views adequately, even admirably, set forth by Hayne.[1] Webster's oratory rose to new heights; indeed, his orations on this occasion are generally conceded to be the greatest ever delivered in an American forum. He attacked point blank the theory that the states were sovereign under the Constitution, or were ever meant to be. The Constitution, he maintained, was created primarily to impose certain restrictions on state sovereignty, and the states were left sovereign only "so far as their sovereignty is not affected by the supreme law." He cited the plain historical fact that if once the thirteen states had created the nation, the nation had since that time created nearly as many new states, and might yet create many more. He pointed out the impracticability of a doctrine which left to each of the twenty-four states individually the right to pass on the constitutionality of an act of Congress, and to the eminent practicability of leaving this power where, as he contended, the Constitution placed it, in the hands of the federal courts, with a right of appeal to the Supreme Court. He warned the South that the nation could never admit that its laws might constitutionally be defied by a state, and that nullification, if attempted, could lead only to a fratricidal war or the disruption of the Union. Finally, in a magnificent peroration, he appealed to the patriotism of the whole American people:

> When mine eyes shall be turned to behold for the last time the sun in heaven, may I not see him shining on the broken and dishonored fragments of a once glorious Union; on States dissevered, discordant, belligerent; on a land rent with civil feuds, or drenched, it may be, in fraternal blood! Let their last feeble and lingering glance rather behold the glorious ensign of the

[1] T. D. Jervey, *Robert Y. Hayne and His Times* (1909).

republic, now known and honored throughout the earth, still full high advanced, its arms and trophies streaming in their original lustre, not a stripe erased or polluted, not a single star obscured, bearing for its motto, no such miserable interrogatory as "What is all this worth?" nor those other words of delusion and folly, "Liberty first and Union afterwards"; but everywhere, spread all over in characters of living light, blazing on all its ample folds, as they float over the sea and over the land, and in every wind under the whole heavens, that other sentiment, dear to every true American heart — Liberty *and* Union, now and forever, one and inseparable!

The South had spoken through Hayne, the Northeast through Webster. What would be the verdict of the West? Would it align itself in *The attitude* a natural partnership with the agricultural South and sup-*of the West* port nullification? Or would it throw itself into the arms of the industrial Northeast and admit the supremacy of the Union? The answer was not long in coming. The Union, after all, had been of service to the West. Through repeated and insistent appeals to the national government it had generally obtained nearly everything it had sought. Even on the matter of the public lands the West was by no means ready to despair, for the obnoxious Foot resolution was soon voted down. No one knew better than Jackson the attitude of the West toward the Union, and no one shared its sentiments more fully. In a cleverly staged incident he made himself the mouthpiece of the section he best represented, and of all those who stood for national supremacy. An anniversary dinner was set for Jefferson's birthday, April 13, 1830, which all the leading Democrats were to attend. The nullificationists, with curious lack of insight, believed that the President was with them, and they arranged a program filled with nullification sentiments that they expected him in some fashion to approve. Well advised as to their plans, and fully decided as to what part he would play, the President rose at an opportune moment, and with his eyes on Calhoun proposed a toast:

"Our Federal Union — it must be preserved!"

Calhoun countered skillfully:

"The Union — next to our liberty, the most dear! May we all remember that it can only be preserved by respecting the rights of the states and distributing equally the benefits and burdens of the Union."

But the President's speech had made it clear that his states'-rights views went to no such lengths as those of Calhoun and Hayne. Nor could the attitude of the West, which the President could be depended upon to reflect with rare accuracy, be longer open to doubt. The South must stand alone in its support of nullification; the North and the West would stand together against it.

Such an alliance in defense of the Union could be accomplished, however, only at the cost of a rift in the Democratic Party. From the first, trouble between the supporters of Jackson and the supporters of Calhoun had plagued the administration. Jackson's appointment of his good friend John H. Eaton to be Secretary of War had served as an opening wedge, for Eaton's wife was socially unacceptable to Mrs. Calhoun and the Washington hostesses who took their cue from her. Only a short time before his appointment Eaton, then a Senator from Tennessee, had shocked the prudish by his marriage to Peggy O'Neill, the lively daughter of an Irish tavern-keeper. Jackson's wife, who died before the inauguration, had found no fault with the new Mrs. Eaton, and Jackson as President treated her with marked consideration. So also did Van Buren, who, like the President, was a widower and therefore free to do as he chose. To this strained social situation was soon added the clash of opinions at the Jefferson Day dinner, and finally an open rupture between Jackson and Calhoun. This event came in May, 1830, when Jackson, spurred on by his kitchen cabinet, reminded Calhoun that as Secretary of War under Monroe he had warmly advocated the censure of Jackson for the course the latter had pursued in Florida. For this behavior the President now demanded an explanation. Calhoun explained at length, but, to the delight of the kitchen cabinet, the President refused to have anything further to do with him. The chief political significance of the break was that (Van Buren, not Calhoun, would receive the President's support for the succession when Jackson's term of office came to a close.)

Party dissensions

To clear the now badly overheated atmosphere, Van Buren and Eaton resigned from the Cabinet, and left the Calhoun members no choice but to follow their example. Jackson then appointed a cabinet composed entirely of his own friends, and retained only one member of the first Cabinet. Among the new appointees were at least three men of some distinction, Secretary of State Edward Livingston of Louisiana, Secretary of War Lewis Cass of Michigan, and Attorney-General Roger B. Taney of Maryland, but the President still looked mainly to his kitchen cabinet for counsel. Jackson sought to reward Van Buren's magnanimity by an appointment as minister to England, but the Senate, with Vice-President Calhoun casting the deciding vote, refused to confirm the nomination. This rebuke was the more pointed because Van Buren had already sailed for England, but Benton of Missouri read the future aright when he remarked, "You have broken a minister and elected a Vice-President." Eaton was made governor of Florida, then minister to Spain. During the rest of Jackson's ad-

Cabinet reconstruction

ministration the hostility between the adherents of Jackson and the adherents of Calhoun was bitter and unconcealed.

Calhoun soon had occasion to marshal his forces for a final test of the doctrine of nullification. In December, 1831, Jackson urged Congress, in view of the rapid reduction of the national debt that the heavy revenues had made possible, to undertake a revision of the tariff. The South insisted upon radically lower duties, but the Northeast and the Northwest, standing together under the leadership of John Quincy Adams, now a member of the House, and Henry Clay, now a member of the Senate, achieved in July, 1832, another victory for protection. Most of the abominations that had characterized the Tariff of 1828 were removed, however, and the measure was so much better than the old that many representatives from Virginia and North Carolina supported it. Nevertheless, the South Carolina delegation in Congress promptly issued an address of protest to the people of their state. Since protection must "now be regarded as the settled policy of the country," they insisted that the time had come to use the weapon that Calhoun had forged, to decide whether "the rights and liberties you received as a precious inheritance from an illustrious ancestry shall be tamely surrendered, or transmitted undiminished to your posterity." The response of the state was all that Calhoun could have asked. Nullification became the issue upon which a legislature was chosen in the fall of 1832, and, upon the recommendation of the governor, the new legislature promptly called a convention to deal with the emergency that confronted the state. Delegates were chosen, the convention met, and on November 19, 1832, by a vote of 136 to 26, it declared the tariffs of 1828 and of 1832 "null, void, and no law, nor binding upon this State, its officers, or citizens." Furthermore, federal officers were forbidden to collect customs in South Carolina after February 1, 1833, and any federal action designed to coerce the state into obedience of the nullified laws was declared to be not only null and void, but also "inconsistent with the longer continuance of South Carolina in the Union." Calhoun now resigned as Vice-President, was chosen once more to the Senate, and made ready to defend the course of action that he had led his state to pursue.

Jackson did not hesitate to take up the gauntlet that the nullificationists had thus thrown down. He sent a warship and seven revenue *Jackson* cutters to Charleston Harbor, reinforced the garrisons of *and the* the forts that commanded it, and even let it be known that *nullifiers* in case a clash came he might take the field personally. On December 10, 1832, he issued a proclamation that left no slightest doubt as to his constitutional views. "I consider," he said, "the power to annul a law of the United States, assumed by one State, incompatible with the existence of the Union, contradicted expressly by the letter of the Constitution, unauthorized by its spirit, inconsistent with every principle on which it was founded, and destructive of the great object for which it was formed." A month later he asked Congress for more specific authority to deal with the crisis, and a "force bill," enabling him, if he saw fit, to change the location of customs houses and to enforce federal law and the decisions of federal courts by the use of military might, was promptly introduced in the Senate. Here it met the inflamed opposition of Calhoun, Tyler, and other states'-rights advocates, and its passage was delayed until the crisis was over.

It was not Jackson's intention, however, to use force if he could help it. His December proclamation had contained a long appeal to the South Carolinians to reconsider their action, and in the interest of national harmony to "snatch from the archives of your State the disorganizing edict of its convention." Moreover, he was ready to concede that the existing tariff rates, *The Compromise Tariff of 1833* although constitutional, were inexpedient, and he encouraged his friends in Congress to seek a revision downward. It was not, however, until Henry Clay, arch-protectionist and leading exponent of the "American system," assumed leadership of the movement for tariff reduction that any real progress was made. On February 12, 1833, he introduced a compromise tariff bill, which was rushed through Congress in three weeks' time. This measure, which even Calhoun supported, somewhat enlarged the free list, and provided for the gradual reduction of such duties as remained until at the end of nine years no rate should exceed twenty per cent. This compromise, it was generally conceded, would satisfy South Carolina and put an end to nullification, but on the same day that it was signed by the President the force bill also became law.

A peaceful solution of the controversy was now possible. Nothing had yet been done by the South Carolina authorities toward the enforcement of the nullification ordinance, and on March 11, 1833, it was formally withdrawn by the same convention, reassembled for the purpose, that had passed it. The convention, however, to show that it was making no retraction of the constitutional rights it claimed, formally nullified the force bill that had just been passed. Both sides now claimed the victory. The nullificationists pointed out that their firm stand had won a concession on the tariff that could otherwise never have been obtained. The nationalists maintained that through Jackson's firm course the doctrine of the supremacy of the Union had been singularly vindicated. In a sense both contentions were correct. But it was the threat of secession and the danger of Civil War rather than the resort to nullification that had led to the passage of the Compromise Tariff; while Jackson's ardent defense of the Union was somewhat qualified by his increasingly evident desire to interpret strictly the powers conferred upon it by the Constitution.

CHAPTER XXIII

THE REIGN OF ANDREW JACKSON

ALMOST as spectacular as his conflict with the Nullificationists was Jackson's war on the Bank of the United States. This institution, operating after 1822 under the presidency of Nicholas Biddle,[1] a wealthy and aristocratic Philadelphian, was in a flourishing condition when Jackson took office. Its cautious conservatism satisfied the eastern industrialists and silenced the criticism of many states'-rights Southerners, who on principle could not bring themselves to approve it. Its charter rights would last until 1837, and the chances that the privileges it enjoyed would be renewed for another twenty years seemed excellent. The bank, however, did not lack for critics, particularly in the West. It had unhesitatingly made use of its powerful position to restrain state banks from indulging in dubious practices, such as issuing more paper money than their resources warranted and lending freely on insufficient security. This restrictive policy won the deep resentment of all potential "wildcatters," whose resources were meager and whose profits were being curtailed. It won the resentment also of the many disappointed customers of state banks, who were given to understand that the real reason they could not renew old loans or negotiate new ones lay in the policy of the Bank of the United States. The bank was itself a good collector, and by its numerous foreclosures had raised up an equally numerous company of enemies.

The Bank of the United States

Indeed, many people who had had unhappy experiences with banks had begun to think that the whole banking business was essentially dishonest. State banks, in spite of the watchful attitude of the Bank of the United States, sometimes closed their doors and inflicted heavy losses on their depositors. All banks, by virtue of the special privileges the law conferred upon them, were prone to charge unreasonable interest rates and to exact unreasonable profits. Furthermore, there was no such thing as "free banking"; that is to say, a man, simply because he had

---

[1] *The Correspondence of Nicholas Biddle Dealing with National Affairs, 1807–1844*, edited by R. C. McGrane (1919), supplements admirably the numerous secondary accounts that deal with the bank.

the means, could not become a banker. In the states political influence, doubtless reinforced at times by downright bribery, was necessary to obtain the special law of incorporation under which, and under which only, a bank was permitted to do business; while the Bank of the United States was an outright monopoly. By the terms of its charter no other such bank was to be permitted. Jackson represented a fairly well-defined anti-bank sentiment when he told Biddle: "I do not dislike your bank more than all banks, but ever since I read the history of the South Sea Bubble, I have been afraid of banks."

When he first took office, however, Jackson did not seem disposed, whatever his private views, to make immediate trouble for the Bank of the United States. In his first three annual messages to Congress he pointed out the wisdom of deciding early upon the expediency of re-chartering the bank, and he made it clear enough that he would prefer an institution whose powers would be confined primarily to handling the business of the United States government. But he issued no declaration of war, while among his supporters, both in the Cabinet and in Congress, there were many outspoken friends of the bank. Twice in 1830 congressional committees controlled by Democrats upheld the constitutionality of the bank, and urged its continuance.

Nevertheless, Biddle found it impossible to view the future without anxiety. Not only did Jackson consistently refuse to state precisely the *The bank in politics* terms of a new charter which he would be willing to sign, but he also made thinly veiled hints that places for good Jacksonian Democrats should be found on the bank's pay-roll. Biddle did not hesitate to make a number of Jackson men directors of branch banks, but he was unwilling to subject the welfare of the bank more fully to the hazards of the spoils system. His nervous apprehension, however, led him to seek the favor of Congress in a way almost equally open to question. Previous to the election of Jackson, the bank had lent to congressmen only when such a course seemed warranted as a strictly business proposition; but, beginning with 1829, this policy was unmistakably relaxed. That year thirty-four members of Congress found it possible to borrow a total amount of $192,161 from the bank; in 1830 fifty-two congressmen borrowed a total of $322,199; in 1831 fifty-nine congressmen borrowed a total of $478,069. Thus the bank was almost as definitely in politics as even the introduction of the spoils system could have made it. Also, it lent with similar freedom to powerful newspaper editors, and it paid each year a generous retainer to Daniel Webster, who, as its attorney and a member of its board of directors, saw nothing improper in representing its interests both in and out of Congress.

Jackson's war on the bank was precipitated by the ill-advised action of Webster and Clay, who persuaded Biddle to bring forward a request for the recharter of the bank along existing lines well before the election of 1832. They were convinced — correctly, *A new charter vetoed* as the event proved — that Congress would pass such a bill, and they thought it shrewd politics to force upon Jackson the alternative of signing a measure he disliked, or taking the responsibility for what, in their opinion, would be an unpopular veto. Clay was early in the field as the candidate of the National Republican Party in 1832, and he felt especially confident of victory in case he could make an issue of the President's antagonism to the bank. All went substantially as the conspirators had planned. In the summer of 1832 the Senate, by a vote of 28 to 20, and the House by a vote of 109 to 79, passed the bank bill, and Jackson's veto was quickly forthcoming. The bank, he argued, was un-American, undemocratic, and unconstitutional.

> More than a fourth part of the stock is held by foreigners and the residue is held by a few hundred of our own citizens, chiefly of the richest class. . . . Should the stock of the bank principally pass into the hands of the subjects of a foreign country, and we should unfortunately become involved in a war with that country, what would be our condition? . . . If we must have a bank with private stockholders, every consideration of sound policy and every impulse of American feeling admonishes that it should be purely American.

In support of his contention that the bank was undemocratic, he pointed to the dangers which "might flow from such a concentration of power in the hands of a few men irresponsible to the people," and deplored the requests of rich men to be made "richer by act of Congress." He professed alarm at the way in which the bank made profits from the debtor West for the benefit of eastern and European creditors, and he denounced all further "grants of monopolies and exclusive privileges" for the "advancement of the few at the expense of the many." He maintained, also, that the President and Congress, no less than the Supreme Court, were entitled to an opinion on the constitutionality of laws, and he made it clear that on this score the President, at least, felt the gravest doubts about the measure before him.[1]

Jackson's message, with its ringing appeal to the patriotism and self-interest of the masses, and its deliberate deference to the states'-rights prejudices of the South, may not have shown a keen understanding of banking and finance, but it was far shrewder politics than the more

---

[1] In addition to Catterall's *Second Bank of the United States*, already cited, see for details of Jackson's "war on the bank": J. T. Holdsworth and D. R. Dewey, *The First and Second Banks of the United States* (1910); W. L. Royall, *Andrew Jackson and the Bank of the United States* (1880); and von Holst, *Constitutional and Political History of the United States*, III.

elaborate schemes of Webster and Clay. The issue in the election became for the ordinary voter not so much the success or failure of the bank, as Clay had intended, but rather the success or failure of Andrew Jackson, champion of the common man. Jackson and his advisers had grasped the fact, far more clearly than their opponents, that elections were won by the votes of the people rather than by the good opinion of thoughtful men. Issues must be dramatized and simplified. The great importance of a national bank to the financial system of the country, a tenet which Clay now welcomed into his increasingly complicated American system, could not possibly compete in popular appeal with the Democratic demand that Andrew Jackson, the people's friend, should be sustained in his struggle to defend their rights against the attacks of rich aristocrats.

In this campaign, for the first time in American history, an organized third party put in its appearance. The Anti-Masonic Party, as it was

Anti-Masonry called, originated in western New York, a region still distinctly frontier in character. Secret societies in this democratic community were regarded with much disfavor, partly, no doubt, because only a few could afford membership in such organizations, and partly because of the fantastic exaggerations that gained currency with regard to the oaths sworn and the secrets kept. In 1826 one William Morgan, a citizen of Batavia, New York, and a former Mason, published a pamphlet in which he claimed to have revealed the secrets of Masonry. When, shortly afterwards, he disappeared under conditions that suggested foul play, the Masons were held responsible and a furor of protest arose against the Masonic fraternity in particular and, for good measure, all other secret societies also. The contagion spread rapidly throughout central and western New York, across the borders into Pennsylvania and Vermont, as far east as Massachusetts and as far west as Ohio. For a time Anti-Masonry was a social upheaval rather than a political movement, but shrewd politicians — former Federalists, defeated National Republicans, and unrewarded Democrats — were not slow to make it serve their purposes. They found flaws in state and local administrations that were dominated by Masons. They appealed to religious prejudice, and saw in even the small number of Catholic immigrants who were coming to the United States (most of whom voted the Democratic ticket) a menace to the liberty of the Republic. They further widened their program to advocate assistance for "domestic manufacture, internal improvements, the abolishment of imprisonment for debt, repeal of our militia system, and all other measures calculated to promote the general interest and welfare of the people." Some of these principles were taken over bodily from Henry Clay's American system, but they had a strong popular appeal in the sections where Anti-Masons were most numerous.

The democratic spirit that had given rise to Anti-Masonry should normally have drawn it toward the support of Jackson and the national administration, but circumstances decreed otherwise. In the first place, success for the politicians who headed the movement, such men as Thurlow Weed and William H. Seward in New York, and Thaddeus Stevens in Pennsylvania, depended upon their ability to overthrow the existing Democratic control of their respective states; and, secondly, Jackson was himself a Mason who consistently refused to forswear an innocent allegiance he had long avowed. Cheered by many local victories, the Anti-Masonic leaders were eager to enter the arena of national politics, and as the election of 1832 approached they began an intensive search for a presidential candidate around whom they might rally all the forces opposed to Jackson. They would gladly have supported Clay, but he like Jackson was a Mason who refused to retract. Perhaps also he underestimated the strength of the Anti-Masonic movement, and showed it too little deference. At length the Anti-Masonic leaders took the unprecedented step of calling a national nominating convention to select their candidate for the Presidency, and in September, 1831, their convention, meeting at Baltimore, chose William Wirt of Virginia to lead them, and Amos Ellmaker of Pennsylvania for second place. Wirt's friendship and admiration for Clay were well known, and it was the Anti-Masonic hope that all anti-Jackson men would support him.

But the Anti-Masonic movement failed completely to divert attention from the main contest, which was between the National Republicans, with Clay as their candidate, and the Democrats, with Jackson as theirs.[1] Both parties, however, followed an Anti-Masonic precedent in calling together national nominating conventions for the selection of presidential and vice-presidential candidates. Such a direct consultation of the popular will was quite in line with the current conception of democracy, and neither party dare overlook the opportunity of thus cultivating the favor of "King Numbers." In December, 1831, the National Republicans, also meeting at Baltimore, nominated Clay for President, and John Sergeant of Pennsylvania for Vice-President; and in May, 1832, the Democrats, at the same place, endorsed the "repeated nominations" which Jackson had received "in various parts of the Union," and chose Martin Van Buren of New York as their candidate for Vice-President. The nomination of Van Buren was in strict

Election of 1832

[1] Charles McCarthy, *The Antimasonic Party: A Study of Political Antimasonry in the United States, 1827–1840* (1903); S. R. Gammon, *The Presidential Campaign of 1832* (1922).

accordance with Jackson's desires, but was so lacking in popular appeal that in the hope of giving a contrary impression, a rule was devised whereby a candidate to be nominated must receive "two thirds of the whole number of votes in the convention." Van Buren, thanks to the persuasive efforts of the President's friends, received well over this number, and for a hundred years the "two-thirds rule" remained the practice of Democratic national conventions. Each state, in these early conventions, was assigned as many delegates as it had senators and representatives in Congress, but the methods employed for the choosing of delegates were somewhat irregular. In time a complete system of state and local conventions was devised which, theoretically, at least, made the voters of any given party the ultimate source of all party authority.

The election resulted in an overwhelming victory for Jackson. In New York, Ohio, and elsewhere the National Republicans and the Anti-*Jackson's* Masons supported the same electoral tickets, and in general *victory* the Wirt candidacy was used to promote Clay's chances of victory. Nevertheless, in the popular vote Jackson triumphed by 687,502 to 530,189 for Clay and Wirt combined, while in the electoral college the vote was 219 for Jackson to 49 for Clay. Only half the states of New England stood by Clay; Vermont cast her seven votes for Wirt, while Maine and New Hampshire gave comfortable majorities for Jackson. In South Carolina, where the legislature still chose presidential electors, the Nullificationists retained their majority, and gave the eleven votes of the state to John Floyd of Virginia. Jackson's re-election was essentially an endorsement of the popular principles of government for which he stood. This was not due to any lack of specific issues, for the Anti-Masonic and the Democratic conventions had made sufficiently definite commitments in formal addresses to the people, while the National Republicans had set the precedent for party platforms by adopting a series of resolutions that embodied the whole "American system" of Henry Clay. Furthermore, during the campaign both major parties gave much attention to Jackson's veto of the bank bill, and doubtless swayed some voters by the arguments over this issue. Nevertheless, it seems reasonable to suppose that Jackson would have won by about the same majority had he signed the bill instead of vetoing it. The common people liked him as an individual, they believed in him as the peculiar champion of their rights, and his political lieutenants had already learned how to "get out the vote." Among the innovations in campaigning used by both sides was the political cartoon, which was quite as intelligible even to the voters who could not read as to those who could.

Jackson naturally interpreted his re-election as a mandate against the

BORN TO COMMAND.

OF VETO MEMORY.

HAD I BEEN CONSULTED.

VETO

CONSTITUTION
of the
UNITED STATES

KING ANDREW THE FIRST.

Culver Service

AN ANTI-JACKSON CARTOON

recharter of the bank, but he was far too impatient to await its orderly *Jackson's* demise in 1836, the year in which its charter rights expired. *war on the* He feared, too, that Biddle might somehow use the power of *bank* the bank to rebuild its popularity, and to force its continuance, even over the opposition of the President. Jackson determined, therefore, to cripple the bank by withdrawing from it the deposits of the United States government — a truly formidable blow, for the treasury balance was rarely less than ten or twelve million dollars. Power to withdraw the deposits was vested, however, not in the President, but in the Secretary of the Treasury, who was authorized to take such action only in the event that he considered the bank an unsafe place for the government's funds. Jackson's current Secretary of the Treasury, Louis McLane of Delaware, refused to remove the deposits, whereupon Jackson made him Secretary of State to succeed Livingston, who became minister to France. Jackson assumed that his new Secretary of the Treasury, William J. Duane of Pennsylvania, knew why he had been appointed and would take action against the bank at once, but Duane, too, refused to remove the deposits and was summarily dismissed. His successor, Roger B. Taney of Maryland,[1] was a states'-rights Jeffersonian Democrat of the old school who believed the bank unconstitutional, and did not hesitate to issue the order which Jackson desired. Thereafter the United States drew upon its deposits in the bank to meet its obligations, but placed all newly collected tax money in selected state banks — "pet banks," as they were called — whose importance increased as that of the Bank of the United States declined. Jackson's action was received with a storm of criticism from the National Republicans, and the Senate actually passed a resolution of censure, which, however, Benton at length induced it to expunge from the record.

Jackson's war on the bank ushered in a period of great financial uncertainty.[2] Biddle did not entirely give up hope of securing a recharter before 1836, but the withdrawal of government deposits obliged him to curtail his business drastically. This, in turn, caused serious embarrassment to many of his former customers in the Northeast, for a disproportionate number of the pet banks were located in the agricultural West, while the industrial centers found it extremely difficult for a time to obtain the money and credit they needed. During the year 1834 this money famine in the Northeast was so acute as to cause a sharp panic, but the West prospered as never before. The administration made an

---

[1] Taney was later chosen by Jackson to succeed Marshall as Chief Justice. See C. B. Swisher, *Roger B. Taney* (1936); C. W. Smith, Jr., *Roger B. Taney: Jacksonian Jurist* (1936).

[2] R. C. McGrane, *The Panic of 1837* (1924), treats of the depression and its causes with commendable directness and brevity.

effort to select only the soundest state banks as federal depositories and to hedge them about with strict regulations, but the urgent pleas for funds made by state bankers who had supported Jackson were hard to ignore. Too many of these bankers were Westerners; too much federal money drifted into the West. Moreover, the declining power of the Bank of the United States emboldened state bankers of wildcat tendencies to indulge their long-suppressed desires to issue more currency and to extend their loans. Eastern state bankers were for the most part conservative, and refused to expand their business more than their resources warranted, but the number of wildcatters in the West steadily increased. Here many new state banks were chartered, some of them with the flimsiest of financial backing, but they nevertheless added generously to the amount of money and credit available. What was happening can best be set forth as follows:

STATE BANKING IN THE UNITED STATES

Year	Number of Banks	Capital*	Circulation*	Loans*
1829	329	110.2	48.2	137.0
1834	506	200.0	94.8	324.1
1836	718	251.9	140.3	457.5
1837	788	290.8	149.2	525.1

* In millions of dollars.

So marked an inflation of money and credit was certain to result in some form of speculation, and with the chief incidence of inflation in the West this meant primarily speculation in land. Even be- *Speculation* fore inflation set in, western land prices were on the rise. *in land* The demand for new cotton land in the Southwest steadily increased, while throughout the interior the improved means of transportation promised such profits from western agriculture as had never been known before, and at the same time greatly facilitated long-distance migration. Land speculators bought up choice locations far in advance of settlement, and sold their holdings at a good profit to actual settlers, or to other speculators. The effect of inflation on such a situation was certain to be disastrous. Purchases of government land far outran any reasonable demand, and the same plots were often sold and resold several times without once being held by anyone who expected to till them. There is no way of measuring the full scope of the speculation, but a fair idea of what was going on can be gathered from the fact that the government sales of public lands rose from four million acres in 1834 to fifteen millions in 1835, and to twenty millions in 1836. It was during this period that the phrase "doing a land-office business" entered the American vernacular.

The changed banking habits of the United States government served to add unneeded fuel to the flames. Receipts from public lands had contributed to the treasury only $4,857,000 in 1834; but in 1835 this item rose to $14,757,000, and in 1836 to $24,877,000. To care for these funds more and more pet banks were designated, until instead of the twenty-nine depositories of January, 1835, the government by November, 1836, had its accounts distributed among eighty-nine state banks. These banks had nothing better to do with the funds that poured into their vaults than to lend them out again, and in far too many instances the borrowers were mere speculators who bought more land. Thus an endless chain was fashioned; payments made by the speculators to the United States were deposited in pet banks, then lent again to other speculators to buy more land, then paid once more into the treasury, then redeposited, then lent again, and so on in a vicious circle.[1]

The unhealthiness of a situation which, as Jackson said, served "to transfer to speculators the most valuable public lands and pay the gov-*The "Specie* ernment by a credit on the books of the banks," could not *Circular"* long be ignored. Jackson finally decided that the universal practice among government land agents of accepting bank notes in payment for public lands must stop, and in July, 1836, his Secretary of the Treasury embodied this policy in an official statement known as the "Specie Circular." This document announced that after August 15 land purchased of the government would have to be paid for in gold or silver, except in the case of actual settlers who were permitted until December 15, on purchases of three hundred and twenty acres or less, "the same indulgences heretofore extended." The Specie Circular, timed carefully to take effect after, rather than before, the election of 1836, virtually ended for a number of years the purchase of land directly from the government.

Meantime the treasury was seriously embarrassed by its mounting receipts. In 1835 the last dollar of the public debt was paid off, and the treasury needed only enough money to pay current expenses. At the peak of the speculation, however, the revenues from the public lands were alone sufficient to meet the entire cost of the national government, but by that time the tariff was also bringing in startlingly large sums. The Compromise Tariff of 1833, because it provided for a gradual scaling-

---

[1] A. M. Sakolski, *The Great American Land Bubble* (1932); M. S. Wildman, *Money Inflation in the United States: A Study in Social Pathology* (1905).

down of rates, was expected to produce less revenue as time went on rather than more; but the exact reverse proved to be true. The huge speculative profits that were being made in western lands, and the stimulating effects of inflation on business generally, fostered a spirit of extravagance that was reflected in the heavy purchases of foreign goods. Such a luxury item as silk, for example, rose from an import value of under six millions in 1831 to over ten millions in 1834, and in 1836 to nearly twenty-three millions. Tariff receipts which had stood at only about sixteen millions in 1834 were half again as large by 1836, and therefore, like the receipts from the public lands, sufficient in themselves to pay the full costs of the national government. A reduction in the revenue from public lands seemed impracticable, for eastern sentiment strongly opposed any further cut in the sale price, while western sentiment was equally hostile to the restriction of land sales. Likewise, a reduction in tariff receipts could not easily be made, for such a plan would involve a revision of the rates agreed upon in the Compromise Tariff of 1833, a course which all who had supported that measure wished earnestly to avoid. Furthermore, schemes for extravagant spending by the government were sure to be opposed by the President on some such grounds as he advanced in his Maysville veto.

Various projects were brought forward to rid the treasury of its surplus revenue.[1] Most debated was Clay's plan for the distribution of the proceeds of the sales of public lands among all the states, but *Distribution* the President's known antagonism to such a measure pre- *of the* vented its adoption. Others took seriously a suggestion *surplus* that Jackson himself had once made, and urged that all the surplus funds of the government, regardless of their origin, should be distributed among the states; but again the President objected, not because he opposed such a course on principle, but because he questioned whether Congress had the necessary authority under the Constitution to take such action. Finally, to satisfy the President, it was agreed that the money should be distributed among the states as a loan rather than as a gift, and in June, 1836, such a bill became law. According to this act, whatever money in excess of five million dollars was in the treasury on January 1, 1837, was to be apportioned among the states in accordance with their representation in the electoral college, and paid over to them during the year in four quarterly installments.

The national government might far better have held on to its funds. Already many of the states, particularly the new states in the West, had embarked upon extensive programs of internal improvement, and had

[1] E. G. Bourne, *The History of the Surplus Revenue of 1837* (1885).

borrowed heavily for this purpose. Unfortunately they found a ready market for their securities among foreign investors, who were misled by the excellent credit of the United States government into thinking that *State* the credit of the various American states was equally good. *extravagance* As a matter of fact, some of the states had not only contracted obligations for far more than their taxable resources warranted, but had also lent their credit freely in aid of dubious private enterprises. Now, dazzled by the prospect of receiving generous subsidies from the national government, many of them were tempted to increase their extravagance; by 1837 the total of state indebtedness had reached $170,000,000, for the times a prodigious sum.

English exporters, who furnished the bulk of the goods sent to the United States, were among the first to observe that the phenomenal prosperity of their customers might have a disastrous ending. By 1836 the balance of trade was running strongly against the United States, for in addition to much extravagant spending by Americans on manufactured articles, a crop failure in 1835 necessitated the heavy importation of high-priced European wheat. When, as a result of the unfavorable trade balance, American drafts and bills of exchange began to sell at a discount in England, the Bank of England promptly raised its discount rates. Thereupon exporters took fright, refused new credits to American customers, and demanded the immediate settlement of old accounts. To meet their foreign obligations American importers in turn tried to make immediate collections, and, since the foreign balance could be met only in hard money, the American banks were deluged with requests for specie, requests they could not possibly hope to meet.

For the American banking system, even without this blow, was tottering to its fall. Unaccustomed to doing business with gold and silver, *The panic* neither the banks nor the public they served had been fully *of 1837* aware of the fact that much of the nation's slender store of specie had already gone abroad to redress unfavorable trade balances. But the inadequacy of the bank reserves was made abundantly apparent by Jackson's Specie Circular. Thereafter land speculators who tried to get hard money from the banks found out that the banks had no hard money to lend; moreover, Jackson's order also revealed clearly that the United States treasury no longer regarded state bank notes as of face value. To make matters still worse, the pet banks, supposedly the strongest in the country, were given a body blow by the Distribution Act, which required them to return the surplus government funds they held on deposit. Payment of the first installment, January 1, 1837, caused them great embarrassment, and the second, on April 1 following, brought almost immediate disaster. Bank failures now came thick and fast, and in May, 1837, every bank in the United States suspended specie payment. Notes of the failed or failing banks became virtually worthless, and the public took enormous losses. Meantime, many English exporters, unable to collect on the debts owed them by Americans, had also been forced into bankruptcy. Their failure brought down, in turn, the English merchants and manufacturers who furnished goods for the American market. Soon both England and the United States were plunged into the depths of a thoroughgoing economic depression. English cotton mills closed down, and the American planter saw his best market evaporate. The ensuing distress of the cotton planter similarly affected the western farmer, who had sold great quantities of foodstuffs to the South. The loss of buying power in the South and West meant the strangulation of manufacturing in the Northeast. By the summer of 1837 business was almost at a standstill, and for many years its normal activity was not resumed.

It would not be fair to say that Jackson's war on the Bank of the United States was wholly responsible for the panic of 1837. Doubtless the West would have developed with dangerous rapidity *Causes of* under any circumstances; internal improvements, particu- *the panic* larly the building of canals, were already an obsession when the "war" began; over-expansion of cotton planting in the South and of manufacturing in the Northeast could hardly have been forestalled. But Jackson's crude handling of public finance certainly stimulated the boom, and accentuated the crash. Fortunately for his popularity, he left office a few weeks before the panic broke. As for the Bank of the United States, it secured a charter from the state of Pennsylvania, and continued in operation until 1841, when it failed. Its management during these later years showed little of the restraint for which the bank had once been famous, and the speculations that it promoted probably served to prolong the depression.

Jackson's administration witnessed an abrupt break with the past in the handling of American foreign relations. Most of Jackson's predecessors in the Presidency had represented their country for *"Shirt-* long periods abroad, and were thoroughly versed in the arts *sleeve"* of diplomacy, but neither Jackson nor many of the men *diplomacy* whom he appointed to office had had the benefit of any such training. By 1833 the state department was cleared of all but two of the officials who had served before Jackson took office, while diplomatic posts were parceled out as the exigencies of party politics required. The resulting lack of finesse in dealing with foreign countries has sometimes been described as "shirt-sleeve" diplomacy; but the new methods, if exasperating to Europeans, were often singularly effective.

Among the diplomatic problems that Jackson inherited was the impasse between the United States and Great Britain over American trade *British* with the British West Indies. Repeated efforts to secure *West Indian* for American shippers the same rights to trade with these *trade* islands as British subjects enjoyed had failed to produce results, and during the administration of John Quincy Adams irritating reprisals had been adopted by both governments. Jackson was determined to secure the opening of the West Indian trade on the best terms he could get, and he lost no time in notifying the British authorities that a new administration was in power which was ready to adopt a new policy. Such a reference to internal politics, however precisely in accordance with the facts, was regarded by experienced diplomats as extremely improper, but Jackson soon found out that he could make good progress if only the law discriminating against British trade could be eliminated. Accordingly, he asked from Congress, and in May, 1830, received, authority to withdraw the existing·discriminations against British ships coming from the West Indies to the United States, and to admit them upon whatever terms West Indian ports were open to American ships. This satisfied the British, and in a short time an agreement was reached that gave the United States full freedom of trade with the British West Indies, although the right of American ships to trade between these islands and Great Britain was still withheld. Probably, however, the British concession was not so much a victory for Jacksonian diplomacy as a revelation that the British government was about ready to remove the last of the shackles it had once placed on colonial trade.[1]

Another problem that confronted Jackson was the non-payment by France of the so-called "spoliation claims." These the United States *The* had long held against France in consideration of the losses *"spoliation* which Napoleon, in his vain effort to enforce the Conti- *claims"* nental System, had inflicted upon American shipping. French governments after Napoleon were usually willing to acknowledge the justice of the American demand, but they pleaded poverty and asked for delay. Also, they advanced counterclaims for American damages to French shipping, and for the failure of the United States to grant to French vessels in the ports of the Louisiana Purchase the "most-favored

---

[1] F. L. Benns, *The American Struggle for the British West India Carrying Trade, 1815-1830* (1923).

nation" treatment stipulated by the treaty of cession. Under strong pressure from Jackson an agreement was reached in July, 1831, whereby the United States was to be paid twenty-five million francs, less one and one half millions for the French claims against the United States, in six equal installments beginning in February, 1833. Also, the French gave up their interpretation of the Louisiana treaty in return for a ten-year reduction of the American duty on French wines. This settlement fully satisfied American public opinion, and Congress made prompt provision for carrying it out, but the payments required were so strongly resented in France that the French Chamber refused to appropriate the necessary funds. Completely disgusted, Jackson, in a message to Congress, denounced the French government in plain words for its failure to live up to a solemn agreement, and asked for authority to make reprisals if necessary. Among European nations so frank a statement was generally regarded as a prelude to war, and throughout France the already heated feeling against the United States was fanned to a flame. Responsible French officials were honestly desirous of meeting the American obligation in full, but the popular clamor forced them to break off diplomatic negotiations with the United States and to make ready for war. Finally, however, the Chamber was induced to vote the necessary sums on condition that a suitable apology should be made for the President's blunt threats. Jackson was not given to apologies, but a statement he made to Congress that he had no desire to harm, insult, or menace France was construed in that light, and the money was at length paid over.[1]

Jackson also was confronted with the difficult task of maintaining peaceful relations with Mexico while the independent state of Texas was in process of formation. Unfortunately the south- *Texas* western boundary of the United States, as defined by the treaty of 1819 with Spain, was set at the Sabine River just at a time when the southwestern pioneers were beginning to look with longing upon the practically unoccupied lands of Texas, lands which for a good third of the way to the Rio Grande were admirably suited to cotton-growing. In Spanish times Moses Austin, a resident of Missouri, sought and obtained permission to lead a group of colonists to Texas, and a few years later his son, Stephen F. Austin, won from the new revolutionary government of Mexico confirmation of the privileges the Spanish had extended to his father. A nucleus of settlement from the United States speedily appeared at San Felipe de Austin, and in 1824 a general colonizatian law welcomed other American settlers in. By 1830 about

[1] G. A. King, *The French Spoliation Claims* (1912)

twenty thousand former citizens of the United States, owners of perhaps a thousand Negro slaves, were residents of Texas.[1]

Inevitably trouble developed between the Texans and their Mexican overlords. The former were constantly irritated by the fact that Texas was not a separate and self-governing state of Mexico, but was joined to the neighboring state of Coahuila on terms that ensured to the native Mexicans a permanent majority in the state legislature. They were skeptical, too, of Mexican land titles, which were semi-feudal in character, and beyond the comprehension of the ordinary American pioneer. Also they were presumed by the terms of the law under which they were admitted to Texas to be good Catholics, whereas only occasionally was this the case. But most important of all, the sentimental attachment of the Texans for their native land was not destroyed merely because they had crossed an international border, and a great many of them looked forward confidently to the time when Texas would become a part of the United States. With this ambition the government of the United States seemed fully sympathetic, for it made repeated efforts, both before and after Jackson became President, to purchase Texas from Mexico. These efforts, however, the Mexicans deeply resented, and, far too late, the Mexican government began to repent of having admitted so large a foreign element within the borders of its country. In 1830 further immigration into Texas was prohibited and the importation of Negro slaves was forbidden. Practically prohibitive duties were placed on imports from the United States, and Mexican officials supported by Mexican soldiers were sent to the border to enforce the regulations.

Inasmuch as during this period Americans within the United States were not above attempts to nullify the acts of their own Congress, it is *The Texan revolt* not difficult to understand how their kinsmen in Texas were ready to revolt against the far more unpopular rule of Mexico. At first the Texans took sides with a Mexican revolutionist, Santa Anna, whose promises seemed fair enough, but when he triumphed they found themselves no better off than they had been before. Finally, they decided to follow the well-known precedents of the American Revolution, and in March, 1836, declared their independence of Mexico. By this time war had already begun, and Santa Anna was sweeping northward with so many troops at his command that the Texans should have been easily overwhelmed. But at San Jacinto, on April 21, 1836, Santa Anna was disastrously defeated by a Texas army under the command of General Sam Houston, and from this time forward Mexican authority in Texas was at an end.

[1] E. C. Barker, *The Life of Stephen F. Austin, Founder of Texas, 1793–1836* (1925).

The government of the United States, meanwhile, preserved an air of neutrality, but made little effort to restrain the American public from giving great aid and comfort to the Texans. American volunteers joined the Texan army, and American money and supplies kept the war for independence going. There is little reason to doubt that, had Santa Anna rather than Houston won at San Jacinto, public opinion in the United States would have forced the administration to come openly to the defense of the Texans. Indeed, for a little time, on the pretense of danger from the Indians, a detachment of American troops under General Edmund P. Gaines was actually on Texas soil, and because of this and other allegedly unneutral acts of the United States, the Mexican minister left Washington.

Annexation, however, proved to be a different matter. The Texans, supported by many citizens of the United States, urged it strongly, and probably Jackson would have been glad to comply with their wishes. He was restrained by the growing opposition *Recognition of Texas* both within and without his party to such a course. Annexation meant the ultimate admission from the new territory of one or more slave states, and many Northerners, among them ex-President John Quincy Adams, were by this time on record against the acquisition of any new territory open to slavery. Also, there was the practical certainty that annexation would involve the United States in a war with Mexico, and many Southerners as well as Northerners were eager to avert such a calamity. Jackson, therefore, with an eye to the effect of anything he might do on the Democratic chances of victory in 1836, wisely decided to take no action whatever on this subject. He even delayed the opening of diplomatic relations with Texas until after he could consult Congress, and not until the day before he left office was the Republic of Texas officially recognized by the United States.

When Jackson became President there was little agreement as to the policies for which his party stood, but by the end of his administration he had committed both himself and his followers on a wide variety of issues. His interpretation of the slogan, "Let the people rule," had led to the adoption of the spoils system with its useful corollary, rotation in office. His whole-hearted espousal of Calhoun's plan for the removal of the Indians to the trans-Mississippi West had constituted in effect a party pledge that the settled portions of the United States must become a "white man's country." His conflict with the South Carolinians over nullification had left no doubt that under his leadership the Democratic Party proposed to maintain the supremacy of the Union at all costs; but his Maysville veto and his war on the Bank of the United

States had set equally strong precedents in favor of the drastic limitation of the scope of national powers. On the critical questions of the public lands and the tariff, the clash of sectional interests had forced upon him compromise solutions, but the unmistakable trend of his administration had been toward the generous treatment of actual settlers on the public domain, and the reduction of the tariff to a strictly revenue basis. In his conduct of foreign affairs he had taken an aggressive, strongly nationalistic attitude, and had seemed at times on the verge of plunging his country into war. These various commitments won for the President and his party much support, but also much opposition.

The National Republicans, led by Henry Clay, unceasingly denounced the administration and sought to encompass its defeat. This party *Jackson's* included within its membership the "better classes" of the *opponents* Northeast — the aristocratic and the moderately well-to-do — most of whom were interested, directly or indirectly, in manufactures, and were therefore in favor of a high protective tariff. Moreover, they believed, practically to the last man, in a strong banking system, headed by just such a national bank as Jackson had made it his business to destroy. The National Republicans had also a strong following in the West, where Jackson's Maysville veto was extremely unpopular and his attitude toward the bank by no means universally admired.

Anti-Masons, following the failure of their party to achieve national prominence in the election of 1832, very generally went over to the National Republicans. Indeed, the doctrines of Anti-Masonry, except on the subject of secret societies, were from the beginning the doctrines of Henry Clay. This accretion to the National Republican strength was of great importance, for it gave the party an enthusiastic rural following and an atmosphere of democracy that it otherwise would have lacked.

Southerners who were opposed to Jackson were somewhat at a loss to know what to do. Conservatives for the most part, they resented the open flouting of states' rights that had characterized Jackson's utterances during the nullification controversy, they regarded his inept handling of public finance as an even worse calamity than an unconstitutional Bank of the United States, and they objected strenuously to the excesses of democracy that the spoils system introduced. On the other hand, they could have little sympathy for National Republicanism as long as its cardinal tenets were a national bank, a protective tariff, and a national program of internal improvements.

As the election of 1836 approached, it became the fashion for Jack-

Brown Brothers

MARTIN VAN BUREN

son's opponents, who had long denounced as "Tory" the autocratic powers the President had assumed, to refer to themselves as "Whigs." The Whigs, to be sure, had little in common except their hostility to "King Andrew I," but they at least agreed that another such "reign" must be prevented. They accused the President of desiring to found a dynasty; for he was determined that the Vice-President, Martin Van Buren, should succeed to the Presidency, and practically dictated his nomination to the Democratic National Convention. The weakness of the Whigs lay in their lack of cohesion. They did not themselves dare to have a national convention, for their leaders doubted whether they could agree either on candidates or on platform. Ultimately they decided, almost of necessity, that there should be many candidates, as in 1824, and that each section should be encouraged to support its favorite son. In this fashion enough electoral votes might be drawn from Van Buren to ensure his defeat, and the House of Representatives could choose Jackson's successor.

Thus the election of 1836 became a kind of free-for-all. Before the Democratic National Convention met, the Tennessee legislature had *Election of 1836* presented Judge Hugh L. White as a candidate for the Presidency, and in spite of the action of the convention, White's name was not withdrawn. Whether White was a Whig or an Independent Democrat was open to speculation, but two years later he declared himself to be a Whig. The legislature of Massachusetts nominated Daniel Webster, and a Pennsylvania state convention, William Henry Harrison. In South Carolina, where the legislature still chose electors, the Nullificationists would indubitably support some anti-Jackson Democrat. Hence there were to all intents and purposes four candidates in the field against Van Buren. But in the fall of 1836 the country was still prosperous, Jackson was still popular, and Van Buren won with 170 electoral votes against 73 for Harrison, 26 for White, 14 for Webster, and 11 (from South Carolina) for Willie P. Mangum. The selection of the Vice-President, for the first and only time in the history of the United States, went to the Senate, which chose Richard M. Johnson of Kentucky, the Van Buren candidate. Jacksonian Democracy had triumphed, but the margin of victory was uncomfortably narrow.

CHAPTER XXIV

A PERIOD OF DEPRESSION

MARTIN VAN BUREN (1782–1862),[1] to whose lot fell the task of guiding the United States government through the period of depression, was by no means lacking in political experience. He was of Dutch *Martin* descent, but hardly of the Hudson Valley aristocracy, for *Van Buren* his father was only a poor farmer and tavern-keeper of Kinderhook, New York. Young Van Buren's formal education was confined to such instruction as he could obtain from the common schools of Kinderhook and from a local academy. He read law, however, under a prominent New York City lawyer, and he won such success as a practitioner that his financial independence was quickly assured. Unusually adroit in his dealings with men, he was irresistibly drawn into the factional political struggles of his native state, and held a succession of minor offices. After 1816 he made Albany his residence, and was soon recognized as the leader of a little group known as the "Albany Regency" which dictated the policies of the Republican, or as it was later known, the Democratic Party, in the whole of New York. The Regency made good use of such political devices as the spoils system to maintain its hold upon the party, and the party's hold upon the state; indeed, Van Buren's clever manipulations won for him a title that followed him all his life — "the Little Magician." In 1821 he went to the United States Senate, where, however, he made no very profound impression. He lacked the gift of dramatic oratory, then deemed so essential to success as a senator; moreover, his chief interest still lay in state rather than national politics, and his attitude toward such national issues as the tariff and internal improvements was vacillating.

In 1824 Van Buren supported Crawford for President, but shortly afterward he identified himself with the partisans of Andrew Jackson,

---

[1] *The Autobiography of Martin Van Buren*, edited by John C. Fitzpatrick (1920), is a document of great value, although it was never completed.   The standard biography of Van Buren is E. M. Shepard, *Martin Van Buren* (1888).   See also Holmes Alexander, *The American Talleyrand; The Career and Contemporaries of Martin Van Buren* (1935).

and had much to do with the successful termination of Jackson's campaign in 1828. That same year Van Buren was elected governor of New York, but he resigned in order to enter Jackson's Cabinet as Secretary of State. In his personal relationships he was far more conciliatory than his chief, and he made fewer enemies among the professional politicians; but he lacked the popular appeal that made so many votes for Jackson, and it was only because of the President's favoritism that the Little Magician could be chosen Vice-President in 1832 and President in 1836. Indeed, the popular vote in the latter contest was extremely close, for Van Buren's majority over all his opponents was less than twenty-seven thousand out of a total vote cast of over a million and a half.

Jackson left the Presidency in a blaze of glory, but Van Buren had barely taken office when the panic of 1837 broke, and his whole administration was affected by the economic depression that gripped the country. Brought up, however, on the Jeffersonian principle of the "less government the better," he regarded the afflictions of the business world as entirely removed from the proper scope of governmental activity. His chief concern as President, therefore, was not to restore prosperity to the people of the United States as a whole, but rather to put the United States government on a sound financial basis. Business would have to look out for itself.

To deal with the situation Van Buren called a special session of Congress for September, 1837. With the revenues of the government at the *The Independent Treasury Bill* vanishing point, the law calling for the distribution of the surplus was quickly repealed, and an issue of treasury notes to meet current expenses was authorized. But Van Buren's most cherished plan, the establishment of an independent treasury, was violently opposed, and its adoption long delayed. Van Buren recommended that for the future the United States Treasury should have no dealings whatever with banks, whether national or state. Strong vaults, or sub-treasuries, should be constructed in the various cities and placed in charge of government officials, who should receive and disperse government funds on a strictly specie basis. Thus the government would run no risk of losing its money by depositing it in banks, nor would it contribute indirectly and unintentionally to such an overexpansion of bank credit as had preceded the panic of 1837.[1]

The Sub-Treasury Bill, as it was popularly called, furnished the Whigs a much-needed issue. Some of them believed that a third Bank of the

[1] David Kinley, *The Independent Treasury of the United States and its Relations to the Banks of the Country* (1910).

United States should be chartered, and some of them did not, but they could all agree that the sub-treasury system would merely deal one more diastrous blow to the already reeling business *Whig opposition* interests of the country.   Partisans of the state banks declared that Van Buren's measure, if adopted, would affect not only the deposit banks (that is, the pet banks), but all other state banks also, for their notes would no longer be receivable by the United States government.   Henry Clay thought that the sub-treasury system would drive the country to the use of a strictly metallic currency, "reduce all property in value two thirds," and force the debtor to pay back in effect three times as much as he had borrowed.   Webster unleashed his eloquence against a measure that was designed exclusively for the relief of the United States government, and contained not one single clause for the relief of the American people.   Nevertheless, the bill passed the Senate in 1837 and again in 1838, only to meet defeat both times at the hands of a hostile House of Representatives.

Van Buren's championship of a "divorce bill" that would sever the connection between the government of the United States and the banking business did not lack for popular appeal.   Among the first to come to his support was a noisy popular faction in the *The "Loco-Focos"* Democratic Party of New York State, known as the Loco-Focos, whose activities had for several years been a thorn in the flesh of conservative citizens.   The Loco-Focos blamed the panic of 1837 upon the reckless activities of banks and bankers, and they looked upon Jackson's war on the Bank of the United States as only the beginning of a war against all banks and monopolies.   Their curious name came from an episode that occurred in 1835 when the conservatives at a Democratic convention in New York City put out the lights to prevent a radical victory, only to be discomfited in turn when the radicals produced a new invention called "loco-focos," or matches, and rekindled the lights.   Anti-banking sentiment was not confined to New York, but was strong wherever individuals had lost heavily from bank failures, and in all such circles the news that Van Buren had gone "loco-foco" was received with great enthusiasm.   More than ever the Democratic Party could claim to be the party of the people, and could charge that the Whigs were out to obtain special privileges for the favored few.   Finally, in 1840, the advocates of the Sub-Treasury Bill succeeded in obtaining a majority in both houses of Congress, and the long-debated measure became a law.

With the national government completely removed from the banking field, it became necessary for the states and private individuals to work

out a banking system that could meet the needs of the country.[1]
Banking   Several western states experimented with state-owned banks,
reform   patterned after the Bank of the United States, but with
a few exceptions these banks soon met disaster. They were too easily
involved in partisan politics, they were rarely well managed, and their
provisions for redeeming note issues were generally inadequate. Better
results were obtained by instituting reforms in the existing system of
privately owned state banks. Indeed, many precedents for reform were
set even before the panic of 1837. New England, for example, through
the "Suffolk Bank system," so called from the bank that first introduced
it, had succeeded fairly well in establishing a currency of standard value
throughout that section. The notes of the smaller country banks, which
tended ordinarily to circulate at a varying discount away from home,
were redeemed at par by the large Boston banks out of funds deposited
with them for the purpose by the country banks. Thus a kind of
clearing-house system was evolved which ensured, at least for the region
concerned, that one bank's notes would ordinarily be as good as another's.

To New York, however, goes the credit for the most important innovations in the state banking system. There, ever since 1829, a state
law had required each newly chartered bank to contribute a certain
percentage of its income to a common safety fund, the purpose of which
was primarily to ensure that all the notes of failed banks should be
redeemed at par. When the panic of 1837 proved that the amounts so
collected were apt to be inadequate, another law was passed, which
obliged every bank in the state to deposit with the comptroller sufficient
United States, state, or other designated bonds to protect all the notes
it proposed to circulate. If the bank failed, then the securities so
deposited could be sold, and the noteholders indemnified. More important still was the adoption in 1838 of the principle of free banking.
Before that time the only way an individual or company could enter the
banking business was to secure from the legislature a special law granting
the desired privilege. But the New York statute now specified certain
conditions which, if properly met, permitted any individual or group
of individuals to establish a bank. Free banking appealed strongly to
the democratic sentiment of the time, and was very generally adopted

[1] D. R. Dewey, *State Banking before the Civil War* (1910); Robert E. Chaddock, *The
Safety Fund Banking System in New York, 1829–1866* (1910); J. J. Knox, *History of Banking in the United States* (1900). A short account of the money and banking situation in the
United States during these years is available in Horace White, *Money and Banking, Illus-
trated by American History* (1895). This book has been repeatedly revised, and has gone
through many editions.

by other states. By thus substituting a general law of incorporation for special laws, and by insisting on such devices as safety funds and bond deposits, the states were soon able to provide a banking system which, if not wholly satisfactory, at least enabled the country to carry on its business.

Many of the states, however, were long troubled by the debts they had incurred during the boom period. Little of the money they had so freely lavished upon canals and other works of internal improvement had been raised by taxation; most of it had been borrowed on the assumption that profits from the works undertaken would ultimately pay off the debt. Also, some western and southern states, notably Louisiana, Alabama, and Mississippi, had borrowed the capital for their ill-fated state-owned banks. As previously noted, the credit of the American states among English investors was excellent, and little difficulty was experienced in floating these huge loans. Repayment, however, with the depression persisting year after year, was a different matter. Indeed, many of the states found themselves unable so much as to meet the interest on their indebtedness. Heavy taxation for this purpose was politically inexpedient, and in many instances such a policy would have availed little because of the inadequacy of the state's taxable resources. With a few exceptions the projects upon which the borrowed money had been spent failed to bring in a revenue. Some of these projects had to be abandoned half finished and entirely unproductive, while others proved all too frequently to be unnecessary and premature and could be operated only at a loss. Overwhelmed by their calamities, several states, notably Mississippi, Louisiana, Maryland, Pennsylvania, Indiana, and Michigan, frankly repudiated their indebtedness. The blow which this action dealt to American credit abroad was long felt. Some of the defaulting states repented and paid off their obligations in whole or in part, but others remained obdurate, and their debts were never paid. Urgent pleas, emanating mainly from the solvent states, that the federal government save American credit by assuming all state debts, came to nothing.[1]

Repudiation of state debts

The reverses experienced by the states in their efforts to finance banks and internal improvements made a lasting impression upon the public mind. One after another the projects so initiated found their way into private hands or were abandoned altogether. The conviction grew that the state might better withdraw completely from the field of business, and leave the carrying-out of

State withdrawal from business

[1] For details on this subject see W. A. Scott, *The Repudiation of State Debts* (1893); and R. C. McGrane, *Foreign Bondholders and American State Debts* (1935).

even such expensive enterprises as canals and railroads to private initiative. Prior to the panic of 1837 sentiment generally regarded state sponsorship of such large projects as preferable to the formation of powerful private corporations, but during the depression a complete reversal of opinion took place. Provisions were inserted in the constitutions of many states which limited to a specified sum the total indebtedness that the state might incur, and forbade outright the lending of the state's credit for any purpose whatsoever. On the other hand, less objection was raised than formerly to the formation of private corporations large enough to finance needed projects. Indeed, the public had little choice but to encourage private capital to do the work which both nation and state now refused to do. General laws of incorporation, not only to extend banking privileges but for other purposes as well, became increasingly common, the principle of limited liability for stockholders was reluctantly conceded, and in a general way the corporation came to enjoy the same rights and immunities before the law that generations of precedents had built up for the protection of the individual.

The political effect of depression is usually adverse to the party in power, whichever it is and whatever it does. The Whig orators, led by *Attacks on* Clay, Adams, and Webster, pointed to the hundreds of *Van Buren* closed factories, the thousands of unemployed men, the collapse of cotton prices in the South and of land prices in the West as evidence of the mistaken policies that the Democratic Party had pursued. Not an opportunity was lost to discredit the unfortunate Van Buren. For his advocacy of an independent treasury he was likened to the captain of a ship at sea who seizes the lifeboats to save himself and his crew, but permits the passengers to drown. The corruption of government officials, mostly land agents who had speculated with the funds that passed through their hands, was charged against the administration, and the cry raised that the "Goths and Vandals" must be driven from power. An expensive Indian war, fought to effect the removal of the Seminoles from Florida, was branded as a pro-slavery extravagance, designed mainly to punish runaway Negroes who had joined the Indians. On the other hand, the President's failure to work for the annexation of Texas was cited as unmistakable proof of his anti-slavery views.

The success of the Whig propaganda was already apparent in the elections of 1838, when the administration lost control of both houses of Congress; hence the Whig leaders looked forward with confidence to a complete victory in 1840. Northern and southern Whigs were as far apart as ever on political principles, but they had discovered some interests in common. The northern manufacturers of cotton, for example, had necessary business contacts with the southern producers of cotton. Both types were essentially conservative, and socially they got on well together. Moneyed men everywhere tended to unite under the Whig banner as a means of protecting themselves from further Democratic experimentation in the realm of banking and finance. Agreement upon a Whig platform might still be impossible, but the results of the campaign of 1836, when the Whig policy of encouraging many favorite son candidacies served only to bring about the election of Van Buren, indicated clearly the necessity of agreement upon a common candidate. To do this a national convention was essential, and accordingly one was called to meet at Harrisburg, Pennsylvania, in December, 1839.

At this gathering union and harmony were the watchwords. Henry Clay was the outstanding Whig leader, but his chances were sacrificed upon the altar of availability. His long political career had *The Whig* netted him many enemies, and his political principles were *nominees* too well known. He himself sensed these facts, and well in advance of the convention he advised his friends to "discard all attachment or partiality to me, and be guided solely by the motive of rescuing our country from the dangers which now encompass it." If the convention decided to name another candidate, Clay promised that, "far from feeling any discontent, the nomination will have my best wishes and receive my cordial support." The delegates, perhaps somewhat to his surprise, took Clay at his word, and cast about for a man whose name would arouse the least possible opposition. Daniel Webster obviously would not do, for he was too closely identified with the conservative East to have much vote-getting power in the West. John Tyler of Virginia was satisfactory to the southern Whigs, but to no one else. Once Clay was passed by, the choice seemed to lie between two military heroes, General Winfield Scott, whom Thurlow Weed had persuaded the New York delegation to favor, and General William Henry Harrison. Both candidates had seen service in the War of 1812 and in Indian wars, but the greater glamour had come to attach to the name of Harrison, and in the campaign of 1836 his ability to win support had already been demonstrated. Clay led in the early balloting, but the convention finally turned to Harrison. For Vice-President, John Tyler was chosen, not only as an appropriate concession to the South, but also as a gesture of friendship to his close personal friend, Henry Clay, whose disappointment at being passed over in favor of Harrison was extreme.

William Henry Harrison (1773–1841) was the son of Benjamin Harrison, an early governor of Virginia and a signer of the Declaration of Independence. The younger Harrison's whole career, however, was

associated with the West. He was one of General Wayne's aides
William during the campaign against the Northwest Indians, and
Henry at the close of that struggle was placed in command of Fort
Harrison Washington, near Cincinnati. He married a daughter
of John Cleves Symmes, the purchaser of the Symmes tract. He was
made secretary of the Northwest Territory in 1797, delegate to Congress
in 1799, and governor of Indiana Territory — an office which he held for
a dozen years — in 1800. His clash with the Indians at Tippecanoe,
and his participation in the Canadian campaign which ended in the
battle of the Thames, have already been noted. After the War of 1812,
for short periods each, he represented an Ohio district in Congress,
served in the Ohio State Senate, and was a United States Senator from
Ohio. In 1828 he was appointed by President Adams minister to
Colombia, but was promptly recalled at the beginning of the Jackson
administration. Throughout his long career he had distinguished himself for little else than his dealings with the Indians, both in peace and
in war, but his reputation as an Indian fighter was second only to that of
Jackson himself, and constituted an unmistakable political asset. After
Jackson became President, Harrison retired to his farm at North Bend,
Ohio, and would doubtless have been content to stay there had not the
Whig leaders determined to capitalize upon the popular enthusiasm
which they believed his name would evoke.

The Democrats renominated Van Buren and in a long series of resolutions stood by the record he and his predecessor in office had made.
The Whig They were thus subject to attack in a fashion that the Whigs,
strategy who had no platform, escaped. But issues of any sort or
kind were soon forgotten. It was a part of the Whig strategy to commit
their party only in the matter of opposition to the Democrats. "If
General Harrison is taken up as the candidate," Nicholas Biddle had
said, "it will be on account of the past. Let him say not one single word
about his principles, or his creed — let him say nothing — promise
nothing. Let no committee, no convention, no town meeting ever
extract from him a single word about what he thinks now or will do hereafter. Let the use of pen and ink be wholly forbidden." This advice
was followed in so far as it was humanly possible, not only by Harrison
but also by the Whig orators. Their campaign speeches were long and
numerous, but confined primarily to denunciations of Van Buren and
laudations of Harrison. The observation of a disappointed adherent
of Henry Clay's, that if Harrison could only be given a pension and
a barrel of cider he would gladly retire to a log cabin for the rest of his
days, produced a text for the Whig orators. This quip, repeated in

a Democratic paper, made it possible for Harrison's supporters to feature the plainness of their candidate in comparison with the fastidiousness of Van Buren. The votes of common men, many of whom themselves still lived in log cabins and drank cider, were solicited for the "log-cabin, hard-cider candidate." Van Buren was attacked as a lover of old silver and good wine who wore cologne-scented whiskers and laced up in corsets. Daniel Webster regretted that he himself had not been born in a log cabin, but rejoiced that his brothers and sisters had had that advantage. Seward campaigned the country districts of New York State in a green farm-wagon. Log cabins, cider barrels, and coonskin caps furnished the *motifs* for innumerable badges, floats, and songs. Enthusiasm replaced argument, and emotion put reason to flight. In this bizarre fashion the Whig candidates, "Tippecanoe and Tyler too," came to be identified, as once the name of Andrew Jackson had been, with the common man's crusade against the aristocrats.

> Let Van from his coolers of silver drink wine,
> And lounge on his cushioned settee;
> Our man on his buckeye bench can recline
> Content with hard cider is he!

The success of the Whig tactics was complete, and Van Buren was defeated by an electoral vote of 234 to 60. The popular vote, however, was surprisingly close, for Harrison received less than 150,000 majority out of over 2,400,000 votes cast.[1]

The Whig leaders, particularly Webster and Clay, took it for granted that they would be called upon to guide the new administration, and all started off well enough. Harrison chose Webster to be Secretary of State, and gave most of the other places in his Cabinet to the friends of Henry Clay. Clay himself retained his seat in the Senate, and prepared to push through a Congress that the election had made overwhelmingly Whig his long-delayed American system. Unfortunately, however, the President, who was more than sixty-eight years of age at the time of his inauguration, did not long survive that event. Thousands of Whig office-seekers, bent upon replacing the "rascally Democrats" at once, thronged into the capital and gave him no peace. With his strength thus overtaxed, he failed to throw off a severe cold contracted the day of his inauguration, and a month later he was dead.

Death of Harrison

[1] A. B. Norton, *The Great Revolution of 1840* (1888), preserves much of the picturesque character of this campaign. The troubled career of the Whig Party is entertainingly set forth in John Fiske, *Essays Historical and Literary* (2 vols., 1902), i. See also A. C. Cole, *The Whig Party in the South* (1913); and H. R. Mueller, *The Whig Party in Pennsylvania* (1922).

John Tyler (1790–1862) [1] was a Virginia aristocrat who had long been known for the pronounced views he held and the determination with
John Tyler which he held them. As a member of the Virginia state legislature, of the national House of Representatives, and finally of the United States Senate, he had gone on record repeatedly on all the important issues of the day. He was uncompromisingly opposed to a protective tariff, to a national bank, and to internal improvements at national expense; and he was equally ardent in his defense of states' rights, slavery, nullification, and expansion. He had, too, a kind of vanity in his views and a touchiness about them that made it extremely difficult for him to compromise. In 1838, for example, he had resigned from the Senate rather than obey instructions sent him by the Virginia legislature. Possibly no man of his generation was less fitted to play the rôle of figurehead for which his predecessor, Harrison, had been cast. Dismayed at the prospect before them, some of the Whig leaders hoped to restrict Tyler's powers on the theory that he was merely a Vice-President acting as President. But Tyler promptly assumed the same title and the same prerogatives as had always been accorded to elected Presidents. He retained Harrison's Cabinet, however, and was as conciliatory toward the Whig leaders as he knew how to be.

The Whigs had been elected to save the country from the depression, and with this in view a special session of Congress was called to meet the
The Whig last of May, 1841. Unfortunately, there was no platform
program to which either the President or the Whig members of Congress could be held, but Clay attempted to supply this deficiency by an elaborate series of resolutions which he presented to the Senate. The Whig program, according to these resolves, would be (1) repeal of the Sub-Treasury Bill, (2) a third Bank of the United States, (3) a higher tariff to produce a revenue adequate to the needs of the government, and (4) the distribution among the states of the proceeds from the sales of public lands. That Clay stated accurately the views of the National Republican wing of the Whig Party there can be no doubt, and Whigs of this persuasion probably constituted a majority in Congress. But there was much about the program that the southern Whigs did not relish, and unfortunately for harmony Tyler was a southern Whig. He had never been a National Republican, and never could have been one. Clay was hopeful, nevertheless. "Tyler dares not resist me," he is reputed to have said. "I will drive him before me."

---

[1] L. G. Tyler, *The Letters and Times of the Tylers* (3 vols., 1884–96), defends Tyler stoutly. Undoubtedly many early writers accepted too readily the opinion of Tyler that was held by Clay and his followers.

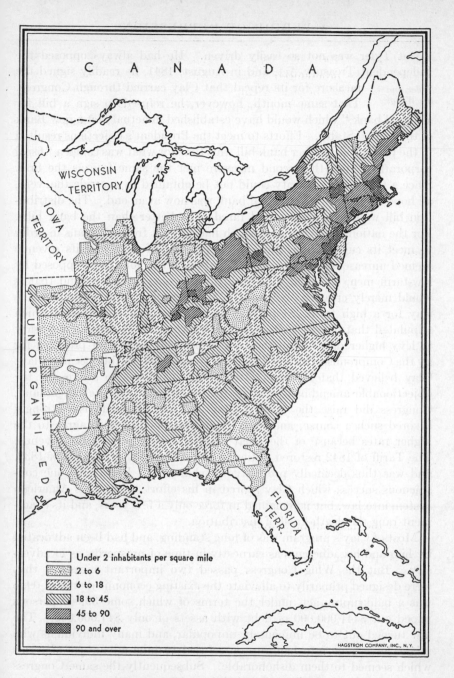

DENSITY OF POPULATION IN 1840

Legend:
- Under 2 inhabitants per square mile
- 2 to 6
- 6 to 18
- 18 to 45
- 45 to 90
- 90 and over

CANADA

WISCONSIN TERRITORY

IOWA TERRITORY

UNORGANIZED

FLORIDA TERR.

HAGSTROM COMPANY, INC., N.Y.

But Tyler was not so easily driven. He had always opposed the Independent Treasury Act, and in August, 1841, he readily signed the measure for its repeal that Clay carried through Congress. *Tyler and the Whigs* That same month, however, he refused to sign a bill for a "fiscal bank," which would have established in actual fact a new Bank of the United States. Efforts to meet the President's objections resulted in the passage of another bank bill, this time for what was called a "fiscal corporation," but the second measure met the same fate as the first. Since a two-thirds majority could not be obtained to override the veto, all hope of chartering a national bank was now at an end. The distribution bill which Clay sponsored fared little better than the bank bills. For the national government, which had to float frequent loans in order to meet its current obligations, to deprive itself of any of its revenue seemed unreasonable; moreover, distribution had long been opposed by low-tariff men, of whom the President was one, on the ground that it would merely create a "vacuum in the treasury," and so prepare the way for a high tariff. Finally Clay agreed to an amendment which stipulated that distribution should cease whenever it became necessary to levy higher duties than the twenty per cent maximum provided for by the Compromise Tariff of 1833; and so modified, the bill became a law. Clay believed that he could later induce Congress to strike out the objectionable amendment, but in this he failed. On the other hand, Congress did raise the tariff. Clay and the protectionists strongly favored such a course, and even Tyler was persuaded to agree to the higher rates because of the great necessity of increasing the revenue. The Tariff of 1842 restored duties to about the level of the Act of 1832, and was thus decidedly protective in character. It was the one conspicuous success which Clay scored in his effort to turn his American system into law, but it remained in force only a few years, and its enactment rang the death-knell of distribution.

Most of Clay's program was of long standing, and had been advocated by him and his adherents as earnestly in time of prosperity as in adversity. But the Whig Congress passed two important measures that were designed primarily to alleviate the existing economic distress. One was a bankruptcy act, under the terms of which some 39,000 persons wiped out $441,000,000 of debt with assets of only $44,000,000. The law turned out to be immensely unpopular, and many individuals who might have gone into bankruptcy refused to take advantage of terms which seemed to them dishonorable. Subsequently the same Congress that had passed the law repealed it. A pre-emption act, however, which western members of Congress succeeded in attaching to Clay's distribution bill, was generally regarded as a reasonable measure of relief. This law made legal at last the pioneer practice of settling upon public lands in advance of their being offered for sale. Pre-emptors, or squatters, were assured that, in case they were actual residents on their claims and had made slight improvements, they might, when the government offered the land for sale, buy it in at the minimum price. By this measure not only was the stigma of law-breaker removed from the squatters, but in reality a bid was made for more squatters to go West and seek new homes. The old theory that the land was to be so administered as to produce a revenue received a fatal blow, and the western theory that the land should be used to provide homes for the needy millions was tacitly acknowledged. Pre-emption had been advocated often enough before 1841, but it was adopted at that particular time primarily as a means of encouraging those who suffered from the depression to seek their salvation in a move to the West.[1]

The West as a haven of refuge was discovered, however, long before it received this legislative blessing. During the boom period two new western states, Arkansas (1836) and Michigan (1837), were *Growth of* admitted to the Union, and in the next few years their *the West* population increased with great rapidity. So also did the population of all the western states where cheap lands were still available. But the most startling development occurred in the territories that were soon to become the states of Wisconsin, Iowa, and Minnesota. Here land was still to be found that government surveyors had not entered, and here squatters by the thousands took claims which for the time being cost them nothing. Also, the new territories had escaped the heavy expenditures for internal improvements that had characterized the boom period, and their rates of taxation were low. Steamboats on the Mississippi River and the Great Lakes, and covered wagons across the prairies, brought the population in. The rapid growth of the West during the early forties, of which this movement into the New Northwest was an important part, had much to do with alleviating the distress felt by the country as a whole. Here many of the unemployed found employment, and at the same time created by their efforts a new market for the goods which the older sections so much needed to sell.

Tyler's obstinate refusal to sign a bank bill brought disaster not only to Clay's program but to the Whig Party itself. All pretense of party harmony was now thrown to the winds. At Clay's behest Tyler's entire

[1] G. M. Stephenson, *The Political History of the Public Lands from 1840 to 1862* (1917), begins about where Wellington's book leaves off (see page 403). Less detailed is Shosuke Sato, *History of the Land Question in the United States* (1886).

Cabinet, with the exception of Webster, resigned, and the President *Whig* was formally read out of the party. Naturally the un*dissensions* seemly dissension at Washington had an adverse effect on the voters, and in the elections of 1842 the Whigs lost their majority in the House of Representatives, although they still controlled the Senate. Clay himself dramatically retired to private life. His farewell speech to the Senate moved many of his auditors to tears, and even won a warm handclasp from his arch-enemy, Calhoun. Everyone knew, however, that in spite of his apparent renunciation of politics he would be a candidate for the Presidency in 1844. Meanwhile, with Congress divided, Clay in retirement, and John Tyler still President, legislation, except on routine matters, was at a standstill.

Webster's decision to remain in Tyler's Cabinet was due in part, no doubt, to his unwillingness to have it appear that Clay could tell him *Foreign* what to do; but he also believed that he was well fitted to *policy* effect a settlement of the serious difficulties that had arisen between the United States and Great Britain. Beginning with the Canadian insurrection of 1837, the relations between the two nations had taken an unfortunate turn.[1] Thereafter for a number of years disorder and unrest rather than actual revolt marked the history of Canada, but many citizens of the United States expressed freely their hope that the great British colony to the north would become first independent of the mother country, and then a part of the United States. Some Americans went so far as to assist the Canadian revolutionists in every possible way to obtain money, men, and supplies. Under the strain of this situation, chronic and long-standing diplomatic differences between the United States and Great Britain became suddenly matters of vital consequence, and were magnified, particularly on this side of the Atlantic, out of all reasonable proportion to their importance. Fortunately, Sir Robert Peel, who became the British Prime Minister in 1841, was eager to restore good relations between the two countries, and sent as special envoy to Washington Lord Ashburton, a man well versed in American matters with whom Webster found it easy to cooperate.

The *Caroline* affair, a particularly disconcerting incident of the *The Caro-* Canadian insurrection, occurred late in 1837. Some Can*line affair* adian rebels, with headquarters at Navy Island on the Canadian side of the Niagara River, had chartered a small American

---

[1] On Anglo-American relations during this period the following books should be consulted: O. E. Tiffany, *Relations of the United States to the Canadian Rebellion of 1837–1838* (1905); J. F. Sprague, *The Northeastern Boundary Controversy and the Aroostook War* (1910); and H. S. Burrage, *Maine in the Northeastern Boundary Controversy* (1919).

steamship, the *Caroline*, to bring to their rendezvous volunteers and supplies from the United States. The Canadian authorities planned to seize and destroy the vessel while she was at the island, and therefore in Canadian waters, but owing to some miscalculation they sent troops for the purpose when the vessel was tied up at a wharf on the American side. Undeterred by this development, the troops crossed the river, boarded the *Caroline*, and overpowered her crew, killing one man and injuring several others. They then set fire to the craft and turned her adrift to float over the falls. The United States government, which was really making an effort to maintain a correct neutrality, took the *Caroline* incident seriously, and demanded an explanation of the British government. When the British reply proved unsatisfactory, President Van Buren let it be known that he was determined to seek redress.

The matter was further complicated in November, 1840, when a Canadian named Alexander McLeod boasted in a New York saloon that he had been a member of the party which had boarded the *Caroline*, and that it was he who had killed a member of her crew. Thereupon McLeod was promptly arrested, indicted for murder, and brought to trial in a New York state court. The British minister to the United States made it clear that his government accepted full responsibility for what had happened to the *Caroline*, and demanded that McLeod be released; also the American minister in London was told that the execution of McLeod would mean war. This was the situation when Webster became Secretary of State. Unfortunately, the new secretary was almost powerless to act in the matter, for the state of New York had complete jurisdiction in the McLeod case; but he kept a watchful eye on the proceedings, and was not surprised when the prisoner was acquitted on an alibi. The international tension was further eased by concessions on both sides. The United States officially agreed that the British were right in contending that in military affairs individuals were not responsible for carrying out orders issued by their government, and Congress, at Webster's request, passed a law which provided that in the future the accused in all such cases should have the right of appeal to the federal courts. The British, on the other hand, while maintaining that their part in the *Caroline* affair was strictly defensible, expressed regret that it had ever occurred.

Another dispute which Lord Ashburton and Webster were called upon to settle concerned the boundary line between the United States and Canada. The northeastern, or Maine, boundary had been fixed by the Treaty of 1783 at "the Highlands which divide those rivers which empty themselves into the St. Lawrence from those which fall into the At-

lantic Ocean." Unfortunately, there were several sets of highlands that
The Canadian boundary answered this description, and an area of approximately twelve thousand square miles was claimed by both countries. In 1827 this dispute had been referred to the King of the Netherlands, who suggested a compromise line, but his decision had been rejected by the United States. In the eighteen-thirties American and Canadian lumberjacks began to clash in the disputed territory, and by the end of the decade the so-called "Aroostook War" had broken out. For a time the situation threatened to get out of hand. Maine voted several hundred thousand dollars for forts, Congress authorized the President to call out the militia and accept fifty thousand volunteers, and General Winfield Scott was sent to the border. Fortunately, however, the governors of Maine and New Brunswick were able in 1839 to agree upon a *modus vivendi*, pending the settlement of the dispute, and early in 1842 Webster and Ashburton began their negotiations. After much jockeying they agreed upon a settlement which gave approximately seven twelfths of the disputed area to the United States, and five twelfths to Great Britain. These terms were included in the famous Webster-Ashburton Treaty, signed August 9, 1842, and subsequently ratified by both nations.

Two minor boundary disputes were also settled by the treaty. The forty-fifth parallel, which supposedly marked the northern boundary of the United States between the Connecticut and St. Lawrence Rivers, had been incorrectly surveyed in 1774 to swing northward, over a considerable part of the distance, as much as three quarters of a mile. This inaccurate line, which had long been regarded as the correct boundary, was confirmed as such by the treaty. Also, the boundary west from Lake Superior to the Lake of the Woods, inadequately defined by earlier negotiations, was brought into harmony with existing geographic information. The Canadian-American boundary from the Atlantic Ocean to the Rocky Mountains thus took the form that it still retains. It was perhaps unfortunate that Webster and Ashburton felt no call to extend their efforts to include a settlement of the Oregon question.

Probably as a result of the *Caroline* affair, it was decided to include in the treaty an article on extradition. Jay's treaty had provided for
Extradition the mutual return of fugitives who were accused of murder or forgery, but after its expiration there had been no agreement whatever on the subject. As a consequence, criminals on both sides of the Canadian-American boundary found it altogether too easy to escape from punishment by flight across the international border. The Webster-Ashburton Treaty listed seven crimes, "murder, or assault

to commit murder, or piracy, or arson, or robbery, or forgery, or the utterance of forged paper," for which extradition was to be required. Embezzlement, unfortunately, was not included, and for a long time the phrase "gone to Canada," implied in the American vernacular that the traveler was guilty of this crime. Later, however, the list of extraditable offenses was greatly extended.

Another subject that the treaty dealt with was the international slave trade. In 1807 Great Britain, and the following year the United States, had declared this trade illegal, and in a short time *The slave* practically all the other civilized nations of the world had *trade* done likewise. But as long as slavery existed anywhere, there were bound to be those who were willing to take the risk of breaking the law. Ships designed to engage in the slave trade were elaborately outfitted with concealed slave decks, carried falsified papers, and used at will the flags of all nations. Slave cargoes could be easily and cheaply obtained at the numerous stations along the western coast of Africa where native chiefs brought in their captives, and exchanged them for liquor and trinkets. The slaver, if he escaped capture on the high seas, could then dispose of his booty at a stiff profit in Porto Rico, Cuba, Brazil, or the United States. Great Britain, with a navy far superior to that of any other power, took the lead in efforts to suppress this nefarious trade, and succeeded in obtaining from many countries permission to visit and search suspected vessels, regardless of the flag they happened to fly. This policy, however, ran counter to a strong American prejudice, and when American ships were so molested the United States entered vigorous protests. Repeatedly the British government tried to come to an understanding with the United States on the subject, but all such efforts ended in failure, and the Stars and Stripes became, in consequence, the chief protection of the slaver. Webster and Ashburton at first wrestled in vain with this knotty problem, but at length they agreed to a suggestion made by President Tyler that both powers should keep strong naval forces off the coast of Africa, the two squadrons to co-operate whenever occasion demanded. This agreement was reasonable enough, but the United States failed to maintain its proper quota of ships in African waters, and until the time of the Civil War the American flag continued, unfortunately, to be used freely by ships engaged in the slave trade.

Webster and Ashburton were also forced by circumstances to try to smooth out irritations that had arisen because of the practice, common along the Atlantic seaboard, of transporting slaves by sea *The Creole* from one part of the United States to another. On several *affair* occasions ships engaged in this maritime domestic slave trade were compelled because of storms or other exigencies to put in at some British West Indian port, whereupon the slaves they carried were promptly set free by the British authorities. In 1841 the *Creole* case brought this matter to a dramatic head. The *Creole* was an American ship bound from Virginia to New Orleans with a cargo of one hundred and thirty-five slaves. During the voyage the slaves engaged in a successful mutiny, killing one person and wounding several others, and then took the ship into the British port of Nassau, where, with the exception of those held responsible for the murder, they were given their freedom. In the United States this incident aroused great excitement, and Webster voiced in no uncertain terms the American objection to what the British had done. The ship, he argued, had entered the British port in distress, and under such circumstances the laws of the United States were not suspended. The slaves were therefore still slaves, and should be returned to their owners. Lord Ashburton claimed that he had no authority to deal with the *Creole* case, and asked that it be excluded from the scope of the treaty. He agreed, however, that for the future "there shall be no officious interference with American vessels driven by accident or by violence" into British ports. There the matter rested for the time being, but in 1853 the case was submitted to the arbitration of a British umpire, Joshua Bates, who upheld Webster's reasoning, and awarded to the United States damages of $110,330.

CHAPTER XXV

THE AWAKENING OF THE AMERICAN MIND

THE United States during and immediately following the Jacksonian era was the scene of a series of remarkable transformations. Democracy in government became for the nation and for most of the states a fact as well as a theory; the multiplication of canals, turnpikes, steamboats, and railroads wrought a revolution in transportation; the industrialization and consequent urbanization of the Northeast progressed with startling rapidity; the triumph of "King Cotton" was duly celebrated in the South; the advance of the western frontier continued through good times and bad. Quite as striking, and quite as characteristic of the age, were the stirrings that the new scene awakened in the American intellect. During this period inventive genius was strangely stimulated, literary talent rose to unprecedented heights, and many crusades for the righting of ancient wrongs swept through the land.[1]

It is easier to produce evidence of this spiritual ferment than to explain how it came about. The growing wealth of the young nation may have had something to do with it. Wealth meant, at least *Intellectual* for a few, freedom from ordinary labor, and the leisure to *activity* read and think. And yet comparatively little of consequence was accomplished directly by the leisure class; most of the striking achievements of the period were made by men and women who had to earn their own livings. Possibly the chief contribution of the well-to-do was to create demands, spiritual no less than material, that others less favored would seek to supply. Closer contacts with European culture had also an invigorating influence upon trends of thought in the United States. Foreign travel, which had been at low ebb from the time of the American Revolution to the close of the War of 1812, slowly revived; more European books were imported and read; European criticisms of the United States, while seemingly scorned, were nevertheless taken deeply to heart;

[1] A general picture of the period is given in C. R. Fish, *The Rise of the Common Man, 1830–1850* (1927). More colorful, but marred somewhat by their flippant style, are E. Douglas Branch, *The Sentimental Years, 1836–1860* (1934); and Meade Minnigerode, *The Fabulous Forties, 1840–1850* (1924).

European ideas that were applicable to American conditions were quickly detected and freely appropriated. But the seething, restless, growing American nation was, after all, its own irresistible challenge to thought. The physical needs of so vast and so new a country commanded the best that inventive genius could supply; and the unique character of the American experiment ensured that alert and inquiring minds would seek to understand it, to explain its implications, to direct its course for the future.

Fortunately the United States was not wholly without an intellectual tradition. New England from its beginnings had had a high regard for *Leadership of New England* learning; it had taken great pride in its schools and colleges; it had required its clergy to become masters of an intricate system of theology. New-Englanders, moreover, were not confined to New England, for in every generation their migratory propensities had taken some of them to nearly every part of the country. Tenacious of their views and born propagandists, they introduced wherever they went New England ideas, New England ways of doing things. Particularly in the West, where a materialistic point of view was naturally prevalent, the New England emigrants exerted a strong leavening influence. Nor were they content merely to uphold the cultural traditions they had inherited; they kept in constant touch with developments in their old homes, and passed on to the rest of the country the new impulses they received. Thus New England became a kind of intellectual capital toward which the whole country looked for leadership.

The thoroughgoing democratization of the newspaper, which took place during this period, helped immeasurably to facilitate the spread *Newspapers* of new ideas. In an earlier age only the upper classes could afford the luxury of a newspaper subscription, but from the eighteen-thirties on almost anyone who could read could enjoy that privilege. No one editor could claim the chief credit for this revolutionary change, but a New-Yorker named Benjamin H. Day, who began in 1833 to sell his paper, the *Sun*, at a penny a copy, had something to do with it. Day further extended his subscription list by making the *Sun* sensational enough to interest even the dullest-witted reader, and because his paper reached so many people he could exact a heavy tribute from the advertisers. His methods were imitated by James Gordon Bennett, who in 1835 began the publication of the *New York Herald*, and by Horace Greeley, who six years later established the *New York Tribune*. Conservative editors and readers at first held the penny papers in great contempt, but the efforts of the latter to increase their

TWO ILLUSTRATIONS FROM "GODEY'S LADY'S BOOK"

circulation led them to present controversial news with an impartiality that even the intelligent public came to respect. In time the higher-priced newspapers were forced either to suspend publication or to reduce their prices. It is also worth noting that the rapid improvement of the national system of transportation enabled the leading papers to extend greatly the radius of their circulation. Not only the New York journals, but such papers also as the *Boston Evening Transcript*, the *Philadelphia Ledger*, and the *Springfield* (Massachusetts) *Republican* exerted far more than a merely local influence. Very often for the distant readers weekly editions took the place of the ordinary daily.[1]

Magazines as well as newspapers enjoyed an astonishing vogue. Possibly a hundred such publications existed in 1825, but a generation later there were six or eight times that number. Most of *Magazines* these periodicals, like their predecessors, were both local in character and extremely short-lived, but a few of them, *Graham's Magazine*, the *Knickerbocker Magazine*, and the *Southern Literary Messenger*, for example, were during many years widely read. They printed articles of nearly every sort and kind — critical essays, sermons, stories, poems, and travel accounts — and played an important part in the formulation of American taste and opinion. Through the magazines American readers made the acquaintance of such writers as Edgar Allan Poe, William Cullen Bryant, Henry Wadsworth Longfellow, and James Fenimore Cooper, not to mention many contemporary English authors whose works, for lack of an international agreement as to copyrights, were frequently pirated. Of especial appeal to American women was *Godey's Lady's Book*, founded in 1830, which supplied not only a somewhat saccharine type of literature, but also the latest word on feminine fashions, good morals, and good manners. Its publisher, Louis A. Godey, became for his times a very rich man. His magazine and many others, also, were plentifully supplied with really excellent woodcut or metal illustrations.[2]

Lyceums vied with newspapers and magazines in giving the public something to think and talk about. Inaugurated at Millburg, Vermont, *Lyceums* in 1826, the lyceum movement soon became nation-wide in its scope, and successfully stimulated the presentation of lecture courses far and wide. Some of the lyceums — for example,

---

[1] Of recent years the history of American journalism has attracted much attention. Useful manuals are W. G. Bleyer, *Main Currents in the History of American Journalism* (1927); and J. M. Lee, *History of American Journalism* (1917). On the value of the newspapers as historical sources see Lucy M. Salmon, *The Newspaper and the Historian* (1923).

[2] F. L. Mott, *A History of American Magazines, 1741–1850* (1930), brings out clearly the importance of the magazines from the point of view of the social historian. See also Algernon de Vivier Tassin, *The Magazine in America* (1916).

he Lowell Institute of Boston, which received in 1836 a bequest of
a quarter of a million dollars — were well supplied with funds, but most
of them depended for their support upon the willingness of large numbers
of citizens to pay small sums to hear the addresses of famous men and
women.   The stipends which the lecturers received, while often ex-
remely modest, were sufficient to aid many intellectuals in the sometimes
difficult task of eking out a living.   Naturally not every lecturer had
a worth-while contribution to make, but such a man as Ralph Waldo
Emerson, whose lecture tours were frequent and extensive, was known to
accept as little as five dollars for delivering an address in some remote
frontier village.   It is difficult to estimate the influence of the lyceum
movement, but it must have been considerable.   The lyceums offered
a platform to every celebrity with a talent for public speaking, and to
every earnest apostle of reform.   Like the newspapers and the magazines, they were both a cause and a result of the intellectual and moral
awakening that was so characteristic of the age.

Not in America alone, but throughout the civilized world, this period
was remarkable for its inventions.[1]   One by one the machines that were
necessary to complete the Industrial Revolution were *Inventions—*
brought to a fair degree of perfection and started on their *the telegraph*
course.   In this work Americans, well aware of the need of annihilating
distance in a country so large as their own, and faced by a chronic
shortage of labor, played an honorable and important part.   Outstanding
among them was Samuel F. B. Morse, a painter and sculptor of New
England origin who had twice spent long periods abroad.   In 1832, as
he was returning to the United States the second time, he talked with
his fellow passengers aboard the ship *Sully* about some electrical experiments then being made in France, and conceived the idea of the electro-
magnetic telegraph.   On his arrival in the United States he assumed
a professorship to which he had recently been elected in the University
of the City of New York, but he spent much of his time in experimentation.   By 1835 he had a mile of telegraph wire in a room at the university,
over which he was transmitting messages successfully.   It was not until
1843, however, that he obtained an appropriation of thirty thousand
dollars from Congress to build an experimental line from Washington to
Baltimore.   On May 1, 1844, with the line complete to Annapolis, the
first news message was sent over the wires.   The invention met so obvious a need that its use became general almost at once.   By 1850 the
settled portions of the country were well supplied with telegraphic com-

[1] George Iles, *Leading American Inventors* (1912); E. W. Byrn, *The Progress of Invention
in the Nineteenth Century* (1900): Holland Thompson, *The Age of Invention* (1921).

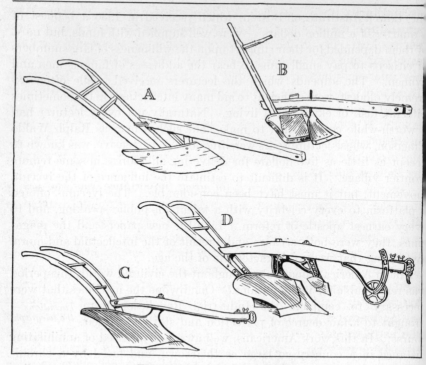

EVOLUTION OF THE PLOW

A. Colonial plow made of wood.   B. One-handled colonial plow with iron point and iron-protected side.   C. First iron plow cast in more than one piece.   D. Plow with first chilled steel mold-board.

munications, and in 1858 a cable was successfully laid across the Atlantic.

Of tremendous importance to agriculture was the work of Cyrus Hall McCormick,[1] a back-country Virginian of Scotch-Irish descent, who in 1831 produced a successful reaper. His father, Robert McCormick, had long sought to construct an improved harvesting machine, and had made extensive experiments which his more successful son had been able to utilize. In 1834 young McCormick patented his device, but he was not well enough satisfied with it to attempt its manufacture and sale until he had worked for several years upon improvements. With better business ability than is given to most inventors, he succeeded ultimately in putting on the market a machine which contributed greatly to the revolution in methods of farming that characterized the middle years of the nineteenth century. Sound judgment led him to establish his headquarters in the West, first

The McCormick reaper

[1] W. T. Hutchinson, *Cyrus Hall McCormick* (2 vols., 1930–35).

at Cincinnati (1845) and then at Chicago (1847), where the demand for agricultural machinery would be greatest and the opposition to new devices least. By 1850 he was manufacturing three thousand machines each year, and by 1860 twenty thousand. Nor was the reaper the only new tool that during this period inventors provided for the farmer. Dozens of other useful devices were constructed, each of which in time was to play a part in freeing the farmer from the bondage of hand labor. It should be observed, however, that the full effect of these inventions was long delayed. Not until the time of the Civil War did the life of the average American farmer begin to be seriously affected by the new machines.

Another American invention of great importance was the sewing machine, which Elias Howe, a manufacturer of cotton-mill machinery at Lowell, Massachusetts, produced in 1845. While Howe *The sewing* was in England, seeking to obtain financial backing for the *machine* manufacture and sale of his machine, some American capitalists put just such a device as he had invented on the market. Fortunately, however, Howe had taken out a patent in 1846, and he was able to protect his rights by legal processes. By the early fifties the manufacture of sewing machines was being carried on extensively, and a decade later the extraordinary demands of the Civil War made the industry extremely prosperous. Ultimately Howe, who himself engaged in the business and received also a royalty on the machines made by other manufacturers, reaped a rich reward. But the sewing machine, like the reaper, was of far greater benefit to a subsequent generation than to the one that produced it.

Several other products of the American inventive genius deserve to be mentioned. In 1830 Samuel Colt, a sixteen-year-old Connecticut lad who had shipped as a sailor from Boston to Calcutta, whiled away his time on the voyage by whittling out a wooden model of a revolving pistol. In 1835 he patented his "revolver" in England, and next year in the United States. By 1838 a company at Paterson, New Jersey, had begun its manufacture. It is difficult to imagine what the history of the Great Plains, just then beginning, would have been like without Colt's invention. In 1836, another Connecticut Yankee, Charles Goodyear, made his first important discovery of an improved treatment for the surface of Indian-rubber products. Some years later he perfected the vulcanizing process, and thus "gave a substantial basis to an industry built on American brains rather than material resources."[1] In 1846

[1] Fish, *Rise of the Common Man*, p. 102. By permission of The Macmillan Company, publishers.

Richard M. Hoe, a New York City manufacturer of printing materials, produced for the use of the *Philadelphia Ledger* the first steam cylinder press. Faster presses were an absolute necessity if the demand for more and more newspapers was to be met, and improvements upon Hoe's invention made during the next few years, enabled the publishers to print an almost incredible number of papers in a minimum length of time.[1]

Americans also showed great resourcefulness in improving and adapting to different conditions inventions that were introduced from abroad. This was true of the English locomotive, which had to be made lighter and speedier to meet American needs, and of numerous details in the way of railroad equipment. It was true of most of the machinery used in American factories and foundries, of the development of the photograph from the French "daguerreotype," of the "loco-focos," or friction matches, which were invented in Europe but first patented in America. Heating and cooking stoves, which had ancestors on both sides of the Atlantic, were made sufficiently practical during the period to cause the closing-off of many handsome fireplaces. By the middle of the century furnaces and plumbing were being installed, whale-oil lamps were replacing candles, gas-lighting systems were spreading from city to city, tinware was being substituted for costlier copper and iron kitchen utensils, woven carpets were sharing the honors with the old-fashioned rag rugs, and wallpaper was coming into general use. At least for the city dweller, life was becoming increasingly comfortable.

Most American inventions were made to meet an obvious need, and the inventors achieved results, as a rule, only by a persistent application *Scientific* of the trial-and-error method. More scientific advances, *advances* however, were by no means lacking.[2] Chief among these should be listed the use of anesthetics in surgery, which a Georgia physician, Doctor Crawford W. Long, proved to be practicable as early as 1842. He did not publish his findings for some years, however, and in the meantime two New England dentists, Doctor Horace Wells of Hartford, Connecticut, and Doctor W. T. G. Morton of Boston, achieved similar results. Useful descriptive data were also made available by American scientists. During these years Louis J. R. Agassiz, a French-Swiss immigrant who became a Harvard professor, made important contributions, based upon observations in America, to the world's knowledge of geology and zoology. J. J. Audubon, born in Haiti, the son of a French naval officer, and educated as an artist in France, made

---

[1] Robert Hoe, *A Short History of the Printing Press and the Improvements in Printing Machinery* (1902).

[2] E. S. Dana and others, *A Century of Science in America* (1918).

the United States his home, and devoted his life to the observation and description of the birds of America.   Notable also was the work of Joseph Henry, a physicist, and the first head of the Smithsonian Institution, a foundation made possible by an Englishman's eccentric bequest of a half million dollars to the United States government "for the increase and diffusion of knowledge among men."   Other American scientists who won distinction were Asa Gray in botany, James Dwight Dana in mineralogy, Ormsby M. Mitchell in astronomy, and Benjamin Silliman in geology.   Silliman, a professor at Yale, was not content merely with his teaching and research, but carried to the country by means of popular lectures information about the work the scientists were trying to do.

The period witnessed also a remarkable outburst of literary activity. Foremost among the writers of the time was Ralph Waldo Emerson (1803–82), a philosopher and poet whose influence upon *Emerson* his fellow men was little short of phenomenal.[1] Emerson was descended on his father's side from a long line of New England preachers, and was thus "born to be educated."   He attended the Boston Latin School, was graduated in 1821 from Harvard College, taught school, studied theology, and accepted a Unitarian pulpit.   He was soon convinced, however, that "to be a good minister one must leave the ministry," and acted accordingly.   Late in 1832 he sailed for Europe, where he met many prominent men of letters, among them Coleridge, Wordsworth, and Carlyle.   On his return to America a few years later he began to formulate, first in sermons and lectures, and then in books of essays, his doctrine that "God is in every man."   Through his reading and his European contacts he had absorbed the philosophy of the German idealists.   Like them, he deduced from the teachings of Kant that the world of experience revealed a realm of the spirit.   The visible world of the senses was, as he expressed it, only an "apparition of God."   There was much to be learned from nature, for whose teachings he sought to be a "transparent eyeball."   The deepest truths, he held, came unbidden and unsought to the receptive human soul.   "To believe in your own thought . . . is genius."   Always professing confidence in the infinite possibilities of man, Emerson found a firm basis for his reasoning in the society he saw about him.   Here man was accomplishing new things, building a new civilization.   Material progress must be matched by spiritual progress.   American thinkers, like American

[1] A satisfactory biography is O. W. Firkins, *Ralph Waldo Emerson* (1915), but the interested reader will examine also *The Journals of Ralph Waldo Emerson, with Annotations*, edited by E. W. Emerson and W. E. Forbes (10 vols., 1909–14).

men of action, must strike out for themselves along original lines. "Our day of dependence, our long apprenticeship to the learning of other lands, draws to a close," he told the Phi Beta Kappa Society of Cambridge in 1837. "Let us have done with Europe and dead cultures, let us explore the possibilities of our own new world."

Other young Americans of this generation were profoundly influenced by German idealism, some from having read Coleridge and Carlyle, *The "tran-* its leading English proponents, some from having studied *scendental-* in the German universities. In Boston, from 1836 to *ists"* 1843, a small group of these like-minded men, Emerson among them, met together informally in what they called the Symposium, or sometimes, after Henry Hedge, their leader, "Hedge's Club." To outsiders, however, members of the group were generally known as "transcendentalists," and their version of Kant's philosophy as "transcendentalism." [1] In 1838 they brought out a series of volumes known as *Specimens of Foreign Standard Literature,* and in 1840 they began the publication of a magazine called the *Dial,* through which many of Emerson's writings reached the public. Nearly all of the original transcendentalists became nationally prominent: Henry Thoreau as one of the few really great masters of English prose; Bronson Alcott and Theodore Parker as preachers and lecturers; George Ripley and Margaret Fuller as editors and literary critics; James Freeman Clarke and George Bancroft as historians. The transcendentalists dreamed of an America which should live up to its opportunities, and, because they thought that it so often failed to do so, they criticized it scathingly. In 1840 some of them, hoping to show how "a system of brotherly co-operation" might be substituted for "one of selfish competition," took part in the establishment of Brook Farm, near West Roxbury, Massachusetts. Here all property was held in common, labor was equally shared, and much time was allotted to social and literary activities. The experiment lasted for several years, and, because of the prominence of its originators, it attracted much attention. The transcendentalists, however, should not be thought of as communists. Their interest was primarily in the individual, and in the full development of his capabilities. Their emphasis upon the dignity of human nature and the perfectibility of man was generally regarded with favor by the

[1] O. B. Frothingham, *Transcendentalism in New England: A History* (1876); H. C. Goddard, *Studies in New England Transcendentalism* (1908). Among the most useful general treatises on American literature are Barrett Wendell, *A Literary History of America* (1900); W. J. Long, *American Literature* (1913); and Bliss Perry, *The American Spirit in Literature* (1918). *The Cambridge History of American Literature,* edited by W. P. Trent and others (4 vols., 1917–21), is more exhaustive.

RALPH WALDO EMERSON
From a sculpture by Daniel Chester French

public, for it was easy enough to see in such doctrines a kind of justification of American democracy.

The writings of the transcendentalists constituted only a fraction of the literary achievements of New England during the middle decades of the nineteenth century. Indeed, the contrast in this *The "New England Renaissance"* respect between the years before and the years following 1830 was so striking that the term "New England Renaissance" soon came to be applied to the literary activities of the period. The blight of Calvinistic theology, which assured mankind of its total depravity and its helplessness without the saving grace of God, is generally regarded as the chief reason for the stifling of nearly every creative impulse in the earlier years of the century. So Emerson maintained when he wrote that "from 1790 to 1820 there was not a book, a speech, a conversation or a thought" in the whole state of Massachusetts. But Emerson exaggerated. New England under the sway of the Calvinists may have reflected chiefly upon its sins, but at least it reflected. Out of these reflections came the Unitarian and Universalist revolts in religion, the New England renaissance in literature, and a remarkable drive for social reform. New England minds may have been slow to open to new ideas, but at least the minds were there, and ultimately some of them did open. The soil which produced such men as Emerson, Thoreau, Longfellow, Whittier, Holmes, Hawthorne, Lowell, Bancroft, Prescott, Motley, Garrison, and Phillips could hardly have been as barren as it has been pictured.

Whatever Americans of the present time may think, Henry Wadsworth Longfellow (1807–82) was a great poet to Americans of his own age. *Longfellow* Longfellow was born in Portland, Maine, and was graduated from Bowdoin College, where he soon became a professor of modern languages. In 1835 he was appointed to a similar post at Harvard University, and from that time on he was closely identified with the aristocracy of Cambridge and "Back Bay" Boston. Longfellow's poetry was much affected by the cloistered life he led. Twice he made long visits to Europe, but most of his time he spent in the spacious mansion at Cambridge which Washington had used as headquarters during the first year of the American Revolution. In his poetic forms Longfellow followed European precedents, and he often made use of European themes; indeed, some of his best work is to be found in his translations of European writers. But he also used American themes, such, for example, as in *Evangeline*, the *Courtship of Miles Standish*, and *Hiawatha*, although in such a restrained, drawing-room manner that the principals concerned could hardly have recognized themselves.

Longfellow's incurable romanticism, his aloofness from the sometimes painful realities of life, and his gentle, soothing rhymes appealed greatly to the American masses. His poetry matched exactly the popular conception of what poetry should be; ordinary men were deeply gratified to see how easily they could understand and appreciate it.

Less able than Longfellow, but freer from the charge of artificiality, was the Quaker poet John Greenleaf Whittier (1807–92). He was born in Haverhill, Massachusetts, of Quaker parents, and he was *Whittier* himself a lifelong member of the Society of Friends. As a boy he worked on his father's farm and sometimes sent verses to the local newspaper. His first publication of consequence, *Legends of New England* (1831), exploited themes with which he had a natural intimacy, but he was soon caught up in the anti-slavery crusade, and turned his talent to the furthering of that cause. He advocated, as a Quaker would, the overthrow of slavery by pacific means, but he portrayed its evils in verse vivid enough to gratify the most earnest believer in more direct action. His "Ichabod," a scathing denunciation of Webster for supporting the Compromise of 1850, reveals clearly his intransigeance. Once the battle for abolition was won, Whittier grew pleasantly reminiscent of by-gone days in New England, and preserved his memories in such poems as *The Barefoot Boy*, *Snow-Bound*, and *The Tent on the Beach*. His output was more limited than Longfellow's, and his poetic competence less marked, but his influence upon the course of events was far greater.

Among the other outstanding writers of the New England Renaissance were Nathaniel Hawthorne (1804–64), Oliver Wendell Holmes (1809–94), and James Russell Lowell (1819–91). Hawthorne *Hawthorne,* began his literary career with *Twice-Told Tales*, a modern *Holmes,* version of classical myths which he published in 1837, but *Lowell* his later works centered about American themes. In *The Scarlet Letter*, a story of early New England Puritanism, he drew a powerful indictment of the moral values of his ancestors; in *The House of the Seven Gables* and *The Blithedale Romance* he dealt with the influences that had shaped the lives of those about him. His artistry with words and his deep psychological insight gave his writings a permanent value, although he was unable to make a living from them, and had to piece out his income by holding minor political offices. Holmes is known for his poetry no less than for his prose, but for his wit and humor most of all. He hated Calvinism cordially, but he could still celebrate its collapse in the perennially amusing *Wonderful One-Hoss Shay*. His *Autocrat of the Breakfast-Table*, and its numerous sequels, showed him to be a past master of the worldly lore and native drollery of the Yankees. Lowell, like Holmes, was remarkable for his versatility. A New England Brahmin, he nevertheless expressed himself admirably in dialect poems, such as the *Biglow Papers*, many of which, like the poems of Whittier, had a definite anti-slavery bias. But Lowell was also a political essayist of note, a professor in Harvard University, editor for several years of the *Atlantic Monthly*, and later one of the editors of the *North American Review*. His services to letters and politics were recognized after the Civil War by two diplomatic appointments, first as minister to Spain, and later as minister to Great Britain.

Any survey of literary New England during the middle period would be incomplete without mention of its able group of historians.[1] The *New England historians* name of Jared Sparks (1790–1866) naturally heads this list. Like so many scholars of his time, Sparks turned his hand to many things. He occupied a Unitarian pulpit, edited the *North American Review*, was for ten years a professor of history at Harvard University and for three years its president. He was one of the first to recognize in the history of the United States a theme of consequence that must no longer be neglected, and he early set himself the task of collecting the records from which at least an important part of this history could be written. In 1830 he published twelve volumes of the *Diplomatic Correspondence of the American Revolution*; several years later twelve more, the *Writings of George Washington*; then within the decade another dozen, the *Works of Benjamin Franklin*. He also found time during his busiest years to edit a twenty-five-volume *Library of American Biography*, for which he himself wrote many of the sketches, and later in life to bring out four valuable volumes of *Correspondence of the American Revolution*. As an editor he took greater liberties with an original text than would now be regarded as proper, but the debt historians owe him is very great.

George Bancroft (1800–91), like Sparks, saw significance in the history of his own country. A graduate of Harvard, he spent five years in the universities of Germany and came back to the United States well grounded in the principles of historical method. But Bancroft's love of country, and his devotion to the principle of democracy in government for which it stood, led him to saturate his work with a patriotic fervor that today would be regarded as bad form. For half a century he occupied himself with the writing of a monumental *History of the United States*, which from the first volume, published in 1834, to the twelfth, published in 1882, idealizes and overstates the American case on nearly every page. Throughout the colonial period, with which Bancroft was

---

[1] J. S. Bassett, *The Middle Group of American Historians* (1917).

chiefly concerned, the colonists in all contentions with the mother country were always right, the British always wrong. The reader gets the unmistakable impression that Bancroft wrote primarily to justify American democracy, to prove the success of the American experiment. For historians of a later generation such a work has little value; but for Americans of Bancroft's time this flattering point of view gave great satisfaction, and Bancroft's popularity was tremendous.

Two other New England historians, William H. Prescott (1796–1859) and John Lothrop Motley (1814–77), looked beyond the borders of the United States in search of more romantic materials than the history of their own country afforded. Prescott found what he wanted in the history of Spain and of the Spanish empire in America. His *History of Ferdinand and Isabella*, published in 1838, won him an enviable reputation both at home and abroad, a reputation which grew as one important work — the *Conquest of Mexico*, the *Conquest of Peru*, and a *History of Philip II of Spain* — succeeded another. Motley interested himself in the history of Holland, and after a long period of research produced in 1856 his *History of the Rise of the Dutch Republic*, and in 1861 the first half of his *United Netherlands*. Greater than either was Francis Parkman (1823–93), who, after an initial work, the *Oregon Trail* (1846), in which he related his own experiences during a trip to the West, fixed upon the French in North America as the theme he wished to develop. But most of Parkman's books were written and published in the years following the Civil War, and they belong, therefore, in point of time, if not in spirit, to the later period.

While the leadership of New England in the world of American letters was incontestable, writers of distinction were also to be found in other parts of the country. Washington Irving (1783–1859), who *Writers of* returned to New York in 1832 after a residence of seventeen *the middle* years abroad, sought with some success to catch the spirit *states* of the untamed West in his *Tour of the Prairies, Astoria,* and *Adventures of Captain Bonneville.* During his later years he wrote a monumental *Life of Washington,* which was more admired by his contemporaries than by their descendants. James Fenimore Cooper (1789–1851), another New-Yorker, found a field for his imagination in the North American Indian, and his *Leather-Stocking Tales* are still read. William Cullen Bryant (1794–1878), a New England boy who won fame in New York and for half a century was editor of the New York *Evening Post,* wrote verse of enduring charm. Walt Whitman (1819–92) more than any other writer caught the spirit of his times, and reflected it in verse forms that were as new and unpredictable as the civilization he delighted to honor. His *Leaves of Grass* registered a more complete break with European tradition than anything that had come out of New England, and the freedom and gusto with which he expressed himself set important precedents for the coming age.

Edgar Allan Poe (1809–49) defies classification both as to time and place. He was not much concerned with the problems of his own, or any *Edgar Allan* other, generation, and while the South claims him, he was *Poe* born in Boston and spent much of his time in New York. Virginia was his home, however, as nearly as he had one, and for a number of years he edited the *Southern Literary Messenger.* Undoubtedly a psychopathic case himself, he was interested in the weird and abnormal to a startling degree, but he had such a sure eye for beauty and for perfection of form that he ultimately won the admiration of even the most conventional. Although he mastered better than any of his predecessors the technique of the short story, particularly the detective story, his chief title to fame rests upon his poetry. Such poems as the *Raven*, the *Bells*, and *Annabel Lee* seem destined never to be forgotten.

The ante-bellum South produced no other writer even faintly comparable to Poe, but it did not lack for stars of a lesser magnitude. Wil- *Southern* liam Gilmore Simms (1806–70), a persistent and often *writers* successful imitator of such English writers as Byron and Scott, published over a hundred volumes of verse and prose before the Civil War. Like so many other Southerners of his time, he turned whatever talent he possessed to a militant defense of the institution of slavery. Henry Timrod (1829–67) and Paul Hamilton Hayne (1830–86) wrote enchanting, but not very enduring, poetry. William J. Grayson (1788–1863) defended slavery in a long poem, *The Hireling and the Slave*, which effectively contrasted the unhappy lot of the wage-slave in the northern mines and factories with the carefree life of the bond-slave of the South. John Pendleton Kennedy (1795–1870) revealed in vivid prose pictures the charm of plantation life in Old Virginia, but he held no brief for slavery.

It is a curious fact that the literary activities of the years following 1830 were in nowise paralleled by similar successes in the realm of the arts. Indeed, the period witnessed a definite decline in such fields as painting and architecture, fields in which during the early years of the Republic promising beginnings had seemingly been made. The blame for this state of affairs is usually placed on the triumph of democracy — a triumph which exalted the taste of the ordinary man, however execrable it might be, to a parity with the taste of the élite. But this

CAPITOL OF THE UNITED STATES IN 1840

From an old engraving

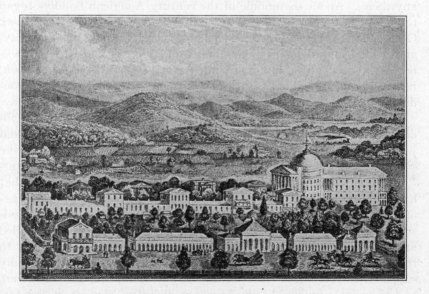

THE UNIVERSITY OF VIRGINIA

From an old engraving

explanation is not entirely satisfying, for by the same reasoning a dearth of good literature should also have developed. One might rather suppose that the artists found it more difficult than the men of letters to keep abreast of the Industrial Revolution. The traditions that bound them were more rigid than literary forms; the materials they worked with were less plastic than words. Not only in the United States, but throughout the civilized world, the arts were at low ebb during the middle decades of the nineteenth century. Everywhere those who looked only to the past for guidance failed to catch the spirit of the new age, while those who broke with the past and began to experiment made many false starts.

American architecture throughout this period was strikingly free from originality. The classical vogue that Jefferson had done so much *Architecture* to introduce still flourished, and totally irrelevant replicas of early Greek temples were everywhere in evidence. For public buildings the favorite design was a combination of dome and portico that was not often strikingly successful. Dwelling-houses were apt to reveal the old Georgian influence of the colonial period, although there was much rule-of-thumb modification, and, as time went on, an unmistakable tendency to copy anything that anybody had ever done anywhere. About the middle of the century American builders began to follow European architects in a furious revolt against classicism. Gothic forms were revived, excessive ornamentation replaced simplicity, and a kind of general pandemonium broke loose. This freedom was necessary, no doubt, if any really important new note was to be struck, but at least until well toward the end of the century the search was conducted in vain.[1]

Buildings are a necessity, and architecture of a kind is therefore indispensable in any age, but the same can hardly be said of painting and *Painting and sculpture* sculpture, which throughout the period under review were almost non-existent in the United States. Portrait painters there were, but they showed little of the distinction that had characterized the post-Revolutionary artists, and the beginnings of photography soon dealt their craft a serious blow. A group of landscape painters, known generally as the "Hudson River School," called attention to the beauty of American scenes, and genuinely sought to reproduce what they saw rather than what artists were traditionally supposed to see. But their technique was European, not American, and their achievements hardly above mediocrity. American sculptors had even less to their credit. What few of them there were clung tena-

[1] T. E. Tallmadge, *The Story of Architecture in America* (1927).

ciously to the classical traditions, and did their best to make American politicians look like Roman emperors in disguise. Horatio Greenough, designer of the Bunker Hill Monument, carved from Italian marble a heroic statue of Washington, scantily clad and seated on a throne, which fortunately was soon relegated to storage in the Smithsonian Institution. The "Greek Slave" by Hiram Powers attracted much attention, mainly perhaps because it was a nude female figure, and most Americans had been taught to identify nudity with naughtiness. Powers's extraordinary daring came doubtless from his long residence in Florence, Italy. A fad for waxwork was widely followed, and some really exquisite modeling was done, mostly by women of leisure, who also busied themselves successfully with many other varieties of "fancy work." [1]

Americans of the period were by no means uninterested in music, although in this respect dependence on Europe remained marked. Musical societies were common to the larger cities, European artists often made American tours, a few symphony orchestras were organized, and attempts to produce opera, mainly Italian, were not unknown. But American composers of music were neither numerous nor of profound ability, although some of their work lives on. The hymns of Lowell Mason (1792–1872), for example, are familiar to nearly every American churchgoer, and their publication contributed materially to the popularity of congregational singing. Mason is also to be remembered for his success in introducing the teaching of music into the public schools. Stephen C. Foster (1826–64), a native of Pennsylvania who knew little of the South or, for that matter, of formal music, wrote both the melodies and the words of dozens of songs which reflected admirably the tempo of southern plantation life, and won an enduring popularity in all parts of the country. Foster's songs, and many others like them, frequently reached the public first through black-face minstrel shows, which then enjoyed a great vogue. The Negroes themselves, who sang while they worked, and whose talent for music was very great, were doubtless the originators of many of the melodies that these songwriters exploited. [2]

Music

Owing partly to frontier conditions and partly to the hostility of New England Puritanism, the American theater was slow to develop. During the colonial period small beginnings were made in some of the coast

[1] Suzanne La Follette, *Art in America* (1929); Charles H. Caffin, *The Story of American Painting* (1907); Lorado Taft, *The History of American Sculpture* (1903); Porter Butts, *The Art Experience of the Middle-West Frontier — Art in Wisconsin* (1936).

[2] J. T. Howard, *Our American Music, Three Hundred Years of It* (1931); N. I. White, *American Negro Folk-Songs* (1928); Carl Wittke, *Tambo and Bones* (1936).

cities, but both the plays and the players were English, and the response *The theater* to their efforts was not always cordial. Even after the Revolution the theater in the United States was for a long time an alien rather than a native institution. By the thirties and forties, however, most of the large towns and cities had stock companies with which well-known actors or actresses on tour co-operated in the production of plays. The tendency to rely mainly upon English stars was a serious handicap to the development of native talent, but a few Americans rivaled the best of the visitors in popularity. Chief among the American stars were Edwin Forrest and Edwin Booth, whose greatest successes were in Shakespearean rôles, and Charlotte Cushman, whom the public liked best as Lady Macbeth or Meg Merrilies.

The theater of this period was more famous for its actors than for its playwrights. Ears attuned to the resonant oratory of Daniel Webster and Henry Clay asked nothing better than to listen to the long declamations of Shakespearean characters, and the steady devotion of theatrical patrons to the classics tended to discourage the writing of new plays. To this rule, however, there were important exceptions. George Henry Boker's *Francesca da Rimini*, for example, won an enduring place in dramatic literature, and Cora Mowatt's *Fashion, or, Life in New York*, burlesqued so successfully the social pretensions of the times that it has had numerous popular revivals. Current English plays also enjoyed a considerable popularity in the United States. One of them, Tom Taylor's *Our American Cousin*, ran one hundred and forty nights at Laura Keene's New Theater in New York. It was during a performance of this play at Ford's Theater in Washington that Abraham Lincoln was assassinated. His assassin, John Wilkes Booth, a younger brother of Edwin Booth, and also an actor, fancied that by this deed he would redress the wrongs done the South.[1]

Possibly an acute sensitiveness to music and the arts was too much to expect of an age that centered so much attention upon the lot of the *The idea* common man. Above all else this was a period which pro-*of progress* claimed his importance and sought to meet his needs. Jacksonian democracy was founded on the principle that one man was as much worth while as another; Unitarian theology saw in even the humblest of God's children a spark of the divine; and, long before the publication of Darwin's *Origin of Species* in 1859, the idea of evolution, at least in so far as it implied the doctrine of human progress, was beginning to find able defenders on both sides of the Atlantic. "Progressive

[1] O. S. Coad and Edwin Mims, Jr., *The American Stage* (*The Pageant of America*, xiv, 1929).

development does not end with us," wrote Theodore Parker, the transcendentalist divine, "we have seen only the beginning; the future triumphs of the race must be vastly greater than all accomplished yet." Society in an age that believed so intensely in the capacity of mankind for improvement could not fail to become increasingly aware of the evils with which it was afflicted, and to seek for remedies. In precisely the same spirit religion discarded some of its formalism and "otherworldliness" in order to concern itself more with the necessity of making this world "a better place to live in." Writers developed their talents, more often than otherwise, as the advocates of worthy causes. Humanitarian reformers of every kind got a hearing, and with surprisingly few exceptions a following as well.

The rapid advance of the factory system in the American Northeast presented the country with a serious labor problem. Under the vanishing domestic system apprentices and journeymen could hope *The labor* to rise ultimately to the status of master craftsmen and *problem* employers, but only rarely was it possible under the new system for a workman to climb into the capitalist class. As the number of employees under a single management grew greater, the line of cleavage between the two classes grew deeper. Moreover, the employer was no longer aware of the conditions under which his employees lived, and he was often little concerned about the conditions under which they worked, so long as the profits of the factory remained good. Competition among manufacturers was keen, and the need of keeping down labor costs led frequently, especially in the textile mills, to the employment of women and children. Long hours of labor were required in the early factories — "from dawn to dark," or from thirteen to fifteen hours a day, was not unusual. Since most of the original "hands," or operators, had been recruited from the farms, where these long working hours had been the rule, the laborers at first saw no reason to protest. But some of them, at least, soon came to realize that the varied outdoor labor of the farm was one thing, and the monotonous indoor labor of the factory quite another. Many of the factories were badly lighted, poorly ventilated, and dangerous to life and limb. Children were given little if any opportunity for schooling, women were kept away from the duties of the home, heads of families were often unemployed because of the unfair competition of women and children.

As the lot of the laborer grew harder, the strength of the employer grew greater. During the decade of the twenties American manufacturers increased their output six times over, while by 1830, with a total investment about one fifth as great as that of all the southern plantations combined, they were turning out goods worth one and one half times as much. Their importance to the society in which they lived won quick acclaim. To the wealthy manufacturers the lawyers looked for fees, the ministers for salaries, the colleges for endowments, the shopkeepers for goods on credit. For all such dependents the prosperity of the manufacturers was a matter of vital importance. Even the farmers, who supplied the foodstuffs to the factory towns, and the laborers themselves, who had no other means of subsistence than their factory jobs, generally accepted the manufacturer's point of view. His will became the will of the community. If protective tariffs were required to make him prosperous, then protective tariffs must be obtained. If the cost of labor must be cut, then the laborer must somehow bear the burden.

Such a thoroughgoing denial in practice of the democratic tenets of the age should have aroused criticism sooner than it did. But the right of individual freedom was a heritage no less prized by Americans than democracy itself. An employer, according to this tradition, must be left free to conduct his business as he chose; an employee must be equally free to accept or reject the contract he was offered. When, early in the nineteenth century, artisans in some of the larger cities sought through unions to force their employers to raise wages, public opinion rallied strongly to the support of the employers. Courts which made use of the English common law to punish strikers for "conspiracy to raise wages" were applauded. Labor organizations of every kind were bitterly condemned, but associations of employers, designed to keep the laborers in their places, won hearty approval.

In spite of these obstacles the country witnessed during the decade that preceded the panic of 1837 a well-defined and relatively successful *A Labor movement* labor movement.[1] The leadership of this movement came from the artisans rather than from the factory hands, but the benefits were shared quite generally by all types of laborers. Prior to 1827 a few labor organizations patterned upon those of England had been formed in the United States, but they were merely local trades unions; that is, membership in a union was confined to a single city and a single craft. But in the year mentioned the failure of a carpenter's strike in Philadelphia led to the formation of the Mechanics' Union of Trade Associations, a federation of many trades unions. By thus combining forces the Philadelphia workingmen found that their power to exert pressure upon their employers was enormously increased. Strikes,

[1] Useful summaries are contained in Mary R. Beard, *A Short History of the American Labor Movement* (1920); and Selig Perlman, *A History of Trade Unionism in the United States* (1922). For fuller accounts see J. R. Commons and Associates, *History of Labour in the United States* (4 vols., 1918–35).

when supported by the city federation, had a good chance to win, and the political influence of so large a group of voters was not to be despised. Soon other cities were similarly organized, and from 1834 to 1837 a somewhat imperfect national federation held annual meetings.

The city federation revealed a strong penchant for political action. The recent widening of the suffrage had made voters of the workingmen, and the possibility of turning this newly won weapon to good purpose was too obvious to be overlooked. The laws, laboring men held, had long been made by the well-to-do, or by their satellites, and the law-makers had shown little concern for the workers. Mechanics' lien laws, free schools supported by public taxes, the abolition of imprisonment for debt, and the abolition of chartered monopolies were among the demands of the Philadelphia workingmen, who for four years, beginning in 1828, regularly nominated candidates for office. During the same period a Workingman's Party was active in New York, and in 1830 its candidate for governor polled a total of three thousand votes. Not only in Philadelphia and New York, but in many other cities also, workingmen's parties existed, and steps were even taken toward the formation of a national labor party. This promising third-party movement was undermined and defeated by the old parties only at the cost of taking over and putting into effect many of the reforms which the workingmen demanded.

To supplement their political activities the workingmen resorted also to strikes. These were particularly numerous during the four years of lush prosperity, 1833–37, when, according to Professor *Strikes* Channing, there were no less than one hundred and sixty-eight such conflicts in the United States. Of this number one hundred and three were held to secure higher wages, and twenty-six for a ten-hour day. Strikers also demanded what came later to be called the "closed shop"; that is, the employment of union men only, and the exclusion of non-union men. Even the factory operatives, who had at first taken little part in the labor movement, now began to strike. Through these direct methods the workingmen gained some victories, although the courts remained on the whole hostile, and could be used by employers to hamper the strikers. In 1842, however, the Massachusetts Supreme Court relaxed the rule of conspiracy to the extent of holding that labor organizations might legally seek to advance wages "by rules binding solely on members." By this time, however, strikes were infrequent and the labor movement at low ebb; indeed, lack of employment after the panic of 1837 led to the disintegration of many unions and the temporary cessation of labor activities.

The untimely decline of this first American labor movement did not

[481]

prevent it from winning many substantial victories for the workingmen. *Labor reforms* A number of the strikes for a ten-hour day were successful, and the demand for shorter hours attracted much favorable comment, even outside labor circles. Politicians were not slow to catch the drift of public opinion. In 1840 President Van Buren proclaimed the ten-hour day in effect on all public works conducted by the national government. In 1847 the state of New Hampshire legalized the ten-hour day "except in pursuance of an express contract requiring greater time." Other states followed this precedent, employers reluctantly swung into line, and by the time of the Civil War the ten-hour day was general throughout the country, although longer hours were by no means unknown, particularly in New England, where in most of the factories a twelve-hour day was still required. During these same years several other labor demands were materially advanced. In nearly all the states new mechanics' lien laws were passed which gave the claims of laborers for wages precedence over the claims of those who merely furnished materials. Imprisonment for debt, a practice still so common that in 1830 there were, according to reliable estimates, no less than seventy-five thousand persons thus imprisoned in the United States, was abolished throughout the North by 1840, although in the South it continued down to the time of the Civil War. Also, laws designed to safeguard the life and health of factory workers were enacted with increasing frequency.

Many thoughtful Americans (among them most of the New England transcendentalists), although not themselves of the laboring class, sympathized deeply with the efforts of the workers to help themselves, but feared that the remedies proposed would prove to be mere palliatives, and of no permanent value. These high-minded observers sought instead to find some formula by which society could be remade with the evils from which it suffered left out. Since the Industrial Revolution, which was mainly responsible for the existing state of affairs, had come sooner to Europe than to America, Europeans had anticipated Americans in thinking and writing about this problem. American reformers, therefore, were not obliged to rely wholly upon their own observation and reflection in the formulation of their ideas. Borrowing freely from such European theorists as Saint-Simon, Fourier, Robert Owen, and Karl Marx, they attacked the principle of competitive individualism, and sought to substitute for it some collectivist scheme that would improve the lot of the ordinary man. They watched with eager eyes the results of the communistic experiments which Robert Owen staged at New Lanark, Scotland, New Harmony, Indiana, and elsewhere. They tried many experiments of their own, such, for example, as the one at Brook Farm, already noted. As utopian reformers they failed, but as agitators for the amelioration of the workingman's lot they made a notable impression. Individualism was too deeply rooted in the American mind to be eradicated, but Emerson's contention that "a man has a right to be employed, to be trusted, to be loved, to be revered," was quite in keeping with the currents of the age.

Both the workingmen and their allies, the humanitarian reformers, were earnest advocates of free public education. To the workingmen the necessity of equal educational opportunities for the *The demand* children of rich and poor alike seemed absolutely essential; *for free* otherwise the caste lines between the two classes, already *schools* marked, would soon become complete and thoroughgoing barriers. The ordinary workingman, however, could not afford to pay for the education of his children; indeed, he often found it necessary to put them to work because he needed their wages, and thus to compound the evils from which he suffered. For child labor, at least in certain industries, kept wages low, and even deprived adults of the opportunity to labor. Workingmen, therefore, united in the demand that the state accept the full responsibility of providing schools at public expense. Taxes for such a purpose, they claimed, were quite as just a public obligation as taxes for any other purpose. The humanitarian reformers carried the argument even further. From their point of view, every man had a right to an education; moreover, in a democracy such as the United States, where, at least in theory, the people ruled, obviously the government must take pains to ensure that its rulers were educated. On the strength of this argument even taxpayers were persuaded that the taking of one man's property to educate another man's children was not so bad as it seemed.

As a matter of fact, the old idea that education was a class prerogative to which ordinary men had no right to aspire had always been somewhat on the defensive in America. Even in the seventeenth century, the Puritans in New England, the Dutch in New York, and the Quakers in Pennsylvania had in varying degrees accepted the responsibility of providing education for the masses, and had passed the tradition down to later generations. In the time of the Confederation the original states had not hesitated to include in the Northwest Ordinances of 1785 and 1787 provisions that obliged the new western states to establish, at least on paper, systems of free public schools. But in every part of the country the difference between precept and practice was considerable. Elementary schools, supported in whole or in part, did exist in the Northeast, particularly in Massachusetts and New York, but they were rarely as good as the private schools to which those whose means permitted preferred to send their children. Moreover, the public schools were often regarded as charity, or "pauper," schools, provided out of tax money (as also were poorhouses) only for those who had no alternative but to use them. In the South, country life made the problem of schooling difficult at best, and the planters were usually content to solve it in their own way for their own children, and to let the rest do without. In the West, the generous grants of school lands were received with much favor, and the obligation to provide free schools was cheerfully accepted, but the schools were slow to materialize. School lands brought slender revenues, and the taxable resources of the new states were always overstrained.

There was need, therefore, of a crusade to secure free public instruction, in fact as well as in theory, and the crusaders were not lacking. *Educational reformers* Two principles had to be established; first, that the maintenance of a school system must be required of every community; and second, that the schools so established must be equally open to all children, regardless of the ability or the inability of their parents to pay tuition. The second principle was embodied in a law which passed the legislature of Pennsylvania in 1834, and which the young Anti-Masonic leader, Thaddeus Stevens, helped save from repeal. The first principle, long established in Massachusetts, was there made thoroughly effective by the work of Horace Mann, who from 1837 to 1848 was secretary of the state board of education. Henry Barnard of Connecticut pioneered in the study of European educational systems with a view to their application in the United States.[1] From such beginnings as these, particularly from the activities of Horace Mann, whose annual reports were studied far and wide, the American system of public schools was soon to grow. Well before the Civil War every northern state was attempting to provide elementary schools at public expense in every community, and important experiments were being made with public high schools. In general, however, private "academies" bridged the gap between elementary and college education, while the zeal of religious denominations, more often than otherwise, provided the colleges. In the South, where both elementary and secondary schools were frequently lacking, the efforts of Thomas Jefferson in behalf of nonsectarian higher education bore fruit when the University of Virginia opened its doors in 1825. Not until 1842, however, was the first of the

[1] B. A. Hinsdale, *Horace Mann and the Common School Revival in the United States* (1898); Will S. Monroe, *The Educational Labors of Henry Barnard* (1893).

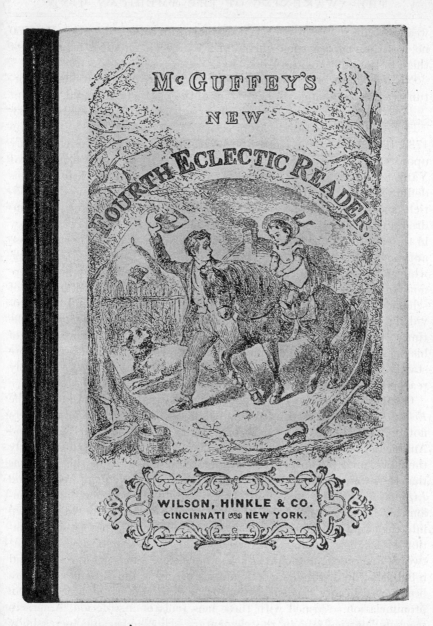

MCGUFFEY'S FOURTH READER — OUTSIDE COVER

western state universities, Michigan, able to receive students. By 1850 no less than fifteen such universities had been founded, nearly all of them in the South or the West.

No less important than the wider extension of educational opportunities was the change in the content of the instruction offered. Except *Schoolbooks* for Noah Webster's *American Speller*, published in 1783, and Jedediah Morse's *American Geography*, published in 1789, the schools of the United States had been compelled to rely mainly upon reprints of European textbooks. When, therefore, a Connecticut Yankee named Samuel Griswold Goodrich began to publish in 1827 his definitely American "Peter Parley" texts, they filled a real need. Goodrich, according to Professor Channing, wrote or edited about one hundred and seventy volumes, most of which bore the name Peter Parley in the title. Among his collaborators was Nathaniel Hawthorne, whose authorship of *Peter Parley's Universal History on the Basis of Geography*, which appeared in 1837, is well attested. The Peter Parley books were not notable, as a rule, either for literary merit or for high standards of scholarship, but they covered a wide variety of subjects, and they provided a medium of instruction precisely fitted to the requirements of the times. Goodrich estimated that not less than seven million copies of his books were sold in the United States, a record that would seem more startling but for the fact that the total sales of Webster's *Speller* probably reached fifty millions.

Competition for the Peter Parley readers was soon furnished by the *Eclectic Series*, compiled by William Holmes McGuffey.[1] These readers not only introduced the youth of America to the best in English and American literature, but contrived at the same time to drive home deftly the moral precepts of the Victorian Age. So popular were the selections that they were repeated in other series, such as the *National Readers* and *Lippincott's Readers*, and probably Mark Sullivan is correct in his opinion that they did much to set the pattern of American thought far down into the twentieth century. In 1828 Noah Webster, whose standardization of English spelling was already taking effect, published his great two-volume *Dictionary of the English Language*. This work, revised and republished in 1840, defined thousands of words that had never before been noted in any English dictionary, and set important precedents in pronunciation. Armed with these new tools of instruction, American teachers, particularly in the elementary schools, became increasingly effective. Largely through the leadership of Horace Mann, who in 1839 induced the state of Massachusetts to establish a normal school at Lex-

[1] H. H. Vail, *A History of the McGuffey Readers* (1910).

ington, efforts were even begun to provide at state expense for the professional training of teachers.

The strongly classical bent of the academies, high schools, and colleges was destined to endure with but slight variation until the time of the Civil War.[1]   Classes in Latin, Greek, and mathematics *Higher* absorbed the bulk of the student's time, although such new *education* subjects as modern languages and natural science won places of importance in some curriculums.   The instruction was often mediocre or worse.   College students, eager to concern themselves with topics of current interest, sometimes learned more from the debates and oratorical contests which literary societies and fraternities delighted to sponsor than from their classroom exercises.   Few went to college except those who wished to enter one of the three learned professions, the ministry, the law, and medicine; and many entered these professions without the benefit of college, or even secondary, training.   Separate divinity, law, and medical schools were fairly common among the older colleges and universities by the middle of the century, but the instruction offered, particularly for the medical students, was extremely meager.   In general, the importance of higher education was not fully recognized by Americans before the Civil War.   Students with a real thirst for learning found it necessary, as a rule, to spend some time in Europe.

The emancipation of women from the restriction that a man-made world had placed about them enlisted the efforts of a notable company of American reformers.   On both sides of the Atlantic *Women's* custom had long decreed that woman's place was in the *rights* home.   The education of women, therefore, except in so far as it might be of use in better fitting them for their domestic duties, was regarded as unnecessary, and even unwise.   Girls who were fortunate enough to receive more than an elementary education attended female seminaries or finishing schools, where religion, morality, and the social graces, including music and art, were given primary consideration.   Before the eighteen-thirties not a college or university in the United States had opened its doors to women, and every other approach to the learned professions was similarly restricted to men.   Also, the legal status of woman was definitely inferior to that of man: she might not vote; control of her property passed at the time of marriage to her husband; in certain matters the husband answered to the law for the conduct of his wife; legal responsibility for the children of a marriage was vested exclusively in the father.

[1] C. F. Thwing, *A History of Higher Education in America* (1906); D. G. Tewksbury, *The Founding of American Colleges and Universities before the Civil War* (1932).

While American men treated women with a deference that excited the comment of European travelers, the women themselves had to take the *Women as reformers* lead in the crusade for women's rights. And of these women many were led to embrace the feminist cause mainly through their interest in other reforms. So deep-seated was the prejudice against women in any public capacity that male reformers sometimes refused to accept the assistance of women, except in a definitely humble and secondary capacity. For example, eight women delegates to a World's Anti-Slavery Convention, held in London in 1840, were denied admission solely because they were women. Two of the excluded delegates were Lucretia Mott and Elizabeth Cady Stanton, both of whom then realized that if women were ever to accomplish anything as reformers they must first achieve a more honorable status for themselves. In this sentiment they were supported strongly by such other able women as Frances Wright, a Scotswoman who on her second trip to America in 1825 had remained to work against slavery and on behalf of the emancipated slave; Lucy Stone, one of the first to demand equal suffrage; Margaret Fuller, the brilliant literary editor of the *New York Tribune*, who in 1844 published a scandalously frank book, *Women in the Nineteenth Century*; Doctor Elizabeth Blackwell, who won admission to the medical profession against almost insuperable obstacles; Dorothea L. Dix, whose primary passion was the reform of prisons and insane asylums; and Mrs. Antoinette Louisa Brown Blackwell, pioneer woman preacher.

While the feminist movement was greeted with much ridicule and was not wholly successful until well after the Civil War, some promising beginnings were made.[1] High schools and normal schools for girls became increasingly common, and teaching in the elementary schools was soon recognized as almost a woman's monopoly. In 1833 Oberlin College, a Congregationalist institution, recognized two reform movements at once by opening its doors to women and Negroes. Coeducation was permitted by Antioch College in 1853, by the University of Iowa in 1858, and in due time by most of the state-supported schools. A little later many strictly women's colleges were founded. Women also made definite headway against the prejudice which had so long barred them from appearance on the public platform. A few of them were licensed to

[1] This subject is best approached through its plentiful biographic and autobiographic literature. See, for example, Katharine S. Anthony, *Margaret Fuller; A Psychological Biography* (1920); Margaret Fuller [Ossoli], *Women in the Nineteenth Century* (1855); Elizabeth Blackwell, *Pioneer Work for Women* (1914); W. R. Waterman, *Frances Wright* (1924); Francis Tiffany, *Life of Dorothea Lynde Dix* (1890); and Elizabeth Cady Stanton, Susan B. Anthony, and others, *History of Woman Suffrage* (6 vols., 1889–1922). The last mentioned is an important source-book for all the major reform movements of the nineteenth century.

preach; and by persistent effort many more won toleration, then approval, as lecturers. In their contest for equality before the law the women scored victories in a few states, mainly with respect to the right of married women to hold property separately from their husbands. For the most part, however, the reforms they sought were delayed until after the Civil War, and the suffrage cause was not won until the adoption of the Nineteenth Amendment in 1920.

Among the causes, other than that of their own emancipation, to which the women reformers were deeply devoted was temperance.[1] Hard drinking was an English tradition which had been easily *Temperance* transplanted to America and had flourished in the new en- *reform* vironment. There was some variation, however, in the types of beverages consumed. English ale, which was of limited potency and required considerable skill to brew, was discarded in favor of the remarkably effective whiskey, which almost any frontiersman knew how to distill. Likewise imported wines, except for the use of the very rich, gave way to more primitive drinks, such as hard cider. Statistics on the consumption of liquor in the United States during these early years are not available, and the testimony of temperance reformers is not to be trusted, but it is safe to say that drinking was almost universal, among women as well as men, and that public drunkenness, at least for men, was no disgrace. Even ministers were apt to exhibit a degree of conviviality at ordination ceremonies, conferences, and college commencements that later generations would have regarded with astonishment.

In its early phases the temperance movement was directed against obvious excesses. Scripture was abundantly available for quotation against drunkenness, and preachers, particularly in the evangelical churches, were fond of quoting it. Women who suffered because of the intemperance of their mates, or who saw the suffering which intemperance inflicted upon other women, bestirred themselves against the evil. A few far-seeing humanitarians connected drunkenness with poverty and crime, and sought by promoting temperance to effect a more fundamental reform. Even before 1830 many local temperance societies had been formed, particularly in New England, and by 1833 a United States Temperance Union joined these locals into one national organization. These early reformers, as the name they took indicated, were primarily interested in temperance rather than in total abstinence; but views of so moderate a nature could hardly survive in an age which responded so cordially to the teachings of extremists. During the eighteen-thirties the temperance movement was practically taken over by the teetotalers.

[1] J. A. Krout, *The Origins of Prohibition* (1925).

[489]

For more than twenty years orators such as John B. Gough and Father Theobald Matthew denounced drinking as a crime against society; writers such as Lucius M. Sargent, with his six volumes of *Temperance Tales*, and Timothy Shay Arthur, with his even more effective *Ten Nights in a Bar-Room*, portrayed the decay of the individual who indulged in drink; and artists, more numerous than talented, provided pictures and cartoons that left nothing to the imagination. This campaign of education was strikingly successful. Individuals by the tens of thousands gave up the use of liquor, churches set more rigorous standards of conduct for the clergy and often also for the laity, and excessive drinking fell into general disrepute.

Efforts to diminish the temptation that led to the downfall of so many youths, and that made so difficult the regeneration of addicts, suggested *Prohibition* naturally an appeal to the power of the state. To the New-Englanders, who stood in the vanguard of the movement, such an appeal was no confession of failure. Brought up, as most of them were, on the tradition that the state was properly charged with the duty of protecting the morals of the people, they could not overlook so effective an ally. Laws were demanded, and were frequently obtained, to license the liquor traffic, to hamper it with heavy taxation, and even to prohibit it altogether. State-wide prohibition of a sort was first adopted by Maine in 1846, under the influence of Neal Dow. Ohio followed in 1850, and perhaps a dozen other northern states had enacted prohibition laws before the Civil War. None of these laws was as effective as its advocates had hoped, and most of them were repealed during the Civil War period. The South, which in later years was to champion the prohibition cause so enthusiastically, was at this time totally uninterested.

It would be difficult to call the roll of the reform movements of the eighteen-thirties and forties with any assurance that all of them would *A reform* be included. During these years the very word "reform" *era* had an almost irresistible charm for multitudes of Americans, and the mere adoption of that label was sufficient to secure a following. Not only in the United States, but throughout the civilized world, the "man of sensibility" was at the crest of his power, seeking out wrongs, striving earnestly to right them. Many reform movements came to America from Europe; others originated on both sides of the Atlantic at about the same time. The rigors of penal codes, although much modified since colonial times, were still open to attack by reformers, who objected to the long sentences meted out for trivial offenses, and to the overfree use of the death penalty. The barbarities common to prisons, insane asylums, and almshouses needed only to be revealed to arouse a feeling of horror, and a demand for change. Probably Dorothea L. Dix, the leading advocate in the United States of this type of reform, saw more of her ambitions realized than any other reformer of the period. New plans of dealing with convicts, designed not so much to punish as to reform them, were tried out with some success, and the idea that the mentally afflicted were entitled to hospitalization and medical treatment was almost universally accepted.

The sufferings incidental to war, while somewhat disguised by the glamor of patriotism, were also recognized, and the problem attacked at its source by concerted efforts to prevent the outbreak *The peace* of war. As early as 1815, the formation of local organiza- *movement* tions devoted to the cause of peace had begun in the United States, and in 1828 about fifty of them joined hands to found the American Peace Society, which for decades not only carried on within the United States a steady propaganda for peace, but co-operated also with similar organizations abroad. An American peace plan was formulated which called for regular world congresses to codify international law, and a world court to apply it.[1] Unhappily the peace movement was unable to sustain the shock of the wars which soon engulfed both Europe and America, and naturally the interest of reformers turned during the war-torn decades of the eighteen-fifties and sixties from the highly academic problem of world peace to the more pressing necessity of ameliorating the horrors of the battlefield.

With the spirit of humanitarian reform so thoroughly unleashed, it was unthinkable that the continued existence of African slavery in the American South could long be overlooked. Ever since the *Slavery a* time of the French Revolution slavery had been generally *natural* frowned upon by world opinion, and its extinction had pro- *target* ceeded with such rapidity that by the middle of the nineteenth century the southern states of the United States shared only with Brazil and the Spanish colonies the doubtful honor of being the last strongholds of slavery in the civilized world. That many people in the United States were opposed to slavery became abundantly apparent during the debate on the admission of Missouri, and the Missouri Compromise, which actually permitted the further spread of slavery, by no means satisfied them. Benjamin Lundy, a Quaker emancipationist, published from 1812 to 1836 a periodical known as *The Genius of Universal Emancipation.*

[1] Two excellent books on this subject are Merle E. Curti, *The American Peace Crusade, 1815-1860* (1929); and W. Freeman Galpin, *Pioneering for Peace: A Study of American Peace Efforts to 1846* (1933). More general in scope is Merle E. Curti, *Peace or War — The American Struggle, 1636-1936* (1936).

Lundy's Fabian tactics and mild manners, however, did not satisfy William Lloyd Garrison, a young enthusiast of Newburyport, Massachusetts, who proposed instead a crusade "as harsh as truth" and "as uncompromising as justice." With the first issue of Garrison's newspaper, the *Liberator*, published in Boston on January 1, 1831, the abolitionist movement may properly be said to have begun. So completely did this reform take the center of the stage that all others soon seemed insignificant in comparison; indeed, the slavery issue was destined to shape the course of American politics for more than a generation, and to leave a legacy of unsolved problems that were to plague many generations to come.

CHAPTER XXVI

SLAVERY AND ABOLITION

By THE time Garrison had opened his abolitionist crusade the institution of slavery, which had once seemed well on the way toward extinction, was more deeply entrenched in the South than ever before. The chief reason for this change, as already noted, was the *The "Cotton South"* insatiable demand for American cotton, an article which, as experience had amply demonstrated, could be profitably grown by means of slave labor. Under pressure of the world's need for cotton, the South produced nearly twice the amount of that commodity in 1830 that it had produced in 1820, fully twice the amount in 1840 that it had produced in 1830, and more than three times the amount in 1860 that it had produced in 1840. Cotton exports during these years showed similar gains, until by the time of the Civil War well over half the value of American goods shipped abroad was in cotton. A broad belt of southern land, ranging in width from about five hundred miles in the Carolinas and Georgia to six or seven hundred miles in the Mississippi Valley, was devoted primarily to cotton culture. Other crops were grown in this region, particularly foodstuffs, and not all the land was suited to cotton-growing; but the chief wealth of the "lower South" came from cotton. In this region, too, the majority of the Negro slaves were congregated. Such states as Virginia and Kentucky, for example, which depended far more upon tobacco-growing and general agriculture for their prosperity than upon cotton, sold great numbers of their slaves "down South," where the demand for "cotton hands" was always good. Slaves were used profitably also, although in smaller numbers, in the Carolina-Georgia rice fields along the coast, and in the production of Louisiana sugar-cane.[1]

The demand for slave labor in the lower South led both to an increase

[1] M. B. Hammond, *The Cotton Industry* (1897), is an excellent short treatise. On slavery the literature is voluminous, but the two books by U. B. Phillips, *American Negro Slavery* (1918), and *Life and Labor in the Old South* (1929), summarize the principal results of recent scholarship.

in the southern slave population and to an advance in the price of slaves.

Growth of slavery   Between 1820 and 1860 the number of slaves in the South grew from about a million and a half to nearly four million, but in spite of the increased supply the price of a good field hand mounted in the same years from three or four hundred dollars to a thousand dollars or more. So great, indeed, was the demand for slaves that their importation, although forbidden by law, was carried on surreptitiously until the outbreak of the Civil War, while freed Negroes living in the South were in some danger of being kidnaped and sold back into slavery. The greatest increases in slave population were naturally in the states of the new Southwest, where cotton culture was making its most rapid strides.

The ownership of slave property in the South was confined to a relatively small number of whites. On the eve of the Civil War probably not more than four hundred thousand southern families — approximately one in four — held slaves. Furthermore, at least two thirds of these families held fewer than ten slaves each. The number of great planters — men who owned fifty or more slaves and proportionately large holdings of land — was probably not above six or seven thousand. Some planters numbered their slaves by the thousand and their acres by the tens of thousands, although such instances were the exception rather than the rule.

The small farmers who lived in the cotton belt, both those who owned slaves and those who did not, raised a considerable part of the cotton crops; but the chief profits of the industry were reserved for the great planter. He was in a far better position than his less prosperous neighbors to practice scientific agriculture, his expenditures bulked less than theirs in proportion to his receipts, and he generally owned the most fertile lands. The farmers, however, saw eye to eye with the planters in all matters pertaining to slavery. Poor men looked forward to the time when they would become slaveholders; and the owners of a few slaves aspired to be the owners of many. What seemed good to the great planter seemed good, therefore, to the rank and file of southern farmers, for they tended to think of themselves not so much as what they were but as what they aspired to become. Thus the great planter and his ways occupy a place in the history of the South quite out of proportion to the numerical strength of the planter class.

The plantation owner was first and foremost a manager. Ordinarily a single plantation, which rarely exceeded a thousand acres in size, *The planta-* commanded his entire energies; but if, as sometimes was *tion system* the case, he owned many plantations, he delegated authority to a hierarchy of stewards and overseers who carried out his orders. Altogether too many of these underlings possessed faults of character which unfitted them to be farmers and planters in their own right, and the relations between master and slave were apt to be far more pleasant than the relations between these white employees and the slaves whose work they supervised. Practically all of the manual labor of a plantation was done by the slaves. Most of the slaves, of course, were field hands, but every plantation had its quota of skilled workers, such as blacksmiths and carpenters, while a favored few were selected for domestic service in and about the master's house. Sometimes Negro foremen, or "slave drivers," were placed in charge of small gangs of slaves. Frequently these drivers, themselves freed from the necessity of labor and empowered to inflict corporal punishment upon those who worked under them, were more oppressive than the whites. Field labor was accomplished by the gang system, in which a driver kept a group of slaves at work on a given task under fear of the lash, or by the task system, in which each individual was given a certain amount of work to do in a given period of time and left free to finish it as he chose, provided only that he did his work well. Any extra time the slave earned by rapid work was his to while away.

The lot of the slave on the southern plantation was ordinarily quite tolerable. As a valuable piece of property, his good health was a matter of considerable consequence to his master. He was well *The slave* fed, although no particular pains were taken to vary his diet from the standard corn bread and fat pork that was regarded as entirely adequate to sustain life. In case of illness he was usually cared for by the same physician that attended the master and his family. His living quarters, usually located not far from the "big house" of the planter, were apt to be primitive, but they afforded protection from the wind and the rain, and were ordinarily provided with fireplaces and a plentiful supply of fuel for use in cold weather. The slave's clothing was coarse enough, and in summer he was not expected to wear very much, but he was about as well clad as southern whites of the lower class. By and large, the conditions of his life represented a distinct advance over the lot that would have befallen him had he remained in Africa.

Indeed, the slaves got much positive enjoyment out of life. Extremely gregarious, they delighted in the community life of the plantation, and on special occasions were permitted to indulge in picnics, barbecues, and various other types of celebration. They loved to sing and dance, and contributed ideas along both lines that the whites, at least of a later generation, were not too proud to appropriate. They were generally blessed with a keen sense of humor; they rarely fretted, when treated well, because of their state of bondage; and they were often deeply devoted to their master and his family. Small children, regardless of color, played together freely, and the affection of white boys and girls for their Negro nurses, or "mammies," was proverbial. The slaves were deeply religious, and almost universally accepted Christianity, usually as interpreted by one of the more emotional denominations, such as the Methodists and the Baptists, whose camp-meetings, revivals, and baptizings gave them unbounded joy. A few Negroes were taught to read, but most of them acquired by word of mouth rather than by reading a considerable knowledge of the Bible and of Christian theology. Their devotions were extremely picturesque, and their moral standards sufficiently latitudinarian to meet the needs of a really primitive people. Heaven to the Negro was a place of rest from all labor, the fitting reward of a servant who obeyed his master and loved the Lord. Negroes sometimes worshiped separately from the whites, and sometimes they were assigned seats in the galleries of the white people's churches. More or less formal marriages among slaves were encouraged by some masters, although cohabitation without marriage was regarded as perfectly normal, and a certain amount of promiscuity was taken for granted. Slave women rarely resisted the advances of white men, as their numerous mulatto progeny abundantly attested.

Nevertheless, the privileges of the slave were strictly limited. Each southern state had a "slave code," which gave the sanction of law to *Slave* the practices that experience had proved to be of value in *discipline* keeping the slave population in order. Even minor offenses were punishable by law, but in all save the most exceptional cases the master usually chose to mete out justice himself. Whippings were permissible at his discretion, or at the discretion of those to whom he delegated authority, although it was a punishable crime to beat a slave to death. Some masters, and many of their subordinates, were excessively cruel, although punishment so severe as to unfit the slave for labor was an expensive indulgence which not many masters would either practice or permit. Slave crimes of a serious nature, such as murder, rape, theft, and conspiracy to revolt, were punishable by death, but their concealment by masters who feared the inconvenience and possible property loss involved was not uncommon. Exacting masters were much troubled by runaways, or so the advertisements in southern papers seem to show. Attempts at insurrection were extremely rare, although in the regions where the blacks far outnumbered the whites, the latter sometimes suffered acutely from an unconfessed fear of what their slaves might do. In 1831 a serious slave uprising, led by a trusted Negro preacher named Nat Turner, occurred in Virginia. Some fifty-five whites, mostly women and children, were killed. Turner, and nearly all the other participants in this insurrection, suffered death or worse for their crime, but the incident served to unsettle the good relations between many southern masters and their slaves for years to come.

Undoubtedly the most unlovely aspect of slavery was the slave trade.[1] As already noted, the international slave trade was outlawed in 1808, and after 1820 it was punishable as piracy, but the *The slave* right to buy and sell slaves within the United States, and *trade* to transport them from one slave state to another, remained unimpaired. During the years that the cotton lands of the newer South — from Alabama to Texas — were being opened up, this domestic slave trade came to assume extraordinary importance. Not only did the planters of the Gulf states need more and more slaves, but it was also a fact that the upper South was being confronted with an oversupply of slave labor. Tobacco-raisers in such states as Maryland, Virginia, and Kentucky were suffering from the continued exhaustion of the soil, from the decline of their export trade which began with the embargo and the War of 1812, and from the competition of Latin-American producers. Under such circumstances the natural increase of their slave population would have amounted almost to tragedy except for the opportunity to sell their surplus hands down South to work in the cotton fields. Except in the case of refractory and objectionable slaves, however, reputable masters often hesitated to dispose of their human property by sale, and many cases are on record where planters allowed themselves to become "slave poor." Other slaveholders were not so squeamish, and bankruptcy or death often accomplished what the best-intentioned master hoped to avoid. Sometimes planters or farmers went as permanent emigrants from the old South to the new, and took their slaves along to be disposed of in whole or in part as necessity required; but far more frequently the slaves were transported from the one region to the other by slave-traders, who bought and sold them strictly with an eye to profit. In 1836, the peak year of this traffic, the number of slaves sold South, or taken there by their masters, from Virginia alone reached the astounding figure of one hundred and twenty thousand. In the eighteen-forties and fifties a revival of agriculture took place in the upper South, due in part to the discovery of better methods of curing tobacco, and in part to the introduction of new and superior varieties. This served to check the domestic slave trade to some extent, but by no means to destroy it.

[1] Frederic Bancroft. *Slave-Trading in the Old South* (1931).

Down to the time of the Civil War there were many planters in the upper South who, whether they would admit it or not, were engaged primarily in the business of raising slaves for sale.

The slave-trader was nevertheless an object of well-nigh universal disdain throughout the South. His business was brutalizing in the *The* extreme, for he was called upon constantly to engage in *slave-trader* the separation of families, and to maintain discipline under adverse circumstances over slaves who in many instances were selected for sale precisely because they were hard to discipline. Few high-minded men would engage in such a business, and those who did were usually corrupted by its demands. The typical slave-trader was coarse and ill-bred, intemperate of speech and habits, and callous to the opinions of his fellow men. To succeed among ruthless competitors he learned to drive close bargains and became as adept at covering up the defects of his Negroes as ever was the Yankee horse-trader in making light of blemishes in horseflesh. Slave-traders were rarely accepted into polite southern society; indeed, they were treated as outcasts even by those who had to deal with them. The social status of bootleggers during the prohibition era was, on the whole, well above that of the slave-trader in the pre-Civil War South.

The collection of a group of slaves and their shipment to the lower South afforded many painful spectacles. Pending shipments, they might be herded together in stockades, locked up in warehouses, or jails, or occasionally cared for decently in taverns. Frequently they were marched overland in coffles to their destination, although the trader also made good use of river steamers and ships engaged in the coastwise trade.

In the final disposal of slaves, the auction-block was frequently resorted to. The slave-trader availed himself, however, of every opportunity to sell, and stops along the route of march, or at wharves, were duly utilized for the cultivation of purchasers. Sometimes slaves were hired out for long or short periods of service, in which case the employer succeeded to the disciplinary authority of the master. Hired slaves were more apt to be overworked and mistreated than slaves directly under the control of their masters.

Such was the institution upon which Garrison and the abolitionists opened their attack.[1] They knew little about it at first hand, but they

[1] The work of Garrison is told in detail, and probably with overemphasis on his importance to the movement, by Wendell Phillips Garrison and Francis Jackson Garrison, *William Lloyd Garrison* (4 vols., 1885–89). The significance of the western group of abolitionists is set forth, perhaps with equal overemphasis, by Gilbert H. Barnes, *The Anti-Slavery Impulse, 1830–1844* (1933). For further evidence on the subject, see also the *Letters of Theodore Dwight Weld, Angelina Grimké Weld, and Sarah Grimké, 1822–1844*, edited by Gilbert H. Barnes and Dwight L. Dumond (2 vols., 1934).

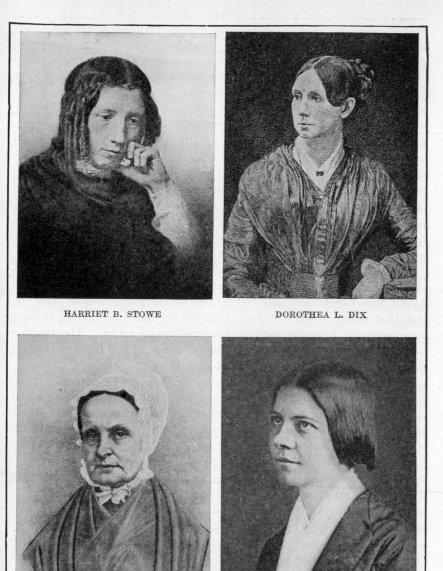

HARRIET B. STOWE   DOROTHEA L. DIX

LUCRETIA MOTT   LUCY STONE

FOUR WOMEN REFORMERS

sought and found an abundance of ammunition to use. Stories of *The abolitionist attack* atrocities committed against slaves, such as brutal whippings, the breaking up of slave homes, enforced immorality, and the like were constantly drifting northward, stories which lost nothing in the telling. These tales were picked up indiscriminately by abolitionist editors and orators who were eager to believe the worst about slavery and who used, as if they were typical, stories which had to do with highly exceptional occurrences. The abolitionists were not limited, however, to the recital of wrongs done the slaves. They regarded the institution at its best as morally indefensible. Slaves were men, and no man, according to the abolitionist argument, had the right to hold a fellow man in bondage. On this ground the abolitionists rejected totally the idea of compensated emancipation. The slave-owner was a criminal; why pay him for his crime?

The abolitionist doctrines struck a responsive chord in many northern hearts. Humanitarian reformers could not logically resist them. Many New-Englanders, angered by the vicious attacks upon their section that nullificationist orators delighted to make, retaliated, perhaps unconsciously, by going over to the abolitionist camp. The Quakers had always regarded slavery as immoral, and great numbers of them found the transition from passive to active opposition extremely easy to make. Most of the northern evangelical churches, particularly the Methodist and the Baptist, began to lean in the direction of abolition. Among the abolitionist orators, Wendell Phillips, scion of an aristocratic Boston family, was pre-eminent. Not since the days of Patrick Henry had American audiences been treated to such fervid appeals as fell from his lips. Two South-Carolinians, Sarah and Angelina Grimké, went North to Philadelphia, joined the Society of Friends, and devoted their lives to the anti-slavery crusade. Theodore Dwight Weld, a Westerner who became the husband of Angelina, is thought by many to have done more for the cause of abolition than Garrison himself. Lucretia Mott, a Philadelphia Quakeress, overcame valiantly the obstacles placed in the way of women orators, and lectured far and wide in behalf of abolition. Gerrit Smith, an up-state New-Yorker of considerable wealth, devoted both his time and his fortune to the cause. Unnamed hundreds of workers spread the abolitionist doctrines among their neighbors, and, translating word into deed, established many lines of secret stopping-places, or "underground railroads," by means of which fugitive slaves could be passed along from the southern states to Canada and freedom.[1]

[1] The abolitionist leaders have nearly all attracted biographers, among them Lorenzo Sears, *Wendell Phillips, Orator and Agitator* (1909); Catherine H. Birney, *The Grimké*

The abolitionists lost no time in perfecting an organization. Their first local association was formed in 1831. The next year a New England Anti-Slavery Society was functioning, and in 1833 a convention at Philadelphia launched the American Anti-Slavery Society. A division in this society occurred in 1840, however, mainly because Garrison and a few other extremists were unwilling to stoop to the level of party politics. Slavery was recognized by the Constitution of the United States, a fact which, according to Garrison, made that document "a covenant with death and an agreement with hell." Theodore Parker, ardent abolitionist and the most eminent preacher of his time, prided himself on his unwillingness even to cast a vote under the authority of such a government. But to the rank and file of abolitionists, the obvious way to promote their cause was through united political action. The actual abolition of slavery was conceded to depend upon the individual states where anti-slavery majorities could not soon be achieved, but the national government had authority to abolish slavery in the District of Columbia and to put an end to the interstate slave trade. To promote these ends, as well as to work toward the eventual abolition of slavery in every state, the Liberty Party was formed shortly before the election of 1840, and James G. Birney was selected as its candidate for President. Birney was a Kentuckian by birth, who after spending many years as a planter in Alabama, had freed his slaves and come North to work against slavery. For a time he published an abolitionist paper, *The Philanthropist*, at Cincinnati, but in 1837 he became secretary of the American Anti-Slavery Society and removed to New York. In the election of 1840 he polled a total of about seven thousand votes.

Abolitionist organization

The abolitionists had made greater progress, however, than this small vote seemed to indicate. Their arguments had stirred up much feeling against slavery throughout the North, and had convinced many people who were unwilling to vote the abolitionist ticket that the slavery system must ultimately be overthrown. Furthermore, the prestige of the southern planters, who traditionally had occupied a prominent place in national affairs, was seriously damaged. Northern farmers came to suspect southern leadership of working against the interests of the small free farmer and solely for the interests of the slaveholding planter.

Sisters, Sarah and Angelina Grimké (1885); Anna D. Hallowell, *James and Lucretia Mott, Life and Letters* (1884); O. B. Frothingham, *Gerrit Smith* (1878); H. S. Commager, *Theodore Parker: Yankee Crusader* (1936); and William Birney, *James G. Birney and his Times* (1890). For more general accounts, see A. B. Hart, *Slavery and Abolition* (1906); Jesse Macy, *The Anti-Slavery Crusade* (1919); and W. H. Siebert, *The Underground Railroad from Slavery to Freedom* (1898).

More and more the conviction grew that slavery at least ought not to expand, that the newly opened lands of the West should be reserved for the use of free farmers and should be denied forever to slaveholders. Partly with this idea in view, and partly also because of the obvious evils it bred, opponents of the domestic slave trade also increased steadily in numbers.

Perhaps the abolition of slavery in the District of Columbia won more support than any other abolitionist tenet. Northern members *Slavery in* of Congress were increasingly sensitive to the existence of *the District* slavery in the national capital, and to the necessity of wit- *of Columbia* nessing day by day the public buying and selling of slaves. Floods of abolitionist petitions, most of them praying that slavery be abolished in the district, cluttered up their mail, and many congressmen took pleasure in presenting them. The southern members, however, were deeply offended at these memorials, and in 1836 they persuaded the House to pass a "gag rule" that required all such petitions to be laid on the table without debate. This action was construed by ex-President John Quincy Adams, who still represented a Massachusetts district in Congress, as a direct violation of the constitutional right of petition, and he fought against it with all his might. While not himself actually an abolitionist, his constant appearance as a defender of abolitionist petitions tended to identify him with the anti-slavery movement, and to clothe it with increasing respectability. In 1844 his efforts were crowned with success, and by a vote of 108 to 80 the obnoxious rule was repealed. But the abolition of slavery in the District of Columbia awaited the verdict of the Civil War.

Regardless of the headway they made, the abolitionists were cordially disliked in the North as well as in the South. As individuals they were, *Opposition* like so many professional reformers, apt to be extremely *to the* irritating to their less conscience-smitten fellow men. *abolitionists* Moreover, the indifference of the extremists among them to the Constitution, and their openly expressed willingness to see the slave-owning South outside the Union, was thoroughly resented by a generation which held both the Constitution and the Union in the deepest reverence. Business interests took fright at the abolitionist propaganda. Northern manufacturers were making good profits from southern trade; with higher tariffs, they stood a chance to make even better profits. Abolitionist activities might imperil the trade relations between the sections, lessen the chance of raising duties against foreign goods, destroy the business value of the Union. Many Northerners, moreover, were themselves ex-Southerners or the descendants of Southerners, and they agreed whole-heartedly with the southern contention that the only proper status for the Negro was slavery. With this view many other Northerners, not themselves of southern descent, were inclined to agree, because of unpleasant contacts they had had with freed Negroes in the North. In fact, most of the anti-slavery crusaders, particularly in the early years of the movement, were subjected to frequent outrages, the offices of abolitionist newspapers were repeatedly sacked, and at least one abolitionist editor, Elijah P. Lovejoy of Alton, Illinois, was put to death at the hands of a pro-slavery mob.

But the unpopularity of the abolitionists in the North was a mild thing indeed compared with the venomous hatred they provoked in the South. Losses from runaway slaves became increasingly *Southern* serious, and for these losses southern masters, with good *reaction to* reason, held the abolitionists responsible. Abolitionist *abolitionism* literature, some of which deliberately suggested to the slaves, by means of cartoons and otherwise, the possibility of running away, flooded the South in spite of the best efforts of Southerners to keep it out. The efficiency of the underground railroad, over which unnumbered thousands of Negroes traveled to freedom every year, was spread assiduously by word of mouth. Southerners believed also that the abolitionists were doing their best to promote Negro insurrections in the South, and occasional unguarded utterances on the part of a few extremists gave color to this charge. The *Liberator*, for example, once wished "success to all slave insurrections," and quoted approvingly the statement of an Englishman who said, "Southern slaves ought, or at least have a right, to cut the throats of their masters." Nat Turner's Rebellion, occurring as it did at about the same time that the abolitionist crusade began, was soon very generally, although quite incorrectly, ascribed to northern anti-slavery propaganda. But more galling even than property losses or the fear of insurrection were the abolitionist denunciations of slaveholders as the lowest type of criminals. Slavery, according to Garrison, was a "damning crime," and slaveholders were the "meanest of thieves and the worst of robbers. . . . We do not acknowledge them to be within the pale of Christianity, of republicanism, or humanity." The southern planter, who was traditionally proud of his reputation and resented hotly any charge against his personal honor, could not let such epithets pass unchallenged; and he was particularly incensed to have them flung at him by un-Christian Unitarians from a region notorious for its tight-fisted money-changers.

Coincident with the rise of abolitionism came the almost complete subsidence of southern interest in emancipation. It was generally

[503]

alleged that this change of sentiment in the South was due mainly to resentment against the northern anti-slavery propaganda, but a better argument can be made in support of the theory that the increasing profits of slavery had already sapped the vitality of southern emancipationism. Whatever the reason, such projects as compensated emancipation and the return of freed Negroes to Africa no longer received southern approbation. The last significant southern debate on the subject of slavery occurred in the Virginia legislature of 1832, immediately following Nat Turner's Rebellion, an incident which few Southerners had as yet thought to blame on the northern abolitionists. During the debate the institution of slavery was subjected to the most searching criticism; slavery, according to one member, was "the heaviest calamity which has ever befallen any portion of the human race," and according to another was "a curse upon him who inflicts as upon him who suffers it." But the legislature finally refused to take action, and within a few years hardly a Southerner of consequence could be found who would not spring to the defense of slavery.

Furthermore, every possible effort was made throughout the South to suppress all agitation in favor of emancipation, and in particular to prevent the delivery of the abolitionist tracts that the mails of the United States brought in. In 1835, after a Charleston, South Carolina, mob had burned a sack of abolitionist literature, the Postmaster-General ruled that local postmasters might refuse to deliver such mail if they believed it to be of an incendiary nature. Although this ruling was soon rescinded, many southern postmasters continued to abide by it, and many other obstacles to the spread of abolitionist propaganda in the South were devised. The individual who failed to destroy such literature immediately on its receipt was subjected to social ostracism, northern states were threatened with an economic boycott if they permitted its publication within their borders, and efforts were made, more spectacular than successful, to secure the extradition for trial in the South of objectionable northern editors.

At length, arguments were adduced to prove that slavery, far from being an evil, was actually a positive good. Of all the pro-slavery *The pro-slavery argument* philosophers probably Thomas Roderick Dew, professor of history, metaphysics, and political law in the College of William and Mary, and afterwards its president, was the most systematic and effective. Dew had obtained his education in Germany, where he was impressed by the open recognition of the inequalities of man, and the inevitability of a stratified society. Instead of apologizing for what he found in the South, he defended it. The great planters, because of their superior education, ability, and property, stood rightly at the head of southern society; next to them in rank were the small landowners, the traders, and free laborers; at the bottom of the ladder were the slaves. "It is the order of nature and of God," he claimed, "that the being of superior faculties and knowledge, and therefore of superior power, should control and dispose of those who are inferior. It is as much the order of nature that men should enslave each other as that other animals should prey upon each other." Dew's arguments were set forth in pamphlet form as early as 1832, and were repeatedly reprinted.[1] He was ably seconded by Chancellor William Harper of the Supreme Court of North Carolina, who published in 1838 a *Memoir on Slavery* that was quoted as authority throughout the South. About the same time John C. Calhoun gave it as his opinion that the South had no reason to be ashamed of slavery, and added that "There never has yet existed a wealthy and civilized society in which one portion of the community did not in fact live on the labor of the other." Professional men of every kind, particularly the preachers and the politicians, took up the argument, and boldly proclaimed the virtues of the South's most distinctive institution.

The idea that slavery was ordained of God was particularly comforting to the people of the South, most of whom were devoutly orthodox in their religious views. The Fourth and the Tenth Commandments, which referred to man-servants and maid-servants as of the same status as slaves, clearly gave the stamp of divine approval to slavery. Abraham, Isaac, and the other patriarchs had held slaves. Jesus himself had enjoined servants to be obedient to their masters. Moreover, it was a particularly happy dispensation of Providence which brought heathen Africans to America, where they might learn the truths of Christianity. But for the institution of slavery they might still be outside the pale of Christian influence.

Slavery was also defended as a benevolent institution in which the relationship between capital and labor was more kindly than could be found anywhere else in the world. The master must care for the slave in sickness as well as in health, in childhood and old age no less than in his prime. The master must not overwork his slave, for to do so would impair the slave's value. Compared with the wage-slave system of the

---

[1] Chancellor Harper and others, *The Pro-Slavery Argument* (1852), contains Dew's Essay. See also William S. Jenkins, *Pro-Slavery Thought in the Old South* (1935). By all odds the best brief treatment of this subject is William E. Dodd, *The Cotton Kingdom* (1919). Of great value also, in this connection, is his *Expansion and Conflict* (1915). W. G. Brown, *The Lower South in American History* (1902), recovers much of the emotional fervor that was characteristic of the defenders of slavery.

[505]

industrial North and of Europe, where, it was asserted, men, women, and children were worked to death in mines and factories, and where the aged, the ill, and the incompetent were ruthlessly discharged, the slavery system could be made to appear as "a beautiful example of communism, where each one receives not according to his labor, but according to his wants."

The claim that slavery as an economic device was also ideally suited to the South was continually made. Dew was not in the least embarrassed

The economics of slavery by the fact that Virginia piled up excellent profits each year from slave-breeding. Without that prop to its economic structure, he maintained that the Old Dominion would soon become a "howling wilderness." Less specious were the arguments of the eminent southern agriculturalist, Edward Ruffin, who pointed out the economic advantage in large-scale production and in the wholesale purchasing of supplies made possible by the slavery plantation system.[1] Furthermore, slave labor could be specialized at the will of the planter and in accordance with the aptitudes of the slaves, while the expensive struggles between capital and labor that had come to be characteristic of the free-labor system could be avoided. Some insisted that the drudgery required for the production of tobacco, rice, sugar-cane, and cotton could never be provided in sufficient amount by free men; and according to one observer, the North was as much benefited by the slave-labor system of the South as ever was the South itself. Northern manufacturers could count on the plantation South both as a steady source of supply for raw materials and as a market for northern goods.

As a matter of fact, the economic disadvantages of slave labor were becoming plain enough to those who wished to observe them. The South, thanks in considerable part to the limitations of the slave, was overspecialized. It produced only what the slave could produce profitably, and to an increasing extent this meant cotton. Even foodstuffs, which could be, and ordinarily were, grown on every southern farm and plantation, were frequently produced in such meager quantities that importations from the North had to be made. The prosperity of the South thus rose and fell with the proceeds from its money crops. Cotton was "King," but an off year, or a serious drop in price, meant widespread disaster. Moreover, the returns of the southern planter were far too small in proportion to his investment. Much of his capital was tied up in the ownership of labor, a situation which the northern employer of

[1] Avery O. Craven, *Edmund Ruffin, Southerner, A Study in Secession* (1932), is of broader scope and interest than the title indicates. See also, by the same author, *Soil Exhaustion as a Factor in the Agricultural History of Virginia and Maryland, 1606–1860* (1926).

free labor did not confront. Much capital had to be invested also in land, the price of which, thanks to the competition among planters for good cotton land, soared frequently to absurd figures. On a much smaller investment the successful northern industrialist made far greater profits.

Doubtless the worst feature of the system of slavery was that its rather scanty profits were absorbed by so small a number of planters. Ruffin was right in his contention that large-scale production was more profitable economically than small-scale pro- *Effect of slavery on the whites* duction. But the bulk of the people of the South belonged to the small planter and the farmer class. They had no choice but to compete with the large planter on terms that made him comfortable, but made them permanently poor. It was on this account that tens of thousands of Southerners who had no slaves or only a few slaves fled to the free states of the old Northwest, or to such portions of the slave states as the plantation system was unable to follow them. Not only did the South lose a steady stream of emigrants to the North; it failed also, because of slavery, to attract immigrants, as the North was doing, from outside the United States. The effect of slavery upon the rank and file of the native southern whites was also unfortunate. They tended to regard physical labor, because it was the customary lot of slaves, as essentially menial and degrading. The leisure class thus came to include many who might have fared far better had they been less opposed to work, and who made little or no contribution to the welfare of their section.

Undoubtedly the flaws in the slave-labor system were too numerous and too serious for slavery to have survived indefinitely. The leaders of southern opinion were temporarily deceived, however, by the advent of King Cotton, and as a consequence came boldly to the defense of the South's "peculiar institution." The attack of the abolitionists gave them an excellent opportunity to transform their apologies for slavery into a determined insistence on its righteousness and the desirability of its permanence. Thus the scene was being rapidly set for an "irrepressible conflict" between North and South -- a conflict that would soon rock the Union to its very foundations.

CHAPTER XXVII

MANIFEST DESTINY

UNTIL the late eighteen-thirties and the early eighteen-forties, the people of the United States took it for granted that the growth of the populated *The Ameri-* area of their country would be hedged in by certain obvious *can frontier* limits. They had foreseen for some time that the frontier of population would advance steadily into the upper Mississippi Valley and that it would reach, and perhaps cross, the international border to the southwest, but they had no idea that the region west of Missouri, which was labeled on the maps the "Great American Desert," would ever be desired for settlement. Indeed, it was because of this conviction that the policy of Indian removals, carried out in Jackson's time, met with such whole-hearted approval. Public opinion demanded that the eastern half of the continent be cleared for the use of the white man, but the Indian was welcome to the rest of it. To be sure, the boundaries of the United States might still be altered, and what they would ultimately become no one was ready to say. The title to the Oregon country was in dispute between the United States and Great Britain, and the settlement of the southwestern boundary, made in 1819, might, owing to the Texas problem, be subjected to generous revision. But the idea that any considerable number of persons would soon have their hearts set upon making their homes in the Far West seemed palpably absurd.[1]

One of the circumstances that served to provide Americans with a new vision of expansion was the opening of the Santa Fe Trail. On the upper *New Mexico* Rio Grande, separated by a long desert trip from Mexico City, the Spanish had established outposts at about the same time the English were founding Jamestown. Settlement in such a far-away spot, however, had been extremely slow to take root, and two hundred years later the American explorer, Zebulon M. Pike, found Santa Fe only a cluster of one-story adobe houses that reminded him of a

---

[1] T. M. Marshall, *A History of the Western Boundary of the Louisiana Purchase, 1819-1841* (1914); W. C. Macleod, *The American Indian Frontier* (1928). On the general subject of expansion during this decade, the best work is G. P. Garrison, *Westward Extension* (1906).

"fleet of flatboats . . . descending the Ohio," and that offered shelter for a "supposed population" of only forty-five hundred. These people, and the inhabitants of the lesser Spanish villages of the region, depended mainly upon agriculture, particularly cattle-raising, for their subsistence, but they carried on a far-flung trade with the Indians, and they sent each year a large shipment of their own and the Indians' products by caravan down the long trail toward Mexico City to be exchanged for greatly needed articles of European manufacture.

Pike was quick to observe, and to point out for the benefit of his countrymen, that a thriving trade might be established between the American and the Spanish frontiers. Imports into Mexico came by way of Vera Cruz, fifteen hundred miles distant from Santa Fe, and the cost of transportation so far into the interior was prohibitive except for the barest necessities. The distance to the bend of the Missouri, on the other hand, to which steamboats could easily bring articles needed for the trade, was not half as great. Thus an excellent market seemed only to await the taking. Early efforts on the part of the Americans to seize this opportunity were thwarted by the Spanish authorities in New Mexico, who rigorously enforced the regulations of the home government against colonial trade with foreign nations, but all this was changed by the Mexican Revolution. After 1822, when William Becknell returned to the Missouri settlements from the first profitable trip to Santa Fe, the caravans of American traders crossed the "Desert" each year for more than two decades. Sometimes their profits were excellent. The expedition of 1824, for example, consisting of eighty-one men with thirty thousand dollars' worth of merchandise in twenty-five wagons, brought back one hundred and eighty thousand dollars in gold and silver, in addition to ten thousand dollars' worth of furs, and some mules.[1]

The men who engaged in the Santa Fe trade were as a rule merely pioneer farmers or merchants with a taste for adventure. Each individual outfitted one or more wagons with hardware, *The Santa* needles and thread, cotton and silk goods, mirrors, glass- *Fe trade* ware, china, and dozens of other articles that his frontier experience recommended as easily salable. For convenience and protection the traders united soon after leaving the "jumping-off place," which most of the time was Independence, Missouri, and traveled as a caravan. A leader, elected by the traders for the purpose, then took command, assigned to each man his duties, and, unless deposed, guided the long

[1] Josiah Gregg, *Commerce of the Prairies, or the Journal of a Santa Fe Trader* (1844), is a classic on this subject. For a recent popular account see R. L. Duffus, *The Santa Fe Trail* (1930).

procession of wagons to its destination. When, however, after a journey of about six weeks, the goal was near at hand, all pretense of order was given up, and a mad rush began to see who could arrive first. Import duties as high as sixty per cent were levied against the trade by the Mexican government, but because the Mexican officials could usually be bribed, such high charges were rarely paid. For the inhabitants of Santa Fe the arrival of the caravan was the event of the year, and the goods brought were quickly disposed of. Most of the traders made all possible haste to return to the United States, but a very few stayed on, the forerunners of the American occupation.

The total volume of trade down the Santa Fe Trail was never very large, and the number of traders engaged in it probably did not average many more than a hundred a year. Nevertheless, the opening of a new trail into the Far West was, at least to the people of the Mississippi Valley, an event of real significance. Traders who were themselves farmers were not slow to observe that the land along the first lap of the journey was good land, and that heavy rainfall sometimes impeded their progress. In 1825, Thomas Hart Benton persuaded Congress to appropriate funds for the survey of the trail, and ardent believers in internal improvements talked even of extending the National Road far out along this new southwestern route. Military escorts that cost the government sums almost as large as the annual profits of the traders occasionally accompanied the caravan to the international border, and United States Commissioners to the Indians, blissfully unconcerned about the promise that the Far West was never to become a white man's country, attempted to purchase immunity for the white man's trade. Nor was the romance of the Santa Fe Trail lost upon a people that had long looked to the West for its tallest tales. In 1843, when Santa Anna, the Mexican leader, put a stop to the trade, the country was ready to be shocked, and even its reopening a year or two later did not serve to destroy the impression that "manifestly" this whole region ought to be a part of the United States.

Meantime, the Oregon Trail had opened to American eyes a new vision of the possibilities of the Far Northwest.[1] The origins of this *The Oregon* route to the West are far more obscure than the origins of *Trail* the Santa Fe Trail. After the explorations of Lewis and Clark and the journey of Astor's Overlanders, numbers of Indian

[1] Joseph Schafer, *A History of the Pacific Northwest* (1905), furnishes an excellent guide to the history of this section. Katharine Coman, *Economic Beginnings of the Far West* (2 vols., 1912), is interesting and informative. Francis Parkman, *The California and Oregon Trail* (1849), has gone through innumerable editions under a shorter title, *The Oregon Trail*, and is as authentic as it is interesting. A recent account is W. J. Ghent, *The Road to Oregon* (1929).

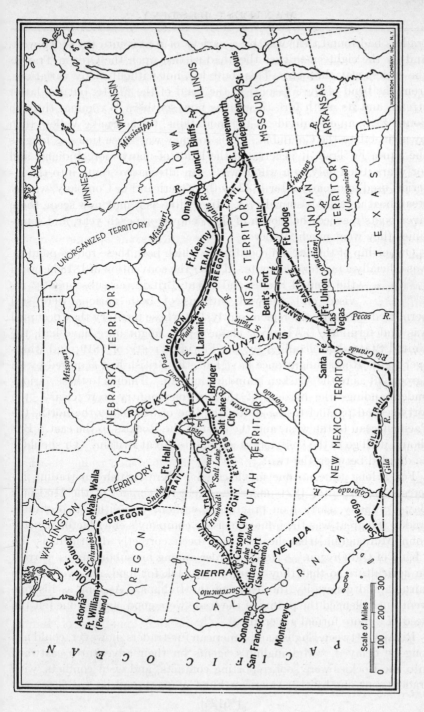

THE WESTERN TRAILS

traders had found their way by a variety of routes into the Northwest, and by the eighteen-thirties they had settled upon the Oregon Trail as the easiest way through. This route led, not without many variations, from the bend of the Missouri to the bend of the Platte, out the latter stream and its north fork to what is now southern Wyoming, through South Pass, an easy divide in the mountains, to the Snake Valley, then by a cut-off to the Columbia. This journey was three times as long as the Santa Fe Trail, it penetrated the lands of many more Indians, and for years it led only to a wilderness. An alternative route into the interior, used frequently after 1832 by the American Fur Company, was by steamboat up the Missouri River. Incredible as it may now seem, these river boats reached the mouth of the Yellowstone each year, and sometimes they went much farther.

Ownership of the Oregon country, to which both these routes pointed, was officially a matter of dispute. Under the convention of 1818 between *The Oregon* the United States and Great Britain, as subsequently re-*country* vised and renewed, citizens of both nations were still permitted to occupy the region jointly, but whose territory they occupied was undetermined. Whatever claims Spain might once have had, the United States had acquired by the Florida Treaty of 1819; and whatever rights Russia might once have had, the British had acquired by an agreement as to the Alaskan boundary in 1825. Thanks to these various understandings the borders of the Oregon country were clear — the forty-second parallel to the south, the line of 54° 40′ to the north, the Pacific Ocean to the west, and the crest of the Rockies to the east. But should it all go to the United States, or all to Great Britain? Or should it be divided between the two?

For a long time no one much cared. Here British fur-trading interests, united after 1821 under the exclusive control of the Hudson's Bay Company, carried on practically without opposition a profitable trade. So great was the influence of the company's chief factor, Doctor John McLoughlin, that he has since been correctly described as the "King of Old Oregon." He kept order among his subordinates, carried on agriculture so that they would never lack for food, and won by his fairness and generosity the fealty of the Indians. As long as his rule went unchallenged the profits of the trade were good, and no one felt the need of a more formal government.

Rivalry between English and American fur-traders, however, could not long be delayed. McLoughlin's agents on their adventures eastward into the Rockies were soon reporting contacts, and even conflicts, with traders sent out by the American Fur Company and its ruthless competitor, the Rocky Mountain Fur Company.[1]   McLoughlin would not permit the use of rum in dealing with the Indians, but the *Anglo-American rivalry* Americans, particularly the Rocky Mountain traders, had no scruples on this score, and the Indians were corrupted accordingly.   Private adventurers also, among them Captain Benjamin L. E. Bonneville, a regular army officer on leave, and Nathaniel J. Wyeth, a Boston ice merchant, both of whom led expeditions into the Far Northwest, brought to McLoughlin's attention the imminence of strenuous American competition.   By the year 1832 it was abundantly evident that "joint occupation" was soon to be given a real test.

And yet the conflict, when finally it came, was less the work of fur-traders than of missionaries.   By the eighteen-thirties most American religious denominations had developed a keen interest in *Missionaries to Oregon* foreign missions, and had recognized, somewhat belatedly, that the Indian tribes offered a suitable field for such labors.   So far as the Indians of the Far Northwest were concerned, a clear call to action was sounded when the news came out that a deputation of Flatheads had crossed the plains to St. Louis and had asked General William Clark to send them a Bible and a "black-robe."   Whether such a request was ever made is a matter of doubt, but the Methodists, undeterred by the obvious reference to the garb of a Catholic priest, promptly responded, and in 1833 sent out their first missionary to the Oregon country, Jason Lee.   Close on the heels of the Methodists came the Presbyterians, whose ablest representative, Marcus Whitman, appeared on the scene in 1836. By the end of the decade the American Catholics also were represented in the person of Father Pierre Jean de Smet, a Belgian Jesuit from St. Louis.

McLoughlin extended to all good men a hearty welcome, but since the Methodists had established a mission in the Willamette Valley, he strongly advised the Presbyterians to make their headquarters much farther in the interior at the junction of the Columbia and the Snake. Father de Smet of his own accord confined his activities largely to the Indians of the mountains and the western plains, who lived still farther to the east.   Thus conflict between the American missionaries was largely avoided.   The great majority of McLoughlin's traders, however, were Catholics, and the French-Canadian priests who came out at about this same time to minister to their needs worked at will among all the Indians. Religious rivalry thus began to take on a nationalistic bias.   In a general

---

[1] H. M. Chittenden, *The American Fur Trade of the Far West* (3 vols., 1902), is the standard authority on this subject.   Useful, also, is K. W. Porter, *John Jacob Astor, Business Man* (2 vols., 1931).   For McLoughlin's career see F. V. Holman, *Dr. John McLoughlin, the Father of Oregon* (1907).

sort of way the British subjects were Catholic and favorable to the Catholic missions, while the Americans were mostly Protestants.

The real trouble, however, came from the fact that many of the Methodist and Presbyterian missionaries, who were nearly all married men with families, soon became actively engaged in agriculture. In this they had the example of McLoughlin himself; but McLoughlin had no desire to carry on agriculture except as a necessary adjunct to his main business, the fur trade, whereas the missionaries sometimes became so absorbed in their farms that they almost forgot the spiritual needs of the Indians. In 1844 the Methodists, convinced that the sending of missionary money to Oregon under these circumstances was a scandal, closed down their Willamette mission. Well before this time, however, the far more interesting news that there was good farming land in Oregon had been spread far and wide, and after 1841 hundreds of emigrants gathered each spring at Independence, Missouri, to make the long journey by covered wagon into the new frontier. Such of them as completed it were often cared for considerately by McLoughlin himself, who in welcoming in the Americans was actually giving the country away. In 1842 the United States government sent out Doctor Elijah White, ostensibly as an Indian agent, but actually to take charge of the growing American colony in Oregon. That same year John C. Frémont, son-in-law of Thomas Hart Benton, began a survey of the Oregon Trail, and a year later the Americans in Oregon held a convention to inaugurate the well-known frontier process of establishing a means of local self-government. By the next election year, 1844, the whole United States was aware of the Oregon question. Joint occupation had run its course. Should Oregon be British or American?

Even in California the workings of "manifest destiny" were becoming apparent.[1] Here the Spanish outposts were not so old as in New *California* Mexico, but even so they dated back to the period when Daniel Boone was leading the advance guard of American settlement into the Ohio Valley. At about that time Spanish officials in the New World, fearful that Russian and British traders might advance too far down the Pacific coast toward Mexico, sought to forestall them by

---

[1] California before the Forty-Niners is excellently portrayed in H. E. Bolton, *The Spanish Borderlands* (1921). A longer account is C. E. Chapman, *A History of California: The Spanish Period* (1921). Mention should be made also of the voluminous writings of H. H. Bancroft, whose interest in western history spread from California to the regions north, east, and south of it. His *History of California* (7 vols., 1884–1900) is but a fraction of his total output. Much of the actual writing, however, was done for him by subordinates, and it is very unequal in value. Himself an early resident of California, Bancroft became interested in the social beginnings he witnessed, and set out to collect the documents from which a history could be written of what was going on.

sending missionaries, soldiers, and colonists from Mexico to California. Before the American Revolution had come to a close, these Mexican frontiersmen had established themselves firmly at San Diego, Santa Barbara, Monterey, and San Francisco. Mexico had few colonists to spare, however, and the number of civilians who made California their home during the next half-century was not very great. Those who came prospered in a fashion, for the climate was easy and the soil was rich. They adopted ranching as their chief occupation, but they had no adequate market for the vast herds they could raise, and the lives they led, while picturesque, were fairly primitive.

The missions, under the able direction of Franciscan friars, fared rather better. Not only did the friars win the Indians over to the Christian religion; they also persuaded great numbers of them to give *The* up their tribal ways, and to attach themselves as laborers to *missions* the missions. Thus it was possible for each mission to expand its grain-fields, to plant vineyards, olive groves, and orchards, to raise great herds of cattle, horses, and sheep, and to build the handsome churches and living quarters that in some instances still stand. A score of prosperous missions soon dotted the fertile coast valleys from San Diego to San Francisco. The natives also learned numerous arts and crafts from the friars, whose benevolent rule they accepted with increasing contentment.

To some extent before and to a greater extent after the Mexican Revolution, the Californians suffered from the ineptitude of their political rulers. Governors and their subordinates were usually venal, and their authority was supported by garrisons of unsavory soldiers who corrupted the Indians, hampered the work of the missionaries, and sometimes drove the civilians to revolt. Moreover, both the Spanish and the Mexican governments insisted upon regarding the missions as merely temporary affairs which, whenever the Indians were sufficiently civilized, should be broken up. When that time came the lands and the herds that the friars had amassed were to be divided among the Indians, and the religious duties of the friars were to be taken over by parish priests. Soon after the revolt from Spain the Mexican government attempted to put this policy into effect, but the Indians, who failed to see that they were to be its chief beneficiaries, shared the resentment of the friars and resisted vigorously. So great was the disorder that the government finally tried to restore the old system, but in this also it failed. Many of the missions were abandoned, their livestock destroyed, and their land appropriated by anyone who chose. Deprived of the protection of the friars, the Indians were ultimately forced to revert to the wild life whence they had come.

[515]

The uneasiness of California society was not lessened by the presence of a constantly increasing number of non-Mexican residents. Some of
Americans in California these came in to profit from the overseas trade which, regardless of hampering regulations, soon began to enliven the remote harbors of the Pacific coast. One such was Thomas O. Larkin, a former citizen of Massachusetts and of South Carolina, who in 1832 opened a store in Monterey. Larkin from the first seems to have cherished the hope that the United States would some day annex California, but he was careful to keep in the good graces of the Mexican officials, even at the cost of lending money to the governor at twelve per cent interest. Occasionally, also, the whalers and merchant-men that put into California harbors left behind deserters who preferred the salubrious climate of that region to the long voyage around the Horn or across the Pacific. More important still were the emigrants from the American frontier who were lured in by the spreading tales of California's fertile unclaimed acres. In 1841, a caravan of forty-eight left the Missouri border with California instead of Oregon as their goal. Following the Oregon Trail to the vicinity of the present Wyoming-Idaho boundary line, they successfully pushed southwestward through the alkaline plains and the Sierra Nevada mountains to their destination. They were not the first to find such a way through, but after their well-advertised journey the trail to California was as much a fact as the trail to Oregon. By 1845 there were no less than seven hundred Americans in California out of a total white population of about ten times that number.

After 1839 Sutter's Fort on the American River, a tributary of the Sacramento, furnished a convenient haven of refuge for the American
Sutter's Fort emigrants. Johann Augustus Suter[1] was a German by birth who served for several years in the Swiss army, emigrated in 1834 to the American frontier, and shortened his name to John A. Sutter. In five years' time he had engaged in the Santa Fe trade, had made the long trip overland to Oregon, had sold at a comfortable profit in Alaska a shipload of freight acquired in the Sandwich Islands, and had sailed into San Francisco Bay seeking yet another world to conquer. By embracing Mexican citizenship he made himself eligible to hold land, and obtained a magnificent grant of eleven square leagues, which he determined to transform into a kind of feudal barony. Here he gathered about him such of the Indians as would accept his protection, supervised their prosecution of the fur trade so successfully that he was soon a recognized rival of the Hudson's Bay Company factor in Oregon, taught his wards many useful skills such as the weaving of baskets and blankets, and gave them charge

[1] Julian Dana, *Sutter of California* (1936).

SUTTER'S FORT

SCENE AT THE POST OFFICE, SAN FRANCISCO

During the days of the Gold Rush

over his lands and his increasing herds of cattle, horses, and sheep. Besides his "fort," Sutter built himself a capacious house, a blacksmith shop, a grist mill, and even a tannery and a distillery. These evidences of civilization were ordinarily the first of their kind to greet the Americans who had successfully crossed the Sierra Nevada, and Sutter never failed to give the tired travelers the aid and encouragement they needed. He even pointed out to them the lands they might safely appropriate, regardless of the Mexican regulations designed to prevent alien land-ownership. Sutter himself was more or less above all law. Armed retainers of an astonishing variety of nationalities protected him from the wrath of the constituted authorities, who sat idly by while he parceled out the lands of California to the American invaders.

Naturally, the American government was not unmindful of the prospect that California might some day become a part of the United States. In 1841, Commodore Thomas ap Catesby Jones, commander of the American squadron in the Pacific, was instructed to seize Monterey in the event of war between the United States and Mexico. Excited by rumors that a British fleet also had designs on California, and convinced that the United States was already at war with Mexico, Commodore Jones decided in October, 1842, that the time had come to carry out his instructions. Accordingly he landed a force at Monterey, took possession of the public property, and ran up the American flag. When Larkin produced evidence to show that Jones's fear of the British was groundless and that the United States and Mexico were still at peace, there was nothing for the American officer to do but apologize and withdraw. His precipitate action revealed, however, all too plainly the ultimate goal of his government. By 1844 Larkin had been designated American consul at Monterey, and the responsiveness of the American colony in California to the idea of annexation was abundantly apparent.

American interest in California

Much as the American public was interested in New Mexico, Oregon and California, the place where "manifest destiny" was most clearly at work was Texas.[1] Here in the "Lone Star State" lived far more Americans than in all the other coveted regions combined. Furthermore, the United States had had a claim to Texas before 1819, and had renounced it only in order to obtain Florida. The issue could therefore be made to appear not so much annexation as reannexa-

Texas

---

[1] N. W. Stephenson, *Texas and the Mexican War* (1921), is an adequate short account. On the diplomatic side, see Jesse S. Reeves, *American Diplomacy under Tyler and Polk* (1907). More exhaustive is G. L. Rives, *The United States and Mexico, 1821–1848* (2 vols., 1913). A special phase of the subject is treated in E. D. Adams, *British Interests and Activities in Texas, 1838–1846* (1910).

tion. Texas had made good its independence, and had been recognized by the other governments as well as by the United States. It was in actual fact no longer a part of Mexico, whatever the Mexican officials might claim. The Texans themselves, with relatively few exceptions, desired annexation, and stood ready to see it accomplished on any reasonable terms. Why should the United States hesitate to add to the wealth and resources of the nation a region that ought never to have been alienated? Still further point was given to this argument by the fear, not wholly groundless, that an alliance between Texas and Great Britain might be consummated that would not only give preference in English ports to Texas cotton, but might also encourage Texas to expand her borders west and south to such an extent as to create for the United States a dangerous southwestern rival.

Probably the annexation of Texas would have been accomplished without serious opposition but for the growing distaste in the North for slavery and the conviction that no more slave territory *Slavery* should be added to the Union. These considerations were *and Texas* sufficient to restrain Van Buren, who refused throughout his term of office to give the slightest encouragement to the annexationists. John Tyler, however, was ardently in favor of annexation, and was undeterred by opposition. Accordingly, as soon as Webster had retired from the State Department Tyler reopened negotiations with Texas, first through Abel P. Upshur, Webster's successor as Secretary of State, and later, after Upshur's untimely death, through John C. Calhoun, whose appointment to the State Department was due mainly to his well-known interest in annexation. On April 12, 1844, a treaty between the United States and the Republic of Texas was signed which provided that Texas should become a territory of the United States, but not yet a state. This treaty, however, was overwhelmingly rejected by the United States Senate. The Mexican government had made it clear that the annexation of Texas would be regarded as good grounds for war, and some senators who might otherwise have favored the treaty voted against it on this account. Moreover, the election of 1844 was close at hand, and it seemed proper to await the verdict of the people; for, even at the time the Senate took its vote, annexation had become a dominant issue in the campaign.

The emergence of this issue took place, however, in spite of the best efforts of Henry Clay, the prospective Whig candidate, and Martin Van Buren, the prospective Democratic candidate, to head it off. *The issue of* Shortly before the nominating conventions met, Clay and *annexation* Van Buren issued separate statements on the subject so similar as to leave little doubt that their action had been previously agreed upon.

Both opposed the annexation of Texas without the consent of Mexico on the ground that it would be dishonorable and would lead to war. Clay went even farther, and pointed to the financial obligations that the acquisition of Texas, with its large war debt, would entail, and to the strong opposition to annexation among the people of the North. But the conventions were by no means satisfied with these pronouncements. The Whigs nominated Clay unanimously, but they made no mention of Texas in their platform, while the Democrats, after much fruitless balloting, passed over Van Buren in favor of James K. Polk of Tennessee, whose devotion to the cause of annexation was unquestioned. Their platform maintained, moreover, that "our title to the whole of the territory of Oregon is clear and unquestionable," and urged both "the reoccupation of Oregon and the reannexation of Texas." The introduction of the Oregon question was shrewdly devised to appeal to the people of the Northwest, whose interest in Oregon was as great as, or greater than, their interest in Texas. Also, by advocating the acquisition of free territory as well as slave territory, the Democrats freed themselves from the charge of sectionalism. With Oregon no less coveted than Texas, they could not so easily be denounced as seeking merely to promote the spread of slavery. Unmentioned, but by no means overlooked, was the further possibility of acquiring New Mexico and California.

As the campaign wore on, it became evident that the Democratic strategy had been wisely planned. To many voters, Northerners as well *Campaign* as Southerners, but to Westerners most of all, it seemed both *of 1844* reasonable and in line with precedent that the borders of the United States should now be expanded. No one was seriously deceived by the pretense of campaign orators that the United States wished only to obtain what was already rightfully hers. The real issue was whether or not the electorate was willing to follow the dictates of "manifest destiny," beginning with Texas and Oregon, and ending no one knew quite where. Clay himself soon realized that he had underestimated the strength of the annexationists, and began to qualify his prenomination statement. Ultimately his position became so equivocal that neither side knew precisely where he stood, and a number of anti-slavery men who had expected to support him turned instead to James G. Birney, the Liberty Party candidate. The attitude of the Democrats, on the other hand, was so plainly revealed throughout the campaign that they attracted practically all the expansionists to their standard. Their battle-cry, "The reannexation of Texas and the reoccupation of Oregon," struck the popular fancy, and was reinforced by such threatening slogans as "Fifty-four-forty or fight," and "All of Oregon or none."

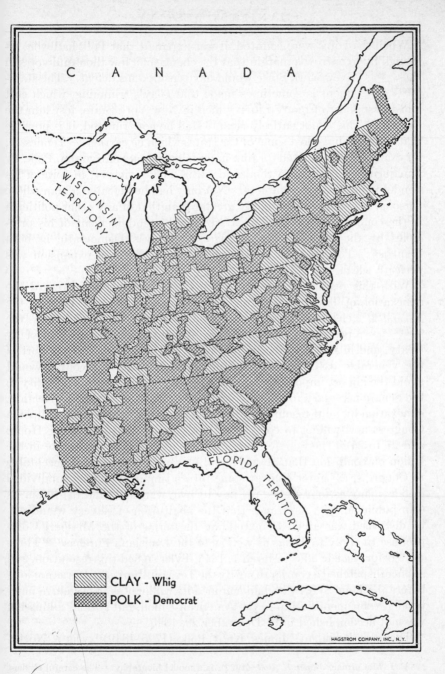

CLAY - Whig
POLK - Democrat

ELECTION OF 1844, BY COUNTIES

When the votes were counted, it was apparent that Polk had won, although by so narrow a margin that the change of a few thousand votes in

Polk's victory New York State would have ensured his defeat. The statement is sometimes made that Clay's trimming, which cost him the support of many Liberty men in New York State, lost him the election. This is not entirely clear. Had he not trimmed, it is possible that he might have lost some of the states which he carried — Tennessee, for example, which voted for him in preference to its native son, Polk, by a majority of less than a thousand. But Polk's victory, in spite of his slender majority, was complete. Not only had he defeated a man whose personal following was probably greater than that of any other politician in the country, but he had received a further endorsement of his principles by the selection of a Congress that was Democratic in both branches. The mandate of the electorate in favor of expansion was perfectly clear.

With this reassuring popular verdict, steps were taken toward the annexation of Texas even before Polk became President. Prior to the

Annexation of Texas election Tyler had already suggested to Congress the possibility of annexation by joint resolution instead of by treaty, and in this position he had received the enthusiastic support of the venerable ex-President, Andrew Jackson. Such a course would avoid the almost impossible task of obtaining the two-thirds majority in the Senate necessary for the ratification of a treaty. After the election, annexation by joint resolution was again pressed by the President upon a Congress now willing to comply. By a vote of 120 to 98 in the House and 27 to 25 in the Senate, Texas was invited to become a state in the Union on condition that (1) it should present a constitution acceptable to Congress, (2) agree that at some future time it might be subdivided into as many as four states, (3) pay its own war debt, and (4) retain its own public lands. Assurance that the institution of slavery would not be disturbed was given by extending the terms of the Missouri Compromise to apply to Texas as well as to the Louisiana Purchase. Three days before he left office, March 1, 1845, Tyler signed this resolution, and at once dispatched a courier to notify the Texas authorities. It was not long before the Lone Star State had signified its willingness to exchange independence for membership in the American Union, but formal admission was not accomplished until December 29, 1845.

The new President, James Knox Polk (1795–1849),[1] was a North-

---

[1] E. I. McCormac, *James K. Polk* (1922), is a model biography. The careful student will wish to examine also *The Diary of James K. Polk, during his Presidency, 1845 to 1849*, edited by M. M. Quaife (4 vols., 1910).

Carolinian by birth, of Scotch-Irish ancestry. He was not widely known, and for the preceding three or four years had been *James* out of office, but his obscurity was much overemphasized by *K. Polk* his contemporaries, who had never before witnessed the nomination of a "dark horse" — that is, a candidate for the Presidency who had not been long groomed for the race. For fourteen consecutive years, 1825–39, Polk had represented a Tennessee constituency in the House of Representatives, and during much of that time he was the recognized leader of the Democratic forces. The last four years he was Speaker of the House. From 1839 to 1841 he was governor of Tennessee, and, although he twice failed of re-election, his prominence in the political life of the state was hardly surpassed by any other man. Thanks to the fact that during the time he was President Polk kept a detailed diary, which subsequently was published, historians now know far more than his contemporaries knew about him. He was a hard-working, conscientious executive who believed it his foremost duty to carry out the will of the people as expressed in the late election. He had no taste for war, and earnestly sought to avoid it; but the annexation of Texas he regarded as both a necessity and a right. The United States and Texas, he maintained, were "independent powers competent to contract, and foreign nations have no right to interfere with them or to take exceptions to their reunion." As for Oregon, he pointed out that

> But eighty years ago our population was confined on the west by the ridge of the Alleghanies. Within that period — within the lifetime, I might say, of some of my hearers — our people, increasing to many millions, have filled the eastern valley of the Mississippi, adventurously ascended the Missouri to its headsprings, and are already engaged in establishing the blessings of self-government in valleys of which the rivers flow to the Pacific. The world beholds the peaceful triumphs of the industry of our emigrants. To us belongs the duty of protecting them adequately wherever they may be upon our soil.

The virtual certainty of trouble with Mexico over the annexation of Texas led Polk to trim his sails materially with regard to Oregon. As early as 1826, plans for the division of the Oregon country *The Oregon* had been discussed between the United States and Great *settlement* Britain, and at that time the American government had indicated its willingness to accept an extension to the Pacific of the forty-ninth parallel as the international boundary line. This was more than the British were then willing to concede, for the Hudson's Bay fur trade had long centered in the region south of the proposed line. Polk, however, hopefully renewed the offer, for Americans were now entering the

Columbia Valley by the thousands, and the Oregon fur trade, whether British or American, had seen its best days. When the British again rejected this plan of division, Polk asked Congress for permission to give notice, in accordance with the terms of the treaty, that after one year joint occupation must come to an end. He wished also the right to erect forts in the American zone and to extend the laws of the United States over Oregon. Probably the President had in mind only to threaten the British and so hasten negotiations along, but Congress feared he might involve the country in war, and agreed only to the termination of joint occupation, refusing the rest. More drastic action was unnecessary, however, for the British then offered to accept the line Polk had so recently proposed. After some diplomatic sparring, this was done; a treaty was signed on June 15, 1846, which extended the forty-ninth parallel as proposed in the negotiations, but gave to Great Britain all of Vancouver Island, to which the British fur-traders had recently shifted their headquarters. The Hudson's Bay Company retained also full freedom to navigate the Columbia River.

Meantime the relations between the United States and Mexico had grown steadily worse.[1] Mexican protests against the proposed annexation of Texas came thick and fast, and when her admission as a state was finally accomplished the Mexican government once again, as in 1836, withdrew its representative at Washington. The situation was still further complicated by the extravagant boundaries that the Texans claimed. While Texas was a part of Mexico, its southwestern border was generally conceded to be the Nueces River, but on becoming independent the new state laid claim to a new border, the Rio Grande from its mouth to its source, and thence due north to the forty-second parallel. This meant that much of New Mexico, including Santa Fe itself, would fall within Texas, a claim so palpably without foundation that the United States in the resolution offering statehood to Texas had definitely reserved the right to adjust "all questions of boundary that may arise." Nevertheless, Polk, in June, 1845, as soon as he had received assurance that Texas would accept statehood, had promptly ordered General Zachary Taylor to occupy territory "on or near the Rio Grande del Norte" in order to be able to "protect what, in event of annexation, will be our western frontier." The United States had also a list of grievances against Mexico that were not connected with Texas. For years the Mexican government had persistently hampered the easy

Relations with Mexico

---

[1] Justin H. Smith in his two books, *The Annexation of Texas* (1911), and *The War with Mexico* (2 vols., 1919), covers this phase of American history in detail. He is at pains to show that the United States was not wholly to blame for the war.

interchange of commerce between the two countries; it had failed miserably to protect the lives and the property of American citizens in Mexico; and it had habitually disregarded its promises to pay damages for the losses Americans had suffered. Unfortunately, Polk was wholly ignorant of Mexican psychology, and failed to realize that the Mexican leaders were really eager for war. They genuinely doubted that the people of the United States would adequately support a war of invasion, and they felt confident that in a defensive contest they would win.

Polk hoped for peace, but he was determined to obtain not only the part of New Mexico claimed by Texas, but all the rest of it as well, and in addition California. Accordingly he sent a minister to *The Slidell* Mexico, John Slidell of Louisiana, with orders to acquire the *mission* desired territory by purchase if he could. For full acknowledgment of the Texas boundary claim, the United States would assume all damages due American citizens from Mexico. For the rest of New Mexico, the United States would pay five million dollars in cash. As for California, "money would be no object," and the United States stood ready to pay from twenty to twenty-five millions, depending upon the exclusion or inclusion of Lower California. But Slidell's mission was doomed to disappointment. He arrived in Mexico just as a revolution was about to take place, and with public opinion intensely anti-American neither Herrera, who was in office when Slidell reached Mexico, nor Paredes, the successful revolutionist, dared receive him. Accordingly, in March, 1846, he returned to the United States with nothing accomplished.[1]

Long before Slidell's return, Polk had decided that war was inevitable, and in January, 1846, Taylor's troops, which for several months had been encamped just west of the Nueces River, were ordered to the Rio Grande. This movement was regarded by the Mexican President as an act of war, but he was unable to make a formal declaration to that effect until the Mexican Congress should meet. Polk, however, grew tired of delay, and early in May, 1846, he prepared a message to Congress in which he recited the failure of the Slidell mission, and recommended war to bring the Mexicans to terms. Before this message was sent, news arrived in Washington that fighting had broken out between Taylor's troops and the Mexicans along the border. Polk, therefore, rewrote his message in such a way as to put the blame for starting hostilities upon the enemy. On May 11, 1846, he told Congress that

> The cup of forbearance had been exhausted even before the recent informa-
> tion from the frontier of the Del Norte. But now, after reiterated menaces,

[1] L. M. Sears, *John Slidell* (1925).

Mexico has passed the boundary of the United States, has invaded our territory and shed American blood upon the American soil ... war exists and, notwithstanding all our efforts to avoid it, exists by the act of Mexico herself.

Congress came with alacrity to the President's support. A declaration of war was carried in the Senate by a vote of 40 to 2 and in the House by *War* 174 to 14. To ensure the successful prosecution of the war, *declared* ten million dollars were appropriated and a volunteer army of fifty thousand men was authorized. At first the country seemed genuinely enthusiastic about the war, but before many months strenuous opposition began to develop. The attack upon a weaker neighbor was criticized as unworthy of the national honor. The Democrats were charged with fomenting war in order to gain glory enough to enable them to win the next election. Anti-slavery men, already deeply distressed at the annexation of Texas, were sure that a southern conspiracy existed to extend still further the area open to slavery. The Whig Party, always in danger of dissolution because of the discordant views of its members, found a new source of dissension. The "cotton" Whigs, mostly from the West and South, supported the war now that it had begun, while the "conscience" Whigs, mainly from the Northeast, branded it as an inexcusable blunder that ought to be abandoned at once, with apologies and reparations to Mexico.

To Zachary Taylor, known in the army as "Old Rough and Ready," was assigned the task of advancing southwestward into Mexico from the *Taylor's* Texas border. He captured Matamoras without much *campaign* difficulty, then with a handful of regulars and several thousand volunteers he advanced toward Monterey. Hampered not only by the enemy, but also by the outbreak of disease among his poorly conditioned recruits, and by almost insuperable obstacles in the matters of transportation and supplies, Taylor nevertheless pushed on to his objective and in three days' hard fighting, September 21–23, took it; although to the intense disgust of President Polk he did not insist on unconditional surrender, and permitted the enemy troops to evacuate. From this time forward Polk lost all confidence in Taylor, but because the General, in the eyes of the people, had become a hero, his removal was politically impossible. Meantime Santa Anna, whose return to Mexico from exile in Cuba Polk had unwisely facilitated, had once again emerged as the Mexican President and war leader. With an army which outnumbered Taylor's by three to one, he marched rapidly northward to repel the invader. Taylor prepared for the attack at Buena Vista, and owing far less to his strategy, which was singularly defective,

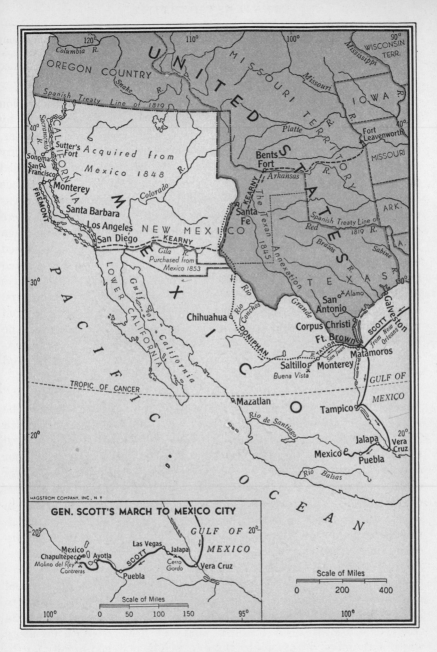

THE WAR WITH MEXICO

FLORIDA STATE COLLEGE FOR WOMEN
TALLAHASSEE, FLORIDA

LIBRARY
FLORIDA STATE COLLEGE FOR WOMEN
TALLAHASSEE, FLORIDA

than to the superior morale of the American soldiers, the Mexicans were repulsed (February 22–23, 1847).

But Polk had already determined to shift the main attack on Mexico from the international border to Vera Cruz on the eastern coast. To carry out this plan, General Winfield Scott was placed in *Scott's* charge of an expeditionary force at New Orleans, and Taylor *campaign* was notified, shortly before the battle of Buena Vista, that henceforth he must subordinate himself to Scott. Before Santa Anna could recover from his defeat by Taylor, Scott had successfully invested Vera Cruz, and with an army of more than ten thousand men was working his way westward, without much opposition, toward Mexico City. Not until the expedition had neared Jalapa, well up in the mountains, did Santa Anna appear with a newly collected army to dispute its advance. But Scott was a far better general than Taylor, and Santa Anna's troops were not very dependable. At Cerro Gordo the Mexicans suffered a disastrous defeat (April 17–18, 1847), Jalapa was soon occupied, and then Puebla. Here Scott rested for several months in preparation for the final climb to Mexico City, but by the middle of August he was again on the march. To the surprise of the Americans, who expected to be attacked in the difficult mountain passes, Santa Anna offered no resistance until the central plateau on which Mexico City is located had been reached. Then he fought, and fought hard, but he was no match for Scott, who won a succession of victories: Contreras (August 19), Churubusco (August 20), Molino del Rey (September 8), and Chapultepec (September 13). On September 14, 1847, the Americans were in possession of the Mexican capital.

The war was won by the campaigns of Taylor and Scott, but the conquest of New Mexico and California clearly foreshadowed the terms of the peace. Early in the summer of 1846, Colonel Stephen *Conquest of* W. Kearny left Fort Leavenworth, near the Missouri border, *New Mexico* bound for Santa Fe. He had with him a force of about seventeen hundred men, but he made no effort to maintain a line of communications, and carried only enough supplies to last until he reached his objective. He counted on a minimum of opposition and, as he had anticipated, the city was abandoned to him without a battle, August 18, 1846. After proclaiming all New Mexico a part of the United States, he set out with a small force for California, leaving the greater part of his troops at Santa Fe with orders to proceed southward under the command of Colonel A. W. Doniphan to join Taylor in Mexico. The garrison left at Santa Fe was soon reinforced by the arrival of a regiment from Missouri under Colonel Sterling Price, who took command. In 1847 Price had to put down a small revolt, but his adventures were slight in comparison with those of Doniphan and Kearny. The former, after weeks of wandering and much irregular warfare, established connections with Taylor's right wing; the latter arrived in southern California in time to bear the brunt of the fighting in that area, and to carry on an interesting dispute with the American officers who had preceded him as to which was in supreme command.

Certainly California had no dearth of conquerors. On the eve of the war an officer of the United States Army, John C. Frémont, who was *Conquest of* already famed as the "Pathfinder of the West," had led a *California* party of explorers across the Sierra Nevada into California, only to be warned out by the Mexican authorities. At first Frémont was defiant and refused to go, but at length he withdrew northward to Oregon, although slowly and with obvious reluctance. Here he was overtaken by a dispatch-bearer from Washington, A. H. Gillespie, who had already delivered messages to Commodore J. D. Sloat, commander of the American squadron in California waters, and to T. O. Larkin, the American consul at Monterey. All these documents were subsequently published, and they sound harmless enough; but something persuaded Frémont to advance once more into California. At about this same time a number of Americans who resided in the Sacramento Valley became excited by rumors that they were to be driven out, and precipitated the so-called "Bear Flag Revolution" at Sonoma (June 14, 1846). They asked Frémont to lead them, but this he refused to do until he learned, some two weeks later, that war had been declared between the United States and Mexico. He then enlisted most of the revolters in a "California battalion," and continued his advance. On July 7 Commodore Sloat hoisted the American flag over Monterey and proclaimed the annexation of California to the United States. Soon afterward Sloat was succeeded by Commodore R. F. Stockton, whose instructions gave him authority over "the forces and operations on shore." Stockton accepted Frémont as his subordinate, and even appointed him military governor of California. But Kearny, who after some sharp skirmishes with the Californians, had appeared on the scene, claimed that he was rightfully in command and had documents to prove it. Kearny finally forced Stockton and Frémont to accede to his authority, and took the latter back to Washington virtually a prisoner. Presently a court-martial found the Pathfinder guilty of insubordination and ordered him dismissed from the army, and although pardoned by the President he resigned his commission.[1]

[1] Allan Nevins, *Frémont, The West's Greatest Adventurer* (2 vols., 1928), makes as good a case for Frémont as the evidence will permit.

Thus, long before Mexico City had fallen, the United States was in possession of the territory Polk had sought to purchase before the war began. Indeed, while Scott was on his way from Vera Cruz *Treaty of* to the Mexican capital, he was joined by Nicholas P. Trist, *Guadaloupe* an employee of the state department whom the President *Hidalgo* had authorized to open negotiations for peace on terms only a little less generous than those once offered through Slidell. As a diplomat Trist left much to be desired, and his sole accomplishment up to the time Mexico City was taken was a contribution of ten thousand dollars to Santa Anna, the price demanded by the wily Mexican for his co-operation, something that failed to materialize. Polk was so incensed by the failure of his emissary that he deprived him of all authority and ordered him to return to the United States. But Trist cheerfully disregarded the President's instructions, and, with the war finally won, negotiated the treaty of Guadaloupe Hidalgo, February 2, 1848. By its terms Mexico accepted the Rio Grande boundary, and ceded New Mexico and California, including all the territory that lay between them, to the United States. The United States, in return, made a cash payment of fifteen million dollars to Mexico, and agreed to the cancellation of all claims due from Mexico to American citizens, claims which the United States government itself now undertook to satisfy to the extent of three and a quarter million dollars. It was an expensive peace, considering that the United States was in position to demand what it liked, but Polk accepted it, and sent the treaty to the Senate, where it was ratified by a vote of 38 to 14. Among those who voted against the treaty was Daniel Webster, who was opposed to the addition of any foreign territory, and E. A. Hannigan of Indiana, who believed that the United States should annex all of Mexico. A majority of the members of both parties voted for the treaty.

It was the irony of fate that the treaty added to the United States a colony of religious refugees who had sought to put persecution behind them by crossing the American border into Mexico. The *The* Mormons had originated in western New York during the *Mormons* late eighteen-twenties when that region was still sparsely settled. The prophet of the new religion, Joseph Smith, proclaimed doctrines that differed only a little from the numerous other Christian sects that during this same period were springing up all along the frontier. His "Church of Jesus Christ of the Latter Day Saints" accepted the teachings of the Bible, but received added inspiration from the *Book of Mormon*, which had been revealed to Smith in a miraculous fashion, and from other "revelations" which came to him from time to time. The chief distinction of the church was its centralized economic life, which contrasted markedly with the "rugged individualism" of the ordinary frontiersmen. Indeed, the close co-operation of the Mormons gave them a certain economic advantage over their neighbors that was resented far more than their religious idiosyncrasies. Retreating before this opposition, the Mormons first made Kirtland, Ohio, their residence, then Independence, Missouri, then a station they called "Far West" in Clay County, Missouri, then Nauvoo, Illinois, a small city on the left bank of the Mississippi River nearly opposite the mouth of the Des Moines. At Nauvoo the Mormons prospered quite consistently until 1844, when Smith announced himself a candidate for the office of President of the United States. This annoyed both Whigs and Democrats, for each party had counted on Mormon support, and the customary outbreak of antagonism was soon in evidence. To add to the confusion, there was talk of polygamy among the Mormon leaders, and schism rent the church. Smith was arrested, then taken from jail and lynched. His successor, Brigham Young, decided, reasonably enough, that the only hope of peace for the Mormons lay outside the boundaries of the United States.[1]

The Mormon migration is one of the outstanding episodes of American frontier history. During the spring and summer of 1846, about twelve *Migration* thousand of the Mormons, four fifths of their total member-*to Utah* ship, left their homes, including such of their property as they were unable to take with them, and crossed through Iowa to the Council Bluffs, a place-name then given to the region on both sides of the Missouri River adjacent to the present city of Omaha. Early in 1847 Young and a small company of his associates pushed on farther west to "spy out the land," and determined on the Great Salt Lake basin as the best available site for the colony they meant to establish. In September, 1847, the first detachment arrived, 1553 in number, and others followed with such rapidity that by 1850 the Salt Lake settlement numbered over eleven thousand. The "Mormon Trail" usually followed the north bank of the Platte River, continued westward through what is now Wyoming to South Pass, then turned southward to the Great Salt Lake. It was not so long or so difficult as either the Oregon or the California Trail, but the endurance of Mormon emigrants was nevertheless severely taxed, and the large volume of the migration made necessary the most systematic organization. Salt Lake City grew with astonishing rapidity, and soon became, to the very great profit of the Mormons, a convenient stopping-point on the way to California. The success of the colony,

---

[1] M. R. Werner, *Brigham Young* (1925); W. A. Linn, *The Story of the Mormons* (1902). Two general histories of the American frontier, not previously cited, are R. E. Riegel, *America Moves West* (1930); and E. Douglas Branch, *Westward* (1930).

LIBRARY
FLORIDA STATE UNIVERSITY
TALLAHASSEE, FLORIDA

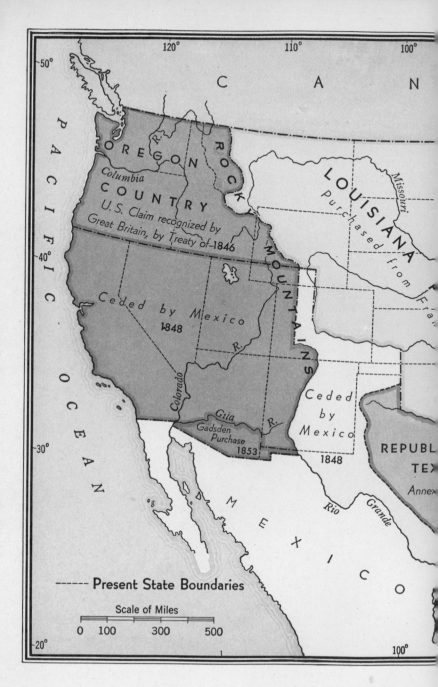

THE EXPANSION

Map showing:

CANADA

L. Superior
L. Michigan
L. Huron
L. Ontario
L. Erie
St. Lawrence R.

Limit of British Claim

Mississippi

THE UNITED STATES
1783

ORIGINAL THIRTEEN STATES

ATLANTIC OCEAN

TENNESSEE R.

Claimed by Spain to 1795
1810   1813
Perdido R.
Purchased from Spain 1819

St. Marys R.

FLORIDA

GULF OF MEXICO

BAHAMA ISLANDS (British)

CUBA

90°   80°   70°   40°   30°   20°

FLORIDA STATE COLLEGE FOR WOMEN
TALLAHASSEE, FLORIDA

LIBRARY
FLORIDA STATE COLLEGE FOR WOMEN
TALLAHASSEE, FLORIDA

however, was due primarily to the sound judgment and the extraordinary executive ability of its leader, Brigham Young. He it was who planned the migration, supervised the settlement of the newcomers, introduced irrigation, and in many other ways warded off the misfortunes that might otherwise have befallen so large a company in so difficult an environment. His dictatorship was virtually unquestioned.

Polk's policy of expansion was carried through well before his term of office was over, and without a serious failure. He obtained all of Oregon to which he could reasonably lay claim, insured the per- *Polk's* manence of the annexation of Texas, and took one third of *achievement* the territory of Mexico in order to advance the boundary of the United States to the Pacific in the Far Southwest, as it had already been advanced in the Far Northwest. Important settlements had been made in every section of the new acquisitions — in Oregon, in California, in New Mexico, and, thanks to the Mormon migration, in what was soon to be known as Utah. Well-defined trails crossed the continent to the Southwest, to the Northwest, and in between. Much of the western country was still regarded as uninhabitable, but such guides as Kit Carson, who accompanied Frémont on some of his explorations and showed Kearny the way from Santa Fe to California, and Jim Bridger, who helped Brigham Young locate the Great Salt Lake basin, were fast dispelling its mysteries. Polk was a man of mediocre ability somewhat lacking in imagination, but by his persistence in the face of obstacles, and by his unconcern for other people's scruples, he had accomplished a work in which many an abler man might have failed.

CHAPTER XXVIII

THE COMPROMISE OF 1850

POLK'S main concern as President was expansion, but during the first half of his administration he was able to redeem two of his party's pledges that had to do primarily with domestic affairs. The first of these was the enactment of a lower tariff than the measure Clay had persuaded Tyler to accept in 1842. Polk's Secretary of the Treasury, Robert J. Walker of Mississippi,[1] had so much to do with the framing of the new law that it became known as the Walker Tariff. It met the customary opposition from the industrial interests in New England and the middle Atlantic states, but it was warmly supported in the South and in the West, passed both houses of Congress with comfortable majorities, and was signed by the President, July 30, 1846. Walker was deeply impressed with the success England was having in abandoning protection, and looked forward confidently to a world movement for free trade. The tariff which bore his name, however, proved to be an excellent revenue measure, for it produced on an average nearly forty per cent greater receipts than the Whig Tariff of 1842. The second of the Democratic pledges which Polk carried through was the re-establishment by act of Congress, signed August 6, 1846, of the independent, or subtreasury, system that had been discontinued early in the preceding administration. Not until the time of the Civil War did the national government abandon its policy of complete aloofness from the banking business, and the subtreasury system as a means of handling treasury receipts continued in force until the passage of the Federal Reserve Act in 1913.

Legislation under Polk

The outbreak of the Mexican War soon provided the country with a much more exciting issue than either the tariff or the subtreasury. It was obvious that the success of the United States in the war would mean the acquisition of more territory; the administration made not the slightest pretense to the contrary. Naturally, therefore, the question was raised, Should slavery be per-

The debate over slavery expansion

[1] An interesting interpretation of Walker's career is given by W. E. Dodd, *Robert J. Walker, Imperialist* (1914).

mitted to expand into the territory soon to be acquired? The anti-slavery forces were convinced that only for this express purpose had the war been precipitated; the southern slaveholders, in spite of their success in annexing Texas, were not yet satisfied. As Lowell wrote,

> They just want this Californy,
> So's to lug new slave states in.

When in August, 1846, Polk asked Congress to appropriate two million dollars to be used in purchasing territory from Mexico, David Wilmot, an anti-slavery Democrat from Pennsylvania, introduced in the House a resolution that "as an express and fundamental condition" to any such acquisition "neither slavery nor involuntary servitude shall ever exist in any part of said territory.") After heated debate the House passed the resolution, but the Senate refused to concur.[1]

The "Wilmot Proviso," as it came universally to be called, was debated, not only in Congress, where for years it was proposed as an amendment to any relevant measure, but with equal ardor *The Wilmot* throughout the country. In the North Wilmot Proviso *Proviso* Leagues were organized to work for the exclusion of slavery from all further territorial acquisitions; in the South mass meetings were held to denounce the Northerners for the stand they were taking. The issue was one which tended to become strictly sectional; party lines had nothing to do with it. Northern anti-slavery men maintained that Congress was legally competent to exclude slavery from the territories of the United States, and should exercise its right at once. Southern extremists took the opposite view, and held that the Constitution, because it recognized and protected slavery in some of the states, must be construed to protect slavery also in the territories, for otherwise the property rights of slave-owners would be discriminated against in a region which was the joint possession of all the states. According to this argument neither Congress, nor a territorial legislature that derived its authority from Congress, had any right to interfere with slavery in any territory of the United States. Congress should therefore keep hands off, and slave-owners should be permitted to take their slaves at will into any of the territories.

There were many, however, who were ready to compromise. One such group accepted the doctrine of "squatter sovereignty" that Lewis Cass of Michigan had first suggested, but that came later to be intimately associated with the name of Stephen A. Douglas of Illinois, who

---

[1] At this point the scholarly and exhaustive work of James Ford Rhodes, *History of the United States from the Compromise of 1850* (9 vols., 1893–1922), begins to be of use. While Rhodes has been corrected at many points, his history of the Civil War period is still indispensable for the serious student.

renamed it "popular sovereignty." Adherents of this theory argued that
Plans of the people of a territory had the right to decide for them-
compromise selves whether the territory should be free or slave, and that
Congress should concede that privilege to whatever new territories it
might create. Still another group had no constitutional argument, but
pointed merely to the practical wisdom of dividing the acquired territory
between the slave states and the free states. This could be done conveniently, and with good historical precedent, by extending the line of
the Missouri Compromise to the Pacific.

But evidence accumulated, month by month and year by year, that
the North as a section was determined to prevent the expansion of slavery. Practically every northern legislature urged Congress to prohibit
slavery in the territories; some of them urged also that slavery be abolished in the District of Columbia; some even went so far as to prohibit
state officials from aiding in the return of fugitive slaves. At the same
time the South, stung by the implication in the northern attitude that
slavery was morally wrong, and fearful that the increasing weight of
the North in the Union might lead to an attack on slavery where it already existed, was equally determined that slavery should expand.
Southern fears were not wholly without foundation. In population the
North was drawing farther and farther away from the South, while unless new territory open to slavery could be acquired, the balance of the
sections in the Senate would soon be broken. Iowa and Wisconsin, admitted in 1846 and 1848, respectively, would serve as numerical offsets
to Florida and Texas, admitted in 1845, but Minnesota could not long be
held out of the Union, and the Oregon country offered a still further opportunity for the creation of new free states. Southern members of Congress, in a vain attempt to extend the Missouri Compromise line to the
Pacific, held up the organization of a territorial government in Oregon
for two years, but were at length compelled to capitulate, and Oregon
became a free territory in 1848, with no pledges given. Thereafter
threats of secession were made with ever-increasing boldness.

The debate on the Wilmot Proviso was interrupted to some extent by
the election of 1848. Both parties were threatened with disruption by
Election the one issue in which the country seemed genuinely inter-
of 1848 ested. For the Democrats to come out openly in favor of
the expansion of slavery meant the alienation of a large northern element in the party; for the Whigs to embrace the free-soil doctrine meant
for them equally serious losses in the South. Moreover, many sincere
patriots in both parties were alarmed at the rapid deepening of the sectional line of cleavage between North and South, and they feared for the

safety of the Union if the two major parties lost their national character and became sectional. It was not merely expediency that led both Whigs and Democrats to avoid the slavery issue in the campaign of 1848; it was also the sincere desire on the part of their most influential leaders to keep the Union intact. The Democrats, therefore, made no reference in their platform to the status of slavery in the territory acquired from Mexico, and turned to the North for their presidential candidate, Lewis Cass of Michigan.[1] The Whigs, even more cautious, adopted no platform, and presented as their candidate General Zachary Taylor, the "hero of Buena Vista," who by a lucky chance happened to be from Louisiana, and to own three hundred slaves. Before his Mexican exploits brought him into the limelight, General Taylor had apparently taken no interest in politics, and his willingness to accept the Whig nomination was at first conditioned upon his being left free to maintain his independence of parties. Later, however, under pressure from the politicians, he admitted that he was "a Whig, but not an ultra Whig." For second place on their ticket the Whigs chose Millard Fillmore, an obscure politician from western New York.

However well-intentioned the actions of the old party leaders may have been, the situation that they created called insistently for the formation of a new third party.[2] All anti-slavery men, whether *Agitation* outright abolitionists, or moderates who would be content to *for a third* prevent the expansion of slavery, could agree to the Wilmot *party* Proviso, which both Democrats and Whigs had so completely ignored. It seemed only reasonable, therefore, that with this as their platform the various dissatisfied groups should join forces. Two abolitionist candidates were early in the field, John P. Hale of New Hampshire, whom the Liberty Party had nominated in 1847, and Gerrit Smith of New York, the choice of a somewhat visionary "Liberty League." At the other extreme was the faction of New York Democrats once known as "Loco-Focos," but now generally termed "Barnburners," because in their determination to overcome all opposition they were willing, some said, to imitate the Dutchman who burned down his barn to get rid of the rats in it. The Barnburners were the devoted followers of Martin Van Buren, whose defeat by Polk for the Democratic nomination in 1844 they had never been able to forgive. Since Van Buren's failure had been due chiefly to his refusal to countenance the annexation of Texas, he and his followers were regarded, more or less correctly, as the element in the Democratic Party most opposed to the expansion of slavery. During

[1] A. C. McLaughlin, *Lewis Cass* (1891).
[2] T. C. Smith, *The Liberty and Free-Soil Parties in the Northwest* (1897).

the Polk administration the Barnburners were denied all patronage favors, and the federal offices in New York went instead to the opposing faction, or "Hunkers," so called because of their notorious "hunkering" after office. When the Democratic National Convention of 1848 assembled, the Barnburners and the Hunkers sent contesting delegations. The convention, although essentially friendly to the Hunkers, sought to compromise by dividing the vote of the state between the two factions, but this offer was indignantly rejected by the Barnburners, who returned home to hold a convention of their own, and to nominate their leader, Martin Van Buren, for the Presidency. Obviously, if the abolitionists and the Barnburners could unite, a strong third party could be formed.

The effort was made at a convention held in Buffalo, August 9, 1848, and presided over by Charles Francis Adams, the son of ex-President *The Free-* John Quincy Adams. The convention adopted a ringing set *Soil Party* of resolutions which insisted that "there must be no more compromise with slavery," that "the soil of our extensive domains" must be "ever kept free for the hardy pioneers of our own land, and the oppressed and banished of other lands," and that the free grant of land "to actual settlers, in consideration of the expenses they incur in making settlements in the wilderness . . . is a wise and just measure of public policy." The clear intent of the platform was to emphasize the contest between the slaveholder and the small free farmer for the lands of the West. There was no lack of moral indignation against slavery, but the strength of the economic appeal, particularly among the working classes of the East, whose interest in free lands was tremendously accentuated by the panic of 1837, was not overlooked. As a final resolve the convention voted to "inscribe on our banner 'Free Soil, Free Speech, Free Labor and Free Men,'" and the new party became known, accordingly, as the "Free-Soil" Party. The nomination of Martin Van Buren over John P. Hale was a further gesture in the direction of expediency, for Van Buren's opposition to slavery was of the most moderate variety. For Vice-President, however, Charles Francis Adams was named, and the ticket received the enthusiastic support of practically all the anti-slavery men.

The strength of the Free-Soil movement was revealed when the election returns came in. The new party had polled nearly three hundred thousand votes, had won the balance of power in a dozen states, and, for good or ill, had drawn enough votes from the Democratic column in New York to throw that state, and the election, to Taylor. The thirteen Free-Soilers chosen to the National House of Representatives were a power to be reckoned with, for no party had a majority in that branch of Congress. In the Senate, which was Democratic, John P. Hale already represented

New Hampshire, and the legislature of Ohio sent Salmon P. Chase, whose anti-slavery views were almost equally radical, to join him. The one lesson that the election seemed to teach was that the effort to avoid the slavery issue could not long be successful.

Nor was it. The nation was at last face to face with the necessity of deciding upon the status of slavery in the territory acquired from Mexico. Already the unreasonable delay of Congress in providing civil government for the regions annexed was causing difficulty. In California and New Mexico the military conquerors, under authority of the President of the United States as commander-in-chief of the army, kept order and, with the assistance of the former Mexican *alcaldes*, or local magistrates, carried on the most essential of the peace-time duties of government. But the arrangement was extremely unsatisfactory: land titles were in dispute, and the legality of any important action was open to question. The Mormons, by means of their closely knit church organization, were adequately governed, but the existence of this peculiar frontier theocracy was hardly compatible, to say the least, with the American democratic tradition.

The discovery of gold in California and the subsequent "gold-rush" introduced a new element into the situation. Early in 1848, James Marshall, a carpenter whom Sutter had employed to con- *Gold in* struct a sawmill not far from his fort, found flakes of gold *California* in the mill-race, and immediately reported the fact to his employer. Sutter tried to keep the news from spreading, for he feared the effect of a gold-rush upon his industries, and believed that the quantity of gold must be small. His efforts were unavailing, however, and by the end of the summer the whole world knew that there was gold — much gold — in California. Polk himself, in his annual message to Congress, December, 1848, confirmed the news. Long before this, Californians had dropped whatever work they were doing and rushed to the gold-fields. They were speedily joined by other residents of the Far West, by sailors who deserted their ships in San Francisco Bay, and even by pioneers who had heard the news on their way to Oregon and had "branched off" on the California Trail. While the "free gold" lasted, anyone, however inexperienced, with only a pick, a shovel, and a wash-pan as tools, could become a successful miner. Claims were staked out, informal records were made, and rules of ownership based upon common sense rather than upon legal precedents were agreed upon.[1]

[1] R. G. Cleland, *A History of California: The American Period* (1922), is excellent. Readable, and probably true enough in the picture, is S. E. White, *The Forty-Niners* (1920). The hardships of the pioneers who traveled overland to California are graphically told by means of a synthetic diary in A. B Hulbert, *Forty-Niners* (1931).

Comparative peace reigned in the "diggings" until the inrush of the "Forty-Niners" made good claims scarce. Then everything was *The "Forty-Niners"* changed. Thousands of men in every part of the United States left for California at the earliest possible opportunity. Those who could not afford to do otherwise took the long journey overland by covered wagon; others took ship around Cape Horn; still others went expensively and with great danger to their health by way of the Isthmus of Panama. Not the United States alone, but the whole world caught the gold-fever, and a huge polyglot population descended upon California. San Francisco, a city of tents and shacks, grew prodigiously; burned down, and grew again. To handle so bewildering a situation, the temporary military government was totally inadequate. Men went armed as a matter of course, fatal shootings were common and rarely investigated, voluntary associations kept what order they could. The need of an adequate and authoritative civil government was obvious, and was keenly felt.

It devolved naturally upon the new President, Zachary Taylor (1784–1850), to take the initiative in seeking a solution for this pressing problem. Taylor was a Virginian by birth, but he grew to manhood in frontier Kentucky, whither, as an infant, he had accompanied his father on the customary move to the West. Early in his twenties he was commissioned a lieutenant in the United States Army, and for forty years before his election to the Presidency he was a soldier. He had fought with vigor in the War of 1812, the Black Hawk War, and the Seminole War, as well as in the war with Mexico. He was not a great tactician, as his record in the Mexican War abundantly proved, but he was honest and forthright, well accustomed to meeting emergencies, and unembarrassed by the necessity of making a sudden decision. As President, he had a somewhat exaggerated opinion of the confidence that the nation reposed in him, and showed little respect for the opinions of Henry Clay, who had long since come to identify the Whig Party with himself. Taylor's Louisiana residence was acquired in 1840 when the General, as commander of the Department of the Southwest, had purchased a sugar plantation near Baton Rouge.

With reference to the problem of government in the newly acquired territory Taylor was ready to act. His solution was to encourage the *Taylor and state sovereignty* organization of state governments that would decide for themselves on the question of slavery, and with this end in view he urged both the Californians and the New Mexicans to draw up state constitutions at once and to seek admission to the Union. This advice the Californians promptly followed. Indeed, by the end of

1849 they had not only drawn up a constitution, but they had also elected a full quota of state officers, who, with the consent of the military governor, had taken over the government of the self-created "state." To the great chagrin of pro-slavery politicians, the California constitution definitely excluded slavery. The New Mexicans, with less reason for haste, were not ready with their constitution until May, 1850, but when it appeared, the chagrin of the pro-slavery men was still greater, for New Mexico, like California, proposed to enter the Union as a free state. Even the Mormons drew up an anti-slavery constitution for a proposed state of Deseret, and with Brigham Young as their duly elected governor applied for admission to the Union.

When, in December, 1849, Congress assembled for the first time after Taylor's inauguration and listened to the President's recommendation that California and New Mexico be promptly admitted, re- *Threats of* gardless of what their constitutions might say on slavery, *secession* the anger and resentment of the southern extremists knew no bounds. Said Robert Toombs of Georgia:

> I do not hesitate to avow before this House and the country, and in the presence of the living God, that if by your legislation you seek to drive us from the territories of California and New Mexico, purchased by the common blood and treasure of the whole people, and to abolish slavery in this District, thereby attempting to fix a national degradation upon half the states of this Confederacy, *I am for disunion.*[1]

Many genuine patriots, both Northerners and Southerners, on listening to such outbursts felt grave doubt for the safety of the Union.

Possibly the President might better have consulted Congress before committing himself so freely. Had he lived, however, there is some reason to believe that his capacity for decisive action might have preserved the Union, even without the compromise measures of 1850, some of which he would doubtless have refused to sign. On one occasion, when it was intimated that the Texans might seek by force to maintain their claims to the upper Rio Grande boundary, and so add materially to the territory open to slavery, the President announced that if any such effort were made he would take the field in person at the head of the United States Army to prevent it.

The Thirty-First Congress was one of the ablest that had ever been chosen. This was in part due to the fact that it was a kind of meeting-point of two generations. In it sat the three great statesmen of the preceding era: Daniel Webster, John C. Calhoun, and Henry Clay. But its roster contained also the names of many men whose careers were

[1] U. B. Phillips, *The Life of Robert Toombs* (1913).

before them, such as Salmon P. Chase, William H. Seward, Thaddeus Stevens, Stephen A. Douglas, Jefferson Davis, Alexander H. Stephens, and Robert Toombs. That so distinguished a group would sit idly by while a military hero with no experience in politics settled offhand the gravest problem, perhaps, that had ever confronted the nation was more than could be expected. Congress proposed to have a hand in the matter, and all eyes turned naturally to the aged Henry Clay, whose reputation as a compromiser was justly great. Throughout his life he had never held so tenaciously to any principle that under sufficient pressure he had found himself unable to give it up.

It is not fair, however, to assign the whole credit for the Compromise of 1850 to Henry Clay. Other men, notably Stephen A. Douglas, had *The Compromise of 1850* an important part in its making, and during the long debate over the Wilmot Proviso a multitude of political theorists had set forth the various possibilities of compromise. It was Clay, however, who presented to the Senate the elaborate series of resolutions that was to form the basis of compromise, and it was Clay's well-established reputation that won for them an instant hearing. The resolutions sensibly did not stop with the question of slavery extension, but included also all the other phases of the slavery problem with which the public mind was vexed. Clay hoped that his plan would restore "the peace, concord, and harmony of the Union" for another thirty years, the length of time that the Missouri Compromise had lasted. On January 29, 1850, he asked the Senate to consider the following suggestions:

1. Permit California to enter the Union as a free state.
2. Establish territorial governments without any restriction as to slavery in the rest of the territory acquired from Mexico.
3. Set reasonable limits to the western boundary of Texas.
4. Assume the public debt of Texas contracted prior to annexation, on condition that Texas relinquish her claim to any part of New Mexico.
5. Agree that slavery in the District of Columbia may not be abolished without the consent of Maryland, and of the people of the district, and without just compensation to the owners of slaves.
6. Prohibit the slave trade in the District of Columbia.
7. Enact a more stringent fugitive slave law.
8. Assert that Congress has no power to interfere with the slave trade between the states.

The debate that these resolutions precipitated in the United States Senate ranks justly as one of the greatest in American legislative history. Clay led off in defense of the Compromise with a speech which for the most part was eminently conciliatory. He pointed out that the admission of California under the free-state constitution already proposed was entirely in line with historical precedent and could scarcely be avoided. He urged that the organization of territorial governments in the rest of the territory acquired from Mexico be no longer delayed by insistence on the Wilmot Proviso, and reminded the North that it could count on "what is worth a thousand Wilmot provisos. You have got Nature itself on your side." As for the other provisions, they offered a sensible solution of the Texas boundary dispute, they made balanced concessions to both sides in dealing with slavery in the District of Columbia, and they assured the South that the rights of slave-owners should no longer be threatened, either by the inadequacy of the present laws for the rendition of fugitive slaves, or by the continued threat of congressional interference with the domestic slave trade. Possibly because so much of the Compromise was favorable to the North, possibly because he was himself from the upper South, where the problem was most acute, Clay was particularly outspoken as to the necessity of a stricter fugitive slave law. Upon this subject he declared that he was ready to "go with the senator from the South who goes furthest." On the whole, however, his speech was less an exposition of the provisions of the Compromise than an appeal to Congress and the country to quiet the clamor over slavery, and thus to save the nation from the unnecessary chaos of civil war.

Clay's appeal was insufficient, however, to win over the southern extremists. John C. Calhoun,[1] so old and ill that his address against the Compromise had to be read to the Senate by a colleague, *Southern views on the Compromise* Senator Mason of Virginia, recited the repeated encroachments of the North upon the South, and declared that the admission of California would serve notice that the North intended to destroy "irretrievably the equilibrium between the two sections." In a posthumous essay he proposed that two Presidents should be elected, one from the North and one from the South, each with a veto on congressional legislation, but his address on the Compromise asked only that a constitutional amendment be submitted "which will restore to the South, in substance, the power she possessed of protecting herself before the equilibrium between the two sections was destroyed by the action of this government." This vague proposal, while courteously received by the other southern extremists, left them unsatisfied. Most of them believed in the doctrine of non-intervention, according to which all the property of emigrants to new territories, including their slave property, was entitled to equal protection; but Jefferson Davis probably reflected their sentiments accurately when he announced his willingness to "agree

[1] A sympathetic view of Calhoun is given in W. E. Dodd, *Statesmen of the Old South* (1911).

to the drawing of a line of 36° 30′ through the territories acquired from Mexico, with the condition that in the same degree as slavery is prohibited north of that line, it shall be permitted to enter south of the line."

The ablest northern defender of the Compromise was Daniel Webster, whose "Seventh of March speech" on the subject ranks among the great-

Northern views est of American orations.[1] Webster, like Clay, appealed to the North to forego its insistence on the Wilmot Proviso. By the "law of nature," he maintained, it was settled forever, "with a strength beyond all terms of human enactment, that slavery cannot exist in California or New Mexico. . . . I would not take pains uselessly to reaffirm an ordinance of nature, nor to re-enact the will of God. I would put in no Wilmot Proviso for the mere purpose of a taunt or reproach." Webster also denounced the abolitionists for the furor they were creating throughout the country, and conceded that "the injunction of the Constitution for the delivery of fugitive slaves" had not been properly obeyed. He wished above all else to save the Union. Peaceable secession he branded as a delusion:

> Sir, he who sees these states, now revolving in harmony around a common center and expects them to quit their places and fly off without convulsion, may look the next hour to see the heavenly bodies rush from their spheres, and jostle against each other in the realms of space, without causing the wreck of the universe.

His peroration closed with a solemn charge:

> Never did there devolve on any generation of men higher trusts than now devolve upon us for the preservation of this constitution, and the harmony and peace of all who are destined to live under it. Let us make our generation one of the strongest and brightest links in that golden chain which is destined, I fondly believe, to grapple the people of all the states to this Constitution for ages to come.

If Clay was unable to win over the southern extremists to the compromise, Webster was no more successful with those of the North. Probably the speech of William H. Seward, the young Senator from New York, best represents the northern opposition to the Compromise. Seward was a Whig, but his views on slavery were as radical as those of many Free-Soilers. "Slavery can be limited to its present bounds," he told an audience in 1848, "it can be ameliorated; it can and must be abolished, and you and I can and must do it." In his speech on the Compromise he urged the immediate admission of California, and objected strenuously to the delays which came from connecting this question with any other. He charged, also, that the failure of the existing Fugitive Slave Law was not due to any fault of the law, but rather to a

---

[1] C. M. Fuess, *Daniel Webster* (2 vols., 1930), is a recent attempt to re-evaluate Webster.

hostile public sentiment in the North, something that a more drastic law would tend only to aggravate. He professed to believe, in spite of Webster's argument, that slavery might actually be transplanted to New Mexico, and he invoked "a higher law than the Constitution" as the authority of Congress to prevent so great a calamity. "The territory is a part, no inconsiderable part, of the common heritage of mankind, bestowed upon them by the creator of the universe. We are his stewards, and must so discharge our trust as to secure in the highest attainable degree their happiness." Emancipation he held to be inevitable and near, and its peaceful consummation would be made more difficult if new laws for the strengthening of slavery should be passed. Unwarrantedly optimistic, he declared that "there will be no disunion and no secession."

Meantime, majority sentiment throughout the country began to assert itself unmistakably in favor of some sort of compromise. Business men, thanks to the flow of gold from California and the in- *Sentiment* creasing demand for railways, enjoyed a degree of prosperity *for the* unparalleled since the panic of 1837. Farmers benefited *Compromise* materially from the strong foreign demand for American grain that followed the repeal of the Corn Laws in England, and commercial interests, already flourishing because of the pre-eminence of the American-built clipper ship, were still further stimulated by the low rates of the Walker Tariff. Laborers drew high wages and could count on steady employment. Such prosperity was far too precious to be disturbed by an academic dispute over slavery. Particularly were the northern manufacturers eager to ensure the permanence of their southern markets by conciliating the South; while southern producers were by no means happy at the prospect of secession, with its inevitable disruption of their normal lines of trade. A convention of southern delegates, called together on the advice of Calhoun, met at Nashville, Tennessee, in June, 1850, but failed to display the radicalism in its resolutions that had been expected of it, and adjourned to await the final action of Congress. Webster's Seventh of March speech made a powerful impression on the public mind, and brought many to the support of the Compromise who might otherwise have wavered. Abolitionists, not without some reason, branded him as a traitor to their cause, and read with approval the lines of Whittier's *Ichabod*:

> All else is gone; from those great eyes
> The soul has fled:
> When faith is lost, when honor dies,
> The man is dead!

[543]

Consideration of the Compromise occupied the chief attention of Congress from the end of January to the middle of September. The Senate referred the proposals to a select committee of thirteen, headed by Clay, which reported back three separate measures. The first, which was promptly termed the "Omnibus Bill," provided for the admission of California as a free state, the creation out of the rest of the Mexican cession of two new territories, New Mexico and Utah, without the Wilmot Proviso, and the payment of ten million dollars to Texas as an indemnity for her surrender of title to New Mexican territory. The second measure proposed the drastic fugitive slave law that the South demanded. The third prohibited the slave trade in the District of Columbia. As the favorable reaction of the country was sensed, the desire of Congress to accept the Compromise became increasingly apparent. Even so, there were serious obstacles to be surmounted. Most baffling, apparently, was the unrelenting opposition of President Taylor, who seemed determined to pursue his own course without regard for the wishes of Congress. But in July, 1850, the President was taken suddenly ill, probably of typhoid fever, and within a few days he was dead.

The new President, Millard Fillmore (1800–74), was known only as a successful lawyer from Buffalo, New York, who had served several terms *Millard* in the state legislature and in Congress. Early in his *Fillmore* career he had won some distinction by pushing through the New York legislature an act for the abolition of imprisonment for debt; later, as a member of Congress, he had much to do with the writing of the Tariff of 1842. When nominated for the Vice-Presidency he was generally regarded as an anti-slavery man, but the debates in the Senate on the Compromise measures, to which he listened as presiding officer, seem to have impressed upon him the urgent necessity of conciliating the South. On succeeding to the Presidency he at once put himself into the hands of Clay, formed a new cabinet with Webster at its head, and gave his undivided support to the proposed plan of compromise.

But opposition in Congress to various features of the Omnibus Bill also threatened for a time to wreck the Compromise. Fortunately, *The Com-* however, while passage of the measure as a whole would *promise* probably have been impossible, its friends soon observed *accepted* that if it were properly subdivided different majorities could be obtained for its several component parts. It thus came about that the Compromise of 1850, as finally passed by Congress and signed by the President, was complete in five laws: (1) California was admitted as a free state; (2) New Mexico was created a territory without the Wilmot Proviso, and the claim of Texas to New Mexican territory was indemnified by the payment of ten million dollars from the federal treasury; (3) Utah was created a territory without the Wilmot Proviso; (4) more stringent provision was made for the rendition of fugitive slaves; and (5) the slave trade was abolished in the District of Columbia. Actually only four senators voted for every one of the five measures, although several others, including Clay and Douglas, would have done so had they not been unavoidably absent when some of the votes were taken. Indeed, in both houses of Congress the majorities in favor of the various compromise bills were in no two instances identical.

For a time it seemed that the Compromise might fail to conciliate the South.[1] Particularly did the admission of California, an act which definitely upset the balance of slave and free states in the Union, arouse resentment and alarm. The adjourned session of the Nashville convention, held in November, 1850, condemned the Compromise, and urged that a general convention of the southern states should be called to safeguard southern rights within the Union, if possible, but if that could not be done, to prepare the way for independence.

Reception of the Compromise in the South

In four states, Georgia, Mississippi, Alabama, and South Carolina, special state conventions were held to consider the advisability of immediate secession. On second thought, however, the people of the South decided in favor of the Compromise. The recommendation of the Nashville "rump" convention — it was attended by only one third as many delegates as had composed the original session — went virtually unheeded, and not one of the state conventions came out in favor of secession. Except in South Carolina, those who wished to give the Compromise a trial were in the majority, and the South-Carolinians were unwilling to risk secession without the support of other southern states. "To secede now," as one of them observed, "would be to secede from the South." Probably the "Georgia Platform," as the resolutions adopted by the Georgia convention were generally called, best expressed the southern point of view. This document admitted freely that Georgia derived many advantages "from her adherence to the confederacy"; it accepted the Compromise "as a permanent adjustment of the sectional controversy"; and it warned the North that "upon the faithful execution of the Fugitive Slave Bill depends the preservation of our much-loved union."

In the North the chief obstacle to acceptance of the Compromise was the harshness of the Fugitive Slave Act. Even legally free Negroes had

[1] The persistence of secessionist sentiment is well set forth in the following works: P. M. Hamer, *The Secession Movement in South Carolina, 1847–1852* (1918); M. J. White, *The Secession Movement in the United States, 1847–1852* (1916); and R. H. Shryock, *Georgia and the Union in 1850* (1926).

good reason to fear for their safety when its provisions went into effect.

The Fugitive Slave Act Under the new law the fugitive, or anyone accused of being a fugitive, was denied the right of trial by jury and his status was determined either by a United States judge, or by one of the many commissioners appointed by the federal circuit courts for the more rapid disposal of such cases. In this hearing the fugitive, who was not allowed to testify in his own behalf, might be turned over to his claimant on no other evidence than the affidavit of his supposed master, or his master's attorney or agent. The act, moreover, was *ex post facto*, for its provisions applied to slaves who had fled from their masters at any time in the past; and it contained an outright bribe, for if the commissioner decided in favor of the master, his fee was to be ten dollars, whereas if he decided in favor of the fugitive, it was to be only five dollars. Federal marshals and their deputies were required, under threat of heavy penalties, to make unusual exertions to capture fugitives, and anyone aiding in the escape of a slave was liable to a fine of not more than one thousand dollars or imprisonment not to exceed six months, in addition to civil damages of one thousand dollars to the owner of the slave. These terms, quite obviously, were not dictated merely by the desire to secure the return of fugitive slaves. They were, and they were meant to be, as Rhodes says, "a taunt and reproach to that part of the North where the anti-slavery sentiment ruled supremely."

But even this thoroughly obnoxious act was insufficient to keep the North from rallying to the support of the Compromise. "Business interests," says Rhodes, "were well satisfied with the conclusion of the matter, for trade loves political repose." Mass meetings were held in Boston, New York, Philadelphia, and elsewhere to voice enthusiastic approval of the Compromise. The Fugitive Slave Act was defended by able lawyers as constitutional throughout, and was generally accepted as a necessary, if irritating, part of the price of peace. Partisans of the Compromise shrewdly proclaimed it as a *final* settlement of the slavery dispute. The question was, by common consent, to be forever outlawed from politics. In January, 1851, forty-four members of Congress, representing both major parties and both North and South, signed a pledge to oppose any candidate for public office who did not accept the Compromise as a *finality*. More Southerners than Northerners signed the pledge, but to Northerners this was especially gratifying, for it put the South even more clearly on record than the North as favorable to a plan which was designed primarily to end the southern threat of secession.

The presidential election of 1852 served as a kind of popular referendum on the Compromise. The Democratic National Convention accepted the Compromise without equivocation, and announced its determination to "resist all attempts at renewing, in Congress or out of it, the agitation of the slavery question, under whatever shape or color the attempt may be made." The Democratic nominee, Franklin Pierce of New Hampshire, was another "dark horse" who captured the nomination after three more prominent leaders, Cass, Buchanan, and Douglas, had each failed in a prolonged contest to win the necessary two-thirds majority. But Pierce's unqualified endorsement of the Compromise measures was well known, and with this in mind the stampede of the convention to his support had been carefully planned. The Whigs, on the other hand, were unable to present so united a front. Many of their ablest leaders in the North had opposed the Compromise, and at heart were still opposed to it. The Whig platform announced that it "acquiesced in" the Compromise laws "as a settlement in principle and substance of the dangerous and exciting questions which they embrace," and promised to "maintain them . . . until time and experience shall demonstrate the necessity of further legislation." Even this lukewarm statement was opposed by one fourth of the delegates, whereas the Democratic convention had adopted its ringing resolutions by an almost unanimous vote. Moreover, the Whigs refused to nominate Millard Fillmore, whose support had so greatly contributed to the adoption of the Compromise, and turned instead to their one remaining Mexican War hero, General Winfield Scott of Virginia, whose views on the Compromise were unknown.

Election of 1852

The issue before the electorate was thus primarily Franklin Pierce and the Compromise, or General Scott and uncertainty. A third alternative was offered by the Free-Soil candidacy of John P. Hale, but four years of Whig supremacy had brought the Van Buren Democrats back into the party fold, so that the Free-Soilers polled little more than half the numbers of votes in 1852 that they had polled four years before. The popular verdict was plain. The Democrats carried twenty-seven states, and the Whigs only four: Massachusetts, Vermont, Kentucky, and Tennessee. Pierce's electoral vote was 254 to Scott's 42. Indeed, the Whig Party, which throughout its existence had rarely been more than an "organized incompatibility," collapsed under the blow, and was never again strong enough to contest a presidential election. For the time being an overwhelming majority, both North and South, chose to believe that the slavery question was permanently settled.

CHAPTER XXIX

PEACE AND PROSPERITY

THE prominent place that the slavery dispute occupied in American politics during the two decades preceding the Civil War has tended to divert the attention of historians from other subjects of equal, or even greater, significance. During these same years transportation was revolutionized by the construction of railways, industry and commerce expanded with phenomenal rapidity, agriculture began its far-reaching shift from traditional to more business-like methods, a new flood of European immigrants swept over the country, and the final conquest of the Far West was definitely assured. Contemporary political leaders, who, in the light of these momentous changes, sought to bury the slavery issue, hardly deserve the scorn that some historians have heaped upon them. Could their efforts have been crowned with success instead of failure, the public mind would have been left free to recognize and wrestle with the issues precipitated by the economic revolution, while slavery in time might well have disappeared without resort to war.

Undoubtedly the greatest factor in transforming American society during this period was the railroad.[1] Up to about 1840 this means of transportation was still in the experimental stage, and the building of a railroad was a choice of desperation to be resorted to only where engineering difficulties made a canal impossible. Among these unwilling experiments were the Baltimore and Ohio, which opened a few miles to traffic in 1830, and the Charleston and Hamburg, which in 1833, with its 137 miles of track across the state of South Carolina, was the longest railroad in the world. Short lines were built, also, to facilitate trade between the principal cities of the country and their respective outlying districts. Philadelphia, for example, was soon connected by rail with the coal-mining regions of central Pennsylvania. By

The railroad

---

[1] An excellent short history of American railroad-building is John Moody, *The Railroad Builders* (1919). An early assessment, still useful, is C. F. Adams, Jr., *Railroads: Their Origin and Problems* (1878). See also B. H. Meyer, C. H. MacGill and others, *History of Transportation in the United States before 1860* (1917); Edward Hungerford, *The Story of the Baltimore and Ohio Railroad, 1827–1927* (1928); F. W. Stevens, *The Beginnings of the New York Central Railroad* (1926).

THE EVOLUTION OF LAND TRANSPORTATION IN AMERICA

the year 1840 the total railroad trackage of the country had reached 2818 miles.

From the operation of these early railroads, short and disconnected as they were, many valuable lessons were learned. The use of horses and sails for motive power was quickly discarded in favor of steam locomotives similar to those built by George Stephenson, the English inventor, but lighter and speedier. Unsubstantial wooden rails, protected only by thin iron straps, gave way to far more durable iron rails. Dizzy curves and steep grades, so characteristic of the early roadbeds, tended to disappear, while wooden cross-ties, designed to ensure that the two lines of rails should remain at all times equidistant, replaced the more uncertain separate foundations. Low four-wheeled trucks, pivoted beneath each end of a freight or passenger car, made the rounding of curves less hazardous, and pointed the way to a complete abandonment of the stage-coach and rail-wagon appearance of the first "rolling-stock." Coal began to replace wood as fuel, partly to save the time consumed in "wooding-up" at frequent intervals, partly to allay the irritation of passengers whose clothing caught fire from the steady stream of sparks that a wood-burner always emitted. Also, the necessity of railroad companies to manage the traffic was quickly demonstrated. On some of the early roads anyone with a proper conveyance was permitted to use the rails just as he might have used a toll road, but endless confusion resulted; moreover, the cost of locomotives and cars was beyond the means of the ordinary individual. It soon became the practically universal custom, therefore, for the owners of the road also to own and operate the equipment. For this service they exacted whatever charges they saw fit, but as "common carriers" they were under obligation to accept for shipment anything within reason presented to them for that purpose.

The second decade of railroad history saw the mistrust with which the new means of transportation had at first been viewed replaced by a deep *Through* and abiding faith. Accidental connections — such, for ex- *routes* ample, as made possible all-rail transportation from Boston to Albany after 1841 — added tremendously to the business of the connecting lines, and pointed the way to future development. The significant part that the railroads might play in linking the East and the West together became apparent in 1842, when a series of seven or eight local lines furnished an alternative route to the Erie Canal across the state of New York. The combinations of all such roads into one through route, while delayed in this case until the emergence of the New York Central in 1853, was a logical next step. By that year three other lines connected the eastern seaboard with the West: the Erie, completed through south-

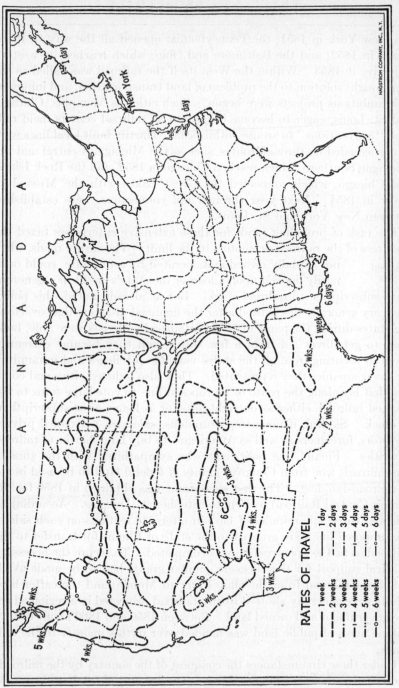

RATES OF TRAVEL

—————— 1 week	——— 1 day
———————— 2 weeks	— — — 2 days
—·—·—·— 3 weeks	—·—·— 3 days
—··—··— 4 weeks	—··—··— 4 days
———————— 5 weeks	···········5 days
—ooo—ooo— 6 weeks	—o—o—o— 6 days

RATIO BETWEEN TIME AND DISTANCE OF TRAVEL FROM NEW YORK IN 1860

Courtesy of the Carnegie Institution of Washington and the American Geographical Society of New York.

HAGSTROM COMPANY, INC., N.Y.

ern New York in 1851; the Pennsylvania, opened all the way to Pittsburgh in 1852; and the Baltimore and Ohio, which reached its western objective in 1853. Within the West itself the railroad was hailed as the long-sought solution to the problem of land transportation, and innumerable ambitious projects were begun. Such cities as Memphis, Chicago, and St. Louis, eager to become important as railroad centers, held railroad "conventions" to arouse enthusiasm. Hastily built local lines were soon succeeded by through routes, such as the Michigan Central and the Michigan Southern, which reached Chicago in 1852, and the Rock Island and Chicago, which connected the Great Lakes with the Mississippi River in 1854. Next year through rail connections were established between New York and St. Louis.

The task of providing funds for these extensive enterprises taxed the resources of the railroad promoters to the limit. The earlier roads, when *Railroad* not actually owned and operated by some state, could ordi-*finance* narily depend upon a loan of the state's credit or a generous state subscription to railroad stock. But as already noted, this policy was very generally discredited after the financial disasters that overtook the states during the panic of 1837. Railroad lobbyists were able, however, to get direct aid from a few states, and they became extremely adept at securing from all the states valuable privileges and immunities for the companies they represented. They also induced cities and counties that lay along the route of a proposed line to vote large sums to the coveted railroad, either as outright gifts, or as loans, or as subscriptions to stock. Skillful, if none too scrupulous, salesmen persuaded private investors, foreigners as well as Americans, to buy large blocks of railroad securities. Finally, the politicians who sympathized with the aims of the railroads won from Congress grants of federal land to be used in aid of railroad-building. The first such grant was obtained in 1850 for the Illinois Central Railroad by Senator Stephen A. Douglas. According to this act, three square miles of land in alternate sections on each side of the proposed line were granted to the state of Illinois for transfer to the railroad as fast as construction was completed. To secure the necessary political support for this measure, similar grants had to be made available for a railroad from the Ohio River to Mobile; and thereafter land grants were generally allotted to any railroad projected in a region where the government still owned land. Between 1850 and 1860 about twenty million acres of public land was handed over in this manner to the railroads.

Under these circumstances the conquest of the country by the railroads proceeded with astonishing rapidity. The amount of trackage increased from 2818 miles in 1840 to 9021 miles in 1850 and to 30,626 miles in 1860. By the last-mentioned year the Northeast alone had 9500 *Railroad* miles of railroad, more than the whole country had pos- *expansion* sessed ten years before. Practically all the important eastern cities were connected by rail, and many of them had also direct connections with the West. The most feverish building, however, had taken place in the Northwest. By 1860 this section, which before the panic of 1837 had hardly a mile of railroad in effective operation, had 11,078 miles to its credit, more than one third of the total trackage of the country. Chicago, thanks mainly to its natural advantages as a railroad center, had grown from a town of 4000 inhabitants in 1840 to 29,000 in 1850, and to 109,000 in 1860. Inland cities, such as Indianapolis, had achieved an importance that without the railroads could scarcely have been imagined. Railroad connections between the Great Lakes and the Ohio–Mississippi River system put the western canals virtually out of business, and stimulated tremendously the growth of such cities as Cleveland, Cincinnati, and Milwaukee, which could serve as links between the waterways and the rails. By 1855 the Mississippi River had been bridged; by 1857 the railroad frontier had reached the Missouri River at St. Joseph. In the South, railroad-building lagged perceptibly.[1] This section, with its extensive coastline and its numerous navigable rivers, stood far less in need of railroads than the Northwest; moreover, whatever surplus capital the South could command was generally invested in plantations and slaves. Nevertheless many short lines were built, and a few of sectional importance. By 1860, both Norfolk, Virginia, and Charleston, South Carolina, were connected through Chattanooga, Tennessee, with the Mississippi River at Memphis; and the Mississippi itself was paralleled from the Ohio to the Gulf. With 10,048 miles of railroads the South was slightly ahead of the Northeast in total mileage, although, in view of its greater distances, the effectiveness of its railroads was far less marked. The Northeast on the eve of the Civil War had about twice as much railroad trackage per square mile of land as the Northwest, and four times as much as the South.

RAILROAD MILEAGE IN THE UNITED STATES, 1830–1865

Year	Miles	Year	Miles
1830	32	1850	9,021
1835	1,098	1855	18,374
1840	2,818	1860	30,626
1845	4,663	1865	35,085

[1] U. B. Phillips, *A History of Transportation in the Eastern Cotton Belt to 1860* (1908).

One of the most striking developments that a railroad map of 1860 reveals is the drawing together of the Northeast and the Northwest. So closely connected, indeed, were the railroads of these two sections that they appear to be, as to all practical purposes they were, one network. With ever-increasing ease the produce of the Northwest found its way to the consumers of the East and to the eastern seaports for transshipment to Europe. Similarly the eastern manufacturers found in the expanding Northwest a gratifying market for the output of their factories. The southern railroads, on the other hand, were not yet integrated with the railroads of the rest of the country. Because so many of them had been built primarily as a means of supplementing the southern waterways, they lacked even sectional unity, and they made contact with the northern railroad system at only three widely separated points.

The revolution in means of communication that took place during this period was almost as marked on the high seas as on the land. To this *Ocean trans-* end American shipbuilders contributed during the eighteen-*portation* forties the fleet clipper ship, which with a fair breeze could make better time than the early steamships, and under normal circumstances could make three trips to Europe while an ordinary ship was making two.[1] Partly because of the superiority of these ships, partly because of recurring wars both in Europe and in Asia, American ships for a few years carried a far greater proportion of the world's commerce than had ever been the case before. During the decade 1850–60, about seventy per cent of the total foreign trade of the United States was carried in ships that flew the American flag, while in the year 1853 alone, according to a reliable estimate, the total tonnage carried by American ships exceeded that of the British by no less than fifteen per cent. About 1855, however, the American clipper ship began to be superseded by the British-built iron steamer, which could cross the Atlantic in less than two weeks' time. Backed by adequate government subsidies, the British steamers soon made heavy inroads upon the American carrying trade. To meet this competition several American steamship companies, which had been organized during the forties, were for a few years voted subsidies by Congress, but they proved to be unable to hold the trans-Atlantic trade against the British. Their importance in the coastwise trade, however, which was closed to foreign vessels, became very great. From the point of view of efficiency in transportation, it mattered little whether the commerce of the United States was carried in British or

[1] A. H. Clark, *The Clipper Ship Era, 1843–1869* (1910); C. C. Cutler, *Greyhounds of the Sea: The Story of the American Clipper Ship* (1930); Ralph D. Paine, *The Old Merchant Marine* (1919).

American bottoms. What was of far greater significance was the fact that ocean lanes were being multiplied, and the time of transit was being lessened. Just as the railroads within the country were bringing its various sections closer together, so the clipper ships and the steamers tended to bring the United States into closer contact with the outside world.

Easier means of communication had much to do with the growth of industry in the United States during this same period.[1] The use of power machinery in manufacturing had made steady prog- *Manufac-* ress during the first four decades of the nineteenth century, *turing* but the difficulties experienced in transporting goods to market had kept down the size of American factories and the amount of their output. Not until the advent of the steam locomotive did the full effects of the Industrial Revolution begin to be felt in the United States. Then factories that had previously depended on serving only a local market began suddenly to expand, while others, less fortunately situated, began to decline materially in importance, and even to disappear. Regardless of the number of factories, the total annual output of manufactured goods mounted rapidly. By 1850, the first year in which the federal census attempted to ascertain accurately the amount of manufacturing that went on in the United States, the total value of manufactured goods, $1,055,500,000, exceeded slightly the total value of agricultural products, $994,000,000. Ten years later the figures were $1,885,862,000 for manufacturing and $1,910,000,000 for agriculture; but the ascendancy that agriculture thus seemed to have regained proved short-lived, for all subsequent census statistics showed manufacturing far in the lead.

Not only improved means of transportation, but many other factors also tended to promote the growth of American industry. The liberal patent system of the United States, which guaranteed to patent-holders a long-time monopoly upon the manufacture, use, and sale of their inventions, encouraged American inventors to devise many labor-saving machines for use in the factory or on the farm, as well as a great variety of articles for the comfort and satisfaction of individuals. A rising standard of living meant also the manufacture and sale in quantities to the ordinary man of the one-time luxuries of the rich. Moreover, the United States was growing rapidly in population, both from the ordinary

---

[1] All of the short manuals of economic history are full at this point. See especially E. C. Kirkland, *A History of American Economic Life* (1932). V. S. Clark, *History of Manufactures in the United States, 1607–1860* (2 vols., 1916–28), is a good general account. Particular industries have also attracted writers, for example: M. T. Copeland, *The Cotton Manufacturing Industry of the United States* (1912); J. V. Woodworth, *American Tool Making and Interchangeable Manufacturing* (1905); J. M. Swank, *History of the Manufacture of Iron in all Ages* (1884).

natural increase and from a new wave of immigration; hence the needs of ever greater numbers of people had to be met. Prosperity meant that nearly everyone had the means with which to buy. Wages were good; agricultural products, thanks in part to the repeal of the Corn Laws in England and in part also to the mid-century European wars, brought high prices; newly mined gold and silver paid the bills of the Far West.

American manufacturing, in spite of its rapid growth, still showed many of the characteristics of youth. The concentration of factories at *Manufactur-* strategic centers had only begun, and there was in conse-*ing practices* quence a far greater diffusion of manufacturing industries than was later the case. While New England and the Middle Atlantic States maintained their early lead in manufacturing, small factories of one kind or another were apt to be found in any part of the country, even in the South and along the frontier. A second characteristic of youth was the close restriction of American manufacturing to the use of such raw materials as were produced within the country: comparatively little was imported in order to be manufactured. American grain was turned into flour and meal, American forests into sawed lumber, American cotton into cotton goods, American wool into woolen goods, American iron ore into iron products, and so on. Also, with some minor exceptions, the entire output of the American factories was consumed in the United States, and that without fully satisfying the demand. American cotton mills turned out enough cotton goods of the coarser grades, and a little to spare, but the finer grades still had to be imported from Europe. American woolens fell still further short of supplying the domestic demand, for the American woolens manufacturers were handicapped not only by their inability to compete with the English in producing fine fabrics, but also by an inadequate American supply of raw wool. The use of anthracite coal and of coke as fuel greatly stimulated the iron industry and pointed the way to a phenomenal development, but the heavy demands of the railway age were greater than the American supply could meet. With reference to many minor industries the situation was not far different.

The high degree of prosperity that American manufacturers enjoyed during these years was achieved in spite of the relatively low duties of *The tariff* the Walker Tariff. Naturally, the fact that importers were able to throw upon the American market a plentiful supply of foreign-made goods was not at all relished by the manufacturing interests. Demands for higher duties in order to promote the more rapid expansion of American industry were persistently voiced, particularly by

THE LOCATION OF FACTORIES IN NORTHERN UNITED STATES, 1860

representatives of the northeastern states, where most of the factories were located. Until the time of the Civil War, however, all such demands were foredoomed to failure. Both the South and the West profited from the low duties, and a coalition of southern and western politicians ruled the country. Indeed, in 1857 the rates of the Walker Tariff were still further reduced.

Circumstances conspired to make this period one of extraordinary prosperity for the cotton-growers of the South.[1] The steady fall in the price of cotton that had at first accompanied the expansion of cotton-growing was arrested in the forties and reversed in the fifties. From an all-time low of less than six cents a pound in 1845, the price of cotton rose to an average of between ten and eleven cents throughout the fifties, and to nearly fourteen cents in 1857. Nor was this change in price due to any curtailment of production, for each year saw a sizable increase in the acreage devoted to cotton culture. Rather, the world demand for cotton had been immensely accelerated. Improvements in textile machinery now made possible the manufacture of cotton goods for sale at so low a price that even the humblest Asiatic or African could afford to buy. American

The profits of cotton-growing

[1] L. C. Gray, *History of Agriculture in the Southern United States to 1860* (2 vols., 1933).

[557]

manufacturers, after meeting practically the entire domestic demand for cheap cotton cloth, were able to export a considerable excess to the Orient; English manufacturers, ensured by the repeal of the Corn Laws against the danger of having to pay high wages to their operatives, sought and found new markets everywhere in the world; French manufacturers, while definitely less flourishing than their British competitors, were by no means idle. Manufacturers everywhere turned to the American South for their raw cotton, for nowhere else could they find an abundant supply of comparable quality. To meet this tremendous demand practically all the land of the South that was suited to cotton culture was used for that purpose. Indeed, except for cotton and tobacco the production in the South of every important crop failed during the fifties to keep pace with the growth of the population. But the cotton crop, which had risen from 1,500,000 bales in 1840 to 2,500,000 bales in 1850, reached the enormous total of 5,300,000 bales in 1860 — seven eighths of the world's supply.

Less frequently noted is the fact that during these same years a renaissance of tobacco-growing made the states of the upper South more *Tobacco- growing* prosperous than they had been for years.[1] This was due in part to the increased demand of a growing world population, in part to the introduction of new species and to improved methods of cultivation and manufacture. In 1849 the tobacco crop of the United States amounted to less than 200,000,000 pounds; ten years later it was nearly 430,000,000 pounds. Virginia and Kentucky were the greatest tobacco-growing states, but other states also, notably Maryland, Tennessee, and Missouri, contributed large quotas. Indeed, every state in the Union, North as well as South, grew some tobacco, although the cotton states during this decade grew proportionately less tobacco than they had ever grown before.

While tobacco was second in value only to cotton among the crops that the South produced, it was a rather poor second. Throughout that section the saying that "Cotton is King!" went unchallenged. Southerners were proud of the fact that the world depended upon them almost exclusively to supply one of the primary necessities of civilization; they relished the thought that without their help the wheels of industry in the North and in England would scarcely turn; they never forgot that the export of cotton paid more than half the bills contracted by the United States abroad. On one score, however, they confessed some embarrassment. The world's need for cotton would continue to mount, but by the end of the fifties the South's ability to meet that need would

[1] Meyer Jacobstein, *The Tobacco Industry in the United States* (1907).

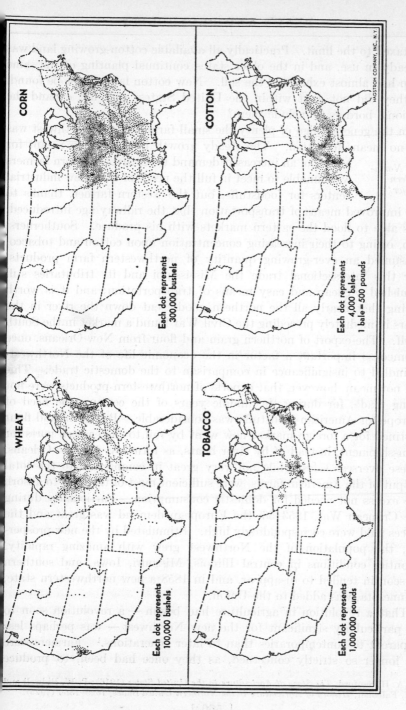

THE DISTRIBUTION OF FARM PRODUCE IN THE UNITED STATES, 1859

be taxed to the limit. Practically all available cotton-growing land was already in use, and in the older states continual planting of the same crop had almost exhausted the soil. New cotton lands must be found. If they did not exist within the United States, why not expand the national borders to include them?

In the general reign of plenty the small farmer of the Northwest was by no means forgotten. The steady growth in population meant for *The North-* him, too, an increased demand to satisfy. Eastern farmers *western* were unable to meet in full the needs of their new industrial *farmer* centers for foodstuffs, but the western farmer, thanks to the improved means of transportation that the railway age introduced, was able to flood the eastern markets with his produce. Southerners, also, owing to their increasing concentration upon cotton and tobacco, consumed an ever-growing quantity of northwestern farm products. For this intersectional trade the Mississippi and its tributaries still furnished a cheap and easy means of transportation; and it is worth noting that nearly all the northern goods sent down the river in the years immediately preceding the Civil War found a market in the South itself. The export of northern grain and flour from New Orleans, once deemed so important a factor in the economic life of the Northwest, dwindled to insignificance in comparison to the domestic trade. This did not mean, however, that exports of northwestern products were not being made, for during the middle years of the century the need of Europe for American foodstuffs was considerable. But grain and flour destined for a foreign market now went by rail to the eastern ports for transshipment, instead of by river boats, as formerly, to New Orleans. These overseas sales, while not very great in comparison to the total output of the American farms, were sufficient most of the time to absorb the excess not needed for domestic consumption. Particularly during the Crimean War, 1853–56, the European demand was great and the prices paid were correspondingly high. Stimulated by the new prosperity, the population of the Northwest grew with amazing rapidity. Frontier conditions in central Illinois, Missouri, Iowa, and southern Wisconsin tended to disappear, and in 1858 a new northwestern state, Minnesota, was added to the Union.

That a revolution in agriculture had begun — a revolution soon to be particularly significant for the new Northwest — was perhaps less apparent to contemporaries than to later generations.[1] Farmers were no longer so strictly concerned, as they once had been, to produce

[1] A. H. Sanford, *The Story of Agriculture in the United States* (1916); P. W. Bidwell and J. I. Falconer, *History of Agriculture in the Northern United States, 1620–1860* (1925).

upon their own farms all the necessities of life for themselves and their families.   In earlier times they had taken their own corn *The revolu-* and wheat to a near-by mill to be ground into the very flour *tion in* from which the bread they ate was to be made.   They *agriculture* had shot or butchered their own meat, had clipped with their own hands the wool that ultimately through home manufacture provided the clothes they wore, had built their own houses, sheds, and fences from timber cut on their own property, and in a great variety of other ways also had met their own needs without help from the outside.   But the self-sufficient farmer was rapidly becoming a thing of the past.   New agricultural machines, such as the reaper, enabled him to produce far more of certain commodities than he could hope to use.   New means of transportation, especially the railroads, enabled him to ship his excess to market.   With the proceeds from the sale of his crop he could now buy many of the things he had formerly found it necessary to make for himself or go without.   He could, and did, begin to specialize in farming, even to the extent of producing only one kind of crop.   His farm became a kind of factory from the profits of which he lived.   No longer was he independent of the rest of the world, for he must sell to it, and he must buy from it.   His purchases stimulated manufacturing, and the growth of manufacturing provided him with new markets.   Northwestern farmers, while grateful for the markets that the cotton- and tobacco-growers of the South were also providing, were increasingly conscious of the greater purchasing power of the industrial Northeast.   The bond of union that was being cemented between these two sections would soon be strong enough to meet the test of civil war.

The rich natural resources of the United States were already contributing generously to what President Pierce chose to call "the light of our prosperity."   Precious metals had much to do, although *Exploitation* by no means everything, with making the population of *of mineral* California four times as great in 1860 as it had been in 1850. *resources* California prospectors pushed throughout the Rocky Mountain area in search of other gold-fields, and made some strikes.   In 1859 the Pike's Peak gold-rush duplicated many of the scenes of ten years before in California, and laid the foundations of the future state of Colorado. That same year discoveries along the famous Comstock Lode made Nevada possible.   Magnificent virgin forests in the upper Mississippi Valley furnished an almost limitless supply of lumber to the prairie states below.   The lead mines of northwestern Illinois and southwestern Wisconsin, once worked by the Indians, now made profits for the whites. Coal and iron ore were found conveniently close together in central

[561]

and western Pennsylvania. The first oil well was drilled in 1859, near Titusville in northwestern Pennsylvania.

It is not surprising that the United States, as "the land of opportunity," attracted during these prosperous years a great host of European immigrants. The impact of the Industrial Revolution *Immigration* upon Europe had not been without its unfortunate aspects. Those left unemployed by the introduction of labor-saving devices found great difficulty in obtaining re-employment. Also, profound political disturbances, such as the Chartist movement in England and the Revolutions of 1848 on the Continent, accompanied the changing economic order. For those who wished to flee this turmoil, Europe had no adequate outlet of its own, but this defect the United States was fortunately in good position to remedy. Its industries were new, and could profitably absorb both skilled and unskilled European workmen. Its frontier, capable seemingly of an almost indefinite expansion, could give homes not only to its own needy millions, but to millions of Europeans as well. Before 1840 the number of immigrants who came to the United States each year was an almost negligible figure, twenty-three thousand in 1830, and eighty-four thousand in 1840; but between 1845 and 1855 the average number of newcomers admitted annually had risen to not less than three hundred thousand. They came from many lands, but, owing to special circumstances, from Ireland and Germany far more than from all other countries combined.[1]

Unlike the Scotch-Irish who came to the United States from the north of Ireland during the eighteenth century, the new Irish immigrants came from the southern counties of Ireland; they were *The Irish* Celtic in origin rather than Teutonic, and Roman Catholic in religion rather than Presbyterian. Their incentives for leaving Ireland were numerous: political oppression, whether real or fancied, absentee landlordism, overpopulation, and above all a series of devastating famines that began with the failure of the potato crop in 1845. Deaths by starvation during these hard seasons were pitifully frequent, and those who were able to leave for a land of plenty such as America availed themselves of the first opportunity. Shipping companies cut the cost of transportation to a figure lower than had ever been known before, herded the immigrants together in stifling holds, and made a rich harvest from their enterprise. The Irish landed virtually destitute at Boston, New York, and other eastern ports, and went to work at

[1] G. M. Stephenson, *A History of American Immigration, 1820–1924* (1926), is the most satisfactory book on this subject. A special study of unusual merit is T. C. Blegen, *Norwegian Migration to America, 1825–1860* (1931).

small wages in the factories, on the railroads, or wherever their help was needed. Thousands of Irish girls found employment as domestics. Soon nearly every city had its "Shantytown" where the newly arrived Irish lived in quarters even more squalid than those they had known in Ireland, and prospered on incomes that to the native Americans seemed ridiculous.

The reasons for the German migration were somewhat analogous. In the vanguard were the political refugees, liberals who had taken a part in the revolutions of 1848 only to lose out in the end before the forces of reaction. Some men of this type, Carl *The Germans* Schurz and Franz Sigel, for example, soon achieved a greater prominence in their adopted land than they had ever known in Germany. Still others left to avoid the compulsory military service required by most German princes, and others to get away from distressing economic conditions for which no remedy seemed available. The success of the English manufacturers with factory-made textiles brought ruin to the numerous German household producers of linen, while crop failures in the Rhine Valley and a losing struggle to hold the English grain market meant critical times for agriculture.

The average German immigrant was a little higher in the social scale than his Irish contemporary, and had often saved enough money to get a start in the new land. Sometimes he went into business, and whole cities, such as Cincinnati, St. Louis, and Milwaukee, soon exhibited many of the characteristic qualities of the Germans. More frequently he bought himself a farm and, unaccustomed to the thriftless methods into which an abundance of rich soil had betrayed the native Americans, he farmed carefully and prospered inordinately. Unlike the Irish, the Germans rarely settled in the East, but went instead to the Middle West, where lands were cheaper and opportunity more abundant. For a generation or more they continued to speak the German language, and they clung tenaciously to the manners and customs of their European homes. Great lovers of music and of good-fellowship, each German community was apt to have its *Liederkranz*, its *Turnverein*, and its *Biergärten*. In Wisconsin the German influence was so pronounced that there was talk of making the state over into an ideal German commonwealth.

Politicians in search of new issues, after the Compromise of 1850 had made a truce over slavery, were quick to discover in the immigrant a menace to American institutions. Port cities and the dis- *Native* tricts adjacent to them complained bitterly of the pauper *Americanism* population that the immigrant tide forced upon them. Religious zealots professed alarm at the presence of a rapidly growing Roman Catholic element in a country that had always before been dominantly Protestant. American workmen complained that their wages were being beaten down and their jobs actually taken away from them by their alien competitors. Southerners were deeply concerned because the foreigners, unaccustomed to slavery in their former homes, consistently avoided the slaveholding South and helped to swell the already alarming lead of the North in population. Good citizens generally recognized the natural prejudices that must be overcome in order to assimilate fully the clannish Irish and the self-sufficient Germans. Not only must the difficult barriers of race and religion be surmounted, but different political traditions must somehow be reconciled. Some of the Germans, thoroughly imbued with the revolutionary doctrines that had precipitated the revolutions of 1848, even dared to propose radical changes in the American form of government.

The first impulse of the politicians, however, was to cater to the foreign vote. In many states the law permitted aliens to vote if they had resided in the United States for a year and had declared their intention of becoming citizens, but the lax polling system of the time made the restrictions in practice even less consequential. To curry favor with the foreigners, German and Irish names were often placed on the ballots, while naturalized citizens were showered with political favors. In the contest for foreign support, however, the Democrats completely eclipsed the Whigs, who were convincingly portrayed by their opponents as the American conservatives. The Irish, almost to the last man, accepted the Democratic Party as the "poor man's party," and therefore their rightful place. Similarly, the liberals among the German leaders saw little to hope for from the Whigs, and encouraged their countrymen to vote for Democratic candidates.

Logically the Whigs might well have seized upon the anti-foreigner issue, but their party was already too moribund to take a pronounced *The Know-* stand upon anything. It fell out, therefore, that a new *Nothings* party was formed precisely for this purpose. Its origins lay in a succession of secret societies, such as the American Brotherhood, the American Protestant Association, the Order of United Americans, and finally the Order of the Star-Spangled Banner, the purpose of which was to combat the alien menace. While not at first admittedly political, these organizations soon sought to correct such "evils" as alien voting or office-holding, too easy means of naturalization, and the admission of foreigners to the same advantages as natives in the acquisition of public lands. Fear of Roman Catholic interference with the public school systems, then being formed, led also to a demand that no Roman Catholic should ever be elected to any public office. Decisions of the anti-foreigner groups were kept secret, and members who were asked what they intended to do replied simply, "I know nothing," whereupon they were promptly dubbed "Know-Nothings." On election days the Know-Nothing vote, particularly in Massachusetts, Pennsylvania, and New York, sometimes assumed astonishing proportions, and candidates were elected whose chances had been regarded as poor. By the middle fifties openly announced Know-Nothing, or American, Party tickets were winning many local victories.[1]

In their search for an attractive issue to keep the mind of the public off the slavery question, the Democrats tried repeatedly to rekindle the interest in expansion that had brought them such success *Expansion* in the election of 1844. This was a favorite idea with *as a political* President Pierce, who declared in his inaugural address *issue* that the policy of his administration would "not be controlled by any timid forebodings of evil from expansion." "Indeed," he continued, "it is not to be disguised that our attitude as a nation and our position on the globe render the acquisition of certain possessions not within our jurisdiction eminently important for our protection."

Most coveted by Pierce and his advisers was the island of Cuba, which still belonged to Spain, and in spite of the efforts of many fili- bustering expeditions from the United States declined to *Cuba* take an abiding interest in revolt. Pierce probably hoped to make the acquisition of Cuba the outstanding achievement of his administration, even if it cost a war with Spain. In 1854 the seizure by Cuban officials of an American merchantman, the *Black Warrior*, on the charge that the vessel had violated some port regulation, almost gave the President the opportunity he needed, but the island authorities receded from their position too soon to permit him to take any drastic action. Disorders in Spain that same year, however, seemed to offer a better pretext, and the ministers from the United States to Great Britain, France, and Spain (James Buchanan, John Y. Mason, and Pierre Soulé) were charged with the task of formulating the American program. Their handiwork, the so-called "Ostend Manifesto," pro- posed that Spain should be offered one hundred and twenty million dollars for Cuba. If this offer were refused, the United States would be justified in taking the island by force on the ground that "our internal

---

[1] Two useful state studies of this subject are L. F. Schmeckebier, *History of the Know-Nothing Party in Maryland* (1899); and L. D. Scisco, *Political Nativism in New York State* (1901).

"THE OSTEND DOCTRINE"

From a contemporary cartoon in the New York Historical Society

peace and the existence of our cherished union" would otherwise be threatened. But this bit of international bad manners came to nothing. Spain refused to sell, and the United States, already embroiled with the slavery issue and in no position to fight a foreign war, disavowed the action of its ministers.[1]

Efforts were also made to acquire more territory on the mainland. James Buchanan, to whose advice Pierce usually listened with respect,

The Gadsden Purchase

had favored the annexation of all of Mexico in 1848, and many others had felt that at best Trist's failure to obtain Lower California had been an inexcusable blunder. Some ardent expansionists felt that the United States should even have a foothold in Central America, and they especially deplored the terms of the Clayton-Bulwer Treaty of 1850 by which the United States conceded to Great Britain an equal interest in any interoceanic canal that might there be built. But the sole tangible result of this expansionist propaganda was the purchase in 1853 from Mexico for ten million dollars of a sandy triangle south of the Gila River. Surveyors claimed that this territory, generally called the "Gadsden Purchase," would be needed

[1] J. M. Callahan, *Cuba and International Relations* (1899).

[566]

in case the United States ever wished to construct a railroad along a southern route to California.

More successful were the efforts of the administration to smooth the way for American traders in the Far East. Ever since 1784, when the *Empress of China* set sail under the Stars and Stripes from New York for Canton, a small but lucrative oriental trade had been maintained, and in 1844, following the Opium *Commerce with the Orient* War between England and China, the United States had been accorded by formal treaty the same commercial privileges that the English had won by force. But American trade in China had always operated at a disadvantage in competition with the long-established connections maintained by Europeans; and it was in part to offset this handicap that the American government determined to open up a new field for commercial exploitation in the so-called "Hermit Kingdom" of Japan. Except for the Dutch, who were allowed limited privileges of trade at Nagasaki, Japan was virtually closed to the outside world, and so mistrustful were the natives of foreigners that shipwrecked sailors were often treated with extreme cruelty. To end this unfortunate situation, Commodore Matthew Perry visited Japan in 1854 with the largest fleet the United States had ever assembled in Asiatic waters. Overawed by so great a show of force, the Japanese government agreed to open two ports to American traders, to permit an American consul to reside at one of them, and to accord protection to American seamen left in distress upon Japanese shores. Elsewhere in the Pacific also the administration sought new advantages for American traders. A treaty with Siam, concluded in 1856, enlarged upon trade privileges that had been obtained twenty years earlier; and an attempt to annex Hawaii, although unsuccessful, called attention to the dominance of American influence in the Middle Pacific.

Meantime, the impossibility of keeping the vexatious slavery question in abeyance was becoming increasingly apparent. Know-Nothingism won a foothold in the South, where there were no foreigners, because the inrush of immigrants was strengthening the free states, and loomed up, therefore, as a possible *Persistence of the debate over slavery* menace to slavery. Expansion was ardently championed in the South, particularly with respect to Cuba, for only in such a fashion could new lands suited to the slave-labor system be obtained; but expansion was quite as heatedly denounced in the North, where it was correctly regarded as a thinly veiled disguise for the acquisition of more slave territory. Efforts to enforce the newly enacted Fugitive Slave Law added to the difficulties of the situation, and Charles Sumner in a four-hour address to the United States Senate called eloquently for its repeal. Abolitionists brought forth evidence to prove that under the terms of this act free Negroes were being kidnaped from their northern homes and sold into slavery; but Southerners had quite as convincing evidence of the success with which anti-slavery men in the North were assisting runaway slaves from the South over the underground railroad to Canada. In spite of the Compromise of 1850 the debate over the morality of slavery did not cease. On this question the leading Protestant churches had already split — the Presbyterians in 1838, the Methodists in 1844, and the Baptists in 1845 — and seemingly the more pronounced the views of any given sect on the slavery question, the more it prospered.[1]

Doubtless the most important document in the history of the antislavery crusade was Harriet Beecher Stowe's *Uncle Tom's Cabin, or,* *"Uncle* *Life Among the Lowly,* a simple and moving story of Negro *Tom's* life. Mrs. Stowe was the daughter of one New England *Cabin"* clergyman, Lyman Beecher, the wife of another, and the sister of seven others, among whom was Henry Ward Beecher. For many years her husband, Calvin Stowe, taught at Lane Theological Seminary in Cincinnati, Ohio, and it was here that she came into intimate contact with the institution of slavery, as it existed across the river in Kentucky. She saw something, too, of the plight of the fugitive slave, and with the strong humanitarian urge that was her birthright she felt impelled to attack what she believed to be an unmitigated evil. Her weapon was her pen, for by her writing she added each year a few hundred dollars to the family income. In 1850 her husband became a professor in Bowdoin College, Brunswick, Maine, and it was here, far removed from the scenes of which she wrote, that *Uncle Tom's Cabin* took form. Published first as a serial in the *National Era,* an anti-slavery paper of Washington, D.C., it attracted little attention, but in 1852 when it appeared in book form its popularity was immediate and great. Three thousand copies were sold the first day, and three hundred thousand copies before the end of a year. As a novel, the book left much to be desired, but as a moral indictment of slavery it was tremendous. Dramatized, and played before enthusiastic audiences throughout the North, it made converts for the anti-slavery cause even among those who could not or would not read. Years later when President Lincoln first met Mrs. Stowe he is said to have remarked, "So

[1] J. N. Norwood, *The Schism in the Methodist Episcopal Church, 1844* (1923), shows the disruptive forces at work in a single denomination. See also H. K. Rowe, *The History of Religion in the United States* (1924).

STEPHEN A. DOUGLAS

you're the little woman who wrote the book that made this great war!" For the popularity which the book achieved in the North was matched only by its unpopularity in the South.

Under these circumstances it is hardly fair to place the entire blame for the reopening of the slavery dispute upon the shoulders of Stephen A. Douglas of Illinois. It is a fact, however, that in 1854 Douglas did sponsor a measure, the Kansas-Nebraska Act, which embodied a plan for the further expansion of slavery, and which could therefore be construed as unsettling the delicate balance that the compromise measures of 1850 had established. But the time was ripe for such a step, and if Douglas had not been the first to suggest it, in all likelihood someone else would have done so at a not much later date.

Stephen A. Douglas (1813–61) [1] was born in Brandon, Vermont, but at the age of twenty he went to Illinois, where he began the practice *Stephen A.* of law. Law led naturally to politics, an occupation for *Douglas* which Douglas had great natural aptitude. He knew how and when to be shrewd and calculating, he mastered easily the oratorical technique required by his time, and he put no restraints upon his ambition. By 1847 he was a member of the United States Senate, and the idol of the boastful, untutored, expansionist Illinois Democracy. Sensitive to the necessity of keeping the southern and western wings of his party together, he supported the Compromise of 1850 with telling effectiveness, and that same year he won the consent of both sections to his policy of liberal land grants to the states in aid of railroad-building. Thereafter the rapid construction of the Illinois Central and other western roads greatly enriched the state of Illinois, converted Chicago from a frontier village into the "metropolis of the West," and made it abundantly clear to Douglas that in befriending the railroads he had made no mistake. Short of stature, but possessed of a magnificent head and massive shoulders, he was called by his admirers the "Little Giant."

The idea of a transcontinental railroad was almost as old as railroads in the United States. In the thirties Asa Whitney, a merchant *The trans-* who was engaged in the China trade, had begun to *continental* advocate that such a road should be built as a means *railroad idea* of shortening the route to the Orient. Whitney had also suggested that the government might aid in financing the project by endowing the road with a strip of land sixty miles wide along the right

[1] The histories of the period all give much attention to Douglas. T. C. Smith, *Parties and Slavery* (1906), is extremely useful. The most scholarly biographies of Douglas are Allen Johnson, *Stephen A. Douglas: a Study in American Politics* (1908); and George Fort Milton, *The Eve of Conflict: Stephen A. Douglas and the Needless War* (1934).

of way. Even before the Mexican War Whitney's arguments had won some support in Congress; after the war, with California a part of the United States and gold discovered in the newly acquired territory, converts came thick and fast. It soon became apparent, however, that there would be grave difficulty in choosing the route over which such a road was to be built. Every enterprising city in the Mississippi Valley aspired to become its eastern terminus, and the claims of New Orleans, Vicksburg, St. Louis, Chicago, and Milwaukee were elaborately set forth. In 1853 Congress, unwilling and unready to choose among so many aspirants, appropriated one hundred and fifty thousand dollars to be used by the Secretary of War in surveying a number of alternative railroad routes across the western half of the continent. In due time the surveyors reported that, at least so far as the engineering problem was concerned, a northern, a southern, and one or more central routes were equally feasible.

Douglas naturally hoped that Chicago, his official residence and the center of his somewhat extensive real-estate speculations, would be in line with the route to the West finally selected. But un- *Objections* fortunately there were serious objections to every northern *to a northern* or central way through. Such a route necessarily trav- *route* ersed much unorganized Indian territory, where the savages were none too tractable, and where the government owned no lands to grant. The proposed southern route, on the other hand, led through the state of Texas and the now fully organized territory of New Mexico. No serious Indian menace embarrassed the advocates of this route, and land grants, either from the state of Texas or from the United States, would be available for its entire length. But there was an obvious way to overcome the serious handicap from which partisans of a northern or central route suffered. The legend of the "Great American Desert" was fast breaking down, and demands that the good agricultural lands directly west of the bend of the Missouri should be opened to settlement were already insistent. Indeed, by the summer of 1853 the Commissioner of Indian Affairs had begun negotiations for the removal of the Indians from the coveted region, and a bill for the erection of the unorganized Indian country into the territory of Nebraska had passed the House of Representatives. If the Senate could only be persuaded to concur in this measure, the relative advantages of the southern railway route would be materially lessened.

Douglas, who as chairman of the Senate Committee on Territories, was beyond a doubt fully conversant with this situation, championed, early in January, 1854, the creation of the new territory. His views

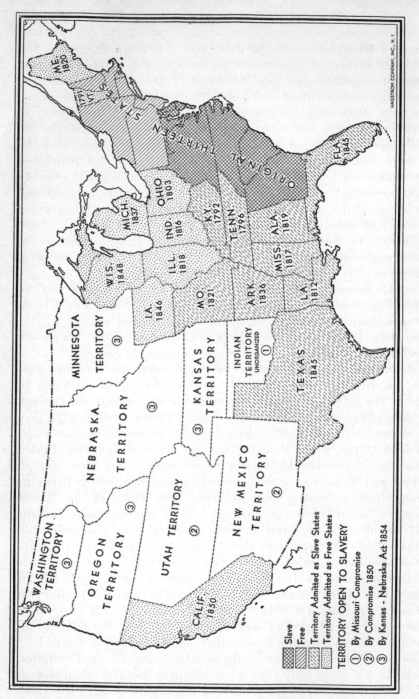

TERRITORIAL ORGANIZATION OF THE UNITED STATES IN 1854

HAGSTROM COMPANY, INC., N. Y.

TERRITORY OPEN TO SLAVERY

① By Missouri Compromise
② By Compromise 1850
③ By Kansas - Nebraska Act 1854

Slave
Free
Territory Admitted as Slave States
Territory Admitted as Free States

were set forth in an elaborate report to the Senate, a report that was fraught with far graver consequences than he could have *The Kansas-* dreamed. Knowing full well that the South would never *Nebraska* favor the creation of a new territory without some *Act* concession to slavery, he artfully suggested that the Compromise of 1850, which had left New Mexico and Utah free to decide for themselves whether they would or would not legalize slavery, had superseded the Missouri Compromise of thirty years before. The proposed new territory might, therefore, be free or slave, not as Congress should determine, but as the people of the territory should determine. Douglas's championship at this juncture of "popular sovereignty," as he called it, was shrewdly conceived, for it appealed both to the democratic instincts of the West and to the persistent hopes of the South for the extension of slave territory. Nevertheless, before the bill could pass its sponsor had to accept important amendments. Instead of one territory, two were authorized, Kansas to the west of Missouri, which presumably would be slave, and Nebraska to the west of Iowa, which presumably would be free. Also, the repeal of the Missouri Compromise, which Douglas would have preferred merely to take for granted, was specifically stated.

The debate over the Kansas-Nebraska Bill revived all the bitterness that had preceded the Compromise of 1850. Southern members of Congress, almost to the last man, supported the meas- *The undoing* ure, while practically all the northern Whigs and many *of the sec-* northern Democrats opposed it. Douglas was accused *tional truce* of deliberately undoing the sectional truce in order to obtain support from the South for his presidential candidacy in 1856, and it would be difficult to prove that no such thought ever crossed his mind. He had no aversion to slavery or to slavery extension, and his second wife, a North-Carolinian, held slaves. Moreover, he must have foreseen that the truce over slavery could not last long, and he may well have believed that the principle of popular sovereignty would furnish a better solution of the problem of slavery extension than the Missouri Compromise. Perhaps a grateful country might make its proponent President. But there is good reason to believe that the idea of a Pacific railroad west from Chicago was never long absent from his mind. Possibly, too, he was no less impressed by the demands of pro-slavery Missourians, who were greatly concerned lest their state be surrounded on three sides by free territory, than by the wishes of the South as a whole.

Whatever Douglas's motives may have been (a subject upon which historians seem destined never to agree),[1] the fires of sectional controversy once more burned bright. The Democratic Party of the North was rent violently in twain. Those who defended the act were known as Pro-Nebraska Democrats; those who opposed it as Anti-Nebraska Democrats. The Whig Party lost its last vestige of unity. Northern Whigs were almost unanimously anti-Nebraska; southern Whigs were quite as unanimously pro-Nebraska. Even the Know-Nothings were forced to take sides, and anti-Nebraska and pro-Nebraska factions brought discord to their lodges. Division of opinion, however, was for the time being confined to the North. Southerners, whether Whigs, Democrats, or Know-Nothings, stood solidly together in favor of the act.

[1] P. O. Ray, *The Repeal of the Missouri Compromise* (1909), challenged the traditional interpretation; but his views were in turn attacked by F. H. Hodder, "Genesis of the Kansas-Nebraska Act," in Wisconsin State Historical Society, *Proceedings*, 1912, pp. 69–86.

CHAPTER XXX

THE HOUSE DIVIDED

THE united front achieved by the opponents of slavery extension during the debate on the Kansas-Nebraska Act was not destined to disappear. In fact, the men who had fought together against the opening of new territory to slavery were about ready, as events proved, to forsake their old party loyal- *Birth of the Republican Party* ties, and to join in the formation of a new party that would reflect accurately the stand they had taken. So general was this sentiment that it is somewhat difficult to designate an exact time and place for the birth of the Republican Party. The superior claims of the Middle West, however, must be conceded, for in this section action was both immediate and vigorous. Here opposition to slavery on moral grounds was rife, but the western small farmers felt also that the lands of the new frontier should belong to them and their kind, and not to the southern slaveholders. At Ripon, Wisconsin, February 28, 1854, an "Anti-Nebraska" mass meeting revived the name Republican; at Jackson, Michigan, July 6, 1854, the first state-wide Republican organization was launched. By November, when the mid-term state and congressional elections were held, Republican tickets, or their equivalent under a different name, challenged the Democrats in every northwestern state, and won far more often than they lost.[1]

In the Northeast, although both Maine and Vermont voted Republican in 1854, the emergence of the new party was not quite so speedily accomplished. The decision of Seward, who was up for reelection to the United States Senate from New York and feared to change his party allegiance, did much to postpone a little longer the day of Whig dissolution. Also Know-Nothingism, by an astonishing victory in Massachusetts and a large vote in Pennsylvania and New York, proved that the anti-foreigner issue had not yet run its course. Shortly after the election the Republican tide set in. By the fall of 1855 Seward, who was generally recognized as the outstanding leader of the anti-slavery Whigs, was safe in the new party fold.

[1] A. W. Crandall, *The Early History of the Republican Party, 1854–1856* (1930).

[575]

and although the Whig Party in the Northeast died hard, it died. Know-Nothingism likewise was unable to survive the inevitable split upon the rock of slavery extension, and ultimately the bulk of the northern Know-Nothings became Republicans. Eastern Republicans, it should be noted, while embracing within their number many former abolitionists, were often quite as much motivated by their resentment against the existing southern domination of the national government as by their dislike of slavery as an institution. New slave states meant more pro-southern votes in Congress, votes that were certain to be used in favor of policies desired by the agricultural South — the low tariff, for example — but against such policies as would enhance the prosperity of the industrial Northeast.

In all sections of the North the rise of the Republican Party did serious damage to the Democrats. According to a compilation made *Decline of* by the *National Intelligencer*, the northern wing of the *the northern* Democratic Party polled nearly three hundred and fifty *Democracy* thousand fewer votes in 1854 than in 1852. Of the forty-two northern Democrats who voted for the Kansas-Nebraska Act in the House, only seven were re-elected. Both in 1854 and in 1855 states that had once been Democratic strongholds elected Republican legislatures and Republican state officers. Eager to clear himself of responsibility for the calamity that had befallen his party, Douglas blamed these results mainly upon the rise of the Know-Nothings. But the statistics did not bear him out; neither did his own alarming loss of popularity throughout the North. Denounced as a traitor for his reopening of the slavery dispute, he was compared to Benedict Arnold and Judas Iscariot. He could have traveled, he later admitted, "from Boston to Chicago by the light of his own burning effigies." In Chicago, where his popularity had once been unbounded, he was greeted with groans and hisses by an unruly audience that finally drove him in a temper from the platform.

Democratic losses in the North, however, were not duplicated in the South. There the passage of the Kansas-Nebraska Act was regarded as a defeat for the hated abolitionists, and a timely recognition of southern rights. Even if Kansas did not become a slave state, as some Southerners had begun to fear, the doctrine of popular sovereignty might be used to advantage elsewhere, in Cuba, for example. Not only did the southern Democrats hold their party lines intact after the passage of the act; they made substantial gains. The Whig Party of the South, like the Whig Party of the North, was in process of liquidation, and many southern Whigs became Democrats. Others, unable to join hands so suddenly with their traditional enemies, broke the fall by becoming Know-Nothings, or "Americans," for a season. Some of the Know-Nothing leaders were shrewd enough to try to make a new issue for their party by requiring of their members an oath to protect and defend the union of the states. Most Southerners, however, chose to interpret this oath as meaning merely that the North should cease its opposition to slavery expansion, hence the difference in principle between southern Democrats and southern Know-Nothings was slight. Perhaps the "Solid South" had not yet arrived, but it was on the way.

The real test of popular sovereignty as a remedy for the sectional controversy over slavery came in Kansas. Under the terms of the Kansas-Nebraska Act territorial governments were set *Kansas and* up both in Kansas and in Nebraska, but the beginnings *Nebraska* of Nebraska Territory attracted little attention. Southerners as well as Northerners conceded that the Iowans who were moving over into Nebraska would be certain to exclude slavery from the territory; and this they promptly did. Nor did many settlers come; indeed, for a time Nebraska was less a place of abode than a highway to the Far West. From its river towns — Omaha, Plattsmouth, and Nebraska City — traders and emigrants set off for Oregon, Utah, and California, but only a few remained to take lands and settle down. With Kansas it was quite otherwise. No sooner was this territory authorized than rivalry broke out between North and South to see which section should settle it, and thus be in position to determine whether it should be free or slave. In the normal course of events Missourians would have taken the lead in the settlement of Kansas, just as Iowans without much outside interference were moving slowly into Nebraska. And, whether correctly or otherwise, it was generally assumed that these Missourians would make Kansas a slave territory and ultimately a slave state. But northern anti-slavery men set themselves the task of heading off this "normal course of events." Organizations to aid emigrants were formed in New England and elsewhere with the avowed intention of putting enough anti-slavery men in Kansas to ensure the defeat of the pro-slavery element when the new government should be organized. In such a competition the South was at a distinct disadvantage, for it had far less man-power to mobilize than the North. Pro-slavery Missourians, however, organized themselves into secret lodges and prepared to march over into Kansas, whenever occasion should demand, to stuff the ballot-boxes. With instinctive common sense the pro-slavery and anti-slavery emigrants to Kansas settled at a considerable distance from each other. Most of the pro-slavery men settled close to the Missouri River, and founded such towns as Atchison and Leavenworth. The anti-slavery men, on the other hand, went farther into the interior, where they founded Lawrence and Topeka.[1]

Popular sovereignty in Kansas President Pierce, recognizing that the rôle of a Kansas governor would be difficult, had chosen an able Pennsylvania lawyer, Andrew H. Reeder, for the place. Reeder was a Douglas Democrat of good reputation, but without scruple as to the morality of slavery. In November, 1854, soon after his arrival in Kansas, an election for territorial delegate was held that resulted in an easy victory for the pro-slavery faction. The reasons for this were obvious. Some seventeen hundred Missourians had crossed the border and cast their votes for the pro-slavery candidate, while many of the anti-slavery men, believing that little was at stake in the election, did not bother to vote. The next spring, however, the real test came with the selection of a territorial legislature; for this body, under the terms of the Kansas-Nebraska Act, might vote to establish or prohibit slavery in the territory. After the election was over it was found that with less than fifteen hundred legal voters in all of Kansas over six thousand votes had been cast. Every resident knew that the election was a fraud. Missourians in armed bands had taken possession of the polls and had voted in the pro-slavery candidates. Governor Reeder was outraged, and set aside the returns in every district where a protest was made, but lack of time and threats of violence kept down the number of protests so that a pro-slavery majority was safely seated. As soon as the legislature met, it enacted a drastic slave code, which Reeder promptly vetoed, only to have the obnoxious measures passed over his veto. Completely disgusted with popular sovereignty as it worked out in practice, Reeder did not hesitate to make his views public. Had the President stood behind his appointee, no doubt the latter would have done his best to obtain an honest vote and an honest count at the earliest opportunity.

Franklin Pierce on Kansas But Franklin Pierce (1804–69)[2] was not to be depended upon in such an emergency. Handsome, a good lawyer, and a polished public speaker, he had entered the Presidency with the hearty good-will of almost the entire American public. Judging from his record as a member for short terms each in both houses of Congress and as a volunteer officer in the Mexican War,

---

[1] W. E. Miller, *The Peopling of Kansas* (1906); L. W. Spring, *Kansas: the Prelude to the War for the Union* (1885).

[2] R. F. Nichols, *Franklin Pierce* (1931). See also, by the same author, *The Democratic Machine, 1850–1854* (1923).

there was good reason to suppose that, in spite of his relative obscurity, he would rise to the requirements of his high office. But these expectations were doomed to quick disappointment. Eager to please, he was always in an agony of indecision, for whichever way he decided someone would be offended: he was known, on occasion, to promise the same office to two different applicants. Such a weakling was bound to be at the mercy of the strongest-willed among his advisers. When the Kansas-Nebraska Act was before Congress, the pressure exerted by Douglas and his friends brought the President, after much wavering, to the support of the measure. Now, with the southern influence strongly dominant among his advisers, he was soon persuaded that the pro-slavery cause in Kansas deserved his support. The fair-minded Reeder must go, and in his place a man more satisfactory to the pro-slavery element must be chosen. When Reeder, after a long correspondence with the President, refused to resign, the President removed him, to make way for an Ohio politician, Wilson Shannon, whose pro-slavery sympathies were well known.

When the anti-slavery Kansans realized the hopelessness of trying to win a territorial election, they decided to follow the precedent recently set by California for establishing a state government in advance of congressional permission. Accordingly they elected delegates to a constitutional convention which met, October 23, at Topeka, and drew up a free state constitution. Before the end of the year this document was submitted to the people at the polls, and, since the pro-slavery faction did not participate in the election, was adopted by a one-sided vote. Under its terms a governor and legislature were promptly chosen, and Congress was petitioned to admit Kansas as a state. This action President Pierce denounced as treasonous. The pro-slavery territorial government, he told Congress, was the only lawful government in Kansas, and as such was deserving of the full support of the United States.

Douglas had claimed that popular sovereignty would exile the debate over slavery from the halls of Congress, and put it where it belonged, in the territories concerned. The speciousness of his reasoning was now fully apparent, for in spite of Pierce's contention Congress, not the President, had authority *The Sumner–Brooks episode* over the admission of new states, and Congress, not the President, must decide whether to leave the pro-slavery territorial government in control, or heed the request of the free-state party and admit Kansas as a state. After a prolonged struggle over the Speakership, the House of Representatives voted in March, 1856, that the new Speaker, a

Republican, should appoint a committee of three to inquire into the trouble in Kansas, and report back to the House. In midsummer the committee presented majority and minority reports, neither of which helped toward a solution of the vexing problem, and both of which added fuel to the flames. The debate on Kansas in the Senate reached its climax on May 19–20, when Charles Sumner of Massachusetts spoke at great length on the "Crime against Kansas." During this address he denounced Senator Andrew P. Butler of South Carolina in the most offensive language, and charged the state he represented with "shameful imbecility" during the American Revolution. For such abuse, according to the southern code, he might possibly have deserved a caning, but the attack made upon him afterward by Preston Brooks, a relative of Butler's and a member of the House, far exceeded any code of proprieties. Brooks, who was a young man, approached Sumner while the latter was seated at his desk in the Senate Chamber, upbraided him for his libelous language, and then, while the Senator was still sitting, beat him over the head with a heavy gutta-percha cane until he fell to the floor covered with blood. The injuries inflicted were so serious that Sumner was unable to resume his regular duties for five years, and his health was permanently impaired.

While the futility of popular sovereignty as a remedy for the dispute over slavery expansion was thus being revealed in Washington, its *Violence in Kansas* results in Kansas were no less unfortunate. There the "border ruffians" who crossed over from Missouri from time to time in order to carry elections did not hesitate to use violence, and they were soon met in kind by the free-state men from the North. Collections were taken up at public meetings throughout the northern states, not only to send more anti-slavery emigrants to Kansas, but also to arm them with the rifles they might need to defend themselves. According to Henry Ward Beecher, who addressed many such meetings, these Sharps rifles might be "a greater moral agency" in Kansas than the Bible, hence such weapons were generally referred to as "Beecher's Bibles." The day before the assault on Sumner a proslavery posse of about a thousand men, consisting mainly of border ruffians, was assembled by the federal marshal for Kansas territory to assist him in serving writs upon the "treasonous" anti-slavery officers of the free-state government at Lawrence. The arrests were made without resistance, but the "posse" did not withdraw until it had destroyed all the local newspaper offices, set fire to a number of buildings, and thoroughly sacked the city.

The self-appointed avenger of this outrage was John Brown of Osawatomie, an abolitionist fanatic whose family was strongly tainted with insanity. Brown reckoned that from first to last five free-state men had been killed in Kansas by their opponents, and that an equal number of pro-slavery men must die. Three days after the raid on Lawrence he and four of his sons, a son-in-law, and two neighbors murdered in cold blood five pro-slavery settlers who lived along Pottawatomie Creek. This wild deed most of the free-state men in Kansas were at pains to disavow, but reprisals were in order, and they were not long in coming. Attempts to arrest Brown failed, but soon armed bands of free-staters and border ruffians were wandering about, attacking each other at sight, and making life for the peaceful settler a nightmare. The "Civil War in Kansas" which thus began was ended presently by a new governor, John White Geary, who did not hesitate to invoke the proffered aid of federal troops. But altogether probably two hundred lives were lost.

It was in an atmosphere surcharged with excitement over the attack on Sumner and "Bleeding Kansas" that the presidential campaign and election of 1856 took place. The logic of the situation *Presidential* demanded that the Democrats should renominate Pierce, *campaign* who had stood as firmly by popular sovereignty as he was *of 1856* ever able to stand by anything; or, if not Pierce, then Douglas, the foremost champion of the doctrine. But both Pierce and Douglas had made a host of enemies, particularly among the Democrats of the North; hence the nomination went to James Buchanan of Pennsylvania, whose absence as minister to England had saved him from too close identification with any point of view. Despite the overwhelming evidence from Kansas to the contrary, the Democratic National Convention maintained in its platform that the doctrine of popular sovereignty was "the only sound and safe solution of the slavery question." The Republicans, as eager to serve availability as the Democrats, overlooked the claims of Seward and Chase, their best-known leaders, to choose as their standard-bearer John C. Frémont, the glamorous "Pathfinder of the West." Their platform revived the Free-Soil doctrine that Congress had the constitutional right and the moral duty to prohibit the expansion of slavery into any of the territories of the United States. The Americans, or Know-Nothings, and a remnant of the Whigs held separate conventions, but nominated the same candidate, ex-President Fillmore, and adopted platforms that sought in the main to avoid sectionalism by an insistent demand for the preservation of the Union.

The Democrats won an unexpectedly easy victory. Their party

alone, as events soon proved, was truly national, and it profited materially from that fact. The Republican Party was so definitely a northern organization that in eleven southern states the names of its candidates did not even appear on the ballot. The Know-Nothings were almost as strictly southern, for their convention, under pressure from the southern delegates, had declared that territories should be permitted "to regulate their domestic and social affairs in their own mode." This could mean only one thing: popular sovereignty. Northerners who believed in Douglas's doctrine generally preferred to vote the Democratic ticket, while those who were opposed to it lined up with the Republicans. Overconfident as a result of their successes in 1854, the Republicans really expected to win. They made a whirlwind campaign, patterned on the Whig tactics of 1840, with "Bleeding Kansas" as their principal issue. But the country was frightened by the specter of disunion, and preferred a national party to one that represented only a section. Eleven northern states cast 114 votes for Frémont, but five northern states and every southern state but one cast a total of 174 votes for Buchanan. While the American Party furnished strong opposition to the Democrats in the South, Fillmore carried only one state, Maryland, with 8 electoral votes. Both houses of Congress were safely Democratic.

James Buchanan (1791–1868)[1] was nearly sixty-five years of age when he assumed the Presidency, and, unlike Pierce, he had had ample *James Buchanan* experience in politics. Curiously, he had begun his political career as a Federalist, and had moved over into the Democratic Party only when the Federalist Party had ceased to exist. After he had served for ten years in the House as a representative from Pennsylvania, he was sent by President Jackson in 1832 as minister to Russia, but returned two years later to enter the United States Senate. Here he remained for more than two decades. Afterward he was Secretary of State under Polk, minister to England under Pierce, and at all times a persistent aspirant to the Presidency. His opposition to the Wilmot Proviso and his ardent championship of expansion marked him as a "dough-face," that is, a "northern man with southern principles." Beyond a doubt he was devoted to the Union, but the conservatism of old age tended to confirm him in the belief that the only way to preserve the Union was to permit the southern leaders to have their way.

---

[1] G. T. Curtis, *Life of James Buchanan* (2 vols., 1883). Many interesting letters bearing on the Buchanan administration are printed in *Robert Tyler, Southern Rights Champion, 1847–1866*, edited by Philip G. Auchampaugh (1934).

Two days after Buchanan's inauguration the Supreme Court of the United States handed down a decision in the case of *Dred Scott vs. Sandford* that put a new aspect upon the dispute over slavery in the territories. This decision did not come un- solicited. The Kansas-Nebraska Act had assumed that the Supreme Court might have a final word to say on the subject; and Southerners, confident that the Court would be on their side, were eager for its pronouncement. Even the President-elect, shortly before his inauguration, seems to have used his influence to swing a wavering justice into line. Seven of the justices were Democrats, one was a Whig, and one a Republican; and of the seven Democrats five were from the South. Surely such a Court would end for all time the Republican pretension that Congress had a right to exclude slavery from the territories. No doubt the majority of the Court, including the venerable Chief Justice Taney, were genuinely persuaded that the weight of their opinion would be sufficient to bring the heated controversy to an end.

The Dred Scott case

The Dred Scott case offered a satisfactory opportunity for the Court to declare itself.[1] Dred Scott was a Negro who until 1834 had legally been held in bondage in the slave state of Missouri. After that date his master, an army surgeon, removed, taking Dred with him, first to Illinois, a free state, and then to Minnesota Territory, where, under the terms of the Missouri Compromise, slavery was also forbidden. Ultimately Dred was brought back to Missouri. Here he was induced by some interested abolitionists to bring suit for his freedom on the ground that his residence in free territory had set him free. Evidence that there was connivance between the defense and the prosecution appears from the fact that during the litigation the ownership of Dred was transferred to a New-Yorker named Sandford. A federal court was then asked to assume jurisdiction on the ground that the suit lay between the citizens of different states. Thus the case could be, and was, promptly passed on up to the United States Supreme Court, where it was argued first in the spring of 1856, and, because of the sharp divergence of views it evoked among the justices, a second time in December of the same year. Naturally these proceedings had won for the case much publicity, and President Buchanan, who knew in advance what the decision would be, saw nothing improper about venturing the hope in his inaugural address that the forthcoming opinion

---

[1] G. T. Curtis, *Constitutional History of the United States* (2 vols., 1889–96), contains a chapter on this subject. The traditional account is significantly amended by F. H. Hodder, "Some Phases of the Dred Scott Case," in the *Mississippi Valley Historical Review*, vol. XVI, pp. 3–22. See also E. S. Corwin, "The Dred Scott Decision," in the *American Historical Review*, vol. XVII, pp. 52–69.

of the Court would settle with finality the status of slavery in the territories.

Chief Justice Taney spoke for the seven Democratic justices. First of all, he denied emphatically the right of the lower federal court to *Taney's* assume jurisdiction in the case. Dred Scott, said the Chief *opinion* Justice, was not a citizen of Missouri within the meaning of the Constitution; hence he could neither sue nor be sued in the federal courts. This opinion the Court might have based, as some of the assenting justices would have been more content to do, on the ground that Dred Scott, whatever his status in Illinois or Minnesota, was at the time he brought suit a slave in Missouri, and so not a citizen. But the Chief Justice had no notion of dodging what to him appeared to be an important issue. Negroes who were of the African race and the descendants of slaves, he asserted, were not and could not become citizens of a state in the sense in which the word citizen was used when the Constitution of the United States was adopted. At that time, according to the Chief Justice, such persons were commonly regarded as of an inferior order of beings who had no rights that a white man need respect. So far as the Constitution of the United States was concerned, their status had not changed during the intervening years. The inference was clear, therefore, that Dred Scott's suit would have been thrown out even if he had been free, and not a slave.

But the Chief Justice took great pains to point out that Dred was not free, that neither his residence in a free state nor in territory north of the Missouri Compromise line could possibly have made him free. Precedent was cited to prove that each state had the right to determine for itself the status of a slave who had resided temporarily in a free state, and the Missouri courts had held that Dred was still a slave. As for the territorial residence, the Chief Justice aligned himself and the Court with the most extreme of the southern extremists. Congress, he said, had exceeded its authority in forbidding slavery in that part of the Louisiana Purchase north of 36° 30′. Slave property in the territories was as much protected by the Constitution as any other kind of property. The Missouri Compromise was therefore unconstitutional, and Dred Scott had been no less a slave in Minnesota than in Missouri.

While the opinion of the Chief Justice was officially regarded as the opinion of the Court, each of the nine justices submitted a separate *Lack of* argument. Five of the Democratic members agreed in the *unanimity* main with the reasoning of the Chief Justice, but one of *in the Court* them, Justice Nelson of New York, held that the case should have been decided strictly on the ground that the highest court of

CHIEF JUSTICE ROGER B. TANEY

Missouri, by ruling that Dred was a slave and not a citizen, had already settled the only point that the Court need consider. Justice Curtis of Massachusetts and Justice McLean of Ohio in dissenting opinions presented much historical evidence to controvert the argument that Negroes had not been regarded as eligible to citizenship at the time the Constitution was adopted, and cited also a long list of precedents to uphold the right of Congress to forbid slavery in the territories. Indeed, the certainty that Justice McLean, who was known to be an ardent Republican with presidential ambitions, would include in his dissenting opinion the contentions of his party on the subject of slavery in the territories had undoubtedly had much to do with persuading the majority of the Court to present the other side of the argument.

It was idle to suppose that a decision so partisan from a Court so divided could settle anything with finality. The Republicans refused to concede that the status of slavery in the territories had actually been before the Court at all. If Dred Scott was not a citizen, that fact alone required demonstration. All the rest of the argument was irrelevant and gratuitous, or as the lawyers put it, *obiter dicta*. Thus the opinion of the Court that slavery in the territories was protected by the Constitution had no legal standing, and could not be regarded as binding precedent. According to a writer for the strongly Republican *New York Tribune* the arguments of the Chief Justice deserved "no more respect than any pro-slavery stump-speech made during the late presidential canvass." Some future Court should, and must, decide otherwise. The duty of the Republicans was clear. They must obtain control of the national government, and then so alter the personnel of the Court as to make sure of a correct decision.

Southern Democrats, on the other hand, were greatly elated by the stand the Court had taken. They denied indignantly, and with fair *Southern* logic, the argument that the status of slavery in the terri- *approval of* tories had not properly been before the Court. The deci- *the decision* sion, they insisted, had settled that matter for all time. The Republicans, in standing out against the highest court in the land, were showing their true colors. To gain their partisan ends they would willingly subvert the Constitution itself. Slavery, said the Southerners, must now be allowed to spread. It must henceforth be regarded as legal in Kansas and in every other territory of the United States. Northern Democrats were by no means so pleased with the decision. Many of them realized that Douglas's doctrine of popular sovereignty, to which they had pinned their faith, could not easily be reconciled with the Dred Scott decision. If slavery could not be excluded from a territory by law of Congress, how then could the legislature of a territory, which owed its authority to Congress, exclude slavery? For the moment, however, they refused to admit the contradiction and said little about it.

Once more the attention of the country turned to Kansas. Eager to prevent a recurrence of trouble in that quarter, President Buchanan persuaded Robert J. Walker of Mississippi, a man of far *Events in* greater ability than could ordinarily be obtained for such *Kansas* a post, to accept the governorship of the new territory. Walker promptly called an election for delegates to a constitutional convention, and urged the free-state men to participate. This, however, they refused to do, for they felt little confidence in the fairness of the Buchanan administration, whose agent Walker was. In consequence, the pro-slavery element carried the election overwhelmingly, and in October, 1857, a convention held at Lecompton framed a pro-slavery constitution. Determined to take no chances, the Lecompton convention failed to give the voters an opportunity to reject the document it had framed, but provided merely that they might vote for or against the further introduction of slaves. Whichever way the vote went, slavery in Kansas would be fully protected. Undeceived by this ruse, the free-state men again refused to vote, so that the constitution was carried with the more extreme pro-slavery clause. In the fall elections for a territorial legislature, however, the free-state men not only voted, but thanks to the rejection by Governor Walker and the territorial secretary of many fraudulent votes, they won. Thereupon the legislature resubmitted the Lecompton constitution, this time with the full alternative of adoption or rejection. Now the pro-slavery men refused to vote, so that the constitution that had just been so easily ratified was almost unanimously rejected. But the relative strength of the two sides was clearly revealed. In support of the Lecompton constitution the pro-slavery forces had cast only 6226 votes, whereas the free-state men only a few weeks later had cast 10,226 votes against it. That Kansas wished to be free and not slave was fully apparent to any unprejudiced observer.

Unhappily, President Buchanan could not be so described. His most trusted advisers were Southerners, and ordinarily he reflected their views. In November, 1857, he forced Walker out *Douglas* of office because the governor's rejection of fraudulent pro- *on Kansas* slavery votes had given the legislature of Kansas to the free-state men. Moreover, in December, 1857, when Congress convened, the President made clear his desire to see Kansas admitted promptly as a slave state. Two months later he submitted to Congress the now thoroughly dis-

NEW YORK TO PHILADELPHIA BANK:
"Going to suspend yourself, eh?
Is that your Brotherly Love?"

A CARTOON OF THE PANIC OF 1857

credited Lecompton constitution, and urged its acceptance. All this was too much for Douglas. His doctrine of popular sovereignty rested upon the assumption that a majority, even in a territory, had the right to decide for or against slavery, and now the President proposed to make Kansas a slave state against its clearly expressed will. This travesty upon popular sovereignty Douglas denounced with all the vigor at his command. Such a course required courage of a high order, for it meant for the Illinois senator not only a break with the administration, but also the certain loss of his recently won popularity in the South. Many other northern Democrats agreed with him, however, and while the President was able to force his policy upon the Senate, he failed with it in the House.

At length a compromise measure, known as the English Bill, was adopted. According to its terms Kansas might vote for a third time on the Lecompton constitution, and in case a majority of the voters approved that document, might be immediately admitted as a state.

[588]

In case the constitution was rejected, statehood would be delayed until the population of Kansas should reach the figure set by the congressional ratio for a representative in Congress, then 93,600. This unsavory threat was insufficient to overawe the free-staters in Kansas, who again voted down the Lecompton constitution, and in consequence saw their chance of winning statehood delayed until after a number of southern states had withdrawn from the Union.

Meantime the panic of 1857 had burst upon the country, and had left in its train a trying period of economic depression.[1] The prosperity of the early years of the decade had carried with it the germs *The panic* of its own dissolution. The success of the railroads tempted *of 1857* them to an unreasonable overexpansion. Lines were built into unsettled areas where for years to come there could be little hope of profits. Manufacturers, likewise, eager to keep pace with the ever-growing markets, were soon well ahead of them. Producers of foodstuffs were lulled into a false sense of security by the abnormal demand of a war-torn Europe for American grain. At best the prices that the farmers received were none too good, and the loss of the European market when the Crimean War came to an end was calamitous. Moreover, the boom period, like every other of its kind, was accompanied by an enormous amount of speculation. To a great extent this took the same form that it had taken before the panic of 1837, speculation in land. Town sites along the lines of projected railroads, city lots in the rapidly growing industrial centers, desirable farm lands everywhere, but particularly in the West, tempted investors to over-buy.

The situation was seriously aggravated by the weakness of the banking system upon which the country was forced to depend. Ever since Jackson's successful war on the Bank of the United States, *Weakness of* the country had been without a national bank, and while *the banking* numerous state-chartered banks existed, they were of *system* widely varying merit. While some of the banks were sound, most of these were eastern institutions, and even in that section the reserves required by law were often too small and the credit extensions too great. There was much confusion, too, because of the plentiful, variegated, and easily counterfeited bank-note currency. A *Bank-Note Reporter*, issued at frequent intervals, undertook to keep subscribers posted on the fluctuating values of the numerous issues of state bank-notes, but with indifferent success. That the currency of the country, as a whole, was seriously inflated, no one could doubt. During the winter of 1856–57 business interests became acutely conscious of the economic breakers

[1] C. F. Dunbar, *Economic Essays* (1904), contains a study of the panic of 1857.

ahead, and when in August, 1857, a supposedly powerful financial house, the Ohio Life Insurance and Trust Company, closed its doors, the panic was on. The news of this failure, and of the numerous others that followed it, was spread more rapidly than could have been possible but for the electric telegraph, and a truly "psychological" panic developed. Even financially sound businesses went into bankruptcy. The panic was soon over, but the depression lasted for several years. During this period railroad-building was at a standstill, many factories remained closed, speculators took heavy losses, farmers were unable to pay their debts, and unemployed workmen thronged the city streets.

Strange as it may seem, the economic depression accentuated to an extraordinary degree the bitterness of the sectional controversy. Because of the hard times the pro-southern administration of President Buchanan lost ground throughout the North. Particularly aggrieved were the northeastern industrialists, to whose demand that the hard-pressed American manufacturer should be aided by a higher tariff the southern leaders turned deaf ears. Southerners generally regarded the additional revenues that such a tariff would bring as unnecessary and undesirable, for the government had accumulated a surplus during the period of prosperity and these funds, locked safely away in sub-treasury vaults while the panic was on, seemed sufficient to outlast the lean years. More and more the conservatives of the North, who had long tolerated the leadership of the South only because it had seemed the only way to secure national harmony, swung their support to the new and sectional Republican Party. But if the North drew more closely together, so also did the South. Strangely, the Cotton Kingdom had almost escaped the depression. Naturally some economic distress was felt in the South, but all through the years that brought such calamity to the North, the world demand for cotton continued to mount, and the price of cotton remained high. Mindful of the reproaches that had long been hurled against them, the southern leaders now claimed that the superiority of their economic system had won singular vindication. "The wealth of the South," said *De Bow's Review*, a New Orleans journal, "is permanent and real, that of the North fugitive and fictitious." And yet the uneasiness of the South at the continued expansion of the North, in spite of the depression, was ill-concealed. The advance of the northern frontier went on through good times and bad. Minnesota was admitted to the Union early in 1858, statehood for Oregon could not possibly be long postponed, and northern emigrants seemed destined to take both Kansas and Nebraska.

The mid-term elections of 1858 revealed clearly how deep the sectional line of cleavage had become. Throughout the North the pro-southern national administration was disastrously defeated. In *Elections* Pennsylvania, the President's own state, a coalition of *of 1858* Republicans, Know-Nothings, and anti-Lecompton Democrats carried all but three of the twenty-five congressional districts, a loss of twelve seats for the administration. This result was due in considerable part to the stagnation in the Pennsylvania iron industry, a condition which, according to the Republicans, the low rates of the Democratic Tariff of 1857 had made inevitable. In New England, New York, and the Northwest, where the tariff issue was not so prominent, the rebuke to the administration was more pointedly upon its handling of affairs in Kansas. In the South, however, the President's pro-slavery policy was cordially supported. "The abolitionists," said Senator Hammond of South Carolina during the campaign, "have at length ... compelled us into a union — a union not for aggression, but for defense." Nevertheless, the solid support of the South was not enough to save the day. While the Senate remained safely Democratic, the administration lost its majority in the House.

Undoubtedly the most spectacular contest of the campaign took place in Illinois, where Stephen A. Douglas fought desperately to retain his seat in the United States Senate. Douglas's break *The senato-* with the Buchanan administration over its policy in Kansas *rial contest* had served to rehabilitate his reputation in the North. *in Illinois* Popular sovereignty, it appeared, would, if honestly applied, ensure that Kansas, and practically every other western territory also, would be free. What more could even a Republican ask? So pleased were many of the eastern Republicans with Douglas's new stand that they openly urged their Illinois friends not to oppose him for re-election. Some went so far as to say that Douglas would ultimately join the Republicans, and that he might possibly be their candidate for the Presidency in 1860. But the Illinois Republicans, who knew Douglas for himself as well as for the enemies he had made, had no notion of permitting the election to go by default. To oppose Douglas they settled upon Abraham Lincoln, a Springfield lawyer who was well known throughout the state for his political sagacity and his forceful public speaking.[1] Lincoln had served one term in Congress during the Polk administration, he had barely missed election to the United States Senate by an anti-Nebraska legislature in 1855, and he had received strong

[1] A. J. Beveridge, *Abraham Lincoln, 1809–1858* (2 vols., 1928), is the most scholarly study of Lincoln's early career.

support for the vice-presidential nomination on the Frémont ticket in 1856. Far from being an obscure backwoodsman, he was the best man the Republicans of Illinois could put forward against Douglas, as the Senator himself well knew.

The choice of Douglas's successor rested, of course, with the Illinois legislature, and so deep was the antagonism of the Buchanan administration for Douglas that administration Democrats were nominated to oppose the Douglas candidates in nearly every legislative district of the state. Ostensibly the administration sought to win seats enough to hold the balance of power in the legislature, and thus be in position to force the election of some other Democrat than Douglas. But no one was deceived. The Buchanan following in Illinois was negligible, and, except for the patronage at the disposal of the President, would have been non-existent. Actually, the only possible effect of the administration tickets upon the contest would be to draw enough votes from the Douglas candidates to ensure that in a majority of the districts their Republican opponents would win. Had the administration openly announced its support of Lincoln, it could hardly have helped him as much.

Lincoln, in accepting his nomination, made a prophetic statement:

> "A house divided against itself cannot stand." I believe this government cannot endure permanently half slave and half free. I do not expect the Union to be dissolved — I do not expect the house to fall — but I do expect it will cease to be divided. It will become all one thing or all the other. Either the opponents of slavery will arrest the further spread of it, and place it where the public mind shall rest in the belief that it is in the course of ultimate extinction; or its advocates will push it forward till it shall become alike lawful in all the States, old as well as new — North as well as South.

The radicalism of this statement pleased Douglas greatly, and on his return to Illinois, after a "magnificent welcome" in Chicago, he accused Lincoln of urging a "war of sections until one or the other shall be subdued." As against this fratricidal doctrine Douglas reaffirmed his faith in "the great principle of the Kansas-Nebraska Bill, the right of the people to decide for themselves." Lincoln was at once put on the defensive, and the better to cope with his skillful adversary he challenged Douglas to a series of joint debates. The challenge was promptly accepted, and arrangements were made for seven different meetings, one in each of the seven congressional districts of the state.

The Lincoln-Douglas debates attracted widespread notice, not only in Illinois, where eager throngs attended them, but throughout the nation at large. Douglas was the outstanding northern Democrat, and

[592]

ABRAHAM LINCOLN

his political life was at stake. More than that, if he lost, the northern
The Lincoln– Democracy had little chance to retain a place in the party
Douglas councils; if he won, his title to the Democratic nomination
debates in 1860 could scarcely be denied. Lincoln was hardly
known outside of Illinois, but his bold words, and his temerity in challenging the able Douglas to a joint debate, awakened an interest in him
that grew as the debate went on. Accounts of its progress, and long
excerpts from the speeches delivered, appeared in nearly every metro-
politan paper, and in many lesser journals as well. Douglas, in his
immediate effect upon an audience, clearly had the advantage, and his
re-election to the Senate occasioned no surprise. On the other hand,
the smashing attacks that Lincoln made upon his opponent's "great
principle" carried conviction to many thoughtful hearers and readers.

Two points Lincoln succeeded in making with telling effectiveness.
One was that Douglas did not regard slavery as morally wrong. Repeatedly Lincoln forced from his adversary the statement, "I don't
care whether slavery is voted down, or voted up." The Republican
Party did care. If Douglas did not care, if he could not agree that
slavery was an evil that must not be allowed to spread, then he had no
title whatever to consideration for the Republican presidential nomination in 1860. With uncanny skill Lincoln also brought to the attention
of the country the contradiction between the doctrine of popular sovereignty and the Dred Scott decision. "Can the people of a United
States territory," he asked Douglas at Freeport, "against the wish of
any citizen of the United States, exclude slavery from its limits prior
to the formation of a state constitution?" If popular sovereignty
meant anything at all, Douglas must answer in the affirmative, and this
he promptly did. By "unfriendly legislation" or even by a refusal to
enact friendly legislation, he declared, a territorial legislature might
effectively exclude slavery, whatever the Supreme Court might say "as
to the abstract question whether slavery may or may not go into a territory." In short, the Dred Scott decision in its practical effect meant
nothing at all.

Douglas's "Freeport Doctrine" satisfied the northern Democrats
and had much to do with his success in winning re-election to the Senate,
but the South, already deeply incensed by his stand on the Lecompton
constitution, was now completely alienated. To the pro-slavery leaders
popular sovereignty had been pleasing enough when it furnished an
unexpected avenue for the expansion of slavery, but popular sovereignty
as an obstacle in the way of the far more gratifying doctrine of the Dred
Scott decision was wholly devoid of charm. "We have a right of pro-

tection for our slave property in the territories," Senator Brown of Mississippi maintained. "The Constitution, as expounded by the Supreme Court, awards it. We demand it, and we mean to have it." Perhaps unwittingly, Lincoln had driven home the wedge between the northern and the southern wings of the Democratic Party that was to make Republican victory a certainty in the next presidential election.

After the elections were over, the sectional dispute raged on with ever-increasing acrimony. Whatever the North desired, Congress, unchanged in personnel until after the fourth of March, was at great pains to deny. President Buchanan, deeply impressed by the defeat his party had received in Pennsylvania, urged a revision of the tariff upward, but southern opposition prevented the adoption of such a conciliatory course. The Pacific railroad project, upon which the North had now set its heart, was likewise done to death, for the South feared that such a measure might result in the further aggrandizement of the North. A homestead bill, long demanded by the small farmers and free laborers of the North, met an identical fate, for Southern leaders contended that its primary purpose was to promote the emigration of free-state settlers to the territories. In the House the bill passed with only three southern members voting for it; in the Senate southern influence prevented it from coming to a vote at all. Southern orators waxed eloquent over the fact that throughout the North the Fugitive Slave Law had virtually become a dead letter. In many northern states "personal liberty laws," artfully contrived by Republican legislatures to "nullify" the federal law, hampered the federal officers; nearly always a hostile public opinion did the rest. In Oberlin, Ohio, several respectable citizens cheerfully stood trial and went to jail for their open rescue of a fugitive from his captors. Northern orators found cause for alarm at the repeated violations in the South of the federal law against the importation of slaves. Douglas placed the number of slaves illegally brought into the country during the preceding year at fifteen thousand. A convention of prominent Southerners, held in May, 1859, at Vicksburg, warmly advocated the reopening of the African slave trade.

Growing intensity of the sectional dispute

As if matters were not already bad enough, John Brown of Osawatomie now re-emerged.[1] By one means or another he had escaped arrest for the Pottawatomie murders, and had even conducted a successful expedition into Missouri to liberate some slaves who were about to be sold. A far more ambi-

John Brown at Harper's Ferry

[1] Of the many lives of John Brown, few escape bias. Probably the most satisfactory is O. G. Villard, *John Brown, 1800–1859* (1910).

tious project now took form in his ill-balanced mind. He would put himself at the head of a small body of trusted men, fortify a rendezvous in the mountains of western Virginia, and from time to time make raids into the neighboring plantation area to free slaves. These slaves would then be armed, and from this small beginning would grow at length a powerful war on slavery throughout the South. Slave property would soon lose its value; all the slaves would have to be freed. The scheme was fantastic, and destined to certain failure, but to every criticism Brown would reply, "If God be for us, who can be against us?" He traveled East, laid his plans before some of the leading abolitionists, and actually got from them considerable financial aid. Without their consent or knowledge, however, he finally decided to make his first blow an attack on the United States Arsenal at Harper's Ferry. The capture of this well-known arsenal, he reasoned, would not only provide him with arms, but would serve also "as a trumpet" to rally the slaves to his standard. On the night of October 16, 1859, with only eighteen followers, he struck, and since the arsenal was virtually without military defense succeeded easily in taking it. Next morning fighting broke out between Brown and the citizens of Harper's Ferry. Soon militia companies from neighboring towns joined in the fray, and presently Colonel Robert E. Lee, with a detachment of United States marines, restored order by capturing Brown and four of his men. Ten others of the attacking party lay dead, and four had escaped.

The reaction of the country to this extraordinary event was ominous in the extreme. The South refused to regard it as the act of an irre-
Reaction of the country sponsible madman, but insisted instead that such an outrage was precisely what was to be expected from the teachings of the abolitionists and their Republican allies. Stories that influential members of the Republican Party had been in conference with Brown were assiduously circulated. The North, on the other hand, was less shocked than it should have been. To incite slave insurrection with all its attendant horrors was indefensible, and yet John Brown's plan, despite his protestations to the contrary, could at best have succeeded in nothing else. When Brown, after a fair if somewhat early trial for treason, was found guilty, sentenced, and executed, he became to thousands of Northerners a martyr to the anti-slavery cause. In some towns bells were tolled and guns fired in honor of the dying saint, while many agreed with the verdict of Emerson that Brown's death would "make the gallows glorious like the cross." Responsible Republican leaders, however, gave voice to no such expressions. Seward, who a

few months before had foretold "an irrepressible conflict" between the systems of slave and free labor, now denounced Brown for his resort to violence, and pointed to the ballot-box as the only proper avenue of reform in a democracy, while the next Republican national platform classed Brown's exploit as "among the gravest of crimes." That there existed in the North, nonetheless, a powerful undercurrent of sympathy for Brown seems evident from the fact that within so short a time northern soldiers were marching south to the tune of

> John Brown's body lies a-mouldering in the grave,
> But his soul goes marching on.

On December 5, 1859, three days after the death of John Brown, the Congress elected in 1858 convened for its first session. In the House of Representatives, where the Republicans had a plurality but not a majority, a contest for the Speakership developed that lasted for nearly two months. After the first ballot *Helper's "Impending Crisis"* Representative John B. Clark of Missouri introduced a resolution, aimed at John Sherman of Ohio, the leading Republican candidate, to the effect that anyone who had endorsed a book by Hilton R. Helper, *The Impending Crisis of the South*, was unfit to be Speaker of the House. Helper was a non-slaveholding white of North Carolina, and his book, published in 1857, was an attempt to demonstrate by means of somewhat unreliable statistics that the deep poverty of the class to which he belonged was due to slavery. Naturally the slaveholders were outraged by such an argument, coming as it did from the South itself, and when in 1859 the obnoxious book was reprinted with approval from high Republican quarters for circulation as an anti-slavery tract their anger knew no bounds. The Republican Party had always claimed that its policy was merely to prevent the expansion of slavery, and not to attack it where it already existed. But Helper's book urged both the abolition of slavery in the southern states and the overthrow of the "oligarchical despotism," based on slavery, that ruled the South. To the pro-slavery leaders it was an incendiary document "precisely in the spirit of the act which startled us a few weeks since at Harper's Ferry." During the contest for the Speakership they could think or talk of little else. Sectional feeling became increasingly tense. According to one congressman, "The members on both sides are mostly armed with deadly weapons, and it is said that the friends of each are armed in the galleries." According to another, "I believe every man in both houses is armed with a revolver — some with two — and a bowie-knife." At length the Speakership went to a conservative Republican from New Jersey,

William Pennington, but the contest had aroused much bad blood, and southern threats of secession had become almost commonplace.

The session of Congress that began thus tempestuously enacted few measures of consequence. Only a presidential veto, however, prevented *A homestead* the passage of a homestead act. With the election of 1860 *act vetoed* in sight, even the southern Democrats hesitated to antagonize further the northern wing of their party, which was as fully committed to the homestead policy as the Republicans themselves. At least one Southerner, Senator Andrew Johnson of Tennessee, had long urged the granting of homesteads because of the benefit the poor whites of the South might derive from such a policy; but Johnson was a man of humble antecedents, and no more representative of the plantation aristocracy than the author of *The Impending Crisis*. During the summer of 1860 both the Senate and the House agreed to a measure that would permit heads of families, whether citizens of the United States or aliens who had declared their intention of becoming citizens, to occupy one hundred and sixty acres of government land for five years, and then buy it at the nominal price of twenty-five cents per acre. But Buchanan promptly denounced the bill in a veto message that recited all the traditional arguments against it. Such a measure, he claimed, would depopulate the older states, strike a blow at the frontiersman's "noble spirit of independence," and "proclaim to all the nations of the earth" that a farm awaited every immigrant to American shores, virtually free of charge, if he would only declare his intention of becoming a citizen.

Few presidential campaigns have aroused the intense interest that extended to every section of the country during nearly the entire year of *Democratic* 1860.[1] From the outset the likelihood of a split in the *dissensions* Democratic Party was well understood. Senator Jefferson Davis of Mississippi, speaking for the southern wing of the party, had served notice on Douglas that if he wished southern support for his candidacy he must agree to the enactment by Congress of a territorial slave code. This complete abandonment of popular sovereignty, designed to protect slavery in every territory whether the people of the territory wanted it or not, Douglas refused utterly to make. When, therefore, the Democratic convention met at Charleston, South Carolina, in April, 1860, the battle was on. Douglas, it transpired, controlled a majority of the delegates and could write the platform, but he lacked the two-thirds majority necessary to achieve the nomination. As soon as the

---

[1] E. D. Fite, *The Presidential Campaign of 1860* (1911), is a convenient account, although open to question on matters of interpretation.

platform was adopted, the delegations of four southern states withdrew from the convention, and were followed by most of the delegates from four other states. After ten days of fruitless balloting, with Douglas far in the lead on every ballot and sometimes in a clear majority, the convention adjourned to meet again in Baltimore on the eighteenth of June. But the adjourned session was no more successful than the original in reconciling northern and southern delegates, so after a few preliminaries the convention divided. One faction, composed mainly of northern delegates, nominated Douglas and stood by popular sovereignty. The other, composed almost exclusively of Southerners, nominated John C. Breckinridge of Kentucky, and called for the protection of slavery in all the territories.

During the interval between the Democratic sessions at Charleston and at Baltimore the Republicans met at Chicago — a significant recognition of the rôle the West was expected to play in the com- *The Republicans at Chicago* ing election. Their platform was intensely nationalistic, not only in its denunciation of southern threats of disunion, but also in its advocacy of national action to satisfy the demands of its adherents. The advance of slavery into the West must be halted, imposts "to encourage the development of the industrial interests" must be levied, a satisfactory homestead law must be enacted, the existing liberal naturalization policy must be maintained, and a railroad to the Pacific (advocated also by both Democratic platforms) must be built — all by authority of the national government. While the "right of each state to order and control its own institutions according to its own judgment" was expressly affirmed, the Chicago platform clearly served notice on the South that, according to Republican principles, a minority section had neither the right to rule the nation nor the right to withdraw from it. If, on the other hand, the new party by uniting the industrial Northeast and the agricultural Northwest could command a majority, it proposed to make full use of the national power for the benefit of the interests it represented.

The nomination of Abraham Lincoln for the Presidency was to a considerable extent a surrender to expediency. The foremost Republican of the time was William H. Seward of New York, who confidently expected the nomination. But Seward had been long in the public eye, and had won the reputation of being an extremist. Everyone knew that he had predicted "an irrepressible conflict," and that in his speech against the Compromise of 1850 he had appealed to "a higher law than the Constitution." Lincoln's utterances, particularly in his "house divided" speech, were equally radical, but they were not so widely

[599]

known. Lincoln also represented the West, which was regarded as far more debatable territory than the East, and he came from the same state as Stephen A. Douglas, who would be his chief opponent. Deals made by Lincoln's subordinates to give Indiana and Pennsylvania representation in the Lincoln Cabinet, and the packing of the galleries of the improvised "Wigwam" where the convention was held with ardent Lincoln men, also had some part in the result. Seward had a lead on the first ballot, but on the third ballot Lincoln won the nomination.

A fourth-party ticket was placed in the field by the remnant of the Whig–Know-Nothing combination that had supported Fillmore in

The Constitutional Union Party 1856. Meeting at Baltimore early in May, they gave their organization a new name, the Constitutional Union Party, and a new platform that was chiefly notable because it recognized "no political principle other than the Constitution of the country, the union of the States, and the enforcement of the laws." To this negative standard they sought to rally all those who wished to preserve the Union by compromise and conciliation — the way it had always been preserved before. In order to ensure an intersectional appeal, they chose as their candidate for the Presidency a Southerner, John Bell of Tennessee, and as their candidate for the Vice-Presidency a Northerner, Edward Everett of Massachusetts. Much ridicule was heaped upon the "Bell-Everetts," or the "Bell-Ringers," as they were generally called, during the campaign, but the party had a strong appeal for thoughtful conservatives who could see in a more forthright stand only disunion and conflict.

The campaign and election served only to emphasize how deep the line of cleavage between the sections had become. For all practical *The contest in the North* purposes two separate contests were being held, one in the North and another in the South. The only candidates to figure seriously in the northern balloting were Lincoln and Douglas, and the issue between them was clearly: Should the North use its numerical majority to force upon the South the nationalistic program called for in the Republican platform? With this program Douglas and the northern Democrats found little fault. Their doctrine of popular sovereignty had proved to be only another way of preventing the spread of slavery into the territories; they had little objection to a higher tariff; they believed in the Homestead Law; they had long defended the immigrants from the attacks of the Know-Nothings; they, too, favored a Pacific railroad. But Douglas and his followers realized, as seemingly the Republicans did not, the serious consequences that might result from forcing the northern point of view upon the South.

They knew that the southern threats of secession were far from meaningless, and that if the North insisted upon pressing its advantage a disruption of the Union was in sight. Sobered by the calamity that had overtaken the Democratic Party at Baltimore, they were now ready, like the Constitutional Unionists, to use caution, restraint, and denial in order to preserve an undivided nation.

In contrast with this attitude, the Republicans stood ready to give the North what it wanted. They denounced with the utmost intemperance the "slave-power" that with the aid of conscienceless "doughfaces" had so long ruled the country. They offered tariffs to please the industrial East, "homes for the millions" to please the agricultural West, and equality of treatment for aliens and citizens to please the immigrants. Against such a forthright attack Douglas fought valiantly, but in vain. Even the generous contributions of a few northern men of means, who feared the disastrous effects of secession on business, availed him nothing. Lincoln carried every northern state but one, New Jersey, and from that state he received four out of seven electoral votes. With the admission of Oregon in 1859, the free states numbered three more than the slave states and cast half again as many electoral votes. Thus Lincoln was elected, even though he had received not a single electoral vote from a southern state. In ten southern states his name had not appeared on the ballot.

In the South the contest lay between Breckinridge on the one hand and either Bell or Douglas on the other. Here the question at issue was, Should "southern rights" be maintained, even at the *The contest* cost of secession and possible civil war? "Southern rights" *in the South* meant vaguely whatever the individual who used the term wished it to mean, but the fundamental idea was the right of the South to some kind of constitutional protection from the tyranny of a northern majority. The election of Lincoln, southern extremists contended, would in itself constitute so flagrant an invasion of "southern rights" as to justify the southern states in seceding immediately from the Union. The party that supported Lincoln lay wholly in the North, and its triumph, they genuinely believed, would be but a prelude to the complete domination of the South by the North. Against this radical point of view the adherents of Bell and of Douglas urged an intermediate course that would ensure the preservation of the Union. But in the South as in the North the more aggressive policy won. Eleven out of the fifteen slave states voted for Breckinridge; only four, all in the Upper South, for his opponents. The verdict of the South was almost as clear as that of the North. It would insist upon its "rights" at whatever cost.

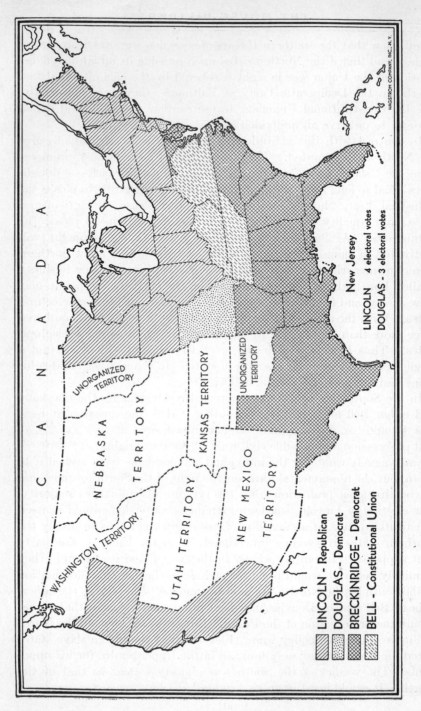

New Jersey

LINCOLN - 4 electoral votes

DOUGLAS - 3 electoral votes

LINCOLN - Republican

DOUGLAS - Democrat

BRECKINRIDGE - Democrat

BELL - Constitutional Union

ELECTION OF 1860, BY STATES

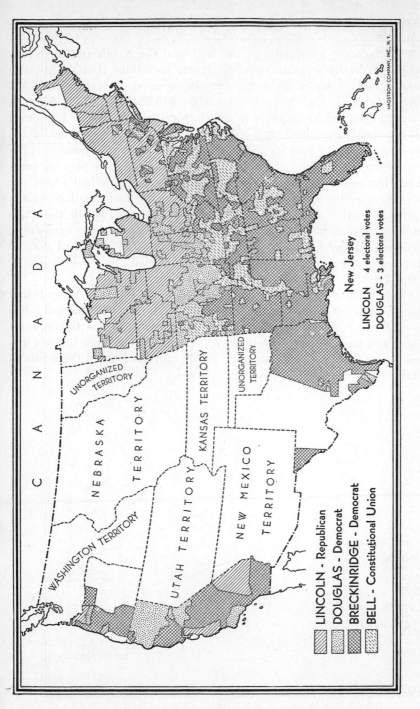

ELECTION OF 1860, BY COUNTIES

New Jersey

LINCOLN - 4 electoral votes
DOUGLAS - 3 electoral votes

LINCOLN - Republican
DOUGLAS - Democrat
BRECKINRIDGE - Democrat
BELL - Constitutional Union

HAGSTROM COMPANY, INC., N. Y.

With so many candidates in the field, and the North and the South holding virtually separate elections, it was inevitable that the popular vote should be badly divided. Lincoln received a total of 1,866,452 votes, Douglas 1,376,957, Breckinridge 849,781, and Bell 588,879. Thus Lincoln's clear majority in the electoral college, 180 to 123 for all his opponents combined, was obtained with only forty per cent of the popular vote being cast for the Republican candidate. Lincoln's opponents actually received all together nearly a million more popular votes than their successful rival. But the really significant fact about the election was that both the North and the South had voted decisively for radical action. Except for a few states of the upper South, the whole nation was in a radical mood. The combined vote of the extremists, Lincoln and Breckinridge, was 2,716,233, while the combined vote of the candidates who urged a middle course, Douglas and Bell, was only 1,965,331.

Could a house so divided against itself hope to stand? Many feared that it could not, but others pointed out that the Republicans had failed to capture a majority in either house of Congress, and that the Supreme Court still had its southern majority. Thus the North was not yet in a position to force its views upon the South, and the fears of the southern "fire-eaters" might for a season be allayed.

CHAPTER XXXI

SECESSION

THAT every state possessed the constitutional right to secede at will from the Union had long been regarded as sound doctrine throughout the South. The argument in support of this contention, sim- *The doctrine* plified and standardized by constant repetition, was by no *of secession* means illogical. History was recited to prove that the states were sovereign, not the nation; and just as the individual states, each acting in its sovereign capacity, had once joined the Union, so now, if they chose, they might leave it. A precise formula by which secession could be accomplished had been evolved. The legislature of a state that contemplated withdrawal from the Union must call for the election of a constituent convention — the same kind of convention that had been held in the original states to ratify the Constitution. On assembling, such a convention might by a majority vote recall all the powers that the state had delegated to the central government, and so declare the state outside the Union.

Was the election of Lincoln a serious enough violation of "southern rights" to justify resort to secession? After the returns were known, this was the question above all others that agitated the South. Many felt that the day of expostulation and protest was done, and that the time had come for action. The North, they said, had harbored and protected the abolitionists, it had openly flouted the Fugitive Slave Act, it had sung the praises of John Brown and his "band of midnight assassins," and it proposed now through a sectional party and a sectional President to subordinate the South to northern interests. The southern states ought not, therefore, even to await Lincoln's inauguration. They should leave the Union at once. But there were many Southerners also who counseled a more moderate course. Why not wait, they asked, until the new régime had actually committed some overt act of oppression? After Lincoln's inauguration, only one out of the three departments of government would be in Republican hands, and years might well elapse before any direct invasion of southern rights could take place. In the meantime constitutional changes or legislative compromises might be adopted that would satisfy the South. At the very least, individual states ought not to secede one by one, and so precipitate a series of crises. Time should be taken for all the southern states to consult together, and to plan for concerted action.

The overwhelming vote that the states of the lower South gave Breckinridge in the election indicated clearly that in this region the counsels of moderation would not prevail. Nor did they. In South Carolina, traditionally the most radical of the southern states, the legislature, in order to be ready to take prompt action, had remained in session until after the election was over. Without the slightest hesitation it summoned a convention which, at a meeting held in Charleston December 20, decided by a vote of 169 to 0 to dissolve the ties that bound the state of South Carolina to the Union. Within six weeks similar action had been taken by all the states that bordered on the Gulf of Mexico: Mississippi on January 9, Florida on January 10, Alabama on January 11, Georgia on January 19, Louisiana on January 26, and Texas on February 1.[1] Only in South Carolina, however, was the vote in favor of immediate secession unanimous. In every other state convention a determined minority stood out steadfastly for delay. Doubtless these minorities might in some cases have been majorities had not the precipitate action of South Carolina tended to identify the theory and the practice of secession. On this account southerners who heartily regretted that South Carolina had left the Union felt obliged to work for the secession of other states. Obviously one small state, acting alone, could not maintain its independence, and if a seceding state should be forced back into the Union, the whole doctrine of secession would be correspondingly discredited.

The seceding states left the Union one by one, but none of them had the slightest intention of maintaining a separate existence. Secession was *The Confederate States of America* but a means to an end, and the end was a united southern confederacy. Early in February a "congress" of delegates, chosen for the purpose by the several secessionist conventions, met at Montgomery, Alabama, to establish the new nation. On February 8 this congress adopted for the Confederate States of America a hastily devised provisional constitution; next day it chose as President and Vice-President, respectively, Jefferson Davis of Mississippi and Alexander H. Stephens of Georgia; and thereafter it remained in session long enough to act as a legislature for the provisional government and to draw

[1] The decision of the Texas convention was referred to a popular vote taken February 23, so that technically Texas was not out of the Union until that time. Dwight L. Dumond, *The Secession Movement, 1860-1861* (1931), treats the movement for secession comprehensively and sympathetically.

JEFFERSON DAVIS

up a permanent constitution. Throughout these proceedings the delegates were acutely conscious of the parallel between what they were doing and what their forefathers had done in severing the ties that had bound the colonies to the mother country. They issued no common declaration of independence, but in spite of their lip service to the doctrine of secession they found the real justification of their course in the right of an oppressed people to revolt.

Jefferson Davis

Jefferson Davis (1808–89),[1] upon whose shoulders now devolved the political leadership of the Confederacy, was a Kentuckian by birth, a graduate of West Point who had seen active military service on the frontier and in the war with Mexico, and a Mississippi cotton planter who shared most of the prejudices of his class. As United States Senator from 1847 to 1851, and again from 1857 to 1861, he had participated in the two great debates of the decade on the preservation of the Union. His views on southern rights had thus been fully stated, and they were known to be far less radical than those of many other Southerners, notably R. B. Rhett of South Carolina, who as one of the most persistent advocates of secession was bitterly disappointed not to be the first President of the Confederacy. But Davis, far more than Rhett, was a southern nationalist. Although the Confederate President believed in states' rights and accepted the doctrine of secession as good constitutional law, he set himself the task of building a new nation. His failure was due in part, no doubt, to his own shortcomings. He had an exaggerated idea of his military ability, and often gravely handicapped his generals by dictating to them, or interfering with their plans. He was not a good judge of men, and surrounded himself with mediocre subordinates when he could have had the best talent of the South for the asking. He was proud to the point of arrogance, and his overbearing attitude toward those who held opinions at variance from his own often cost him dear.

The Confederate Constitution

The permanent constitution of the Confederacy turned out to be a frank adaptation of the Constitution of the United States. The familiar preamble was revised to read, "We, the people of the Confederate States, each State acting in its sovereign and independent character," but instead of guaranteeing to each state the right of secession, the new federal government was described as "permanent." Several provisions were reminiscent of recent sectional disputes. The right of citizens to take their slave

---

[1] Probably the best biography of Davis is W. E. Dodd, *Jefferson Davis* (1907). In this connection, however, it is well to consult such sources as Mrs. Jefferson Davis, *Jefferson Davis, Ex-President of the Confederate States of America; a Memoir* (1890); and Jefferson Davis, *Rise and Fall of the Confederate Government* (2 vols., 1881).

property with them from state to state, and to hold it anywhere as such, was expressly affirmed; Congress was granted full authority to acquire new territory, but in any such territory the institution of slavery must be "recognized and protected"; new states could be admitted only by a two-thirds majority of both houses of Congress; bounties, protective tariffs, and appropriations for internal improvements were forbidden. A few changes, dictated by experience, were made in the machinery of government. The presidential term was lengthened to six years, and the President was made ineligible for re-election; single items in appropriation bills could be separately vetoed by the President; cabinet members, at the option of Congress, might be permitted seats upon the floor of either house; and a modified executive budget was contemplated. On March 11 the constitution was submitted to the seven seceding states, and by the end of April it had been ratified by all of them.

The North, meantime, observed what was going on in the South without fully comprehending it. Many Northerners refused utterly to believe that the secessionists meant what they said. South- *Northern* ern tempers, always easily overheated, would presently *opinion on* cool off, and the states that now seemed so determined to *secession* leave the Union would soon be trying to forget their folly. Others maintained, not without some justification in southern opinion, that a reconstruction of the Union would soon take place. This might possibly be accomplished through the calling of a constitutional convention, or more likely through some great congressional compromise as in 1850. Throughout the winter of 1860–61 northern sentiment definitely rejected the idea of coercion. Greeley's powerful *New York Tribune* repeatedly set forth this point of view. "If the fifteen slave States," ran a typical *Tribune* editorial, "or even the eight cotton States alone, shall quietly, decisively, say to the rest, 'We prefer to be henceforth separate from you,' we shall insist that they be permitted to go in peace. War is a hideous necessity at best, and a civil conflict — a war of estranged and embittered fellow-countrymen — is the most hideous of all wars." Abolitionists professed delight to see the Union purged of so many slave states, and agreed with Greeley that the best policy was to "let the erring sisters go in peace." Quakers and other pacifists read with approval the lines penned by John Greenleaf Whittier:

> They break the bonds of Union: shall we light
> The fires of hell to weld anew the chain
> On that red anvil where each blow is pain?

Nevertheless, most Northerners were deeply dissatisfied with the

weakness displayed by the national administration in its handling of
Buchanan   the secessionist movement. When in earlier years Andrew
on secession   Jackson and Zachary Taylor had been confronted by somewhat similar situations, they had met the southern threats, although
themselves from the South, with equally bold words, and even with
deeds. Had James Buchanan shown less timidity, had he talked back
to the secessionists in their own language, many felt that the headlong
flight of the southern states from the Union might have been checked.
But the President, old and ill, and the discredited representative of a
discredited party, showed himself to be utterly incapable of aggressive
action.[1]   When, early in December, 1860, he sent his annual message
to Congress, not a state had left the Union, although the intentions of
South Carolina were well enough known. This was the time, if ever,
for the President to warn the South of the grave consequences that might
result from secession. Instead, he told them that while secession, in
his opinion, was unconstitutional, so also was the coercion of a state.
If, therefore, the southern states seceded, they need fear nothing as long
as Buchanan remained in office, for, as Seward rephrased the presidential pronouncement, "It is the duty of the President to execute the
laws — unless somebody opposes him; and . . . no State has the right to
go out of the Union — unless it wants to."

Buchanan did not fail to tell Congress, however, what it should do.
The whole blame for the existing sectional controversy he placed upon
the North, and the only way to make amends, as he saw it, was for the
North to yield completely to the southern contentions. Let Congress
submit an "explanatory amendment" to the Constitution on the subject of slavery. Let this amendment guarantee in so many words the
right to hold slave property in all the states where slavery then existed,
and in all the territories of the United States as well. Let it also definitely recognize the right of the master "to have his slave who had
escaped from one state to another restored and 'delivered up' to him."
Then, for good measure, let it declare the existing Fugitive Slave Law
valid, and the existing "personal liberty" laws of the northern states
invalid. Perhaps with these assurances the South might be persuaded
to remain in the Union.

With the secession of South Carolina an accomplished fact, the President was faced by a situation in Charleston Harbor that called insistently for action. Such of the property of the United States within South

---

[1] A sincere, and at points convincing, apology for Buchanan is made by Philip G. Auchampaugh, *James Buchanan and his Cabinet on the Eve of Secession* (1926). On the attitude of the North, in general, toward secession, see Mary Scrugham, *The Peaceable Americans of 1860–1861* (1921).

Carolina as was undefended was promptly taken over by the seceding state, but the forts that protected Charleston Harbor were *Fort Sumter* occupied by a small federal garrison under the command of Major Robert Anderson. Foreseeing the probable course of events, Anderson had long urged the authorities in Washington to reinforce him, and in this request he had been strongly supported by General Scott. The President, however, fearful of irritating the South-Carolinians, sought to maintain the *status quo* in the harbor, and left Anderson to his own devices. A few days after the ordinance of secession was adopted, Anderson, on his own authority, abandoned the indefensible Fort Moultrie and removed his entire garrison to Fort Sumter, an island fortification in the mouth of the harbor. This action deeply enraged the South-Carolinians, who interpreted it as a threat of war, but the President sustained Anderson.

For a time, indeed, it seemed that Buchanan might attempt to play the Jacksonian rôle that some of his advisers desired. A reorganization of his Cabinet brought strong Unionists to the fore, particularly Jeremiah Sullivan Black,[1] the new Secretary of State, and Edwin M. Stanton, the new Attorney-General. Under their urging, Buchanan finally decided to reinforce Sumter and on January 8 he sent the *Star of the West*, a merchant steamer, to Charleston Harbor, with two hundred soldiers aboard. But when three days later the vessel attempted to enter the harbor, she was met by the fire of state batteries, and turned back to New York without discharging her errand. This attack on the *Star of the West* was in reality an act of war, but the President chose to ignore it, and during the remainder of his administration he made no further effort to aid Anderson.

Congress, meantime, was hard at work on a plan of compromise by which the Union might be preserved. The leadership of this movement was assumed, appropriately, by Senator John J. *The* Crittenden of Kentucky, the successor to Clay's seat in *Crittenden* the Senate, and to the Clay tradition of compromise. Two *compromise* days before the secession of South Carolina, Crittenden introduced into the Senate an elaborate set of resolutions not unlike those Clay had presented to the same body ten years before. By amendment to the Constitution he proposed that:

1. Slavery should be prohibited in all the territory of the United States now held, or hereafter acquired, north of 36° 30′, and protected south of that line.
2. Congress should have no power to abolish slavery in places under its

[1] W. N. Brigance, *Jeremiah Sullivan Black* (1934).

exclusive jurisdiction, and situate within the limits of states that permitted the holding of slaves.

3. Congress should have no power to abolish slavery within the District of Columbia without compensation, and without the consent of Maryland, Virginia, and the people of the District.
4. Congress should have no power to prohibit or hinder the transportation of slaves between slaveholding states and territories.
5. The owners of rescued fugitive slaves were to be compensated for their losses by the United States government.

Additional recommendations urged (1) the faithful observance and execution of the Fugitive Slave Law, which, however, should be made less obnoxious to the North, (2) the repeal of all "personal liberty" laws, and (3) the thorough suppression of the African slave trade.

A Senate committee of thirteen, headed by Crittenden, was at once constituted to consider these and other plans of compromise. Care was taken in the selection of the committee to give representation to every section and party. Six members, including Crittenden and Douglas, were open advocates of compromise; Seward, Wade, and three other Republicans spoke for the northern extremists; Toombs and Davis, whose states had not yet seceded, effectively represented the lower South. At first it seemed probable that the committee might agree upon substantially the plan of compromise that Crittenden had proposed. The chief bone of contention was the 36° 30′ dividing line between free and slave territory, a proposition that Toombs and Davis were known to be ready to accept, provided only that a majority of the Republicans would also agree to it. Seward seems to have flirted with the idea, but before committing himself definitely he sent his friend, Thurlow Weed, to Springfield, Illinois, for a conference with the President-elect. Weed reported that Lincoln was willing to make almost unlimited concessions with regard to the enforcement of the Fugitive Slave Law and the repeal of the "personal liberty" laws, but that he was unalterably opposed to any yielding on the question of slavery expansion. Lincoln's opinion seems to have been conclusive, for the Republicans voted unanimously against the proposed dividing line, and the committee reported back to the Senate that it could not agree.

Later Crittenden and his supporters argued that the compromise in which they were interested should be submitted to the people of the country for approval or rejection at the polls. But the machinery for obtaining such a referendum vote did not exist, and all efforts looking toward its creation failed, largely because of Republican opposition. Had there been such a possibility, however, there is some reason to suppose that during the winter of 1860–61 a popular majority for the compromise might have been obtained. The vote of November, 1860, showed the extremists in the majority, both North and South, but at that time the actual specter of secession was not before the voters as they marked their ballots. Faced by the direct alternative of compromise or secession, many who had voted for Lincoln or Breckinridge a few weeks before might well have changed their minds and voted for Crittenden's solution.

If so eminent and representative a group as the Senate committee of thirteen could not propose a successful plan of compromise, it seemed unlikely that any other group could do so. Nevertheless, *House* a House committee of thirty-three continued to struggle *efforts at* with the problem, and early in January, 1861, it brought *compromise* forth an alternative plan, which had substantial support even among the Republicans. The House plan called for (1) an amendment to the Constitution that would safeguard slavery in the states where it already existed, (2) a recommendation that the "personal liberty" laws be repealed, and (3) the admission of New Mexico, "with or without slavery." That this last-mentioned provision would mean a new slave state, few could deny, for in 1859 the territorial government of New Mexico, under pressure from the South, had definitely legalized slavery. But not many slaves were held in the territory, and even Lincoln admitted that he did not "care much about New Mexico." Neither, it seemed, did the representatives of the cotton states, for they were as quick to reject the House plan as the Republicans had been to reject the Crittenden plan; and so nothing came of it. Both houses of Congress voted, however, by two-thirds majorities, to submit a thirteenth amendment to the Constitution that would forever deny to Congress the right to abolish or interfere with slavery in any of the states. This amendment was never ratified, although Lincoln in his inaugural address expressly approved of it. By a curious irony the Thirteenth Amendment that presently was ratified abolished slavery.

Convinced as time went on that Congress would not succeed in working out a satisfactory compromise, the legislature of Virginia invited the various states to send delegates to a great peace convention *The peace* to be opened in Washington, February 4. Twenty-one *convention* states responded favorably, and with ex-President Tyler in the chair the convention made a sincere effort to save the Union. After three weeks of deliberation it recommended to Congress an amendment to the Constitution that would have made latitude 36° 30' the dividing line between slave and free territories, but would also have provided that in the acquisition of any new territory by the United States concurrent majorities of the free-state senators and of the slave-state senators should be required. Unfortunately this provision received far from unanimous support in the convention, and it reached Congress at a time when the secession movement had proceeded too far to be turned back. The resolves of the peace convention were duly presented to the Senate by Senator Crittenden, but they were promptly rejected.

As the time for Lincoln's inauguration approached, all eyes turned toward the ungainly Westerner upon whose shoulders the crisis was so soon to devolve. Abraham Lincoln (1809–65) [1] was born in Kentucky, the descendant of several generations of American frontiersmen. His father, Thomas Lincoln, was only a child when his grandfather, Abraham Lincoln, met death at the hands of the Indians. Grown and married, Thomas Lincoln made two typical pioneer "moves" to the West, first to Indiana, and later to Illinois. Thus repeatedly transplanted, the boy Abraham obtained only the slightest schooling, but he read all the books he could get hold of, and he ultimately learned enough law to meet the modest requirements of the West for admission to the bar. He possessed a native shrewdness that stood him in good stead on all occasions, and he developed a capacity for logical thinking and for the accurate expression of his thought that would have been remarkable in any age or place. On the frontier, politics and law went hand in hand, and Lincoln's political ambitions were not slow in materializing. At first as a Henry Clay Whig, and later as a Republican, he demonstrated his skill in state and local politics; later, particularly by his utterances during the Lincoln-Douglas debates, he won recognition throughout the nation as a leading exponent of Republican doctrine. A thoroughgoing Westerner, he instinctively idealized both nationalism and democracy, and he resented deeply the determination of the southern leaders to rule the nation with or without a majority, or else to ruin it. Well above the average height and homely to the point of fascination, he affected the stoop-shouldered posture and the loose-jointed shambling gait that western lawyers generally mistook for dignity. He knew little or nothing of the polite usages of eastern society, and to those who were more sophisticated the essential gentility of his nature was often obscured by his uncouth manners, his off-color jokes, and his easy familiarity.

During his months as President-elect, Lincoln had studiously avoided

Lincoln

[1] The most useful historical biography of Lincoln is Lord Charnwood, *Abraham Lincoln* (1916). This may be supplemented on the personal side by N. W. Stephenson, *Lincoln* (1922); and W. E. Barton, *The Life of Abraham Lincoln* (2 vols., 1925). The most voluminous biography of Lincoln, John G. Nicolay and John Hay, *Abraham Lincoln: A History* (10 vols., 1890), is a detailed chronicle of the political events of the Civil War period. Carl Sandburg, *Abraham Lincoln, the Prairie Years* (1926), presents a picture of the youth of Lincoln that is convincing in spite of the author's indifference to accuracy in detail.

any public expression of opinion, and the country awaited eagerly his announcement of policy. This statement he properly de- *Lincoln's* cided to reserve for his inaugural address, but when crowds *inaugural* gathered around his train on the long journey to Washington *address* he unfortunately felt obliged to talk to them. Unskilled in the art of concealing his thoughts, and yet strongly desirous of setting the public mind at ease, he resorted to ambiguous and sentimental remarks that made some men wonder if he really understood the situation at all. Also, he was persuaded by those responsible for his personal safety to deviate from his announced schedule in order to enter Washington at a time when he was not expected. Was Lincoln afraid? This suspicion seemed to receive confirmation on Inauguration Day, for on that occasion the city of Washington fairly bristled with bayonets. But the President's inaugural address was reassuring. He reviewed the history of the crisis in such a way as to leave no doubt that he fully understood it, and he presented a calm, cogent argument against the constitutional right of secession that could scarcely have been improved upon. More than that, he left the South no alternative but to return to the Union, or else fight to stay out. He declared it his intention to execute the federal laws in all the states, to "hold, occupy, and possess the property and places" belonging to the United States, and to collect as usual the duties and imposts. "In doing this," he reasoned, "there needs to be no bloodshed or violence; and there shall be none, unless it be forced upon the national authority."

Lincoln had stated his policy with perfect candor, but for the first few weeks after the inauguration his administration was in a too chaotic condition to do more than mark time. The President him- *Lincoln's* self, never an efficient administrator, allowed office-seekers *policy* and their sponsors to throng the White House, and to interfere seriously with his consideration of graver matters. Moreover, the election and the subsequent secession of the lower South had worked a veritable revolution in the official personnel of Washington; new and inexperienced hands had hold of every important post. Members of the Cabinet, whom Lincoln had chosen primarily to appease the various elements that made up the Republican Party, were not only lacking in experience, but what was far worse, some of them were not fully loyal to their chief. Four out of the seven, Secretary of State Seward, Secretary of the Treasury Chase, Secretary of War Cameron, and Attorney-General Bates, had hoped for the nomination that Lincoln had won. Two of them, Seward and Chase,[1]

[1] Frederic Bancroft, *The Life of William H. Seward* (2 vols., 1900); A. B. Hart, *Salmon Portland Chase* (1899).

were fully convinced that in ability they far outranked the new President; and Seward, in an amazing document written four weeks after the inauguration, actually offered to take over the government. "We are at the end of a month's administration," he told the President, "and yet without a policy, either domestic or foreign." Then, after suggesting that the domestic crisis might be cleared by declarations of war against both France and Spain, he demanded that "whatever policy we adopt, there must be an energetic prosecution of it. Either the President must do it himself, or devolve it on some member of his cabinet. It is not in my especial province. But I neither seek to evade nor assume responsibility." Fortunately Lincoln did not choose to abdicate his duties to Seward, and with that extraordinary magnanimity for which he soon became famous he made no effort to discipline his presumptuous subordinate.

But Lincoln could not much longer postpone action. Either he must furnish Major Anderson at Fort Sumter with supplies or else permit the *The bombardment of Sumter* evacuation of the post; and approximately the same situation existed at Fort Pickens in the harbor of Pensacola, Florida. Increasingly it became clear that any attempt to relieve these garrisons would precipitate war, while the failure to do so, with their consequent surrender, would amount to a tacit recognition of the Confederacy. At length Lincoln, in spite of the disapproval of most of his Cabinet, ordered relief expeditions to both garrisons. The one sent to Fort Pickens was entirely successful, and that southern outpost was retained by the North all through the War, but the mere news that Sumter was to be reprovisioned led the Davis government to order its bombardment. On the morning of April 12 this order was executed, and after defending his post gallantly for more than a day Major Anderson surrendered. On Sunday afternoon, the fourteenth of April, with the relief ships standing helplessly by, he abandoned the fort "with colors flying and drums beating, bringing away company and private property, and saluting my flag with fifty guns." No one had been killed on either side, but the South had served notice by the incident that it meant to accept Lincoln's challenge, and would fight to stay out of the Union.

The reception in the North of the news from Charleston made it equally apparent that the North would fight to keep the South in. Three *Response of the North* months before, when under almost identical circumstances the *Star of the West*, flying the national flag, had drawn the fire of Charleston batteries, there had been no answering wave of resentment from the North, and no uprising of the masses. Now there were both. Almost with one voice the people of the free states, irrespective of party, proclaimed their approval of the call for seventy-five thousand militia that Lincoln issued the day after Sumter fell. Douglas sought an interview with the President, and then came out with the ringing statement: "There are only two sides to the question. Every man must be for the United States government or against it. There can be no neutrals in this war; only patriots or traitors." Edward Everett accused the South of inaugurating an "unprovoked and unrighteous war." Ex-Presidents Pierce and Buchanan let their sympathy for the Union cause be known, and Benjamin F. Butler of Massachusetts, an ardent Breckinridge supporter in the campaign of 1860, proclaimed dramatically: "Our faces are set South, and there shall be no footstep backwards. The day of compromise is past."

During the first three months of 1861 the North had thought the problem of secession through, and like Lincoln had made up its mind to prevent it, even at the cost of war. Not every individual had been swayed by the same considerations. To some the economic argument was strong. The Northeast needed southern cotton for its mills, southern markets for its manufactured goods. Both might be imperiled if the South were permitted to leave the Union. The Northwest drove a thriving intersectional trade with the South, and believed, although there was no longer good ground for such an impression, that the Mississippi outlet was essential to its economic life. Many thoughtful men were convinced of the impracticability of secession. After all, it would settle none of the problems that had harassed the good relations of North and South. The territorial question would remain, for how would the two nations divide the territories between them? The fugitive slave problem would be more irritating than ever before. Furthermore, if secession were permitted, to what extent might it not go? Why not next a Pacific confederacy, or a northwestern confederacy? Fernando Wood, mayor of New York City, had actually suggested the desirability of that city's leaving the Union — a project that Lincoln described as not unlike "the front-door setting up housekeeping by itself."

There were numerous other arguments in favor of the North's supporting the war. Some saw in the coming struggle a long-coveted opportunity to strike a death-blow to African slavery. Probably some were influenced by fear of the diplomatic weakening that the division of the United States into two nations would involve. Such a separation would put an end to American isolation, promote alliances with European nations, destroy the Monroe Doctrine. But possibly more potent than anything else was the pride which so many people felt in the American democratic experiment. The United States was practically the only successful republic in the world. Could it survive in the face of such internal dissension as that from which it now suffered? Was democracy a failure? Certainly this question agitated Lincoln far more than any other.

> For my own part [he told his private secretary], I consider the central idea pervading this struggle is the necessity of proving that popular government is not an absurdity. We must settle this question now, whether, in a free government, the minority have the right to break up the government whenever they choose. If we fail, it will go far to prove the incapability of the people to govern themselves.

Before the bombardment of Sumter the eight slave states of the upper South had steadfastly refused to leave the Union. Ties of blood and of *The border* interest bound them no less to the North than to the South; *slave states* war, if it came, would surely make them a battle-ground. From their point of view the retention of the Union as it was, or its "reconstruction" in such a way as to satisfy the seceding members, was far preferable to dismemberment. In all of them, however, the right of secession was generally conceded, and a strong minority favored putting the right into practice. When war between North and South became a certainty, this minority was quickly transformed into a majority in four of the border states — Virginia, North Carolina, Tennessee, and Arkansas. Three others — Delaware, Maryland, and Missouri — decided definitely to remain with the North. Kentucky for a time attempted an impossible neutrality, but Lincoln, with excellent judgment, allowed the Confederacy to trespass first upon its soil, whereupon Kentucky also fell to the Union. Another important victory for the North was won when a block of forty-six counties in the mountains of northwestern Virginia refused to follow the rest of the state out of the Union, and by somewhat irregular methods became the independent loyal state of West Virginia, which Congress in June, 1863, belatedly admitted to the Union.

It must not be supposed that these decisions of the border states reflected in every instance the will of the majority. The federal government took pains to ensure that Maryland, whose territory surrounded the District of Columbia on three sides, had no chance to secede; and the little state of Delaware had perforce to do what Maryland did. Similarly, the Confederacy could not risk the loss of Tennessee because of its important railroad connections, and, with the earnest co-operation of the governor and other state officials, made its secession a certainty. In all the border states sentiment was divided, and most of them furnished recruits for the armies of both North and South. While in a

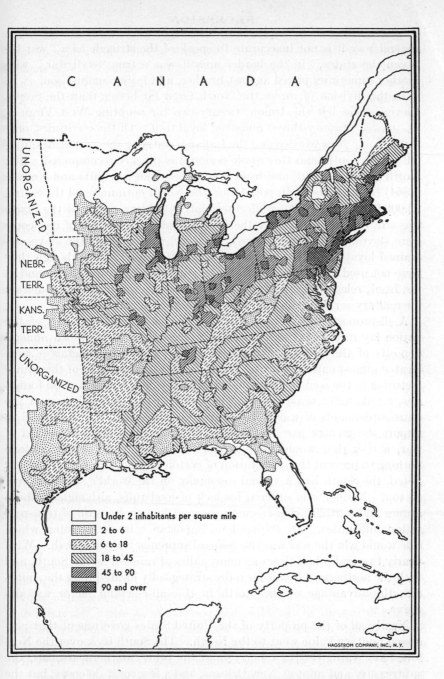

DENSITY OF POPULATION IN EASTERN UNITED STATES, 1860

CANADA

UNORGANIZED

NEBR.
TERR.

KANS.
TERR.

UNORGANIZED

Under 2 inhabitants per square mile
2 to 6
6 to 18
18 to 45
45 to 90
90 and over

HAGSTROM COMPANY, INC., N.Y.

general way it is not inaccurate to speak of the struggle as a "war between the states," in the border area it was a true "civil war," with brother sometimes pitted against brother, and father against son.

In the division of forces the North fared far better than the South. Eleven states left the Union; twenty-two (or counting West Virginia, *The division* twenty-three) remained loyal to it. Of the territories, only *of forces* New Mexico and the Indian country to the west of Arkansas fell to the South, and this whole region was quickly reconquered. The North got all the rest, and from it admitted Kansas (1861) and Nevada (1864) to statehood. In population the North outnumbered the South, 22,000,000 to 9,500,000, while the relative fighting power of the South was still further lessened by the fact that about 3,500,000 of its people were slaves. As events proved, however, nearly all of the slaves remained loyal to their masters throughout the war, and, although they were not used by the South as soldiers, their labor, both at home and at the front, released a far larger proportion of southern white population for military service than could otherwise have been available.

A disproportionately large share of the economic resources of the nation lay in the northern states and territories. The known mineral deposits of the country — coal, iron, copper, precious metals — were located almost entirely in the North. Ninety-two per cent of the manufacturing of the country was carried on in the North, and its iron foundries, textile mills, tanneries, etc., had only to be expanded to meet the unusual demands of war. The South, on the other hand, expected to import the greater part of its manufactures, including the *matériel* of war, a task that would have been easy enough had the North done nothing to prevent the exportation of cotton in payment; for, as already noted, the South had a virtual monopoly on the world's supply of raw cotton. Neither side suffered for lack of foodstuffs, although southern armies and southern cities sometimes went hungry because of transportation difficulties. Of tremendous importance in determining which side would win the war was the railroad supremacy of the North. With nearly two and a half times as many miles of railroad as the South, and with the northern railroads far more strategically located than the southern, the advantage of the North in this all-essential factor was decisive.

Nearly all of the property of the United States government that possessed military value went to the North. The South took over the Norfolk navy yard, Harper's Ferry, and the other southern arsenals, the subtreasury and mint at New Orleans, and a few coast defenses; but the North got practically all the rest, including almost every ship in the

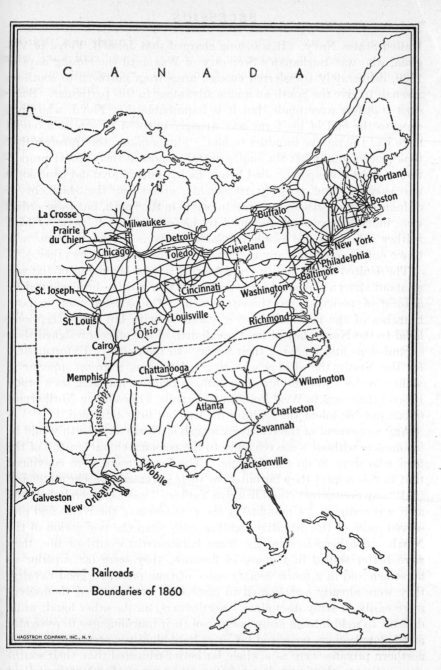

RAILROADS IN THE UNITED STATES, 1860

United States Navy. It was long charged that John B. Floyd of Virginia, who was Buchanan's Secretary of War until the closing days of 1860, deliberately transferred enough arms from northern to southern arsenals to give the South an undue advantage in this particular. Some such transfers were made, but it is improbable that Floyd, who until close to the end of his term was strongly opposed to secession, could have had the motive imputed to him. Furthermore, the transfers that took place actually left the southern states short of their proper proportion of federal weapons. Just before he left office Floyd did issue some unreasonable, and possibly treasonous, orders for the shipment of ordnance from northern factories to points in the South, but these orders were immediately countermanded by his successor. In point of fact, neither side possessed enough reliable weapons at the time the war broke out to constitute any real menace to the safety of the other.

The United States had a regular army at the beginning of the war of about sixteen thousand men, and a navy of ninety ships manned by a total of perhaps nine thousand men. The enlisted men in both branches of the national defense remained, with but rare exceptions, loyal to the North, but at least one fourth of the officers resigned their commissions and tendered their services to the South. Unfortunately for the North, the officers who resigned were as a group superior in ability to those who did not, for southern planters had long been proud to send their sons to West Point or Annapolis, while among Northerners of comparable talent the military life was but little esteemed.

Any assessment of the relative strength of North and South would be incomplete without some reference to the personal characteristics of the men who were to do the fighting. The Southerners were convinced that in this respect they far outshone their adversaries. The statement that "any Southerner could lick five Yankees" was as sincerely believed as it was common. Undoubtedly the population of the South had preserved more of the primitive fighting spirit than the population of the North. Southerners were the more habituated to outdoor life, they were better skilled in the use of firearms, they were far superior as horsemen and in a much shorter space of time produced good cavalry, they were already accustomed to caste lines and adjusted themselves more easily to army discipline. Northerners, on the other hand, while difficult to weld into an army because of their unwillingness to recognize and follow leaders, possessed far more individual resourcefulness. The northern privates were as a whole far better educated than their southern opponents, they were drawn from a wider range of occupations, they possessed greater mechanical skill, they were less embarrassed by an

ROBERT E. LEE

unusual situation. All of which was hardly sufficient to overcome the handicap of fighting in an alien climate and over terrain that neither they nor their officers knew anything about.

The "preponderating asset of the North" turned out to be Lincoln himself. This was not because he possessed any intuitive military un-
Lincoln   derstanding that was of use to his generals; indeed, his ideas on strategy were quite as naïve as those of any other civilian. Nor was he at first a notably good judge of military men. His strength lay in his extraordinary understanding of the feelings and prejudices of the masses, without whose support the war could never have been won. He realized, more fully than most of his advisers, that when a democracy goes to war military efficiency is of no avail without the backing of public opinion. Every such war has, therefore, its political no less than its military side; and it was in the management of the political side of the struggle that Lincoln's genius was mostly clearly manifest.

What Abraham Lincoln, the politician, was to the North, Robert E. Lee (1807–70),[1] the soldier, was to the South. The two men could
Lee   hardly have stood in greater contrast with each other. Lee was of the Virginia gentry, a patrician to his fingertips, and a military genius. The son of General Henry Lee, who had served under Washington during the Revolution, his "strong hereditary claims on the country" had helped him obtain a cadetship at West Point in 1825, where four years later he was graduated, second in his class. As Captain Lee, he was General Scott's chief of staff in Mexico, and out of that campaign he won no less than three brevets — major, lieutenant-colonel, and colonel — for gallant service in the field. Always a favorite with General Scott, who believed him the ablest officer in the army, he was undoubtedly the first choice of both Scott and Lincoln for the active command of the United States Army; a week before the bombardment of Sumter, Francis P. Blair, speaking unofficially for the President, actually offered Lee this post. But Lee, to use his own words, "declined the offer he made me, stating as candidly and as courteously as I could, that though opposed to secession and deprecating war, I could take no part in an invasion of the Southern States." He was deeply distressed at the thought of fighting against the United States, but he regarded it as his duty, in case Virginia seceded, to draw his sword in defense of his native state. As handsome as Lincoln was

---

[1] W. E. Dodd, *Lincoln or Lee* (1928), is an interesting interpretation. Sir Frederick B. Maurice, *Robert E. Lee, the Soldier* (1925), is useful, but has been supplanted, together with all other biographies of Lee, by Douglas Southall Freeman, *R. E. Lee: a Biography* (4 vols., 1934–35), a work of extraordinary merit.

homely, and steeped in the chivalry of the Old South, he was the perfect embodiment of the rôle he was chosen to play. Had he cast his lot with the North instead of the South, it is hard to see how the struggle could have been so long drawn out.

CHAPTER XXXII

THE CIVIL WAR

HAD lack of preparedness alone been a sufficient deterrent, there would have been no war between North and South in 1861.[1] In a military

Lack of preparedness

sense neither side was ready for war; indeed, except for some eleventh-hour activities in the South, it could almost be said that neither side had given any very serious consideration to the military problem. The regular army of the United States was not only insignificant in size; it was divided up into a multitude of tiny garrisons, most of which were located along the Indian frontier, and could be withdrawn only at the risk of an Indian uprising. The organized state militia, which was the second line of defense for the North and the beginning and end of southern preparedness, consisted of a few companies of volunteers to each state, imperfectly armed and inadequately drilled. Probably the total number of such militiamen in the loyal states on the eve of the war was less than ten thousand, and in the seceding states even less than that. When Lincoln, on April 15, 1861, issued his call for seventy-five thousand state militia, and Davis shortly afterward countered with a somewhat similar request for one hundred thousand, both men knew that they were asking for units that did not exist. Before there could be any war, volunteers must be obtained, armed, and organized into armies. This situation, more than anything else, accounts for the slow beginning of military operations, and the uncertainty and delay that characterized the first campaigns. Not until well toward the middle of the war did the armies of North and South confront each other as dependable fighting machines.

Lincoln's first call for troops, issued under an antiquated militia law, asked for a specified number of regiments from each state. Since none of the states had anywhere nearly enough organized militia to fill its assigned quota, each loyal governor was forced in turn to issue his own

[1] F. L. Huidekoper, *The Military Unpreparedness of the United States* (1915), is amply convincing on this point. For the creation of the armies of the Civil War, see F. A. Shannon, *The Organization and Administration of the Union Army, 1861–1865* (2 vols., 1928); and A. B. Moore, *Conscription and Conflict in the Confederacy* (1924).

state-wide call for troops. He was in no better position, however, than the President to accept individual volunteers, so he in turn *How the* passed on this task to the various communities of the state. *armies were* There local leaders promptly assumed the responsibility *raised* thrust upon them, called patriotic mass meetings where "muster-rolls" could be started, and as soon as a company was filled offered its services to the state. Company officers were invariably elected by the volunteers themselves, but regimental officers were usually chosen by the governor. At the state capitol, or some other prescribed rendezvous, the companies were assembled into regiments, furnished with whatever equipment the state was able to obtain, and then promptly turned over to the national government. Within a remarkably short space of time the troops thus raised far exceeded the number Lincoln had called for; but in spite of frantic purchases abroad by both state and national governments, the supply of arms was totally inadequate, and the uniforms, whenever they existed at all, presented an astonishing variety of colors and patterns. Few of the recruits knew even the barest rudiments of military drill, and the officers, selected usually because of their political or social prominence, were almost as ignorant of military matters as the men they attempted to command.

The law cited by Lincoln to authorize his call for state militia limited their term of national service to ninety days, but the President was not so short-sighted as to believe that in that time the war would be over. Encouraged by the response of the country to his first call, he issued another on the third of May following which asked for forty-two thousand volunteers to serve for three years, and directed an increase of eighteen thousand men in the regular army. Since the Constitution gives to Congress, rather than to the President, the right to raise armies, it is hard to see how this second call could have been constitutional. Lincoln himself was under no illusions about his action, and when Congress met on July 4 he asked (and subsequently received) its official ratification of what he had done. Convinced by that time more than ever that the war would be a serious struggle, he asked also for a volunteer army of at least four hundred thousand three-year men. Congress granted him five hundred thousand.

The public, however, expected a speedy conclusion of the war, and called for a battle to end it. With the secession of Virginia, the Confederate capital was removed to Richmond, about a hun- *"On to* dred miles from Washington, while Confederate soil was *Richmond"* no farther away than just across the Potomac. Only a few weeks were required to assemble at Washington a Union army of some thirty-six thousand men, and inevitably the battle-cry was raised, "On to Richmond!" General Scott, who in spite of his seventy-five years was still in high command of the Union forces, counseled delay until the troops could be better trained, but Lincoln felt compelled to yield to the popular pressure for action. Most of the Union troops were three-months men whose term of enlistment would be over before the end of July; moreover, sadly in need of training as they were, they were little if any worse off in this respect than the enemy. A council of war, held in the White House on June 29, decided in favor of an immediate battle, and assigned to General Irvin McDowell, a West Point graduate, the task of striking the blow.[1]

Meantime General Robert E. Lee, first as the commander-in-chief of the Virginia militia, and later as the chief military adviser of President Davis, had made what preparations he could for the defense of his native state. The methods used by the South in raising an army did not vary markedly from the methods of the North, and a plentiful supply of raw recruits was available. General Pierre G. T. Beauregard, with about twenty-two thousand men, was stationed at Manassas Junction, an important railway point some thirty miles to the west of Washington. Half as many men under General Joseph E. Johnston were at Winchester, not less than fifty miles to the northwest of Manassas, guarding the entrance to the Shenandoah Valley. That these two forces might be united in case of an emergency was a part of the Confederate strategy. Knowing full well the limitations of his untrained troops, Lee refused to consider taking the offensive.

McDowell's plan was to attack Beauregard, but in accepting the command he expressly stipulated that the two Confederate forces must not *The Union advance* be permitted to unite. This seemed easy to prevent, for General Robert Patterson had a Union army of at least fourteen thousand men at Martinsburg, Virginia, only a few miles from Winchester, and was already under orders to keep Johnston fully engaged. On the sixteenth of July, amidst almost indescribable confusion and with no slightest attempt at concealment, McDowell's columns began to advance. Only six miles were made the first day, most of the second day was spent in rounding up stragglers, and five days altogether were consumed in reaching the enemy's lines. Unaccustomed to discipline, and oppressed by the delays, the dust, and the heat, the men

[1] The military history of the Civil War is covered briefly in William Wood, *Captains of the Civil War* (1921). The best technical history of the battles and campaigns of the war is J. C. Ropes and W. R. Livermore, *The Story of the Civil War* (4 vols., 1894–1913). Briefer, but also strictly military, are T. A. Dodge, *A Bird's-Eye View of Our Civil War* (1883); and W. B. Wood and J. E. Edmonds, *A History of the Civil War in the United States* (1905).

LIBRARY
FLORIDA STATE COLLEGE FOR WOMEN
TALLAHASSEE, FLORIDA

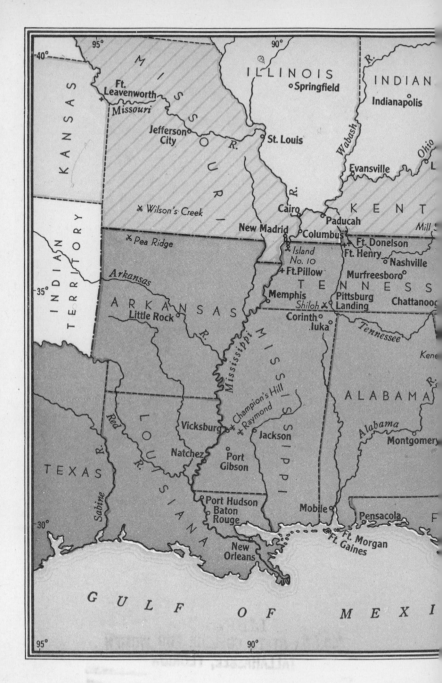

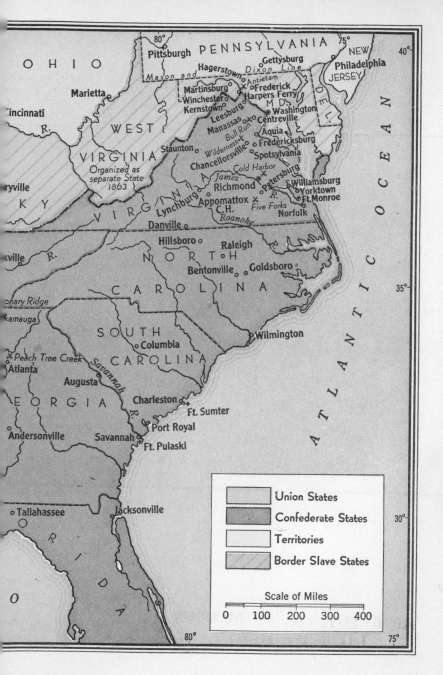

Union States
Confederate States
Territories
Border Slave States

Scale of Miles

0   100   200   300   400

1860–1865

LIBRARY
FLORIDA STATE COLLEGE FOR WOMEN
TALLAHASSEE, FLORIDA

wandered away in search of water, stopped along the roadside to pick blackberries, and generally followed their own devices. Baggage-wagons in charge of unruly civilians brought up the rear, and throngs of sight-seers, including newspapermen, politicians, and even Washington society matrons, all of whom were determined to witness the impending battle, got in everyone's way.

Since McDowell had not less than thirty thousand men under his command, he counted on an easy victory. But unfortunately for these hopes, Johnston was able to give his none-too-clever oppo- *Bull Run* nent, Patterson, the slip, and thanks to a conveniently located railroad succeeded in joining forces with Beauregard on the eve of the Union attack. On the morning of the twenty-first, with the contestants nearly equal in numbers, the battle opened at Bull Run, a few miles north of Manassas. The Confederates had meant to be the first to attack, but an unhappy confusion in orders delayed them and permitted McDowell to develop his admirably devised plan of battle. The men on both sides fought bravely, in spite of their lack of training, and for a time it seemed that the northern troops must surely win. At about three o'clock in the afternoon, however, a Confederate charge, in which the last of Johnston's troops to arrive were just in time to participate, threw the Union right into confusion. Still further dismayed by the rumor, all too true, that the enemy had been heavily reinforced, the same men that had stood their ground bravely all day long now broke and ran. In less than an hour the whole Union army was utterly demoralized, and in full retreat toward Washington. Except for a few hundred regulars, who covered the retreat, all semblance of order was lost, and it was as a panic-stricken mob rather than as a defeated army that McDowell's troops returned to the capital.

On the whole the North was fortunate to have lost at Bull Run. The fear expressed by some of Lincoln's advisers that the Confederates would follow up their victory by the destruction of the Union army and the capture of Washington was wholly unwarranted, for, to use the words of Johnston himself, "the Confederate army was more disorganized by victory than that of the United States by defeat." What the North learned from the humiliating experience was that the war was not to be won by untrained volunteers in a short summer campaign. Only by careful preparation could ultimate success be assured. The South, on the other hand, suffered from a feeling of overconfidence. The southern leaders were not deceived. "I have no idea that the North will give up," wrote Stephens. "Their defeat will increase their energy." But among the masses the conviction grew that the Yankees could not or would not fight. After Bull Run some of the Confederate soldiers went home thinking the war was over.

The "second uprising of the North," which followed closely on the heels of the battle, soon gave Lincoln all the three-year men he asked for, *The Union volunteers* and many more. In raising and organizing these troops, the precedents already set in calling out the state militia were closely followed. Quotas were assigned to the various states, upon whom the primary task of obtaining recruits thus devolved. Communities then vied with one another in the heartiness of their response to the governor's call. Officers from the grade of colonel down were commissioned by the governors, although in practice company officers were usually chosen by the men themselves, and their choices merely ratified by the governor. Care was taken to obtain if possible at least one officer to a regiment who had had some military training, and for this purpose the presence in the northern states of many immigrants who had seen service in Europe proved to be a great advantage. General officers were appointed by the President, by and with the advice and consent of the Senate. This system of recruiting was admirably devised to capitalize fully the existing mass enthusiasm, for the young men of each community could enlist together with the knowledge that they would probably serve together throughout the war. Often they even knew in advance the officers under whom they would serve. But the system also had its disadvantages. When, as frequently happened, certain units took most of the punishment in a given engagement, it followed that the communities from which the men came were correspondingly hard hit. Had the men for each unit been drawn from many different places, the losses would have been more evenly distributed. The problem of replacements was still more perplexing. New companies and new regiments, with a whole new complément of officers, were far easier to raise than an equal number of men for old units that had been decimated by battle losses or disease. Another misfortune was that the War Department chose to keep the regular army intact rather than to distribute it among the volunteer troops to assist in their training. But the President chose many regular army officers for high command in the volunteer army, and it was due mainly to their work that the raw recruits ultimately attained a fair degree of military efficiency. By the spring of 1862, with well over six hundred thousand volunteers accepted, the War Department felt that enough troops had been raised to win the war, and stopped recruiting.

To reorganize the badly beaten "Grand Army of the Potomac," General George B. McClellan was called to Washington. McClellan was a

LINCOLN AND GENERAL McCLELLAN AT ANTIETAM

former regular army officer who as a major-general of Ohio volunteers
McClellan had scored some small but spectacular successes in the occupation of West Virginia. He proved to be an admirable
drill-master, and in a short time brought order out of chaos. By the end
of the summer he had no less than one hundred thousand men at his
disposal, all well disciplined, well equipped, and reasonably well drilled.
The pride of the North in its new army, and in the general who had produced it, was very great. When Scott resigned in November, McClellan
was made commander-in-chief of all the Union forces, and confidence
that he would soon bring the war to a successful conclusion was high.
But as month after month wore on, and nothing was accomplished, the
watchword "All quiet along the Potomac" began to sound like a reproach
to the entire country. McClellan's great defect, it soon appeared, was
his excess of caution.[1] While he was developing a Union army, General
Johnston was doing the same thing over in Virginia for the Confederates. But whereas Johnston's army was never anywhere nearly as
strong as his own, McClellan always insisted that the exact opposite
was true, and, fearful of another Bull Run, he steadfastly refused to
move. Not until March, 1862, after the President had issued express
orders commanding it, did he begin his advance.

The general strategy of the war soon became fairly obvious to all the
participants. Since the South could ask nothing better than to be
Strategy of left alone, the North, in order to win, must take the ag-
the war gressive and wage a war of conquest. The existence of the
Appalachian mountain barrier ensured that there would be two battle-
fronts, one to the east, and one to the west. A third, and extemely important, theater of war lay on the high seas. The South, because of its
primarily agricultural economy, must depend to a great extent for its
munitions of war upon importations from Europe. To pay for these
supplies, it would seek to export cotton, and possibly to a lesser extent
tobacco and sugar. If, therefore, the North could blockade the South,
and could effectively prevent trade between the Confederacy and the
outside world, victory would soon crown the northern arms. The
armies of the East and of the West, advancing simultaneously into the
lower South, would ultimately join forces, crush out the last vestige of
opposition, and restore the supremacy of the Union. The hope of the
South, on the other hand, lay in breaking the blockade, and in maintaining armies in the field large enough to hold the invaders at bay. The

---

[1] This judgment is confirmed, rather than confuted, by McClellan's autobiography,
McClellan's Own Story (1887). An interesting character sketch of McClellan is in Gamaliel
Bradford, *Union Portraits* (1916). See also W. S. Myers, *George Brinton McClellan: a
Study in Personality* (1934).

South did not so much need to win victories as to keep the North from winning victories.

Events on the western front during the first year of the war strikingly paralleled what went on in the East. About a month before Bull Run, General Nathaniel Lyon with a handful of regulars *The western* drove the Confederates from the Missouri state capital and *front* defeated a small secessionist force under General Sterling Price at Boonville, Missouri. This victory virtually ensured control of the northern half of Missouri for the Union, but Lyon's valiant efforts to expel the enemy from the southern part of the state ended with his defeat and death at the battle of Wilson's Creek, on August 10 following. Thereafter the fighting ceased, and in the West as in the East the main concern was the creation of an army. For this purpose two headquarters were established, one at St. Louis on the Mississippi, the other at Cincinnati on the Ohio. Unfortunately the command at St. Louis was given to one of Lincoln's "political" generals, John C. Frémont, who in spite of his former connection with the army had far more exploration than military training to his credit, and proved to be totally lacking in administrative ability. In November, 1861, when his incompetence and the corruption it bred could no longer be tolerated, Lincoln removed him; and a little later he gave the post to General Henry W. Halleck, a middle-aged and uninspiring West Pointer, who had left the army to become a lawyer. Halleck's administration was business-like, but in his excess of caution he was more than a match for McClellan. General Don Carlos Buell, whom Lincoln placed in charge of the "Army of the Ohio," was a more fortunate choice, although Buell regarded his command as wholly independent of Halleck's, and friction between the two became chronic. Fortunately for the North, the decision of Kentucky to remain loyal enabled the Union forces to occupy Louisville, Frankfort, and most of the northern part of that state, and lost for the Confederacy the highly defensible boundary of the Ohio River. But until the spring of 1862 the amount of actual fighting on this front was negligible.

The blockade of the southern coast was decided on immediately after the fall of Sumter. Davis conveniently prepared the way for the introduction of this policy by a proclamation of April 17, 1861, *The* in which he authorized privateers to prey upon the com- *blockade* merce of the United States. Two days later Lincoln retaliated by declaring a blockade of all the ports from South Carolina to Texas, and when Virginia and North Carolina seceded, he added their ports also. With a total of only ninety ships in the United States Navy, and a Confederate coastline of over three thousand miles to be guarded, this proclamation amounted at first to nothing more serious than a "paper blockade." But the Secretary of the Navy, Gideon Welles of Connecticut,[1] although totally ignorant of nautical affairs, developed executive ability of a high order, while his Assistant Secretary, Gustavus Vasa Fox, had been a naval officer, and possessed the necessary technical qualifications. Ships of every sort and kind were converted into blockaders, and before the war was six months old the South had begun to feel the results. Such items as tea, coffee, soap, candles, and matches brought extremely high prices, and were hard to get at any price. Medical supplies fell desperately short of the demand. Because of the lack of print paper, newspapers found it necessary to reduce the size of their issues, and sometimes to print them on brown wrapping paper. Because of the shortage of drygoods, homespun gained steadily in popularity, and women accepted as a patriotic duty the necessity of wearing out-of-date garments.

To make the blockade one hundred per cent effective was, until the very close of the war, wholly outside the realm of possibility. Fleet *Blockade-* blockade-runners, usually of British origin, repeatedly got *runners* through the blockading squadrons under cover of night or fog, and easily outsailed the nondescript ships that the North had pressed into service. Muskets, ammunition, artillery, and nearly all the necessary *matériel* of war were obtained by the South in this fashion. At first, ports in the West Indies and the Bahamas served admirably as headquarters for the blockade-runners, for here the produce of the Confederacy could readily be exchanged for European goods. Irritated by this procedure, the United States government finally advanced the theory that the shipment of goods from European ports to the Confederacy was one "continuous voyage," even if the goods were unloaded and reloaded at neutral ports on this side of the Atlantic. American sea-captains were therefore given orders to seize ships suspected of being engaged in this traffic whether they were found on the "long lap" or the "short lap" of the voyage. This ruling served to tighten up the blockade to some extent, but certainly not to make it entirely effective. Otherwise Lee at Gettysburg, after two years of war, would not have had almost, if not quite, as good artillery as his northern opponent.

Another method used by the North to increase the effectiveness of

[1] *The Diary of Gideon Welles, Secretary of the Navy under Lincoln and Johnson* (3 vols., 1911), gives an intimate account of Welles's activities, and of the whole political history of the times. On the effect of the blockade, see F. B. C. Bradlee, *Blockade Running during the Civil War and the Effect of Land and Water Transportation on the Confederacy* (1925). For the picturesque naval heroes of the war, see Jim Dan Hill, *Sea Dogs of the Sixties* (1935).

the blockade was the capture of southern ports and coast fortifications. As early as August, 1861, the Confederate forts at Hatteras *Amphibious* Inlet, which controlled the best entrance to the waters of *expeditions* North Carolina, were taken by a joint army and navy expedition. The following November a similar attack lost for the Confederacy Port Royal, South Carolina, one of the finest harbors on the southern coast. These "amphibious" expeditions, kept up for the duration of the war, finally closed every Confederate port except Charleston and Wilmington. Although far less spectacular than the great land engagements, they were of tremendous significance; for the success of the blockade, more than any other single factor, brought about the breakdown in southern military efficiency and the collapse in southern civilian morale that enabled the North to win.

Hopeful that the need of the outside world for cotton would bring European nations, particularly England, to their aid, the Confederate leaders were at first inclined to regard the blockade with *The clash of* a certain degree of equanimity. The old illusion that cot- *ironclads* ton was king died hard; surely the navies of England and France must soon break the blockade and open the southern ports. When this hope failed to materialize, however, and the pressure of the blockade became increasingly irksome, the South began to take steps to help herself. The hasty, and probably quite unnecessary, abandonment by the North of the Norfolk navy yard had involved the firing and sinking of the *Merrimac*, a forty-gun steam frigate. This hulk the Confederates raised, remodeled into a low-lying ironclad with ten guns and a cast-iron ram, and dispatched (renamed the *Virginia*, but rarely so called) in March, 1862, against the blockading squadron at Hampton Roads. There on the afternoon of March 8 the *Merrimac* sank the *Cumberland*, a sloop-of-war, forced the *Congress*, a sailing frigate, to strike her colors, and planned to finish off the remaining Union warship, the *Minnesota*, next morning. Well advised from the beginning of the work being done on the *Merrimac*, the Union navy had long had under construction at Brooklyn an ironclad of its own, the *Monitor*, designed by John Ericsson, a Swedish engineer. By an extraordinary coincidence the *Monitor* reached Hampton Roads the night of March 8, so that when the *Merrimac* resumed the fray on the following morning she was met by another ironclad. The *Monitor* was much smaller than the *Merrimac*, and in appearance resembled a "cheese-box on a raft," or a "tin can on a shingle." Her flat, heavily armored deck was surmounted only by a revolving iron tower that carried two powerful guns. In the duel that followed neither ship was able to do serious damage to the other, and the *Merrimac* at length withdrew, never again to figure in the war. The engagement marked a turning-point in naval history, for it proved that the old-fashioned wooden ships were obsolete. But it did nothing to aid the Confederacy, for the North was able to multiply the number of *Monitors* at will, while the South could not produce another *Merrimac*.[1]

The South did succeed, however, in harassing the trade of the North by means of commerce-destroyers. Nineteen of these vessels, of which *Commerce-* the most famous was the *Alabama*, got to sea. Nearly all *destroyers* of them were British-built, manned chiefly by British subjects and outfitted from British ports, but they were officered by the Confederacy, and, acting on its authority, they destroyed a total of over two hundred and fifty northern merchant ships. Their exploits struck an almost fatal blow to the American merchant marine, for the risk of destruction and the consequent high insurance rates led American shipowners to dispose of the bulk of their holdings to foreigners, whereupon the ships were transferred to foreign registry. Commerce between the United States and the outside world was not seriously interrupted, but because of the commerce-destroyers such trade tended increasingly to be carried on under a foreign flag.

The commerce-destroyers were built for speed rather than for heavy fighting, and they proved to be of no value in breaking the blockade. *The Laird* In the spring of 1863, however, it became known that the *rams* same English firm that had built the *Alabama* for the Confederacy was now engaged in the building of two heavy ironclad rams for use in bringing the blockade to an end. Had these "Laird rams" been permitted to sail, they might well have succeeded in opening up a number of southern ports, but the vigorous protests that the United States launched with the British government, backed up by the threat of a war that the British ministry had decided to avoid, caused orders to be issued for their restraint. With the failure of this scheme, the last serious effort of the South to break the blockade came to nought.

The impatience of the northern public with the slow start of the war finally vented itself upon the person of the Secretary of War, Simon Cameron, a Pennsylvania politician whom Lincoln had felt obliged to include in his Cabinet. While Cameron was by no means wholly, or even chiefly, to blame for the existing inertia, his shortcomings as an administrator were soon painfully apparent. Contracts were awarded to political hacks at fantastic figures, the efficiency of the army was

---

[1] The definitive work on this subject is J. P. Baxter, 3d, *The Introduction of the Ironclad Warship* (1933). On the naval activities of the Confederacy, see J. T. Scharf, *History of the Confederate States Navy* (1887).

threatened by the acceptance of inferior goods, and railroads were permitted to make ridiculous overcharges for their services. In January, 1862, Lincoln removed Cameron from office and nominated him to be minister to Russia, an appointment which he accepted and held for a time. Among the loudest of the critics of the administration was another Pennsylvanian, Edwin M. Stanton, who talked freely of "the painful imbecility of Lincoln" and the discreditable record of his subordinates. Stanton was a Democrat, and had served as Attorney-General under Buchanan, but his loyalty to the Union was unquestioned and his ability to serve it had already been demonstrated. Lincoln by a master stroke made him Secretary of War, in which capacity, despite his incorrigibly bad manners, his dangerous habit of interfering in strictly military matters, and his deep-seated personal prejudices, he became a tower of strength to the northern cause. His opinion of Lincoln soon changed.

Less than ten days after Stanton took office, the news of active fighting on the western front began to come in. Lincoln had long urged that something should be done to free the mountaineer Unionists *Fighting in* of eastern Kentucky and eastern Tennessee from Confed- *the West* erate control. From the military point of view, this seemed scarcely worth the pains, for railroads to facilitate such a movement were lacking, whereas farther to the West the existence of navigable waterways, as well as railroads, made the transportation problem much simpler. Nevertheless, a small detachment of Buell's army under General George H. Thomas penetrated as far south as Mill Springs, in southeastern Kentucky, and on January 19–20 won a decisive victory over a slightly superior Confederate force. The way was now open to Cumberland Gap, but the difficulties of maintaining a line of communications into this region were so great that Thomas's victory was not followed up, and his command was soon withdrawn.

Of far greater importance was the beginning of the "river war" in eastern Tennessee. General Albert Sidney Johnston, whom Davis had placed in supreme command of all the Confederate forces in the West, was an abler officer than either Halleck or Buell, and was unharassed by any conflict in authority. He had fewer troops than his opponents, however, and was compelled to fight mostly on the defensive. The natural line of the Union advance was by way of the Mississippi, the Tennessee, and the Cumberland, which almost parallel each other for nearly a hundred miles south of the Ohio. At Columbus and Island No. 10 on the Mississippi, at Fort Henry on the Tennessee, and at Fort Donelson on the Cumberland, Johnston had made every effort to prepare for the

Union attack. Early in February General Ulysses S. Grant, supported by a Union flotilla of gunboats under Flag-Officer Andrew H. Foote, advanced against Fort Henry. On February 6, after hard fighting, the fort surrendered to Flag-Officer Foote an hour and a half before Grant's army arrived on the scene. On February 16 another joint army and gunboat attack under the same officers brought a like fate to Fort Donelson. These victories forced Johnston to abandon his northernmost hold on the Mississippi River at Columbus, and his headquarters at Nashville on the Cumberland. The way seemed well prepared for a Union invasion of eastern Tennessee. Meantime, far out in the Osarks at Pea Ridge, Arkansas, March 5–8, another Union victory drove the Confederates from southern Missouri and northern Arkansas. The North was overjoyed at the success of its arms, and took particular pride in General Grant, whose victory at Fort Donelson was regarded as a kind of offset for the defeat at Bull Run the year before.

Ulysses S. Grant (1822–85)[1] was the son of an eccentric and unprosperous Ohio tanner. Accident rather than ability won him an appoint-

Grant
ment to West Point in 1839, where, to use his own words, he "never succeeded in getting squarely at either end of my class, in any one study, during the four years." Among the thirty-nine members of the graduating class of 1843, reputed to have been unusually weak as a whole, he ranked twenty-first. Commissioned a second lieutenant of infantry, he planned soon to leave the army, but changed his mind with the outbreak of the Mexican War. That conflict, however, brought him only the rank of first lieutenant, and no such distinction as came to Lee, Davis, and many others. The monotony of army life in the Far West, to which he was assigned soon after the war was over, drove him to drink, and in 1854 rather than face a court-martial on the charge of drunkenness he resigned his commission. The year before he had been made a captain. Years of poverty and failure followed, and when the war broke out in 1861 Grant was a clerk at fifty dollars a month in a leather store owned by his two brothers at Galena, Illinois.

In spite of the lack of confidence in himself that had deepened with the years, Grant hoped that his military training and experience fitted him for a colonelcy, and for that rank he applied both at Washington and at Springfield. His applications were ignored until a regiment of

[1] *The Personal Memoirs of U. S. Grant* (2 vols., 1885–86) give a remarkably clear picture of Grant's military career. A satisfactory biography, both military and political, is L. A. Coolidge, *Ulysses S. Grant* (1917). W. B. Hesseltine, *Ulysses S. Grant, Politician* (1935), is primarily concerned with the period after the war, but it contains an excellent chapter on Grant's career as a soldier.

ULYSSES S. GRANT

Illinois volunteers grew mutinous under its "political" colonel and Governor Richard Yates asked Grant, who was almost the only military man available, to accept its command and straighten it out. This task he gladly undertook, and accomplished with ease. Shortly after, when Lincoln asked the Illinois congressmen to make nominations for the rank of brigadier-general, Elihu B. Washburne, from whose district Grant came, sent in Grant's name because Grant was the only colonel from his district who had had military experience. The commission was soon forthcoming, and in August, 1861, Grant took command at Cairo, a village in Frémont's department at the southern tip of Illinois. Without waiting for instructions, Grant forestalled the Confederates in the occupation of Paducah, on the Kentucky side of the Ohio River, and in November, 1861, he successfully attacked a Confederate outpost on the west bank of the Mississippi at Belmont, Missouri, opposite Columbus. These exploits, as well as the location of his command, pointed him out as the natural leader when the time came for the attacks on Forts Henry and Donelson.

The test of time proved that Grant had qualities of tremendous importance to the Union cause. He knew sound advice when he heard it, and was humble enough to accept it. He had a dogged determination, amounting almost to an obsession, never to turn back once he had decided on a given course of action. He chose his subordinates with skill, made his decisions with a degree of speed and accuracy that increased as the war wore on, and accepted without hesitation every new responsibility that was thrust upon him. A member of his staff, General John A. Rawlins, supplemented Grant's qualities admirably, and did much to bring out the best that was in his chief. Among other things, Rawlins saw to it that Grant did not fall again into the liquor habit, which had caused him such sorrow years before. Grant's victory at Donelson, where he refused to accept any terms except "unconditional surrender," won him a sobriquet that followed him all through the war. In "Unconditional Surrender" Grant the North found its first and most authentic hero. He was promptly promoted to the rank of major-general.

Grant seems to have thought that the river war in the West could be won in 1862. He was for following up his initial victory at once, and while somewhat handicapped in this resolve by the cautious and now thoroughly jealous Halleck, he was permitted to advance up the Tennessee River to Pittsburg Landing, a point near the Tennessee-Mississippi border where the river makes a sharp turn to flow north instead of west. With perhaps as many as forty-five thou-

Shiloh

sand men spread out between the river and Shiloh Meeting House, two miles to the southwest, he awaited the arrival of reinforcements under Buell before attacking Johnston's army, known to be near-by at Corinth, Mississippi. Many of Grant's troops were raw recruits, and more attention was paid to making them over into soldiers than to preparing the encampment for an attack. Grant himself spent the nights at Savannah, seven miles away. Sensing the opportunity, Johnston launched an attack on the early morning of April 6 that by nightfall had driven Grant's army out of its camp and to the very banks of the river. The Confederate triumph, however, was short-lived. The death of Johnston, whose refusal to leave the field at the time he was wounded doubtless cost him his life, was a severe blow to Confederate morale, and the arrival of Buell's troops in time to participate in the next day's fighting gave Grant a decided advantage. Beauregard, who had succeeded Johnston in command of the Confederates, was forced back in an orderly retreat to Corinth. But Grant's battle-scarred troops were unable to pursue the retreating enemy, and both sides claimed the victory. The battle of Shiloh, as this engagement is generally called, was a serious setback to Grant's hope of concluding the river war in a single season. A Confederate army of forty thousand men had almost defeated a Union army of sixty thousand, and had inflicted injuries so serious that the advance could not be immediately resumed.

General Halleck, with ill-concealed satisfaction at Grant's discomfiture, now announced that he would take personal command of the army at the front. Grant was supposed to be second in *Evacuation* command, but he was studiously snubbed by his superior, *of Corinth* who prepared cautiously for an advance on Corinth. Here Beauregard collected all the troops he could get, for the capture of the village meant not only the cutting of the important railroad connection between the Confederate capital in Virginia and the port of Memphis on the Mississippi, but also the loss of another link in the north-and-south railroad from the Ohio to the Gulf. But by the end of May he had only sixty thousand men to oppose Halleck's army, which was now swollen to more than double that number. Convinced that to offer battle would be to take unreasonable chances on the loss of his army, Beauregard decided on retreat. When at last Halleck was ready to move, he crawled forward at the rate of a mile a day, and gave Beauregard ample time to withdraw in safety. On the thirtieth of May the Union forces occupied Corinth without a battle.

While all this was taking place, an effort was being made to clear the Mississippi River of Confederates for its entire length. The same day

that Grant was driving Beauregard's troops from the Shiloh battle-
River field, Flag-Officer Foote and his gunboats, aided by troops
fighting under General John Pope, forced the Confederates to
abandon Island No. 10. Soon after this Foote retired from the command because of injuries, but his successor, Flag-Officer Charles Henry
Davis, continued the campaign, and won a spectacular victory over a
Confederate flotilla near Memphis, which became Grant's headquarters.
Meantime a naval squadron under Admiral David Glasgow Farragut
ran the strong defenses that guarded the mouth of the Mississippi, took
New Orleans on April 28 (while Halleck was advancing toward Corinth),
and penetrated up the river as far as Vicksburg.[1] That important
point, however, and some others, could not be taken without a larger
number of troops than Farragut had at his disposal. Nor did it prove
to be of great avail to have swept the Confederates from a large part of
the river as long as the river banks remained in Confederate hands. One
of the chief purposes of this campaign was to cut off the Confederate
states west of the Mississippi from any chance of aiding the Confederate
armies east of the river. That purpose, the northern government tardily
learned, could never be realized by the activities of river boats, here
today and gone tomorrow. The ports along the river had also to be
occupied, and before this could be done the Confederate "Army of the
Mississippi" would have to be reckoned with.

After these spring and early summer campaigns, the river war in the
West reached a stalemate. Halleck dispersed his troops over so wide
an area and under so many different commands that aggressive tactics
were out of the question. Fortunately, however, his presence was
soon required elsewhere than in the West. By accepting full credit for
the successes of his subordinates, and by blaming them for his failures,
he had made for himself an excellent reputation in Washington, whither
he was called in July to become general-in-chief of all the Union armies.
The offensive now passed to the Confederates, who made two brilliant
efforts to regain the territory they had lost. General Braxton Bragg
advanced from Chattanooga through Tennessee and Kentucky with the
Ohio River as his goal, but at Perryville, Kentucky, October 8, 1862, he
was checked by a Union army under Buell. Although neither side won
a victory, the Confederate leader felt obliged to retreat toward Chattanooga. The other Confederate attack was made in western Tennessee,
where Generals Earl Van Dorn and Sterling Price sought to oust the
Union army from its hold on the railroad from Corinth to Memphis.
This campaign ended with a Confederate defeat, October 4, near Cor-

[1] A. T. Mahan, *Admiral Farragut* (1892).

inth. Late in the year Grant resumed the offensive, with the Confederate army before Vicksburg as his goal, but he accomplished nothing, and the year ended with the Union-Confederate lines about where they had been in midsummer.

East of the mountains the North had far less to congratulate itself upon. While Grant was moving on Donelson, McClellan, with two hundred thousand men at Washington to Johnston's fifty *The eastern* thousand at Manassas Junction, let slip the opportunity to *front* strike his adversary a telling blow. Even when ordered by the President to begin an advance on February 22, in honor of Washington's birthday, he delayed long enough on account of bad roads to permit Johnston to withdraw his army to the south bank of the Rappahannock. The middle of March had passed before the cautious Union commander got under way. His plan was to transport his army by sea to Fortress Monroe at the mouth of the Chesapeake, and then to advance up the peninsula between the York and the James Rivers toward Richmond. To satisfy Lincoln and his civilian advisers, who feared that, with McClellan's army gone, the Confederates might somehow attack Washington, McDowell with an army of forty thousand men was to march overland to the peninsula, keeping between Washington and the enemy. At first everything went as planned, but Lee suggested to General "Stonewall" Jackson, who commanded a few thousand "foot cavalry" in the Shenandoah Valley, that a diversion was needed in his area to create the impression that Washington might soon be attacked. On guard in the lower Shenandoah was General Nathaniel P. Banks with at least twenty thousand Union troops, and more near at hand. Nevertheless, Jackson brought on an engagement at Kernstown, March 23, and, although he failed to win the battle, he created the impression that he had with him a powerful army. Fear that Washington might be in danger led Lincoln to cancel McDowell's marching orders and keep him close at hand, near Centreville, Virginia.

McClellan, always overestimating his enemy, was much discomfited at this turn of events, and delayed accordingly. Not until the end of April, when he had 110,000 men on the peninsula, did he dare to begin his advance. Then for a time it seemed as if nothing could stop him. The Confederates, unable to muster more than 65,000 men to meet the invader, evacuated Yorktown on May 3, lost a rear-guard engagement at Williamsburg two days later, and by the middle of the month were preparing to remove their government from Richmond. McDowell, once again on the march, had reached Fredericksburg. But Lee, meantime, had decided to try the same strategy that had worked so well two months before. He increased Jackson's little army in the Shenandoah to 17,000 men, and ordered it to make another diversion. Once more Jackson rose to the occasion. He marched first toward an army of 9000 men under Frémont that was advancing through West Virginia to join Banks, and on May 8, at the village of McDowell, won a decisive victory over its advance guard. Then, after destroying the bridges and blocking the roads over which Frémont meant to march, he returned to the Valley, and in three days' hard fighting, May 23–25, decisively defeated Banks at Winchester. Again the civilian strategists at Washington were sure that the Union capital was in danger, and again, as Lee had hoped, McDowell was called back to protect it. Every effort was then made to entrap Jackson, but repeatedly he defeated in detail the superior forces sent against him, and escaped in safety to the upper Shenandoah.

While all this was going on, the Union army on the peninsula stood still, awaiting the time when McDowell's corps could join it. Richmond *The penin- sular campaign* was only four and a half miles away and the Union forces were overwhelmingly superior, but McClellan dared not attack. Finally the offensive passed to the Confederates. On May 31 Johnston attacked a part of the Union army at Seven Pines, and on the first day's fighting seemed to have won. But on the second day the Union superiority in numbers asserted itself, and he fell back on Richmond. In this battle Johnston himself was severely wounded, and Lee left his post as chief adviser to Davis to become the active commander of the "armies in eastern Virginia and North Carolina." Davis should have made him commander-in-chief of all the Confederate armies, but he long failed to realize that Lee's genius far outmatched his own. On the twelfth of June Lee sent his ablest cavalry officer, J. E. B. Stuart, with twelve hundred men to reconnoiter the Union positions. Finding his retreat cut off, Stuart accomplished the remarkable feat of riding clear around the Union army. Fortified with the information Stuart had brought him, Lee sent word to Jackson to join him for a combined attack on McClellan's army. Jackson obeyed with alacrity, and even succeeded in keeping his destination unknown to the Union scouts. Then, beginning on June 25, there followed the famous Seven Days' Battles, in which Lee forced McClellan to retreat twenty miles to the protection of the Union gunboats on the James River.

This reverse need not have been so serious, for McClellan's army was in good condition and ready to continue the campaign. McClellan now suggested a plan that Grant was to follow successfully later on. He wished to remove his army to the south of the James River, and, by threatening the railroads that brought supplies from the south into Richmond, force the Confederates to abandon the city. But by this time Halleck was in Washington as general-in-chief, and his advice, rather than McClellan's, was followed. Halleck brought with him from the West the brash and boastful General John Pope, whose services in the capture of Island No. 10 both he himself and his superior had much overrated. Pope superseded McDowell; and McClellan, without actually being removed from command, was ordered to embark his army at Harrison's Landing for Aquia Creek on the Potomac. He was then to join Pope, whose "Army of Virginia" lay along the Rappahannock with its principal base at Manassas. No greater blunder could have been made. By a single stroke the pressure on Richmond was removed and McClellan's army was tied up in an operation that would last for a month. Naturally Lee turned his attention to Pope, whom he completely outmaneuvered and defeated at the second battle of Bull Run, August 30. The rout of the Union forces was almost as complete as McDowell's army had suffered at the same place the year before.

Lee now decided that the time had come to carry the war into the enemy's territory, and early in September he crossed the Potomac from Leesburg, Virginia, to Frederick, Maryland. He had no *Battle of* intention of attacking Washington, but meant rather to cut *Antietam* some of the important railroad connections between the East and the West and then invade Pennsylvania. McClellan, who after Pope's disaster resumed command of all the troops about Washington, was compelled to give chase, and on September 12, two days after the Confederates had withdrawn to the northwest, Union troops occupied Frederick. Next day by a lucky chance one of McClellan's soldiers found, wrapped around three cigars, a copy of Lee's "Special Orders No. 191" to his division commanders. These orders divulged the fact that Lee had sent a part of his army back across the Potomac to capture Harper's Ferry and Hagerstown, so that if McClellan had been capable of prompt action he might have won a magnificent victory. But Lee soon found out what had happened, took up a strong position on Antietam Creek, and trusted that McClellan's caution would give him time to reunite his army. In this he was not disappointed, and when the battle came, on September 17, it could hardly be said that either side had won. On September 19 Lee crossed back into Virginia unpursued. Three weeks later Stuart repeated his previous performance, and rode completely around McClellan's army. It was on this occasion that Lincoln remarked: "When I was a boy we used to play a game called 'Three times round and out.' Stuart has been round McClellan twice. The third time McClellan will be out."

But McClellan never had his third time, for in November he was superseded by one of his corps commanders, General Ambrose E. Burnside.

Fredericks- It was a choice of desperation, and Burnside himself not *burg* only protested his unfitness for so great a responsibility, but soon proved it. His plan was to advance southward from a secure base on navigable water at Aquia Creek. But Lee forestalled him in the occupation of Fredericksburg, only twelve miles from Aquia, and from an impregnable position beat off the rash frontal attack that Burnside launched on December 13. Before the winter was over, Burnside followed McClellan into the discard, and like his predecessor was succeeded by one of his own subordinates. This time Lincoln's choice fell on "Fighting Joe" Hooker, an able soldier whom the men liked, but a caustic critic of his superiors. Lincoln's letter to Hooker, entrusting him with the command, set forth clearly the President's misgivings:

> I have heard, in such a way as to believe it, of your recently saying that both the army and the government needed a dictator. Of course it was not for this, but in spite of it, that I have given you the command. Only those generals that gain successes can set up dictators. What I now ask of you is military success, and I will risk the dictatorship.... And now beware of rashness. Beware of rashness, but with energy and sleepless vigilance go forward and give us victories.

Hooker took hold with vigor, and by spring had instilled into the discouraged and defeated Army of the Potomac a feeling of confidence and *Chancel-* buoyancy. His numbers were overwhelming: against Lee's *lorsville* 62,000, still encamped at Fredericksburg, he had fully 130,000 men spread out along the left bank of the Rappahannock. By the end of April the Union army was on the move. Fully conscious of his superiority, Hooker thought it safe to divide his forces. General John Sedgwick with 35,000 men was ordered to attack below Fredericksburg, while Hooker himself with the rest of the army crossed the Rappahannock above the city, near the village of Chancellorsville, and prepared to turn Lee's left flank. The Union cavalry had now reached a fair degree of efficiency, and in imitation of Stuart's tactics General George Stoneman was sent on a raid back of Lee's lines to cut his communications with Richmond. Stoneman succeeded in his task, but his raid was a mistake, for the damage he did was soon repaired, and, as events proved, he was absent when Hooker needed him most. Lee was not deceived by Hooker's plans, and met the Union attack at Chancellorsville, May 2, with all but 10,000 of his troops. A brilliant fourteen-

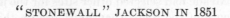
Culver Service

"STONEWALL" JACKSON IN 1851

mile march by Jackson's command around the rear of the Confederate army and then across the Union front enabled the Confederates to surprise the Union right wing and win an astounding victory. On May 5 Hooker, defeated and dazed, retired to his own side of the Rappahannock. The Confederate victory, however, was dearly bought, for Jackson himself was mortally wounded.[1]

Once more Lee determined on taking the war into the enemy's country. Early in June he left Fredericksburg, crossed the Blue Ridge into *Lee again* the Shenandoah Valley, and marched northward toward *crosses the* Maryland and Pennsylvania. Hooker curiously wanted *Potomac* to invest Richmond at once, but Lincoln, who had learned something with the years, wisely observed that "Lee's army and not Richmond is your sure objective point"; so Hooker's army advanced in a northerly direction almost parallel with Lee's, but on the east side of the Blue Ridge. Crossing the Potomac above Harper's Ferry, Lee advanced through the Maryland panhandle, and by the end of June had his entire army, now seventy-five thousand men, on Pennsylvania soil. Both the Confederate and the Union cavalry did excellent work during these weeks in screening the movements of each army from the other. Lee probably blundered, however, in permitting Stuart to make one of his famous distant raids, for while the cavalry was gone, Lee was virtually in the dark as to his opponent's whereabouts. He did not know for three days that on June 27 Hooker had crossed the Potomac, and was hard-by at Frederick. Throughout this trying period Hooker had conducted himself well, but he had constant trouble with Halleck, still general-in-chief, and on the very eve of what turned out to be the most important battle of the war he resigned his command. Almost as surprising, Lincoln accepted his resignation, and gave the command to another Army of the Potomac corps commander, General George G. Meade.

Both Lee and Meade had selected other sites for the impending battle, but the convergence of the roads they must use on the little village of *Gettysburg* Gettysburg, Pennsylvania, took the decision out of their hands. Here on the first of July two brigades of Union cavalry under General John Buford were driven back by a detachment of the Confederate advance guard under General A. P. Hill. Before noon the Union troops were reinforced by the First Corps under General John F. Reynolds, who stemmed the tide of the Confederate advance and chose the positions that the Union army must defend. Reynolds

[1] G. F. R. Henderson, *Stonewall Jackson and the American Civil War* (2 vols., 1898), is one of the best military biographies ever written.

was shot dead long before the day was over, but General Winfield S. Hancock, whom Meade sent forward to replace him, fell in with his plans and established the Union lines along Cemetery Ridge, to the southeast of Gettysburg. By this time both Lee and Meade were concentrating their forces on the scene of the battle. The Confederates occupied Seminary Ridge, to the west of the Union lines, and almost parallel with them. Both battle-lines ran almost directly north and south, and both had natural heights to defend. The advantage, however, lay with the Union army, for it had a numerical superiority of over twenty thousand men, and it could afford to fight on the defensive. Lee, on the other hand, must attack and win, or else order a rapid retreat to Confederate soil.

The battle of Gettysburg lasted two days more. Meade speedily proved himself to be by far the most dangerous adversary Lee had met, and handled his troops with skill and precision. His subordinates, too, executed his orders faithfully and well, while Lee sorely missed the brilliant support of Stonewall Jackson and was hampered by the halfhearted co-operation of Longstreet. Of the fighting on July 2, Lee reported: "We attempted to dislodge the enemy, and, though we gained some ground, we were unable to get possession of his position." Next day at three o'clock, after an extensive artillery preparation, Lee sent General George E. Pickett with ten thousand men directly against the Union center. But Pickett's valiant troops suffered frightful losses from the Union artillery, and were turned back after a brief period of hand-to-hand fighting at the top of Cemetery Ridge. Three fourths of Pickett's men fell dead or wounded, and only a pitiful remnant reached the shelter of the Confederate lines. Next day Lee began his retreat to the Potomac. Forty per cent of his men were killed or wounded, but his cavalry was able to cover his movements, and Meade, whose losses were about thirty per cent of his command, was unable to follow up the victory he had won. Still it was a victory, and with the failure of Pickett's charge at Gettysburg the scales seemed to have tipped definitely in favor of the North.

From the West also came news of a Union triumph. There Grant had been wrestling for months with the difficult problem of taking Vicksburg, the most serious obstacle to northern control *Vicksburg* of the Mississippi River. After all other means had failed, he finally transported his army, in April, 1863, to the west bank of the river above the city, then marched it thirty miles to the south, where, with the help of a flotilla of Union gunboats that had successfully passed the Confederate batteries at Vicksburg for the purpose, he recrossed to the east bank of the river. Then, after dislodging the Confederates from Port Gibson on May 1, he marched northward to invest the city. This movement gave the Union troops the advantage of high ground on which to operate, but it meant that for weeks Grant was without a secure land base, and that his men had to live off the country.

Opposed to Grant's army of forty-three thousand men were forty thousand Confederates under General J. C. Pemberton at Vicksburg, and nearly fifteen thousand more under General J. E. Johnston at Jackson, Mississippi. Perceiving the necessity of defeating Johnston before he could join Pemberton, Grant turned aside from his main objective, and in two battles, at Raymond, May 12, and at Jackson, May 14, won decisive victories. With the city of Jackson now safely in Union hands, Grant headed again toward Vicksburg, only to meet Pemberton, who was vainly seeking to cut his adversary's non-existent line of communications. At Champion's Hill on May 16, and at Big Black River on May 17, Grant won easily, and on the eighteenth Pemberton took refuge within the defenses of Vicksburg. Then followed a long, wearisome siege with Grant's army on one side of the city and the Union gunboats on the other. On July 3, while Meade was winning at Gettysburg, Pemberton met Grant and arranged terms for the surrender of Vicksburg next day — the "Glorious Fourth." On the eighth following, when the news of Grant's victory at Vicksburg had reached Port Hudson, Louisiana, its commander surrendered to General N. P. Banks, who had brought troops up from New Orleans to invest it. A few days later the safe descent of a commercial steamboat from St. Louis to New Orleans justified Lincoln's observation that "the Father of Waters again goes unvexed to the sea." More important still, the Confederate states to the west of the Mississippi were now virtually out of the war.

Meantime General William S. Rosecrans, who had succeeded Buell after the battle of Perryville, was campaigning with another Union *Murfreesboro* army in eastern Tennessee. The Union objective was Chattanooga, which, if taken, would cut squarely in two the only continuous railroad from the East to the West that the Confederacy possessed. At the desperate and bloody battle of Murfreesboro, fought on the last day of 1862 and the first two days of 1863, a Confederate army under General Braxton Bragg successfully halted the Union advance, although Rosecrans claimed the victory. Then, during the rest of the winter and on into the spring and summer, the two armies did little more than keep a close watch on one another. In June Bragg sent General John H. Morgan with twenty-five hundred cavalry on a raid into Kentucky, Indiana, and Ohio that caused some physical and much mental anguish to the loyal civilians along the line of march. Morgan was ultimately captured, and his raid had no military significance, except, perhaps, to divert attention from the retreat of Bragg's army into the strong defenses of Chattanooga. By somewhat the same type of maneuvers that Grant had used at Vicksburg, Rosecrans almost trapped Bragg in Chattanooga, but the Confederate general chose rather to abandon the city to his opponent, who entered it on September 9. Shortly before, General Burnside with a much smaller army had occupied Knoxville, so that Lincoln's hope of rescuing the loyal Unionists of the Tennessee mountains from Confederate control seemed at last to have been realized.

But Bragg was not the man to give up without a battle. Collecting reinforcements from every possible source, he soon had under his command or on the way to join him no less than sixty-six thousand men, while Rosecrans had only fifty-eight thousand. Indeed, the tables were soon completely turned, for Rosecrans was badly beaten at Chickamauga, September 19–20, and his communications with the outside world cut off, except for one narrow wagon-road through the mountains. Real want descended upon the Union camp in Chattanooga, but the administration acted with celerity in coming to the rescue. The discredited Rosecrans was succeeded by General George H. Thomas, whose conduct during the recent battle had won him undying fame as the "Rock of Chickamauga." A division under Hooker was detached from the Army of the Potomac and sent by rail to the West. More important still, General Grant, whose success at Vicksburg had captured the national imagination, was given supreme command in the West, and on October 23 arrived at Chattanooga, soon to be followed by his former army, now under General William T. Sherman. Grant and Thomas quickly opened a road over which the greatly needed supplies could be obtained, and before long, with the troops of Sherman and Hooker converging on his lines, it was Bragg's turn to be beleaguered. The battle of Chattanooga, which followed on November 23–25, was a decisive Union victory, and Bragg was sent in full retreat toward Atlanta. Once again Grant had opened a way to the lower South.

Grant's victories at Vicksburg and Chattanooga marked him as the man so sorely needed to take supreme command of all the Union armies, East as well as West. Congress, therefore, promptly revived the grade of lieutenant-general, and Lincoln as promptly nominated Grant for the place. By March, 1864, the nomination had been confirmed, and the new commander-in-chief was in Washington to assume his responsibili-

Chicka-mauga and Chattanooga

ties. His modesty and tact won him many friends. Halleck was consoled for the loss of his title as general-in-chief by being made Grant's chief of staff, and Meade, who after Gettysburg had spent the rest of the year in a fruitless game of hide and seek with Lee, was left in command of the Army of the Potomac. Grant made it clear, however, that he had no intention of remaining in Washington as an "armchair" general, and the first hard fighting of the spring found him riding side by side with Meade to direct the operations of the Army of the Potomac. If the war was to be won, Lee must be beaten, and Grant rightly concluded that his first duty was to match his wits with Lee's.

The first results were far from reassuring. Grant, with more than one hundred and twenty thousand men to Lee's sixty-five thousand, felt *Grant* justified in advancing overland directly toward Richmond. *vs. Lee* On May 3 he crossed the Rapidan at the Germanna Ford and entered a tangled thicket generally known as the Wilderness. His plan was to cross through this region before fighting a battle, but Lee decided that the now definitely superior Union artillery would be less effective at such a spot than elsewhere, and on May 5 opened the battle of the Wilderness, which raged on for two days, with appalling losses on both sides. Unable to dislodge Lee's army, Grant first wheeled his columns to the left, and then, amidst shouts of joy from troops that had known so many retreats, began again the southward march. But Lee, disregarding the damage that General Phil Sheridan with ten thousand Union cavalry was doing in the Confederate rear, again blocked Grant's way. For five days more, May 8–12, the two armies fought desperately near Spotsylvania. Both here and in the Wilderness Grant's losses far exceeded Lee's, but Grant could count confidently on his government for replacements, whereas Lee could not. Conscious of this advantage, the Union commander unhesitatingly forced the fighting. On May 11 he sent back word to Halleck, "I propose to fight it out along this line if it takes all summer." After Spotsylvania, beaten or not, he advanced again, only to find that in three weeks' intermittent fighting Lee's "living screen" was always between the Union army and Richmond. At Cold Harbor the Confederate army occupied a position so impregnable that Grant's order to attack, as he afterward admitted, was sheer folly. But the defeat he suffered, June 1–3, did not cause him to give up, nor did the administration at Washington supersede him, as it had so frequently done with his predecessors when they were beaten. The heavy fighting, after all, had not been wholly in vain, for Lee's battered army was never the same again, while Grant, in spite of battle losses of over fifty thousand men in a month's campaign, could and did remake his army. For future fighting, however, he chose the south bank of the James, to which he removed his army with such skill and celerity that Lee for a long time did not know what his adversary was about, and made no move to check him. Grant then began the advance toward Richmond by way of Petersburg that McClellan had once recommended in vain, and that ultimately was to end the war.

Grant's plans for the campaigns of 1864 had called for a concerted Union attack on all fronts. While he himself reckoned with Lee's main army, Butler was to lead a small force up the James River and strike at Richmond from the rear, Banks was to co-operate with Farragut in the capture of Mobile, the only Gulf port still remaining in Confederate hands, and Sherman was to advance southeastward from Chattanooga toward Atlanta. Butler had a brilliant opportunity, for his movement was unsuspected, but he was not a good enough general to take full advantage of the situation, and was soon completely checked. Banks, unfortunately, was in no position to play the part assigned to him, for his army, before Grant took command, had been sent by the civilian authorities in Washington on an ill-starred and wholly unnecessary expedition up the Red River, and had not yet returned. Only Sherman succeeded measurably in carrying out the orders he had received.[1]

Indeed, Sherman had already made an extensive raid through Mississippi before the time set for his advance on Atlanta. Wherever his troops went, public property was destroyed, railroads were *The Atlanta* torn up, and many buildings were burned. Later he was *campaign* given credit for the statement, "War is hell," and whether or not he used precisely that phrase, it well describes his tactics. One of the best ways to shorten the war, he believed, was to bring its horrors home to the people of the lower South, who, for the most part, knew war only at a distance. In May, 1864, acting under orders from Grant, he advanced with 100,000 men along the railroad line that led from Chattanooga to Atlanta. His adversary, General J. E. Johnston, who had succeeded Bragg after the battle of Chattanooga, artfully impeded the invader's progress; but Johnston had only 55,000 men at his command, and he wisely avoided a general engagement. Sharp fighting occurred from time to time as Johnston clung tenaciously to carefully prepared positions, and at Kenesaw Mountain, June 27, the exasperated Sherman lost 3000 men in a rash frontal attack. Ordinarily, however, he used his superior numbers to outflank the Confederates, and in two months' time his battle losses were only 16,800 men to 14,500 for Johnston — heavy enough, except when compared with what was going on in Virginia.

[1] Lloyd Lewis, *Sherman, Fighting Prophet* (1932), is an excellent popular biography.

Bleak desolation accompanied the Union advance, and Johnston's defensive tactics, while wholly justified, soon aroused a storm of criticism in the South. With the Union army almost in sight of Atlanta, President Davis removed Johnston on the ground that he had "failed to arrest the advance of the enemy," and put in his place General John B. Hood, who promptly gave battle at Peach Tree Creek, July 20, near Atlanta, July 22, and at Ezra Church, July 28. Each time he lost, but it was not until September 2 that he abandoned Atlanta to the enemy.

Sherman speedily expelled the civilian population from Atlanta, and made the city over into a fortified Union camp. "If the people raise a *Sherman's* howl about my barbarity and cruelty," he told the authori- *march to* ties at Washington, "I will answer that war is war, and not *the sea* popularity-seeking. If they want peace, they and their relatives must stop the war." Hood's army was still intact, and was used by its commander with great skill to threaten Sherman's long line of communications with Chattanooga. Finally Sherman, with Grant's consent, embarked upon a bold course of action. Thomas, with headquarters at Nashville, and an army that was soon strengthened by new recruits to seventy thousand men, was left behind to account for Hood. Atlanta, which not only because of Hood's activities, but also because of the desolation that surrounded it had become a liability rather than an asset, was abandoned and destroyed; and Sherman, with sixty thousand picked men, cut loose from his base and started southeastward toward Savannah, where the United States Navy had already taken Fort Pulaski. "I propose," he said, "to demonstrate the vulnerability of the South and make its inhabitants feel that war and individual ruin are synonymous terms." On the fifteenth of November Sherman left on his long march "from Atlanta to the sea"; on the tenth of the following month he arrived at Savannah. He had been as good as his word. In his wake lay a devastated area nearly three hundred miles long and sixty miles wide. While his army invested the city, news came that on December 15–16 Thomas had defeated and scattered Hood's army near Nashville. Four days after Thomas's victory Sherman received the surrender of Savannah.

The utter hopelessness of the Confederate cause was now apparent. Just as the operations of Grant and Farragut had served the year before to isolate the trans-Mississippi West, so now the campaigns of Sherman and Thomas had taken the lower South out of the war. Only the Carolinas and a part of Virginia remained to be conquered. Moreover, the relative superiority of the North in man-power grew steadily as time went on. By 1865 the southern armies totaled less than two hundred thousand men all told, and the South had no reserves from which to replace battle losses and desertions. The North, on the other hand, had a million men under arms and at least an additional million subject to call. But neither Davis nor Lee was ready to give up. Finally, a few months before the end of the war, Davis made Lee commander-in-chief of all the Confederate forces. This action came far too late to do much good, but Lee promptly restored Johnston to his command, and the two together did what could be done to impede the progress of the northern armies.

Sherman now turned northward with his sixty thousand men to march through the Carolinas and join Grant in Virginia. "God pity South Carolina!" he wrote, as he entered the state which his thor- *Sherman in* oughly efficient army of pillagers regarded as responsible for *the Carolinas* the war. Columbia, the capital, was burned, and the depredations along the march generally exceeded those done by his "dashing Yankee boys" in Georgia. As he advanced, he obtained reinforcements, whereas his opponent, Johnston, who could muster a Confederate army of only forty thousand men, was utterly unable to replace his losses. Sherman's march through the Carolinas, however, was no such easy promenade as his march through Georgia. The country was much more difficult, and in Johnston he had a worthy opponent. At Bentonville, North Carolina, March 19–21, Johnston gave battle, but with such odds against him that he had no chance to win. A few days later Sherman had made Goldsboro, North Carolina, his headquarters. He was now within one hundred and fifty miles of Grant's army in Virginia, and had more than twice as many men as Johnston.

Ever since the summer of 1864 Grant had been engaged in the dreary business of besieging Petersburg and Richmond. For a while Lee used the Shenandoah Valley successfully for diversions, but *Sheridan in* General Phil Sheridan, acting under Grant's orders, finally *the* put an end to that. Twice, at Opequon Creek, September *Shenandoah* 19, 1864, and at Cedar Creek, exactly a month later, he won notable victories over his opponent, General Jubal Early, but his chief contribution was the devastation of the Shenandoah Valley. On October 7, 1864, he reported to Grant: "I have destroyed over 2000 barns filled with wheat, hay, and farming implements; over 70 mills filled with flour and wheat; have driven in front of the army over 4000 head of stock, and have killed and issued to the troops not less than 3000 sheep. . . . Tomorrow I will continue the destruction of wheat, forage, etc., down to Fisher's Hill. When this is completed, the Valley from Winchester up to Staunton, ninety-two miles, will have but little in it for man or beast." Not only was it impossible for the Confederate cavalry to operate in a region so denuded of forage, but it was likewise impossible for Lee to depend any longer upon the Valley to furnish supplies for his army at Richmond.

Only because the Union lines about Richmond and Petersburg did not encircle the cities had Lee been able to withstand Grant's siege so long. *The* Railway connections leading to the west were still open, and *Petersburg* over them came the supplies on which the Confederate *campaign* army lived. By the spring of 1865, however, Lee's position had become extremely precarious. He had less than 50,000 men to Grant's 113,000, and with Sherman approaching from the South the odds threatened soon to be even worse. Late in March Grant began to extend his lines to the west from below Petersburg. A battle followed at Five Forks, April 1, in which the Confederates were badly beaten, and next day Lee abandoned both Petersburg and Richmond. Lee's plan was to get away to the mountains, where he thought he might continue the war indefinitely, but he experienced great difficulty in obtaining supplies and moved too slowly. By the seventh Grant's army was upon him; two days later Sheridan's cavalry, well supported by infantry, was in front of him. "There is nothing left me but to go and see General Grant," he said, when he heard the news, "and I would rather die a thousand deaths."

The same day in the village of Appomattox Court House, Lee and Grant met for a conference that virtually ended the war. Grant, who *Lee's* had discussed with Lincoln a few days before the terms on *surrender* which Lee's surrender should be accepted, was magnanimous. All the Confederate troops, officers as well as men, were to be paroled under promise not to serve against the United States again until exchanged; all military stores and arms, except the sidearms of officers, were to be surrendered; the mounted Confederates, who unlike the Union cavalry owned the horses they rode, were to be allowed to keep their mounts. Learning that Lee's men were desperately short of food, Grant also ordered that rations for twenty-five thousand men, approximately the number of troops Lee had surrendered, should be sent to the former enemy at once. Johnston, whose army was now "melting away like snow before the sun," realized that further resistance was useless and soon surrendered to Sherman on the same terms that Grant had given Lee. One by one the lesser bodies of Confederate troops laid down their arms, and on May 10 Jefferson Davis himself was captured. The Confederate States of America had ceased to exist.

The Union was saved, but at a fearful cost. For four years great numbers of men had been taken by both sides from productive employment and had been turned into efficient engines of destruction. The total number of enlistments in the Union army had been about 2,900,000; in the Confederate army about 1,300,000. But because *Losses of the war* these figures take no account of short-term enlistments they fail to give an accurate picture of the relative strength of the two armies. A careful student of the subject, Thomas L. Livermore, computes that the Union army was equivalent to about 1,500,000 men serving for three years, and the Confederate army on the same basis, to about 1,000,000 men. These statistics are doubtless inaccurate, and the confused state of the records makes it virtually impossible to estimate the actual number of individuals who served on one side or the other. The death-toll was terrific. For the Union army, counting those killed or mortally wounded in battle, and those who died from sickness or other causes, Livermore sets the figure at about 359,000 and for the Confederate army at about 258,000. Among the survivors were thousands who were maimed for life, and other thousands whose health was permanently undermined.[1]

In spite of the enthusiasm that had at first moved more men to join both armies than the two governments were able to make over into soldiers, the volunteering principle failed, unaided, to supply the huge armies that had somehow to be raised. Loath to resort to conscription, both North and South first tried to encourage enlistments by offering bounties. Many of the southern troops had enlisted for one year only, and late in 1861 they were offered a bounty of fifty dollars and a sixty-day furlough to re-enlist. The North went much further. From the beginning of the war it offered a cash bounty of one hundred dollars to every volunteer, and in 1863 it raised the sum to three hundred and two dollars for new recruits, and four hundred and two dollars for veterans who would re-enlist. Even so, conscription was not to be forestalled for long.

The South invoked it first. Comparatively few of the twelve-months troops accepted the bounty-furlough offer, and in the spring of 1862, with the northern drives beginning, something had to be *Conscription in the South* done to keep them in the army. Accordingly, on March 28, 1862, President Davis was authorized to disregard all short-term enlistments and retain everyone then in the service for three full years from the date of his original enlistment. Also, he might conscript for a like period all white males between the ages of eighteen and thirty-five. Six months later the age limit was raised from thirty-five to forty-five, and

---

[1] T. L. Livermore, *Numbers and Losses in the Civil War in America, 1861–1865* (1901). These figures, it is only fair to state, are hotly contested. Probably it is impossible to compile anything like exact statistics.

in February, 1864, conscription was made applicable to all between seventeen and fifty. In the closing months of the war many Southerners, including General Lee, believed that the slaves should be offered their freedom to enlist, and on March 13, 1865, the Confederate Congress actually passed such a law. But the measure came too late to be of any use. In the earlier conscription laws, liberal exemptions were permitted, but toward the end these were whittled down to extremely narrow limits.

The North was a year later than the South in resorting to conscription, and when on March 3, 1863, a draft act was finally passed, it differed *The northern draft* materially from the southern conscription laws. The purpose of the northern act was primarily to stimulate enlistments. Only when a given district had failed to produce its assigned quota of troops by volunteering was the draft to be applied. It was thus made a point of honor for a state or a city or a county to supply all the soldiers required of it by means of volunteering, and without resort to the draft. All the able-bodied citizens, and all aliens who had declared their intention of becoming citizens, between the ages of twenty and forty-five were enrolled by districts, roughly resembling the congressional districts, and in assigning quotas to each district the President was to take into consideration the number of volunteers it had already furnished. Many whole states were able to escape the draft altogether, and the number of men forcibly inducted into the northern army was trifling.

But the stimulation to enlistment was very real. Bounties were raised to fantastic figures as states, counties, and cities vied with one another for volunteers. In some districts the total amount of bounty-money that a man who enlisted could claim ran to over a thousand dollars. Immigrants, particularly those coming from Ireland, were often persuaded to enter the army as a means of getting a start in the new land. So generous were the rewards that a class of "bounty-jumpers" arose, whose business it was to enlist and collect the bounty, then desert and re-enlist as often as possible.[1] Lincoln's tender-heartedness caused him to pardon many such deserters, and deeply irritated the draft authorities. But whatever the defects of the system, the draft and the bounties worked relentlessly to keep the Union armies full. Generous exemptions were allowed, and at first a man who was drafted could escape service either by paying three hundred dollars or by hiring a substitute. This provision, which led to the charge that the struggle was a "rich man's war but a poor man's fight," was soon abolished, and a like provision in the southern conscription law went the same way.

[1] Ella Lonn, *Desertion during the Civil War* (1928).

In both North and South the attempts to enforce conscription met forcible resistance. In the North serious "draft riots" occurred in New York City and elsewhere during the summer of 1863. In the South resistance was strongest in the mountain regions where the Confederate cause was never popular, and among the states'- rights extremists, who thought that in conscripting an army the southern government was exceeding its powers. In several southern states, particularly in Georgia, where Governor J. E. Brown definitely branded the conscription law as unconstitutional, and in North Carolina, where the legislature added at will to the exempted classes, the execution of the law was somewhat impeded. On the whole, however, resistance to conscription, both North and South, was ineffective. Thanks to these measures the South put practically its entire man-power into the field, and the North drew as heavily upon its man-power as was necessary to win the war.

Resistance to conscription

CHAPTER XXXIII

BEHIND THE LINES

WHEN the Civil War broke out the North had not fully recovered from the depression that had followed the panic of 1857, and for a time business interests were more frightened than stimulated by the clash of arms. By the summer of 1862, however, a surge of prosperity had put in its appearance that was to outlast the war. The returns of agriculture were phenomenally good, manufactures flourished as never before, railroads rolled up huge wartime profits, and business generally enjoyed a "boom." [1]

Prosperity for the northern farmer was in part a result of the abnormal demands of war. With millions of men under arms the government *War and* became a dependable and generous purchaser of every kind *prosperity* of foodstuff, and its equally great need of woolen goods and leather strengthened the market also for raw wool and hides. Probably the sales that the farmers made directly or indirectly to the government more than offset the losses sustained by wartime interference with sales to the South. And, as a matter of fact, much of this intersectional trade persisted in spite of the war, and in spite of the half-hearted efforts of the government to suppress it.

Almost equally important, however, was the chance that forced Great Britain during these critical years to import from the United States a large proportion of its wheat. For some time the British farmer had failed to supply the United Kingdom with all the wheat it needed, but in the early years of the Civil War a succession of crop failures made the

---

[1] E. D. Fite, *Social and Industrial Conditions in the North during the Civil War* (1910), is an excellent analysis of the causes of northern prosperity. A. C. Cole, *The Irrepressible Conflict, 1850–1865* (1934), is of equal merit and wider scope. It covers the social and economic history of both North and South in the decade before as well as during the war. All phases of the conflict, but with the emphasis on politics, are covered in Channing, VI; Rhodes, III–V; and Schouler, VI. The same can be said also of J. B. McMaster, *History of the People of the United States During Lincoln's Administration* (1927). Useful short accounts are F. L. Paxson, *The Civil War* (1911); J. F. Rhodes, *History of the Civil War* (1917): and N. W. Stephenson, *Abraham Lincoln and the Union* (1918).

deficiency abnormally large. Ordinarily the British shortage in wheat had been made up by importations from the Continent, from South America, or from Egypt, but these sources of supply now proved to be insufficient, and the importation of wheat from the United States became a virtual necessity. During the three-year period 1861–63, northern farmers actually furnished more than forty per cent of the wheat and flour imported into Great Britain, and the total export of wheat from the United States rose to well above fifty million bushels annually, three times the normal amount.

Several circumstances conspired during these same years to make possible the needed expansion of American agriculture. In the first place, it was possible to increase the acreage under cultiva- *Agricultural* tion almost at will. All along the frontier, and elsewhere, *expansion* good land that had remained unworked or unappropriated was pressed into service. Moreover, with the South out of the Union, a homestead law, so long the goal of believers in free land, was speedily enacted (1862). Thereafter any person who was the head of a family, or had arrived at the age of twenty-one years, whether a citizen of the United States or an alien who had declared his intention of becoming a citizen, might take up a quarter section of public land, and, after having lived upon it for five years and improved it, might receive full title to it virtually free of charge. Comparatively little use was made of this law during the war, although under its terms thousands of acres of new land were placed under cultivation, immediately after the war ended, all along the "middle border," in Iowa, Kansas, Nebraska, and Minnesota.

Very important also was the rapid introduction of labor-saving farm machinery. Such valuable aids to farming as the improved plow, the corn-planter, the two-horse cultivator, the mower, the reaper, and the steam thresher had all been invented before the Civil War, but it took the acute shortage of man-power that resulted from placing millions of men under arms to induce farmers to give up their old-fashioned methods and make use of the new tools. Before the war, with farm labor relatively cheap and plentiful, the farmer had seen little point to labor-saving machinery. But when he was faced with the alternative of losing his crops or using the machines, he used the machines. A reaper operated by one man could cut ten or twelve acres of grain in a day, whereas the best a man could hope to do with an old-fashioned back-breaking cradle was an acre and a half. By utilizing the new implements the northern farmer was able to take care of a vastly increased acreage without serious difficulty. Even women and children could operate many of the machines, and in innumerable instances they were called upon to do so. By 1865 it was estimated that not less than two hundred and fifty thousand reapers were in use in the United States.[1]

Of some assistance also was the trend toward more scientific methods of farming. The states that lay to the east of the virgin lands of the *The Morrill* frontier were soon aware that they suffered from certain *Land Grant* obvious disadvantages. Their soil would not, unaided, *Act* grow such crops as the newer states could produce. In the older states, particularly, much of the land had been "cropped to death." Discerning men, mostly Easterners, had begun well before the Civil War to advocate the scientific study and teaching of agriculture, but legislative response to their pleas, curiously, came at the outset more from the West than from the East. In 1857 Michigan established the first state college of agriculture, only to be emulated in quick succession by Iowa in 1858, and Minnesota in 1859. By the latter date Justin S. Morrill of Vermont, chairman of the House Committee on Agriculture, had pushed through Congress a measure for the granting of public lands to each of the states as an endowment for agricultural education. But Buchanan vetoed the bill, and it was not until 1862, with Lincoln in the presidential chair, that the Morrill Act was placed on the statute-books. Each state, according to the new law, was granted as many times thirty thousand acres of public land as the number of senators and representatives it elected to Congress. Thus stimulated, the establishment of agricultural colleges, or of agricultural departments in state-supported universities, spread rapidly from state to state. The wartime character of the Morrill Act is attested by the fact that the measure required that courses in military training be offered by each of the educational institutions that received benefits under the terms of the act.

Another factor, probably of far greater importance than agricultural education in promoting the welfare of northern agriculture during the Civil War, was the weather. Year after year ideal climatic conditions prevailed over the greater part of the North. The total wheat production of the loyal states and territories rose from 142,000,000 bushels in 1859 to 187,000,000 in 1862, and to 191,000,000 in 1863. This was the banner year for wheat, but the general level of production for all agricultural commodities remained high throughout the entire war. With inflated prices, and with adequate transportation facilities available both by land and by sea, the American farmer enjoyed a degree of prosperity that he had never known before.

Much as agriculture profited from the war, the stimulus given by the

---

[1] H. N. Casson, *The Romance of the Reaper* (1908); Joseph Schafer, *A History of Agriculture in Wisconsin* (1922), and *The Social History of American Agriculture* (1936).

struggle to manufacturing was even greater. The armies required huge quantities of manufactured goods of every sort and kind — *Wartime* clothing, boots and shoes, hats and caps, blankets, wagons, *manufactur-* arms and ammunition, ready-to-eat rations, and innumer- *ing* able other items. To meet these needs old factories were remodeled and expanded and new factories were built. As was the case with the farmer, the manufacturer had only to make use of inventions already at hand in order to increase his output. Possibly of all machines the sewing machine helped him most. By use of it whole uniforms, and many other types of garments, could be turned out in far greater quantity and with far less hand labor than had ever been possible before. The war, indeed, changed the clothing habits of masculine America completely. For the average male citizen ready-made suits permanently replaced suits made at home or at the local tailor shop. Out of the war, too, came the habit of using such factory-made items as shoes, caps, socks, and prepared foods. It is not too much to say that the war brought to an end the last remaining survivals of the domestic system of manufacture in the United States. Manufacturers whose fortunes were founded on government contracts saw their wealth continue to increase after the war, for the changes in customs that the war promoted enabled them to sell with equal advantage to the civilian population.

What came in later times to be called the "heavy industries" profited enormously from the war. Purchases of munitions abroad practically ceased after the first year because of the rapidity with which American factories supplied the government's needs. The new steel mills, gun factories, and powder plants that came into existence were for the most part the results of private initiative, but the government itself went as deeply into the business of manufacturing war materials as public opinion would permit. Before the end of the war, for example, the government arsenal at Springfield, Massachusetts, was producing a thousand rifles a day. Railroad-building, which was resumed in the North after the outbreak of the war, and the continual need for railroad repairs, did much for the manufacturers of iron and steel. They were helped, also, by the demand for ironclads that set in after the battle between the *Monitor* and the *Merrimac*.

High tariffs ensured the northern manufacturers against the dangers of European competition. A protectionist policy had been demanded by the Republican national platform of 1860, and a higher *The Morrill* schedule of tariffs, sponsored by the same Justin S. Morrill *Tariff Act* who gave his name to the act for the stimulation of agricultural education, was placed upon the statute-books two days before Buchanan left office. This speedy answer to the prayers of the protectionists was made possible by the withdrawal from Congress of the delegations from the seven seceding states of the lower South, and by the fact that President Buchanan was no longer unmindful of the wishes of the manufacturers within his home state. The original Morrill Tariff Act was repeatedly revised upward during the war, until by 1864 the average of duties levied on imports had reached forty-seven per cent, the highest thus far in the history of the nation. The significance of this development can scarcely be overemphasized. A policy which the South had persistently blocked in the years preceding the war became an actuality during it, and, as subsequent events were to prove, remained as a permanent fixture in American political and economic life.

An important component part of northern wartime prosperity was the production of a sufficient quantity and variety of raw materials to satisfy *Exploitation* the needs of the northern manufacturers. The mining of *of natural* coal, which was not only a lucrative industry in itself but *resources* served also as a kind of measuring-stick for the progress of the factory system, increased threefold, and the production of such basic items as iron ore, copper, salt, and petroleum reached unprecedented heights. Lumber also was in great demand, and the forests of the Great Lakes region, of Maine, and of New York were exploited as never before. Wool-growers found a ready market for all the wool they could grow, and by 1865 were producing annually two and one third times as much wool as in 1860. The only commodity that the northern manufacturers experienced serious difficulty in obtaining was cotton, and there was enough trading through the lines, both licensed and illicit, to hold this shortage to a minimum.

Another important source of northern prosperity lay in the output of the gold and silver mines of the Far West. While the flow of precious metals from the mines of California was somewhat diminished during the war, new mines were opened up in various parts of the Rocky Mountains area — particularly in the regions later known as Colorado, Nevada, Arizona, and Montana — that more than made up for this loss. Millions of dollars' worth of gold and silver thus flowed into the national mints at a time when the nation's need for hard money was greatest.

Indeed, from whatever angle the subject is viewed, the wartime prosperity of the North was phenomenal. Its railroads, overbuilt dur- *Business* ing the fifties, were turned into profitable investments by *activities* the heavy traffic of the war, and the railroad mileage of both the Northeast and the Northwest had to be substantially increased to

[664]

carry the load. Internal waterways — the Great Lakes, the western rivers, and the canals — did an enormous volume of business. Financial institutions, which at the outset of the war had seriously missed the patronage of the South, found a more than adequate compensation for this loss in the expanding commercial activity of the northern states. The northern merchant marine, as already noted, was virtually ruined by the war; but this involved little loss of capital, for most of the ships were sold, not sunk, and the proceeds from their sale were invested in such lucrative securities as government bonds, manufacturing concerns, and railroads. From one point of view, American shippers were fortunate in leaving the field of ocean transportation at this particular time. Wooden ships were soon to be replaced by ships of iron and steel, and many American firms sold out just in time to escape the cost of extensive replacements.

The profits of war bred a spirit of extravagance and frivolity among the non-combatants of the North that contrasted oddly with the long casualty lists displayed as a regular part of the daily news. *Wartime* Social life reached a dizzy whirl, with more parties and *extravagance* dances, theaters and circuses, minstrel shows and musicales than ever had been known before. Public interest in sports tended to grow rather than to diminish, and to such standard outlets of the sporting instinct as horse-racing and prize-fighting were added the crude beginnings of baseball, soon to be the favorite game of the nation. The *nouveaux riches*, of whom every community had its quota, spent so lavishly as to win the contempt of more sober-minded citizens. Their purchases of foreign luxuries, rather than imports needed for the prosecution of the war, resulted in an unfavorable balance of trade with Europe that sent $54,000,000 of American gold abroad in 1863 and $91,000,000 in 1864. Prosperity, however, was not evenly divided, and labor in particular failed to obtain its proportionate share. With prices rising steadily throughout the war, wages rose also, but never rapidly enough to keep pace with the cost of commodities. According to a statement published by the *Springfield Republican* in 1864, many of the factories whose profits during the war had been "augmented beyond the wildest dreams of their owners" paid their laborers only from twelve to twenty per cent more than before the war. "There is absolute want in many families, while thousands of young children who should be at school are shut up at work that they may earn something to eke out the scant supplies at home." As a consequence of such tactics on the part of employers labor disorders were frequent, and a strong impetus was given to labor organization.

If the war brought prosperity to the North, it brought little but adversity to the South.[1] With the welfare of the section so intimately

Downfall of "King Cotton" bound up with cotton culture, the failure of southern cotton to find a normal market was simply catastrophic. The southern government, gambling on the hope that European nations would come to the aid of the South whenever European mills faced a serious enough cotton shortage, tried in the early months of the war to prevent the shipment of cotton abroad. Cotton-planters were even urged to destroy their crops as the best insurance against exportation, and it is estimated that this mistaken policy cost the South about a million bales of cotton. Had exportation been stimulated rather than discouraged, the South might have built up credit abroad for subsequent use, but faith in the power of "King Cotton" clouded the judgment of the southern leaders.[2] By 1862 the southern government was ready to reverse its cotton policy, but by that time the northern blockade held shipments to a minimum. The effectiveness of the blockade may be estimated from the fact that the price of cotton in Liverpool rose from fourteen cents in 1861 to fifty cents in 1865. Trade between the lines helped the South and the cotton-planter to some extent, especially after the northern armies had penetrated far into the southern states. In exchange for cotton and tobacco, southern traders received salt, clothing, foodstuffs, and even war materials. Naturally much of this trade was accomplished by means of the most demoralizing bribery and corruption.

The break with the North, followed by the blockade, forced the South to attempt a far greater diversity of economic life, both agricultural and

Southern manufacturing industrial, than it had known before the war. Foodstuffs were grown instead of cotton, salt-works[3] were established wherever the resources justified, while cotton mills, boot and shoe factories, munitions plants, and the like were started up in spite of inadequate capital, defective machinery, and poorly trained workers. The difficulties experienced by the South in its effort to achieve self-sufficiency, however, were too great to be overcome in a short space of time, and as the war wore on, both soldiers and civilians were frequently called upon to endure the greatest extremes of privation. While the North was pushing forward relentlessly to the factory system, the South was compelled to resort more and more to household manufacture. The

---

[1] An important, but difficult, book is J. C. Schwab, *The Confederate States of America, 1861–1865: A Financial and Industrial History of the South during the Civil War* (1901). A simpler story is told in N. W. Stephenson, *The Day of the Confederacy* (1919).

[2] F. L. Owsley, *King Cotton Diplomacy* (1931); James A. B. Scherer, *Cotton as a World Power; a Study in the Economic Interpretation of History* (1916).

[3] Ella Lonn, *Salt as a Factor in the Confederacy* (1933). The trials of the war-torn South are well told in M. P. Andrews, *The Women of the South in War Times* (1920).

breakdown of southern transportation, particularly the railroads, which the South was utterly unable to keep in repair, served to compound the confusion. The suffering endured by northern prisoners in southern prison-camps was due far more to this confused economic situation than to any deliberate intent on the part of the jailers.[1]

But even the hard-pressed South was not without its war profiteers. Most of those who made money out of the war were associated in some fashion or other with blockade-running, from which the *Southern* returns were frequently spectacular. Money inflation *profiteers* tempted also to speculation, a passion which, according to Jefferson Davis, "seduced citizens of all classes from a determined prosecution of the war." The southern *nouveaux riches*, while more limited in their opportunities than those of the North, did not hesitate to make whatever vulgar display of their wealth they could, and the social life of such cities as Charleston and Richmond kept up an appearance of gaiety to the very end.

Once prosperity was in the saddle, the North had little difficulty in financing the war. At the outset, however, the credit of the northern government was at low ebb, the treasury was empty, and *Northern* the banks of the country were so skeptical of the outcome *wartime* that they soon suspended specie payments. Secretary of *finance* the Treasury Chase had little acquaintance with finance, and was so fearful of the political effects of taxation that he proposed to pay the cost of the war mainly from loans. At first he was compelled to pay ruinous rates to obtain money — on one occasion as high as 7.3 per cent — but with the assistance of Jay Cooke,[2] a Philadelphia banker, he succeeded in floating loans that totaled by the end of the war well over two billion dollars. Cooke popularized the bond issues, and besides making the public see that they were a good investment, he played most successfully upon the patriotic motive. People bought bonds to help the government as well as to help themselves. Cooke himself profited considerably from his undertaking, for the government allowed him a commission of one half of one per cent on all the sales he made up to ten million dollars, and three eighths of one per cent on all sales above that amount.

While loans were the chief reliance, the government resorted also to far heavier taxation than the people of the United States had ever before been called upon to pay. In 1862 excises were levied upon a remarkable variety of articles, businesses, occupations, and activities. This tax levy,

[1] W. B. Hesseltine, *Civil War Prisons — a Study in War Psychology* (1930); C. H. Wesey, *The Collapse of the Confederacy* (1922).

[2] E. P. Oberholtzer, *Jay Cooke, Financier of the Civil War* (2 vols., 1907).

according to James Ford Rhodes, "might be briefly described with a near *Northern* approach to accuracy as an act which taxed everything." [1] *taxation* Even lawyers, physicians, and dentists were required to buy licenses, and such articles as liquor, tobacco, carriages, yachts, billiard-tables, and plate carried heavy duties. Manufacturers were required to pay a tax for the privilege of manufacturing, and the articles they manufactured were also taxed. Railroads, steamboats, toll-bridges, savings banks, insurance companies, and the like paid a three per cent duty on their gross receipts. Multifold as these taxes were, they did not produce a great revenue. Even with the help of increased rates, levied in 1864, the total receipts from all such sources during the war barely passed the $300,000,000 mark. An income tax, which began in 1861 as a three per cent tax on all incomes above $800, and was later so modified as to tax incomes between $600 and $5000 at the rate of five per cent, and all higher incomes at the rate of ten per cent, was even less successful as a revenue measure, for it brought in a total of only $55,000,-000. Still these were large sums to a people quite unused to federal taxation. Tariff levies, pushed steadily upward as an offset to the internal taxes that protected interests were required to pay, also netted the government more than $305,000,000 during the four years that the war lasted.

But neither the loans nor the taxes sufficed to keep the government supplied at all times with ready cash, and as a result several issues of *Greenback* paper money were authorized by Congress. Between Feb-*issues* ruary, 1862, when the first of the "legal tender" acts was passed, and March, 1863, the date of the last, a total of no less than $450,000,000 in fiat money was ordered printed. Of this sum $431,000,-000 was outstanding at the close of the war. Back of the "greenbacks," as the public promptly dubbed these notes, there lay no gold reserve, but only the good faith of the government. Since they were by law made legal tender for all debts, public and private, except duties on imports and interest on the public debt, they constituted in fact a forced non-interest-bearing loan that the government as an emergency measure exacted from the people. [2]

A National Bank Act, passed in 1863 and amended in 1864, provided the nation with yet another type of paper money: the national bank-note. According to this measure, any association desiring to do a

---

[1] *History of the United States*, IV, p. 58. By permission of The Macmillan Company, publishers.

[2] W. C. Mitchell, *A History of the Greenbacks with Special Reference to the Consequence of their Issue, 1862–1865* (1903).

national banking business and possessed of the minimum capital ($50,000 for cities of less than 6000 inhabitants, $100,000 for cities of from 6000 to 50,000, and $200,000 for larger cities) was entitled to a national charter of incorporation. Partly *The National Bank Act* as a means of stimulating the market for United States bonds, the law provided that one third of the capital of such a bank must be invested in national securities, but it was also stipulated that, by depositing these bonds with the United States Treasurer as security, the bank should be entitled to receive in exchange "circulating notes equal in amount to ninety per centum of the current market value of the United States bonds so transferred and delivered." It was hoped at first that the state banks would quickly convert themselves into national banks, but when this failed to materialize, Congress levied in 1865 a ten per cent tax on all state bank-notes. While this law did not destroy state banking, it did, as was intended, tax state bank-notes out of existence, so that one of the legacies of the Civil War was a national currency, composed in part of greenbacks and in part of national bank-notes. By the end of 1865 the national bank-note circulation had reached more than $200,000,000. The bank-notes were not "legal tender," as were the greenbacks, but the two types of paper money depended in the last analysis upon the credit of the national government, and circulated at the same value.

Since the government had been forced to suspend specie payments early in the war, none of this paper money was worth its face value in gold. Two main factors controlled the value of a paper dollar: (1) the amount of paper in circulation, and (2) the *Currency depreciation* success or failure of the Union armies at the front. During the dark days of 1864, when it appeared that even the tenacity of Grant might prove insufficient to win the war, the value of the paper dollar, as expressed in terms of gold, dropped to thirty-nine cents, and even at the close of the war it stood at only sixty-seven cents. Even fractional currency was driven out of circulation as the premium on precious metals mounted, and the Treasury was forced to issue paper half-dollars, quarters, dimes, five-cent and three-cent "shinplasters," as the small-sized notes were called. The paper dollars themselves, as well as the notes of larger denominations, were of generous dimensions — about twice the size of the currency now in circulation. Their fluctuating value caused an equivalent fluctuation in prices that netted huge fortunes to speculators. While the wages of laborers rose slowly to meet the new price-levels, the salaries of "white collar" workers proved to be extremely resistant to change. Soldiers, also, fought on at thirteen dollars a month until late in the war, when their pay was raised to sixteen dollars. The generous bounties paid for enlistments served, however, to correct this inequality.

In addition to the official expenditures of the United States government for the winning of the war there was an unknown amount of assist-*Private* ance given to the cause by private individuals. In the early *benevolence* weeks of the struggle the outfitting of soldiers was often paid for by patriotic men or groups, some of whom neglected to bill the government for their expenditures. The families of soldiers were in innumerable instances cared for by relatives and neighbors. Ladies' Aid Societies in nearly every village sewed and knit and made bandages for the "boys in blue." A group of humanitarians, led by Henry W. Bellows and Frederick Law Olmsted, organized early in 1861 the United States Sanitary Commission to aid in the care of the sick and wounded. This society, which the United States government recognized with some reluctance, co-operated effectively with the hopelessly overworked Medical Bureau of the army, and raised millions of dollars in gifts for the purpose.[1] "Sanitary fairs" were held all over the country to stimulate the collection of funds, and from the larger cities and from California huge sums were obtained. Pacific coast communities consciously atoned in this way for their inability to contribute their proper proportion of men to the northern armies. So sustained, the Commission became "a great machine running side by side with the Medical Bureau wherever the armies went." Another private organization, the United States Christian Commission, sought to promote the spiritual well-being of the soldiers by distributing tracts, holding religious services, and relieving in numerous practical ways the "intolerable ennui" of camp life.

The South, in its efforts to finance the war, was driven rapidly from one makeshift to another. The United States mint at New Orleans and *Southern* the United States custom-houses that were seized provided *finance* the Confederacy with perhaps a million dollars in greatly needed specie, and the confiscation of private debts owed by southern citizens to northern creditors also helped. Bond issues were floated, both by the Confederacy and by the several Confederate states, but the limited credit resources of the South were soon dried up. The best results were obtained when the bonds were made payable in produce. In this fashion the southern government came into the possession of large quantities of cotton, tobacco, and other staple commodities, some of which it was able to market, and some of which it pledged as security for

---

[1] Charles J. Stillé, *History of the United States Sanitary Commission* (1866), is almost a contemporary account. See also W. E. Barton, *The Life of Clara Barton, Founder of the American Red Cross* (1922).

a small loan floated in Europe in 1863. Taxation turned out to be almost as fruitless as borrowing. An attempt to levy a direct tax through the instrumentality of the states netted as little real money as the similar efforts of the United States Congress during the Confederation period. Thereafter, the example set by the northern government of levying excises, licensing occupations, and taxing incomes was tried, but with comparatively slight success. One unique feature of the southern taxation program, a ten per cent tax on farm produce, to be paid in kind, proved to be of great assistance to the Confederate armies. It was excessively unpopular, however, and the charge of unconstitutionality was persistently hurled at this and all other effective means of taxation. The total receipts of the Confederacy from all tax sources has been estimated at about one hundred million dollars.

The inadequacy of the sums realized from bond issues and taxation drove the Confederacy early in the war to a chief reliance upon printing-press money. Notes were issued by the Confederate Treasury in a steadily increasing volume until before the end of the war more than a billion dollars of such money was in circulation. In addition, states, municipalities, and private corporations also put out issues of paper that passed for money. The depreciation that inevitably set in as the amount of fiat money increased, and the prospect of Confederate victory dimmed, far outran the depreciation of the northern greenback. By the summer of 1863 the Confederate dollar was worth only twenty-five cents in gold; a year later it was worth less than five cents; by the end of the war it was valueless. Southerners of small incomes suffered the acute distress usually attendant upon such extremes of money inflation, but a few skillful speculators made comfortable fortunes. Northern greenbacks, smuggled through the lines, were eagerly received, and circulated at a tremendous premium.

The confidence of the South that European intervention on behalf of "King Cotton" would be the decisive factor in the war made diplomacy a major concern on the part of both belligerents from the very beginning. Every move of the southern government was designed to promote intervention, while the fondest *"King Cotton" diplomacy* hope of the northern government was to prevent it. In the diplomatic battle of wits the South, with leaders more experienced in international relations than the northern Republicans could command, should have had the advantage, but the southern government failed to live up to its opportunities. Davis's two secretaries of state, R. M. T. Hunter and Judah P. Benjamin, were second-rate men who had no particular aptitude for the post assigned them, and were quite outmatched by Seward.

William L. Yancey, the first Confederate commissioner to England, quickly lost heart and came home. He was succeeded by James M. Mason, who was well received by the British aristocracy, but made little headway with the British government. In France, John Slidell did better, but there was little that France could do to aid the Confederacy without the approval of England, who as "mistress of the seas,"and the chief foreign consumer of southern cotton, had to make the decision for or against European intervention in the American war.[1]

English sympathy at the outset of the war seemed definitely to lean toward the South. The Tory aristocracy, which understood and appre-
English atti- ciated the kindred southern planter class, looked forward
tude toward with satisfaction to the possible downfall of democracy any-
the Ameri-
can Civil where. Many English liberals also favored the South, for
War their favorite doctrine was then free trade, and the South
seemed to be definitely committed to a free-trade policy, while the North had just inaugurated a program of protection. Moreover, the right of revolution was a part of the Whig tradition. By the "Glorious Revolution" England had been freed from the tyranny of the Stuarts, and by the American Revolution the colonies had rightfully won their independence, while at the same time bringing deserved discredit upon the attempt of an English king to establish personal rule. If, therefore, the southern people wished to be free, they had the right to be free. Possibly among Whig manufacturers this argument was duly strengthened by the reflection that a direct exchange of southern cotton for English manufactures would be greatly facilitated by the success of the southern arms. Diplomats of both parties saw a probable advantage for England in the division of the United States into two contending powers.

The North, however, was not without its friends in England. Such reformers as John Bright and Richard Cobden, although distressed at the newly adopted tariff policy of the United States, saw clearly that a northern victory must result in the abolition of slavery. With the issue thus reduced to a struggle between free labor and slave labor, their sympathies could lie only with the North. Lincoln's early insistence that the war was one for the preservation of the Union, and not for the abolition of slavery, was somewhat confusing to many Englishmen, but when at last he issued his Emancipation Proclamation, the number of northern sympathizers was greatly increased, particularly among the lower

[1] Numerous studies have been made on the foreign relations of both North and South. Among the best are the following: E. D. Adams, *Great Britain and the American Civil War* (2 vols., 1925); Donaldson Jordon and E. J. Pratt, *Europe and the American Civil War* (1931); W. R. West, *Contemporary French Opinion on the American Civil War* (1924); J. M. Callahan, *The Diplomatic History of the Southern Confederacy* (1901).

classes. The workingmen of Manchester, in spite of the suffering that the failure of the American cotton supply had caused them, congratulated Lincoln upon his stand, and urged him to complete "the erasure of that foul blot upon civilization and Christianity — chattel slavery." To some extent, perhaps, British sympathy for the North was purchased by the greater need for northern wheat than for southern cotton; and there can be no doubt that the profits of neutrality were widely regarded as preferable to a hazardous war on behalf of southern independence. At all events, well before the end of the war the weight of British opinion had shifted to the side of the North.

Northern anxiety as to the course Great Britain meant to pursue became acute as early as May, 1861, when the British government issued a proclamation of neutrality with respect to the American war. This action, because it accorded to the South the status of belligerent, was regarded by the North as deliberately unfriendly, for at the time the northern government *British recognition of southern belligerency* still maintained that the uprising in the South was no more than an insurrection, and was therefore of no concern to outside nations. The British contention, however, that the struggle was in reality a war was in closer accord with the facts. Indeed, Lincoln himself, in ordering a blockade of the southern coast, had already unwittingly recognized the belligerency of the South. Probably the British proclamation was not meant to be unfriendly, but was designed merely to serve notice that the two contending parties would be expected to observe the customary rules of war. Nevertheless the fact that it was issued just before the arrival in England of Charles Francis Adams,[1] whom Lincoln had sent as minister from the United States, confirmed Northerners in their suspicion that the sympathies of the British government lay with the South. Otherwise, they argued, Adams would at least have been given an opportunity to present the northern point of view. Northern fears that the recognition of southern belligerence would ultimately be followed by the recognition of southern independence proved to be unfounded.

Late in 1861 an incident occurred that almost precipitated war between the United States and Great Britain. When the news reached Captain Charles Wilkes of the United States frigate *San Jacinto* that the two Confederate commissioners, Mason *The Trent affair* and Slidell, were aboard a British mail steamer, the *Trent*, bound from Havana to Southampton, he promptly intercepted the neutral ship, arrested the Confederate commissioners, and took them to Boston. Wilkes's action was totally without official authorization, and was much

[1] C. F. Adams, Jr., *Charles Francis Adams* (1900).

the same sort of high-handed procedure that the United States had protested against when practiced by Great Britain before the War of 1812. But the northern public went wild with joy at the news, and Congress voted Wilkes the thanks of the nation for his exploit. What he had done seemed, in a sense, a fair offset to Great Britain's hasty proclamation of neutrality.

In view of the record of its own admiralty during the Napoleonic wars, the British government should not have been deeply shocked at the capture of Mason and Slidell. But immediately on hearing the news, the Cabinet decided that Wilkes's action was "a clear violation of the law of nations, and one for which reparation must be at once demanded." The British public, also, was fully aroused, and there was much loose talk to the effect that this "insult to the flag" must be avenged. Fortunately for the friends of peace, the Queen's husband, Prince Albert, was enough of an outsider to take a somewhat objective view of the incident. When the ultimatum that the Ministry framed came to the Queen for her approval, he successfully urged that its tone be softened so that the United States might the more easily yield to its demands. The British minister to the United States, Lord Lyons, who was friendly to the North, still further eased the tension by neglecting to refer to the British note as an ultimatum, although he made it clear that Mason and Slidell must be released, and a suitable apology made, or there would be war. To emphasize the gravity of the situation, the British government ordered the navy to be put on a war footing, and sent eight thousand troops to Canada.

Secretary Seward seems to have realized from the first that, in case Great Britain so demanded, the prisoners would have to be released, but because of the superheated state of American public opinion and the divergent views of his colleagues in the Cabinet he was obliged to delay action as long as possible. When at length he replied to the British ultimatum, he neglected to include a formal apology for Wilkes's action, but argued somewhat trickily that the persons of Mason and Slidell were "contraband of war." As such they were justly liable to capture, although Wilkes, Seward held, was clearly at fault in failing to bring the *Trent* as well as its passengers into port. On this account the American government stood ready to deliver up the Confederate envoys to the proper British authorities. Seward's argument, however specious it may have been, served its purpose well, for public opinion on both sides of the Atlantic was appeased, and so the crisis passed.[1]

The blockade of the southern coast that the North maintained caused

[1] T. L. Harris, *The Trent Affair* (1896).

far less friction with the British government than might have been ex-·
pected. After all, Great Britain dared not raise too serious *England*
objections to practices that she herself could follow to ex- *and the*
cellent advantage as a belligerent. Even the American *blockade*
doctrine of continuous voyages, which led at times to the capture of
British ships bound from one British port to another, was allowed to
stand unchallenged. After 1914, when Great Britain was a belligerent
and the United States was a neutral, the precedents of the American
Civil War were followed by the British Admiralty with telling effect.

The lax interpretation that the British government placed upon its
neutral duties sorely taxed the patience of the United States. Commerce-destroyers were built in British ports for the use of the Confederacy, and were allowed to attack the shipping of the United States with-·
out ever having visited a Confederate port. Damaging as this practice
was to northern commerce, the northern government contented itself
with protests that could be, and were, made the basis for collecting damages later on. The Laird rams, however, which might possibly have
raised the blockade had they sailed, were quite another thing. On hearing in September, 1863, that one of them was about to leave port, Charles
Francis Adams wrote to Lord John Russell, the British foreign minister:
"It would be superfluous for me to point out to your Lordship that this
is war." But the British government, well aware of this fact without
being told, had already given orders that the rams be detained. From
this time until the close of the war there was no further danger of British
intervention.

Had the British government approved, there is little reason to doubt
that Napoleon III of France would gladly have come to the aid of the
South. His chief reason for desiring a Confederate victory lay in his
hope that by this means the Monroe Doctrine might be eliminated, and
the expansion of French influence on the American continent made possible. Shortly after Burnside's crushing defeat at Fredericksburg, Napoleon offered mediation between North and South, and when it was
indignantly rejected by the North, he toyed long with the idea of recognizing southern independence. Objections from Great Britain held him
back, however, and he was compelled to content himself with the work-
ing-out of his project for the virtual acquisition of Mexico.

The way was paved for Napoleon's Mexican adventure when in October, 1861, Great Britain, France, and Spain agreed to a *French*
joint intervention in Mexico to secure "protection for the *intervention*
persons and properties of their subjects, as well as the ful- *in Mexico*
fillment of obligations." In accordance with this program the allies

sent troops into Mexico and seized several Mexican custom-houses. By April, 1862, Great Britain and Spain had come to a satisfactory agreement with the Mexican government, and withdrew, but Napoleon ordered his army to Mexico City, called an assembly of pliant "Notables," and with their consent placed the Archduke Maximilian of Austria upon an imperial Mexican throne. A more complete violation of the Monroe Doctrine could scarcely have been imagined, but as long as the United States was torn by civil strife Napoleon knew that he had nothing to fear from north of the Rio Grande. Secretary Seward did not fail to register a vigorous protest, however, and after the defeat of the South, Napoleon found it expedient to recall his troops from Mexico. The fall of Maximilian's government then followed as a matter of course.

Spain, too, attempted to profit from the temporary weakness of the United States, first, by the reannexation of the Dominican Republic, and, *Spanish* secondly, by the occupation of some valuable guano islands *neutrality* off the coast of Peru. These actions were taken in spite of Seward's warning that anything of the kind would meet "with a prompt, persistent, and, if possible, effective resistance" from the United States. The Dominican venture, however, aroused such active native opposition that by 1865 the Spanish were ready to abandon it, while a pointed remonstrance from the United States brought to an end a little later the trespass upon the property of Peru.

Other European nations showed comparatively slight interest in the American Civil War, although the American public got the impression *Russia* that Russia was strongly sympathetic with the northern cause. This opinion was borne out to some extent by the anti-slavery sentiments of the Czar Alexander II, which led him in 1861 to emancipate the Russian serfs, and by the common assumption that both Russia and the United States were in the bad graces of the British government. In anticipation of war with Great Britain, the Russian government, late in 1863, dispatched two fleets to American waters, one to New York and the other to San Francisco. The purpose of this maneuver was to have the Russian ships in readiness for an instant attack on British commerce in case war between Russia and Great Britain should be declared, but the Americans very generally interpreted the presence of the Russian fleets as a gesture of friendship to the North. Several years later the purchase from Russia of Alaska, at a price supposed to be far above its actual value, was justified in the United States on the ground that Russia had once been a friend in time of need.[1]

Left practically alone by European nations, the two American belliger-

[1] B. P. Thomas, *Russo-American Relations, 1815–1867* (1930).

ents found problems of even graver consequence than diplomacy in their own internal dissensions. While the South was far more united than the North, the Davis government lost steadily in popularity, particularly after the defeats at Gettysburg and Vicksburg, and was seriously handicapped by the opposition it encountered behind the lines. In the North, opposition to the Lincoln government was open and defiant almost from the beginning.

One of the most persistent of the problems that arose within the Confederacy was the age-old contest between states' rights and nationalism.[1] Were the southern nationalists, led by Jefferson Davis, merely trying to establish a new tyranny to replace the central government at Washington against which the southern states had revolted? *States' rights in the Confederacy* Accusations that the Davis administration was strongly nationalistic were not without plausibility, for each step that it took in the direction of military efficiency led it farther and farther away from states' rights. Reasonable wartime precaution demanded that the President should have authority to suspend the writ of habeas corpus in the war zones, and yet, when the Confederate Congress granted him this privilege, his opponents accused him of seeking to establish a centralized despotism upon the ruins of the states. Conscription, also, which was assuredly a necessity if southern resistance was to be maintained at all, led to a violent clamor against the administration for its encroachments upon the reserved rights of the states. Likewise, each effective tax measure raised up a crop of enemies who took refuge behind the well-worn screen of unconstitutionality. Party lines were not clearly drawn in the Confederacy, but the congressional elections held in the fall of 1863 placed the Confederate Congress definitely in the hands of the anti-administration forces.

But Davis, in his effort to establish a new nation, had more than merely political opposition to meet. A small proportion of the southern population, probably not above ten per cent, was actually opposed to the war from the beginning, and consistently sought to evade military service and other unpleasant duties. *Southern opposition to the war* Most such individuals were of the lowest class of southern whites, whose imaginations were incapable of grasping either the idea of states' rights or of southern nationalism, and whose interests were strictly local. Moreover, as the horrors of war multiplied and came closer home, the futility of the struggle grew apparent to an increasing number of every class. Why fight on, or hope on, when there was no chance to win? Many did so, loyally and valiantly, but others made ready to give up,

[1] F. L. Owsley, *State Rights in the Confederacy* (1925).

and even to place the blame on Jefferson Davis that their cause was lost.

The unity of northern opinion that had been so apparent immediately after the bombardment of Sumter was not maintained for long. Had *Northern opposition to the war* the war lasted only for a summer, as many seemed to anticipate, and had Bull Run been a resounding northern victory instead of a defeat, the outburst of patriotic ardor in which the war was launched might have been of sufficient duration to see it through. As matters turned out, discontent with Lincoln's administration, and dismay at the prospect of a long fratricidal war, had become abundantly apparent well before the first summer was over. While such sentiments were by no means entirely confined to Democratic circles, the Republicans were generally pro-war, even when anti-Lincoln, and urged that all Union men, regardless of party convictions, stand together. In the fall of 1861, Union rather than Republican tickets were nominated wherever important state elections were to be held, and in New York and Ohio these tickets were even headed by War Democrats. This strategy, while unavailing as a means of heading off the nomination of separate Democratic tickets, did enable the Republicans and their pro-war allies to win by satisfactory majorities.

Opponents of the Lincoln administration were quick to charge the President with indulgence in unconstitutional practices that made him *Criticism of the President* little less than a dictator.[1] His orders of May, 1861, for the increase of the regular army and for the organization of a volunteer army composed of three-year men clearly transcended his constitutional authority. About the same time he suspended the writ of habeas corpus without previously obtaining the consent of Congress, and he deliberately defied the ruling of Chief Justice Taney in *Ex Parte Merryman* (1861) that the President had no right to take such action on his own authority. Also, he permitted citizens to be arrested by military orders and tried by courts-martial, without as well as within the regions where hostilities existed. By such means no less than thirteen thousand arbitrary arrests and imprisonments were made during the war, although, according to a subsequent decision of the Supreme Court (1866), military courts had no lawful authority over civilians where regular civil courts were open for business. In May, 1863, Lincoln even approved of the arrest and conviction by court-martial of Clement L. Vallandigham of Ohio, his leading Democratic critic, on the charge that Vallandigham's utterances tended to "weaken the power of the government in its efforts to suppress an unlawful rebellion." In this case, however, the President ordered that the court-

[1] J. G. Randall, *Constitutional Problems under Lincoln* (1926).

martial sentence of close confinement until the end of the war should be commuted to banishment, and directed that Vallandigham be sent beyond the Union lines to the Confederacy. On the question of freedom of the press, the President's course was less open to criticism. When the military authorities attempted to suppress the New York *World* and the Chicago *Times*, he promptly reversed their orders.

The administration was criticized also for its inefficiency in waging the war. Members of the President's own party were free with criticism on this score, and a strongly Republican Congress created, *The Committee on the Conduct of the War* early in 1862, a joint Committee on the Conduct of the War, the duty of which was to point out to the administration its mistakes, and also, if possible, to force the President to allow Congress a greater voice in the direction of military affairs. The vast amount of waste and corruption that characterized the early months of the war played into the hands of this committee, and the failure of the northern arms to win victories, particularly in the East, helped it still more. But Lincoln refused to be intimidated, and persisted in his assumption that the conduct of the war was an executive, not a legislative, function. Judging from the temper of his "radical Republican" critics, it seems probable that his "presidential dictatorship" was far milder than the "congressional dictatorship" they would have set up had they had the opportunity.

Beyond a doubt the most perplexing problem of public opinion that the administration faced was the debate over Negro emancipation. Abolitionists argued with increasing effectiveness that the *The problem of emancipation* war had been caused by slavery, and that to fight on without removing the root of the evil was ridiculous. They were promptly joined by a host of radical Republicans who were out to punish the "rebels" for carrying secession into effect, and saw in the abolition of slavery a convenient tool. More conservative Republicans, however, were for a considerable time reluctant to abandon the official attitude of their party, which had always been to oppose only the expansion of slavery, and to leave the institution itself alone where it already existed. Sentiment in the loyal slave states, and in Democratic circles generally, was strongly against emancipation, and in many regions merely to suggest that the war was being fought as an "anti-slavery crusade" was a sure means of provoking trouble.

With opinion so divided, Lincoln wisely emphasized the preservation of the Union as the fundamental war aim of the North, for on this ground he could appeal to a far larger number of people than on any other. As late as the summer of 1862, he wrote to Horace Greeley:

My paramount object in this struggle is to save the Union. If I could save the Union without freeing any slaves, I would do it; if I could save it by freeing some and leaving others alone, I would also do that. I shall do less whenever I shall believe what I am doing hurts the cause, and I shall do more whenever I shall believe doing more will help the cause. I shall adopt new views as fast as they shall appear to be true views.

Nevertheless, when Lincoln penned these words he had already made up his mind that emancipation would have to come. From the first of *Slaves as* the war the northern government had been perplexed with *"contra-* the problem of what to do with the Negroes that came *band"* through the lines from the South. When they were ordinary fugitives, orders were usually given, although not always obeyed, for their return. But sometimes Negroes that had been employed in building fortifications or in digging trenches, or in aiding the enemy directly in some such way, either escaped to the Union lines or were captured by Union troops. It was manifestly absurd to return such valuable property to the enemy, and nothing of the kind was done. But what was the legal status of such Negroes? Were they free or slave? If slave, whose property were they? General Benjamin F. Butler answered this question by calling them "contraband of war," but while the term tickled the public fancy, it had little legal significance. Probably before, and certainly after August, 1861, when Congress passed an act for the confiscation of any property, including slaves, that was being used for an insurrectionary purpose, the captured slaves were technically the property of the United States government. To put an end to such an anomalous situation, Congress in July, 1862, passed a second confiscation act, one clause of which specifically declared that whenever the slaves of "rebel" masters should fall into Union hands they should be "forever free of their servitude." Ultimately about one hundred and fifty thousand freed Negroes were enlisted in the Union army, and many of them saw active service.

Meantime the radical Republicans, steadily augmented in numbers as the war wore on, pressed insistently for complete and thoroughgoing *Growing* emancipation. Two of Lincoln's generals, John C. Fré- *sentiment* mont and David Hunter, early yielded to this pressure, the *for emanci-* first with a proclamation issued in August, 1861, which *pation* freed the slaves of disloyal citizens in Missouri, and the second with a proclamation issued in May, 1862, which performed a like service for all the slaves in North Carolina, Georgia, and Florida. Both orders were revoked by the President, who understood far better than his subordinates the opposition within the North that such a course was

ABE LINCOLN'S LAST CARD; OR, ROUGE-ET-NOIR.

A BRITISH VIEW OF THE EMANCIPATION PROCLAMATION
From a cartoon in *Punch*, London, October 18, 1862

sure to arouse. Lincoln would have much preferred a system of graduated emancipation, with compensation to the owners of slaves. In April, 1862, Congress adopted such a policy for the District of Columbia, and at Lincoln's suggestion also offered federal funds to the loyal slave states — which were not accepted — to aid them in working out a similar policy. But to the radicals the idea of waiting until the end of the war to effect the abolition of slavery within the Confederacy was intolerable, and the prospect of compensating former "rebels" for the loss of their slave property was utterly unthinkable.

Ultimately the time came when Lincoln had either to emancipate the slaves or alienate the majority of his own party. He knew, too, that if he proclaimed to the world that the war was being fought *The Eman-* to free the slaves, there would be an immediate end to the *cipation* danger of foreign intervention. His mind made up, he *Proclama-* waited two full months longer before he acted, so that the *tion* winning of a Union victory (Antietam, September 17, 1862) could be cited as proof that his course was not a choice of desperation. Then, on September 22, 1862, he issued his preliminary Emancipation Proclamation. Claiming the right as commander-in-chief of the army and navy,

[681]

he promised that "on the 1st day of January, A.D. 1863, all persons held as slaves within any state or designated part of a state the people whereof shall then be in rebellion against the United States shall be then, thenceforward, and forever free."

The elections of 1862, which took place immediately after this proclamation was issued, offered an opportunity for the voters of the North to *Opposition* express their sentiments with respect to the administration. *to the ad-* While the Republicans were able, as in 1861, to induce many *ministration* Democrats to co-operate with them in the support of "Union" tickets, the Democratic party organization had remained intact, and now furnished vigorous opposition. Among the Democrats there were many ardent supporters of the war. Some of these, indeed, had no serious objection to the course the administration was following, but were for sentimental reasons unable to break from the party to which they had always belonged. Others, while definitely favorable to the war, objected strenuously to Lincoln's dictatorial course, and criticized the administration freely for its failure to achieve military success. Still others, a large and vociferous minority, were definitely opposed to the war and wished to see it brought to an immediate conclusion. In the Emancipation Proclamation this faction had a strong talking point. The war, they said, had ceased to be a struggle to save the Union. If the administration so desired, it could have peace at once with the old Union fully restored. The trouble was that the abolitionists were in control, and were shedding the best blood of the North merely to set free a rabble of Negro slaves.

The death of Douglas, in June, 1861, was a great misfortune, not only for the Democrats, but also for the whole nation. Had Douglas lived, there is little reason to doubt that he would have remained a Democrat, and would have led his party along a course of intelligent and useful criticism of the administration. Unfortunately, after his death no Democrat of like ability arose to take his place. General McClellan, who, on his loss of favor with the administration in the fall of 1862, became a kind of Democratic rallying-point, totally lacked political flair. Horatio Seymour, Democratic candidate for the governorship of New York, was probably the ablest of the Democratic leaders, but he was little known beyond the confines of his own state. Clement L. Vallandigham of Ohio was a more astute politician than either, but he was among the most extreme of the opponents of the war, and for that reason was practically disqualified for a position of national leadership.

With its pacifist element well to the fore, the Democratic Party made an excellent showing in the elections of 1862. Helped along by the

failure of the armies in the East to win a decisive victory, and by the
near escape Grant had had at Shiloh, they easily took the *The elections*
ascendancy in New York, New Jersey, Pennsylvania, Ohio, *of 1862*
Indiana, Illinois, and Wisconsin, all of which, with the exception of New
Jersey, had voted for Lincoln in 1860. Fortunately for the Unionists,
the border slave states, for reasons not wholly unconnected with their
occupation by northern armies, supported the administration; otherwise
the Democrats would have won a majority in the national House of
Representatives. As it was, some of the Democratic legislatures that
were chosen gave the administration serious trouble. The virtual withdrawal of Indiana and Illinois from the support of the war was prevented only by the resourcefulness of the two governors concerned,
Oliver P. Morton of Indiana and Richard Yates of Illinois, each of whom
proved to be more than a match for his recalcitrant legislature.

The passage of the Draft Act in the spring of 1863 added fresh fuel to
the flames of discontent. Peace-at-any-price men banded together into
secret societies with such high-sounding names as "Knights *"Copper-*
of the Golden Circle," "Order of American Knights," *headism"*
"Order of the Star," and "Sons of Liberty." Thus organized, they
plotted much mischief, and performed a little. They were accused of
assassinating enrolling officers, of fomenting draft riots, of encouraging
soldiers to desert, of giving aid and information to the Confederacy, of
helping captured Confederate prisoners to escape. To counteract such
activities, "Union Leagues" were formed, and during the last two years
of the war an unknown number of individual assaults and reprisals took
place. Democrats who were opposed to the war, or lukewarm toward
it, were generally called "Copperheads" by the Unionists, and, inasmuch as the Democratic Party as a whole was somewhat tinctured with
"Copperheadism," the terms Democrat and Copperhead tended, on
hostile lips, to be regarded as synonymous.[1]

The occasional elections that were held in the fall of 1863 revealed,
however, an unmistakable trend back to the support of the administration. In nearly every instance the Unionists showed *The effect of*
greater strength than the Democrats, although by majori- *Union*
ties that were not always large. This change of sentiment *victories*
was due primarily to the victories at Gettysburg and Vicksburg, but
even those successes were insufficient to quiet the peace-at-any-price
men, whose numbers, particularly in the states that bordered on the
Ohio River, were very great. In Ohio a governor had to be chosen, and

[1] An excellent discussion of Copperheadism is contained in W. D. Foulke, *Life of Oliver
P. Morton* (2 vols., 1899).

Vallandigham himself, still an exile but by that time in Canada, won the Democratic nomination. To oppose him the Unionists chose John Brough, a War Democrat, who won the election by a vote of 288,000 to 187,000. Inasmuch as Vallandigham consistently denounced the war and called for an immediate armistice, this vote furnished a fair test of the pacifist forces in the Middle West. The eastern wing of the Democratic Party, which looked to Seymour rather than to Vallandigham for leadership, was far less imbued with pacifist principles.

The dark days of 1864, with their long casualty lists and their infrequent victories, led the critics of Lincoln's administration to redouble *Presidential* their efforts. Among them were the radicals within his own *nominations,* party, who had always objected to his moderation, and now *1864* plotted to deprive him of a renomination. At a mass convention held in Cleveland, May 31, 1864, they called for the suppression of the rebellion "by force of arms and without compromise," urged the "confiscation of the lands of the rebels, and their distribution among the soldiers and actual settlers," and nominated an opposition Republican ticket headed by John C. Frémont. The Democratic National Convention, under the control of the Vallandigham element, went to an opposite extreme in its platform by denouncing the war as a failure, and urging an immediate cessation of hostilities as a prelude to a convention of the states which should restore the federal Union.[1] For their nominee, however, they turned to General McClellan, who accepted the nomination, but denounced the platform. The Union, he declared, must be saved before there could be peace: "no peace can be permanent without union."

The administration forces, to make clear that they represented an alliance of Republicans and War Democrats, not only retained the Union label that had served them so well before, but also nominated as Lincoln's running-mate Andrew Johnson of Tennessee, a War Democrat who had no Republican connections whatever. But for a while it seemed as if the re-election of the President would be impossible. Later generations, accustomed to the veneration of Lincoln, find it difficult to realize that his popularity dates from the end rather than from the beginning of the war, and that many of his contemporaries had the gravest doubt as to his ability. On one occasion during the campaign Lincoln himself went on record as convinced that he could not win. At an August Cabinet meeting he asked the members present to endorse unopened a document he had written. Then, several weeks later when the

---

[1] E. C. Kirkland, *The Peacemakers of 1864* (1927); E. J. Benton, *The Movement for Peace Without Victory During the Civil War* (1918).

MARVELOUS EQUESTRIAN PERFORMANCE ON TWO ANIMALS

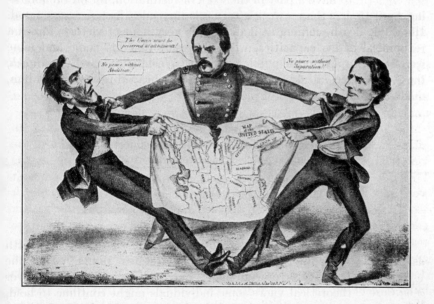

THE TRUE ISSUE, OR "THAT'S WHAT'S THE MATTER."

TWO VERSIONS OF THE ELECTION OF 1864

election was over, he read it to them: "This morning," it ran, "as for some days past, it seems exceedingly probable that this administration will not be re-elected. Then it will be my duty to so co-operate with the President-elect as to save the Union between the election and the inauguration, as he will have secured his election on such grounds that he cannot possibly save it afterwards."

But victories changed the situation again, and the Union ticket won. Three states, New Jersey, Delaware, and Kentucky, cast together only *Election* 21 electoral votes for McClellan, while all the other states *results* that voted were carried by Lincoln, whose total reached 212. In nearly every state, however, McClellan's share of the popular vote was only a little less than Lincoln's, so that the change of a comparatively small number of votes would have given the Democrats the election. In New York, for example, Lincoln's majority was less than 7000 votes out of a total of 730,000.

By Inauguration Day, March 4, 1865, the war was nearly over, and Lincoln promised, "with malice toward none, with charity for all . . . to *Death of* bind up the nation's wounds." But he was not permitted *Lincoln* to have a part in the work of restoration, for on the following April 15, less than a week after Lee's surrender, he was assassinated. His tragic death, coming as it did at the very hour of victory, forced a reappraisal of his capacities, with the result that his name and fame were soon coupled in the public mind with Washington's.[1] Even *Punch*, the English periodical, which had repeatedly heaped ridicule upon him, made the following graceful recantation:

> Beside this corpse that bears for winding sheet
> The Stars and Stripes he lived to rear anew,
> Between the mourners at his head and feet,
> Say, scurrile jester, is there room for you?
>
> Yes, he had lived to shame me from my sneer,
> To lame my pencil and confute my pen;
> To make me own this hind of princes peer,
> This rail-splitter a true-born king of men.

Lincoln and his contemporaries interpreted the victory of the North as primarily a triumph of nationalism over states' rights. That the *Significance* Union was now in fact "one and indivisible," whatever *of the Civil* theoretical views some individuals might continue to hold, *War* was generally acknowledged, even by the defeated South. Incidentally, the institution of slavery, which had made the doctrine of

---

[1] Lloyd Lewis, *Myths after Lincoln* (1929), shows the beginning of the apotheosis of Lincoln; and Roy P. Basler, *The Lincoln Legend* (1935), its continuation.

states' rights its chief constitutional defense, was also brought to an end. While the Emancipation Proclamation had applied only to those states and parts of states that on January 1, 1863, were still at war with the United States, the momentum that Lincoln's action gave to the abolition movement was too great to be stopped. State action in Missouri, West Virginia, Maryland, Tennessee, and Louisiana had abolished slavery within their respective borders by the time the war was over. Meantime, a movement to write abolition into the national Constitution had gathered headway, and in January, 1865, Congress submitted to the states the Thirteenth Amendment, which forbade slavery or involuntary servitude, except as a punishment for crime, within the United States, or any place subject to its jurisdiction. By the end of the year this amendment had become a part of the Constitution. Whether a long civil war was necessary to secure the triumph of nationalism over states' rights and of abolitionism over slavery may well be doubted. Probably, with more skillful handling of a few crises, both ends might ultimately have been achieved without resort to war.

A factor not fully understood at the time, and possibly overemphasized today, was the commanding importance that the new industrial interests won during the course of the struggle. War profits *Industrial* compounded the capital of the industrialists and placed *supremacy* them in a position to dominate the economic life, not only of the Northeast where they were chiefly concentrated, but also of the nation at large. With the southern planters removed from the national scene, the government at Washington tended more and more to reflect the wishes of the industrial leaders. The protective tariff, impossible as long as southern influence predominated in national affairs, became the corner-stone of the new business edifice, for by means of it the vast and growing American market was largely restricted to American industry. Transcontinental railroads, designed to complete the national transportation system, were likewise accorded the generous assistance of the government, while a national banking act and a national currency facilitated still further the spread of nation-wide business.

The Northwest, where industry was definitely subordinate to agriculture, profited less from the war than the Northeast, but the Westerners applauded the passage of the Homestead Act, which threw the national domain wide open to settlers, and they were for a time as eager as the Easterners to accelerate the expansion of the railroads. By assisting in the defeat of the South, however, the Northwest had unknowingly sacrificed a valuable ally. Before the war the two agricultural sections had repeatedly stood together, first against the commercial, and later against the industrial, Northeast. Now, with the weight of the South in the Union immensely lessened, the Northwest was left to wage its battles virtually alone. For more than a generation after the war, with eastern men and eastern policies in the ascendancy, American industry steadily consolidated the gains it had made.

LIST OF BOOKS CITED

(With page references to original citations in the text.)

Abbott, W. C. *New York in the American Revolution.* 1929. 163 n.

Abel, Annie H. *The History of Events Resulting in Indian Consolidation West of the Mississippi* (American Historical Association, *Annual Report*, 1906, I). 401 n.

Abernethy, T. P. *From Frontier to Plantation in Tennessee.* 1932. 376 n.

Adams, C. F., Jr. *Charles Francis Adams* (*American Statesmen*, XXIX). 1900. 673 n.

———— *Railroads: Their Origin and Problems.* 1878. 548 n.

Adams, E. D. *British Interests and Activities in Texas, 1838–1846.* 1910. 518 n.

———— *Great Britain and the American Civil War.* 2 vols. 1925. 672 n.

Adams, H. B. *Maryland's Influence in Founding a National Commonwealth.* 1877. 170 n.

Adams, Henry. *History of the United States during the Administrations of Jefferson and Madison.* 9 vols. 1890–91. 258 n.

———— *John Randolph* (*American Statesmen*, XVI). 1882. 274 n.

———— *Life of Albert Gallatin.* 1879. 225 n.

Adams, James T. *Founding of New England.* 1921. 24 n.

———— *New England in the Republic, 1776–1850.* 1926. 163 n.

———— *Revolutionary New England, 1691–1776.* 1923. 61 n.

———— *The Adams Family.* 1930. 247 n.

Alexander, Holmes. *The American Talleyrand: The Career and Contemporaries of Martin Van Buren.* 1935. 441 n.

Allen, A. V. G. *Jonathan Edwards.* 1889. 78 n.

Allen, G. W. *Our Naval War with France.* 1909. 249 n.

———— *Our Navy and the Barbary Corsairs.* 1905. 266 n.

Alvord, C. W. *The Illinois Country, 1673–1818* (*Centennial History of Illinois*, I). 1920. 104 n.

———— *The Mississippi Valley in British Politics.* 2 vols. 1917. 104 n.

Anderson, T. S. *The Command of the Howe Brothers During the American Revolution.* 1936. 146 n.

Andrews, C. M. *Colonial Folkways* (*Chronicles of America*, IX). 1921. 28 n.

———— *Colonial Self-Government, 1652–1689* (*American Nation*, V). 1904. 55 n.

———— *Connecticut's Place in Colonial History.* 1924. 33 n.

———— *The Colonial Background of the American Revolution.* 1924. 116 n.

———— *The Colonial Period.* 1912. 21 n.

———— *The Colonial Period of American History.* 2 vols. 1934–36. 19 n.

———— *The Fathers of New England* (*Chronicles of America*, VI). 1921. 24 n.

Andrews, M. P. *The Women of the South in War Times.* 1920. 666 n.

Anthony, Katharine S. *Margaret Fuller; a Psychological Biography.* 1920. 488 n.

Ashe, S. A. *History of North Carolina.* 1908. 41 n.

Auchampaugh, Philip G. *James Buchanan and his Cabinet on the Eve of Secession.* 1926. 610 n.

———— *Robert Tyler, Southern Rights Champion, 1847–1866.* 1934. 582 n.

[689]

Babcock, K. C. *Rise of American Nationality, 1811–1819* (*American Nation*, XIII). 1906. 302 n.

Bancroft, Frederic. *Slave Trading in the Old South.* 1931. 497 n.

—— *The Life of William H. Seward.* 2 vols. 1900. 615 n.

Bancroft, H. H. *History of California.* 7 vols. 1884–1900. 514 n.

Barker, E. C. *The Life of Stephen F. Austin, Founder of Texas, 1793–1836.* 1925. 436 n.

Barnes, Gilbert H. *The Anti-Slavery Impulse, 1830–1844.* 1933. 498 n.

Barnes, Gilbert H., and Dumond, Dwight L. *Letters of Theodore Dwight Weld, Angelina Grimké Weld, and Sarah Grimké, 1822–1844.* 2 vols. 1934.

Barnes, Viola F. *The Dominion of New England.* 1923. 93 n.

Barrett, J. A. *Evolution of the Ordinance of 1787; with an Account of the Earlier Plans for the Government of the Northwest Territory* (University of Nebraska, Department of History and Economics). 1891. 182 n.

Barton, W. E. *The Life of Abraham Lincoln.* 2 vols. 1925. 614 n.

—— *The Life of Clara Barton, Founder of the American Red Cross.* 2 vols. 1922. 670 n.

Basler, Roy P. *The Lincoln Legend.* 1935. 686 n.

Bassett, J. S. *Constitutional Beginnings of North Carolina* (Johns Hopkins University, *Studies in Historical and Political Science*, Twelfth Series, III). 1894. 41 n.

—— *Life of Andrew Jackson.* 2 vols. 1911. 376 n.

—— *The Federalist System, 1789–1801* (*American Nation*, XI). 1906. 216 n.

—— *The Middle Group of American Historians.* 1917. 472 n.

Baxter, J. P., 3d. *The Introduction of the Ironclad Warship.* 1933. 636 n.

Beard, Charles A. and Mary R. *The Rise of American Civilization.* 2 vols. 1927. 197 n.

Beard, C. A. *An Economic Interpretation of the Constitution of the United States.* 1913. 197 n.

—— *Economic Origins of the Jeffersonian Democracy.* 1915. 224 n.

—— *The Supreme Court and the Constitution.* 1912. 206 n.

Beard, Mary R. *A Short History of the American Labor Movement.* 1920. 480 n.

Becker, Carl L. *Beginnings of the American People* (*Riverside History*, I). 1915. 14 n.

—— *The Declaration of Independence; a Study in the History of Political Ideas.* 1922. 141 n.

—— *The Eve of the Revolution* (*Chronicles of America*, XI). 1921. 116 n.

Beer, G. L. *British Colonial Policy, 1754–1765.* 1907. 107 n.

—— *Commercial Policy of England towards the Colonies* (Columbia University, *Studies in History, Economics, and Public Law*, III). 1893. 89 n.

—— *The Old Colonial System, 1660–1754.* 1912. 89 n.

—— *The Origins of the British Colonial System, 1578–1660.* 1908. 15 n.

Bemis, S. F. *Jay's Treaty: A Study in Commerce and Diplomacy.* 1923. 239 n.

—— *Pinckney's Treaty* (*Shaw Lectures on Diplomatic History*, XII). 1926. 241 n.

——, ed. *The American Secretaries of State and their Diplomacy.* 10 vols. 1927–29. 235 n.

Benns, F. L. *The American Struggle for the British West India Carrying Trade, 1815–1830* (*Indiana University Studies*, X). 1923. 434 n.

Benton, E. J.   *The Movement for Peace without Victory During the Civil War* (Western Reserve Historical Society, *Collections*, no. 99).   1918.   684 n.

Beveridge, A. J.   *Abraham Lincoln, 1809–1858.*   2 vols.   1928.   591 n.

—— *The Life of John Marshall.*   4 vols.   1916–19.   251 n.   267 n.

Bidwell, P. W., and Falconer, J. I.   *History of Agriculture in the Northern United States, 1620–1860.*   1925.   560 n.

Birney, Catharine H.   *The Grimké Sisters, Sarah and Angelina Grimké.*   1885.   500 n.

Birney, William.   *James G. Birney and his Times.*   1890.   501 n.

Bittinger, Lucy.   *The Germans in Colonial Times.*   1901.   67 n.

Blackwell, Elizabeth.   *Pioneer Work for Women.*   1914.   488 n.

Blegen, T. C.   *Norwegian Migration to America, 1825–1860.*   1931.   562 n.

Bleyer, W. G.   *Main Currents in the History of American Journalism.*   1927.   462 n.

Bogart, E. L.   *The Economic History of the United States.*   1907.   323 n.

Bolton, C. K.   *The Private Soldier under Washington.*   1902.   143 n.

Bolton, H. E., and Marshall, T. M.   *The Colonization of North America, 1492–1873.*   1920.   18 n.

Bolton, H. E.   "Papers of Z. M. Pike, 1806–1807," in *American Historical Review*, XIII, pp. 798–827.   282 n.

—— *The Spanish Borderlands* (*Chronicles of America*, XXIII).   1921.   514 n.

Bond, B. W., Jr.   *The Civilization of the Old Northwest.*   1934.   184 n., 297 n.

—— *The Monroe Mission to France, 1794–1796.*   1907.   242 n.

—— *The Quit Rent System in the American Colonies.*   1919.   47 n.

Boucher, C. S.   *The Nullification Controversy in South Carolina.*   1916.   412 n.

Bourne, E. G.   *Spain in America, 1450–1580* (*American Nation*, III).   1904.   10 n.

—— *The History of the Surplus Revenue of 1837.*   1885.   431 n.

Bowers, Claude.   *Jefferson and Hamilton, the Struggle for Democracy in America.*   1925.   218 n.

—— *Jefferson in Power.*   1936.   256 n.

—— *Party Battles of the Jackson Period.*   1922.   396 n.

Brackenridge, H. H.   *Incidents of the Insurrection in the Western Parts of Pennsylvania.*   1795.   225 n.

Bradford, Gamaliel.   *Union Portraits.*   1916.   632 n.

Bradlee, F. B. C.   *Blockade Running during the Civil War and the Effect of Land and Water Transportation on the Confederacy.*   1925.   634 n.

Branch, E. Douglas.   *Westward.*   1930.   530 n.

Brigance, W. N.   *Jeremiah Sullivan Black.*   1934.   611 n.

Brigham, A. P.   *Geographical Influences in American History.*   1903.   2 n.

Brown, W. G.   *The Lower South in American History.*   1902.   505 n.

Browne, W. H.   *George and Cecilius Calvert.*   1890.   39 n.

—— *Maryland, The History of a Palatinate.*   1884.   39 n.

Bruce, H. A.   *Daniel Boone and the Wilderness Road.*   1910.   113 n.

Bruce, Henry.   *Life of General Oglethorpe.*   1890.   48 n.

Bruce, P. A.   *Social Life of Virginia in the Seventeenth Century.*   1907.   22 n.

—— *The Colonial Period, 1607–1763* (*History of Virginia*, I).   1924.   54 n.

—— *The Economic History of Virginia in the Seventeenth Century.*   2 vols.   1896.   22 n.

Bruce, P. A.   *The Institutional History of Virginia in the Seventeenth Century.* 1910.   22 n.
———— *The Virginia Plutarch.*   2 vols.   1929.   72 n.
Burgess, J. W.   *The Middle Period (American History Series,* IV).   1897.   341 n.
Burrage, H. S.   *Maine in the Northeastern Boundary Controversy.*   1919.   454 n.
———— *The Beginnings of Colonial Maine, 1602–1658.*   1914.   34 n.
Butts, Porter.   *The Art Experience of the Middle-West Frontier — Art in Wisconsin.*   1936.   477 n.
Byrn, E. W.   *The Progress of Invention in the Nineteenth Century.*   1900.   463 n.

Caffin, Charles H.   *The Story of American Painting.*   1907.   477 n.
Calder, Isabel M.   *The New Haven Colony (Yale Historical Publications. Miscellany,* XXVIII).   1934.   33 n.
Callahan, J. M.   *Cuba and International Relations* (Johns Hopkins University, *Studies,* extra vol. XXI).   1899.   566 n.
———— *The Diplomatic History of the Southern Confederacy.*   1901.   672 n.
Carman, H. J.   *Social and Economic History of the United States.*   2 vols.   1930–34.   189 n., 323 n.
Carpenter, E. J.   *Roger Williams.*   1909.   30 n.
Carter, C. E.   *Great Britain and the Illinois Country, 1763–1774.*   1910.   111 n.
Casson, H. N.   *The Romance of the Reaper.*   1908.   662 n.
Catterall, Ralph C. H.   *The Second Bank of the United States.*   1903.   335 n., 423 n.
Chaddock, Robert E.   *The Safety Fund Banking System in New York, 1829–1866.*   1910.   444 n.
Channing, Edward.   *A History of the United States.*   6 vols.   1905–25.   10 n., 256 n.
Chapman, C. E.   *A History of California: The Spanish Period.*   1921.   514 n.
Charnwood, Lord.   *Abraham Lincoln.*   1917.   614 n.
Cheyney, E. P.   *European Background of American History, 1300–1600 (American Nation,* I).   1904.   12 n.
Chinard, Gilbert.   *Thomas Jefferson.*   1929.   256 n.
Chittenden, H. M.   *The American Fur Trade of the Far West.*   3 vols.   1902.   513 n.
Chitwood, O. P.   *A History of Colonial America.*   1931.   18 n.
Clark, A. H.   *The Clipper Ship Era, 1843–1869.*   1910.   554 n.
Clark, B. C.   *John Quincy Adams: "Old Man Eloquent."*   1932.   373 n.
Clark, G. L.   *A History of Connecticut.*   1914.   33 n.
Cleland, R. G.   *A History of California: The American Period.*   1922.   537 n.
Cleveland, C. C.   *The Great Revival in the West.*   1916.   262 n.
Coad, O. S., and Mims, Edwin, Jr.   *The American Stage (The Pageant of America,* XIV).   1929.   478 n.
Cobb, S. H.   *The Rise of Religious Liberty in America.*   1902.   65 n.
Cobbett, William.   *A Year's Residence in the United States of America.*   1818.   326 n.
Cole, A. C.   *The Irrepressible Conflict, 1850–1865 (A History of American Life,* VII).   1934.   660 n.
———— *The Whig Party in the South.*   1913.   449 n.
Coman, Katherine.   *Economic Beginnings of the Far West.*   2 vols.   1912.   510 n.

Coman, Katherine. *The Industrial History of the United States.* 1905. 323 n.

Commager, H. S. *Theodore Parker: Yankee Crusader.* 1936. 501 n.

Commons, J. R., and Associates. *History of Labour in the United States.* 4 vols. 1918–35. 480 n.

Coolidge, L. A. *Ulysses S. Grant.* 1917. 638 n.

Copeland, M. T. *The Cotton Manufacturing Industry of the United States (Harvard Economic Studies,* VIII). 1912. 555 n.

Corwin, E. S. *French Policy and the American Alliance.* 1916. 149 n.

—— *John Marshall and the Constitution (Chronicles of America,* XVI). 1919. 267 n.

—— *The Doctrine of Judicial Review.* 1914. 206 n.

—— "The Dred Scott Decision," in *American Historical Review,* XVII, pp. 52–69.

Coulter, E. M. *College Life in the Old South.* 1928. 331 n.

Coupland, Reginald. *The American Revolution and the British Empire.* 1930. 121 n.

Crandall, A. W. *The Early History of the Republican Party, 1854–1856.* 1930. 575 n.

Crane, V. W. *The Southern Frontier, 1670–1732.* 1929. 48 n.

Craven, Avery O. *Edmund Ruffin, Southerner, A Study in Secession.* 1932. 506 n.

—— *Soil Exhaustion as a Factor in the Agricultural History of Virginia and Maryland, 1606–1860.* 1926. 52 n., 506 n.

Cresson, W. P. *The Holy Alliance.* 1922. 364 n.

Cross, A. L. *The Anglican Episcopate and the American Colonies (Harvard Historical Studies,* IX). 1902. 56 n.

Cubberley, E. P. *Public Education in the United States.* 1919. 331 n.

Curti, Merle E. *Peace or War — the American Struggle, 1636–1936.* 1936. 491 n.

—— *The American Peace Crusade, 1815–1860.* 1929. 491 n.

Curtis, E. E. *The Organization of the British Army in the American Revolution (Yale Historical Publications, Miscellany,* XIX). 1926. 144 n.

Curtis, Edith R. *Anne Hutchinson.* 1930. 30 n.

Curtis, G. T. *Constitutional History of the United States.* 2 vols. 1889–96. 583 n.

—— *Life of Daniel Webster.* 2 vols. 1870. 341 n.

—— *Life of James Buchanan.* 2 vols. 1883. 582 n.

Cushing, H. A. *History of the Transition from Provincial to Commonwealth Government in Massachusetts* (Columbia University, *Studies in History, Economics, and Public Law,* VII). 1896. 163 n.

Cutler, C. C. *Greyhounds of the Sea: The Story of the American Clipper Ship.* 1930. 554 n.

Cutts, Lucia B., ed. *Memoirs and Letters of Dolly Madison.* 1886. 314 n.

Dana, E. S., and others. *A Century of Science in America.* 1918. 466 n.

Dana, Julian. *Sutter of California.* 1936. 516 n.

Darling, A. B. *Political Changes in Massachusetts, 1824–1848.* 1918. 391 n.

Davis, Jefferson. *The Rise and Fall of the Confederate Government.* 2 vols. 1881. 608 n.

Davis, Mrs. Jefferson. *Jefferson Davis, Ex-President of the Confederate States of America; a Memoir.* 1890. 608 n.

Decker, Malcolm. *Benedict Arnold, Son of the Havens.* 1932. 156 n.

Dewey, D. R. *Financial History of the United States.* Revised edition. 1931. 189 n.

—— *State Banking before the Civil War.* 1910. 444 n.

Dexter, E. G. *A History of Education in the United States.* 1904. 331 n.

Dickerson, O. M. *American Colonial Government, 1696–1765: a Study of the Board of Trade in its Relation to the American Colonies.* 1912. 94 n.

Dodd, William E. *Expansion and Conflict (Riverside History, III).* 1915. 505 n.

—— *Jefferson Davis.* 1907. 608 n.

—— *Lincoln or Lee.* 1928. 624 n.

—— *Robert J. Walker, Imperialist.* 1914. 532 n.

—— *Statesmen of the Old South.* 1911. 541 n.

—— *The Cotton Kingdom (Chronicles of America, XXVII).* 1919. 505 n.

Dodge, T. A. *A Bird's-Eye View of Our Civil War.* Revised edition. 1897. 271 n.

Donaldson, Thomas C. *The Public Domain, Its History.* 1884. 271 n.

Downes, R. C. *Frontier Ohio, 1788–1803 (Ohio Historical Collections, III).* 1935. 273 n.

Doyle, John H. *English Colonies in America.* 5 vols. 1880–1907. 19 n.

Du Bois, W. E. B. *Suppression of the African Slave Trade to the United States of America, 1638–1870 (Harvard Historical Studies, I).* 1896. 355 n.

Duffus, R. L. *The Santa Fe Trail.* 1930. 509 n.

Dumond, Dwight L. *The Secession Movement, 1860–1861.* 606 n.

Dunbar, C. F. *Economic Essays.* 1904. 589 n.

Dunbar, Seymour. *A History of Travel in America.* 4 vols. 1915. 347 n.

Dunning, W. A. *The British Empire and the United States.* 1914. 317 n.

Dwight, Theodore. *History of the Hartford Convention.* 1833. 316 n.

Earle, Alice Morse. *Child Life in Colonial Days.* 1899. 62 n.

—— *Colonial Dames and Goodwives.* 1895. 73 n.

—— *Colonial Days in Old New York.* 1896. 73 n.

—— *Customs and Fashions in Old New England.* 1896. 73 n.

—— *Home Life in Colonial Days.* 1898. 73 n.

—— *Stage-Coach and Tavern Days.* 1901. 73 n.

—— *The Sabbath in Puritan New England.* 1891. 61 n.

Egerton, H. E. *Short History of British Colonial Policy.* 1905. 38 n.

—— *The Causes and Character of the American Revolution.* 1923. 116 n.

Eggleston, Edward. *The Beginners of a Nation.* 1896. 21 n.

—— *The Transit of Civilization from England to America in the Seventeenth Century.* 1901. 62 n.

Egleston, Melville. *The Land System of the New England Colonies.* 1880. 58 n.

Elliot, Jonathan, ed. *The Debates on the Federal Constitution.* 5 vols. 1827–45. 209 n.

Emerson, E. W., and Forbes, W. E., eds. *The Journals of Ralph Waldo Emerson, with Annotations.* 10 vols. 1909–14. 467 n.

Faris, J. T. *The Romance of Old Philadelphia.* 1918. 47 n.

Farrand, Livingston. *Basis of American History (American Nation,* II). 1904. 1 n.

Farrand, Max, ed. *Records of the Federal Convention of 1787.* 3 vols. 1911. 198 n.

—— *The Fathers of the Constitution (Chronicles of America,* XIII). 1921. 199 n.

—— *The Framing of the Constitution of the United States.* 1913. 199 n.

Faulkner, H. U. *American Economic History.* 1924. 323 n.

Faust, A. B. *The German Element in the United States.* 2 vols. 1909. 67 n.

Faÿ, Bernard. *Franklin, the Apostle of Modern Times.* 1929. 158 n.

—— *The Revolutionary Spirit in France and America.* 1927. 149 n.

Fearon, Henry B. *Sketches of America.* 1818. 326 n.

Findley, W. *History of the Insurrection in the Four Western Counties of Pennsylvania.* 1796. 225 n.

Firkins, O. W. *Ralph Waldo Emerson.* 1915. 467 n.

Fish, C. R. *American Diplomacy.* 1915. 158 n.

—— *The Rise of the Common Man, 1830–1850 (History of American Life,* VI). 1927. 459 n.

Fisher, S. G. *Pennsylvania; Colony and Commonwealth.* 1897. 47 n.

—— *The Making of Pennsylvania.* New edition. 1932. 47 n.

—— *The Quaker Colonies.* 1921. 44 n.

—— *The Struggle for American Independence.* 2 vols. 1908. 136 n.

—— *The True Benjamin Franklin.* 1899. 80 n.

—— *The True William Penn.* 1899. 44 n.

Fiske, John. *Essays Historical and Literary.* 2 vols. 1902. 449 n.

—— *Historical Writings.* 12 vols. 1902. 23 n.

—— *New France and New England.* 1902. 103 n.

—— *Old Virginia and her Neighbours.* 2 vols. 1897. 23 n.

—— *The American Revolution.* 2 vols. 1891. 136 n.

—— *The Beginnings of New England.* 1889. 24 n.

—— *The Critical Period of American History.* 1888. 168 n.

—— *The Dutch and Quaker Colonies in America.* 2 vols. 1899. 42 n.

Fite, E. D. *Social and Industrial Conditions in the North during the Civil War.* 1910. 660 n.

—— *The Presidential Campaign of 1860.* 1911. 598 n.

Fitzpatrick, John C., ed. *The Autobiography of Martin Van Buren.* 1920. 441 n.

Ford, Amelia C. *Colonial Precedents of our National Land System as it Existed in 1800* (University of Wisconsin, *History Series,* II). 1910. 181 n.

Ford, H. J. *The Scotch-Irish in America.* 1915. 68 n.

—— *Washington and his Colleagues (Chronicles of America,* XIV). 1918. 216 n.

Ford, P. L. *Pamphlets on the Constitution of the United States.* 1888. 209 n.

—— *The Many-Sided Franklin.* 1899. 80 n.

—— *The True George Washington.* 1904. 213 n.

Forman, S. E. *Rise of American Commerce and Industry.* 1927. 60 n.

Foster, J. W. *A Century of American Diplomacy.* 1900. 187 n.

Foulke, W. D. *Life of Oliver P. Morton.* 2 vols. 1899. 683 n.

Fox, Dixon Ryan. *Ideas in Motion.* 1935. 171 n.

Fox, Dixon Ryan. *The Decline of Aristocracy in the Politics of New York* (Columbia University, *Studies in History, Economics, and Public Law,* LXXXVI). 1910. 391 n.

Freeman, D. S. *R. E. Lee: a Biography.* 4 vols. 1934–35. 624 n.

Friedenwald, Herbert. *The Declaration of Independence, an Interpretation and an Analysis.* 1904. 141 n.

Frothingham, O. B. *Gerrit Smith.* 1878. 501 n.

—— *Transcendentalism in New England: A History.* 1876. 468 n.

Frothingham, Richard. *The Rise of the Republic of the United States.* 1872. 36 n.

Fry, W. H. *New Hampshire as a Royal Province* (Columbia University, *Studies in History, Economics, and Public Law,* XXIX). 1908. 34 n.

Fuess, C. M. *Daniel Webster.* 2 vols. 1930. 542 n.

Fuller, Hubert B. *The Purchase of Florida.* 1906. 360 n.

Fuller [Ossoli], Margaret. *Women in the Nineteenth Century.* 1855. 488 n.

Gabriel, R. H., and others, eds. *Pageant of America.* 15 vols. 1929. 54 n.

Galpin, W. Freeman. *Pioneering for Peace: A Study of American Peace Efforts to 1846.* 1933. 491 n.

—— *The Grain Supply of England During the Napoleonic Period* (University of Michigan, *Publications, History and Political Science,* VI). 1925. 285 n.

Gammon, S. R., Jr. *The Presidential Campaign of 1832* (Johns Hopkins University, *Studies in Historical and Political Science,* XL). 1922. 425 n.

Garrison, G. P. *Westward Extension, 1841–1850* (*American Nation,* XVII). 1906. 508 n.

Gay, S. H. *James Madison.* 1884. 289 n.

Ghent, W. J. *The Road to Oregon.* 1929. 510 n.

Gilman, D. C. *James Monroe.* 1883. 339 n.

Gilmore, J. R. *John Sevier as a Commonwealth-Builder.* 1887. 176 n.

Goddard, H. C. *Studies in New England Transcendentalism.* 1908. 468 n.

Goebel, D. B. *William Henry Harrison.* 1926. 298 n.

Gooch, G. P. *English Democratic Ideas in the Seventeenth Century.* 1927. 88 n.

Goodwin, Cardinal L. *The Trans-Mississippi West, 1803–1853.* 1922. 362 n.

Goodwin, E. L. *The Colonial Church in Virginia.* 1927. 56 n.

Goodwin, Maud W. *Dutch and English on the Hudson* (*Chronicles of America,* VII). 1919. 42 n.

Gordy, J. P. *Political History of the United States with Special Reference to the Growth of Political Parties.* 2 vols. 1902. 224 n.

Gray, L. C. *History of Agriculture in the Southern United States to 1860.* 2 vols. 1933. 557 n.

Greene, E. B. *Provincial America* (*American Nation,* VI). 1905. 55 n.

—— *The Foundations of American Nationality.* 1922. 18 n.

Green, F. V. *The Revolutionary War.* 1911. 136 n.

Gregg, Josiah. *Commerce of the Prairies, or the Journal of a Santa Fe Trader.* 1844. 509 n.

Hallowell, Anna D. *James and Lucretia Mott, Life and Letters.* 1884. 501 n.

Hamer, P. M. *The Secession Movement in South Carolina, 1847–1852.* 1918. 545 n.

Hammond, M. B.   *The Cotton Industry: An Essay in American Economic History.* 1897. 493 n.

Hanna, C. A.   *The Scotch-Irish.* 1902. 68 n.

Harding, S. B.   *The Contest over the Ratification of the Federal Constitution in the State of Massachusetts (Harvard Historical Studies, II).* 1896. 209 n.

Harlow, A. F.   *Old Towpaths, The Story of the American Canal Era.* 1926. 386 n.

Harlow, R. V.   *Samuel Adams, Promoter of the American Revolution.* 1923. 125 n.

Harris, T. L.   *The Trent Affair.* 1896. 674 n.

Hart, A. B., and Bolton, H. E.   *American History Atlas.* 1930. 51 n.

Hart, A. B., ed.   *Epochs of American History.* 4 vols. 1891–1929. 51 n.

—— *Salmon Portland Chase.* 1899. 615 n.

—— *Slavery and Abolition, 1831–1841 (American Nation, XVI).* 1906. 501 n.

—— *The American Nation: A History.* 28 vols. 1904–28. 1 n.

Hatch, L. C.   *Administration of the American Revolutionary Army (Harvard Historical Studies, X).* 1904. 143 n.

Hazelton, J. H.   *The Declaration of Independence; its History.* 1906. 141 n.

Henderson, Archibald.   *Conquest of the Old Southwest, 1740–1800.* 1920. 71 n.

Henderson, G. F. R.   *Stonewall Jackson and the American Civil War.* 2 vols. 1898. 648 n.

Hesseltine, W. B.   *Civil War Prisons — a Study in War Psychology.* 1930. 667 n.

—— *Ulysses S. Grant, Politician.* 1935. 638 n.

Hibbard, B. H.   *A History of the Public Land Policies.* 1924. 181 n.

Hill, Charles E.   *Leading American Treaties.* 1922. 276 n.

Hill, Jim Dan.   *Sea Dogs of the Sixties.* 1935. 634 n.

Hinsdale, B. A.   *Horace Mann and the Common School Revival in the United States.* 1898. 484 n.

—— *The Old Northwest; the Beginnings of our Colonial System.* 1899. 184 n.

Hirsch, A. H.   *The Huguenots of Colonial South Carolina (Duke University Publications).* 1928. 41 n.

Hockett, H. C.   *Western Influences on Political Parties to 1825.* (Ohio State University, *Contributions in History and Political Science*, No. 4). 1917. 264 n.

Hodder, F. H.   "Genesis of the Kansas-Nebraska Act," in Wisconsin State Historical Society, *Proceedings* (1912), pp. 69–86. 574 n.

—— "Some Phases of the Dred Scott Case," in *Mississippi Valley Historical Review*, XVI, pp. 3–22.

Hodges, George.   *William Penn.* 1901. 45 n.

Hoe, Robert.   *A Short History of the Printing Press and the Improvements in Printing Machinery.* 1902. 466 n.

Holdsworth, J. T., and Dewey, D. R.   *The First and Second Banks of the United States.* 1910. 423 n.

Holman, F. V.   *Dr. John McLoughlin, the Father of Oregon.* 1907. 513 n.

Holst, Herman Edward von.   *John C. Calhoun.* 1882. 410 n.

—— *The Constitutional and Political History of the United States.* 8 vols. 1876–92. 410 n., 423 n.

Hosmer, J. K.   *Samuel Adams.* 1884. 125 n.

—— *The History of the Louisiana Purchase.* 1902. 276 n.

Hosmer, J. K.   *The Life of Thomas Hutchinson.*   1896.   128 n.

Houston, D. F.   *Critical Study of Nullification in South Carolina* (*Harvard Historical Studies*, III).   1896.   412 n.

Howard, G. E.   *Preliminaries of the Revolution, 1763–1775* (*American Nation*, VIII).   1905.   116 n.

Howard, J. T.   *Our American Music, Three Hundred Years of It.*   1931.   477 n.

Hughes, Rupert.   *George Washington.*   3 vols.   1926–30.   105 n., 144 n., 213 n.

Huidekoper, F. L.   *The Military Unpreparedness of the United States.*   1915.   626 n.

Hulbert, A. B.   *Braddock's Road* (*Historic Highways of America*, IV).   1903.   105 n.

—— *Forty-Niners.*   1931.   537 n.

—— *The Paths of Inland Commerce* (*Chronicles of America*, XXI).   1920.   338 n.

Hulme, Thomas.   *Journal of a Tour in the Western Countries of America, 1818–1819.*   1828.   326 n.

Hungerford, Edward.   *The Story of the Baltimore and Ohio Railroad, 1827–1927.*   1928.   548 n.

Hunt, Gaillard.   *John C. Calhoun.*   1908.   410 n.

—— *The Life of Madison.*   1902.   289 n.

Huntington, Ellsworth.   *The Red Man's Continent* (*Chronicles of America*, I).   1919.   1 n.

Hutchinson, W. T.   *Cyrus Hall McCormick.*   2 vols.   1930–35.   464 n.

Iles, George.   *Leading American Inventors.*   1912.   463 n.

Irving, Washington.   *Astoria.*   1836.   362 n.

Jacobstein, Meyer.   *The Tobacco Industry in the United States.*   1907.   558 n.

James, J. A.   *The Life of George Rogers Clark.*   1928.   154 n.

Jameson, J. F., ed.   *Original Narratives of Early American History.*   19 vols.   1906–17.   19 n.

—— *The American Revolution Considered as a Social Movement.*   1926.   171 n.

Jenkins, W. S.   *Pro-Slavery Thought in the Old South* (University of North Carolina, *Social Study Series*).   1935.   505 n.

Jernegan, M. W.   *The American Colonies.*   1929.   51 n.

Jervey, T. D.   *Robert Y. Hayne and His Times.*   1909.   415 n.

Johnson, Allen, and Malone, Dumas, eds.   *Dictionary of American Biography.*   20 vols.   1928–1936.   78 n.

Johnson, Allen.   *Jefferson and his Colleagues* (*Chronicles of America*, XV).   1921.   256 n.

—— *Stephen A. Douglas: A Study in American Politics.*   1908.   570 n.

—— ed.   *The Chronicles of America Series.*   50 vols.   1919–21.   1 n.

—— *Union and Democracy* (*Riverside History*, II).   1915.   341 n.

Johnson, Amandus.   *The Swedish Settlements on the Delaware, 1638–1664.*   2 vols. 1911.   42 n.

Johnson, G. W.   *Randolph of Roanoke, A Political Fantastic.*   1929.   274 n.

Johnston, Mary.   *Pioneers of the Old South* (*Chronicles of America*, V).   1918.   39 n.

Jones, R. L.   *History of the Foreign Policy of the United States.*   1933.   158 n.

Jones, R. M. *The Faith and Practices of the Quakers.* 1927. 45 n.
——— *The Quakers in the American Colonies.* 1911. 45 n.
Jordan, Donaldson, and Pratt, E. J. *Europe and the American Civil War.* 1931.
672 n.

Kennedy, John P. *Memoirs of the Life of William Wirt.* 2 vols. 1849. 341 n.
King, G. A. *The French Spoliation Claims (American Journal of International
Law, VI).* 1912. 435 n.
King, Rufus. *Ohio: First Fruits of the Ordinance of 1787.* 1888. 273 n.
Kinley, David. *The Independent Treasury of the United States and its Relations
to the Banks of the Country.* 1910. 442 n.
Kirkland, E. C. *A History of American Economic Life.* 1932. 555 n.
——— *The Peacemakers of 1864.* 1927. 684 n.
Knox, J. J. *History of Banking in the United States.* 1900. 444 n.
Krout, J. A. *The Origins of Prohibition.* 1925. 489 n.

La Follette, Suzanne. *Art in America.* 1929. 477 n.
Latané, J. H. *A History of American Foreign Policy.* 1927. 158 n.
——— *From Isolation to Leadership.* 1918. 364 n.
Lecky, W. E. H. *The American Revolution, 1763–1783.* 1898. 130 n.
Lee, J. M. *History of American Journalism.* 1917. 462 n.
Lester, W. S. *The Transylvania Colony.* 1935. 113 n.
Levermore, C. H. *The Republic of New Haven.* 1886. 33 n.
Lewis, Lloyd. *Myths after Lincoln.* 1929. 686 n.
——— *Sherman, Fighting Prophet.* 1932. 653 n.
Lincoln, C. H. *The Revolutionary Movement in Pennsylvania, 1760–1766* (Uni-
versity of Pennsylvania, *Publications, History Series,* I). 1901. 132 n.
Linn, W. A. *The Story of the Mormons.* 1902. 530 n.
Livermore, T. L. *Numbers and Losses in the Civil War in America, 1861–1865.*
1901. 657 n.
Locke, Mary S. *Anti-Slavery in America, from the Introduction of African
Slaves to the Prohibition of the Slave Trade, 1619–1808 (Radcliffe College Mono-
graphs,* no. 11). 1901. 355 n.
Lodge, H. C. *Alexander Hamilton.* 1882. 218 n.
——— *Daniel Webster.* 1883. 414 n.
——— *George Washington.* 2 vols. 1889. 213 n.
——— *Life and Letters of George Cabot.* 1877. 316 n.
Long, W. J. *American Literature.* 1913. 468 n.
Lonn, Ella. *Desertion during the Civil War.* 1928. 658 n.
——— *Salt as a Factor in the Confederacy.* 1933. 666 n.
Lyon, E. W. *Louisiana in French Diplomacy, 1759–1804.* 1934. 276 n.

McBain, H. L. *The Living Constitution.* 1927. 206 n.
McCain, J. R. *Georgia as a Proprietary Province; the Execution of a Trust.*
1917. 48 n.
McCaleb, W. F. *The Aaron Burr Conspiracy.* 1903. 279 n.
McCarthy, Charles. *The Antimasonic Party: A Study of Political Antimasonry
in the United States, 1827–1840* (American Historical Association, *Annual
Report,* 1902). 425 n.

McClellan, George B. *McClellan's Own Story.* 1887. 632 n.

McClellan, W. S. *Smuggling in the American Colonies at the Outbreak of the Revolution.* 1912. 115 n.

McCormac, E. I. *Colonial Opposition to Imperial Authority during the French and Indian War* (University of California, *Publications in History,* I). 1911. 115 n.

—— *James K. Polk.* 1922. 522 n.

McCrady, Edward. *The History of South Carolina under the Proprietary Government, 1670–1719.* 1897. 41 n.

McElroy, R. M. *Kentucky in the Nation's History.* 1909. 177 n.

McGrane, R. C. *Foreign Bondholders and American State Debts.* 1935. 445 n.

—— ed. *The Correspondence of Nicholas Biddle Dealing with National Affairs, 1807–1844.* 1919. 421 n.

—— *The Panic of 1837.* 1924. 428 n.

McIlwain, C. H. *The American Revolution; a Constitutional Interpretation.* 1923. 119 n.

McLaughlin, A. C., and others. *Source Problems in United States History.* 1918. 136 n.

McLaughlin, A. C. *A Constitutional History of the United States.* 1935. 341 n.

—— *Confederation and the Constitution, 1783–1789* (*American Nation,* XX) 1905. 168 n.

—— *Lewis Cass.* 1891. 535 n.

McMaster, J. B. *A History of the People of the United States from the Revolution to the Civil War.* 8 vols. 1883–1913. 185 n.

—— *A History of the People of the United States During Lincoln's Administration.* 1927. 660 n.

—— *Daniel Webster.* 1902. 414 n.

—— *The Acquisition of Political, Social, and Industrial Rights of Man in America.* 1903. 164 n.

M'Nemar, Richard. *The Kentucky Revival.* 1807. 262 n.

MacDonald, William. *Jacksonian Democracy, 1829–1837* (*American Nation,* XV). 1906. 396 n.

Maclay, E. S. *History of the United States Navy from 1775 to 1901.* 3 vols. 1901–02. 308 n.

—— ed. *The Journal of William Maclay.* 1890. 217 n.

MacLear, Anne B. *Early New England Towns* (Columbia University, *Studies in History, Economics, and Public Law,* XXIX). 1908. 58 n.

Macleod, W. C. *The American Indian Frontier.* 1928. 508 n.

Macy, Jesse. *The Anti-Slavery Crusade* (*Chronicles of America,* XXVIII). 1919. 501 n.

Mahan, A. T. *Admiral Farragut.* 1892. 642 n.

—— *Sea Power in its Relation to the War of 1812.* 2 vols. 1905. 283 n.

—— *The Influence of Sea Power upon History, 1660–1783.* 1890. 108 n.

—— *The Major Operations of the Navies in the War of American Independence.* 1913. 150 n.

Maitland, F. W. *Constitutional History of England.* 1908. 82 n.

Major, Howard. *The Domestic Architecture of the Early American Republic.* 1926. 332 n.

Markham, C. R. *Life of Christopher Columbus.* 1892. 9 n.

Marshall, T. M. *A History of the Western Boundary of the Louisiana Purchase, 1819–1841.* 1914. 508 n.

Mason, E. C. *The Veto Power.* 1890. 205 n.

Mathews [Rosenberry], Lois Kimball. *The Expansion of New England.* 1909. 63 n.

Maurice, Sir Frederick B. *Robert E. Lee, the Soldier.* 1925. 624 n.

Meigs, W. M. *Life of John Caldwell Calhoun.* 2 vols. 1917. 410 n.

Melvin, F. E. *Napoleon's Navigation System.* 1919. 285 n.

Mereness, N. D. *Maryland as a Proprietary Province.* 1901. 40 n., 87 n.

Merriam, C. E. *History of American Political Theories.* 1903. 119 n.

Meyer, B. H., MacGill, C. H., and others, eds. *History of Transportation in the United States before 1860.* 1917. 548 n.

Miller, W. E. *The Peopling of Kansas.* 1906. 578 n.

Milton, George Fort. *The Eve of Conflict: Stephen A. Douglas and the Needless War.* 1934. 570 n.

Miner, C. E. *The Ratification of the Federal Constitution by the State of New York* (Columbia University, *Studies in History, Economics, and Public Law*, XCIV). 1920. 209 n.

Minnigerode, Meade. *The Fabulous Forties, 1840–1850.* 1924. 459 n.

Minot, George R. *History of the Insurrection in Massachusetts in the Year 1786.* 1788. 193 n.

Mitchell, W. C. *A History of the Greenbacks with Special Reference to the Consequence of their Issue, 1862–1865.* 1903. 668 n.

Monaghan, Frank. *John Jay, Defender of Liberty.* 1935. 239 n.

Monroe, Will S. *The Educational Labors of Henry Barnard.* 1893. 484 n.

Moody, John. *The Railroad Builders* (*Chronicles of America*, XXXVIII). 1919. 548 n.

Moore, A. B. *Conscription and Conflict in the Confederacy.* 1924. 626 n.

Moore, J. B. *The Principles of American Diplomacy.* 1918. 236 n.

Morgan, J. H., and Fielding, M. *Life Portraits of George Washington.* 1931. 213 n.

Morison, S. E. *Builders of the Bay Colony.* 1930. 27 n.

——— *Life and Letters of Harrison Gray Otis.* 2 vols. 1913. 316 n.

——— *The Founding of Harvard College.* 1935. 63 n.

Morse, J. T., Jr. *Benjamin Franklin.* 1889. 80 n.

——— *John Adams.* 1884. 158 n., 247 n.

——— *John Quincy Adams.* 1882. 373 n.

——— *Thomas Jefferson.* 1883. 256 n.

Mott, F. L. *A History of American Magazines, 1741–1850.* 1930. 333 n., 462 n.

Mowat, R. B. *The Diplomatic Relations of Great Britain and the United States.* 1925. 317 n.

Mueller, H. R. *The Whig Party in Pennsylvania* (Columbia University, *Studies in History, Economics, and Public Law*, CI). 1922. 449 n.

Munro, W. B. *The Seigneurs of Old Canada* (*Chronicles of Canada*, V). 1914. 101 n.

Murdock, K. B. *Increase Mather, the Foremost American Puritan.* 1925. 61 n.

Muzzey, D. S. *Thomas Jefferson.* 1918. 256 n.

Myers, W. S. *George Brinton McClellan: a Study in Personality.* 1934. 632 n.

Namier, L. B.   *England in the Age of the American Revolution.*   1930.   121 n.

Nettels, C. P.   *The Money Supply of the American Colonies before 1720* (University of Wisconsin, *Studies in the Social Sciences and History*, no. 20). 1934.   96 n.

Nevins, Allan, ed.   *American Social History as Recorded by British Travellers.* 1923.   326 n.

────── *Frémont, The West's Greatest Adventurer.*   1928.   528 n.

────── *The American States during and after the Revolution, 1775–1789.*   1924. 161 n.

Nichols, R. F.   *Franklin Pierce.*   1931.   578 n.

────── *The Democratic Machine, 1850–1854* (Columbia University, *Studies in History, Economics, and Public Law*, CXI).   1923.   578 n.

Nicolay, John G., and Hay, John.   *Abraham Lincoln: A History.*   10 vols. 1890.   614 n.

Nock, A. J.   *Jefferson.*   1926.   256 n.

Norton, A. B.   *The Great Revolution of 1840.*   1888.   449 n.

Norwood, J. N.   *The Schism in the Methodist Episcopal Church, 1844: a Study of Slavery and Ecclesiastical Politics* (*Alfred University Studies*, I).   1923.   568 n.

Nussbaum, F. L.   *Commercial Policy in the French Revolution.*   1923.   285 n.

Oberholtzer, E. P.   *Jay Cooke, Financier of the Civil War.*   2 vols.   1907.   667 n.
────── *Robert Morris.*   1903.   147 n.

Ogg, F. A.   *Daniel Webster.*   1914.   414 n.

────── *The Old Northwest* (*Chronicles of America*, XIX).   1919.   184 n.

────── *The Opening of the Mississippi.*   1904.   189 n.

────── *The Reign of Andrew Jackson* (*Chronicles of America*, XX).   1919.   396 n.

Orth, S. P.   *Our Foreigners* (*Chronicles of America*, XXXV).   1920.   68 n.

Osgood, H. L.   *The American Colonies in the Eighteenth Century.*   4 vols.   1924–25.   83 n.

────── *The American Colonies in the Seventeenth Century.*   3 vols.   1904–07. 83 n.

Ostrogorski, M.   *Democracy and the Organization of Political Parties.*   2 vols. 1902.   398 n.

Owsley, F. L.   *King Cotton Diplomacy.*   1931.   666 n.
────── *State Rights in the Confederacy.*   1925.   677 n.

Paine, R. D.   *The Fight for a Free Sea* (*Chronicles of America*, XVII).   1920. 286 n.

────── *The Old Merchant Marine.*   1919.   554 n.

Palfrey, J. G.   *History of New England.*   5 vols.   1858–90.   24 n.

Parkman, Francis.   *Count Frontenac and New France under Louis XIV.*   1877. 98 n.

────── *Half-Century of Conflict.*   2 vols.   1892.   98 n.

────── *La Salle and the Discovery of the Great West.*   2 vols.   1879.   100 n.

────── *Montcalm and Wolfe.*   2 vols.   1884.   98 n.

────── *Pioneers of France in the New World.*   1865.   100 n.

────── *The California and Oregon Trail.*   1849.   510 n.

────── *The Conspiracy of Pontiac.*   2 vols.   1851.   110 n.

────── *Works.*   20 vols.   1897–98.   98 n.

Parrington, V. L. *Main Currents in American Thought*. 3 vols. 1927–30. 29 n., 333 n.

Parton, James. *Life of Andrew Jackson*. 3 vols. 1860. 376 n.

Paullin, C. O. *Atlas of the Historical Geography of the United States*. 1932. 51 n.

────── *Commodore John Rodgers*. 1910. 266 n.

────── *Diplomatic Negotiations of American Naval Officers*. 1912. 266 n.

────── *The Navy of the American Revolution*. 1906. 150 n.

Paxson, F. L. *A History of the American Frontier, 1763–1893*. 1924. 70 n.

────── *The Civil War*. 1911. 660 n.

────── *The Independence of the South American Republics*. 1903. 364 n.

────── *The Last American Frontier*. 1910. 401 n.

Perkins, Dexter. *The Monroe Doctrine, 1823–1826*. 1927. 364 n.

────── *The Monroe Doctrine, 1826–1867*. 1933. 364 n.

Perkins, J. B. *France in the American Revolution*. 1911. 149 n.

Perlman, Selig. *A History of Trade Unionism in the United States*. 1922. 480 n.

Perry, Bliss. *The American Spirit in Literature* (*Chronicles of America*, XXXIV). 1918. 468 n.

Phillips, U. B. *A History of Transportation in the Eastern Cotton Belt to 1860*. 1908. 553 n.

────── *American Negro Slavery*. 1918. 493 n.

────── *Georgia and State Rights* (American Historical Association, *Annual Report*, 1901, II). 400 n.

────── *Life and Labor in the Old South*. 1929. 493 n.

────── *The Life of Robert Toombs*. 1913. 539 n.

Pollard, A. F. *The Evolution of Parliament*. 1920. 82 n.

Porter, K. H. *A History of Suffrage in the United States*. 1918. 391 n.

Porter, K. W. *John Jacob Astor, Business Man*. 2 vols. 1931. 513 n.

Posey, W. B. *The Development of Methodism in the Old Southwest, 1783–1824*. 1933. 262 n.

Powell, E. P. *Nullification and Secession in the United States*. 1897. 412 n.

Pratt, J. W. *Expansionists of 1812*. 1925. 300 n.

Quaife, M. M. *Chicago and the Old Northwest, 1673–1835*. 1913. 297 n.

────── ed. *The Diary of James K. Polk, during his Presidency, 1845 to 1849*. 4 vols. 1910. 522 n.

Ragatz, L. J. *The Fall of the Planter Class in the British Caribbean*. 1928. 49 n.

Randall, E. O., and Ryan, D. J. *History of Ohio*. 4 vols. 1912. 273 n.

Randall, J. G. *Constitutional Problems under Lincoln*. 1926. 678 n.

Raper, C. L. *North Carolina; A Study in English Colonial Government*. 1904. 41 n.

Ray, P. O. *The Repeal of the Missouri Compromise*. 1909. 574 n.

Reddaway, W. F. *The Monroe Doctrine*. 1905. 364 n.

Reeves, Jesse S. *American Diplomacy under Tyler and Polk*. 1907. 518 n.

Rhodes, J. F. *History of the Civil War*. 1917. 660 n.

────── *History of the United States from the Compromise of 1850*. 9 vols. 1893–1922. 533 n., 668 n.

Richman, I. B. *Rhode Island: Its Making and Its Meaning*. 2 vols. 1902. 32 n.

Riegel, R. E.   *America Moves West.*   1930.   530 n.

Rives, G. L.   *The United States and Mexico, 1821–1848.*   2 vols.   1913.   518 n.

Robinson, Howard.   *The Development of the British Empire.*   Revised edition.   1936.   49 n.

Roosevelt, Theodore.   *The Naval War of 1812.*   1882.   308 n.

———— *The Winning of the West.*   4 vols.   1894–96.   112 n.

Root, W. T.   *The Relations of Pennsylvania with the British Government, 1696–1765.*   1912.   94 n.

Ropes, J. C., and Livermore, W. R.   *The Story of the Civil War.*   4 vols.   1894–1913.   628 n.

Rosenberger, J. L.   *The Pennsylvania Germans.*   1923.   67 n.

Rowe, H. K.   *The History of Religion in the United States.*   1924.   568 n.

Royall, W. L.   *Andrew Jackson and the Bank of the United States.*   1880.   423 n.

Sakolski, A. M.   *The Great American Land Bubble.*   1932.   430 n.

Salmon, Lucy M.   *The Newspaper and the Historian.*   1923.   462 n.

Sandburg, Carl.   *Abraham Lincoln, the Prairie Years.*   1926.   614 n.

Sanford, A. H.   *The Story of Agriculture in the United States.*   1916.   560 n.

Sato, Shosuke.   *History of the Land Question in the United States* (Johns Hopkins University, *Studies in Historical and Political Science,* IV).   1886.   453 n.

Schafer, Joseph.   *A History of Agriculture in Wisconsin.*   1922.   662 n.

———— *A History of the Pacific Northwest.*   1918.   510 n.

———— *The Social History of American Agriculture.*   1936.   662 n.

Scharf, J. T.   *History of the Confederate States Navy.*   1887.   636 n.

Scherer, James A. B.   *Cotton as a World Power; a Study in the Economic Interpretation of History.*   1916.   666 n.

Schlesinger, A. M., and Fox, D. R., eds.   *A History of American Life.*   12 vols.   1929–   .   10 n.

Schlesinger, A. M.   *New Viewpoints in American History.*   1922.   67 n., 119 n.

———— *The Colonial Merchants and the American Revolution, 1763–1776* (Columbia University, *Studies in History, Economics, and Public Law,* LXVIII).   1917.   120 n.

Schmeckebier, L. F.   *History of the Know-Nothing Party in Maryland* (Johns Hopkins University, *Studies in Historical and Political Science.*   Series VIII, nos. 4–5).   1899.   565 n.

Schouler, James.   *History of the United States of America under the Constitution.*   7 vols.   1880–1913.   185 n.

Schurz, Carl.   *Henry Clay.*   2 vols.   1887.   374 n.

Schuyler, R. L.   *Parliament and the British Empire.*   1929.   121 n.

———— *The Constitution of the United States; an Historical Survey of its Formation.*   1923.   199 n.

Schwab, J. C.   *The Confederate States of America, 1861–1865: A Financial and Industrial History of the South during the Civil War.*   1901.   666 n.

Scisco, L. D.   *Political Nativism in New York State* (Columbia University, *Studies in History, Economics, and Public Law,* XIII).   1901.   565 n.

Scott, W. A.   *The Repudiation of State Debts.*   1893.   445 n.

Scrugham, Mary.   *The Peaceable Americans of 1860–1861; A Study in Public Opinion* (Columbia University, *Studies in History, Economics, and Public Law,* XCVI).   1921.   610 n.

Searight, T. B. *The Old Pike, A History of the National Road, with Incidents, Accidents and Anecdotes Thereon.* 1894. 338 n.

Sears, Lorenzo. *Wendell Phillips, Orator and Agitator.* 1909. 500 n.

Sears, L. M. *George Washington.* 1932. 213 n.

—— *History of American Foreign Relations.* 1927. 187 n.

—— *Jefferson and the Embargo.* 1927. 288 n.

Sellery, G. C., and Krey, A. C. *Medieval Foundations of Western Civilization.* 1929. 5 n.

Semple, Ellen C. *American History and its Geographic Conditions.* 1903. 2 n.

Shaler, N. S. *Nature and Man in America.* 1891. 2 n.

Shannon, F. A. *Economic History of the People of the United States.* 1934. 323 n.

—— *The Organization and Administration of the Union Army, 1861–1865.* 2 vols. 1928. 626 n.

Shepard, E. M. *Martin Van Buren.* 1888. 441 n.

Shipp, J. E. D. *Giant Days; or, The Life and Times of William H. Crawford.* 1909. 373 n.

Shoemaker, F. C. *Missouri's Struggle for Statehood, 1804–1821.* 1916. 354 n.

Shryock, R. H. *Georgia and the Union in 1850.* 1926. 545 n.

Siebert, W. H. *The Underground Railroad from Slavery to Freedom.* 1898. 501 n.

Skinner, Constance Lindsay. *Pioneers of the Old Southwest (Chronicles of America, XVIII).* 1921. 71 n.

Slosson, E. E. *The American Spirit in Education (Chronicles of America, XXXIII).* 1921. 331 n.

Small, A. W. *The Beginnings of American Nationality (Johns Hopkins University, Studies in Historical and Political Science, VIII).* 1890. 168 n.

Smith, C. W., Jr. *Roger B. Taney: Jacksonian Jurist.* 1936. 428 n.

Smith, Justin H. *Our Struggle for the Fourteenth Colony — Canada and the American Revolution.* 1907. 139 n.

—— *The Annexation of Texas.* 1911. 524 n.

—— *The War with Mexico.* 2 vols. 1919. 524 n.

Smith, T. C. *Parties and Slavery, 1850–1859 (American Nation, XVIII).* 1906. 570 n.

—— *The Liberty and Free-Soil Parties in the Northwest (Harvard Historical Studies, VI).* 1897. 535 n.

Smith, W. H., ed. *The St. Clair Papers.* 1882. 227 n.

Spears, J. R. *The History of Our Navy from its Origin to the Present Day.* 4 vols. 1897. 308 n.

Sprague, J. F. *The Northeastern Boundary Controversy and the Aroostook War.* 1910. 454 n.

Spring, L. W. *Kansas: the Prelude to the War for the Union.* 1907. 578 n.

Stanton, Elizabeth Cady, Anthony, Susan B., and others. *History of Woman Suffrage.* 6 vols. 1889–1922. 488 n.

Stanwood, Edward. *A History of the Presidency.* 2 vols. New edition. 1916. 234 n.

—— *American Tariff Controversies in the Nineteenth Century.* 2 vols. 1903. 336 n.

Stephens, F. F. *The Monroe Doctrine, Its Origin, Development and Recent Interpretation.* 1916. 364 n.
Stephenson, Carl. *Mediaeval History.* 1935. 5 n.
Stephenson, G. M. *A History of American Immigration, 1820–1924.* 1926. 562 n.
—— *The Political History of the Public Lands from 1840 to 1862.* 1917. 453 n.
Stephenson, N. W. *Abraham Lincoln and the Union (Chronicles of America, XXIX).* 1918. 660 n.
—— *Lincoln.* 1922. 614 n.
—— *Texas and the Mexican War (Chronicles of America, XXIV).* 1921. 518 n.
—— *The Day of the Confederacy (Chronicles of America, XXX).* 1919. 666 n.
Stevens. F. W. *The Beginnings of the New York Central Railroad.* 1926. 548 n.
Stillé, C. J. *History of the United States Sanitary Commission.* 1866. 670 n.
—— *Life and Times of John Dickinson.* 1891. 123 n.
Stoddard, T. L. *The French Revolution in San Domingo.* 1914. 276 n.
Stone, W. L. *Life and Times of Sir William Johnson.* 2 vols. 1865. 110 n.
Story, W. W. *Life and Letters of Joseph Story.* 2 vols. 1851. 341 n.
Sumner, W. G. *Andrew Jackson.* 1924. 376 n.
—— *The Financier and the Finances of the Revolution.* 1891. 147 n.
Swank, J. M. *History of the Manufacture of Iron in all Ages.* 1884. 555 n.
Sweet, W. W. *The Story of Religions in America.* 1930. 65 n.
—— *The Baptists.* 1931. 262 n.
Swisher, C. B. *Roger B. Taney.* 1936. 428 n.

Taft, Lorado. *The History of American Sculpture.* 1903. 477 n.
Tallmadge, T. E. *The Story of Architecture in America.* 1927. 476 n.
Tanner, E. P. *The Province of New Jersey, 1664–1738 (Columbia University, Studies in History, Economics, and Public Law, XXX).* 1908. 676 n.
Tansill, C. C., ed. *Documents Illustrative of the Formation of the Union of the American States.* 1927. 198 n.
Tassin, Algernon de Vivier. *The Magazine in America.* 1916. 462 n.
Taussig, F. W. *The Tariff History of the United States.* Revised edition. 1931. 336 n.
Tewksbury, D. G. *The Founding of American Colleges and Universities before the Civil War.* 1932. 487 n.
Thayer, W. R. *George Washington.* 1922. 213 n.
Thomas, B. P. *Russo-American Relations, 1815–1867 (Johns Hopkins University, Studies in Historical and Political Science, XLVIII).* 1930. 676 n.
Thomas, C. M. *American Neutrality in 1793; A Study in Cabinet Government (Columbia University, Studies in History, Economics, and Public Law, no. 350).* 1931. 236 n.
Thomas, D. Y. *One Hundred Years of the Monroe Doctrine, 1823–1923.* 1923. 364 n.
Thompson, Hallard. *The Age of Invention (Chronicles of America, XXXVII).* 1921. 463 n.
Thorpe, F. N. *A Constitutional History of the American People, 1776–1850.* 2 vols. 1898. 392 n.
Thwaites, R. G., and Kellogg, L. P., eds. *Documentary History of Dunmore's War, 1774.* 1905. 113 n.

LIST OF BOOKS CITED

Thwaites, R. G.   *Brief History of Rocky Mountain Exploration.*   1904.   281 n.
—— *Daniel Boone.*   1902.   113 n.
—— ed.   *Early Western Travels, 1748–1846.*   32 vols.   1904–07.   326 n.
—— *France in America, 1497–1763 (American Nation, VII).*   1905.   101 n.
—— *How George Rogers Clark Won the Northwest.*   1903.   154 n.
—— *The Colonies.*   1891.   51 n.
Thwing, C. F.   *A History of Higher Education in America.*   1906.   487 n.
Tiffany, Francis.   *Life of Dorothea Lynde Dix.*   1890.   488 n.
Tiffany, O. E.   *The Relations of the United States to the Canadian Rebellion of 1837–1838* (Buffalo Historical Society, *Publications,* VIII).   1905.   454 n.
Tocqueville, Alexis de.   *Democracy in America.*   2 vols.   1862.   391 n.
Tower, Charlemagne.   *Marquis de La Fayette in the American Revolution.*   2 vols.   1895.   156 n.
Treat, P. J.   *The National Land System, 1785–1820.*   1910.   181 n.
Trent, W. P., and others, eds.   *The Cambridge History of American Literature.*   3 vols.   1917–21.   468 n.
Trevelyan, Sir George Otto.   *The American Revolution.*   3 vols.   1905.   136 n.
Tryon, R. M.   *Household Manufactures in the United States, 1640–1860.*   1917.   69 n.
Turner, F. J.   *Rise of the New West, 1819–1829 (American Nation,* XIV).   1906.   346 n., 363 n.
—— *The Frontier in American History.*   1920.   4 n.
—— *The Significance of Sections in American History.*   1932.   175 n., 232 n., 371 n.
—— *The United States, 1830–1850.*   1935.   396 n.
Turner, F. M.   *Life of General John Sevier.*   1910.   176 n.
Tyler, L. G.   *England in America, 1580–1652 (American Nation,* IV).   1904.   21 n.
—— *The Letters and Times of the Tylers.*   3 vols.   1884–96.   450 n.
Tyler, M. C.   *Literary History of the American Revolution, 1763–1783.*   2 vols.   1897.   140 n.
—— *Patrick Henry.*   1887.   119 n.

Updyke, F. A.   *Diplomacy of the War of 1812.*   1915.   283 n.

Vail, H. H.   *A History of the McGuffey Readers.*   1910.   486 n.
Van Tyne, C. H.   *The American Revolution, 1776–1783 (American Nation,* IX).   1905.   136 n.
—— *The Causes of the War of Independence.*   1922.   116 n.
—— *The Loyalists of the American Revolution.*   1902.   142 n.
—— *The War of Independence.*   1929.   142 n.
Vignaud, Henry.   *Toscanelli and Columbus.*   1902.   9 n.
Villard, O. G.   *John Brown, 1800–1859.*   1910.   595 n.
Vincent, Francis.   *A History of the State of Delaware.*   1870.   47 n.
Volwiler, A. T.   *George Croghan and the Westward Movement, 1741–1782.*   1926.   111 n.

Wallace, D. D.   *The Life of Henry Laurens.*   1915.   158 n.
Wandell, S. H., and Minnigerode, Meade.   *Aaron Burr.*   2 vols.   1925.   279 n.

[707]

Ward, A. W., ed. *Cambridge History of British Foreign Policy.* 3 vols. 1922–23. 317 n.

Warfield, E. D. *The Kentucky Resolutions of 1798.* 1894. 254 n.

Warren, Charles. *The Making of the Constitution.* 1928. 199 n.

—— *The Supreme Court in United States History.* 2 vols. 1932. 267 n.

Waterman, W. R. *Frances Wright.* 1924. 488 n.

Webb, W. P. *The Great Plains.* 1931. 4 n.

Weeden, W. B. *Economic and Social History of New England, 1620–1789.* 2 vols. 1890. 28 n.

Wellington, R. G. *The Political and Sectional Influence of the Public Lands, 1828–1842.* 1914. 403 n.

Wendell, Barrett. *Literary History of America.* 1900. 468 n.

Werner, M. R. *Brigham Young.* 1925. 530 n.

Wertenbaker, T. J. *The First Americans, 1607–1690 (A History of American Life, II).* 1927. 21 n.

Wesley, C. H. *The Collapse of the Confederacy* (Howard University, *Studies,* no. 2). 1922. 667 n.

West, W. R. *Contemporary French Opinion on the American Civil War* (Johns Hopkins University, *Studies in Historical and Political Science,* Series XLII). 1924. 672 n.

Wheeler, O. D. *The Trail of Lewis and Clark, 1804–1904.* 1904. 281 n.

Whitaker, A. P. *The Mississippi Question, 1795–1803.* 1934. 276 n.

—— *The Spanish American Frontier, 1783–1795.* 1927. 189 n.

White, Horace. *Money and Banking.* Revised edition. 1914. 444 n.

White, M. J. *The Secession Movement in the United States, 1847–1852.* 1916. 545 n.

White, N. I. *American Negro Folk-Songs.* 1928. 477 n.

White, S. E. *The Forty-Niners (Chronicles of America, XXV).* 1920. 537 n.

Whitford, N. E. *History of the Canal System of the State of New York.* 2 vols. 1906. 386 n.

Whitlock, Brand. *La Fayette.* 1929. 156 n.

Wildman, M. S. *Money Inflation in the United States: A Study in Social Pathology.* 1905. 430 n.

Winsor, Justin, ed. *The Narrative and Critical History of America.* 8 vols. 1884–89. 1 n.

—— *The Westward Movement.* 1897. 176 n.

Wittke, Carl. *History of Canada.* 1928. 103 n.

—— *Tambo and Bones.* 1936. 477 n.

Wood, W. B., and Edmonds, J. E. *A History of the Civil War in the United States.* 1905. 628 n.

Wood, William. *Captains of the Civil War (Chronicles of America, XXXI).* 1921. 628 n.

—— *Elizabethan Sea-Dogs (Chronicles of America, III).* 1918. 12 n.

—— *War with the United States (Chronicles of Canada, XIV).* 1915. 302 n.

Woodward, W. E. *George Washington, the Image and the Man.* 1926. 213 n.

Woodworth, J. V. *American Tool Making and Interchangeable Manufacturing.* 1905. 555 n.

Wright, C. D. *Industrial Evolution of the United States.* 1895. 323 n.

Wrong, G. M. *The Conquest of New France (Chronicles of America*, X). 1918. 103 n.

—— *The Rise and Fall of New France.* 2 vols. 1928. 103 n.

—— *Washington and his Comrades in Arms (Chronicles of America*, XII). 1921. 144 n.

Zimmerman, J. F. *Impressment of American Seamen* (Columbia University, *Studies in History, Economics, and Public Law*, CXVIII). 1925. 286 n.

INDEX

Abolitionists, early efforts of, 491; underground railroad, 500; movement organized, 501; opposition to, 502; in Kansas, 577; during Civil War, 609, 679, 682

Adams, Charles Francis, candidate for Vice-President (1848), 536; minister to England, 673

Adams, John, on Boston Massacre, 126; favors independence, 140; Treaty of Paris, 158; mission to England, 186; Vice-President, 234; President, 245; X Y Z affair, 248; peace with France, 250

Adams, John Quincy, minister to Russia, 317; library, 333; Secretary of State, 360; treaty with Spain, 361; on Monroe Doctrine, 368; sketch of, 373; elected President, 380; on Indian affairs, 382; on internal improvements, 385; defeated for re-election, 393; member of Congress, 418; opposed to "gag rule," 502

Adams, Samuel, sketch of, 125; "committees of correspondence," 128

Agassiz, Louis J. R., 466

Agriculture, in plantation area, 52; in early New England, 58; in the Middle Colonies, 69; after War of 1812, 325; aided by inventions, 464, 661; in upper South, 497; effects on, of improved means of transportation, 555; revolution in, 560; stimulated by Civil War, 660; Morrill Land Grant Act, 662

Alabama, admission, 346; threats of secession (1850), 545; secession, 606

Alabama, Confederate commerce-destroyer, 636

Albany Conference, 106

Albany Regency, 441

Albemarle Sound, settlement, 41

Alcott, Bronson, 468

Alert, surrendered to *Essex*, 309

Alexander II, of Russia, emancipates serfs, 676

Alexandria (Va.) Conference, 194

Alien Acts, 252

Allen, Ethan, in American Revolution, 138

Amendments, provisions for, in state constitutions, 166; in Constitution of the United States, 208; necessary to secure ratification, 211; Eleventh, 244; Twelfth, 255; Thirteenth, 687

American Anti-Slavery Society, formed, 501

American Brotherhood, formed, 564

American Fur Company, founded, 362; trades in Oregon, 512

American Geography, by Jedediah Morse, 486

American Party, rise of, 576; in election of 1856, 581; merges with Constitutional Union Party, 600

American Peace Society, founded, 491

American Protestant Association, formed, 564

American Speller, by Noah Webster, 486

American system, Clay's, beginnings, 379; distribution of land revenues, 406; national bank, 424; platform of National Republicans, 426

Amusements, among the colonials, 76; early nineteenth century, 477

Anderson, Major Robert, at Charleston Harbor, 610

André, Major John, executed as a spy, 156

Andros, Sir Edmund, heads Dominion of New England, 92

Anesthetics, early use of, 466

Annabel Lee, by Edgar Allan Poe, 474

Annapolis, Convention, 194; first telegraph line, 463

Anne, Queen of England, "Queen Anne's War," 103

Antietam, battle of, 645

Anti-Federalists, oppose Constitution, 210

Anti-Masonic Party, formed, 424; candidates in 1832, 425; absorbed by National Republicans, 439

Anti-Slavery Society, organized, 501

Appalachians, historical significance of, 3

Appomattox Court House, scene of Lee's surrender, 656

Architecture, in colonies, 73; classical revival, 332; in eighteenth century, 476

Aristocracy, in colonial America, 77; decline of, 328

Ark and *Dove*, reach Maryland, 39

Arkansas, territory, 354; admission, 453; secession, 618

Armed Neutrality (1798), 151

Army, in Revolutionary War, 143; in 1799, 249; in War of 1812, 304; increase, 334; in Mexican War, 526; in Civil War, 622, 626, 630

Arnold, Benedict, leads expedition against Canada, 138; treason, 155

Aroostook War, 456

Arthur, Timothy Shay, *Ten Nights in a Bar-Room*, 490

Articles of Confederation, provisions, 167; problem of western lands, 169; ratification, 170; defects, 171, 193; attempts to amend, 190

Ashburton, Lord, negotiations with Webster, 454

Astor, John Jacob, fur dealer, 362

Astoria, founded, 362; Washington Irving on, 473

Atchison (Kan.), founded, 578

Atlanta, in Civil War, 653

Atlantic Monthly, ed. by James Russell Lowell, 472

Audubon, J. J., 466

Austin, Stephen F., founder of Texas, 435

Autobiography, by Benjamin Franklin, 81

Autocrat of the Breakfast-Table, by Oliver Wendell Holmes, 471

Aztecs, conquered by Cortez, 10

"Bacon's Rebellion," 72 n.

Bainbridge, William, sea captain, 309

Baltimore, population in 1800, 261; attacked

INDEX

Charleston (S.C.), founded, 41; growth of, 54; attacked by British during Revolution, 139; population (1800), 261; southern metropolis, 409; Charleston and Hamburg railroad, 548; railroad connections to Memphis, 553; Democratic convention (1860), 598; Fort Sumter, 610, 616; Confederate port, 635

Charters, Colonial, Virginia, 20, 22; Rhode Island, 32; Connecticut, 34; Maryland, 39; Pennsylvania, 45; Georgia, 48; Somers Islands Company, 49; Hudson's Bay Company, 50

Chase, Salmon P., elected to the Senate (1848), 537; Compromise of 1850, 540; Secretary of the Treasury under Lincoln, 615, 667

Chase, Samuel, Associate Justice, impeachment (1805), 270

Chattanooga, battle of, 651

"Checks and balances," in state constitutions, 164; in Constitution of the United States, 207

Cherokee Indians, treaty at Hard Labor, 111; *Cherokee Nation vs. State of Georgia*, 400

Cherry Valley, scene of Indian massacre, 153

Chesapeake, attacked by the *Leopard*, 286; insult avenged, 295; lost to the *Shannon*, 310

Chesapeake and the Ohio Canal, 389

Chicago, headquarters of Cyrus H. McCormick, 464; railroad center, 552; growth of population, 553; interest in transcontinental railroad, 571; Republican convention (1860), 599

Chickamauga, battle of, 651

China, trade with America, 567

Chippawa, battle of, 312

Chisholm vs. Georgia, 244

Church of England in America, established in Maryland, 40; in the South, 55; disestablishment, 172; Protestant Episcopal Church organized, 173

Church of Jesus Christ of the Latter Day Saints, 529

Churubusco, in Mexican War, 527

Cincinnati, founded, 183; capital of Northwest Territory, 184; western land office, 272; first western headquarters of Cyrus H. McCormick, 464; the *Philanthropist*, 501; railroad center, 553; Union army headquarters, 633

Circular Letter, by Samuel Adams, 125

Civil War, lack of preparedness, 626; battle of Bull Run, 629; training the armies, 630; strategy of, 632; blockade of southern ports, 633; blockade-runners, 634; part played by the navy, 634; commerce-destroyers, 636; in the West, 637; Shiloh, 640; river fighting, 641; on the eastern front, 643; peninsular campaign, 644; Antietam, 645; Chancellorsville, 646; Gettysburg, 648; Vicksburg, 649; Murfreesboro, 650; Chickamauga, 651; Chattanooga, 651; Grant vs. Lee in Virginia, 652; Atlanta campaign, 653; Sherman's march to the sea, 654; through the Carolinas, 655; devastation of the Shenandoah Valley, 655; Petersburg campaign, 656;

Lee's surrender, 656; losses of the war, 656; conscription, 657; stimulus to agriculture, 660; to manufacturing, 662; breeds extravagance, 665; Northern methods of finance, 667; Southern methods of finance, 670; diplomacy of, 671; opposition to, 677; Committee on Conduct of the War, 679; Emancipation Proclamation, 681; significance of, 686

Civilization in America, European origins, 1; the colonial South, 53; New England, 56; Middle Colonies, 63; frontier, 71; effects of the Revolution, 171; conditions about 1800, 260; after War of 1812, 325; during the middle period, 459; cotton South, 493

Claiborne, William C. C., governor of New Orleans, 279

Clark, George Rogers, western campaign during Revolution, 153; agent of Genêt, 232

Clark, William, Lewis and Clark expedition, 281; Missouri Fur Company, 362

Clarke, James Freeman, historian, 468

Clay, Henry, Speaker of the House, 301; a "War Hawk," 301; peace commissioner at Ghent, 317; favors Second Bank of U.S., 336; second Missouri Compromise, 359; candidate for the presidency (1824), 372; sketch of, 374; American system, 379; Secretary of State (1824), 380; duel with John Randolph of Roanoke, 381; Panama Congress, 382; favors distribution of revenue from lands, 406, 431; Compromise Tariff of 1833, 419; favors re-charter of Second Bank of U.S., 423; nominated for presidency (1832), 425; opposes Sub-Treasury Bill, 443; Congressional program (1841), 450; breaks with Tyler, 453; views on annexation of Texas, 519; nominated for presidency (1844), 520; member Thirty-First Congress, 539; Compromise of 1850, 540

Clayton-Bulwer Treaty (1850), 566

Clermont, early steamboat, 347

Cleveland, Ohio, canal terminal, 389; growth stimulated by railroads, 553

Clinton, DeWitt, defeated candidate for presidency (1812), 303; governor of New York, 386; opens Erie canal, 387

Clinton, George, elected Vice-President (1804), 278; (1808), 288

Clinton, Sir Henry, in charge of British expedition in the Carolinas, 139; succeeds General Howe, 152; captures Savannah, 154

Clipper ships, activities, 554

Coal, early use by manufacturers, 323; Pennsylvania deposits, 561; production during Civil War, 664

Coastal plain, significance, 2

Cobden, Richard, English reformer, 672

Cohens vs. Virginia, 343

Coke, Thomas, superintendent of American Methodists, 173

Cold Harbor, battle of, 652

Colleges, in the South, 56; in New England, 62; in the Middle Colonies, 69; Marietta, 183; Harvard in 1800, 261; University of Virginia, 331, 484; curricula, 487; agricultural, 662

with Indians, 104; French and Indian War, 105; American alliance with, 149; French Revolution, 228; Genêt's mission, 230; doctrine of retaliation, 242; X Y Z affair, 248; Naval War of 1798, 249; Convention of 1800, 250; Treaty of San Ildefonso, 274; sale of Louisiana, 276; Continental System, 284; Berlin and Milan Decrees, 285; Bayonne Decree, 293; Rambouillet Decree, 294; downfall of Napoleon's empire, 312; admitted to European Alliance, 365; supression of Spanish revolution, 366; settles spoliation claims, 435; intervention in Mexico, 675

Francesca da Rimini, by George Henry Boker, 478

Franciscan friars, direct missions in California, 515

Frankfort (Ky.), occupied by Union forces, 633

Franklin, Benjamin, founds Academy at Philadelphia, 69; aids in establishment of public library, 77; sketch of, 80; Albany Plan of Union, 106; views on Stamp Act, 118; on Boston Tea Party, 130; obtains aid from France, 149; member of Peace Commission, 158; on Articles of Confederation, 167; in Federal Convention of 1787, 198; *Works*, ed. by Jared Sparks, 472

Franklin, State of, 176

Frederick William II, King of Prussia, joins in Declaration of Pillnitz, 229

Frederick (Md.), occupied by Union forces, 645

Fredericksburg, battle of, 646

Free land, along the colonial frontier, 70

Free-Soil Party, election of 1848, 536; of 1852, 547

"Freeport Doctrine," expounded by Stephen A. Douglas, 594

Frémont, John C., survey of Oregon Trail, 514; exploits in California, 528; nominated for the presidency (1856), 581; in command at St. Louis (1861), 633; defeated at McDowell, 644; emancipation proclamation, 680; opposes Lincoln (1864), 684

French and Indian War, 105

French Revolution, outbreak, 228; Jefferson's view of, 230; Genêt's mission, 232; admirers in America, 244. *See also* France

Frenchtown, battle of, 311

Frolic, lost to the *Wasp*, 309

Frontenac, Count, governor in New France, 101

Frontier, in colonial times, 70; advanced to the Ohio, 111; Indian wars on, 112; during the Revolutionary War, 152; of 1780's, 196; problems in 1790, 225; northwestern (1809), 297; southwestern (1810), 300; after War of 1812, 346; effect of the Erie Canal on, 388; views on land problem, 405; expansion during the 1830's, 435, 453; during the 1840's, 508; during the 1850's, 560; during the Civil War, 661

Fugitive Slave Act (of 1850), 545

Fuller, Margaret, transcendentalist, 468; interest in reform, 488

Fulton and Livingston, steamboat firm, 347

Fundamental Orders of Connecticut, 33

Fur trade, Dutch interest in, 13; Hudson's Bay Company, 50; in Middle Colonies, 70; in New France, 102; in the Northwest, 186; Canadian opposition to American advance, 226; as a cause of War of 1812, 299; in the Far West, 362; in Oregon, 512

Gadsden Purchase, 566

Gage, General Thomas, in command of British forces at Boston (1774), 131; attempts to seize military supplies at Concord, 136; victory at Bunker Hill, 138

"Gag rule," 502

Gaines, General Edmund P., crosses Texas border, 437

Gallatin, Albert, in Whiskey Rebellion, 225; Secretary of the Treasury, 264; in War of 1812, 303; on Peace Commission at Ghent, 317

Gallipolis, settlement, 183

Galloway, Joseph, plan of colonial union, 133

Gama, Vasco da, Portuguese explorer, 8

Gang system, on Southern plantations, 495

Gardoqui, Don Diego de, first Spanish minister to the United States, 188

Garrison, William Lloyd, abolitionist activities, 492, 503

Gaspee incident, 128

Gates, General Horatio, at Saratoga, 149; at Camden, 154

Genêt, Edmond Charles, mission to the United States, 230; failure, 233

Genius of Universal Emancipation, by Benjamin Lundy, 491

George II, King of England, grants Georgia charter, 48; "King George's War," 103

George III, King of England, determines on personal rule, 121; rejects American petition for redress of grievances, 139; the "King's friends" in control, 142; end of personal rule, 157

Georgia, founded by James Oglethorpe, 47; growth retarded by charter, 48; state constitution of, 167; western land claims, 175; ratifies Constitution, 211; Yazoo Land Companies, 273; cedes western lands to Congress, 274; case of *Fletcher vs. Peck*, 274; difficulties with Creek Indians, 382; with Cherokees, 400; debate on secession (1850), 545; secedes, 606

Germans, in colonial times, 66; known as Pennsylvania Dutch, 67; nineteenth century immigrants, 563

Germantown, founded, 67; battle of, 148

Gerry, Elbridge, at Philadelphia Convention, 199, 202; mission to France, 247

Gettysburg, battle of, 648

Ghent, peace negotiations at, 318; treaty of, 319

Gibbon vs. Ogden, 344

Gila River, 566

Gilbert, Sir Humphrey, colonization project, 19

Gillespie, A. H., carrier of dispatch to Frémont, 528

Gist, Christopher, land prospector, 103; delivers warning to French, 104

Globe, The, Washington journal, 397

INDEX

claims by states, 175; State of Franklin, 176; Cumberland settlements, 177; Northwest Ordinances, 178; early settlement of Ohio, 183; need of Mississippi River trade, 188; problems in 1790, 225; religious revival in 1800's, 262; growth stimulated by Land Law of 1800, 272; loses "right of deposit," 275; desires war with England, 300; democracy in, 329; western state banking, 335; why people went West, 346; aided by steamboats, 347; Land Law of 1820, 353; favors tariff of 1824, 383; affected by Erie Canal, 388; views on public land policy, 403; attitude toward nullification, 416; pre-emption act, 452; growth during the forties, 453; connected with East by railroads, 550

West Indies, trade with continental colonies, 41; British possessions in, 49; Molasses Act of 1733, 95; violations of American neutrality in, 286; British discriminations continued, 319; British restrictions on American trade removed, 434

West Point, proposed betrayal by Benedict Arnold, 156

West Point Academy, authorized, 305; reorganized, 334

West Roxbury, location of Brook Farm, 468

West Virginia, admitted to the Union (1863), 618

Western Engineer, steamboat, 361

Wethersfield (Conn.), founded, 32

Wheat, failure of American crop (1835), 432; exported to England during Civil War, 661

Whig Party, formed, 438; national convention at Harrisburg, 447; dissensions, 454; split over Mexican War, 526; decline of, 547; split over Kansas-Nebraska Act, 574; dissolution, 575

Whiskey Rebellion, 224

White, Doctor Elijah, American leader in Oregon, 514

White, Judge Hugh L., candidate for presidency (1836), 440

Whitman, Marcus, missionary sent to Oregon, 513

Whitman, Walt, poet, 473

Whitney, Asa, advocates trans-continental railroad, 570

Whitney, Eli, inventor of cotton gin, 261

Whittier, John Greenleaf, abolitionist poet, 471

"Wigwam," convention place of Republicans (1860), 600

Wilderness, battle of the, 652

Wilderness Road, route to Boonesborough (Ky.), 113

Wilkes, Captain Charles, intercepts the *Trent*, 673

Wilkinson, James, advocates the West join New Spain, 188; receives pay from Spain, 279; reveals Burr's conspiracy, 280; sends Pike on expedition, 282

Willamette mission, in Oregon, 513

William III, King of Great Britain, "Glorious Revolution," 92; "King William's War," 103

William and Mary, joint rulers of Great Britain, 92

William and Mary College, founded, 56; curriculum, 331

Williams, Roger, settlement on Narragansett Bay, 30

Williamsburg, battle of, 643

Wilmington (N.C.), British plan to attack, 139; Confederate port, 635

Wilmot, David, Representative from Pennsylvania, 533

Wilmot Proviso, provisions, 533

Wilson, James, views on representation, 202

Wilson's Creek (Mo.), battle of, 633

Winchester (Va.), occupied by General Johnston, 628; battle of, 644; destruction near, 655

Winchester, General James, American military officer, 311

Winder, General William Henry, American military officer, 313

Windsor (Conn.), founded, 32

Winthrop, John, Puritan leader, 27; removed as governor, 27

Wirt, William, Anti-Masonic candidate for presidency (1832), 426

Wisconsin, Fox River waterway, 389; admitted to the Union, 534; lead mines, 561; German settlement in, 563

Witchcraft delusion, 61 n.

Wolfe, James, British officer, 108

Women, status of, 328; movement for women's rights, 487; as reformers, 488; work in the Civil War, 670

Wood, Fernando, mayor of New York City, 617

Wool-growing, in Northeast, 325; demand for protection, 384; inadequate production of in America, 556; increased production during the Civil War, 664

Worcester vs. Georgia, 400

Workingmen's Party, 481

Wright, Frances, anti-slavery agitator, 488

Writs of Assistance, 122

Wyoming Valley, massacre, 153

X Y Z dispatches, 248

Yale College, founded, 62

Yancey, William L., Confederate commissioner to England, 672

Yazoo Land Companies, 273

York, Duke of, grants proprietary rights over New Netherland, 43; fosters religious toleration, 65

York (Toronto), American raid on (1813), 311

Yorktown, surrender of Cornwallis, 157; evacuated by Confederates, 643

Young, Brigham, Mormon leader, 530; elected governor of Deseret, 539